January 5-9, 2011,
Schwarzenberg, Austria

**Association for
Computing Machinery**

Advancing Computing as a Science & Profession

FOGA'11

Proceedings of the 2011 ACM/SIGEVO

Foundations of Genetic Algorithms XI

Sponsored by:
ACM SIGEVO

Supported by:
Vorarlberg University of Applied Sciences (FHV)

Edited by:
Hans-Georg Beyer & William B. Langdon

Association for Computing Machinery

Advancing Computing as a Science & Profession

The Association for Computing Machinery
2 Penn Plaza, Suite 701
New York, New York 10121-0701

ISBN: 978-1-4503-0633-1

Additional copies may be ordered prepaid from:

ACM Order Department
PO Box 30777
New York, NY 10087-0777, USA

Phone: 1-800-342-6626 (USA and Canada)
+1-212-626-0500 (Global)
Fax: +1-212-944-1318
E-mail: acmhelp@acm.org
Hours of Operation: 8:30 am – 4:30 pm ET

ACM Order Number: 910114

Printed in the USA

Preface

Welcome to the eleventh Foundations of Genetic Algorithms (FOGA XI) workshop proceedings. This time, FOGA was held in the Gasthof Hirschen, Schwarzenberg, Austria, (5–9 January 2011). It was supported by the Vorarlberg University of Applied Sciences (FHV).

FOGA has a long standing tradition of a two stage review process. During the summer of 2010 the submitted papers went through a first round of reviewing to select the papers to be presented at the workshop. The authors of selected papers then had several months during the autumn of 2010 to revise their work, taking into account the feed back generously provided by their three reviewers. After the workshop there was a second round of reviewing and the authors had a final opportunity to revise their papers. Whilst the second round allows the papers to be made clearer and further improvements to their presentation, it also allows the reviewers to check whether errors have been rectified.

The final proceedings is published by the Association for Computing Machinery (ACM) and the final papers are in the ACM digital library.

Introduction

As you can see from the table of contents, FOGA has retained its tradition of addressing theoretical issues in all aspects of evolutionary computation.

History – 20 Years of Mathematical and Theoretical Analysis of Evolutionary Algorithms

The first workshop on the foundations of genetic algorithms was held 15-18 July 1990 in Indiana University, USA. Since then it has been held every two years, both in the USA and elsewhere. FOGA 2 (26–29 July 1992) was in Vail, Colorado, FOGA 3 (31 July to 2 August 1994) Estes Park, Colorado. FOGA 4 (2–5 August 1996) in San Diego and then FOGA 5 (24–28 September 1998) marks the first move outside the USA. It was held in a small castle-hotel in Leiden, The Netherlands. With FOGA 6 (21–23 July 2000) the workshop returned to the USA, actually Charlottesville in Virginia (the first time on the East Coast). FOGA 7 (2–4 September 2002) saw the workshop return to Europe, this time to Torremolinos on the southern Spanish coast.

FOGA 7 was the last of seven highly successful (and still widely cited) proceedings to be published by Morgan Kaufmann. MKP withdrew totally from the business of publishing conference proceedings. The next workshop was again held outside the USA. Not only was FOGA 8 held in Japan but it also marks a change to the calendar, since it was hosted 28 months later in the winter (5–9 January 2005, rather than the summer) by the University of Aizu in Aizu-Wakamatsu City. Both FOGA 8 and FOGA 9 are published by Springer (as LNCS 3469 and LNCS 4436). FOGA 9 (8–11 January 2007) was hosted by the Instituto de Ciencias Nucleares of Universidad Nacional Autonoma de Mexico, in Mexico city. FOGA 10 (9–11 January 2009) marked a return to the USA and was hosted by the University of Central Florida in Orlando.

Twenty years ago, FOGA was started by the International Society for Genetic Algorithms (ISGA) specifically to provide a theoretical complement their ICGA conferences. Over the years ICGA grew and then combined with other newer evolutionary computation conferences to form the GECCO conference. Similarly (although it retains the name – FOGA) the workshop's scope grew to encompass the theoretical foundations of all types of evolutionary computation. As GECCO became the most preeminent conference in the field, the Society itself changed and joined the ACM to form the ACM Special Interest Group on Evolutionary Computation, SIGEVO. And so it is SIGEVO which is responsible for FOGA and so the ACM has published the FOGA proceedings since FOGA 10.

Keynote

In addition to the twenty one papers, Prof. Karl Sigmund delivered a lecture. He chose as his title: "Sanctions and Public Goods". He dealt with forming and maintaining co-operative links in an adaptive and changing society, including discussing many economic experiments and simulations.

W. B. Langdon, Hans-Georg Beyer, Jeff Bassett, Karl Sigmund, Guenter Rudolph, Anne Auger, Nikolaus Hansen, Dirk Arnold, Anthony Bucci, Andrew Sutton, Alberto Moraglio, Daniel Johannsen, Karl Bringmann, Christine Zarges, Dirk Sudholt, Luigi Malago, Per Kristian Lehre, Elena Popovici, Karsten Weicker, Nataliya Sokolovska, Kenneth De Jong, Markus Wagner, Una-May O'Reilly, Robb Wilcox, Steffen Finck, Patrick Spettel, Alden Wright.

Acknowledgments

We thank Martin Hefel and Hannelore Nagel for their support.

Hans-Georg Beyer
FH Vorarlberg GmbH, FZ PPE
Hochschulstr. 1
A-6850 Dornbirn, Austria

W. B. Langdon,
Department of Computer Science,
University College London
Gower Street, London WC1E 6BT, UK

Table of Contents

FOGA 2011 Organisation

Organisers: Hans-Georg Beyer *(Vorarlberg University of Applied Sciences, Austria)*
W. B. Langdon *(University College London, UK)*

Programme Committee: Dirk V. Arnold *(Dalhousie University, Canada)*
Anne Auger *(INRIA, France)*
Anthony Bucci *(Icosystem Corporation, USA)*
Carlos A. Coello Coello *(Cinvestav, Mexico)*
Benjamin Doerr *(Max Planck Institute, Saarbrucken, Germany)*
Anton Eremeev *(Sobolev Institute of Mathematics, Russia)*
Steffen Finck *(Vorarlberg University of Applied Sciences, Austria)*
Ivan Garibay *(University of Central Florida, USA)*
Robert B. Heckendorn *(University of Idaho, USA)*
Jeff Horn *(Northern Michigan University, USA)*
Christian Igel *(University of Copenhagen, Denmark)*
Thomas Jansen *(University College Cork, Ireland)*
Colin Johnson *(University of Kent, UK)*
Nic McPhee *(University of Minnesota, Morris, USA)*
Silja Meyer-Nieberg *(Bundeswehr University of Munich, Germany)*
Frank Neumann *(University of Adelaide, Australia)*
Martin Pelikan *(University of Missouri in St. Louis, USA)*
Riccardo Poli *(University of Essex, UK)*
Adam Prugel-Bennett *(University of Southampton, USA)*
Colin Reeves *(Coventry University, UK)*
Jon Rowe *(The University of Birmingham, UK)*
Marc Schoenauer *(INRIA, France)*
Jonathan Shapiro *(University of Manchester, UK)*
Dirk Sudholt *(The University of Birmingham, UK)*
Olivier Teytaud *(INRIA, France)*
Lothar Thiele *(ETH, Switzerland)*
Darrell Whitley *(Colorado State University, USA)*
Paul Wiegand *(University of Central Florida, USA)*
Stephan Winkler *(Upper Austria University of Applied Sciences)*
Carsten Witt *(Technical University of Denmark)*
Alden H. Wright *(University of Montana, USA)*
Xin Yao *(The University of Birmingham, UK)*
Eckart Zitzler *(Pedagogical Hochschule, Bern, Switzerland)*

FOGA 2011 Sponsors & Supporters

Sponsor:  SIGEVO

Supporters: **Vorarlberg University of Applied Sciences (FHV)**

Analysis of Evolutionary Algorithms: From Computational Complexity Analysis to Algorithm Engineering

Thomas Jansen
Dept. of Computer Science
University College Cork
Cork, Ireland
t.jansen@cs.ucc.ie

Christine Zarges
Fakultät für Informatik, LS 2
TU Dortmund
44221 Dortmund, Germany
christine.zarges@tu-dortmund.de

ABSTRACT

Analyzing the computational complexity of evolutionary algorithms has become an accepted and important branch in evolutionary computation theory. This is usually done by analyzing the (expected) optimization time measured by means of the number of function evaluations and describing its growth as a function of a measure for the size of the search space. Most often asymptotic results describing only the order of growth are derived. This corresponds to classical analysis of (randomized) algorithms in algorithmics. Recently, the emerging field of algorithm engineering has demonstrated that for practical purposes this analysis can be too coarse and more details of the algorithm and its implementation have to be taken into account in order to obtain results that are valid in practice. Using a very recent analysis of a simple evolutionary algorithm as starting point it is shown that the same holds for evolutionary algorithms. Considering this example it is demonstrated that counting function evaluations more precisely can lead to results contradicting actual run times. Motivated by these limitations of computational complexity analysis an algorithm engineering-like approach is presented.

Categories and Subject Descriptors

F.2.2 [**Analysis of Algorithms and Problem Complexity**]: Nonnumerical Algorithms and Problems
; I.6.4 [**Simulation and Modeling**]: Model Validation and Analysis

General Terms

Algorithms, Design, Measurement, Performance, Theory

Keywords

Runtime analysis, algorithm engineering, performance measures

1. INTRODUCTION

Evolutionary algorithms (EAs) are general randomized search heuristics that are often used for optimization when there is not enough time or expertise to develop a problem-specific algorithm. They are usually easy to apply and often deliver solutions of acceptable quality in reasonable time. For better solutions or faster performance, however, normally modifications need to be made and it is not at all obvious how these can be done in an informed and efficient way. This motivates the desire for a better understanding of evolutionary algorithms, the way they work, their limitations and potentials. Consequently, this motivates research in evolutionary algorithm theory. In the last fifteen years one branch of EA theory that has become increasingly important, established, and elaborate is the analysis of the optimization time of EAs for concrete problems or classes of problems. By now, methods are available [1, 15] and many results for relevant problem classes are known (see [10, 11] for an overview). This is also often referred to as run time analysis or computational complexity analysis. The performance of an EA is measured by means of the number of function evaluations T it makes until an optimal solution is found for the first time. The reason is that evolutionary algorithms tend to be algorithmically simple and each step can be carried out relatively quick. Thus, a function evaluation is assumed to be the most costly operation in terms of computation time. Most often, results about the expected optimization time $\mathrm{E}(T)$ as a function of n are derived where n is a measure for the size of the search space. If a fixed-length binary encoding is used n denotes the length of the bit strings (and the size of the search space equals 2^n). Results are usually given in asymptotic form. For an upper bound this is often given as $\mathrm{E}(T(n)) = O(f(n))$ for some function $f\colon \mathbb{N} \to \mathbb{R}_0^+$. Formally, this means there exist some constants $n_0 \in \mathbb{N}$ and $c \in \mathbb{R}^+$ such that $\mathrm{E}(T) \le cf(n)$ holds for all $n \ge n_0$. The constants n_0 and c need not be explicitly stated but often they can be derived from the proofs. We see that this gives some bound on the performance that may be quite loose. Even in the case of an asymptotically tight bound $\mathrm{E}(T) = \Theta(f(n))$ we only know that for all $n \ge n_0$ we have $c_1 f(n) \le \mathrm{E}(T) \le c_2 f(n)$ for some constants $0 < c_1 \le c_2$. Depending on the gap $c_2 - c_1$ predictions about the actual average run time (number of function evaluations in fact) can be vary vague. Remember that the motivation for EA theory is to come up with better EAs for practical applications. For this purpose such asymptotic results may be too imprecise or even misleading. While in some case such rough results lead to valuable insights (consider [6] for a positive example) they can lead to incorrect conclusions even if the results about the computational complexity are precise. This motivates a different approach that adds empirical analysis to the analytical one. We do not argue against computational complexity analysis in general. We make the point that, like algorithm engineering [14] adds to the run time analysis of algorithms [4], careful empirical analysis and an analysis that is more faithful to the concrete implementation of the algorithm can yield insights that a pure theoretical optimization time analysis cannot. It is important to point out that our approach is in the spirit of algorithm engineering, bringing together theoretical and empirical analysis. This is quite different from an experimental approach (e. g. [2]).

We introduce the evolutionary algorithm and fitness function under consideration in the next section. In Section 3 we discuss one recently published example for an computational complexity analysis that leads to an incorrect impression. This motivates a more detailed analysis that incorporates empirical findings in Section 4. In order to broaden the perspective we briefly present results on other example functions in Section 5. We conclude and discuss possible future research in Section 6.

2. EA AND FITNESS FUNCTIONS

The EA under consideration, known as (1+1) EA [5], is a very simple one with a population size of 1, an offspring population size of 1, strict deterministic plus-selection, and standard bit mutations. As the analysis investigates the first point of time an optimum is found one neglects the choice of a stopping criterion and lets the algorithm run forever. We restrict ourselves here to fixed mutation rates $p(n)$ that may (and should) depend on n but are fixed during a run. We remark that it is known that varying the mutation probability during a run may speed up the optimization dramatically [8]. The most recommended fixed choice is $p(n) = 1/n$ so that in expectation exactly one bit flips. We remark that it is known that this choice is far from optimal for some problems [7]. We give a formal algorithmic description in Algorithm 1.

Algorithm 1 (1+1) EA

Initialization
Select $x \in \{0,1\}^n$ uniformly at random and compute its function value $v_x = f(x)$.
loop
  Mutation
  Create $y \in \{0,1\}^n$ by copying each bit of x and, independently for each bit, flip this bit with probability $p(n)$. Compute $v_y = f(y)$.
  Selection
  If $v_y \geq v_x$ Then set $x := y$ and $v_x := v_y$.
end loop

Many asymptotic analyses have been performed for the (1+1) EA, for example functions as well as for combinatorial optimization problems. The consideration of example functions is useful since they are usually structurally simple and help to illustrate properties of an algorithm, they can exhibit typical structures, and they are often useful first steps in the development of new analytical tools. One such

example function introduced in the context of the analysis of unimodal functions is LEADINGONES [12]. The function value is given by the number of consecutive 1-bits counting from left to right. A formal definition is given in Definition 2.

DEFINITION 2. *For $n \in \mathbb{N}$, $x = x[1]x[2]\cdots x[n] \in \{0,1\}^n$, the function* LEADINGONES: $\{0,1\}^n \to \mathbb{R}$ *is defined by*
$$\text{LEADINGONES}(x) = \sum_{i=1}^{n} \prod_{j=1}^{i} x[j].$$

The optimization time T is defined as the number of times the fitness function f is evaluated until a global optimum of f is found. According to Algorithm 1 the initialization requires 1 function evaluation to compute v_x and each time the loop is executed 1 function evaluation is made to compute v_y.

3. ON COMPUTATIONAL COMPLEXITY ANALYSIS

It is known that the expected optimization time of the (1+1) EA on LEADINGONES is $\text{E}(T) = \Theta(n^2)$ [5] for any mutation probability $p(n) = \Theta(1/n)$. For the (1+1) EA on LEADINGONES, however, much more is known. In particular, given the current function value $v_x \leq n-2$ we know the complete probability distribution for the current bit string x. A simple inductive proof [5] shows that

$$\text{Prob}(x = x') = 2^{-(n-(v_x+1))}$$

holds for any $x' \in \{0,1\}^n$ with $x[1] = x[2] = \cdots = x[v_x] = 1$ and $x[v_x + 1] = 0$. This can be exploited to derive a much more precise result.

Böttcher, Doerr, and Neumann [3] prove for the (1+1) EA with fixed mutation probability $p(n)$ that its expected optimization time equals

$$\text{E}(T) = \frac{(1 - p(n))^{1-n} - (1 - p(n))}{2p(n)^2}. \tag{1}$$

This is an exact, precise result for the expected optimization time of an evolutionary algorithm for a non-trivial fitness function. Using this result Böttcher, Doerr, and Neumann derive an optimal fixed mutation rate for the (1+1) EA on LEADINGONES by observing that the optimal mutation rate that minimizes (1) converges to $1.59362/n$. For not too small values of n all significantly other mutation probabilities yield larger expected optimization times. Note that this is only true in an asymptotic sense – exactly speaking, it is false. The exact equation eq. (1) is correct and the optimal mutation probability depends on n and only converges to $1.59362/n$ for increasing n. For this value the expected optimization time is $0.772n^2$. For realistic values of n very slightly smaller mutation probabilities are better (e. g., $1.58105/n$ for $n = 100$ and $1.59235/n$ for $n = 1000$). We compute the actual optimal values using eq. (1) for subsequent experiments. A graphical representation of the optimal mutation probabilities due to Böttcher, Doerr and Neumann [3] is given later in Figure 3 (together with much smaller values that are derived using a different cost model).

Remember that this cost model counts only the number of function evaluations since it assumes those to be most costly. However, at the end of the day time is wall clock time. This is even more true for EAs since the only motivation for considering them is in practical applications. Let us assume that the assumption that the function evaluations account for the majority of the actual run time is correct. In this case we will be careful with these function evaluations. Considering the (1+1) EA, we see that with probability $(1 - p(n))^n$ no bit is flipped at all and $y = x$ holds. Using the common choice $p(n) = 1/n$ we have $(1 - p(n))^n \approx e^{-1} > .35$ and we see that in expectation in more than 35% of the generations no bit is flipped. In these cases no function evaluation is necessary and will be omitted in any sensible implementation. Note, that this is typical for evolutionary search in discrete search spaces and completely different from evolutionary search in continuous domains. If we want to be precise we need to take this resampling into account. We keep the very simple cost model where we assign cost 1 for a function evaluation but take into account that no function evaluation is made if no bit is flipped. Let $T_{>0}$ denote the cost in this modified cost model. The following holds.

THEOREM 3. *Let $p(n)$ with $0 < p(n) < 1$ denote the mutation probability of the (1+1) EA, $c > 0$ a constant.*

$$p(n) = c/n \Rightarrow \lim_{n \to \infty} E(T_{>0})/n^2 = \frac{(e^c - 1)^2}{2c^2 e^c} > .5 \quad (2)$$

$$p(n) \geq \frac{1}{n} \Rightarrow \lim_{n \to \infty} E(T_{>0})/n^2 \geq \frac{(e-1)^2}{2e} > .54 \quad (3)$$

$$p(n) = o\left(\frac{1}{n}\right) \Rightarrow \lim_{n \to \infty} E(T_{>0})/n^2 = \frac{1}{2} = .5 \quad (4)$$

PROOF. We present only a short proof containing the most important steps. A very similar proof is carried out in Section 4.3 with a more general cost model. The cost model employed here actually is a special case of this more general cost model. Thus, a complete proof including all major intermediate steps can be found in Section 4.3. We remark that most computations are similar or even identical to the corresponding proofs in [3].

Let x be the current bit string of the (1+1) EA and $v_x = \text{LEADINGONES}(x) < n$. Let G_{v_x} denote the number of generations until an offspring y with $\text{LEADINGONES}(y) > v_x$ is generated for the first time. Let T_{v_x} denote the number of function evaluations in these generations. For $i \in \mathbb{N}$ let $T_{v_x,i} \in \{0, 1\}$ denote the number of function evaluations in the i-th generation. Applying the law of total probability we have $E(T_{v_x}) = \sum_{t=1}^{\infty} \text{Prob}(G_{v_x} = t) \cdot E(T_{v_x} \mid G_{v_x} = t)$. By definition $T_{v_x} = \sum_{i=1}^{G_{v_x}} T_{v_x,i}$ holds and

$$E(T_{v_x}) = \sum_{t=1}^{\infty} \text{Prob}(G_{v_x} = t) \cdot \sum_{i=1}^{t} E(T_{v_x,i} \mid G_{v_x} = t)$$

follows by linearity of expectation. For $i = G_{v_x}$ we have $E(T_{v_x,i}) = 1$ since in this final mutation at least the leftmost 0-bit flips. For $i < G_{v_x}$ all $E(T_{v_x,i})$ are equal for symmetry reasons and thus

$$E(T_{v_x}) = \sum_{t=1}^{\infty} \text{Prob}(G_{v_x} = t)((t-1)E(T_{v_x,1} \mid G_{v_x} = t) + 1) \quad (5)$$

holds. We have $G_{v_x} = t$ if and only if on the one hand in the t-th generation the left-most v_x bits do not flip and $x[v_x + 1]$ flips and, on the other hand, this does no happen in the $t-1$

preceding generations. Thus

$$\text{Prob}(G_{v_x} = t) = (1 - p(n)(1 - p(n))^{v_x})^{t-1} \cdot p(n)(1 - p(n))^{v_x} \quad (6)$$

holds. For $i < G_{v_x}$ we consider one single mutation. Let S denote the event that in this mutation the function value is increased. Let Z denote the event that in this mutation no bit is flipped. Since we consider $T_{v_x,i}$ for $i < G_{v_x}$ we know that the function value is not increased. Thus,

$$E(T_{v_x,i}) = \text{Prob}(\overline{Z} \mid \overline{S}) = \frac{\text{Prob}(\overline{Z} \wedge \overline{S})}{\text{Prob}(\overline{S})}$$

holds. We already know that $\text{Prob}(\overline{S}) = 1 - \text{Prob}(S) = 1 - (1 - p(n))^{v_x} \cdot p(n)$ holds. For $\text{Prob}(\overline{Z} \wedge \overline{S})$ we observe $\text{Prob}(\overline{S}) = \text{Prob}(\overline{Z} \wedge \overline{S}) + \text{Prob}(Z)$ and $\text{Prob}(\overline{Z} \wedge \overline{S}) = \text{Prob}(\overline{S}) - \text{Prob}(Z)$ follows. With $\text{Prob}(Z) = (1 - p(n))^n$ we obtain

$$E(T_{v_x,i}) = 1 - \frac{(1 - p(n))^n}{1 - (1 - p(n))^{v_x} \cdot p(n)}.$$

Inserting the equations for $\text{Prob}(G_{v_x} = t)$ and $E(T_{v_x,i})$ into eq. (5) we obtain

$$E(T_{v_x}) = \sum_{t=1}^{\infty} (1 - p(n)(1 - p(n))^{v_x})^{t-1} \cdot p(n)(1 - p(n))^{v_x}$$

$$\cdot \left((t-1)\left(1 - \frac{(1 - p(n))^n}{1 - (1 - p(n))^{v_x} \cdot p(n)}\right) + 1\right)$$

$$= \frac{1 - (1 - p(n))^n}{p(n)(1 - p(n))^v}. \quad (7)$$

For the expected number of function evaluations we take random initialization into account and obtain

$$E(T_{>0}) = \sum_{v_x=0}^{n-1} 2^{-(v_x+1)}\left(E(T_{v_x}) + \frac{1}{2}\sum_{i=v_x+1}^{n-1} E(T_{v_x})\right)$$

$$= \sum_{v_x=0}^{n-1} \frac{E(T_{v_x})}{2} = \frac{(1 - (1 - p(n))^n)^2}{2p(n)^2(1 - p(n))^{n-1}}. \quad (8)$$

First we consider the case $p(n) = c/n$ and make use of $\lim_{n \to \infty}(1 - c/n)^n = e^{-c}$. Hence, we have

$$\lim_{n \to \infty} E(T_{>0})/n^2 = \frac{(1 - e^{-c})^2}{2c^2 e^{-c}} = \frac{(e^c - 1)^2}{2c^2 e^c}$$

and (2) follows. We observe that $E(T_{v_x})$ grows with growing $p(n) \geq 1/n$ and thus (3) holds. For $p(n) = o(1/n)$ we have $p(n) = 1/(n\alpha(n))$ for some function α with $\lim_{n \to \infty} 1/\alpha(n) = 0$. Making use of $\lim_{n \to \infty}(1 - p(n))^n = \lim_{n \to \infty} 1 - (1/\alpha(n)) = 1$ in this case we obtain (4). $\square$

We visualize the limit terms $(e^c - 1)^2/(2c^2 e^c)$ from (2), $(e - 1)^2/(2e)$ from (3), and $1/2$ from (4) in Figure 1 (as a function of c). We also include the constant term 0.772 for the expected number of function evaluations $0.772n^2$ that results from using the fixed mutation probability $1.59362/n$ from [3]. Note that in the context of Figure 1 this mutation probability is fixed and independent of the parameter c.

Theorem 3 tells us that we minimize the number of function evaluations by making the mutation probability arbitrarily small. For example, the mutation probability $p(n) = 2^{-n}$ implies a smaller number of function evaluations than

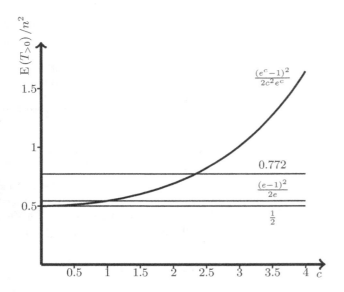

Figure 1: Limit terms for $\lim\limits_{n\to\infty} \mathbf{E}\left(T_{>0}\right)/n^2$ for different values of the mutation probability $p(n)$ as given in Theorem 3 together with 0.772 from [3].

$p(n) = 1/n$ or $p(n) = 1.59362/n$. This, of course, does not imply that one should set the mutation probability so small. It demonstrates that the simple cost model is inadequate. While function evaluations may be costly the other operations of the (1+1) EA are definitely not for free. In order to take them into account in an appropriate way the implementation needs to be taken into account. We do this in the following section.

4. ALGORITHM ENGINEERING

In order to be able to analyze the actual optimization time (as opposed to the number of function evaluations) of the (1+1) EA on LEADINGONES we need to know about how the (1+1) EA is implemented. We consider a simple implementation that is neither naive nor sophisticated. In particular, we want an implementation that is organized in modules and can be considered as reasonable from a programming or software engineering point of view. This is useful since in applications evolutionary algorithms often exhibit the need to be modified to better fit the current task. One modification is the application of different kinds of crossover and mutation operators or selection schemes. Such modifications are facilitated when the evolutionary algorithm is implemented using such a module structure.

4.1 Implementation Details

The modules we use are fitness function evaluation, mutation, and selection. The fitness function evaluation receives as input an individual and returns its fitness. The mutation receives an individual to be mutated and sufficient memory to store the mutated offspring. In addition to this offspring it returns the information if at least one bit was flipped. No other information (like the specific bits flipped) is available to the main loop. We remark that use of such additional information may enable one to implement a more efficient fitness function evaluation. The selection receives the par-

ent, the offspring, and their fitness values. It returns the new population together with its fitness.

The implementation is carried out in ANSI C using a `char` to store a single bit. The random decisions of the (1+1) EA are implemented using `drand48()` as pseudo-random number generator. This leads to the following straight-forward implementation of the fitness function LEADINGONES (see Algorithm 4; the string length n is a global variable).

Algorithm 4 Implementation of LEADINGONES

```
long fitness(char *x)
{
    long i;
    for ( i=0; ( i<n ) && ( x[i]==1 ); i++ );
    return i;
}
```

We observe that a fitness evaluation is not at all time consuming. It can be carried out in $O(n)$ steps and actually takes only $\Theta(\text{LEADINGONES}(x))$ steps. Since with high probability in each mutation the number of leading 1-bits is increased by $O(1)$, we have that on average $\Theta\left(\left(\sum_{i=1}^{n} i\right)/n\right) = \Theta(n)$ computation steps are carried out in a function evaluation where the average is taken over the complete run. Being able to carry out one function evaluation in time $O(n)$ is not unusual. Most example functions can be computed in linear time (even more complex ones like the well-known long path function [12]) and the same holds for many combinatorial optimization problems. It is true that fitness evaluations can be time consuming. However, in many cases and in particular for LEADINGONES, they are not.

Considering the rest of the (1+1) EA mutation seems to be a potentially time consuming operator. A naive implementation may perform a random experiment for each of the n bits to determine if this bit is flipped. This would make each mutation an operation that requires $\Theta(n)$ random decisions and thus extremely costly. However, a much more efficient implementation is known. Already Knuth [9] (described for standard bit mutations by Rudolph and Ziegenhirt [13]) pointed out that for small probabilities $p(n)$ it is much more efficient not to perform n random experiments (one for each potential mutation site) but to randomly draw the position of the next mutation site. This does not change the probability distribution but reduces the number of random experiments necessary from n on expectation to $p(n) \cdot n$, thus only 1 for the mutation probability $p(n) = 1/n$. We implement this idea in a straight-forward way using two global variables, `nextPos` to store the next mutation site and `l=log(1.0-p)` where `p` $= p(n)$ is the mutation probability. This variable `l` is needed for the determination of the next mutation site. We initialize `nextPos=-1` to indicate that currently there is no random position available and one has to be determined randomly. The mutation itself is described in Algorithm 5. It makes use of two auxiliary functions described in Algorithm 6 and Algorithm 7, respectively.

What remains is selection. The strict plus-selection employed requires a comparison of the two function values and, in case the offspring is no worse than its parent, replacing the parent by the offspring. In a naive implementation one may copy the offspring to the parent requiring $\Theta(n)$ computation steps. It is, however, quite obvious that it suffices to

Algorithm 5 Implementation of mutation

```
int mutation(char *parent,char *offspring)
{
    long next, start=0; /* start at offspring[0] */
    int mutated=0; / remember if bit is flipped /
    next=getNextPos(n-1); /* get mutation site */
    if ( next != -1 )
    { /* position within current bit string */
        mutated=1; /* remember some bit is mutated */
        /* copy parent to offspring */
        memcpy(offspring, parent, sizeof(char)*n);
        while (next != -1) /* while within string */
        {
            /* mutate bit */
            offspring[start+next]=1-parent[start+next];
            start += (next+1); /* update next pos.   */
            next=getNextPos(n-startindex-1);
        }
    }
    return mutated; /* flag if any bit was mutated */
}
```

Algorithm 6 Implementation of getNextPos (for mutation)

```
long getNextPos(long length)
{ /* deliver next mutation site */
    if (nextPos>=0) /* next position available */
        return savePos(nextPos, length);
    /* randomly choose next position */
    nextPos=(long)floor( log( drand48() )/l );
    return savePos(nextPos, length);
}
```

swap the pointers to parent and offspring so that selection can easily be done in time $\Theta(1)$.

4.2 Data-Driven Cost Model Generation

In theory, it appears to be appropriate to assign cost n to a mutation that flips a bit (due to the fitness evaluation involved) and cost 1 to a mutation where no bit is flipped. It is, however, unclear if this is a reasonable setting when considering the implemented (1+1) EA. One obstacle may be that fitness evaluations involve only simple and fast basic operations whereas mutations involve pseudo-random number generation and the computation of a logarithm, both

Algorithm 7 Implementation of savePos (for mutation)

```
long savePos(long pos, long length)
{ /* update position */
    if (pos>length)
    { /* next position not within string */
        nextPos = pos-length-1; /* subtract used part */
        return -1; /* signal:  end for this string */
    }
    else
    {
        nextPos=-1; /* position used */
        return pos;
    }
}
```

rather costly. We therefore use results of preliminary experiments to assign cost to generations with and without actual mutation.

All experiments reported have been carried out on an iMac with a 2.8GHz quad-core Intel Core i7 processor with 8MB shared L3 cache and 8GB 1066MHz DDR3 SDRAM. The ANSI C implementation has been compiled using gcc 4.2.1 with optimization -O3. The run time is measured using clock() so that the actual time spent in the (1+1) EA is measured. The experiments are all carried out for $n \in \{50, 100, 150, \ldots, 1000\}$ and are repeated 100 times independently, i. e., with independent random seeds for the pseudo-random number generator. The results are always presented using box plots in the following way. The mean of the data is drawn by a thick line. The upper and lower quartile are used to draw a rectangle (or box) around the mean where the upper and lower side of the rectangle are defined by the upper and lower quartile, respectively. Attached to this rectangle are two whiskers, one below and one above, that extend to the two most extreme data points that have a distance to the corresponding side of the rectangle of at most 1.5 times the height of the rectangle. All even more extreme data points are considered as outliers and are depicted by circles.

In order to get an estimate of the time spent in generations without any flipping bit in comparison to generations where at least one bit flips we perform 100 independent runs of the (1+1) EA with mutation probability $p(n) = 1/n$ on LeadingOnes. Clearly, this time is not independent of the mutation probability $p(n)$. In particular, very small mutation probabilities increase the probability to have several consecutive generations where no bit is flipped. In all but the first of the generations of such a sequence the mutation is particularly fast because no random experiment needs to be carried out at all. Preliminary experiments confirmed that the differences are not significant for mutation probabilities $p(n) = c/n$ with $1/4 < c < 4$. Thus, we do these measurements for $p(n) = 1/n$, only. We comment on larger and smaller mutation probabilities later.

We measure the cumulative time for all generations where no bit flips and the cumulative time for all generations where at least one bit flips. For each run we report the quotient of the average times spent in one generation of these two types: the average time for a generation with an actual mutation over the average time for a generation where no bit flips. Note that already one run yields the average over a large random number of generations. We average these averages over 100 runs and present the results in form of box plots in Figure 2. Due to the enormous number of random experiments the results are concentrated around the mean values in an extreme way, the upper and lower quartiles are hardly visible, only the outliers (drawn as small circles) can be seen. They are also still very close to the mean. Computing a least squares fit for the means (using gnuplot) yields that we obtain a reasonable fit (also given in Figure 2) for $0.0011n + 1.18$. We see that the relation between the average run time in generations with and without actual mutation is indeed linear but the factor is really small and hence the ratio grows only slowly with n.

4.3 Application of the New Cost Model

Based on these empirical findings we assign cost $q(n) := 1$ to a generation where in the mutation no bit is flipped and

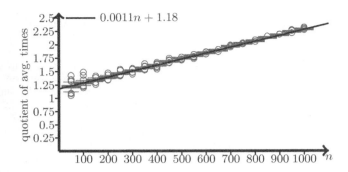

Figure 2: Quotients of measured average run times for generations with and without flipping bit, averaged over 100 runs, using mutation probability $p(n) = 1/n$.

cost $r(n) := 0.0011n + 1.18$ to a generation where at least one bit is flipped. Using this cost model we revisit the proof of Theorem 3. Note, that the cost model used in Theorem 3 corresponds to setting $q(n) = 0$ and $r(n) = 1$. In order to make the calculations also applicable to other cost models, we present results for general $q(n)$ and $r(n)$. We remark that the most useful equation when filling in intermediate steps is the following about the geometric series.

$$\sum_{i=a}^{b} q^i = \sum_{i=0}^{b} q^i - \sum_{i=0}^{a-1} q^i = \frac{1-q^{b+1}}{1-q} - \frac{1-q^a}{1-q} = \frac{q^a - q^{b+1}}{1-q} \quad (9)$$

Recall that (in Theorem 3) G_{v_x} denotes the number of generations until an offspring y with $\text{LEADINGONES}(y) > v_x$ is generated for the first time. Moreover, in Theorem 3 T_{v_x} denotes the number of function evaluations in these generations. For $i \in \mathbb{N}$, $T_{v_x,i} \in \{0,1\}$ denotes the number of function evaluations in the i-th generation. Note, that here in the more general cost model, T_{v_x} and $T_{v_x,i}$ correspond to the costs (instead of the number of function evaluations) with respect to the cost model and, thus, $T_{v_x,i} \in \{q(n), r(n)\}$.

Using the same notation eq. (5) now becomes

$$E\left(T_{v_x}\right) = \sum_{t=1}^{\infty} \text{Prob}\left(G_{v_x} = t\right) \cdot \left((t-1) E\left(T_{v_x,1} \mid G_{v_x} = t\right) + r(n)\right) \quad (10)$$

since the cost for the final generation where the left-most 0-bit is guaranteed to flip is now set to $r(n)$. The other change concerns the expected cost of a generation $E\left(T_{v_x,i}\right)$. Using the notation from the proof of Theorem 3 we obtain

$$E\left(T_{v_x,i}\right) = q(n) \cdot \text{Prob}\left(Z \mid \overline{S}\right) + r(n) \cdot \text{Prob}\left(\overline{Z} \mid \overline{S}\right)$$
$$= q(n) \cdot \frac{\text{Prob}\left(Z \wedge \overline{S}\right)}{\text{Prob}\left(\overline{S}\right)} + r(n) \cdot \frac{\text{Prob}\left(\overline{Z} \wedge \overline{S}\right)}{\text{Prob}\left(\overline{S}\right)}$$
$$= q(n) \cdot \frac{\text{Prob}\left(Z\right)}{\text{Prob}\left(\overline{S}\right)} + r(n) \cdot \frac{\text{Prob}\left(\overline{S}\right) - \text{Prob}\left(Z\right)}{\text{Prob}\left(\overline{S}\right)}$$
$$= q(n) \cdot \frac{(1-p(n))^n}{1 - (1-p(n))^{v_x} \cdot p(n)}$$
$$\quad + r(n) \cdot \left(1 - \frac{(1-p(n))^n}{1 - (1-p(n))^{v_x} \cdot p(n)}\right)$$

for all $i < G_{v_x}$.

Inserting this value for $E\left(T_{v_x,i}\right)$ and $\text{Prob}\left(G_{v_x} = t\right)$ from eq. (6) into eq. (10) we obtain

$$E\left(T_{v_x}\right)$$
$$= \sum_{t=1}^{\infty} (1-p(n)(1-p(n))^{v_x})^{t-1} p(n)(1-p(n))^{v_x}$$
$$\cdot \left((t-1)\left(\frac{q(n)(1-p(n))^n}{1-p(n)(1-p(n))^{v_x}}\right.\right.$$
$$\left.\left. + r(n)\left(1 - \frac{(1-p(n))^n}{1-p(n)(1-p(n))^{v_x}}\right)\right) + r(n)\right)$$

$$= \sum_{t=1}^{\infty} (1-p(n)(1-p(n))^{v_x})^{t-1} p(n)(1-p(n))^{v_x}$$
$$\cdot \left((t-1)\left(\frac{q(n)(1-p(n))^n}{1-p(n)(1-p(n))^{v_x}}\right.\right.$$
$$\left.\left. + r(n)\left(1 - \frac{(1-p(n))^n}{1-p(n)(1-p(n))^{v_x}}\right)\right)\right)$$
$$+ \sum_{t=1}^{\infty} (1-p(n)(1-p(n))^{v_x})^{t-1} p(n)(1-p(n))^{v_x} r(n)$$

$$= p(n)(1-p(n))^{v_x}\left(\frac{q(n)(1-p(n))^n}{1-p(n)(1-p(n))^{v_x}}\right.$$
$$\left. + r(n)\left(1 - \frac{(1-p(n))^n}{1-p(n)(1-p(n))^{v_x}}\right)\right)$$
$$\cdot \sum_{t=1}^{\infty} (t-1)\left(1-p(n)(1-p(n))^{v_x}\right)^{t-1}$$
$$+ p(n)(1-p(n))^{v_x} r(n) \sum_{t=1}^{\infty} \left(1-p(n)(1-p(n))^{v_x}\right)^{t-1}$$

It is easy to see that two series in the above equations converge since we can apply eq. (9). This yields

$$\sum_{t=1}^{\infty} (t-1)\left(1-p(n)(1-p(n))^{v_x}\right)^{t-1}$$
$$= \sum_{t=1}^{\infty} t\left(1-p(n)(1-p(n))^{v_x}\right)^t$$
$$= \sum_{t=1}^{\infty} \sum_{u=t}^{\infty} \left(1-p(n)(1-p(n))^{v_x}\right)^u$$
$$= \sum_{t=1}^{\infty} \frac{\left(1-p(n)(1-p(n))^{v_x}\right)^t}{1 - \left(1-p(n)(1-p(n))^{v_x}\right)}$$
$$= \frac{1}{p(n)(1-p(n))^{v_x}} \sum_{t=1}^{\infty} \left(1-p(n)(1-p(n))^{v_x}\right)^t$$
$$= \frac{1}{p(n)(1-p(n))^{v_x}} \cdot \frac{1-p(n)(1-p(n))^{v_x}}{1 - \left(1-p(n)(1-p(n))^{v_x}\right)}$$
$$= \frac{1-p(n)(1-p(n))^{v_x}}{\left(p(n)(1-p(n))^{v_x}\right)^2}$$

for the first term and

$$\sum_{t=1}^{\infty} \left(1-p(n)(1-p(n))^{v_x}\right)^{t-1} = \sum_{t=0}^{\infty} \left(1-p(n)(1-p(n))^{v_x}\right)^t$$
$$= \frac{1}{1 - \left(1-p(n)(1-p(n))^{v_x}\right)} = \frac{1}{p(n)(1-p(n))^{v_x}}$$

for the second one. Plugging these results into the above

calculations we obtain

$$\mathrm{E}\left(T_{v_x}\right)$$

$$= p(n)(1-p(n))^{v_x}\left(\frac{q(n)(1-p(n))^n}{1-p(n)(1-p(n))^{v_x}}\right.$$

$$+ \left. r(n)\left(1-\frac{(1-p(n))^n}{1-p(n)(1-p(n))^{v_x}}\right)\right)$$

$$\cdot \frac{1-p(n)(1-p(n))^{v_x}}{(p(n)(1-p(n))^{v_x})^2} + \frac{p(n)(1-p(n))^{v_x}r(n)}{p(n)(1-p(n))^{v_x}}$$

$$= \frac{1-p(n)(1-p(n))^{v_x}}{p(n)(1-p(n))^{v_x}}\left(\frac{q(n)(1-p(n))^n}{1-p(n)(1-p(n))^{v_x}}\right.$$

$$+ \left. r(n)\left(1-\frac{(1-p(n))^n}{1-p(n)(1-p(n))^{v_x}}\right)\right) + r(n)$$

$$= \frac{1-p(n)(1-p(n))^{v_x}}{p(n)(1-p(n))^{v_x}} \cdot \frac{q(n)(1-p(n))^n}{1-p(n)(1-p(n))^{v_x}}$$

$$+ \frac{r(n)\left(1-p(n)(1-p(n))^{v_x}\right)}{p(n)(1-p(n))^{v_x}}$$

$$\cdot \left(1-\frac{(1-p(n))^n}{1-p(n)(1-p(n))^{v_x}}\right) + r(n)$$

$$= \frac{q(n)(1-p(n))^n}{p(n)(1-p(n))^{v_x}} + \frac{r(n)\left(1-p(n)(1-p(n))^{v_x}\right)}{p(n)(1-p(n))^{v_x}}$$

$$- \frac{r(n)(1-p(n))^n}{p(n)(1-p(n))^{v_x}} + r(n)$$

$$= \frac{(1-p(n))^n q(n) + \left(1-(1-p(n))^n\right)r(n)}{p(n)(1-p(n))^{v_x}}$$

We denote the complete cost by T_q (instead of $T_{>0}$ like in the proof of Theorem 3). Making use of

$$\mathrm{E}\left(T_q\right) = \sum_{v_x=0}^{n-1} \frac{\mathrm{E}\left(T_{v_x}\right)}{2}$$

from eq. (8) like in the proof of Theorem 3 we obtain

$$\mathrm{E}\left(T_q\right)$$

$$= \sum_{v_x=0}^{n-1} \frac{(1-p(n))^n q(n) + \left(1-(1-p(n))^n\right)r(n)}{2p(n)(1-p(n))^{v_x}}$$

$$= \frac{(1-p(n))^n q(n) + \left(1-(1-p(n))^n\right)r(n)}{2p(n)}$$

$$\cdot \sum_{v_x=0}^{n-1} \frac{1}{(1-p(n))^{v_x}}$$

$$= \frac{(1-p(n))^n q(n) + \left(1-(1-p(n))^n\right)r(n)}{2p(n)}$$

$$\cdot \frac{1-(1-p(n))^n}{p(n)(1-p(n))^{n-1}}$$

$$= \left(1-(1-p(n))^n\right)$$

$$\cdot \frac{(1-p(n))^n q(n) + \left(1-(1-p(n))^n\right)r(n)}{2p(n)^2(1-p(n))^{n-1}}$$

for the expected total cost. Note, that setting $q(n) = 0$ and $r(n) = 1$ yields the same equations as in eq. (7) and eq. (8) from Theorem 3.

We are interested in determining a mutation probability $p(n)$ that minimizes this expected cost. We cannot solve this equation arithmetically for $p(n)$, but we can do so numerically. This way, we obtain optimal mutation probabil-

ities in the sense that they minimize the expected cost derived in this cost model. For the values of n where we explore the algorithm's performance empirically we plot $n \cdot p(n)$ in Figure 3. We observe that the factor to be multiplied with the standard mutation rate $1/n$ in the mutation probabilities that are optimal for our empirical cost model decreases with increasing n. Moreover, it is always strictly smaller than the optimal values derived in the uniform cost model applied by Böttcher, Doerr, and Neumann [3]. In Figure 3, these values and the asymptotic value 1.59362 are given to allow for a comparison. We see that for the range of values of n we are concerned with the optimal mutation probabilities are all $1/n \le p(n) \le 1.5/n$. This is one confirmation that performing our measurements with $p(n) = 1/n$ was indeed sufficient since the differences resulting from using mutation probabilities c/n with $1 < c \le 1.5$ as compared to mutation probability $1/n$ are rather small. We come back to this point again when discussing actual run times. Note that these findings are valid for the range of values n considered here. For much larger values of n one can expect that even smaller mutation probabilities are optimal.

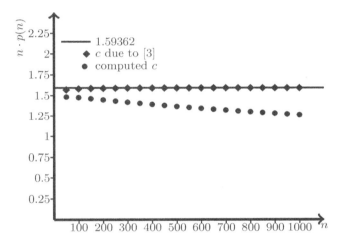

Figure 3: Graph of $n \cdot p(n)$ for mutation probabilities $p(n)$ minimizing the empirical cost model and for mutation probabilities due to [3].

4.4 Experimental Evaluation

To compare the impact of the different mutation probability we perform experiments, again for $n \in \{50, \ldots, 1000\}$. For each value of n and each mutation probability, we perform 100 independent runs and plot the means, upper and lower quartile, as well as outliers using box plots. In addition to the derived optimal mutation probabilities for the empirical cost model (Figure 3) and the optimal mutation probability $\approx 1.59362/n$ for the uniform cost model, we consider the most recommended standard choice $1/n$ and several smaller and larger mutation probabilities. Remember that we consider the (1+1) EA on LeadingOnes. The probability to increase the function value equals $(1-p(n))^{v_x}p(n)$ if v_x denotes the function value of the current bit string. We consider fixed mutation probabilities of the form $c(n)/n$. In most cases $c(n) = c$ is independent of n. For the optimal mutation probabilities, however, $c(n)$ actually depends on n. With mutation probability $p(n) = c(n)/n$ the expected waiting time for increasing the function value equals

$$\frac{n}{c(n)} \cdot \left(1 - \frac{c(n)}{n}\right)^{-v_x} \geq n \cdot \frac{e^{c(n)\cdot(v_x/n)}}{c(n)}.$$

Remember that at some point of time during the run we will have $v_x/n = 1 - O(1/n)$. We see that increasing $c(n)$ beyond 1 increases the expected waiting time exponentially whereas decreasing $c(n)$ below 1 increases it only linearly. Thus, we can expect much more dramatic effects when increasing the mutation probability. Thus, we consider the mutation probabilities c/n and $2^{1-c}/n$ for $c \in \{2, 3, 4, 5\}$ and expect to see a similar increase in optimization time for larger and smaller mutation probabilities. Remember that we report actual run times and *not* the number of function evaluations. In all plots we have on the x-axis the length of the bit string n and on the y-axis computation time in milliseconds.

The results for the different mutation probabilities $p(n) = c/n$ are given as box plots in a number of separate diagrams, all in Figure 4. In addition to the choices $c \in \{1/16, 1/8, 1/4, 1/2, 1, 2, 3, 4, 5\}$, the values due to Böttcher, Doerr, and Neumann [3], and the computed values from Figure 3 we present results for the mutation probability $p(n) = 1/n^2$ (equivalent to setting $c = 1/n$ in the mutation probability $p(n) = c/n$). This very small mutation probability is motivated in the following way. If we follow the reasoning that a generation that does not flip any bit can be carried out in time $\Theta(1)$ and other generations require time $\Theta(n)$ we could assign cost 1 to generations without flipping bits and cost n to other generations. Since increasing the function value has always probability $\Theta(1/n)$ we can expect on average to perform $\Theta(n)$ generations before an improvement occurs. Since in the simple cost model that we consider now these $\Theta(n)$ generations account for a total cost of $\Theta(n^2)$ we can afford to have $\Theta(n^2)$ generations without mutating any bit without increasing the total cost asymptotically. Thus, from an asymptotic and theoretical point of view, $\Theta(1/n^2)$ are the smallest mutation probabilities that are still of optimal efficiency on LEADINGONES.

In Figure 4 we have one plot for each value of c we consider. In order to allow for some comparison in all plots the same scale is used. We notice that with all mutation probabilities the run times are very much concentrated around the mean value, the box plots are almost collapsed to this value. Moreover, we see that all mutation probabilities $p(n)$ with $1/(16n) \leq p(n) \leq 2/n$ lead roughly to the same run time behavior. This includes the two sets of mutation probabilities based on the simple cost model due to Böttcher, Doerr, and Neumann [3] and the empiric cost model developed here. It is noteworthy that smaller mutation probabilities seem to have much less a detrimental effect than larger ones. Since comparisons are difficult to make this way we plot all medians in one common diagram (Figure 5) omitting all data except for the medians for the sake of readability. We caution the reader to infer too much from tiny differences in the mean values. Too small differences are likely not to be statistically significant.

In Figure 5 we have the median run times in milliseconds for different values of c in the mutation probability $p(n) = c/n$ plotted over the length of the bit string n. We observe that the values between $c = 1/16$ and $c = 2$ form a cluster of very similar run times with $c = 1/4$ being fastest and $c = 2$ being slowest within this efficient cluster. This includes the

sets of c-values that are computed depending on n. We notice that there is indeed no advantage for neither of them. If at all, smaller mutation probabilities are to be preferred and the standard choice, $p(n) = 1/n$ does pretty well, too. It is worth mentioning that most small mutation probabilities do remarkably well. With larger mutation probabilities, things start to change. When increasing the mutation probability beyond $2/n$ run time increases considerably as can be seen in the plots for $p(n) = c/n$ for $c \in \{3, 4, 5, 1/n\}$. In particular, the theoretically smallest efficient mutation probability $p(n) = 1/n^2$ turns out to be not efficient at all. Moreover, we point out that with respect to actual run time the result by Böttcher, Doerr, and Neumann [3] points in exactly the wrong direction. For LEADINGONES, increasing the mutation probability above the standard choice $p(n) = 1/n$ is a particularly bad idea. Decreasing it is a by far safer choice. The good news is that performance of the (1+1) EA is quite robust with respect to changes in the mutation probability. The actual run time is not greatly affected as long as some care is taken. Only the extremely small mutation probability $p(n) = 1/n^2$ (corresponding to $c = 1/n$) yields a really bad performance. Given the efficient implementation of mutations it is not surprising that smaller mutation probabilities hurt less than larger ones. Note, however, that all these findings apply to LEADINGONES only, a function where mutations of single bits are sufficient (and even optimal) for optimization. Thus, in the following section, we consider two more example functions where we relax these requirements in two steps.

5. OTHER FITNESS FUNCTIONS

All results derived here (as well as in [3]) apply to the (1+1) EA on LEADINGONES, only. Of course, LEADINGONES is a very special function that has a structure that allows for this kind of very precise analysis. It is interesting to find out if the findings for LEADINGONES apply to other functions, too, even if the analytical proofs do not carry over. We restrict our attention in the following to two other well known example functions. Both share with LEADINGONES that a single function evaluation is not a complex operation and, thus, the average times for single function evaluations are similar.

The first function we consider here is called ONEMAX and it is probably the best known function in the community concerned with the analysis of evolutionary algorithms. The function value equals the number of bits set to 1. The run time for an evaluation of ONEMAX is slightly larger than for LEADINGONES. One needs to see all n bits in order to count the number of 1-bits. For computing LEADINGONES(x), it suffices to look at the first LEADINGONES(x) + 1 bits, i.e., stop at the left-most 0-bit.

DEFINITION 8. *For $n \in \mathbb{N}$, $x = x[1]x[2]\cdots x[n] \in \{0,1\}^n$, the function* ONEMAX: $\{0,1\}^n \rightarrow \mathbb{R}$ *is defined by* ONEMAX(x) $= \sum\limits_{i=1}^{n} x[i]$.

The function ONEMAX shares with LEADINGONES the property that mutations of single bits are sufficient to find the optimum efficiently. The expected number of function evaluations is $\Theta(n \log n)$ for any mutation probability $p(n) = c/n$ where $c \in \mathbb{R}_0^+$ is a constant. We perform the same experiments for the same values of c as we did for LEADINGONES

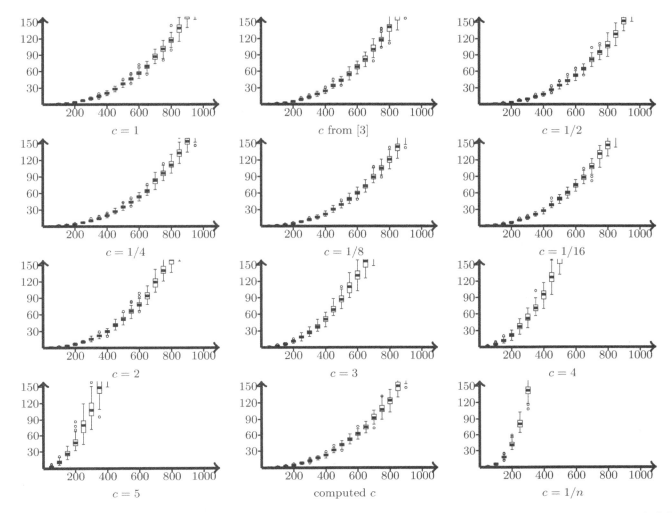

Figure 4: Run times of the (1+1) EA for LeadingOnes **for different values of c in the mutation probability $p(n) = c/n$, averaged over 100 runs. The plots show run times in milliseconds over n.**

and report them in the same way. The single plots or each mutation probability also containing statistical information about the 100 runs in form of box plots are given in Figure 6.

The first striking difference to LeadingOnes is the clearly increased variance and the larger number of outliers. Both could be expected as it is well known that the run time for LeadingOnes is very much concentrated around the expected value [5]. For OneMax, this is not the case in this extreme way. The other plots look roughly similar to the corresponding plots for LeadingOnes (but with smaller overall run times, of course). In order to take a closer look we again consider a plot that contains the median values, only (Figure 7).

Similar to the results for LeadingOnes, the mutation probabilities $p(n) = c/n$ with $1/16 \leq c \leq 2$ form a band of good performance. Within this, again, differentiation makes hardly any sense. We see again the tendency that decreasing the mutation probability below $1/n$ hurts less than increasing it beyond $1/n$. And, again, the standard choice $p(n) = 1/n$ leads to good performance. A noteworthy difference in comparison to LeadingOnes is the performance when the mutation probability $p(n) = 1/n^2$ (cor-

responding to $c = 1/n$) is employed. It is comparable in performance to setting $c = 3$ and thus much more efficient then it is for LeadingOnes. We conclude that even very small mutation probabilities like $p(n) = 1/n^2$ (where with probability $(1 - 1/n^2)^n \approx e^{-1/n} \approx 1 - 1/n$ no bit flips at all) may lead to efficient optimization since generations without mutating bits are computationally cheap and small mutation probabilities increase the probability of single bit mutations and decrease the probability of mutations where several bits flip simultaneously. For OneMax, this is favorable. One may speculate that if the simultaneous mutation of some bits is needed things change. In order to investigate that we consider a third example function, Jump$_k$ [5].

DEFINITION 9. *For $n \in \mathbb{N}$, $x = x[1]x[2]\cdots x[n] \in \{0,1\}^n$, $k \in \{1, 2, \ldots, n\}$, the function* Jump$_k \colon \{0,1\}^n \to \mathbb{R}$ *is defined by*

$$\text{Jump}_k(x) = \begin{cases} n - \sum\limits_{i=1}^{n} x[i] & \text{if } n - k < \sum\limits_{i=1}^{n} x[i] < n, \\ k + \sum\limits_{i=1}^{n} x[i] & \text{otherwise.} \end{cases}$$

Typically, one considers Jump$_k$ for small values of k. In these cases the function is very similar to OneMax. Only

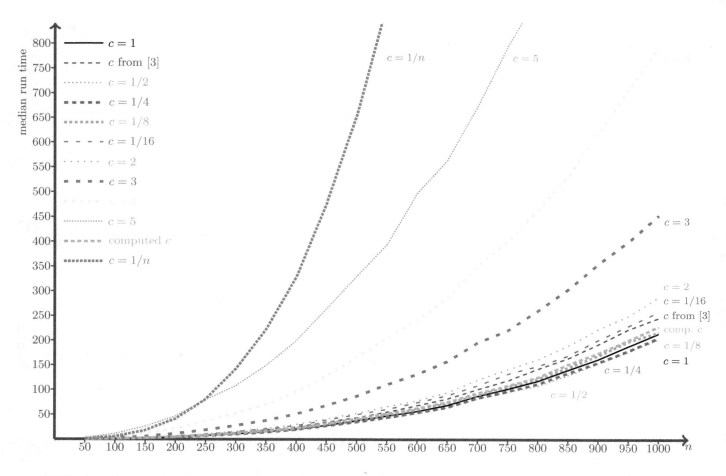

Figure 5: Median run times of the (1+1) EA for LeadingOnes **for different values of c in the mutation probability $p(n) = c/n$, averaged over 100 runs. The plots show run times in milliseconds over n.**

if the number of 1-bits is between $n-k$ and n the function value is very small. Thus, bit strings with exactly $n-k$ 1-bits are easy to locate. From there a direct jump to the unique global optimum, the all ones bit string, is needed. For the (1+1) EA with mutation probability $p(n) = 1/n$ this dominates the expected number of function evaluation that is $\Theta(n^k + n \log n)$ for all $k \in \{1, 2, \ldots, n\}$ [5].

We set $k = 2$ and consider Jump$_2$ here, only. With this setting, for the (1+1) EA with mutation probability $p(n) = 1/n$, the expected number of function evaluations needed and sufficient for optimization of Jump$_2$ equals $\Theta(n^2)$ and is thus asymptotically equal to LeadingOnes. However, a run of the (1+1) EA on Jump$_2$ will be similar to a run on OneMax. Only if some x with OneMax$(x) = n - 2$ is reached things change. At that point a mutation of the two remaining 0-bits is needed to find the global optimum. If mutation probability $p(n)$ is used, this mutation has probability $p(n)^2(1 - p(n))^{n-2}$. The reciprocal of this mutation probability is the expected waiting time for this mutation and dominates the expected run time. This term becomes minimal for $p(n) = 2/(n-2)$. Thus, we should expect to see good performance when using mutation probability $p(n) = 2/n$, in particular since this mutation probability does not slow down the (1+1) EA on the OneMax-part of the function too much. For the very small mutation probability $p(n) = 1/n^2$ (corresponding to $c = 1/n$) the expected waiting time be-

comes $\approx n^4$ and we can expect to see dramatically increased optimization times. As we did for the other two functions we first present the run times together with some statistics in separate plots (see Figure 8).

Things look considerably different for Jump$_2$ in comparison to LeadingOnes and OneMax. First of all, variance in the run times is even larger than for OneMax. This could be expected since here the run time largely depends on the waiting time for one single event. This implies a much larger variation in comparison to LeadingOnes and OneMax, where the run time is the sum of the waiting times for many such mostly independent events. Second, already in these small plots we can recognize a much increased run time when the mutation probability is decreased. Already for $p(n) = 1/(4n)$ (corresponding to $c = 1/4$) the run times seem to be clearly larger. We consider this in some more detail in Figure 9 where only the medians are plotted.

We notice that setting the mutation probability small for Jump$_2$ is a very bad idea. The mutation probabilities corresponding to $c = 1/n$ and $c = 1/16$ are clearly the two worst choices considered. For the mutation probabilities with $c \in \{1/2, 1/4, 1/8\}$ it is very interesting to note that they pair up with larger values: $c = 1/2$ with $c = 3$, $c = 1/4$ with $c = 4$, and $c = 1/8$ with $c = 5$. We see that even for Jump$_2$ where a mutation probability of $2/n$ seems to be indicated setting the mutation probability larger is not a good

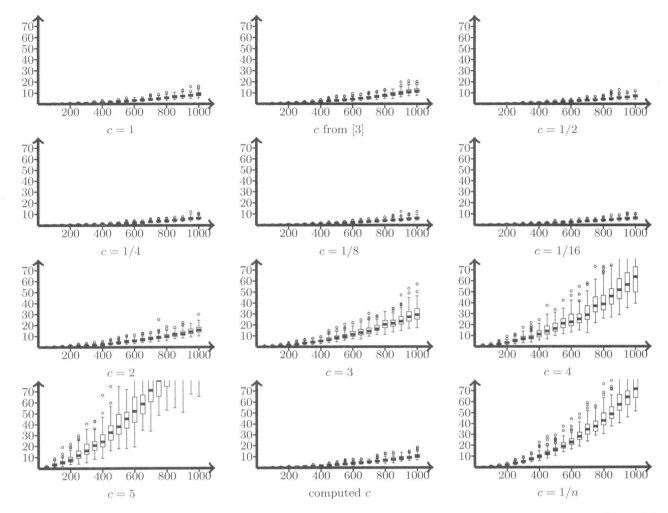

Figure 6: Run times of the (1+1) EA for OneMax for different values of c in the mutation probability $p(n) = c/n$, averaged over 100 runs. The plots show run times in milliseconds over n.

idea. Thus, increasing the mutation probabilities seems to be in general more dangerous with respect to the run time of the (1+1) EA than decreasing them. Considering the other mutation probabilities we see no clear advantage for any of them. In particular, the choice $p(n) = 2/n$ is not superior. Taking into account what we have learned this is easy to explain. Setting the mutation probability slightly smaller than $2/n$ decreases the probability of mutating more than two bits (expensive mutations that are likely to be useless) while slightly increasing the probability for mutations mutating single bits (also expensive, but useful in the OneMax-phase of the optimization) and for mutations mutating no bits at all (cheap mutations).

6. CONCLUSIONS

We studied the actual run times of a simple evolutionary algorithm, the (1+1) EA, on three example functions. Studying the actual run times is different from studying the expected number of function evaluations, a common measure in theoretical studies. While being inspired and motivated by theoretical research our study is a step to bridge the gap between theory and practice. Clearly, practitioners

care more about wall clock time than they care about the number of function evaluations.

Theoretical research most often yields asymptotic results that give valid insights in the performance of the considered evolutionary algorithm on some level but not in arbitrary detail. When theoretical studies try to overcome this limitation and aim at becoming more precise they may arrive at precise results that turn out to be misleading instead of helpful. We demonstrated this exemplarily by re-considering a theoretical analysis of the (1+1) EA on LeadingOnes recently presented by Böttcher, Doerr, and Neumann [3].

When aiming at more precise results one has to keep track of what really matters to people interested in evolutionary algorithms. Most often these people are practitioners trying to solve a concrete problem with evolutionary algorithms and their main concern in addition to the quality of the solution is wall clock time. When aiming at making sensible and correct statements about the actual run time of an evolutionary algorithm its concrete implementation needs to be taken into account and implementation details matter. We considered a 'normal' implementation in C, neither naive nor sophisticated. Combining empirical research and analytical

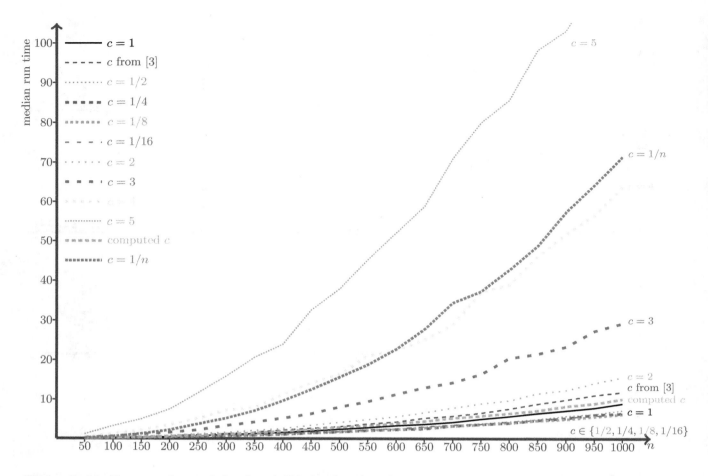

Figure 7: Median run times of the (1+1) EA for OneMax for different values of c in the mutation probability $p(n) = c/n$, averaged over 100 runs. The plots show run times in milliseconds over n.

studies we could gain further insight in the actual run time behavior of the (1+1) EA with different mutation probabilities and derive some ideas about how mutation probabilities should be set. In particular, given that in a sensible implementation mutations that do not flip any bit come cheaper than mutations that do it makes sense to set the mutation probability slightly smaller than one would do otherwise.

This approach that combines analysis of algorithms with empirical findings is similar in spirit to algorithm engineering. We believe that following this approach can enhance, strengthen, and stretch the field of evolutionary computation theory in the same way algorithm engineering did with classical algorithmics.

Even with respect to the (1+1) EA and LeadingOnes by far not all questions are answered. In particular, we do not contribute an analysis of the choice of mutation probability that outperforms other choices with respect to actual average run time. Our model suggests optimal run times for mutation probabilities of approximately $1.3/n$ and does not show that much smaller mutation probabilities like $.25/n$ may be superior. One may speculate that our model that assigns cost 1 to a generation without flipping any bit and cost r to other generations is still too coarse. We derived values for r empirically by measuring the average times u and v for these two kinds of generations and used $r = u/v$. The average times are not independent of the mutation proba-

bility. If the mutation probability is larger than $1/n$ it becomes more likely to flip several bits in one mutation. This increases the cost of a single generation with mutation. On the other hand, setting the mutation probability smaller decreases the cost of these generations but also decreases the average cost of generations that do not flip any bit since in a sequence of such generations in all but the first generations of this sequence no random experiment is carried out at all. Our relative cost measure $r = u/v$ cannot distinguish between mutation probabilities p_1 and p_2 where p_1 leads to average costs u and v while p_2 leads to average costs uw and vw since the quotients u/v and $(uw)/(vw)$ are equal. Thus, one may speculate that taking u and v into account may improve the results. We tested this hypothesis for $p(n) = .25/n$ (not reported here due to space restrictions) and found no recognizable improvement. It is an open problem to enhance the cost model to better reflect the actual average run time implied by different mutation probabilities.

One may wonder how general the very specific results presented here are. In short, the results themselves are not general. But this paper is not about the specific results but about a method of research. This method of research is general and applicable in almost all areas of analysis of randomized search heuristics. By means of a concrete example we investigated the topic of cost models in the analysis of evolutionary algorithms. We demonstrated the limita-

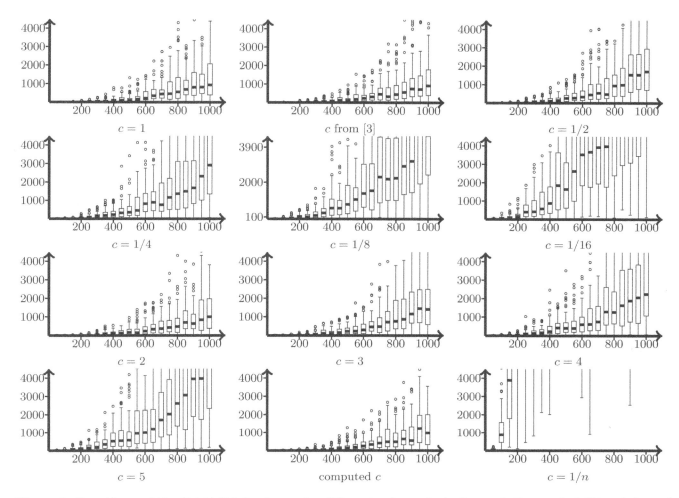

Figure 8: Run times of the (1+1) EA for JUMP₂ for different values of c in the mutation probability $p(n) = c/n$, averaged over 100 runs. The plots show run times in milliseconds over n.

tions of counting function evaluations when aiming at very precise results. More importantly, we demonstrated that developing an appropriate cost model requires incorporating empirical data about the actual implementation if one wants to obtain analytical results that are also meaningful in practice. Such an approach that adds empirical to theoretical analysis is similar in spirit to algorithm engineering. It brings the theory of randomized search heuristics closer to practice and narrows the gap between theory and practice. This makes theoretical results and the theory of randomized search heuristics more practically relevant.

Acknowledgments

This material is based in part upon works supported by the Science Foundation Ireland under Grant No. 07/SK/I1205.

7. REFERENCES

[1] A. Auger and B. Doerr. *Theory of Randomized Search Heuristics*. World Scientific Review, 2011. To appear.

[2] T. Bartz-Beielstein. *Experimental Research in Evolutionary Computation – The New Experimentalism*. Springer, 2006.

[3] S. Böttcher, B. Doerr, and F. Neumann. Optimal fixed and adaptive mutation rates for the LeadingOnes problem. In R. Schaefer, C. Cotta, J. Kołodziej, and G. Rudolph, editors, *Proceedings of the 11th International Conference on Parallel Problem Solving From Nature (PPSN XI)*, volume 6238 of *LNCS*, pages 1–10. Springer, 2010.

[4] T. H. Cormen, C. E. Leiserson, R. L. Rivest, and C. Stein. *Introduction to Algorithms*. MIT Press, 2001. 2nd edition.

[5] S. Droste, T. Jansen, and I. Wegener. On the analysis of the (1+1) evolutionary algorithm. *Theoretical Computer Science*, 276:51–81, 2002.

[6] T. Jansen and D. Sudholt. Analysis of an asymmetric mutation operator. *Evolutionary Computation*, 18(1):1–26, 2010.

[7] T. Jansen and I. Wegener. On the choice of the mutation probability for the (1+1) EA. In M. Schoenauer, K. Deb, G. Rudolph, X. Yao, E. Lutton, J. J. Merelo, and H.-P. Schwefel, editors, *Proceedings of the 6th International Conference on Parallel Problem Solving From Nature (PPSN VI)*, volume 1917 of *LNCS*, pages 89–98. Springer, 2000.

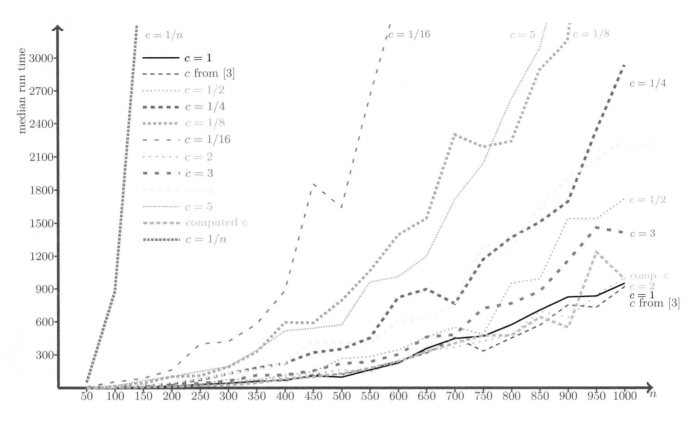

Figure 9: Median run times of the (1+1) EA for JUMP$_2$ for different values of c in the mutation probability $p(n) = c/n$, averaged over 100 runs. The plots show run times in milliseconds over n.

[8] T. Jansen and I. Wegener. On the analysis of a dynamic evolutionary algorithm. *Journal of Discrete Algorithms*, 4(1):181–199, 2005.

[9] D. Knuth. *The Art of Computer Programming. Volume II*. Addison-Wesley, 1969.

[10] F. Neumann and C. Witt. *Bioinspired Computation in Combinatorial Optimization - Algorithms and Their Computational Complexity*. Natural Computing Series. Springer, 2010.

[11] P. S. Oliveto, J. He, and X. Yao. Time complexity of evolutionary algorithms for combinatorial optimization: A decade of results. *International Journal of Automation and Computing*, 4(3):281–293, 2007.

[12] G. Rudolph. *Convergence Properties of Evolutionary Algorithms*. Kovac, 1997.

[13] G. Rudolph and J. Ziegenhirt. Computation time of evolutionary operators. In T. Bäck, D. B. Fogel, and Z. Michalewicz, editors, *Handbook of Evolutionary Computation*, pages E2.2:1–4. CRC Press, 1997.

[14] P. Sanders. Algorithm engineering – an attempt at a definition. In S. Albers, H. Alt, and S. Näher, editors, *Efficient Algorithms – Essays Dedicated to Kurt Mehlhorn on the Occasion of His 60th Birthday*, volume 5760 of *LNCS*, pages 321–340. Springer, 2009.

[15] I. Wegener. Methods for the analysis of evolutionary algorithms on pseudo-Boolean functions. In R. Sarker, X. Yao, and M. Mohammadian, editors, *Evolutionary Optimization*, pages 349–369. Kluwer, 2002.

On the Behaviour of the $(1, \lambda)$-ES for a Simple Constrained Problem

Dirk V. Arnold
Faculty of Computer Science
Dalhousie University
Halifax, Nova Scotia
Canada B3H 1W5
dirk@cs.dal.ca

ABSTRACT

We study the behaviour of the $(1, \lambda)$-ES for a linear problem with a single linear constraint. The algorithm produces offspring until λ feasible candidate solutions have been generated and selects the best of those as the next generation's parent. Integral expressions that describe the strategy's one-generation behaviour are developed and used in a simple zeroth order model for the steady state of the strategy. Implications for the performance of cumulative step size adaptation are discussed and a comparison with the $(1 + 1)$-ES is drawn.

Categories and Subject Descriptors

I.2.8 [**Problem Solving, Control Methods and Search**]; G.1.6 [**Optimization**]: Constrained Optimization

General Terms

Algorithms, Performance

Keywords

Constrained optimisation, evolution strategy

1. INTRODUCTION

Constraint handling techniques used in evolutionary algorithms include penalty approaches, repair mechanisms, and strategies based on ideas from multi-objective optimisation. A recent survey of techniques has been compiled by Coello Coello [10]. Techniques used in the context of evolution strategies include those described by Oyman et al. [17], Runarsson and Yao [20, 21], Mezura-Montes and Coello Coello [15], and Kramer and Schwefel [12]. The approaches differ with respect to the assumptions they make with regard to the nature of the constraints. While some assume only the existence of a black-box function that can be used to determine whether a solution is feasible or not, others depend on geometrical properties of the constraints that make it possible to project infeasible candidate solutions onto the boundary of the feasible region. Some algorithms assume that objective function values can be computed even for infeasible solutions. Many of the approaches that have been proposed depend sensitively on parameters that need to be set appropriately in order to be able to approach an optimum located at the boundary of the feasible region, and a host of adaptive variants has been proposed. See [14] and the references therein for examples.

Despite the existence of a multitude of constraint handling mechanisms used in connection with evolutionary algorithms, there is little analytically based knowledge with regard to their properties. The performance of such techniques is commonly evaluated using large and diverse sets of test functions, such as the benchmark set compiled for the *CEC 2010 Special Session on Constrained Real-Parameter Optimization* [13]. The evaluation criteria used are often relatively complex and involve various parameters, such as the number of function evaluations allowed and different quality thresholds. As a result, the observed outcomes are not always easy to interpret, and if a mechanism fails it often remains unclear why.

In contrast, in the realm of unconstrained optimisation there is a significant body of work employing simple test functions that aims at arriving at a better understanding of the behaviour of evolution strategies. See [2, 5, 8, 19] for examples and further references. Starting from the simplest non-trivial strategies and optimisation environments, the complexity of the scenarios studied has increased over time, and today results are available for adaptive strategies and problems with various degrees of ill-conditioning. The approach complements observations for large and difficult test beds with results that are easy to interpret, and that reveal scaling properties and the influence of parameters on optimisation performance.

Among the sparse references on analytically based results for constrained evolutionary optimisation is the *Handbook of Evolutionary Computation* [6, page B2.4:**11f**], which lists a small number of studies that use simple test functions and derive analytical results in the realm of constrained optimisation with evolution strategies. Rechenberg [18] studies the performance of the $(1 + 1)$-ES[1] for the axis-aligned corridor model. Schwefel [22] considers the performance of the $(1, \lambda)$-ES in the same environment. Beyer [7] analyses

---

[1] See Beyer and Schwefel [9] for an overview of evolution strategy terminology.

the performance of the $(1+1)$-ES for a constrained discus-like function. All of those have in common that the normal vectors of the constraint planes are oriented such that they are perpendicular to the gradient vector of the objective function. First analytically based results for problems that do not have that specific property have been derived by Arnold and Brauer [4], who have studied the behaviour of the $(1+1)$-ES for a simple linear problem with a single linear constraint of general orientation. They describe the distance of the search point from the constraint plane using a Markov chain approach and investigate the limit behaviour of the chain using two simple probabilistic models.

An issue of particular significance in the context of real-valued evolutionary optimisation is that of step size adaptation. In order to achieve good performance, the mutation strength of an evolution strategy needs to be adapted in the course of the search. For a linear problem with a single linear constraint, the optimal long-term strategy is to increase the step size of the algorithm. The mutation strength of the $(1+1)$-ES is typically adapted using the 1/5th success rule [18]. Schwefel [23, page 116f] points out that using that rule, the presence of constraints may lead to the step size being reduced in situations where the angle between the gradient direction and the normal vector of the active constraint is small, leading to convergence to a non-singular point. A quantitative investigation of this behaviour using the above mentioned models has been presented in [4]. Non-elitist evolution strategies, such as variants of the $(\mu/\rho, \lambda)$-ES use other forms of step size adaptation, none of which have been studied analytically for constrained problems other than those with a very specific orientation of the constraint plane.

The goal of this paper is to study the behaviour of the $(1, \lambda)$-ES for the linear, constrained environment considered in [4]. As a constraint handling mechanism, the strategy produces offspring until λ feasible candidate solutions have been generated. This approach is among the simplest possible, and its only underlying assumption is that the feasibility of a candidate solution can be determined.

The remainder of this paper is organised as follows. Section 2 briefly formalises the algorithm and problem and introduces notational conventions used throughout the paper. Section 3 considers the single-step behaviour of the strategy and derives probability distributions that characterise the offspring candidate solutions as well as an expression for the progress rate of the strategy. Section 4 investigates the multi-step limit behaviour of the strategy for a fixed step size employing a simple zeroth-order model for the distribution of distances from the constraint plane. A comparison with the behaviour of the $(1+1)$-ES is also presented. Section 5 considers cumulative step size adaptation. Section 6 concludes with a brief discussion and goals of future research.

2. PROBLEM AND ALGORITHM

Throughout this paper, we consider the problem of maximising[2] a linear function $f : \mathbb{R}^N \to \mathbb{R}$, $N \geq 2$, with a single linear constraint. We assume that the gradient vector of the objective function forms an acute angle with the normal vector of the constraint plane. Without loss of generality, we

---

[2]Strictly speaking, the task is one of amelioration rather than maximisation, as a finite maximum does not exist. We do not make that distinction here.

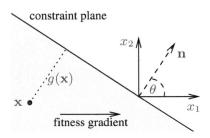

Figure 1: Linear objective function with a single linear constraint. The subspace spanned by the x_1- and x_2-axes is shown. The shaded area is the feasible region. The parental candidate solution x of the $(1, \lambda)$-ES is at a distance $g(\mathbf{x})$ from the constraint plane.

choose a Euclidean coordinate system with its origin located on the constraint plane, and with its axes oriented such that the x_1-axis coincides with the gradient direction ∇f, and the x_2-axis lies in the two-dimensional plane spanned by the gradient vector and the normal vector of the constraint plane. The angle between those two vectors is denoted by θ as illustrated in Fig. 1, and it is referred to as the constraint angle. Constraint angles of interest are in $(0, \pi/2)$. The unit normal vector of the constraint plane expressed in the chosen coordinate system is $\mathbf{n} = \langle \cos\theta, \sin\theta, 0, \ldots, 0 \rangle$. The signed distance of a point $\mathbf{x} = \langle x_1, x_2, \ldots, x_N \rangle \in \mathbb{R}^N$ from the constraint plane is thus $g(\mathbf{x}) = -\mathbf{n} \cdot \mathbf{x} = -x_1 \cos\theta - x_2 \sin\theta$, resulting in the optimisation problem

$$\text{maximise} \quad f(\mathbf{x}) = cx_1 \quad \text{subject to} \quad g(\mathbf{x}) \geq 0$$

for some constant $c > 0$. Notice that due to the choice of coordinate system, variables $x_3, x_4, \ldots, x_N$ enter neither the objective function nor the constraint inequality.

Assuming a feasible initial candidate solution $\mathbf{x} \in \mathbb{R}^N$, the $(1, \lambda)$-ES iteratively generates a sequence of further candidate solutions by performing the following four steps per iteration:

1. Generate λ feasible offspring candidate solutions $\mathbf{x}^{(i)} = \mathbf{x} + \sigma \mathbf{z}^{(i)}$, $i = 1, \ldots, \lambda$, where the $\mathbf{z}^{(i)}$ are independent, identically distributed vectors drawn from an N-dimensional normal distribution with mean zero and unit covariance matrix. Vectors $\mathbf{z}^{(i)}$ are referred to as mutation vectors, and step size parameter σ is referred to as the mutation strength.

2. Evaluate the $\mathbf{x}^{(i)}$ for $i = 1, \ldots, \lambda$ and let $\hat{\mathbf{z}}$ denote the mutation vector of the offspring candidate solution with the largest objective function value.

3. Update the parental candidate solution according to $\mathbf{x} \leftarrow \mathbf{x} + \sigma \hat{\mathbf{z}}$.

4. Modify the mutation strength.

Notice that Step 1 may require generating more than λ offspring as infeasible candidate solutions are rejected immediately. It will become clear in Section 3 that on average, no more than 2λ offspring need to be sampled per iteration.

The probability of a candidate solution being feasible as well as the expected improvement in objective function value per iteration depend on the distance $g(\mathbf{x})$ of the parental

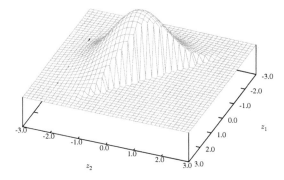

Figure 2: Joint probability density $p_{1,2}(x,y)$ of the z_1 and z_2-components of feasible offspring for $\delta = 0.5$ and $\theta = \pi/4$.

candidate solution from the constraint plane. Simple trigonometry reveals that the evolution of the normalised distance $\delta = g(\mathbf{x})/\sigma$ is described by

$$\delta^{(t+1)} = \delta^{(t)} - \hat{z}_1 \cos\theta - \hat{z}_2 \sin\theta \qquad (1)$$

where superscripts on δ indicate time and $\hat{z}_1$ and $\hat{z}_2$ are the z_1 and z_2-components of vector $\hat{\mathbf{z}} = \langle \hat{z}_1, \hat{z}_2, \dots, \hat{z}_N \rangle$. As a performance measure, we consider the expected progress

$$\varphi = \sigma \mathrm{E}\left[\hat{z}_1\right] \qquad (2)$$

in the direction of the fitness gradient.

3. SINGLE-STEP BEHAVIOUR

This section first characterises the distribution of feasible offspring. It then considers the expected step made by the strategy in a single iteration of the algorithm.

3.1 Distribution of Feasible Offspring

Due to the process of sampling offspring candidate solutions described in Section 2, the joint probability density function of the z_1 and z_2-components of the offspring is proportional to the standard bivariate Gaussian density in the feasible region, and it is zero outside. Computing the integral of the bivariate Gaussian density over the feasible region yields the probability

$$P_{\text{feasible}} = \frac{1}{2\pi} \int_{-\infty}^{\infty} \int_{-\infty}^{(\delta - x\cos\theta)/\sin\theta} e^{-\frac{1}{2}(x^2+y^2)} \mathrm{d}y\,\mathrm{d}x$$
$$= \frac{1}{\sqrt{2\pi}} \int_{-\infty}^{\infty} e^{-\frac{1}{2}x^2} \Phi\left(\frac{\delta - x\cos\theta}{\sin\theta}\right) \mathrm{d}x$$
$$= \Phi(\delta)$$

for a randomly sampled candidate solution to be feasible. Here, $\Phi(x) = (1 + \mathrm{erf}(x/\sqrt{2}))/2$ denotes the cumulative distribution function of the standard normal distribution and the upper bound of the inner integral results from the constraint that the normalised distance from the constraint plane must be non-negative and Eq. (1). The last equality follows from an identity proven in [1, p. 117]. The number of offspring that need to be generated until one is feasible follows a geometric distribution. As for $\delta \geq 0$ (i.e., the parental solution being feasible) the probability of a random offspring candidate solution being feasible is at least

one half, on average no more than two candidate solutions need to be sampled to generate a feasible offspring.

With P_{feasible} as normalisation constant it follows

$$p_{1,2}(x,y) = \begin{cases} \dfrac{e^{-\frac{1}{2}(x^2+y^2)}}{2\pi\Phi(\delta)} & \text{if } \delta \geq x\cos\theta + y\sin\theta \\ 0 & \text{otherwise} \end{cases} \qquad (3)$$

for the joint density of the z_1 and z_2-components of feasible mutation vectors. The shape of that joint density is illustrated in Fig. 2.

The marginal density of the z_1-components of feasible mutation vectors is

$$p_1(x) = \int_{-\infty}^{\infty} p_{1,2}(x,y)\mathrm{d}y$$
$$= \frac{1}{2\pi\Phi(\delta)} e^{-\frac{1}{2}x^2} \int_{-\infty}^{(\delta - x\cos\theta)/\sin\theta} e^{-\frac{1}{2}y^2} \mathrm{d}y$$
$$= \frac{1}{\sqrt{2\pi}\Phi(\delta)} e^{-\frac{1}{2}x^2} \Phi\left(\frac{\delta - x\cos\theta}{\sin\theta}\right). \qquad (4)$$

The corresponding cumulative distribution function

$$P_1(x) = \frac{1}{\sqrt{2\pi}\Phi(\delta)} \int_{-\infty}^{x} e^{-\frac{1}{2}z^2} \Phi\left(\frac{\delta - z\cos\theta}{\sin\theta}\right) \mathrm{d}z \qquad (5)$$

cannot be expressed in closed form. The cumulants κ_k, $k \geq 1$, of the marginal distribution can be computed from the characteristic function

$$\chi(t) = \int_{-\infty}^{\infty} e^{itx} p_1(x) \mathrm{d}x$$
$$= e^{-\frac{1}{2}t^2} \frac{\Phi(\delta - it\cos\theta)}{\Phi(\delta)}$$

where i is the imaginary unit, as

$$\kappa_k = (-i)^k \left.\frac{\mathrm{d}^k}{\mathrm{d}t^k} \log(\chi(t))\right|_{t=0}.$$

The first four cumulants are given in Table 1. Mean κ_1, variance κ_2, skewness $\gamma_1 = \kappa_3/\kappa_2^{1.5}$ and kurtosis $\gamma_2 = \kappa_4/\kappa_2^2$ are plotted against the normalised distance of the parent from the constraint plane in Fig. 3. It can be seen that as δ increases, mean, skewness, and kurtosis tend to zero while the variance tends to one and the distribution of the feasible z_1-components approaches the standard normal distribution. For finite values of δ the distribution is negatively skewed, and for a given value of δ the degree of skewness increases with decreasing constraint angle. The negative values of κ_1 indicate a bias opposite to the direction of the gradient that results from the presence of the constraint.

3.2 Expected Step

The z_1-component of the mutation vector resulting in the best offspring candidate solution is the λth order statistic of the sample of feasible z_1-values. Its probability density is thus

$$\hat{p}_1(x) = \lambda p_1(x) P_1^{\lambda-1}(x). \qquad (6)$$

The expected step in the direction of the x_1-axis is

$$\mathrm{E}\left[\hat{z}_1\right] = \lambda \int_{-\infty}^{\infty} x p_1(x) P_1^{\lambda-1}(x) \mathrm{d}x. \qquad (7)$$

Table 1: Cumulants of the distribution of the z_1-components of feasible mutation vectors.

$$\kappa_1 = -\frac{\cos\theta}{\sqrt{2\pi}\,\Phi(\delta)}\mathrm{e}^{-\delta^2/2}$$

$$\kappa_2 = 1 - \frac{\cos^2\theta}{\sqrt{2\pi}\,\Phi(\delta)}\mathrm{e}^{-\delta^2/2}\left(\delta + \frac{1}{\sqrt{2\pi}\,\Phi(\delta)}\mathrm{e}^{-\delta^2/2}\right)$$

$$\kappa_3 = -\frac{\cos^3\theta}{\sqrt{2\pi}\,\Phi(\delta)}\mathrm{e}^{-\delta^2/2}\left[\delta^2 - 1 + \frac{1}{\sqrt{2\pi}\,\Phi(\delta)}\mathrm{e}^{-\delta^2/2}\left(3\delta + \frac{2}{\sqrt{2\pi}\,\Phi(\delta)}\mathrm{e}^{-\delta^2/2}\right)\right]$$

$$\kappa_4 = \frac{\cos^4\theta}{\sqrt{2\pi}\,\Phi(\delta)}\mathrm{e}^{-\delta^2/2}\left\{\delta(3-\delta^2) - \frac{1}{\sqrt{2\pi}\,\Phi(\delta)}\mathrm{e}^{-\delta^2/2}\left[7\delta^2 - 4 + \frac{6}{\sqrt{2\pi}\,\Phi(\delta)}\mathrm{e}^{-\delta^2/2}\left(2\delta + \frac{1}{\sqrt{2\pi}\,\Phi(\delta)}\mathrm{e}^{-\delta^2/2}\right)\right]\right\}$$

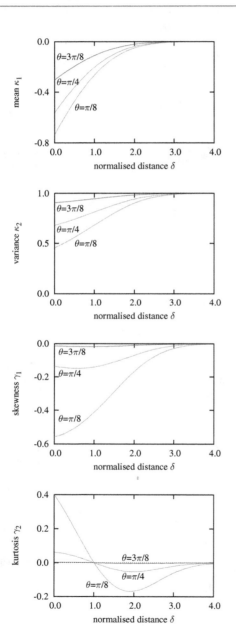

Figure 3: Mean, variance, skewness, and kurtosis of the distribution of the z_1-components of feasible mutation vectors for $\theta \in \{\pi/8, \pi/4, 3\pi/8\}$.

The expected step in the direction of the x_2-axis is

$$\mathrm{E}\left[\hat{z}_2\right] = \int_{-\infty}^{\infty}\int_{-\infty}^{\infty} y\hat{p}_1(x)p_2(y|z_1 = x)\mathrm{d}y\,\mathrm{d}x$$

where $p_2(y|z_1 = x) = p_{1,2}(x,y)/p_1(x)$ is the density of the z_2-components of the feasible mutation vectors conditional on the z_1-component assuming a value of x. Using Eqs. (3), (4), and (6) yields

$$\mathrm{E}\left[\hat{z}_2\right] = \frac{\lambda}{2\pi\Phi(\delta)}\int_{-\infty}^{\infty}\mathrm{e}^{-\frac{1}{2}x^2}P_1^{\lambda-1}(x)$$
$$\int_{-\infty}^{(\delta - x\cos\theta)/\sin\theta} y\mathrm{e}^{-\frac{1}{2}y^2}\mathrm{d}y\,\mathrm{d}x. \quad (8)$$

In Appendix A the inner integral is solved and the remaining integral transformed, resulting in expression

$$\mathrm{E}\left[\hat{z}_2\right] = \tan\theta\left[\lambda\int_{-\infty}^{\infty} xp_1(x)P_1^{\lambda-1}(x)\mathrm{d}x\right.$$
$$\left. -\lambda(\lambda-1)\int_{-\infty}^{\infty} p_1^2(x)P_1^{\lambda-2}(x)\mathrm{d}x\right] \quad (9)$$

for the mean value of the z_2-component of the selected mutation vectors.

3.3 Progress Rate Approximation

Eq. (7) provides an expression that can be used to compute the strategy's progress rate defined in Eq. (2). Defining y implicitly by $\Phi(y) = P_1(x)$ yields after the change of variables

$$\varphi = \frac{\sigma\lambda}{\sqrt{2\pi}}\int_{-\infty}^{\infty} P_1^{-1}(\Phi(y))\mathrm{e}^{-\frac{1}{2}y^2}\Phi^{\lambda-1}(y)\mathrm{d}y. \quad (10)$$

Expanding $P_1^{-1}(\Phi(y))$ into a Cornish-Fisher series as described in [11] results in

$$\varphi = \frac{\sigma\lambda}{\sqrt{2\pi}}\int_{-\infty}^{\infty}\left[\kappa_1 + \sqrt{\kappa_2}\left(y + \frac{\gamma_1}{3!}\mathrm{He}_2(y)\right.\right.$$
$$\left.\left. +\frac{\gamma_2}{4!}\mathrm{He}_3(y) + \dots\right)\right]\mathrm{e}^{-\frac{1}{2}y^2}\Phi^{\lambda-1}(y)\mathrm{d}y$$

where the $\mathrm{He}_k(\cdot)$ are the Hermite polynomials and the cumulants are those of the distribution of feasible z_1-values given in Table 1. Using the "progress coefficients"

$$d_{1,\lambda}^{(k)} = \frac{\lambda}{\sqrt{2\pi}}\int_{-\infty}^{\infty} y^k\mathrm{e}^{-\frac{1}{2}y^2}\Phi^{\lambda-1}(y)\mathrm{d}y$$

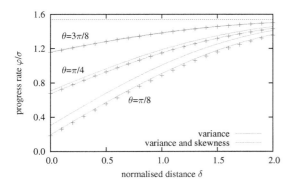

Figure 4: **Progress rate** φ **divided by the mutation strength** σ **plotted against the normalised distance** δ **of the parent from the constraint plane for** $\lambda = 10$ **and** $\theta \in \{\pi/8, \pi/4, 3\pi/8\}$.

introduced by Beyer [8] the progress rate can thus be approximated as

$$\varphi = \sigma \left[\kappa_1 + \sqrt{\kappa_2} \left(d_{1,\lambda}^{(1)} + \frac{\gamma_1}{3!} (d_{1,\lambda}^{(2)} - 1) \right. \right.$$
$$\left. \left. + \frac{\gamma_2}{4!} (d_{1,\lambda}^{(3)} - 3d_{1,\lambda}^{(1)}) + \dots \right) \right]. \quad (11)$$

Fig. 4 shows the progress rate φ normalised by division by the mutation strength plotted against the normalised distance δ of the parental candidate solution from the constraint plane. The curves show results from Eq. (11) using either the variance only or variance and skewness. Curves that additionally use the kurtosis would be almost identical to the latter and are not shown. It can be seen that with increasing distance from the constraint plane the progress rate tends to the value $d_{1,\lambda}^{(1)}$ (represented by a dotted line in the figure) that it would assume in the absence of the constraint. The points mark measurements from Monte Carlo experiments in which the algorithm described in Section 2 is iterated for 10^6 time steps with the distance from the constraint plane artificially held constant. The quality of the approximation provided by Eq. (11) visibly deteriorates with decreasing constraint angle. This is unsurprising as smaller values of θ result in distributions farther from a Gaussian (compare Fig. 3). Presumably, considering further terms in the Cornish Fisher expansion that include higher order powers of the skewness would result in a better approximation.

4. STEADY STATE BEHAVIOUR

All of the results that have been derived thus far consider a single time step only and are conditional on the distance of the parental candidate solution from the constraint plane. Assuming for now that the mutation strength σ is held constant, when the algorithm is iterated, the distribution of δ-values tends to a stationary limit distribution. As a zeroth order approximation, let us assume that the limit distribution is well characterised by its mean, and that higher order moments can be neglected. That is, we model the limit distribution as a (shifted) Dirac delta function and compute the mode of the distribution by requiring that

$$\mathrm{E}\left[\delta^{(t+1)}\right] = \delta^{(t)}. \quad (12)$$

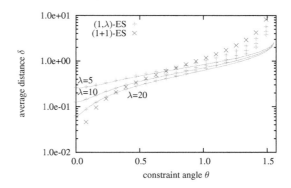

Figure 5: **Average normalised distance** δ **from the constraint plane plotted against the constraint angle** θ **for** $\lambda \in \{5, 10, 20\}$.

According to Eq. (1), the expected normalised distance of the parental solution from the constraint plane at iteration $t + 1$ is

$$\mathrm{E}\left[\delta^{(t+1)}\right] = \delta^{(t)} - \mathrm{E}\left[\hat{z}_1\right]\cos\theta - \mathrm{E}\left[\hat{z}_2\right]\sin\theta.$$

Using Eqs. (7) and (9) in Eq. (12) yields after simplification

$$\int_{-\infty}^{\infty} x p_1(x) P_1^{\lambda-1}(x)\mathrm{d}x$$
$$= \sin^2\theta(\lambda - 1)\int_{-\infty}^{\infty} p_1^2(x) P_1^{\lambda-2}(x)\mathrm{d}x. \quad (13)$$

The curves in Fig. 5 show the result of numerically solving Eq. (13) for δ. The points mark measurements obtained by averaging over 10^6 steps of the strategy described in Section 2. Also shown for comparison are corresponding measurements made in runs of the $(1 + 1)$-ES. It can be seen from the figure that the average distance from the constraint plane decreases with increasing λ, and that it increases with increasing constraint angle θ. Interestingly, the $(1 + 1)$-ES tracks the constraint plane more closely than the $(1, 20)$-ES for small constraint angles while it tracks it at a greater distance than the $(1, 5)$-ES for larger values of θ.

The quality of the zeroth order approximation provided by the Dirac model appears visually good for small constraint angles, but it deteriorates markedly with increasing θ. That is, in situations where the strategy closely tracks the constraint plane the behaviour of the algorithm is quite well described by the model that does not include variations of that distance. As the constraint angle becomes less acute and the strategy tracks the constraint plane at a greater distance, variations in that distance become significant and the Dirac model is inappropriate. Presumably, using an exponential model for the distribution of distances as used in [4] for the $(1+1)$-ES would allow deriving more accurate values.

The curves in Fig. 6 have been obtained by using the δ-value predicted by the Dirac model from Eq. (12) in Eq. (7) in order to compute the progress rate per offspring of the $(1, \lambda)$-ES. It can be seen that the progress rate increases with increasing θ. As in the unconstrained limit case, which is reflected at the right hand edge of the figure, the progress rate per offspring is higher for $\lambda = 5$ than for $\lambda = 10$ and $\lambda = 20$ for all but the smallest constraint angles, and the measurements for the $(1 + 1)$-ES indicate that the elitist

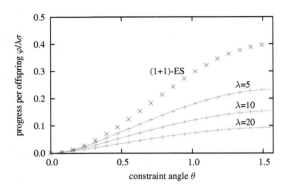

Figure 6: Progress per offspring φ/λ divided by the mutation strength σ plotted against the constraint angle θ for $\lambda \in \{5, 10, 20\}$.

strategy is more efficient for the same value of σ than any of the non-elitist strategies shown. Somewhat surprisingly, the quality of the approximation of the progress rate provided by the Dirac model is visually good for the entire range of constraint angles. While for larger values of θ, Fig. (5) has shown that the approximation of the average value of δ is very inaccurate, the influence of the distances from the constraint plane on the progress rate becomes weaker as the slope of the curves in Fig. 4 decreases with increasing δ.

5. MUTATION STRENGTH ADAPTATION

The mutation strength of the $(1, \lambda)$-ES can be adapted using one of several mechanisms, including mutative self-adaptation, two-point adaptation, and cumulative step size adaptation. The latter mechanism has been introduced by Ostermeier et al. [16] and is popular due to its use in the CMA-ES. It has been studied for the sphere model in [1, 3], for a class of further convex quadratic functions in [2], and for ridge functions in [5]. Cumulative step size adaptation employs a search path $\mathbf{s} \in \mathbb{R}^N$ defined by $\mathbf{s}^{(0)} = \mathbf{0}$ and

$$\mathbf{s}^{(t+1)} = (1 - c)\mathbf{s}^{(t)} + \sqrt{c(2 - c)}\hat{\mathbf{z}} \quad (14)$$

that implements an exponentially fading record of past steps taken by the strategy. Constant $c \in (0, 1)$ is referred to as the cumulation parameter and determines the effective length of the memory implemented in the search path. The mutation strength is updated according to[3]

$$\sigma^{(t+1)} = \sigma^{(t)} \exp\left(c \frac{\|\mathbf{s}^{(t+1)}\|^2 - N}{2DN}\right) \quad (15)$$

where $D > 0$ is a damping constant that scales the magnitude of the updates. Clearly, the sign of $\|\mathbf{s}\|^2 - N$ determines whether the mutation strength is increased or decreased. The underlying idea is that long search paths indicate that the steps made by the strategy point predominantly in one direction and could beneficially be replaced with fewer but longer steps. Short search paths indicate that the strategy steps back and forth and that it should operate with a

---

[3]This update differs from the original prescription in that [16] adapts the mutation strength based on the length of the search path rather than on its squared length. With appropriately chosen parameters both variants often behave similarly. Basing the update of the mutation strength on the squared length of the search path simplifies the analysis.

smaller step size. The search path has a squared length of N if consecutive steps are perpendicular on average, in which case no change in mutation strength is effected.

For the linear, constrained environment considered here, the $(1, \lambda)$-ES with cumulative step size adaptation does not assume a stationary limit state. The mutation strength is either increased or decreased on average. As the progress rate of the strategy is positive and proportional to the mutation strength, increasing σ is desirable while decreasing it leads to stagnation and convergence to a non-singular point. Similarly to [1] we define the logarithmic adaptation response of the strategy as

$$\Delta_\sigma^{(t+1)} = D \log\left(\frac{\sigma^{(t+1)}}{\sigma^{(t)}}\right).$$

Rather than attempting to solve the difficult problem of examining the dynamic behaviour of the non-linear stochastic process generated by the algorithm, we consider the logarithmic adaptation response of the $(1, \lambda)$-ES operating out of a stationary state. That is, we assume that the strategy has been run with a fixed step length until time step t, where t is large, and we compute the logarithmic adaptation response at time step $t + 1$.

From Eq. (14), the search path at time step $t + 1$ is

$$\mathbf{s}^{(t+1)} = \sqrt{c(2 - c)} \sum_{j=0}^{t} (1 - c)^j \hat{\mathbf{z}}^{(t-j)}. \quad (16)$$

Its expected squared length

$$\mathrm{E}\left[\|\mathbf{s}^{(t+1)}\|^2\right] = \sum_{i=1}^{N} \mathrm{E}\left[s_i^{(t+1)2}\right]$$

can be computed from the squares

$$s_i^{(t+1)2} = c(2 - c) \sum_{j=0}^{t} (1 - c)^{2j} \hat{z}_i^{(t-j)2}$$
$$+ 2c(2 - c) \sum_{j=1}^{t} \sum_{k=0}^{j-1} (1 - c)^{j+k} \hat{z}_i^{(t-j)} \hat{z}_i^{(t-k)} \quad (17)$$

of its components. Due to the assumption that the strategy is operating out of a stationary state, the distribution of the $\hat{z}_i$ is independent of time. For brevity, we omit time superscripts and write

$$e_{i,j} = \mathrm{E}\left[\hat{z}_i^j\right]$$

for the jth moment about zero of $\hat{z}_i$. Taking the expectation of Eq. (17) and using identities

$$\sum_{j=0}^{t} a^{2j} = \frac{1 - a^{2(t+1)}}{1 - a^2}$$

and

$$\sum_{j=1}^{t} \sum_{k=0}^{j-1} a^{j+k} = \sum_{j=1}^{t} a^j \frac{1 - a^j}{1 - a}$$
$$= \frac{1}{1 - a}\left[\sum_{j=0}^{t} a^j - 1 - \sum_{j=0}^{t} a^{2j} + 1\right]$$
$$= \frac{1 - a^{t+1}}{(1 - a)^2} - \frac{1 - a^{2(t+1)}}{(1 - a)(1 - a^2)}$$

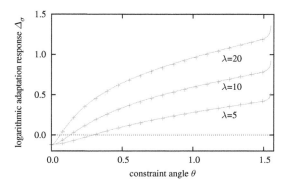

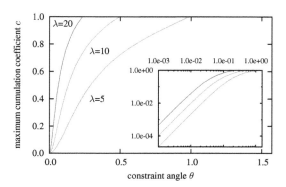

Figure 7: Logarithmic adaptation response Δ_σ plotted against the constraint angle θ for $\lambda \in \{5, 10, 20\}$ and cumulation parameter $c = 0.5$.

Figure 8: Maximum value of the cumulation parameter c for which the logarithmic adaptation response is positive plotted against the constraint angle θ for $\lambda \in \{5, 10, 20\}$. The inset shows a log-log plot of the same curves.

for the geometric series in the limit of large t yields

$$\mathrm{E}\left[s_i^{(t+1)^2}\right] = e_{i,2} + 2\frac{1-c}{c}e_{i,1}^2.$$

For $i = 3, \ldots, N$ the $\hat{z}_i$ are standard normally distributed and thus $e_{i,1} = 0$ and $e_{i,2} = 1$. As a result, from Eq. (16) it follows that

$$\mathrm{E}\left[\|\mathbf{s}\|^2 - N\right] = e_{1,2} + e_{2,2} + 2\frac{1-c}{c}\left(e_{1,1}^2 + e_{2,1}^2\right) - 2. \quad (18)$$

Notice that this result depends on the search space dimensionality only through the cumulation parameter c, which is usually set to an N-dependent value.

Expressions for $e_{1,1}$ and $e_{2,1}$ are given in Eqs. (7) and (9), respectively. It remains to compute $e_{1,2}$ and $e_{2,2}$. The former is

$$e_{1,2} = \mathrm{E}\left[\hat{z}_1^2\right] = \lambda \int_{-\infty}^{\infty} x^2 p_1(x) P_1^{\lambda-1}(x)\mathrm{d}x. \quad (19)$$

The latter equals

$$\mathrm{E}\left[\hat{z}_2^2\right] = \frac{\lambda}{2\pi\Phi(\delta)} \int_{-\infty}^{\infty} \mathrm{e}^{-\frac{1}{2}x^2} P_1^{\lambda-1}(x) \\ \int_{-\infty}^{(\delta-x\cos\theta)/\sin\theta} y^2 \mathrm{e}^{-\frac{1}{2}y^2} \mathrm{d}y\, \mathrm{d}x. \quad (20)$$

In Appendix B it is shown that this can equivalently be written as

$$e_{2,2} = 1 - \tan^2\theta \left[1 - \lambda \int_{-\infty}^{\infty} x^2 p_1(x) P_1^{\lambda-1}(x)\mathrm{d}x \right. \\ + 2\lambda(\lambda-1) \int_{-\infty}^{\infty} x p_1^2(x) P_1^{\lambda-2}(x)\mathrm{d}x \\ \left. - \frac{1}{2}\lambda(\lambda-1)(\lambda-2) \int_{-\infty}^{\infty} p_1^3(x) P_1^{\lambda-3}(x)\mathrm{d}x \right] \quad (21)$$

allowing the computation of the logarithmic adaptation response of the strategy.

Fig. 7 shows results from Eq. (18) where values from the Dirac model have been used for the average distance of the strategy from the constraint plane and the cumulation parameter has been set to $c = 0.5$. The points mark measurements made in runs of the strategy in which δ is free to vary while σ remains fixed. As seen earlier for the progress rate, the logarithmic adaptation response values predicted

using the Dirac model are much more accurate than could have been expected from looking at Fig. 5. It can also be seen that the logarithmic adaptation response is negative for small constraint angles, suggesting that the strategy will converge to a non-stationary point for the parameter settings used.

The maximum value of the cumulation parameter c for which the logarithmic adaptation response is positive can be computed from Eq. (18), which yields

$$c \le \frac{e_{1,1}^2 + e_{2,1}^2}{1 + e_{1,1}^2 + e_{2,1}^2 - e_{1,2}/2 - e_{2,2}/2} \quad (22)$$

when solved for c. That relationship is illustrated in Fig. 8. It can be seen that small values of the constraint angle require small values of c in order to avoid stagnation of the strategy, and that larger values of λ allow using larger values for the cumulation parameter. For very small constraint angles the limit value of c appears to depend quadratically on θ.

An intuitive explanation of the failure of cumulative step size adaptation for small constraint angles can be derived from Fig. 9. The curves in that figure have been generated from Eqs. (7), (19), (9), and (21), where δ has been obtained using the Dirac model. Notice that $e_{1,1}$ and $e_{1,2}$ are shown on a logarithmic scale. For small constraint angles, both are very small as there is little motion in the direction of the gradient of the objective function. Neither $e_{1,1}$ nor $e_{1,2}$ contribute much to the quantity in Eq. (18). Steps in the direction of the x_2-axis more and more resemble a random walk with zero mean and unit variance as the bias toward the direction of the negative x_2-axis disappears with decreasing constraint angle. Thus, in order for the quantity in Eq. (18) to be positive, the cumulation parameter c must be chosen small enough to sufficiently amplify the term in parentheses. As that term tends to zero as θ approaches zero, no value of c is sufficient for preventing stagnation for all constraint angles.

The behaviour of the $(1, \lambda)$-ES for several combinations of values of the cumulation parameter c and the number λ of offspring generated per time step is illustrated in Fig. 10. In all cases, $D = 1$ and $\theta = \pi/16$. For that value of the constraint angle and $\lambda = 5$ the maximum value of c for which

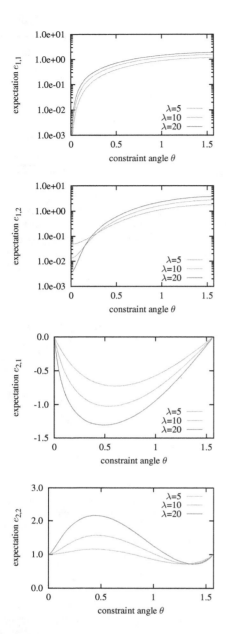

Figure 9: Expectations $e_{i,j}$ plotted against the constraint angle θ for $i, j \in \{1, 2\}$ and $\lambda \in \{5, 10, 20\}$.

stagnation of the strategy is avoided can be computed from Eq. (22) as 0.35. Indeed, it is observed that the mutation strength is decreased for $c = 0.5$ while it is increased for $c = 0.25$. For $\lambda = 10$ the maximum admissible value for c is 0.67, and the strategy is observed to increase the mutation strength as expected.

6.   SUMMARY AND CONCLUSIONS

To conclude, in this paper we have studied the behaviour of the $(1, \lambda)$-ES with cumulative step size adaptation for a simple linear problem with a single linear constraint. The normalised distance of the parental candidate solution from the constraint plane has been seen to be the state variable of the stochastic process that describes the operation of the

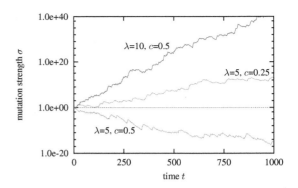

Figure 10: Mutation strength σ plotted against time for three runs of the $(1, \lambda)$-ES with cumulative step size adaptation and different combinations of the number λ of offspring generated per time step and the cumulation parameter c.

strategy. It has been possible to derive exact expressions that characterise the single step behaviour of the algorithm and that are conditional on the normalised distance from the constraint plane. The multi-step behaviour forms a non-linear stochastic process and is not as easily determined. Under the assumption of constant mutation strength a simple model has been used to compute the approximate average normalised distance of the strategy from the constraint plane. That value has been used to compute approximate values of the progress rate of the strategy as well as its logarithmic adaptation response when operating out of the stationary state.

It has been found that for acute constraint angles, cumulative step size adaptation may systematically reduce the mutation strength, resulting in convergence to a non-stationary point. Stagnation can be avoided by generating more offspring per time step or by using a smaller value for the cumulation parameter. The first option is unattractive as it leads to increased computational costs per time step and reduces the efficiency of the algorithm. Moreover, it is unclear what value parameter λ should be set to. The second option is unattractive as well as it prevents fast adaptation of the mutation strength on other functions, and again it is unclear how the parameter should be set in a particular instance. Success probability based step size adaptation for the $(1 + 1)$-ES has been seen in [22, 5] to suffer from problems that are similar in effect, and at this point it is unclear whether other step size adaptation strategies do as well.

Opportunities for extending this work are manifold. The exponential model in combination with the Kullback-Leibler divergence used for modelling the steady state of the $(1+1)$-ES in [4] can be used in an attempt to obtain a better approximation of the distribution or normalised distances from the constraint plane. Also desirable is the simplification of the expression in Eqs. (9), (19), and (21), possibly using an expansion, that would allow reducing the task of numerical integration to one of computing a small number of progress coefficients that do not depend on δ and θ. Further future work includes the extension of the results of the paper to the more general $(\mu/\mu, \lambda)$-ES, which performs recombination of several selected candidate solutions. It also remains to consider other step size adaptation mechanisms, such as mutative self-adaptation, and non-linear objective functions where the local constraint angle is not constant.

ACKNOWLEDGEMENTS

This research was supported by the Natural Sciences and Engineering Research Council of Canada (NSERC) and the Canada Foundation for Innovation (CFI). Helpful comments and questions by the reviewers and the participants of FOGA are gratefully acknowledged.

7. REFERENCES

[1] D. V. Arnold. *Noisy Optimization with Evolution Strategies*. Kluwer Academic Publishers, 2002.

[2] D. V. Arnold. On the use of evolution strategies for optimising certain positive definite quadratic forms. In *Genetic and Evolutionary Computation Conference — GECCO 2007*, pages 634–641. ACM Press, 2007.

[3] D. V. Arnold and H.-G. Beyer. Performance analysis of evolutionary optimization with cumulative step length adaptation. *IEEE Transactions on Automatic Control*, 49(4):617–622, 2004.

[4] D. V. Arnold and D. Brauer. On the behaviour of the $(1 + 1)$-ES for a simple constrained problem. In G. Rudolph et al., editors, *Parallel Problem Solving from Nature — PPSN X*, pages 1–10. Springer Verlag, 2008.

[5] D. V. Arnold and A. MacLeod. Step length adaptation on ridge functions. *Evolutionary Computation*, 16(2):151–184, 2008.

[6] T. Bäck, D. B. Fogel, and Z. Michalewicz. *Handbook of Evolutionary Computation*. Oxford University Press, 1997.

[7] H.-G. Beyer. *Ein Evolutionsverfahren zur mathematischen Modellierung stationärer Zustände in dynamischen Systemen*. PhD thesis, Hochschule für Architektur und Bauwesen, Weimar, 1989.

[8] H.-G. Beyer. *The Theory of Evolution Strategies*. Springer Verlag, 2001.

[9] H.-G. Beyer and H.-P. Schwefel. Evolution strategies — A comprehensive introduction. *Natural Computing*, 1(1):3–52, 2002.

[10] C. A. Coello Coello. Constraint-handling techniques used with evolutionary algorithms. In *Proceedings of the 2008 GECCO Conference Companion on Genetic and Evolutionary Computation*, pages 2445–2466. ACM Press, 2008.

[11] R. A. Fisher and E. A. Cornish. The percentile points of distributions having known cumulants. *Technometrics*, 2(2):209–225, 1960.

[12] O. Kramer and H.-P. Schwefel. On three new approaches to handle constraints within evolution strategies. *Natural Computing*, 5(4):363–385, 2006.

[13] R. Mallipeddi and P. N. Suganthan. Problem definitions and evaluation criteria for the CEC 2010 Competition on Constrained Real-Parameter Optimization. Technical report, Nanyang Technological University, Singapore, 2010.

[14] E. Mezura-Montes, editor. *Constraint-Handling in Evolutionary Optimization*. Springer Verlag, 2009.

[15] E. Mezura-Montes and C. A. Coello Coello. A simple multi-membered evolution strategy to solve constrained optimization problems. *IEEE Transactions on Evolutionary Computation*, 9(1):1–17, 2005.

[16] A. Ostermeier, A. Gawelczyk, and N. Hansen. Step-size adaptation based on non-local use of selection information. In Y. Davidor et al., editors, *Parallel Problem Solving from Nature — PPSN III*, pages 189–198. Springer Verlag, 1994.

[17] A. I. Oyman, K. Deb, and H.-G. Beyer. An alternative constraint handling method for evolution strategies. In *Proc. of the 1999 IEEE Congress on Evolutionary Computation*, pages 612–619. IEEE Press, 1999.

[18] I. Rechenberg. *Evolutionsstrategie — Optimierung technischer Systeme nach Prinzipien der biologischen Evolution*. Friedrich Frommann Verlag, 1973.

[19] I. Rechenberg. *Evolutionsstrategie '94*. Friedrich Frommann Verlag, 1994.

[20] T. P. Runarsson and X. Yao. Stochastic ranking for constrained evolutionary optimization. *IEEE Transactions on Evolutionary Computation*, 4(3):274–283, 2000.

[21] T. P. Runarsson and X. Yao. Search biases in constrained evolutionary optimization. *IEEE Transactions on Systems, Man and Cybernetics — Part C: Applications and Reviews*, 35(2):233–243, 2005.

[22] H.-P. Schwefel. *Numerical Optimization of Computer Models*. Wiley, 1981.

[23] H.-P. Schwefel. *Evolution and Optimum Seeking*. Wiley, 1995.

APPENDIX

A. COMPUTATION OF $\mathrm{E}[\hat{z}_2]$

The mean value of the z_2-components of the selected mutation vectors is described by Eq. (8). Solving the inner integral yields

$$\mathrm{E}[\hat{z}_2] = \frac{-\lambda}{2\pi\Phi(\delta)} \int_{-\infty}^{\infty} \mathrm{e}^{-\frac{1}{2}x^2} P_1^{\lambda-1}(x)$$
$$\exp\left(-\frac{1}{2}\left(\frac{\delta - x\cos\theta}{\sin\theta}\right)^2\right) \mathrm{d}x.$$

The result can be written in a different form by employing integration by parts with

$$u' = \exp\left(-\frac{1}{2}\left(\frac{\delta - x\cos\theta}{\sin\theta}\right)^2\right)$$
$$v = \mathrm{e}^{-\frac{1}{2}x^2} P_1^{\lambda-1}(x)$$
$$u = -\sqrt{2\pi}\tan\theta\, \Phi\left(\frac{\delta - x\cos\theta}{\sin\theta}\right)$$
$$v' = -x\mathrm{e}^{-\frac{1}{2}x^2} P_1^{\lambda-1}(x) + (\lambda-1)\mathrm{e}^{-\frac{1}{2}x^2} p_1(x) P_1^{\lambda-2}(x)$$

resulting in expression

$$\mathrm{E}[\hat{z}_2] = \tan\theta \left[\lambda \int_{-\infty}^{\infty} x p_1(x) P_1^{\lambda-1}(x)\mathrm{d}x\right.$$
$$\left. -\lambda(\lambda-1) \int_{-\infty}^{\infty} p_1^2(x) P_1^{\lambda-2}(x)\mathrm{d}x\right]$$

for the mean value of the z_2-components of the selected mutation vectors.

B. COMPUTATION OF $\mathrm{E}[\hat{z}_2^2]$

The second moment about zero of the z_2-components of the selected mutation vectors is described by Eq. (20). Solving the inner integral yields

$$\mathrm{E}\left[\hat{z}_2^2\right] = A - B$$

with

$$A = \frac{\lambda}{\sqrt{2\pi}\Phi(\delta)} \int_{-\infty}^{\infty} e^{-\frac{1}{2}x^2} P_1^{\lambda-1}(x) \Phi\left(\frac{\delta - x\cos\theta}{\sin\theta}\right) \mathrm{d}x$$
$$= \lambda \int_{-\infty}^{\infty} p_1(x) P_1^{\lambda-1}(x) \mathrm{d}x$$
$$= 1$$

and

$$B = \frac{\lambda}{2\pi\Phi(\delta)} \int_{-\infty}^{\infty} e^{-\frac{1}{2}x^2} P_1^{\lambda-1}(x) \left(\frac{\delta - x\cos\theta}{\sin\theta}\right)$$
$$\exp\left(-\frac{1}{2}\left(\frac{\delta - x\cos\theta}{\sin\theta}\right)^2\right) \mathrm{d}x.$$

Integration by parts with

$$u' = \left(\frac{\delta - x\cos\theta}{\sin\theta}\right) \exp\left(-\frac{1}{2}\left(\frac{\delta - x\cos\theta}{\sin\theta}\right)^2\right)$$
$$v = e^{-\frac{1}{2}x^2} P_1^{\lambda-1}(x)$$
$$u = \tan\theta \exp\left(-\frac{1}{2}\left(\frac{\delta - x\cos\theta}{\sin\theta}\right)^2\right)$$
$$v' = -xe^{-\frac{1}{2}x^2} P_1^{\lambda-1}(x) + (\lambda-1)e^{-\frac{1}{2}x^2} p_1(x) P_1^{\lambda-2}(x)$$

yields $B = C - D$ with

$$C = \frac{\lambda\tan\theta}{2\pi\Phi(\delta)} \int_{-\infty}^{\infty} xe^{-\frac{1}{2}x^2} P_1^{\lambda-1}(x)$$
$$\exp\left(-\frac{1}{2}\left(\frac{\delta - x\cos\theta}{\sin\theta}\right)^2\right) \mathrm{d}x$$

and

$$D = \frac{\lambda(\lambda-1)\tan\theta}{2\pi\Phi(\delta)} \int_{-\infty}^{\infty} e^{-\frac{1}{2}x^2} p_1(x) P_1^{\lambda-2}(x)$$
$$\exp\left(-\frac{1}{2}\left(\frac{\delta - x\cos\theta}{\sin\theta}\right)^2\right) \mathrm{d}x.$$

Using integration by parts with

$$u' = \exp\left(-\frac{1}{2}\left(\frac{\delta - x\cos\theta}{\sin\theta}\right)^2\right)$$
$$v = xe^{-\frac{1}{2}x^2} P_1^{\lambda-1}(x)$$
$$u = -\sqrt{2\pi}\tan\theta\,\Phi\left(\frac{\delta - x\cos\theta}{\sin\theta}\right)$$
$$v' = (1-x^2)e^{-\frac{1}{2}x^2} P_1^{\lambda-1}(x) + (\lambda-1)xe^{-\frac{1}{2}x^2} p_1(x) P_1^{\lambda-2}(x)$$

the first expression can be rewritten as

$$C = \tan^2\theta \left[1 - \lambda \int_{-\infty}^{\infty} x^2 p_1(x) P_1^{\lambda-1}(x) \mathrm{d}x\right.$$
$$\left. + \lambda(\lambda-1) \int_{-\infty}^{\infty} xp_1^2(x) P_1^{\lambda-2}(x) \mathrm{d}x\right].$$

Similarly, using integration by parts with

$$u' = \exp\left(-\frac{1}{2}\left(\frac{\delta - x\cos\theta}{\sin\theta}\right)^2\right)$$
$$v = e^{-\frac{1}{2}x^2} p_1(x) P_1^{\lambda-2}(x)$$
$$u = -\sqrt{2\pi}\tan\theta\,\Phi\left(\frac{\delta - x\cos\theta}{\sin\theta}\right)$$
$$v' = (p_1'(x) - xp_1(x))e^{-\frac{1}{2}x^2} P_1^{\lambda-2}(x)$$
$$+ (\lambda-2)e^{-\frac{1}{2}x^2} p_1^2(x) P_1^{\lambda-3}(x)$$

the second expression can be rewritten as

$$D = \tan^2\theta \left[\lambda(\lambda-1) \int_{-\infty}^{\infty} (p_1'(x) - xp_1(x))\, p_1(x) P_1^{\lambda-2}(x)\mathrm{d}x\right.$$
$$\left. + \lambda(\lambda-1)(\lambda-2) \int_{-\infty}^{\infty} p_1^3(x) P_1^{\lambda-3}(x)\mathrm{d}x\right]$$

where $p_1'(x)$ is the first derivative of $p_1(x)$. Using integration by parts one last time with

$$u' = p_1(x)p_1'(x)$$
$$v = P_1^{\lambda-2}(x)$$
$$u = \tfrac{1}{2}p_1^2(x)$$
$$v' = (\lambda-2)p_1(x) P_1^{\lambda-3}(x)$$

allows rewriting this as

$$D = \tan^2\theta \left[-\lambda(\lambda-1) \int_{-\infty}^{\infty} xp_1^2(x) P_1^{\lambda-2}(x)\mathrm{d}x\right.$$
$$\left. + \tfrac{1}{2}\lambda(\lambda-1)(\lambda-2) \int_{-\infty}^{\infty} p_1^3(x) P_1^{\lambda-3}(x)\mathrm{d}x\right].$$

Altogether, it follows

$$\mathrm{E}\left[\hat{z}_2^2\right] = 1 - \tan^2\theta \left[1 - \lambda \int_{-\infty}^{\infty} x^2 p_1(x) P_1^{\lambda-1}(x)\mathrm{d}x\right.$$
$$+ 2\lambda(\lambda-1) \int_{-\infty}^{\infty} xp_1^2(x) P_1^{\lambda-2}(x)\mathrm{d}x$$
$$\left. - \tfrac{1}{2}\lambda(\lambda-1)(\lambda-2) \int_{-\infty}^{\infty} p_1^3(x) P_1^{\lambda-3}(x)\mathrm{d}x\right]$$

for the second moment about zero of the z_2-components of the selected mutation vectors.

Elementary Bit String Mutation Landscapes

W. B. Langdon

CREST centre, Department of Computer Science,
University College, London, Gower Street, London, WC1E 6BT, UK
w.langdon@cs.uc1.ac.uk

ABSTRACT

Genetic Programming parity with only XOR is not elementary. GP parity can be represented as the sum of $k/2 + 1$ elementary landscapes. Statistics, including fitness distance correlation (FDC), of Parity's fitness landscape are calculated. Using Walsh analysis the eigen values and eigenvectors of the Laplacian of the two bit, three bit, n-bit and mutation only Genetic Algorithm fitness landscapes are given. Indeed all elementary bit string landscapes are related to the discrete Fourier functions. However most are rough ($\lambda/d \approx 1$). Also in many cases fitness autocorrelation falls rapidly with distance. GA runs support eigenvalue/graph degree (λ/d) as a measure of the ruggedness of elementary landscapes for predicting problem difficulty. The elementary needle in a haystack (NIH) landscape is described.

Categories and Subject Descriptors

F.2.m [**Analysis of Algorithms and problem Complexity**]: Miscellaneous; G.2.2 [**Graph Theory**]; G.1.6 [**Optimisation**]: Stochastic programming; G.3 [**Probability and Statistics**]: Probabilistic algorithms; I.2.8 [**Artificial Intelligence**]: Problem Solving, Search

General Terms

Theory

Keywords

genetic algorithms, genetic programming, search, optimisation, graph theory, Laplacian, Hamming cube, Walsh transform, fitness distance correlation, elementary fitness autocorrelation

1. FITNESS LANDSCAPES

An elementary landscape is a special case of a fitness landscape. There are some important combinatorially hard problems, e.g. k-satisfiability and maxsat [21], which have elementary landscapes and where these properties have been

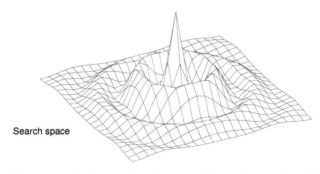

Search space

Figure 1: A fitness landscape where internal nodes have four neighbours. Fitness is plotted vertically.

used to devise improved search techniques. This is the first time genetic programming has been analysed in terms of elementary landscapes. Our motivation is to explore the technique, with a view to further analyse and hopefully improve GP. However to do this we recast GP as a bit string genetic algorithm (GA) and report many problem independent properties of elementary landscapes.

Firstly we recap fitness landscapes then some well known properties of elementary landscapes will be described in the next section. Section 3 describes our simplified version of the genetic programming parity problem. In Section 4 we approximate tree GP parity by a GA where mutation flips exactly two bits. Section 5 gives many properties of the fitness landscapes created by this double bit flip mutation, particularly those relating to GP parity. In Section 6 some of these results are generalised to three and n-bit flip mutation as well as to normal mutation only GAs. Section 7 describes some GP experiments on parity and on two elementary landscapes.

Fitness landscapes (see Figure 1) have often been used to try and explain how optimisation techniques, particularly evolutionary algorithms [1] such as genetic programming [13] work. An optimisation problem can viewed as a search problem where all possible solutions to the problem are nodes in the search space and each has a value. In genetic algorithms [15] this is called a fitness value (more generally an objective value). Optimisation is viewed as sampling from this space with the aim of to finding better points (or even the best point) in the space.

Except for Monte Carlo methods, optimisation techniques use information gathered from previous samples to decide where in the search space to sample next. The goal being to minimise the number of samples that are needed before an acceptable solution is found. In general evolutionary algorithms, and several other optimisation techniques, only use the current search point (or the current population of search points) to guide the choice of where to look next. They do not use previously gained knowledge. Different algorithms can have radically different ways of moving from one point in the search space to the next. A search neighbourhood is the set of points that a specific algorithm can reach in one step from the current search point. A fitness landscape can be thought of as a graph where neighbours are linked by a single edge if and only if our search algorithm can move between the two nodes in the graph. While the height of the node is given by its fitness.

Typically in evolutionary algorithms, the edges in the graph are undirected, because if one node can be reached from another then the reverse move is also possible. Notice that the difficulty of a problem depends not only on how fitness values are decided but also on the way the search algorithm moves across the search space. I.e. problem difficulty also depends on the fitness landscape the search algorithm imposes on the underlying problem [11, Chp. 2].

In genetic algorithms a common fitness landscape is to encode candidate solutions as strings of l bits. Each of the 2^l bit strings is allocated a fitness value. This gives a search space of 2^l candidate solutions. If mutation is restricted to flipping a single bit then each of the candidate solutions is connected in the fitness landscape to l other candidate solutions. This is known as the Hamming neighbourhood or hypercube graph [22]. The fitness landscape metaphor can be extended to population approaches (such as Particle Swarm Optimisation [12]) by allowing multiple sample points (one for each member of the population) in the landscape.

Fitness landscapes are a useful metaphor with simple mutation which has a well defined neighbourhood. However with the canonical mutation only genetic algorithm the analogy starts to fail. Since GA mutation is defined as a probability of each bit flipping, multiple bits can be changed. There is a finite, albeit exponentially small, probability of any string being converted into any other. Thus, in principle, the whole fitness landscape becomes a single fully connected clique.

Fitness landscapes can be extended to allow multi-parent search operations (e.g. crossover). However then the neighbourhood of each member of the population depends upon the location of everyone else in the population and the idea of fixed predetermined links in the graph fails. (Nevertheless Stadler and Wagner extend the idea of fitness landscapes to include crossover by using P-structures [19].)

2. ELEMENTARY LANDSCAPES

2.1 Wave Equation

The following is based on Whitley's (e.g. [25] and [27]) definitions. (See also Grover [6] and Stadler [18, p3].)

In an elementary landscape the fitness function f and the search space neighbourhood graph are related by a wave equation. The search space neighbourhood graph can be represented by a matrix Δ (see Sections 2.2 and 5.3). Only in an elementary landscape do the search space and the fitness function obey

$$\Delta f = \lambda(f - \overline{f})$$

Where $\overline{f}$ is the mean fitness across the whole search space.

That is, zero-mean fitness $f - \overline{f}$ is an eigenvector of Δ with eigenvalue λ. Notice a given search space (e.g. that created by one point mutation acting on a bit string chromosome) will have multiple eigenvectors. Each eigenvector will be the fitness function (up to an additive constant) for a different elementary landscape.

2.2 Average Fitness Change

For simplicity we will deal with regular landscapes. I.e. landscapes where every location has the same number of search neighbours d. In general the mean change in fitness caused by one genetic change depends on the current position in the search space. Treating the mean change as a vector of the same size as the search space gives it as:

$$\frac{1}{d}(Af - f)$$

If we treat the search space as a graph, then d is the degree of each node in the graph. (I.e. the number of links from the node). A is the adjacency matrix. For our purposes, it is a sparse real square matrix where every element corresponding to a link in the graph has the value 1 and all the others are zero.

$$\frac{1}{d}(Af - f) = \frac{1}{d}(A - dI)f = -\frac{1}{d}\Delta f$$

Where Δ is the Laplacian and is defined to be $dI - A$. (I is the identity matrix.)

2.3 Average Neighbourhood Fitness in an Elementary Landscape

The mean fitness of a neighbourhood, $N(x)$, will also depend on the current position in the search landscape x. It is given by the fitness of the current position, $f(x)$, plus the average change in fitness (calculated in the previous section).

$$
\begin{aligned}
\mathrm{avg}_{y \in N(x)}\{f(y)\} &= \frac{1}{d}\sum_{y \in N(x)} f(y) \\
&= f(x) + \frac{1}{d}\sum_{y \in N(x)} f(y) - f(x) \\
&= f(x) - \frac{1}{d}\Delta f(x) \\
&= f(x) - \frac{1}{d}\lambda(f(x) - \overline{f}) \\
&= f(x) + \frac{\lambda}{d}(\overline{f} - f(x))
\end{aligned}
$$

If, for convenience we set $\overline{f}$ to zero, in an elementary landscape the mean fitness of the neighbours of x is:

$$\mathrm{avg}_{y \in N(x)}\{f(y)\} = f(x) - \frac{\lambda}{d}f(x) = (1 - \frac{\lambda}{d})f(x) \qquad (1)$$

Thus, if $\lambda < d$, the mean of the neighbourhood is always closer to the overall average $\overline{f}$ than the centre of the neighbourhood $f(x)$ is. Figure 2 shows a local optimum. By Equation 1, the average of the neighbourhood must lie between $\overline{f}$ and $f(x)$. At a local optimum, by definition, $f(x)$ must be above the fitness of all its neighbours and hence must be above their average fitness. Therefore $f(x)$ must be above $\overline{f}$. Another way of saying this is: in elementary landscapes (with $\lambda < d$) there are no local optima with below average fitness. In special cases, e.g. k-Satisfiability and

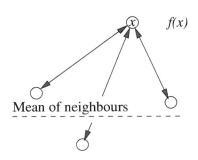

Average Fitness + max step * degree/eigenvalue

f(x)

Mean of neighbours

Average Fitness

Figure 2: By definition at a hill top x the fitness of its neighbours is lower than that of the peak $f(x)$. By Equation 1, provided $\lambda < d$, the average fitness of the neighbours of x is closer to the average of the whole landscape $\overline{f}$ than $f(x)$ is. Therefore $f(x)$ must lie above $\overline{f}$ [6, Thm. 6]. Dimova et al. give an upper bound $f \leq \overline{f} + \epsilon_{\max} d/\lambda$ [5, Crly. 4].

MAXSAT [21], there are tighter bounds on the fitness of local optima and even on the widths of plateaus. (See also [20].)

2.4 Bound on Maximum Fitness

Dimova et al. [5, Crly. 4] prove a global upper bound $f \leq \overline{f} + \epsilon_{\max} d/\lambda$ for the whole search space. Where $\epsilon_{\max}$ is the largest change in fitness for any single step in the landscape [5, 23]. (Remember d is the number of possible moves and λ is Δ's eigenvalue.) For onemax: $\overline{f} = l/2$, $d = l$ and the eigenvalue $\lambda = 2$. Since every move either increments or decrements fitness $\epsilon_{\max} = 1$. Thus in the case of onemax, $f_{\max} = \overline{f} + \epsilon_{\max} d/\lambda$ holds exactly at the global maximum $f_{\max} = l$ and f is strictly less than $\overline{f} + \epsilon_{\max} d/\lambda$ elsewhere.

As a second example, take the needle in a haystack (which will be fully described in Section 5.4). The largest step $\epsilon_{\max}$ is 1, the mean fitness $\overline{f}$ is 2^{-n}, node degree d is 2^n and the eigenvalue $\lambda = 2^n$. Thus $f_{\max} = \overline{f} + \epsilon_{\max} d/\lambda = 1 + 2^{-n}$, which is very close to the global maximum (1).

As a third example, take the concatenated four bit trap like elementary landscape described in Section 7.3. The average fitness $\overline{f} = 2 \times 4 = 8$ and $f_{\max} = 4 \times 4 = 16$. (The full 16-bit fitness function is given by adding together four functions like that given in Figure 5). Since mutation flips exactly two bits, the number of possible moves is $d = C_2^{16} = 16 \times 15/2 = 120$. The eigenvalue $\lambda = 84$. The maximum change in fitness comes when mutation flips two bits in separate traps so each causes the maximum change (3). Adding these together we get $\epsilon_{\max} = 6$. Thus $\overline{f} + \epsilon_{\max} d/\lambda = 8 + 6 \times 120/84 = 16 + 4/7$. Again, as expected, $f_{\max} < \overline{f} + \epsilon_{\max} d/\lambda$ holds everywhere including the global maximum. Notice that the bound can be calculated directly. I.e. without sampling the search space at all.

In the case of 4×Trap-4 we know fitness values have integer values, so if we find a point with fitness 16, Dimova et al.'s bound tells us it is a global optimum. (But not that

it is the unique global optimum.) More generally it places a limit on how much a result can be improved. E.g. if we have found a 4×Trap-4 point with value 15, we know that further search can only improve by at most 1. This could be used as another way of deciding when to stop searching.

3. GENETIC PROGRAMMING PARITY

The classic definition of the GP parity problems was given by Koza [8]. He defined the representation for order-k parity as binary trees whose external leafs are the functions inputs (drawn from $D_0 \cdots D_{k-1}$) and whose internal nodes are drawn from four binary Boolean functions. Initially the first simplification is to use just one Boolean function rather than four. We use either equals (EQ) or exclusive-or (XOR) depending if we are dealing with even or odd parity.

Koza defines the fitness of each tree by testing it on all 2^k possible input patterns and counting the number of times it returns the same answer as parity would. (Even-k-parity is true if the number of inputs which are true is even.) Thus Koza's fitness lies in the range $0 \ldots 2^k$ and a solution to the parity problems has fitness 2^k.

Elsewhere [10, pages 421–423] we have used the symmetries of EQ and XOR to show that with a function set composed only of either EQ or only of XOR, trees will have fitness of either 2^{k-1} or 2^k. These properties also carry over from tree based GP to Cartesian GP and have also been exploited by Yu and Miller [29]. Further a tree is only a solution to parity if it contains an odd number of each type of leaf. (To simplify the text, and since odd parity behaves similarly, from now on we will discuss only even parity.) Since solutions to k-parity have one leaf of each of the k types plus redundant pairs of the same leaf type, they always have $k + 2n$ leafs (for $n = 0, 1, 2, \ldots$). So their total size is $2k + 4n - 1$. Notice neither the shape of the tree nor the order of its leafs matters. All binary trees formed by re-arrangements of the leafs and internal nodes of the tree have identical fitness. The group properties of EQ also mean any pairs of leafs of the same type can be removed. E.g., using = to represent EQ, $(D_1 = (D_2 = D_2))$ is identical to the input D_1 on its own. So if there are an even number any type of leaf (e.g. D_2) then it is as if the input was not connected. A tree missing one or more inputs scores exactly half the maximum score on parity.

We extend our previous analysis of the parity problem [10], which described its fitness distribution, to consider parity's fitness landscape.

4. THE PARITY PROBLEM

4.1 The Mutation Operator

To form a landscape, in addition to the representation and its associated fitness function we need at least one search operator to establish which representations are adjacent to each other. Koza's [8] subtree crossover is a bit complicated to start with so we shall instead start with a mutation operator.

The mutation operator changes exactly one thing in the tree. Since the internal nodes are always EQ, the only possible change is to convert one leaf from one input (D_i) to another (D_j with $j \neq i$). This does not change the size of the tree. In principle more complicated tree size changing mutation operators or indeed crossover operators might also be considered.

4.2 Mutation's Impact on Fitness

The effect of mutation is either to make no difference to fitness (i.e. remain at 2^{k-1}) or to increase it from 2^{k-1} to 2^k or reduce it from 2^k to 2^{k-1}. A solution to parity has an odd number of all k types of leafs. Thus replacing any leaf with another of a different type will always mean it is no longer a solution. So it is impossible to mutate a tree of fitness 2^k into another tree of fitness 2^k.

Now the chance of each of these three things happening depends only on the number of each type of leaf. It does not depend upon the order of the leafs or their placement on the tree. Since these permutations make no difference to either fitness or to any of the changes in fitness we ignore them and initially replace trees with k integer counts d_i. Obviously there is a constraint that all of the tree's leafs must be present. So for a tree of size $2k + 4n - 1$, $\sum_{i=0}^{k-1} d_i$ must be $k + 2n$.

A tree's fitness is only 2^k if the number of leafs of each type (d_i) is odd for all k types. We can further simplify the representation by replacing the d_is with e_is which are 1 if their corresponding d_i is even and 0 if it is odd. Similarly we can simplify Koza's fitness function so that 2^{k-1} is replaced by 0 and 2^k by 1. Under the new scheme fitness = 1 if and only if all e_i are 0 and fitness = 0 otherwise.

Mutation cannot change the total number of leafs, therefore having chosen an initial tree, $\sum d_i$ is fixed. This is a constraint on d_i and so we only need to specify $k - 1$ values for the d_i. (The remaining one can be inferred from the need to supply all the tree's leafs.) In fact, the oddness or evenness of $(k - 1)$ d_i is enough for the odd or evenness of the remaining one to be inferred. Another way of looking at this is to say: although for convenience we have k e_i, mutation can only reach half of their 2^k possible values. The unreachable half of the 2^k values correspond to trees of the wrong size for any of them to be parity solutions and so have zero fitness. We will assume the tree size is $2k + 4n - 1$, which allows one solution in a space of 2^{k-1}.

Mutating a leaf from type i to type j means decrementing d_i and incrementing d_j. Provided $d_i > 0$, this is equivalent to inverting e_i and e_j. I.e. mutation flips exactly two of the k bits. The next section will describe how we ensure $d_i > 0$ so that all mutation are always possible and further they are all equally likely.

4.3 Large Trees Simplify Mutation Analysis

Now it will greatly simplify things later if we assume the type of input we are about to mutate is chosen uniformly at random from the k possible types and that the type of the replacement leaf is chosen uniformly at random from the $k - 1$ remaining types. Obviously this requires the tree to have at least one leaf of each of the k types.

To further simplify the analysis we shall assume that the trees are much bigger than the minimum size $(2k-1)$. So big in fact, that we can assume that the tree has more than one leaf of each type. Further we assume the tree has sufficiently large number of leafs that undirected random drift from an initial random starting point in the search landscape will never cause the number of leafs of any of the k types to fall to one. I.e. random drift will not approach the edge of the k-dimensional simplex. If evolution lasts for G generations then drift will change the number of leafs of a given type by about $\sqrt{G}$. So assuming the tree is also bigger than a constant multiple of $(2k - 1)\sqrt{G}$ will ensure the chance of

any of the k types of leaf approaching extinction is negligible. So mutation is always free to choose any pair of leaf types. This ensures it is always symmetric.

5. THE PARITY FITNESS LANDSCAPE

Treat the landscape as a graph where the nodes are k length bit vectors. As in Section 4.2, if bit i is 1 this indicates the tree has an even number of D_i leafs. Nodes in the graph are directly connected (i.e. the corresponding trees are neighbours) if mutating one node gives the other in exactly one step. We deal with the 2^{k-1} nodes that are indirectly connected to the solution node.

Neighbours in the graph have exactly two bits different. Thus the graph consists of 2^{k-1} nodes each connected by $\frac{1}{2}k(k - 1)$ symmetric links and the probability of moving along each link is the same (i.e. $\frac{2}{k(k-1)}$). Only the single node with none of the k elements are even has fitness 1. All other nodes have zero fitness. Average fitness is $\overline{f} = 2^{1-k}$. The variance of fitness is $\frac{1}{2^{k-1}} \sum f_i^2 - \overline{f}^2 = \frac{1}{2^{k-1}} - \overline{f}^2 = 2^{1-k} - 2^{2-2k}$. So the standard deviation $\sigma_f = \sqrt{2^{1-k} - 2^{2-2k}} \approx 2^{-(k-1)/2}$.

5.1 Fitness Distance Correlation

Jones and Forrest state that the fitness distance correlation based on random sampling of a needle in a haystack fitness function will be near zero [7, page 186]. We confirm this by giving values based on analysing the whole space and thus avoiding noise introduced by random sampling.

Jones and Forrest [7, page 185] define the fitness distance correlation as $r = \mathrm{Cov}(f, d)/\sigma_f \sigma_d$. Where the covariance between fitness and distance (d) to the global optimum is: $\mathrm{Cov}(f, d) = \frac{1}{2^{k-1}} \sum_{i=0}^{2^{k-1}-1} (f_i - \overline{f})(d_i - \overline{d})$ and σ_f is the standard deviation of f (calculated in the previous section) and similarly σ_d is the standard deviation of the number of two bit flips to the origin (i.e. distance to the global optimum).

$$
\begin{aligned}
&\mathrm{Cov}(f, d) \\
&= \frac{1}{2^{k-1}} \sum_{i=0}^{2^{k-1}-1} (f_i - \overline{f})(d_i - \overline{d}) \\
&= \frac{1}{2^{k-1}} \left((1 - \overline{f})(d_0 - \overline{d}) + \sum_{i=1}^{2^{k-1}-1} -\overline{f}(d_i - \overline{d}) \right) \\
&= \frac{1}{2^{k-1}} \left((1 - \overline{f})(d_0 - \overline{d}) - \overline{f} \sum_{i=1}^{2^{k-1}-1} d_i - \overline{d} \right) \\
&= \frac{1}{2^{k-1}} \left((1 - \overline{f})(-\overline{d}) + \overline{f}(d_0 - \overline{d}) - \overline{f} \sum_{i=0}^{2^{k-1}-1} d_i - \overline{d} \right) \\
&= \frac{1}{2^{k-1}} \left((1 - \overline{f})(-\overline{d}) - \overline{f}\,\overline{d} \right) \\
&= \frac{-\overline{d}}{2^{k-1}} \left((1 - \overline{f}) + \overline{f} \right) \\
&= \frac{-\overline{d}}{2^{k-1}}
\end{aligned}
$$

The distance from the optimum is $\approx bc/2$. Where bc is the number of 1s (the bit count). The number of points in

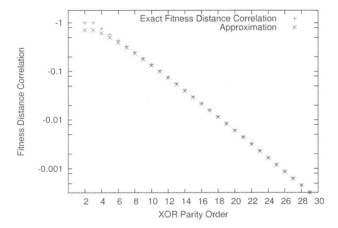

Figure 3: Fitness Distance Correlation for Needle in a Haystack with double flip mutation. Note log scale.

the search space with identical bit count is C_{bc}^{k-1}. C_{bc}^{k-1} are coefficients of the binomial distribution. The mean of the binomial distribution is np and the variance is $np(1-p)$. Here $p = 1/2$ and $n = k-1$. So the mean distance divided by the standard deviation of the distance $\bar{d}/\sigma_d \approx n^{\frac{1}{2}} = \sqrt{k-1}$.

$$
\begin{aligned}
r = \frac{\text{Cov}(f, d)}{\sigma_f \sigma_d} &\approx \frac{-\bar{d}}{2^{k-1}} \frac{1}{2^{-(k-1)/2} \sigma_d} \\
&= \frac{-1}{2^{(k-1)/2}} \frac{\bar{d}}{\sigma_d} \\
r &\approx \frac{-\sqrt{k-1}}{2^{(k-1)/2}}
\end{aligned}
$$

Figure 3 plots this approximation and the exact fitness distance correlation. It shows even for quite modest order, the actual correlation coefficient converges to this large order approximation.

5.2 Walsh Analysis of Fitness Autocorrelation

Jones [7] defined fitness distance correlation in terms of distance from the global optimum. This has a number of problems. Usually one needs to know the location of the best solution in the search space and it is assumed that there is only one solution with the best fitness value. Fitness autocorrelation, for example along a random walk, addresses these problems and can be used as a measure of landscape smoothness and indicator of how easy a problem might be to solve. This section provides an informal argument that fitness correlation between neighbours falls rapidly with distance. It could be argued that in the case of a needle in a haystack landscape, such as parity, the chance of encountering the needle is sufficiently remote that fitness along a random walk will always be zero in practise. Nevertheless the following arguments can be applied to any landscape where the fitness landscapes created by the Walsh functions are elementary landscapes. This includes 1-bit, 2-bit, 3-bit and n-bit flip mutation as well as GA bit string mutation (see Sections 5.6 and 6).

We shall see in Section 5.10 that GP Parity can be represented as a linear sum of elementary landscapes. Dimova *et al.* [4] proved that fitness autocorrelation for a random walk on an elementary landscapes falls exponentially. Since the autocorrelation of all the components of parity fall monotonically, the correlation of parity itself must also fall monotonically with distance. (With increasing distance the actual value will be dominated by the slowest changing exponential term.)

Using Walsh analysis, any discrete fitness landscape can be represented as a sum of Walsh coefficients. If (as is known in many cases) the Walsh basis functions are elementary landscapes and fitness correlation falls rapidly in one step it will continue to fall towards zero for all larger distances.

For simplicity let the mean fitness be zero. Then fitness auto-correlation is essentially given by:

$$\sum_i \sum_{id} f_i f_{id}$$

where $\sum_i$ is the sum over the whole search space and $\sum_{id}$ is the sum over all neighbours of i which are d steps from i. For illustration assume $f = w + v$ where w and v are two Walsh basis elementary landscapes.

$$
\begin{aligned}
\sum_i \sum_{id} f_i f_{id} &= \sum_i \sum_{id} (w_i + v_i)(w_{id} + v_{id}) \\
&= \sum_i \sum_{id} w_i w_{id} + v_i w_{id} + w_i v_{id} + v_i v_{id}
\end{aligned}
$$

Now the first and last terms are simply the auto-correlation of w and v which we know fall exponentially.

$$
\begin{aligned}
\sum_i \sum_{id} v_i w_{id} &= \sum_i \sum_{id} v_i(w_i - (w_i - w_{id})) \\
&= \sum_i D v_i w_i - \sum_i \sum_{id} v_i(w_i - w_{id})
\end{aligned}
$$

where D is the number of neighbours separated by d. Now the first term is zero, since w and v are orthogonal Walsh basis functions.

$$\sum_i v_i \sum_{id} (w_i - w_{id}) \leq v_{\max} \sum_i \sum_{id} (w_i - w_{id})$$

When the separation distance becomes large wrt w's order $\sum_i \sum_{id} w_i - w_{id}$ will become small. Hence the autocorrelation between the sum of two Walsh functions falls rapidly with distance. This argument can be generalised to summing more than two elementary landscapes and holds for any fitness landscape where the Walsh basis functions are elementary landscapes.

Section 6 will show with many mutation operations, the Walsh basis functions are elementary landscapes. As well as parity, well known examples include max-3-sat [25]. Fitness distance correlation will fall rapidly with distance for all of them.

5.3 Laplacian of the Parity Landscape Graph

Form the Laplacian Δ matrix as a real square matrix whose rows and columns correspond to the 2^{k-1} nodes in the parity landscape. Every element is zero except the off diagonal terms corresponding to an edge in the graph and the diagonal. Since the graph's edges are bidirectional and each have the same probability, the graph is symmetric and we can make all the non-zero off-diagonal terms be -1. The diagonal elements are the number of edges connected to the corresponding node in the graph. This is $\frac{1}{2}k(k-1)$ for all nodes. I.e. every node in the graph has the same degree. ($d = \frac{1}{2}k(k-1)$.) Thus every row (and every column) sums to zero.

$\Delta = \frac{1}{2}k(k-1)I - A$ where A is the graph's adjacency matrix.

$$\Delta_2 = \begin{array}{c|cc} & 00 & 11 \\ \hline 00 & 1 & -1 \\ 11 & -1 & 1 \end{array}$$

$$\Delta_3 = \begin{array}{c|cccc} & 000 & 101 & 110 & 011 \\ \hline 000 & 3 & -1 & -1 & -1 \\ 101 & -1 & 3 & -1 & -1 \\ 110 & -1 & -1 & 3 & -1 \\ 011 & -1 & -1 & -1 & 3 \end{array}$$

$$\Delta_4 = \begin{array}{c|cccccccc} & 0000 & 1001 & 1010 & 0011 & 1100 & 0101 & 0110 & 1111 \\ \hline 0000 & 6 & -1 & -1 & -1 & -1 & -1 & -1 & 0 \\ 1001 & -1 & 6 & -1 & -1 & -1 & -1 & 0 & -1 \\ 1010 & -1 & -1 & 6 & -1 & -1 & 0 & -1 & -1 \\ 0011 & -1 & -1 & -1 & 6 & 0 & -1 & -1 & -1 \\ 1100 & -1 & -1 & -1 & 0 & 6 & -1 & -1 & -1 \\ 0101 & -1 & -1 & 0 & -1 & -1 & 6 & -1 & -1 \\ 0110 & -1 & 0 & -1 & -1 & -1 & -1 & 6 & -1 \\ 1111 & 0 & -1 & -1 & -1 & -1 & -1 & -1 & 6 \end{array}$$

$\Delta_5 =$

	00000	10001	10010	00011	10100	00101	00110	10111	11000	01001	01010	11011	01100	11101	11110	01111
00000	10	-1	-1	-1	-1	-1	-1	0	-1	-1	-1	0	-1	0	0	0
10001	-1	10	-1	-1	-1	-1	0	-1	-1	-1	0	-1	0	-1	0	0
10010	-1	-1	10	-1	-1	0	-1	-1	-1	0	-1	-1	0	0	-1	0
00011	-1	-1	-1	10	0	-1	-1	-1	0	-1	-1	-1	0	0	0	-1
10100	-1	-1	-1	0	10	-1	-1	-1	-1	0	0	0	-1	-1	-1	0
00101	-1	-1	0	-1	-1	10	-1	-1	0	-1	0	0	-1	-1	0	-1
00110	-1	0	-1	-1	-1	-1	10	-1	0	0	-1	0	-1	0	-1	-1
10111	0	-1	-1	-1	-1	-1	-1	10	0	0	0	-1	0	-1	-1	-1
11000	-1	-1	-1	0	-1	0	0	0	10	-1	-1	-1	-1	-1	-1	0
01001	-1	-1	0	-1	0	-1	0	0	-1	10	-1	-1	-1	-1	0	-1
01010	-1	0	-1	-1	0	0	-1	0	-1	-1	10	-1	-1	0	-1	-1
11011	0	-1	-1	-1	0	0	0	-1	-1	-1	-1	10	0	-1	-1	-1
01100	-1	0	0	0	-1	-1	-1	0	-1	-1	-1	0	10	-1	-1	-1
11101	0	-1	0	0	-1	-1	0	-1	-1	-1	0	-1	-1	10	-1	-1
11110	0	0	-1	0	-1	0	-1	-1	-1	0	-1	-1	-1	-1	10	-1
01111	0	0	0	-1	0	-1	-1	-1	0	-1	-1	-1	-1	-1	-1	10

For a landscape to be elementary its fitness function must have a special relationship with its move operator; it must obey the "wave equation" $\Delta f = \lambda(f - \overline{f})$ (see Section 2.1). I.e. treat the fitness function as a vector whose elements are the fitnesses of the corresponding nodes in landscape graph. Call this f. If the landscape is to be elementary f (up to an additive constant) must be an eigenvector of Δ with corresponding eigenvalue λ. For parity, f is a vector with 2^{k-1} elements all of which are zero except the first, which has the value 1. Thus Δf is simply the first column of Δ. The first element of the first column of Δ is $\frac{1}{2}k(k-1)$ and there are $\frac{1}{2}k(k-1)$ other elements whose values are -1. Thus the first column of Δ is not a simple scalar multiple of the fitness vector f and so f is not an eigenvector of Δ. Therefore the parity landscape is not elementary.

Section 5.5 and those following it will show not only is parity's landscape not elementary but also it cannot be decomposed into a small number of elementary landscapes.

5.4 The Elementary Needle in Haystack

We use the analysis from the previous section to construct another needle in a haystack (NIH) problem which is elementary. Without loss of generality we can keep the solution at all zeros and give it fitness one (all other points have zero fitness). Thus the NIH has the same fitness function as parity. There are 2^l points in the search space, so $\overline{f} = 2^{-l}$. For an NIH landscape to be elementary it must still obey the "wave equation" $\Delta f = \lambda(f - \overline{f})$ and Δf is again the first column of Δ. An elementary NIH Laplacian is:

$$\Delta_{\mathrm{NIH}} = \begin{pmatrix} 2^l\text{-}1 & -1 & -1 & \cdots & -1 \\ -1 & 2^l\text{-}1 & -1 & \cdots & -1 \\ -1 & -1 & 2^l\text{-}1 & \cdots & -1 \\ \vdots & \vdots & \vdots & \ddots & \vdots \\ -1 & -1 & -1 & \cdots & 2^l\text{-}1 \end{pmatrix}$$

which gives $\lambda = 2^l$. That is we can construct an elementary needle in a haystack landscape with a mutation operator which can move to any point in the search landscape in one step and all such points are equally likely. Next we show that Δ_{NIH} is the only elementary needle in a haystack landscape Laplacian.

Suppose the first row of an elementary needle Laplacian is $(a, b, c, d, \ldots, z)$. Since the Laplacian is symmetric its first column is also $(a, b, c, d, \ldots, z)$. a is the degree of the solution node. Since the solution must be accessible $a > 0$. Now $f = (1, 0, 0, 0, \ldots, 0)$. So Δf is $(a, b, c, d, \ldots, z)$ but since Δ represents an elementary NIH landscape $\Delta f = \lambda(f - 2^{-n})$. Thus $a = \lambda(1 - 2^{-n})$, so $\lambda > 0$. Also $b = -\lambda 2^{-n}$. Since the off diagonal terms of Δ are either 0 or -1, $b = -1$ and so λ must be 2^n. The other elements of the first row of Δ, $c, d, \ldots, z$, must also be -1. Either the wave equation or the fact that Δ's rows sum to zero gives us $a = 2^n - 1$. Notice $b = $ -1, $c = $ -1, $d = $ -1, $\ldots$, $z = $ -1 in any elementary needle in a haystack landscape. That is, in any elementary NIH landscape every point in the search space can reach the global optimum in one move and vice versa.

The last part of the argument, is to say that in a fair needle in a haystack problem, the chance of finding the optimum should be no more than the chance of finding any other point in the search space. Thus the number of paths into that point should not be less than the number into the optimum. We have shown the optimum's degree is $2^n - 1$ and so every row must contain $2^n - 1$ "-1" elements. Since each row has only 2^n elements, every off diagonal element must be -1. I.e. Δ_{NIH} represents the only elementary needle in a haystack landscape.

5.5 Recursive Construction of Parity's Landscape

We use the notation

$$\left(\begin{array}{c|c} A & B \\ \hline C & D \end{array} \right)$$

to indicate a square $n \times n$ matrix that is composed of four square $n/2 \times n/2$ matrices A, B, C and D. (Section 6 will expand the following analysis to 3-bit and multiple bit changing mutation operators.)

This section will show that the Laplacian of the connectivity graph for k order parity (Δ_k) can be recursively created from two Laplacian for (k-1) parity and two Laplacians for the k-2 Hamming graph (H_{k-2}). I.e:

$$\Delta_k = \left(\begin{array}{c|c} (k-1)I + \Delta_{k-1} & H_{k-2} - (k-1)I \\ \hline H_{k-2} - (k-1)I & (k-1)I + \Delta_{k-1} \end{array} \right) \quad (2)$$

Where I is the identity matrix (of the appropriate dimensions). $(k-1)I$ is included in the two on-diagonal submatrices so that all the diagonal elements are $(k-1) + \frac{1}{2}(k-1)(k-2) = \frac{1}{2}k(k-1)$ as required. Since H (like Δ) is a graph Laplacian, its rows sum to zero. By subtracting $(k-1)I$ from the off diagonal matrices we ensure all the rows in $(k-1)I + \Delta_{k-1}|H_{k-2} - (k-1)I$ also sum to zero. (When we look in detail at H_{k-2} we will see that $-(k-1)I$ is exactly the adjustment needed for the Hamming cube adjacency matrix.)

Label the rows and columns of Δ_k with 2^{k-1} integers. These are given by the first 2^{k-1} integers starting from zero plus a kth bit. This most significant bit is set (or cleared) to ensure the number of bits set in the row label is even. Order the rows/columns by the lower k-1 bits, ignoring the top (parity) bit. Elements of Δ are -1 if there are exactly two bits different in the row and column labels. Diagonal elements are $\frac{1}{2}k(k-1)$ and all other elements are zero.

Divide Δ into four equal sub-matrices. Half of Δ is made of the rows whose k-1th bit is zero. The other half is made of the rows whose k-1th bit is one. (Similarly for the columns). In the two on-diagonal sub-matrices the k-1th bit in both the rows and the columns is the same.

If an element of Δ in the on-diagonal sub-matrices is -1, then this means that there are exactly two bits that differ in its row and column labels but the differing bits cannot include the k-1th bit. If we remove the k-1th bit, this is the condition for Δ_{k-1} to be -1. (We have to tidy up the labels by not just removing the k-1th bit but also the kth bits and recalculating the top, parity, bit for the k-2 bits.) As mentioned above, Δ_{k-1} has diagonal elements of $\frac{1}{2}(k-1)(k-2)$ so k-1 has to be added to them to convert the diagonal elements of Δ_{k-1} to those for Δ_k.

In the off diagonal sub-matrices of Δ, either the k-1th bit of the row's label is zero and the k-1th bit of the column's label is one or vice versa. I.e. the row and column's label already differs in one bit. If an element of Δ in the off-diagonal sub-matrices is -1, then, excluding the k-1th and k^{th} bits, its row and column labels must differ by exactly one bit. (Alternatively the k-1th and k^{th} bits both differ and the other k-2 bits are the same.) Ignoring the top two bits for a moment, we see that Δ being -1 in the off diagonals is exactly the same as the Hamming distance between two k-2 bit strings being one. That is, if H_{k-2} is -1 so too are the corresponding off diagonal elements in Δ. The only other non-zero elements of H are on the diagonal.

Since a k-bit string has k neighbours which differ by exactly one bit, the diagonal elements of H are k. I.e., the diagonal elements of H_{k-2} are k-2. These elements correspond to the lower k-2 bits of the row and column labels of Δ being the same. In Δ these elements are -1 (rather than k-2) since the two top bits can be simultaneously changed without changing the lower k-2 bits. Subtracting $k-1$ from the diagonal elements of H_{k-2} (i.e. from k-2) gives -1. Which is the value of the corresponding element in Δ_k. Hence we have proved Equation 2.

Δ_{k-1} can be defined in terms of Δ_{k-2} and H_{k-3} and so on. The base cases are: Δ_2 and H_1 which are both $\left(\begin{array}{cc} 1 & -1 \\ -1 & 1 \end{array} \right)$.

5.6 Eigen Analysis of Parity's Landscape

Using the recursive decomposition of Δ given in the previous section, we shall show if e_{k-1} is an eigenvector of Δ_{k-1} then $e_{k-1}|e_{k-1}$ and $e_{k-1}| - e_{k-1}$ are eigenvectors of Δ_k. It turns out the Walsh functions [24] are eigenvectors of both the Laplacian of the Hamming neighbourhood H and of the that of the Parity neighbourhood Δ. (Indeed, as Section 6 will prove, they are also eigenvectors of the Laplacians of many bit flip mutations.) The eigenvalues of Δ will be given at the end of this section.

$e_k \Delta_k =$

$(e_{k-1}| \pm e_{k-1}) \left(\begin{array}{c|c} (k-1)I + \Delta_{k-1} & H_{k-2} - (k-1)I \\ \hline H_{k-2} - (k-1)I & (k-1)I + \Delta_{k-1} \end{array} \right) =$

$$\left(\begin{array}{cc} (k-1)e_{k-1} + \lambda e_{k-1} & \pm e_{k-1}H_{k-2} \mp (k-1)e_{k-1} \\ e_{k-1}H_{k-2} - (k-1)e_{k-1} \pm & (k-1)e_{k-1} \pm \lambda e_{k-1} \end{array} \right)$$
(3)

Start with the base case (k=2): $\left(\begin{array}{cc} 1 & -1 \\ -1 & 1 \end{array} \right)$ has eigenvectors e_{2+}=(1,1) (eigenvalue 0) and e_{2-}=(1,-1) (eigenvalue 2). Notice that these are eigenvectors of both Δ_2 and H_1. So Equation 3 for k=3 becomes

$(e_2| \pm e_2)\Delta_3 =$
$\left(\begin{array}{cccc} (k-1)e_{k-1} + \lambda e_{k-1} & \pm & \lambda e_{k-1} \mp (k-1)e_{k-1} \\ \lambda e_{k-1} - (k-1)e_{k-1} & \pm & (k-1)e_{k-1} \pm \lambda e_{k-1} \end{array} \right) =$
$\left(\begin{array}{cccc} 2e_2 + \lambda e_2 & \pm & \lambda e_2 \mp 2e_2 \\ \lambda e_2 - 2e_2 & \pm & 2e_2 \pm \lambda e_2 \end{array} \right) =$
$\left(\begin{array}{c} 2\lambda e_2 \\ 2\lambda e_2 \end{array} \right)$ and $\left(\begin{array}{c} 4e_2 \\ -4e_2 \end{array} \right)$

That is $(e_2|e_2)$ are eigenvectors of Δ_3 (with eigenvalue 2λ) and so too are $(e_2| - e_2)$ (with eigenvalue 4). So Δ_3 has four eigenvectors:

$$
\begin{array}{lrrrr}
e_{3++} & =(1, & 1, & 1, & 1) \\
e_{3+-} & =(1, & 1, & -1, & -1) \\
e_{3-+} & =(1, & -1, & 1, & -1) \\
e_{3--} & =(1, & -1, & -1, & 1)
\end{array}
$$

with corresponding eigenvalues: $\lambda_{3++} = 2\lambda_{2+} = 0$, $\lambda_{3+-} = 2\lambda_{2-} = 4$, $\lambda_{3-+} = 4$ and $\lambda_{3--} = 4$. We can see that the four eigenvectors form an orthonormal set and so this is a complete eigen description of Δ_3. The eigenvectors of Δ_3, e_3 are the Walsh basis (on 2 bits).

It can be shown that the Walsh basis (on k bits) are eigenvectors of the Hamming cube H_k, with eigenvalues $2i$ with multiplicity C_i^k for $0 \leq i \leq k$. (See, for example, Dr. Daniel Spielman's lecture notes (Lecture five, 16 September 2009 http://www.cs.yale.edu/homes/spielman/561/lect05-09 .pdf) or [2].) Therefore the eigenvectors of Δ_3 are also eigenvectors of H_2 (albeit with different eigenvalues). We have e_3 are the Walsh basis therefore $e_3|e_3$ and $e_3| - e_3$ are the Walsh basis (3 bits). Let this hold for any higher order. I.e. $e_{k-1}|e_{k-1}$ and $e_{k-1}| - e_{k-1}$ are the Walsh basis on k-1 bits. Then Equation 3 becomes:

$\left(\begin{array}{cccc} (k-1)e_{k-1} + \lambda_{k-1}e_{k-1} \pm & 2ie_{k-1} \mp (k-1)e_{k-1} \\ 2ie_{k-1} - (k-1)e_{k-1} & \pm(k-1)e_{k-1} \pm \lambda_{k-1}e_{k-1} \end{array} \right) =$
$\left(\begin{array}{c} (2i + \lambda_{k-1})e_{k-1} \\ (2i + \lambda_{k-1})e_{k-1} \end{array} \right)$ and $\left(\begin{array}{c} (2(k-1) - 2i + \lambda_{k-1})e_{k-1} \\ -(2(k-1) - 2i + \lambda_{k-1})e_{k-1} \end{array} \right)$

Table 1: Eigenvalues of Laplacian of Parity's landscape graph. The subscripts are the multiplicity of the Δ eigenvalues. Last column is the number of distinct eigenvalues. The total number of eigenvalues and eigenvectors is 2^{k-1}. (Catalogued as A176296 in the on-line encyclopedia of integer sequences.)

$k=$								
2	0_1	2_1						2
3	0_1	4_3						2
4	0_1	6_4	8_3					3
5	0_1	8_5	12_{10}					3
6	0_1	10_6	16_{15}	18_{10}				4
7	0_1	12_7	20_{21}	24_{35}				4
8	0_1	14_8	24_{28}	30_{56}	32_{35}			5
9	0_1	16_9	28_{36}	36_{84}	40_{126}			5
10	0_1	18_{10}	32_{45}	42_{120}	48_{210}	50_{126}		6
11	0_1	20_{11}	36_{55}	48_{165}	56_{330}	60_{462}		6
$\vdots$								
17	0_1	32_{17}	60_{136}	84_{680}	104_{2380}	$\cdots$	144_{24310}	9

Where $2i$ is an eigenvalue of H_{k-2}. So $0 \leq i \leq k-2$. $2i$ and λ_{k-1} are related since they are the eigenvalues of H_{k-2} and Δ_{k-1} for the same eigenvector e_{k-1}.

That is $e_{k-1}|e_{k-1}$ are indeed eigenvectors of Δ_k (with eigenvalues $2i + \lambda_{k-1}$) and so too are $e_{k-1}| - e_{k-1}$ (with eigenvalues $2(k-1) - 2i + \lambda_{k-1}$). Notice since $e_{k-1}| \pm e_{k-1}$ are the Walsh basis, they form a complete orthogonal set of eigenvectors for Δ_k. The eigenvalues of Δ are not as elegant as those of the Hamming cube H but can be rapidly calculated, $O(k^2)$. The first values are given in Table 1. Notice there are rather fewer distinct values than for the Hamming cube. In Section 5.9 we will prove that Δ_k has $k/2+1$ distinct eigenvalues.

The multiplicities shown as subscripts in Table 1 are similar to Pascal's triangle. (I.e. the eigenvalue multiplicities of the Hamming cube's Laplacian.) Firstly they sum to 2^{k-1} in each row. Also, except for the largest eigenvalue, each multiplicity is the sum of the multiplicities immediately above and to the left in the previous row. The multiplicity of the largest eigenvalue depends upon whether k is odd or even. If k is even, the multiplicity of the largest eigenvalue is the same as that in the previous row. If k odd, it is the sum of the multiplicity in the previous row to the left plus *twice* the multiplicity of the largest eigenvalue for k-1.

5.7 Largest Eigenvalue of Double Bit Flip Graph Laplacian

Since Δ is a Laplacian and hence its rows always sum to zero, its smallest eigenvalue is always zero (with multiplicity one). The smallest non-zero eigenvalue corresponds to the lowest Walsh function and has the value $2k-2$. Saying in closed form which Walsh functions have the largest eigenvalue is not straight forward. However we can 1) establish an upper bound on the largest eigenvalue and 2) give a stochastic estimate for large k.

5.7.1 Upper Bound on Largest Eigenvalue of Double Bit Flip Graph Laplacian

Depending upon the Walsh function chosen, an eigenvalue of Δ_k is either $\lambda_{H_{k-2}} + \lambda_{k-1}$ or $2(k-1) - \lambda_{H_{k-2}} + \lambda_{k-1}$. We know $\lambda_{H_{k-2}}$ cannot exceed $2k - 4$ or be smaller than zero. Therefore the largest eigenvalue cannot exceed $2k - 2 + \max(\lambda_{k-1})$. We know $\max(\lambda_2) = 2$. So (for $k > 2$)

$$\lambda_k \leq \sum_{i=3}^{i=k} 2i - 2 + 2$$

$$\lambda_k \leq \sum_{i=3}^{i=k} 2i$$

$$\lambda_k \leq -2 - 4 + 2\sum_{i=0}^{i=k} i$$

$$\lambda_k \leq -2 - 4 + 2k(k+1)/2$$

Rearranging gives $\lambda_k \leq k(k+1) - 6$. However it appears the actual value is $\lceil (k-1)(k+1)/2 \rceil$.

5.7.2 Long Bit String Estimate of the Largest Eigenvalue of the 2-bit Flip Graph Laplacian

For any unit vector u the length of Δu will be no bigger than the largest eigenvalue. Choose a random direction. I.e. let v be a vector of 2^{k-1} components each of which is either $+1$ or -1, chosen uniformly at random. $|v|^2 = 2^{k-1}$ hence $|v| = 2^{(k-1)/2}$ (Eventually we will normalise v to be of unit length by dividing by $|v|$.) The first element of Δv is typical of them all.

$$\Delta v(1) = \pm \frac{1}{2}k(k-1) \qquad \underbrace{\pm 1 \pm \cdots\cdots\cdots \pm 1}_{\frac{1}{2}k(k-1) \text{ terms with random signs}}$$

The square of the length of Δv is given by summing the squares of each of its components in the usual way. Since the elements of v were randomly chosen, each of the elements of Δv (i.e. $\Delta v(i)$) are independent and identically distributed and therefore $|\Delta v(i)|^2$ are also i.i.d. Thus the expected value of $|\Delta v|^2$ is $2^{k-1} \times$ the expected value of any of them, e.g. the first $|\Delta v(1)|^2$. The expected length of $\Delta v(1)$ is approximately $\frac{1}{2}k(k-1)$. (The random signs ensure on average the following terms come to near zero and for large k the sum is dominated by the first (largest) term.) Thus the expected value of $|\Delta v|^2$ is $|\frac{1}{2}k(k-1)|^2 2^{k-1}$ and that of $|\Delta v| = \frac{1}{2}k(k-1)2^{(k-1)/2}$. Taking the ratio $\frac{|\Delta v|}{|v|}$ gives $\frac{1}{2}k(k-1)$ as an upper bound on all the eigenvalues. For large k this will become a tight bound on the largest eigenvalue.

Note the exact bound appears to be within a factor of two of the apparent value, whereas the stochastic upper bound appears to be increasingly tight as k increases. Finally note the eigenvalues of parity's Δ are a factor of k bigger than those of the Hamming cube.

5.8 Elementary Landscape Roughness and the Eigenvalues of the Graph Laplacian

Recall $d = \frac{1}{2}k(k-1)$ so the stochastic bound is needed to ensure $\frac{\lambda}{d} \leq 1$ for all cases (cf. Equation 1). Higher order Walsh functions are considered to be more rugged, since their sign changes more often than lower order Walsh functions. (Rothlauf points out [16, p27] that Walsh order is not a universal indicator of problem difficulty.) Elementary landscapes generated by higher Walsh basis functions have higher eigenvalues than those corresponding to lower order Walsh functions. Using Equation 1, we can see the higher an elementary landscape's eigenvalue the further each point is from the average of its neighbours. Thus we can view $\frac{\lambda}{d}$ as another measure of landscape ruggedness. The larger it is, the less each point tells us about the (average) fitness of its neighbours.

In other regular elementary landscapes eigenvalues can exceed the number of neighbours. I.e. $\frac{\lambda}{d}$ can exceed 1. For example in the Hamming cube the largest eigenvalue of H_k is $2k$ and each node has k neighbours. (So $0 \leq \lambda_H/d_H \leq 2$.) Whitley et $at.$ [26, p589] equates $\frac{\lambda}{d} > 1$ with rugged elementary landscapes. Whereas they suggests if $0 \leq \frac{\lambda}{d} \leq 1$ the elementary landscape is smooth. ([26] uses a constant rather than referring to λ as an eigenvalue.)

We get the same conclusion if we use Whitley's [28] component based model of elementary landscapes. This treats their fitness as being composed of components which are added to and removed from the current trial solution as the search process moves from a point to one of its neighbours. [25, p383] gives $\frac{\lambda}{d} = p_1 + p_2$. Where p_1 is the proportion of components of $f(x)$ that change when we move away from x. p_2 is the proportion of components not included in $f(x)$ that change when we move away from x. Thus we should expect a small value of $p_1 + p_2$ to give a smooth landscape. When $p_1 + p_2$ approaches one, most of the components are being changed at each move, so we expect a more rugged landscape, in keeping with the previous paragraph.

5.9 Number of Distinct Eigenvalues and Parity's Graph Diameter

A graph's diameter is the maximum distance between any two nodes in the graph. (Where the distance is the smallest number of edges that have to be traversed to go between the nodes.) Parity is symmetric so the longest distance between any pair of nodes, is the same as the longest distance between the origin and any node. This is the minimum number of pairs of bit flips between k-1 zeros and the binary string of the target node. This is simply $bc(target)/2$, where bc is the number of 1s (the bit count). Obviously the worst case is when all bits are one. Hence Δ's graph diameter is $k/2$. Whereas the diameter of the Hamming cube is k-1.

Reeves [14, page 598] says the number of distinct eigenvalues is the graph diameter plus one. We can see, from the last column of Table 1, that the number of distinct eigenvalues is indeed $k/2+1$.

5.10 Number of Distinct Elementary Landscapes and Walsh Analysis

Since the eigenvectors form an orthogonal set, any vector, including the fitness f vector, can be represented by its components projected onto the eigenvectors. Remembering Section 5.3, each eigenvector of Δ represents an elementary landscape, so fitness can be represented as a sum of elementary landscapes. One for each eigenvector where it has a non-zero projection. As the Walsh basis functions are eigenvectors of Δ projecting the fitness f vector onto these eigenvectors is equivalent to the Walsh analysis of f. Since f is 1 followed by $2^{k-1} - 1$ zeros it has 2^{k-1} non-zero Walsh coefficients. That is all its Walsh coefficients are non-zero (actually they are all equal to $2^{-(k-1)}$). However eigenvec-

tors with the same eigenvalue form sub-spaces where any linear combination of these eigenvectors is also an eigenvector. Hence any vector can be represented as a sum of eigenvectors, one for each subspace where it has non-zero projection. We know that Parity's fitness vector has non-zero projection into each subspace so all $k/2 + 1$ subspaces must be used. That is, Parity's fitness function can be expressed as $k/2 + 1$ elementary fitness landscapes. Indeed $k/2+1$ is an upper limit on the number of elementary landscapes needed to represent any fitness function (when we use only a 2-bit flip mutation operator).

6. HIGHER BIT FLIP LANDSCAPES

6.1 Construction of 3-Bit Flip Laplacian

We can extend the construction used in Section 5.5 to consider the landscape formed by a mutation operator which flips exactly three bits.

$$\Delta_{3,l} = \left(\begin{array}{c|c} (C_3^l - C_3^{l-1})I + \Delta_{3,l-1} & \Delta_{2,l-1} - (C_3^l - C_3^{l-1})I \\ \hline \Delta_{2,l-1} - (C_3^l - C_3^{l-1})I & (C_3^l - C_3^{l-1})I + \Delta_{3,l-1} \end{array} \right)$$
$$(4)$$

We use $\Delta_{n,l}$ to refer to the Laplacian of the graph formed by flipping exactly n bits in strings of length l. Note, unlike for parity in Section 5, we allow the graph to be disjoint. This simplifies the analysis a little. For example, all strings are of length l rather than being shorter if parts of the search space are inaccessible.

Unlike the double flip operator, every point in the search space can be reached eventually by mutating exactly three bits. Therefore, when using Equation 4, we have to use a version of the Laplacian which includes the half of the search space which (starting from the origin) was previously inaccessible. E.g. for three bits the new Laplacian for flipping two bits (cf. Δ_3 Section 5.3) is:

$$\Delta_{2,3} = \begin{array}{c} \\ 000 \\ 001 \\ 010 \\ 011 \\ 100 \\ 101 \\ 110 \\ 111 \end{array} \begin{array}{cccccccc} 000 & 001 & 010 & 011 & 100 & 101 & 110 & 111 \\ \hline 3 & 0 & 0 & -1 & 0 & -1 & -1 & 0 \\ 0 & 3 & -1 & 0 & -1 & 0 & 0 & -1 \\ 0 & -1 & 3 & 0 & -1 & 0 & 0 & -1 \\ -1 & 0 & 0 & 3 & 0 & -1 & -1 & 0 \\ 0 & -1 & -1 & 0 & 3 & 0 & 0 & -1 \\ -1 & 0 & 0 & -1 & 0 & 3 & -1 & 0 \\ -1 & 0 & 0 & -1 & 0 & -1 & 3 & 0 \\ 0 & -1 & -1 & 0 & -1 & 0 & 0 & 3 \end{array}$$

$$\Delta_{3,3} = \begin{array}{c} \\ 000 \\ 001 \\ 010 \\ 011 \\ 100 \\ 101 \\ 110 \\ 111 \end{array} \begin{array}{cccccccc} 000 & 001 & 010 & 011 & 100 & 101 & 110 & 111 \\ \hline 1 & 0 & 0 & 0 & 0 & 0 & 0 & -1 \\ 0 & 1 & 0 & 0 & 0 & 0 & -1 & 0 \\ 0 & 0 & 1 & 0 & 0 & -1 & 0 & 0 \\ 0 & 0 & 0 & 1 & -1 & 0 & 0 & 0 \\ 0 & 0 & 0 & -1 & 1 & 0 & 0 & 0 \\ 0 & 0 & -1 & 0 & 0 & 1 & 0 & 0 \\ 0 & -1 & 0 & 0 & 0 & 0 & 1 & 0 \\ -1 & 0 & 0 & 0 & 0 & 0 & 0 & 1 \end{array}$$

$$\Delta_{3,4} = \begin{array}{c|cccccccccccccccc} 0000 & 4 & 0 & 0 & 0 & 0 & 0 & 0 & -1 & 0 & 0 & 0 & -1 & 0 & -1 & -1 & 0 \\ 0001 & 0 & 4 & 0 & 0 & 0 & 0 & -1 & 0 & 0 & 0 & -1 & 0 & -1 & 0 & 0 & -1 \\ 0010 & 0 & 0 & 4 & 0 & 0 & -1 & 0 & 0 & 0 & -1 & 0 & 0 & -1 & 0 & 0 & -1 \\ 0011 & 0 & 0 & 0 & 4 & -1 & 0 & 0 & 0 & -1 & 0 & 0 & 0 & 0 & -1 & -1 & 0 \\ 0100 & 0 & 0 & 0 & -1 & 4 & 0 & 0 & 0 & 0 & -1 & -1 & 0 & 0 & 0 & 0 & -1 \\ 0101 & 0 & 0 & -1 & 0 & 0 & 4 & 0 & 0 & -1 & 0 & 0 & -1 & 0 & 0 & -1 & 0 \\ 0110 & 0 & -1 & 0 & 0 & 0 & 0 & 4 & 0 & -1 & 0 & 0 & -1 & 0 & -1 & 0 & 0 \\ 0111 & -1 & 0 & 0 & 0 & 0 & 0 & 0 & 4 & 0 & -1 & -1 & 0 & -1 & 0 & 0 & 0 \\ 1000 & 0 & 0 & 0 & -1 & 0 & -1 & -1 & 0 & 4 & 0 & 0 & 0 & 0 & 0 & 0 & -1 \\ 1001 & 0 & 0 & -1 & 0 & -1 & 0 & 0 & -1 & 0 & 4 & 0 & 0 & 0 & 0 & -1 & 0 \\ 1010 & 0 & -1 & 0 & 0 & -1 & 0 & 0 & -1 & 0 & 0 & 4 & 0 & 0 & -1 & 0 & 0 \\ 1011 & -1 & 0 & 0 & 0 & 0 & -1 & -1 & 0 & 0 & 0 & 0 & 4 & -1 & 0 & 0 & 0 \\ 1100 & 0 & -1 & -1 & 0 & 0 & 0 & 0 & -1 & 0 & 0 & 0 & -1 & 4 & 0 & 0 & 0 \\ 1101 & -1 & 0 & 0 & -1 & 0 & 0 & -1 & 0 & 0 & 0 & -1 & 0 & 0 & 4 & 0 & 0 \\ 1110 & -1 & 0 & 0 & -1 & 0 & -1 & 0 & 0 & 0 & -1 & 0 & 0 & 0 & 0 & 4 & 0 \\ 1111 & 0 & -1 & -1 & 0 & -1 & 0 & 0 & 0 & -1 & 0 & 0 & 0 & 0 & 0 & 0 & 4 \end{array}$$

Using $\Delta_{2,3}$ and $\Delta_{3,3}$ we can easily see that Equation 4 holds for $\Delta_{3,4}$:

$$\Delta_{3,4} = \left(\begin{array}{c|c} 3I + \Delta_{3,3} & \Delta_{2,3} - 3I \\ \hline \Delta_{2,3} - 3I & 3I + \Delta_{3,3} \end{array} \right)$$

To show Equation 4 holds in general we reuse the argument given in Section 5.5. Essentially in the on diagonal quadrants of $\Delta_{3,l}$ the most significant bits of the node labels are the same. I.e. either both 0 or both 1. Thus in these two quadrants, where the node labels differ by exactly three bits (a "-1" element) the different bits must be in the lower $l-1$ bits. Which is exactly the condition for $\Delta_{3,l-1}$ to also have a -1 element. In the off diagonal quadrants, the most significant bits are different. Thus any -1 element must correspond to exactly two bits being different in the lower $l-1$ bits of the search space labels. This is exactly the condition of $\Delta_{2,l-1}$ to also have a -1 element. It only remains to fix up the diagonal elements of the four quadrants.

The diagonal elements in the three bit mutation's Laplacians are C_3^l (where the bit string length is l). Correspondingly the diagonal elements of $\Delta_{3,l-1}$ are C_3^{l-1}. So, in equation 4, we need to add $C_3^l - C_3^{l-1}$ to the main diagonal.

$$\begin{aligned} C_3^l - C_3^{l-1} &= \frac{l(l-1)!}{3!(l-3)!} - \frac{(l-1)!}{3!(l-4)!} \\ &= \frac{(l-1)!}{3!(l-3)!} \times (l - (l-3)) \\ &= \frac{(l-1)!}{3!(l-3)!} \times 3 \\ &= \frac{(l-1)!}{2!(l-1-2)!} \\ &= C_2^{l-1} \end{aligned}$$

Having added to C_2^{l-1} to the two on-diagonal quadrants, to ensure every row of $\Delta_{3,l}$ continues to sum to zero, we must subtract C_2^{l-1} from the diagonal of the two off-diagonal quadrants. Notice, since the diagonal elements of $\Delta_{2,l-1}$ are C_2^{l-1}, the diagonals of the off diagonal quadrants are zero.

6.2 Construction of n-Bit Flip Laplacian

We can extend the construction used in the previous section to consider the landscape formed by a mutation operator which flips exactly n bits.

We start by simplifying the diagonal terms. Again we need to add a multiple of I to the main diagonal and subtract it in the remaining two quadrants. (See previous section.) For the n bit Laplacian we must add $C_n^l - C_n^{l-1}$ to ensure the diagonal of Δ_n^{l-1} is brought up to that of Δ_n^l

$$\begin{aligned} C_n^l - C_n^{l-1} &= \frac{l(l-1)!}{n!(l-n)!} - \frac{(l-1)!}{n!(l-1-n)!} \\ &= \frac{(l-1)!}{n!(l-n)!} \times (l - (l-n)) \\ &= \frac{(l-1)!}{n!(l-n)!} \times n \\ &= \frac{(l-1)!}{(n-1)!(l-1-(n-1))!} \\ &= C_{n-1}^{l-1} \end{aligned}$$

Notice again that this is equal to the diagonal elements of $\Delta_{n,l-1}$, and so in general the diagonal elements of the off diagonal quadrants corresponding to the lower order mutation operator acting on the shorter bit string are zero. This is correct, since n-bit flip mutation cannot simply flip the most significant bit (which correspond to changing only one bit).

$$\Delta_{n,l} = \left(\begin{array}{c|c} C_{n-1}^{l-1} I + \Delta_{n,l-1} & \Delta_{n-1,l-1} - C_{n-1}^{l-1} I \\ \hline \Delta_{n-1,l-1} - C_{n-1}^{l-1} I & C_{n-1}^{l-1} I + \Delta_{n,l-1} \end{array} \right) \quad (5)$$

To give a concrete example, consider the Laplacian for flipping exactly five bits. The example shows it can be decomposed into two lower order five bit and two four bit Laplacians (plus C_4^{l-1} multiples of the identity matrix I). To make the symmetries clearer, we have only printed the non-zero elements.

$$\Delta_{4,5} =$$

$$\begin{array}{c|ccccccccccccccccccccccccccccccccc}
00000 & 5 & & & & & & & & -1 & & & & & & & & & & -1 & & & -1 & -1 & -1 \\
00001 & & 5 & & & & & & & & -1 & & & & & & & -1 & & & -1 & -1 & & -1 \\
00010 & & & 5 & & & & & & & & -1 & & & & & & & -1 & & -1 & & -1 & -1 \\
00011 & & & & 5 & & & & & & & & -1 & & & & & -1 & & -1 & & -1 & -1 & -1 \\
00100 & & & & & 5 & & & & & -1 & & & & & & & -1 & & -1 & -1 & & -1 \\
00101 & & & & & & 5 & & -1 & & & & & & -1 & & & & -1 & -1 & -1 \\
00110 & & & & & & 5 & -1 & & & & & & & -1 & & & -1 & -1 & -1 \\
00111 & & & & & & 5 & -1 & & & & & -1 & & & & -1 & -1 & -1 \\
01000 & & & & & -1 & & 1 & 5 & & & & & & -1 & -1 & -1 & & & & & -1 \\
01001 & & & & -1 & & 5 & & & & & -1 & & & & -1 \\
01010 & & & -1 & & & 5 & & & & -1 & & -1 & & -1 & & -1 \\
01011 & & -1 & & & & 5 & & -1 & & & -1 & -1 & & -1 \\
01100 & & -1 & & & & 5 & & & -1 & -1 & & -1 & & -1 \\
01101 & -1 & & & & & 5 & & -1 & & -1 & -1 & & -1 \\
01110 & -1 & & & & & 5 & -1 & & -1 & -1 & & -1 \\
01111 & -1 & & & & & 5 & -1 & -1 & -1 & & -1 \\
10000 & & & & & & -1 & & -1 & -1 & -1 & 5 & & & & & & -1 \\
10001 & & & & -1 & & -1 & -1 & -1 & & -1 & 5 & & & & -1 \\
10010 & & -1 & & & & -1 & & -1 & & & 5 & & & -1 \\
10011 & & & & -1 & & -1 & -1 & & -1 & -1 & & 5 & & -1 \\
10100 & & -1 & & -1 & -1 & & -1 & & & & & 5 & & -1 \\
10101 & -1 & & & & -1 & -1 & -1 & & & & 5 & & -1 \\
10110 & -1 & & & -1 & -1 & -1 & & & 5 & -1 \\
10111 & -1 & & & -1 & -1 & -1 & & & 5 & -1 \\
11000 & & -1 & -1 & & & & -1 & & & & & -1 & 5 \\
11001 & & -1 & -1 & -1 & & & -1 & & & & -1 & 5 \\
11010 & & -1 & & -1 & -1 & & & -1 & & & & -1 & 5 \\
11011 & -1 & & -1 & -1 & & & -1 & & & -1 & 5 \\
11100 & & -1 & -1 & & -1 & -1 & & & -1 & & 5 \\
11101 & -1 & & -1 & & -1 & & & -1 & & 5 \\
11110 & -1 & & -1 & -1 & & -1 & & & -1 & 5 \\
11111 & & -1 & -1 & -1 & & -1 & & & -1 & 5
\end{array}$$

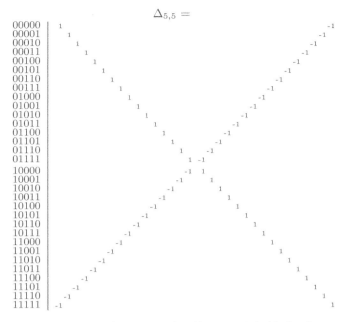

$$\Delta_{5,5} =$$

Using $\Delta_{4,5}$ and $\Delta_{5,5}$ we see that Equation 5 holds for $\Delta_{5,6}$:

$$\Delta_{5,6} = \left(\begin{array}{c|c} 5I + \Delta_{5,5} & \Delta_{4,5} - 5I \\ \hline \Delta_{4,5} - 5I & 5I + \Delta_{5,5} \end{array} \right)$$

The proof of Equation 5 follows that for two and three bit flip mutation (Sections 5.5 and 6.1). In the on diagonal quadrants of $\Delta_{n,l}$ the most significant bits of the node labels are the same, thus in these two quadrants, where there is a -1 element, the node labels must differ in exactly n positions. Since the most significant positions are the same, the n differences must be in the lower part of the node labels. Which is the condition for $\Delta_{n,l-1}$ to have a -1 element. Whereas in the two off diagonal quadrants, the top positions do differ, so each -1 element means there are n-1 differences in the lower parts of the node labels. Which is the condition for $\Delta_{n-1,l-1}$ to have a -1 element. The only other non-zero elements are the diagonals, which (at the beginning of this section) we showed need to be adjusted by $\pm C_{n-1}^{l-1}$.

The base case for flipping exactly n bits is the set of strings of n bits. Here mutation is highly constrained and all it can do is move between each string and its complement. So although there are 2^n strings in the fitness landscape, with n-bit mutation, the landscape falls into 2^{n-1} parts. Each part contains exactly two string. Each part is inaccessible from all the others. Thus $\Delta_{n,n}$ is the $2^n \times 2^n$ sparse symmetric array with exactly one -1 per row (along the trailing diagonal) and 1 on the main diagonal (see $\Delta_{3,3}$ and $\Delta_{5,5}$). Starting from the set of $\Delta_{n,n}$, Equation 5 can be used recursively to construct the Laplacian for mutation of binary strings by flipping exactly n bits.

6.3 Eigen Analysis of n-bit Mutation

Re-using the eigen analysis for the case of flipping exactly two bits (given in Section 5.6) and the recursive decomposition of $\Delta_{n,l}$ given in the previous section, we shall show the Walsh basis are also eigenvectors of the Laplacian describing n-bit mutation's landscape.

The Walsh basis are vectors of length 2^l. The jth Walsh basis vector's components are: $\psi_j(x) = (-1)^{bc(j \wedge x)}$, where x is the index of the vector element (starting from 0) and

bc is again the number of bits set to one. So $\psi_j(x)$ is -1 if $bc(j \wedge x)$ is odd and 1 if it is even.

The base cases for flipping n bits, $\Delta_{n,n}$, can be split into the sum of the identity matrix (of size $2^n \times 2^n$) and a matrix of the same size which is also zero's except for -1 along the reverse diagonal (e.g. $\Delta_{3,3}$ and $\Delta_{5,5}$). Call this matrix N. Thus $\Delta_{n,n} = I + N$. Multiplying a vector by N, reverses the order of its elements and then multiplies them by -1. Notice reversing the elements means replacing element x by element $\overline{x}$, where $\overline{x}$ is the bitwise complement of x. Hence $\psi_j(x)\Delta_{n,n} = \psi_j(x)(I + N) = \psi_j(x) - \psi_j(\overline{x}) = \psi_j(x) - (-1)^{bc(j \wedge \overline{x})}$.

Suppose j has t bits set. (I.e. $bc(j) = t$.) Only the bits of x which match these influence the calculation of $bc(j \wedge x)$. Suppose, in these positions, x has k bits set and m zeros. (Note $k = bc(j \wedge x)$ and $m = t - k$.) Then $\overline{x}$ has k zeros and m ones matching set bits in j. Hence $bc(j \wedge \overline{x}) = m$. $(-1)^{bc(j \wedge \overline{x})} = (-1)^m = (-1)^{t-k} = (-1)^t(-1)^{-k} = (-1)^t(-1)^k = (-1)^t(-1)^{bc(j \wedge x)} = (-1)^{bc(j)}\psi_j(x)$. Hence $\psi_j(x)\Delta_{n,n} = \psi_j(x) - (-1)^{bc(j)}\psi_j(x) = 0$ or $2\psi_j(x)$. I.e. the Walsh basis vectors, $\psi_j(x)$, are eigenvectors of $\Delta_{n,n}$. The corresponding eigenvalue is either zero (if the number of bits set in j is even) or $\lambda = 2$ (if $bc(j)$ is odd). Remember ψ_j are orthogonal and there are 2^n of them. In other words, the Walsh basis form a complete set of eigenvectors for $\Delta_{n,n}$.

To show the Walsh basis are also eigenvectors of $\Delta_{n,l}$ we reuse the fact that the higher order Walsh basis can be constructed by concatenated each vector with itself or with -1 times itself. I.e., $(e_{l-1}|e_{l-1})$ and $(e_{l-1}|-e_{l-1})$. Using Equation 5:

$$e_l \Delta_{n,l} =$$

$$(e_{l-1}| \pm e_{l-1}) \left(\begin{array}{c|c} C_{n-1}^{l-1}I + \Delta_{n,l-1} & \Delta_{n-1,l-1} - C_{n-1}^{l-1}I \\ \hline \Delta_{n-1,l-1} - C_{n-1}^{l-1}I & C_{n-1}^{l-1}I + \Delta_{n,l-1} \end{array} \right)$$

$$= \left(\begin{array}{c} C_{n-1}^{l-1}e_{l-1} + \Delta_{n,l-1}e_{l-1} \pm \Delta_{n-1,l-1}e_{l-1} \mp C_{n-1}^{l-1}e_{l-1} \\ \Delta_{n-1,l-1}e_{l-1} - C_{n-1}^{l-1}e_{l-1} \pm C_{n-1}^{l-1}e_{l-1} \pm \Delta_{n,l-1}e_{l-1} \end{array} \right)$$

$$= \left(\begin{array}{c} (\lambda_{n,l-1} + \lambda_{n-1,l-1})e_{l-1} \\ (\lambda_{n,l-1} + \lambda_{n-1,l-1})e_{l-1} \end{array} \right)$$

or

$$= \left(\begin{array}{c} (2C_{n-1}^{l-1} + \lambda_{n,l-1} - \lambda_{n-1,l-1})e_{l-1} \\ -(2C_{n-1}^{l-1} + \lambda_{n,l-1} - \lambda_{n-1,l-1})e_{l-1} \end{array} \right)$$

Note e_{l-1} is an eigenvector of both $\Delta_{n,l-1}$ (with eigenvalue denoted $\lambda_{n,l-1}$) and of $\Delta_{n-1,l-1}$ (with eigenvalue denoted $\lambda_{n-1,l-1}$). Therefore $(e_{l-1}|e_{l-1})$ is an eigenvector of $\Delta_{n,l}$ with eigenvalue

$$\lambda_{n,l} = \lambda_{n,l-1} + \lambda_{n-1,l-1} \tag{6}$$

and $(e_{l-1}|-e_{l-1})$ is another eigenvector of $\Delta_{n,l}$ (the higher Walsh vector) with eigenvalue

$$\lambda_{n,l} = 2C_{n-1}^{l-1} + \lambda_{n,l-1} - \lambda_{n-1,l-1}. \tag{7}$$

Since $\lambda_{n,n}$ is either 0 or 2, $\lambda_{n,l}$ will always be real, integer and even. Table 2 shows an example where Equations 6 and 7 are used recursively.

Table 3 gives some example eigenvectors of the graph Laplacians formed by various bit flip mutation operators. Notice that, apart from the zeroth order Walsh basis vector, no eigenvector has the same eigenvalue for all mutation operators.

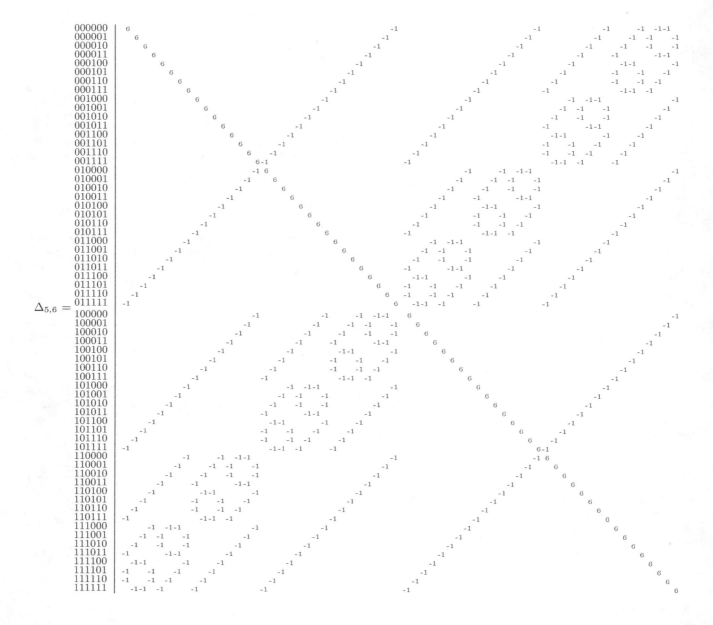

$\Delta_{5,6} =$ (matrix shown above)

6.4 Eigen Analysis Flipping bits Independently

A common mutation scheme in genetic algorithms (GAs) is not to flip a given number of bits but instead to flip each bit independently, albeit at low probability. Often the probability is set to 1/length of the bit string. Thus the mean number of bits flips is one. The actual number of flips follows a Binomial distribution but for long bit strings (i.e. large l) this can be approximated by a Poisson distribution with mean $m = 1.0$, $P(n) = m^n e^{-m}/n! = 0.37/n!$. The first few probabilities are $P(0) = 0.37$, $P(1) = 0.37$, $P(2) = 0.18$, $P(3) = 0.06$. The probabilities fall rapidly with larger changes. A complete graph Laplacian can be constructed by adding (weighted by $P(n)$) together the graph Laplacians for each value of n.

Since each each Walsh basis vector $\psi_j(x)$ is an eigenvector of all of the matrices being added together, $\psi_j(x)$ is also an eigenvector of the matrix for normal GA mutation. The eigenvalue corresponding to the jth Walsh basis vector for a mutation only GA's Laplacian is

$$\lambda_j = \sum_{i=1}^{l} \frac{m^i e^{-m}}{i!} \lambda_{j,i,l} = \frac{1}{e} \sum_{i=1}^{l} \frac{\lambda_{j,i,l}}{i!}$$

(The right hand side applies where $m = 1.0$). $\lambda_{j,i,l}$ is the eigenvalue of the jth Walsh basis vector when applied to the Laplacian for flipping exactly i bits in strings of length l. We set $\lambda_{j,0,l}$ to zero, since it corresponds to flipping zero bits, i.e. making no change. m is the mean number of bits flipped and λ_j is the eigenvalue of the jth Walsh basis vector when applied to the Laplacian for flipping bits independently. The right most column of Table 3 gives λ_j for a mutation only GA which flips on average one bit per child.

Notice that if a fitness function is a Walsh basis functions (or a simple multiple of any) then a mutation only GA using it will have an elementary landscape. Stadler [17] also considers crossover.

36

Table 2: Example recursion. Each n bit Laplacian is followed by the two n-1 bit Laplacians from which it is composed and from which its eigenvectors and eigenvalues can be calculated using Equation 6 or 7. Directly below each Laplacian are its eigenvalues (which are subscripted by their multiplicities). The recursion is halted when the eigen analyse is known. I.e. for the Hamming cube ($n = 1$) or when every bit in the string is flipped ($n = l$).

$$\Delta_{6,7}$$
$$0_2 4_{42} 8_{70} 12_{14}$$

$$\Delta_{6,6} \qquad\qquad \Delta_{5,6}$$
$$0_{32} 2_{32} \qquad 0_1 2_6 4_{15} 6_{20} 8_{15} 10_6 12_1$$

$$\Delta_{5,5} \qquad\qquad \Delta_{4,5}$$
$$0_{16} 2_{16} \qquad 0_2 4_{20} 8_{10}$$

$$\Delta_{4,4} \qquad\qquad \Delta_{3,4}$$
$$0_8 2_8 \qquad 0_1 2_4 4_6 6_4 8_1$$

$$\Delta_{3,3} \qquad \Delta_{2,3}$$
$$0_4 2_4 \qquad 0_2 4_6$$

$$\Delta_{2,2} \qquad \Delta_{1,2}$$
$$0_2 2_2 \qquad 0_1 2_2 4_1$$

6.5 Largest Eigenvalue of n-bit Flip Graph Laplacian

We generalise Section 5.7, for flipping two bits, to flipping n bits. Again the smallest eigenvalue is always zero (with multiplicity one). The smallest non-zero eigenvalue corresponds to the lowest Walsh function for the Hamming cube, which is 2. As before, we can 1) establish an upper bound on the largest eigenvalue and 2) give a stochastic estimate for large l.

6.5.1 Upper Bound on Largest Eigenvalue of n-bit Flip Graph Laplacian

Following, Section 5.7.1 starting from Equation 7 and using $\lambda_{n,l} \geq 0$

$$
\begin{aligned}
\lambda_{n,l} &= 2C_{n-1}^{l-1} + \lambda_{n,l-1} - \lambda_{n-1,l-1} \\
\lambda_{n,l} &\leq 2C_{n-1}^{l-1} + \lambda_{n,l-1} \\
&\leq 2C_{n-1}^{l-1} + 2C_{n-1}^{l-2} + \lambda_{n,l-2} \\
&\leq \lambda_{n,n} + \sum_{i=n}^{l-1} 2C_{n-1}^{i} \\
&= 2 + 2\sum_{i=n}^{l-1} C_{n-1}^{i} \\
&= 2 + 2C_{n-1}^{l-1} \sum_{i=n}^{l-1} \frac{C_{n-1}^{i}}{C_{n-1}^{l-1}} \\
&< 2 + 2C_{n-1}^{l-1} \sum_{i=0}^{\infty} \left(\frac{C_{n-1}^{l-2}}{C_{n-1}^{l-1}} \right)^{i} \\
&= 2 + 2C_{n-1}^{l-1} \frac{1}{1 - \frac{C_{n-1}^{l-2}}{C_{n-1}^{l-1}}}
\end{aligned}
$$

Table 3: Eigenvalues of the graph Laplacian of mutation operators which flip exactly 1, 2, 3, 4 or 5 bits, when acting on strings of 5 bits. λ_j are the eigenvalues for elementary landscapes of a mutation only GA with $p_m = 1/5$.

	$\Delta_{1,5}$	$\Delta_{2,5}$	$\Delta_{3,5}$	$\Delta_{4,5}$	$\Delta_{5,5}$	λ_j
ψ_{00000}	0	0	0	0	0	0.000
ψ_{00001}	2	8	12	8	2	3.124
ψ_{00010}	2	8	12	8	2	3.124
ψ_{00011}	4	12	12	4	0	4.736
ψ_{00100}	2	8	12	8	2	3.124
ψ_{00101}	4	12	12	4	0	4.736
ψ_{00110}	4	12	12	4	0	4.736
ψ_{00111}	6	12	8	4	2	5.351
ψ_{01000}	2	8	12	8	2	3.124
ψ_{01001}	4	12	12	4	0	4.736
ψ_{01010}	4	12	12	4	0	4.736
ψ_{01011}	6	12	8	4	2	5.351
ψ_{01100}	4	12	12	4	0	4.736
ψ_{01101}	6	12	8	4	2	5.351
ψ_{01110}	6	12	8	4	2	5.351
ψ_{01111}	8	8	8	8	0	5.376
ψ_{10000}	2	8	12	8	2	3.124
ψ_{10001}	4	12	12	4	0	4.736
ψ_{10010}	4	12	12	4	0	4.736
ψ_{10011}	6	12	8	4	2	5.351
ψ_{10100}	4	12	12	4	0	4.736
ψ_{10101}	6	12	8	4	2	5.351
ψ_{10110}	6	12	8	4	2	5.351
ψ_{10111}	8	8	8	8	0	5.376
ψ_{11000}	4	12	12	4	0	4.736
ψ_{11001}	6	12	8	4	2	5.351
ψ_{11010}	6	12	8	4	2	5.351
ψ_{11011}	8	8	8	8	0	5.376
ψ_{11100}	6	12	8	4	2	5.351
ψ_{11101}	8	8	8	8	0	5.376
ψ_{11110}	8	8	8	8	0	5.376
ψ_{11111}	10	0	20	0	2	5.121
Largest	10	12	20	8	2	5.376
Upper bound		34	26	12.667		
Aprx. bound	5	10	10	5	1	
No. distinct	6	3	4	3	2	6

The above bound on the largest eigenvalue of the n-bit flip's Laplacian is calculated for various n and strings of length 5 at the end of Table 3.

6.5.2 Long Bit String Estimate of the Largest Eigenvalue of the n-bit Flip Graph Laplacian

Here we generalise the argument given in Section 5.7.2 for two bits. Again, for any unit vector u the length of Δu will be no bigger than the largest eigenvalue. Choose a random direction. I.e. let v be a vector of 2^l components each of which is either +1 or -1, chosen uniformly at random. $|v|^2 = 2^l$ hence $|v| = 2^{l/2}$. Multiply by the Laplacian.

The first element of Δv is typical of them all.

$$\Delta v(1) = \pm C_n^l \quad \underbrace{\pm 1 \pm \cdots\cdots \pm 1}_{C_n^l \text{ terms with random signs}}$$

37

Since the elements of v were randomly chosen, each of the elements of Δv are independent and identically distributed, and therefore $|\Delta v(i)|^2$ are also i.i.d. Thus the expected value of $|\Delta v|^2$ is the number of components in Δv (2^l) multiplied by the expected value of any of them. E.g. the first, $|\Delta v(1)|^2$. The expected length of $\Delta v(1)$ is approximately C_n^l. (The random signs ensure on average the following terms come to near zero and for large l the sum is dominated by the largest term.) Thus the expected value of $|\Delta v|^2$ is $2^l |C_n^l|^2$ and so the expected length $|\Delta v|$ is $2^{l/2} C_n^l$. Taking the ratio $\frac{|\Delta v|}{|v|}$ gives C_n^l as an upper bound on all the eigenvalues. For long strings this will become a tight bound on the largest eigenvalue.

C_n^l is of course the number of strings which n-bit mutation can reach in one step, i.e. the degree. So our roughness measure $\lambda/d \lesssim 1$. The bound is calculated for rather short strings (length 5) at the end of Table 3.

6.6 Number of Distinct Eigenvalues

Referring back to Section 5.9. In the simple case, the string length l is an exact multiple of the number of bits to be flipped n and so the minimum number of steps to reach any point in the search space (the graph diameter) is simply l/n and hence the Laplacian has $l/n + 1$ distinct eigenvalues [14, page 598]. The last line of Table 3 gives some examples.

When l/n is not an integer, calculating the graph's diameter is more complicated. For example, not every point may be accessible. I.e. the graph may fall into separate homogeneous graphs. In which case, we need only calculate the diameter of one of them. This may be slightly smaller than l/n. Secondly, the bit flips and string lengths may not align well, so even the minimum path involves repeated flips of one or more bits. In which case the diameter will be slightly more than l/n. Nevertheless, even with these complications, the number of distinct eigenvalues when flipping n multiple bits will be near $l/n + 1$.

7. COMPARISON WITH REAL GP

7.1 NIH Non-Elementary Landscape

To verify GP does behave similarly to our model, we first ran GP to show it treats EQ-parity as a needle in a haystack problem and to investigate the distribution of jump sizes in a real GP. In the first group of genetic programming runs, GP was run with Koza's 16-even parity fitness function and only EQ in the function set (details given in Table 4).

TinyGP uses the "grow" method [13] to create the initial random programs. Since there are four times as many terminals as functions, despite a large depth limit (8), the grow method produces populations that consist mostly of programs that are too small (mean 17) to solve the 16-EQ parity problem (minimum solution size 31). Note since a needle in a haystack landscape does not provide fitness guidance, the population evolves as though there was no fitness, hence there is no bloat and, excluding drift, on average programs do not change size [9]. Therefore there remains a substantial part of the population which is simply too small to solve the problem. This increases the search time. Also TinyGP does not ensure children are different from their parents. This also increases the search time. And so a large number of programs need to be run before finding a solution. The first hitting time is 2 400 000 (mean of 10 runs, standard devia-

Table 4: TinyGP Parameters for 16 even parity

Function:	EQ
Terminals:	$D_0, \ldots D_{15}$
Fitness:	Number of correct answers on all 2^{16} test cases. However (see Section 3) only fitness 32768 and 65536 are possible.
Selection:	Steady state. 2 members tournaments.
Population:	65 536
Initial pop:	grow (max depth 8),
Parameters:	80% subtree crossover, 20% point mutation (p_m 0.05). Crossover and mutation points are chosen uniformly (i.e. without a function bias [8]) No size limit.
Termination:	100 generations

Table 5: Summary of Experiments

Problem	degree	eigenvalue	λ/d	hitting time
Parity	120	136*	1.1333*	2 400 000
4 Trap-like	120	84	0.7	18 000
1 Max	120	2	0.0167	1 020

*Parity is not elementary. We give the weighted average of all λ.

tion 2 200 000). Also the distribution shows signs of being geometric as expected of a needle problem. This and two other experiments are summarised in Table 5.

Although the programs are rather smaller than assumed in Section 4.3, if we exclude mutations which make no difference (distance 0) the distribution of jump sizes for TinyGP mutation (Figure 4 dashed line) is somewhat similar to that predicted in Section 4.3. That is, most mutations moves cause the child to be exactly two bits different in our search space. The number of 4, 6, 8 etc. moves falls rapidly. (As an anti-bloat mechanism TinyGP uses point mutation with a fixed probability of mutation per program element [13]. Thus not only can zero elements be changed but also a mutant child may differ in multiple places from its mother.) Notice, as expected, mutation only causes jumps by multiples of 2.

Figure 4 also shows the distribution of jump sizes caused by crossover. Note since subtree crossover can change program sizes, it can make arbitrary jump sizes (including odd sized jumps). However the most popular (mode) jump size is two, as assumed for the mutation only model presented in Section 4.3,

Most crossovers take place between trees which were themselves created by crossovers. (Point mutation does not change tree size or shape and so a tree's size and shape are determined by crossover, even if it also undergoes point mutation.) It may be these repeated crossovers that gives the distribution (excluding 0 and 1) its pleasing Zipf like tail. (Falling by about 60% per unit increase in step size.) Note, although the distribution of tree sizes would be expected to rapidly converge to a Lagrange distribution [3], the distribution in Figure 4 refers to jumps in our bit oriented semantic search space. The mapping between it and that of the GP binary trees is not straightforward and we have not attempted to prove a mathematical relationship between random crossover of Lagrange distributed trees and the jumps in our space to accompany the experimental data given in Figure 4. Figure 4 shows there is some truth in our simplification that all moves are of size two. However it shows the full situation is more complex.

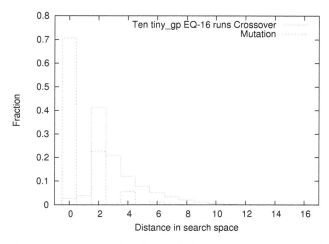

Figure 4: Distribution of jumps in the search space sizes caused by crossover and mutation in ten TinyGP 16-EQ parity runs.

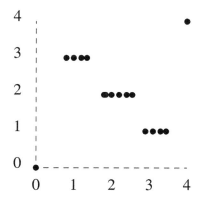

Figure 5: Schematic of the integer valued 4 bit unitation fitness function formed by adding four third order 4-bit Walsh functions. Fitness plotted vertically. Unitation horizontally. Spots indicate the fitness of 16 possible bit values. The full fitness function is formed by concatenating four of these. It has a single global optimum with fitness 16.

7.2 1 Max Elementary GP Landscape

A further ten runs were made where the fitness function is given by the Hamming distance from the optimum in our bit-orientated semantic landscape. (Note in GP terms this is cheating, since we allow the fitness function to look inside the program, rather than simply being based on what the program does when it is run.) The problem is now like ones max and so considerably easier than the parity problem used in the previous section. n^{th} order one-max can be shown to be an elementary landscape by either noting 1) its fitness is composed of n components in Whitley's sense [22] or 2) by noting it can be decomposed into the n first order Walsh coefficients all of which are eigenvectors of Δ with the same eigenvalue and hence any linear combination of them (such as onemax) is also an eigenvector of Δ and therefor onemax is elementary. (The zeroth Walsh coefficient essentially gives the average fitness $\bar{f}$.)

TinyGP was run with a much reduced population size (128). Except for this and the fitness function, the same parameters (cf. Table 4) were used. 85% of runs succeeded in solving EQ-16 on this more friendly landscape. The mean first hitting time was 1020 (standard deviation 430). I.e. the second fitness landscape is about 2000 times easier for GP even though their search spaces are identical.

7.3 4 Trap-like Third Order GP Landscape

A further ten runs were made where the fitness function is given by summing four trap-like functions. Each trap-like function is defined on a group of four non-overlapping bits from the total of 16 in our bit-orientated semantic landscape. Where each four bit function is created by adding together all the third order Walsh coefficients. (See Figure 5. Again in GP terms this is cheating.)

If we retain Section 4's assumption that search proceeds by flipping exactly two bits, then the new fitness landscape is elementary. To show this we start with the four bit (i.e. 16×16) Laplacian Δ_5 and note the fitness function is composed of third order Walsh functions and repeat the argument given in Section 5.6 but for this special case. We have already shown the third order Walsh functions are eigenvectors of the 16×16 Laplacian and have the same eigenvalue (12). The 32×32 Laplacian is formed of four 16×16 matrices as described in Equation 2. Concatenating a 16-bit Walsh function with itself and multiplying by the 32×32 Laplacian gives a vector of 32 elements, whose two 16 elements halves are both equal to a multiple of the original 16-bit Walsh function. I.e. the 32 element vector is an eigenvector of the 32×32 Laplacian. The eigenvalue is λ_{H_3} plus that of the original 16-bit Walsh function. Where λ_{H_3} is the eigenvalue of the third order Walsh function applied to the Laplacian of the Hamming cube (rather than double flip parity). $\lambda_{H_3} = 2 \times 3 = 6$. I.e. the concatenated 32 bit third order Walsh functions have eigenvalues $6 + 12 = 18$. Note this is true of all four original third order Walsh functions and therefore they all have the same eigenvalue. Therefore the 32 element vector formed by adding them together is also and eigenvector with eigenvalue 18.

We keep doubling using this procedure until we form a vector with 2^{16} elements. It will be an eigenvector of the $2^{16} \times 2^{16}$ Laplacian for the 16-EQ search space; with eigenvalue $6 \times (16 - 4) + 12 = 84$. Notice this vector repeats the 16 values of the third order Walsh function 4096 times, corresponding exactly to the repeat of the lower 4 bits of our trap-like fitness function. Since our landscape is symmetric we can rotate the labels by 4, 8 and 12 bits to show that the three other components of the fitness function are also eigenvectors with the same eigenvalue. Since the combined fitness function is the sum of four eigenvectors with the same eigenvalue, it too is an eigenvector of of the $2^{16} \times 2^{16}$ Laplacian (with eigenvalue 84.) Therefor our trap-like fitness landscape is elementary.

The problem is now intermediate between parity and one-max. Therefore TinyGP was run with a intermediate population size (1024). Except for this and the fitness function, the same parameters (cf. Table 4) were used. Nine out of ten runs succeeded. The mean first hitting time was 18 000 (standard deviation 9 000). I.e. this third fitness landscape is about 130 times easier for GP than the first (and about 17 times harder than the second) even though all three search spaces are identical.

8. CONCLUSIONS

We have analysed our [10] genetic programming parity fitness landscape. As well as proving it is not elementary we have calculated its mean fitness and fitness variance and its fitness distance correlation. Also we have argued that existing results on fitness autocorrelation along random walks in elementary landscapes can be greatly extended to show fitness autocorrelation falls rapidly with distance in many bit string mutation GAs.

Section 5.4 gave the elementary needle in a haystack fitness landscape.

We have given a complete eigen analysis of the search space formed by using two bit flip mutation. Showing the eigenvectors of its graph Laplacian are the same as those of the single bit flip Hamming cube (i.e. the Walsh basis functions). The eigenvalues can be rapidly calculated. They are somewhat similar but a factor of about k larger than those of the Hamming cube. Since the graph is connected the smallest eigenvalue is of course zero. The next is $2(k$-$1)$, the next $4(k$-$2)$, then $6(k$-$3)$ and so on. Table 1 gives the eigenvalues and their multiplicities for initial values of k. We provide two proofs (one a bound and the other a tight asymptotic limit) for the largest eigenvalue. The actual values appears to be $\lceil (k-1)(k+1)/2 \rceil$ but we have not proved this. The number of distinct eigenvalues is $k/2$+1 and so the separation between eigenvalues is about $2k$. For large k, multiplying the Laplacian by a unit vector pointed in almost all directions will increase its length by about the number of neighbours of each node $\frac{1}{2}k(k-1)$.

In Section 6 we generalised most of these results to landscapes where neighbours differ by n>2 bits. Indeed we gave the eigen analysis, not only for mutation which flips three or more bits, but also for normal bit string genetic algorithms (without crossover) which flip a variable number of bits independently. This showed the eigenvectors of the Hamming cube are also eigenvectors of two, three and more bit flip mutations and the mutation only GA. Hence any fitness function which is a Walsh function will form an elementary landscape with this set of widely used mutation operators. However most of these have large eigenvalues, corresponding to rough fitness landscapes. Typically an eigenvalue has a large multiplicity (i.e many eigenvectors share the same eigenvalue). Any fitness function which is a linear combination of Walsh vectors which have the same eigenvalue will also form an elementary landscape.

The number of distinct eigenvalues when flipping exactly n bits is approximately $l/n + 1$ and total number of eigenvectors is 2^l. Therefore there is at least one subspace with in the region of $2^l n/l$ eigenvectors. Any linear combination of these is also an eigenvector and each of these corresponds to an elementary landscape. Restricting ourselves to coefficients 0 and 1 means this subspace alone contains at least $2^{2^l/n}$ elementary landscapes. (This is a lower bound, the total number of n-bit flip elementary landscapes is much bigger.)

We compared our simplified [10] genetic programming parity with experiment and showed it does indeed behave as a needle in a haystack. We have run GP on two elementary fitness landscapes of the same size but different fitness functions, and shown, as expected, they behave differently. I.e. elementary landscapes, with identical sizes and connectivity, can represent problems of very different difficulty. Results so far have been in keeping with the ruggedness measure (Section 5.8). However given non-universal results on other proposed indicators of problem hardness (e.g. order of non-zero Walsh coefficients) we cannot be confident of its usefulness.

Acknowledgments

I would like to thank Daniel Spielman, Gylson Thomas for fhtseq.m, Riccardo Poli for TinyGP and Gabriel Peyr for fwt.m. Also many participants at Dagstuhl Seminar 10361 and FOGA 2011 for helpful discussions, including Andrew Sutton, Francisco Chicano, Jon Rowe, Darrell Whitley, Ken De Jong, Una-May O'Reilly, Alden Wright and Nataliya Sokolovska and the FOGA 2011 anonymous reviewers.

Funded by EPSRC grants EP/D050863/2 and EP/G060525/2.

9. REFERENCES

[1] T. Bäck. *Evolutionary Algorithms in Theory and Practice: Evolution Strategies, Evolutionary Programming, Genetic Algorithms*. Oxford University Press, New York, 1996.

[2] T. Biyikoglu, J. Leydold, and P. F. Stadler. *Laplacian Eigenvectors of Graphs: Perron-Frobenius and Faber-Krahn Type Theorems*, volume 1915 of *Lecture Notes in Mathematics*. Springer, 2007.

[3] S. Dignum and R. Poli. Generalisation of the limiting distribution of program sizes in tree-based genetic programming and analysis of its effects on bloat. In D. Thierens, H.-G. Beyer, J. Bongard, J. Branke, J. A. Clark, D. Cliff, C. B. Congdon, K. Deb, B. Doerr, T. Kovacs, S. Kumar, J. F. Miller, J. Moore, F. Neumann, M. Pelikan, R. Poli, K. Sastry, K. O. Stanley, T. Stutzle, R. A. Watson, and I. Wegener, editors, *GECCO '07: Proceedings of the 9th annual conference on Genetic and evolutionary computation*, volume 2, pages 1588–1595, London, 7-11 July 2007. ACM Press.

[4] B. Dimova, J. W. Barnes, and E. Popova. Arbitrary elementary landscapes & AR(1) processes. *Applied Mathematics Letters*, 18(3):287–292, 2005.

[5] B. Dimova, J. W. Barnes, E. Popova, and B. W. Colletti. Some additional properties of elementary landscapes. *Applied Mathematics Letters*, 22(2):232–235, Feb 2009.

[6] L. K. Grover. Local search and the local structure of NP-complete problems. *Operations Research Letters*, 12(4):235–243, 1992.

[7] Terry Jones and S. Forrest. Fitness distance correlation as a measure of problem difficulty for genetic algorithms. In *Proceedings of the 6th International Conference on Genetic Algorithms, ICGA 1995*, pages 184–192. Morgan Kaufmann, 1995.

[8] J. R. Koza. *Genetic Programming: On the Programming of Computers by Natural Selection*. MIT press, 1992.

[9] W. B. Langdon. The evolution of size in variable length representations. In *1998 IEEE International Conference on Evolutionary Computation*, pages 633–638, Anchorage, Alaska, USA, 5-9 May 1998. IEEE Press.

[10] W. B. Langdon. Scaling of program tree fitness spaces. *Evolutionary Computation*, 7(4):399–428, Winter 1999.

[11] W. B. Langdon and R. Poli. *Foundations of Genetic Programming*. Springer-Verlag, 2002.

[12] R. Poli, W. B. Langdon, and O. Holland. Extending particle swarm optimisation via genetic programming. In M. Keijzer, A. Tettamanzi, P. Collet, J. I. van Hemert, and M. Tomassini, editors, *Proceedings of the 8th European Conference on Genetic Programming*, volume 3447 of *Lecture Notes in Computer Science*, pages 291–300, Lausanne, Switzerland, 30 Mar. - 1 Apr. 2005. Springer.

[13] R. Poli, W. B. Langdon, and N. F. McPhee. *A field guide to genetic programming*. Published via http://lulu.com and freely available at http://www.gp-field-guide.org.uk, 2008. (With contributions by J. R. Koza).

[14] C. R. Reeves. Fitness landscapes. In E. K. Burke and G. Kendall, editors, *Search Methodologies: Introductory Tutorials in Optimization and Decision Support Techniques*, chapter 19, pages 587–610. Springer, 2005.

[15] C. R. Reeves and J. E. Rowe. *Genetic Algorithms–Principles and Perspectives: A Guide to GA Theory*. Kluwer Academic Publishers, 2003.

[16] F. Rothlauf. *Representations for Genetic and Evolutionary Algorithms*. Physica-Verlag, 2002.

[17] P. F. Stadler, R. Seitz, and G. P. Wagner. Population dependent Fourier decomposition of fitness landscapes over recombination spaces: Evolvability of complex characters. *Bulletin of Mathematical Biology*, 62:399–428, 2000.

[18] P. F. Stadler. Landscapes and their correlation functions. Technical Report 95-07-067, Santa Fe Institute, USA, 1995.

[19] P. F. Stadler and G. P. Wagner. Algebraic theory of recombination spaces. *Evolutionary Computation*, 5(3):241–275, 1997.

[20] A. M. Sutton, A. E. Howe, and L. D. Whitley. Estimating Bounds on Expected Plateau Size in MAXSAT Problems. In T. Stützle, M. Birattari, and H. H. Hoos, editors, *Second International Workshop, Engineering Stochastic Local Search Algorithms. SLS 2009*, volume 5752 of *Lecture Notes in Computer Science*, pages 31–45, Brussels, 3-4 September 2009. Springer.

[21] A. M. Sutton, A. E. Howe, and L. D. Whitley. A theoretical analysis of the k-satisfiability search space. In T. Stützle, M. Birattari, and H. H. Hoos, editors, *Second International Workshop, Engineering Stochastic Local Search Algorithms. SLS 2009*, volume 5752 of *Lecture Notes in Computer Science*, pages 46–60, Brussels, 3-4 September 2009. Springer.

[22] A. M. Sutton, L. D. Whitley, and A. E. Howe. A polynomial time computation of the exact correlation structure of k-satisfiability landscapes. In *GECCO '09: Proceedings of the 11th Annual conference on Genetic and evolutionary computation*, pages 365–372, Montreal, 2009. ACM.

[23] V. K. Vassilev, T. C. Fogarty, and J. F. Miller. Information characteristics and the structure of landscapes. *Evolutionary Computation*, 8(1):31–60, Spring 2000.

[24] V. K. Vassilev, T. C. Fogarty, and J. F. Miller. Smoothness, ruggedness and neutrality of fitness landscapes: from theory to application. In A. Ghosh and S. Tsutsui, editors, *Advances in evolutionary computing: theory and applications*, pages 3–44. Springer-Verlag New York, Inc., 2003.

[25] D. Whitley, D. Hains, and A. Howe. Tunneling between optima: partition crossover for the traveling salesman problem. In *GECCO '09: Proceedings of the 11th Annual conference on Genetic and evolutionary computation*, pages 915–922, Montreal, 2009. ACM.

[26] D. Whitley, A. M. Sutton, and A. E. Howe. Understanding elementary landscapes. In M. Keijzer, G. Antoniol, C. B. Congdon, K. Deb, B. Doerr, N. Hansen, J. H. Holmes, G. S. Hornby, D. Howard, J. Kennedy, S. Kumar, F. G. Lobo, J. F. Miller, J. Moore, F. Neumann, M. Pelikan, J. Pollack, K. Sastry, K. Stanley, A. Stoica, E.-G. Talbi, and I. Wegener, editors, *GECCO '08: Proceedings of the 10th annual conference on Genetic and evolutionary computation*, pages 585–592, Atlanta, GA, USA, 12-16 July 2008. ACM.

[27] L. D. Whitley and A. M. Sutton. Elementary landscape analysis. In *GECCO '09: Proceedings of the 11th annual conference companion on Genetic and evolutionary computation conference*, pages 3227–3236, Montreal, 8-12 July 2009. ACM. Tutorial.

[28] L. D. Whitley and A. M. Sutton. Partial neighborhoods of elementary landscapes. In G. Raidl, F. Rothlauf, G. Squillero, R. Drechsler, T. Stuetzle, M. Birattari, C. B. Congdon, M. Middendorf, C. Blum, C. Cotta, P. Bosman, J. Grahl, J. Knowles, D. Corne, H.-G. Beyer, K. Stanley, J. F. Miller, J. van Hemert, T. Lenaerts, M. Ebner, J. Bacardit, M. O'Neill, M. Di Penta, B. Doerr, T. Jansen, R. Poli, and E. Alba, editors, *GECCO '09: Proceedings of the 11th Annual conference on Genetic and evolutionary computation*, pages 381–388, Montreal, 8-12 July 2009. ACM.

[29] Tina Yu and J. F. Miller. Through the interaction of neutral and adaptive mutations, evolutionary search finds a way. *Artificial Life*, 12(4):525–551, Fall 2006.

On the Practicality of Optimal Output Mechanisms for Co-optimization Algorithms

Elena Popovici
Icosystem Corp.
10 Fawcett St.
Cambridge, MA, USA
elena@icosystem.com

Ezra Winston
Icosystem Corp.
10 Fawcett St.
Cambridge, MA, USA
ezra@icosystem.com

Anthony Bucci
Icosystem Corp.
10 Fawcett St.
Cambridge, MA, USA
anthony@icosystem.com

ABSTRACT

Co-optimization problems involve one or more search spaces and a means of assessing interactions between entities in these spaces. Assessing a potential solution requires aggregating in some way the outcomes of a very large or infinite number of such interactions. This layer of complexity presents difficulties for algorithm design that are not encountered in ordinary optimization. For example, what a co-optimization algorithm should output is not at all obvious. Theoretical research has shown that some output selection mechanisms yield better overall performance than others and described an optimal mechanism. This mechanism was shown to be strictly better than a greedy method in common use, but appeared prohibitive from a practical standpoint. In this paper we exhibit the optimal output mechanism for a particular class of co-optimization problems and a certain definition of better overall performance, and provide quantitative characterizations of domains for which this optimal mechanism becomes straightforward to implement. We conclude with a discussion of potential extensions of this work to other problem classes and other views on performance.

Categories and Subject Descriptors

G.1.6 [**Mathematics of Computing**]: Optimization; I.2.8 [**Problem Solving, Control Methods, and Search**]: Heuristic Methods

General Terms

Algorithms

Keywords

co-optimization, solution concepts, free lunch

1. INTRODUCTION

Optimization problems involve a search space whose entities, or potential solutions, are assessed via an objective

function, with the goal of finding entities that optimize the function's value. Among the many methods that can be used to attack such problems, heuristic search techniques like evolutionary algorithms have proven particularly effective when the structure of the search space or optimization function are not deeply understood.

By contrast, co-optimization problems involve one or more search spaces, and it is interactions between entities from or within the search spaces, not entities themselves, that are assessed via some measurement function (often called a payoff function or payoff matrix). Potential solutions to co-optimization problems are constructed from one or more entities drawn from one or more of the underlying search spaces. Most importantly, assessing a potential solution requires aggregation of measurements from a large set of interactions. For these reasons, clearly defining and achieving co-optimization goals has proven considerably more challenging than in ordinary optimization. By and large, co-optimization problems have been approached by and studied under the umbrella of coevolutionary algorithms (but see [18] for an example of non-evolutionary co-optimization heuristics). In this paper we focus on some of the difficulties that co-optimization problems pose independently of whether or not evolutionary concepts are used for algorithm design.

To date, a fair amount of work has focused on clarifying what kinds of potential solutions may be of interest and what is meant by "good" potential solutions; that is, defining the *solution concept* of the problem at hand [4]. However, even with a well-defined notion of good potential solutions in place, practically determining whether a certain potential solution is better than another according to the given notion is typically far from trivial or even impossible.

To be more specific, imagine the problem being explored is large enough that no algorithm could feasibly assess all the interactions within it. Chess is a good example, as it is infeasible to enumerate all chess-playing strategies and assess (play) a given strategy against all of them for the purposes of determining how strong a player it represents and whether it is indeed better than some other strategy. Under this assumption, the trace of outcomes of interactions that occurred during the run of an algorithm represents only a sample of the full problem and only a subset of those interactions required to determine which out of the potential solutions at hand is better.

A significant amount of attention has also been paid to the question of how to arrange the search process itself, mainly via selection and the choice of which interactions to assess, to encourage the production of good potential solutions [20, 14]. Surrogate notions of goodness have typically been used.

By contrast, considerably less investigation has been conducted into the question of what potential solutions a co-optimization algorithm should output whenever queried or upon completion. It is this latter research area that our paper is focused on.

Both questions are difficult to answer due to the same underlying cause, namely having to make decisions based on incomplete information. Furthermore, since these questions really pertain to algorithm design, to properly answer them one must first extend the formalization of what a good potential solution is to a formalization of what a good algorithm is.

The seminal work of Wolpert and Macready [23] initiated such a formalization by defining the goodness of an algorithm in the context of incomplete information as an aggregate of the goodness of the algorithm's output, with the aggregate taken over all possibilities for the unseen information. This can also be seen as a means of judging the algorithm over an entire set of problems. Different means of aggregating lead to different notions of what it means for one algorithm to be better than another. For instance, we might prefer an algorithm that outputs best potential solutions on more problems, regardless of how bad its output is when it is not best; or we might prefer an algorithm with a good average of outputted potential solution quality, regardless of on how many problems it outputs suboptimal potential solutions; and we might additionally prefer an algorithm that has low variance in the quality of its output, etc.

In light of no free lunch results the same authors had produced for traditional optimization [22], it is worth asking in the context of co-optimization whether there would even be cases of one algorithm being better than another in a generic way (i.e. over a large set of problems) and, subsequently, whether the notion of a best algorithm would make sense. [23] showed that such free lunches do typically exist in co-optimization. Moreover, with respect to the output question above, Wolpert and Macready showed that, regardless of the notion of aggregation used to define algorithm goodness, an output mechanism, called *Bayes*, can be defined that incorporates that notion and is subsequently optimal with respect to it.

These results were mostly theoretical in nature and implementing *Bayes* in a real algorithm appeared prohibitive. The large body of coevolutionary algorithms developed to solve co-optimization problems were using different output mechanisms, similar to the best-so-far of traditional optimization. The meaning of best was "greedily" defined only on the basis of seen information, and was therefore unreliable, leading to various seemingly counterintuitive and undesirable effects.

A question that arises is whether the *greedy* and *Bayes* output mechanisms really differ in their behavior (in which case *Bayes* would be strictly advantageous). This question is addressed in [12], in the context of two specific solution concepts (best worst case [1] and maximum expected utility [3]) and a certain means of aggregating over unseen information (average value). Under certain assumptions, it was found that *Bayes* is indeed strictly better than *greedy*. And while some light was shed upon it, the practicality of *Bayes* remained questionable.

In this paper, we extend that work by analyzing a different performance aggregation method, *average rank*, in the context of the best worst-case solution concept. We still find *Bayes* to be strictly better than *greedy*. More importantly, we are able to quantitatively characterize certain types of domains for which, at any time during the run of an algorithm on that domain, *Bayes* is equivalent to a criteria that is very easy to implement. Additionally, for domains where implementing *Bayes* is possible but not always simple, we contribute an algorithm that minimizes the amount of computation required. Finally, we discuss domain types for which we do not yet have a means of implementing *Bayes*.

The paper is organized as follows. In section 2 we introduce formal definitions of co-optimization problems, algorithms and performance, including the best worst-case solution concept, the average-rank performance aggregation method, and the *Bayes* and *greedy* output mechanisms. In section 3 we present an analysis comparing *Bayes* and *greedy* and assessing the practicality of *Bayes* as an algorithm mechanism. We wrap up in section 4 with a discussion, conclusions and future work. To benefit the flow, certain detailed mathematical derivations are presented in appendices A, B and C and an example of mapping coevolutionary algorithms to co-optimization algorithms in appendix D. For easy reference, appendix E provides three tables summarizing notation.

2. CO-OPTIMIZATION FORMALISMS

Following on the structure described in detail in [11], in this section we describe interactive domains, co-optimization and co-search problems defined over interactive domains, and the performance of algorithms run on such problems. Simply put, interactive domains describe the space of entities to explore, co-optimization or co-search problems detail which domain entities are most valuable, and algorithms actually seek out valuable entities.

The primary reason for carefully separating these three concepts is to discern which features impact the quality of potential solutions ultimately produced, and how that impact arises. For instance, we will see in section 3 that the sizes of the search spaces and the size of the measurement function's value set, which are features of the interactive domain, impinge on the efficiency of the *Bayes* output mechanism.

We use an example to illustrate the concepts.

2.1 Domains and Problems

Let us consider the real-world application described in [10] and summarized as follows. The design of large ships includes subsystems composed of a network of pipes, valves and pumps, which transport water for purposes such as instrument cooling or putting out fires. Such piping networks must be resilient to damage (e.g. pipes breaking, valves getting stuck, etc.) in the sense that they must reconfigure on the fly (e.g. by closing/opening valves, starting/stopping pumps) to isolate the damage and continue to provide water to as much of the rest of the ship as possible. Both the space of piping network designs and the space of possible damages are very large, and different piping network designs can have different resilience to the same damage. The goal is to find a piping network design that has as high a resilience as possible even when the damage that is worst for it occurs. An alternative goal may be to find a piping network whose average resilience over all possible damages is high. Thus there is a common context (domain) upon which multiple goals (problems) can be defined. We formalize this kind of situation below. The notation introduced in this subsection is summarized in table 1, appendix E.

Consider a specific type of **interactive domain** given by:

- two sets $\mathcal{B}_1$ and $\mathcal{B}_2$, called **entity sets**; we say the domain has to two **roles** and $\mathcal{B}_i$ is the entity set associated with role i;

- a function $f : \mathcal{B}_1 \times \mathcal{B}_2 \to \mathbb{R}$, called a **metric**; we call tuples $e = (b_1, b_2) \in \mathcal{B}_1 \times \mathcal{B}_2$ **interactions** or *events*; we call tuples $(e, f(e))$ measured interactions; for brevity, we will write $\mathcal{E} = \mathcal{B}_1 \times \mathcal{B}_2$.

In our example, $\mathcal{B}_1$ is the set of piping networks, $\mathcal{B}_2$ is the set of damages and f gives a quantification of how resilient a given network is to a given damage.

Note that interactive domains[1] can be significantly more generic, e.g. have more roles, reuse entity sets across roles, have more metrics[2], have stochastic metrics, etc. Consult [12, 4, 9, 11] for further details.

On the above domain we define a specific kind of **co-search problem**, by specifying what we are looking for via two constructs:

- the **space of potential solutions** to the problem, a set $\mathcal{S}$. In our case, $\mathcal{S} = \mathcal{B}_1$;

- the **solution concept**, a function $\mathcal{C} : \mathcal{S} \to \{true, false\}$ that partitions the space of potential solutions into solutions[3] and non-solutions.

In the ship design domain, the piping network designs are the potential solutions and the two different goals listed – best in the worst case or best on average – are examples of solution concepts. For example, if our solution concept is to maximize average, then $\mathcal{C}$ is defined to return *false* for a given design if its average resilience over all damages is less than the average resilience of some other design, and *true* otherwise.

Note that in general $\mathcal{S}$ can be more complex, for instance an aggregation over the different entity sets such as $\mathcal{B}_1 \times \mathcal{B}_2$ or $\wp(\mathcal{B}_1)$. Thus many different kinds of problems can be defined over the same domain. A top-level clustering into meta-classes is based on the nature of the mapping from the entity sets $\mathcal{B}_i$ to $\mathcal{S}$. A meta-class of problems common in the literature are **test-based problems** (such as the one we defined above), for which some of the entity sets are not used in the definition of $\mathcal{S}$. These sets are however used in the definition of $\mathcal{C}$, as we will exemplify next. In other words, their elements can be seen as **tests** helping to determine which potential solutions are actual solutions; hence

the name test-based. For further details and examples of test-based and other kinds of problems, see [4, 9, 11]. In our ship design problems, the damages are the tests.

Many different solution concepts can be defined over the same space of potential solutions. As defined above, a solution concept is a very coarse notion. In practice, solution concepts are more fine grained, in that they specify, via some partial or total order on $\mathcal{S}$, how some potential solutions are better than others. The maximal elements of such an order are then considered solutions.

We consider a solution concept called **best worst case**, which is part of a class of so-called **co-optimization** solution concepts that are defined via a **quality function** $g : \mathcal{S} \to \mathbb{R}$, as follows

$$\mathcal{C}(s) = true \Leftrightarrow g(s) = \operatorname*{opt}_{ps \in \mathcal{S}}(g(ps)),$$

where opt is one of max or min. We call a **co-optimization problem** a problem that has a co-optimization solution concept. Note that g induces an almost[4] total order on $\mathcal{S}$. We consider the *maximin* version of best worst case, which is defined by

$$opt = \max, \text{ and}$$

$$g(ps) = \min_{t \in \mathcal{B}_2}(f(ps, t)).$$

The *minimax* version of best worst case can be defined similarly. For examples of other co-optimization or even more generic co-search problems, see [11, 4, 9, 12].

Revisiting the example, and given that larger values of f denote better resilience of a piping network when confronted with a damage, the quality of a piping network is assessed as resilience to the damage that the network is least resilient to. The *maximin* solution concept maps onto the goal of finding a piping network with the highest least resilience.

Co-optimization problems are more difficult than traditional optimization problems when g is prohibitively expensive to compute. For best worst case this can happen when $\mathcal{B}_2$ is infinite or very large, or when assessing interactions via f is very costly, both of which are common in practice. Solving problems featuring the best worst-case solution concept is thus a valuable research area, featuring theoretical work [23, 12], empirical analysis via synthetic problems [8, 2, 13, 21] and applications to areas such as the illustrated ship design [10], job scheduling [5, 6, 7] and constrained optimization [1]. Yet there are still open questions, some of which we tackle in this paper in a way that narrows the gap between theory and practice. Since our focus is on designing high-performing co-optimization algorithms for solving best worst-case problems, we focus next on defining how co-optimization algorithms operate and what we mean by performance. The notation pertaining to algorithms and performance is summarized in table 2, appendix E.

2.2 Algorithms and Performance

2.2.1 Algorithms

Unlike in traditional search/optimization, an algorithm attempting to solve some co-search/co-optimization problem must sample multiple spaces: the entity sets $\mathcal{B}_i$, the cross product interaction set $\mathcal{E}$, and the set of potential solutions

---

[1] In [12] interactive domains have been termed *multi-actor domains* and entity sets termed *behavior sets*. The phrase *interactive domain* is intended to convey the fact that the domain contains interactions (the domain itself does not interact with anything). This usage of the terminology is also distinct from that in *interactive evolution* or *human-computer interaction*.

[2] Should there be multiple metrics, the measurement of an interaction is simply considered to be a vector (containing the values for all the different metrics) instead of a single value.

[3] Also referred to as actual solutions or true solutions.

[4] In fact, the antisymmetry condition of a total order is typically not satisfied.

$\mathcal{S}$, whose construction from the sets $\mathcal{B}_i$ can vary in complexity. The effort required to draw samples from these spaces is considered negligible, and the cost of such co-search/co-optimization algorithms is typically defined in the field as the number of interactions measured via the domain's metrics[5]. We therefore adopt the view of co-search algorithms introduced in [23], formalized in [12] and summarized in the following.

We call a **history** a finite sequence of *distinct* measured interactions. Let $\mathcal{H}^t$ be the set of all histories of length t, i.e. $\mathcal{H}^t = \{H^t = ((e^1, f(e^1)), ..., (e^t, f(e^t))) \mid \forall i, j, 1 \leq i \neq j \leq t : e^i \neq e^j\}$, with $\mathcal{H}^0 = \{()\}$, and let $\mathcal{H} = \bigcup_{t=0}^{|\mathcal{E}|} \mathcal{H}^t$ be the set of all possible histories.

Then a **co-search algorithm**, A, is a set of two functions:

- the **search heuristic**, $h_A : \mathcal{H} \to \mathcal{E}$; it determines what interaction to assess next, given the interactions assessed so far and their measurements; and

- the **output selection**, $output_A : \mathcal{H} \to \mathcal{S}$; it determines what potential solution to return, given the assessed interactions and their measurements.

The operation of A on a problem given by metric f is equivalent to the following:

```
t ← 0
H⁰ ← ()
if queried, answer outputₐ(H⁰)
repeat {
    t ← t + 1
    e ← hₐ(Hᵗ⁻¹)
    compute f(e)
    Hᵗ ← concat(Hᵗ⁻¹, (e, f(e)))
    if queried, answer outputₐ(Hᵗ)
} until (stop_condition)
```

In words, at every time step the search heuristic is called to decide, based on the current history, what interaction to assess next. For instance, using the ship domain as an example, the search heuristic could decide to pair the piping network design from the last assessed interaction with a damage scenario that this design had not yet interacted with; or it could choose a "new" design (i.e. one for which there are no respective interactions in the history) and pair it with some damage. The chosen interaction would then be assessed via the domain's metric (e.g. determine resilience of design to damage) and, together with the result, added to the history. Whenever an output is desired, the output selection function is invoked and, based on the history, it will return a potential solution (e.g. a piping network design).

For the purposes of this paper we assume both the search heuristic and the output selection to be deterministic, though often in practice at least the former is stochastic, as is the case with coevolutionary algorithms. Appendix D shows an example of how a coevolutionary algorithm can be formalized as a co-optimization algorithm. We believe the current analysis can be extended to address stochastic effects and this is a subject for future work.

---

[5]Should there be multiple metrics, it is assumed that an *outcome* is determined from the interaction, all metrics operate upon this outcome, and the effort of computing the metrics is negligible compared to the effort of determining the interaction outcome.

The question that arises is whether certain co-optimization algorithms are "better" than others. Of course, to be able to answer such a question, one must define what good/better means with respect to algorithms, or in other words detail how to define **algorithm performance** and how to compare the performance of different algorithms. We make these notions precise in the next subsection.

2.2.2 Performance

A first distinction to be made is between performance of an algorithm on a single problem (which we will simply refer to as performance) and **aggregated performance** of an algorithm on a set of problems, which will be derived from its performance on the individual problems using some sort of aggregation. Given the formalisms we have in place, what we mean here by set of problems is problems that share the $\mathcal{B}_i$, $\mathcal{S}$ and $\mathcal{C}$ but differ in the assignment of values to interactions via the metric f. In other words, we equate the notions of problem and metric.

Wolpert and Macready showed in [22] that for traditional search/optimization, if aggregation is over all possible problems (metrics) and some set of assumptions is met, then all algorithms have the same aggregated performance regardless of the definitions of performance and aggregation (that is, there is no free lunch). This was later shown to also hold on any set of problems that is closed under permutation [15].

For co-optimization, Wolpert and Macready later showed in [23] that, for certain types of co-search problems and certain definitions of performance and aggregation, different co-search algorithms can have different aggregated performance even when aggregation is over all problems (i.e. there are free lunches). The same conclusions have been derived in [19, 17, 16] for further types of co-search problems, performance and aggregation. Some of the results were concerned with comparing algorithms that shared the same output selection mechanism but differed in the search heuristic, while others addressed the converse, that is keeping the search heuristic fixed and varying the output selection mechanism.

A generic formalization of these issues and a review of specific results in existence at the time can be found in [12]. In this paper we focus on comparing output selection mechanisms while keeping the search heuristic fixed, and do so in the context of a specific type of problem (the best worst-case solution concept) and specific definitions of performance and aggregation.

Our choice of aggregated performance, called average rank, is detailed next. Average rank is intended to encode a preference towards algorithms that, on average over a set of problems, output potential solutions that rank higher in quality, without concern for the magnitude of quality differences.

Single-problem performance.

We start by defining the performance of an algorithm on a given problem as simply equal to the quality of the potential solution it outputs for that problem. We denote by $\phi_{A,t} \in \mathbb{R}$ the performance of co-search algorithm A at time t (i.e. after having seen a history H^t of length t) on the problem given by metric f, potential solution space $\mathcal{S} = \mathcal{B}_1$ and solution concept $\mathcal{C}$ specified via quality function g, as introduced in section 2.1. We specifically define $\phi_{A,t}$ to be equal to $g(output_A(H^t))$. This is well defined, since $output_A : \mathcal{H} \to \mathcal{S}$ and $g : \mathcal{S} \to \mathbb{R}$. We can alternatively write $\phi = g$ (note that then $\phi : \mathcal{S} \to \mathbb{R}$) and

$\phi_{A,t} = \phi(output_A(\mathrm{H}^t))$ and say that our performance function ϕ is directly mapped to our quality function g.

Note however that the quality of the potential solutions considered for outputting is typically not known to the algorithm; for instance, in our case (the *maximin* solution concept), computing g for a given potential solution may require measuring as many interactions as there are tests in $\mathcal{B}_2$, which the algorithm is unlikely to have done. This also means that, unless we put additional effort into computing g for the outputted potential solution (were that possible) we would not know the *actual* performance of the algorithm on the given problem.

Aggregated performance.

Given a performance function ϕ, we must next specify the means of aggregating ϕ over multiple problems (i.e. over multiple alternatives for the metric f). The aggregation method investigated in this paper is called **average rank**, because it averages over a given set of problems the rank of the algorithm's performance on those problems.

To formally define this, we make the assumption that the set of potential values for the metric f (its codomain) is finite. We will discuss this assumption in sections 3 and 4. We denote the codomain by $V = \{v_1, v_2, ..., v_p\} \subset \mathbb{R}$, $v_1 < v_2 < ... < v_p$ (without loss of generality), with $|V| = p \geq 2$ (otherwise there is nothing to optimize). The case $p = 2$ is of special interest (thus treated separately in section 3.2), as it models domains where only potential solutions pass or fail tests. Then the values g (and therefore ϕ) can take are also restricted to V and if $\phi(ps) = g(ps) = v_i$ we say the V-**rank**[6] of the potential solution ps is i and write $rank_V(\phi(ps)) = rank_V(g(ps)) = rank_V(v_i) = i$.

Given an algorithm A, a time step t, and the performance function $\phi = g$, we define $Agg_{\mathrm{H}^t}(\phi_{A,t})$, the **average-rank aggregated performance** of A at time t having seen history H^t, as the average of $rank_V(\phi(output_A(\mathrm{H}^t)))$, taken over all possible metrics f that are *consistent* with the history H^t.

A metric f is consistent with a history H if for any interaction in H it returns the same measurement as the one the interaction has associated with it in H. To get a better intuition for this, it may help the reader to think of black-box optimization. At the start of the algorithm, the metric f is completely unknown and could be any out of the combinatorial number of metrics that can be defined from $\mathcal{E}$ to V. Every time we sample f by presenting it with an input $e \in \mathcal{E}$ and getting some output $v \in V$ we gain some information, namely the number of alternatives possible for the metric f decreases (those that for e return a value other than v are not consistent with the information we have seen).[7]

---

[6] Note that for a specific metric f (and therefore quality function g), the V-rank of a potential solution ps will be different from the "true" rank of ps among all potential solutions if the image of g is a strict subset of V.

[7] The notion of aggregating over metrics consistent with the history is also present in Wolpert and Macready's work for traditional optimization [22]. There it isn't emphasized as much, because the history only impacts the quality of potential solutions that are part of the history, and the unseen information only impacts the quality of potential solutions not yet seen. In co-search/co-optimization consistency with the history is very important because for many solution concepts (including best worst case) the quality of a potential solution can be impacted by both the seen and the unseen

Note that aggregated performance over a set of problems can also be interpreted as *expected* performance of the algorithm on the problem at hand, given that this problem is part of the set. The nature of the aggregation can reflect various assumptions about the problem set or the domain itself. For instance, taking the average, as for average rank defined above, reflects an implicit assumption that all problems are equally likely. Aggregating ranks instead of raw performance values may reflect knowledge or belief that the metric values are unevenly distributed across the range of V. Extending this research to other performance aggregation methods, including ones incorporating assumptions of non-uniform problem likelihood, is an interesting avenue for future work.

Comparing algorithms.

Given some notion of aggregated performance for an algorithm, we can move on to using it to compare two or more algorithms. The approach we take is to fix t and compare aggregated performance for that t.[8] As previously mentioned, in this work we are only concerned with comparing algorithms that share the same search heuristic but vary in the output selection mechanism.

What Wolpert and Macready [23] made apparent is that given a performance function ϕ and an aggregation method Agg, a specific output selection mechanism which they called **Bayes** is *optimal* in the following sense: $\forall$ search heuristic function h, $\forall$ output selection function $output$, given the algorithms $A = (h, output)$ and $B = (h, Bayes)$, we have $\forall t$: $Agg_{\mathrm{H}^t}(\phi_{B,t}) \geq Agg_{\mathrm{H}^t}(\phi_{A,t})$. $Bayes : \mathcal{H} \to \mathcal{S}$ is defined to take into account Agg and ϕ by returning for a given H that element of $\mathcal{S}$ that has the highest aggregate performance value over all metrics consistent with H. Formally, $Bayes(\mathrm{H}) = s \in \mathcal{S}$ such that $Agg_{\mathrm{H}}(\phi(s))$ is the maximum possible over all $ps \in \mathcal{S}$.

We will refer to the instantiation of $Bayes$ for the average-rank performance aggregation method as the **Bayes average-rank** output selection mechanism. For a given H, it will output that $s \in \mathcal{S}$ for which $avg_{\mathrm{H}}(rank_V(\phi(s)))$ is the maximum possible over all $ps \in \mathcal{S}$ (where avg_{H} denotes averaging over all metrics f consistent with the history H).

$Bayes$ is a very informed output selection function, as it incorporates Agg and ϕ (thus, indirectly, $\mathcal{C}$). It favors a paradigm where one first decides on how an algorithm's performance will be judged, and then constructs a suitable output mechanism. However, $Bayes$ appears problematic from an implementation standpoint, given it involves computing aggregates over a potentially large set of metrics.

In practice, a different output mechanism has widely been used both before and after the introduction of $Bayes$, specifically the so-called **greedy** output selection. For co-optimization solution concepts, *greedy* operates by extending the quality function g from $\mathcal{S}$ to $\mathcal{S} \times \mathcal{H}$, $g(ps, \mathrm{H})$ representing the **current quality** of the potential solution ps given the history H. For instance, for *maximin* g can be extended

---

information. This has been described in terms of the history providing a bias that can be exploited by algorithms, thus, coarsely speaking, it is the reason free lunches exist.

[8] A different approach could be to fix a certain threshold value and compare the algorithms' respective cost t needed to achieve aggregated performance above the threshold.

via $g(ps, H) = \min_{t:(ps,t)\in H} (f(ps, t))$. Then *greedy* outputs the potential solution with the best current quality.

The definitions of *greedy* and *Bayes* already point to a potential difference in behavior. Specifically, *greedy* will only consider for outputting those potential solutions for which it can determine current quality. For best worst case, this means those potential solutions for which at least one interaction with a test has been assessed (i.e. is part of the history). We will call such potential solutions *partially evaluated*. By contrast, *Bayes* would compute aggregated performance both for partially evaluated and for *completely-unevaluated* potential solutions, i.e. ones that have not seen any test. For the best worst-case solution concept the aggregated performance is the same for any completely-unevaluated potential solution (since it does not depend on information about other potential solutions). Should this aggregate be better than any of those for partially-evaluated potential solutions, then *Bayes* would randomly sample a new potential solution and output it without assessing any additional interactions, and would therefore differ in its output from *greedy*. As was shown in [12] for a different aggregation method, and as the analysis in section 3 will show for average-rank aggregation as well, *Bayes* and *greedy* can produce different outputs even when *Bayes* outputs a partially-evaluated potential solution.

3. ANALYSIS

Armed with the framework laid out in section 2, we set out to perform a quantitative investigation of when the outputs of *Bayes* and *greedy* will differ, and also determine if in such situations *Bayes*, which would be strictly better, can actually be implemented.

We start in 3.1 by setting up the analysis through further notations and assumptions, then reviewing and adapting the formulas and results from [12] to the average-rank performance aggregation method. Then we present our extended analysis and new results, broken down into two parts (3.2 and 3.3) corresponding to two different domain types.

During the analysis we use a number of variables and quantities relating to domain properties (like the already introduced $|V| = p$) or algorithm state properties. The respective notation is summarized in table 3, appendix E. The outcome of the analysis exposes which of these variables/quantities one does or does not need to know in order to implement *Bayes*, thus directly impacting practicality.

3.1 Setup

In section 2.2, in order to formalize the average-rank performance aggregation method, we have already assumed that the number of metric values, p, is finite. We now also assume $\mathcal{B}_2$ to be finite, $\mathcal{B}_2 = \{t_1, t_2, ..., t_m\}$, $|\mathcal{B}_2| = m$, and will refer to its elements as tests. These assumptions were introduced by Wolpert and Macready [23], the supporting argument being (just as for traditional optimization) that computers have finite memory and that for domains where these sets are originally of infinite size, bounds and/or discretization need to be put in place for implementation purposes. Note however that there are still real-world domains where these sets are finite to begin with, such as the ship domain evoked in section 2.1, which has $m = 11480$ and $p \leq 959$ [10].

We consider $m \geq 2$ (or else we would be dealing with the case of traditional optimization), and in fact the domains of interest for co-optimization are those with large values of m, so that evaluating a potential solution with all m tests is not feasible in practice.

Note that we do not need to make any assumptions about the size of $\mathcal{S} = \mathcal{B}_1$ (the space of potential solutions).[9]

To compare the outputs of *Bayes* and *greedy* we start by considering the case when the algorithm has partially evaluated only two potential solutions out of $\mathcal{B}_1$. We denote them by a and b. Generalizations of this will be presented later in the section. Suppose potential solution a has interacted with k *distinct* tests, $1 \leq k < m$ and potential solution b has interacted with l *distinct* tests, $1 \leq l < m$.[10] Let H denote the history composed of these interactions and their outcomes and suppose that H is such that the current quality for a and b is, respectively, $g(a, H) = v_i$ and $g(b, H) = v_j$, $1 \leq i, j \leq p$. The *greedy* output mechanism will consider only a and b and output a if $i > j$, output b if $i < j$, and either of a and b if $i = j$. The *Bayes* output function will consider not just a and b, but also all completely-unevaluated potential solutions. Since the latter are all equivalent from an aggregated performance standpoint, we use only one representative, which we denote by c.

To compute the aggregate performance values that the operation of *Bayes* average rank requires, we can build off of the formulas derived in [12]. That work is concerned with a different performance aggregation method, called average value. Where average rank first transforms the performance values ϕ into ranks and then applies averaging, the average-value aggregation method applies averaging directly to the performance values (thus encompassing a paradigm where one has a strong interest in the magnitude of performance differences). We first reproduce the formulas of [12][11]:

$$avg_H(\phi(a)) = E_H(g(a)) = \sum_{q=p-(i-1)}^{p} \delta v_q \cdot \left(\frac{q}{p}\right)^{m-k},$$

$$avg_H(\phi(b)) = E_H(g(b)) = \sum_{q=p-(j-1)}^{p} \delta v_q \cdot \left(\frac{q}{p}\right)^{m-l},$$

$$avg_H(\phi(c)) = E_H(g(c)) = \sum_{q=1}^{p} \delta v_q \cdot \left(\frac{q}{p}\right)^{m},$$

where $\forall q \in 1..(p-1) : \delta v_q = v_{p-q+1} - v_{p-q}$ and $\delta v_p = v_1$.

We can derive the corresponding formulas for average-rank aggregation by simply replacing the metric values $v_1, ...,$

---

[9]If $\mathcal{B}_1$ is finite, then for a given metric f, the cardinality of the image of f would be bounded from above by $m \cdot |\mathcal{B}_1|$. However, when considering a class of metrics with codomain V, such a bound on $|V| = p$ need not necessarily hold.

[10]Being able to fully evaluate some potential solutions (i.e. k or l being equal to m) is uncommon in practice. However, all the statements in the paper still hold if the phrase "partially evaluated" were to be replaced with "partially or fully evaluated". The proofs in appendices A and B are explicitly presented with $k, l \leq m$.

[11]$E_H(g(\cdot))$ is the notation from [12], hinting at the possible interpretation of aggregation as estimation. The summations were derived using counting arguments about the proportion of assignments of values to interactions (i.e. metrics f) that would result in a certain actual worst-case value $g(\cdot)$, followed by summation over all actual worst-case values still possible given the current worst-case value $g(\cdot, H)$, since $g(\cdot) \leq g(\cdot, H)$.

v_p with their ranks, that is, respectively, $1, ..., p$. Making use of $\forall q \in 1..(p-1) : \delta v_q = (p - q + 1) - (p - q) = 1$, we get:

$$avg_{\mathrm{H}}(rank_V(\phi(a))) = \sum_{q=p-(i-1)}^{p} \left(\frac{q}{p}\right)^{m-k},$$

$$avg_{\mathrm{H}}(rank_V(\phi(b))) = \sum_{q=p-(j-1)}^{p} \left(\frac{q}{p}\right)^{m-l},$$

$$avg_{\mathrm{H}}(rank_V(\phi(c))) = \sum_{q=1}^{p} \left(\frac{q}{p}\right)^{m}.$$

For simplicity of notation, instead of $avg_{\mathrm{H}}(rank_V(g(\cdot)))$ we write $AR(\cdot)$ (for average rank, and leaving the history implicit) and refer to it as the average rank of a potential solution. We also apply the transformation $q \to p - q$ and reverse the summation order, yielding:

$$AR(a) = \sum_{q=0}^{i-1} \left(1 - \frac{q}{p}\right)^{m-k},$$

$$AR(b) = \sum_{q=0}^{j-1} \left(1 - \frac{q}{p}\right)^{m-l},$$

$$AR(c) = \sum_{q=0}^{p-1} \left(1 - \frac{q}{p}\right)^{m}.$$

When we want to make explicit some of the variables used in the $AR(\cdot)$ formula we will use notation such as $AR(\cdot|k, i)$ to mean the average rank of a partially-evaluated potential solution that has seen k tests and has current rank i.

Note that the average rank of a potential solution (whether partially evaluated or completely unevaluated) does not depend on information about other potential solutions. This will allow for easy generalization from only two partially-evaluated potential solutions to any number of such potential solutions, which will be presented later in this section. It is also the reason we do not need to make assumptions about the size of $\mathcal{B}_1$, since regardless of how many completely-unevaluated potential solutions there are, the aggregated performance for any of them is given by $AR(c)$.

[12] also proved some relationships between the three summations in their generic form, and these relationships transfer to the average-rank summations. In summary:

- if two partially-evaluated potential solutions a and b have the same current rank ($i = j$), Bayes considers better the potential solution that has seen more tests (i.e. a if $k > l$, b if $k < l$, and either a or b if $k = l$); so Bayes may make a distinction where greedy doesn't; Bayes may still output a completely-unevaluated potential solution c, depending on the actual values of m, p, k, l, i and j;

- if two partially-evaluated potential solutions a and b have different current ranks, and the one that has a strictly better current rank has seen more or the same number of tests, then Bayes agrees with greedy on the relative ordering of a and b, and will output either the potential solution with a better current rank or a completely-unevaluated potential solution c, depending on the actual values of m, p, k, l, i and j;

- if two partially-evaluated potential solutions a and b have different current ranks, and the one that has a strictly better current rank has seen fewer tests, then even which of a and b Bayes considers better is not clear cut, and there is still potential for it outputting a completely-unevaluated potential solution c.

To get an intuition for the first two situations above, it helps to think of aggregation as expectation, as follows. For the best worst-case solution concept, each test not yet seen by a potential solution can be viewed as a chance for the current rank of that potential solution to get worse. If out of two potential solutions the one that has a better current rank also has fewer chances of its rank getting worse (because it has seen more tests so far), then it is more likely this potential solution will end up with a better actual rank once all tests are seen by both potential solutions.

Also note that for the first two situations above, implementing the Bayes relative ordering of a and b in a real algorithm is reasonably practical. It involves comparing numbers of tests seen so far and current ranks.

For the former comparison, the algorithm must maintain accurate counts of *distinct* tests seen by each potential solution, i.e. make sure tests are not counted more than once per potential solution. One way to achieve this is to keep track of all interactions measured so far, and whenever a new interaction is generated by the search heuristic check if it has been measured before or not. This is easy to implement, but can put a strain on memory requirements. Alternatively, the algorithm may use a search heuristic whose operation principle is guaranteed to never output the same interaction twice (e.g. a deterministic enumeration-like algorithm).

For the latter comparison, to determine the relationship between the current ranks, we do not actually need to know the current ranks, we can directly compare current quality. This is good because the size and exact contents of the set V may not be known a priori, in which case it may be difficult or impossible to determine the rank in V of some observed value v. On the other hand, keeping track of a potential solution's current quality is easy for the best worst-case solution concept: whenever interacting with a new test yields a metric value that is worse than the current quality, update the current quality to be the new value.

Determining whether a completely-unevaluated potential solution c should be outputted and even the relative ordering of a and b for the third case above appear to require actual computation of the given summations, which can be rather costly as well as prone to computer precision errors for large values of m and p (see appendix C for details). Therefore, in the following section we explore in more detail how the domain characteristics m and p, and the algorithm-state variables k, l, i and j influence the output of the Bayes average-rank function, and are able to further tease apart some cases when implementing Bayes is practical.

We split the analysis in two cases: domains with binary metric outcomes (i.e. tests are either passed or failed, modeled via $p = 2$) and domains with fine-grained metric outcomes (i.e. $p \geq 3$). In each case we first present the analysis for only two partially-evaluated potential solutions and then generalize to an arbitrary such number. We find that for $p = 2$ Bayes is easy to implement at any point during the algorithm regardless of the value of m, while for $p \geq 3$ additional constraints on the domain and the algorithm state must hold in order for Bayes to be simple.

3.2 Binary Metric Outcomes

In this section we focus on the special case when there are two possible values for the metric, or $p = 2$.

3.2.1 Two Partially-Evaluated Potential Solutions

We have $AR(c) = 1 + \left(1 - \frac{1}{p}\right)^m$. Since i and j can only take values 1 and 2, we distinguish the following cases: $i = j = 1$, $i = j = 2$, $i = 1 < 2 = j$ and $j = 1 < 2 = i$.

Case I. If $i = j = 1$, then $AR(a) = AR(b) = 1 < 1 + \left(1 - \frac{1}{p}\right)^m = AR(c)$, therefore *Bayes* will output c regardless of the values of $m \geq 2$, $l \geq 1$ and $k \geq 1$. This is fairly intuitive. If a potential solution has already been assigned the worst rank in the domain, then by nature of the best worst-case solution concept, that will be this potential solution's actual rank. Therefore, all other potential solutions will be no worse, and by randomly selecting a completely-unevaluated potential solution *Bayes* has a chance of actually outputting something better.

Case II. If $i = j = 2$, then $AR(a) = 1 + \left(1 - \frac{1}{p}\right)^{m-k} > 1 + \left(1 - \frac{1}{p}\right)^m = AR(c)$, since $k \geq 1$. Similarly, $AR(b) > AR(c)$, therefore *Bayes* will not output c, but one of a and b, specifically, as reviewed earlier, the one that has seen more tests (i.e. a if $k > l$, b if $k < l$, and either a or b if $k = l$).

Case III. If $i = 1 < 2 = j$, then $AR(a) = 1 < 1 + \left(1 - \frac{1}{p}\right)^{m-l} = AR(b)$ and $AR(b) > AR(c)$ as for Case II above. Therefore *Bayes* will output b regardless of the values of $m \geq 2$, $l \geq 1$ and $k \geq 1$.

Case IV. $j = 1 < 2 = i$ is like Case III, except with the roles of a and b swapped. Therefore *Bayes* will output a regardless of the values of $m \geq 2$, $l \geq 1$ and $k \geq 1$.

3.2.2 General Bayes Procedure

The above analysis can easily be extended to more than just two partially-evaluated potential solutions, and implementing the *Bayes* average-rank output mechanism can easily be done as follows:

- if all partially-evaluated potential solutions have a current rank of 1, output a randomly-selected, completely-unevaluated potential solution;

- if some partially-evaluated potential solutions have a current rank of 2, output one amongst these that has seen the most tests (disregard potential solutions of current rank 1 and the number of tests they've seen).

Note that for $p = 2$, meaning V has only 2 values, determining the current rank of a potential solution (i.e. whether it is 1 or 2) is trivial. With respect to comparing numbers of tests seen so far, the corresponding remarks from section 3.1 apply: maintaining accurate counts may require ever-increasing memory.

3.2.3 Discussion

The important conclusion of this subsection is that for domains where we only care about passing/failing of tests, we have an easy, practical way of implementing the *Bayes* output selection mechanism that is optimal with respect to the best worst-case solution concept and the average-rank

performance aggregation method. Note that while the total number of tests m was used in the analysis, in fact to implement *Bayes* we need not even know what the value of m is for the given domain. This is a valuable result, since for certain domains determining the value of m may not be straightforward.

Furthermore, note that for $p = 2$ the best worst-case solution concept can be restated as the goal of finding a potential solution that passes all the tests. If such a solution is known to exist, then this solution concept also becomes equivalent to the goal of finding the potential solution that passes the most tests. These goals are specific instantiations of two solution concepts called *simultaneous maximization of all outcomes* [11, 14] and *maximization of expected utility* [11, 3, 12]. While it is beyond the scope of the current paper, it is possible that the analysis could be extended to those solution concepts when applied to domains with binary metric outcomes.

3.3 Fine-grained Metric Outcomes

Here we extend the analysis to value sets with $p \geq 3$; that is, when metrics can take more than two values.

3.3.1 Two Partially-Evaluated Potential Solutions

Again we treat separately the cases involving potential solutions of current rank 1.

Case I. If $i = j = 1$, then $AR(a) = AR(b) = 1 < 1 + \left(1 - \frac{1}{p}\right)^m + \sum_{q=2}^{p-1} \left(1 - \frac{q}{p}\right)^m = AR(c)$, since the summation has at least one term and all its terms are strictly positive. Therefore *Bayes* will output c regardless of the values of $m \geq 2$, $p \geq 3$, $l \geq 1$ and $k \geq 1$.

For cases when at least one of a and b has a current rank strictly greater than 1, we perform the analysis in two steps. First we focus on the relative *Bayes*-ordering of a and b, then we investigate the impact of c on *Bayes*' actual output.

Ordering two partially-evaluated potential solutions.

Case II. One of a and b has current rank 1 and the other has a current rank strictly greater than 1. If $i = 1 < j$ then $AR(a) = 1 < 1 + \sum_{q=1}^{j-1} \left(1 - \frac{q}{p}\right)^{m-l} = AR(b)$, since the summation will have at least one term ($j > i = 1 \Rightarrow j - 1 \geq 1$) and also $AR(a) = 1 < 1 + \sum_{q=1}^{p-1} \left(1 - \frac{q}{p}\right)^m = AR(c)$. So *Bayes* will consider a worse than b, and also worse than c, so it definitely not output a, regardless of the relative values for $m \geq 2$, $p \geq 3$, $l \geq 1$, $k \geq 1$ and $j \geq 2$. Which of b and c is outputted will be addressed further in this section. The case $j = 1 < i$ is equivalent to swapping a and b.

Case III. Neither of a and b has current rank 1 (i.e. $2 \leq i, j \leq p$). As previously summarized in the review of [12] in section 3.1, in some cases the *Bayes* ordering is easy to implement. The case that requires further analysis is when the two potential solutions have strictly different current ranks, and the one that has a strictly better current rank has seen fewer tests. Let us therefore consider $2 \leq j < i \leq p$ (i.e. a has a strictly better current rank than b, therefore *greedy* considers a to be better than b) and $m \geq l > k \geq 1$ (i.e. a has seen fewer tests). The case $j > i$ and $k > l$ is equivalent to swapping a and b.

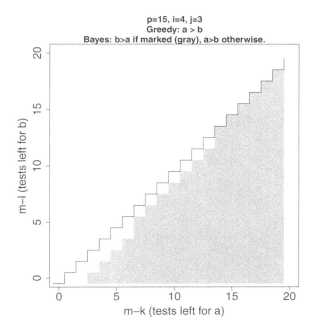

Figure 1: Example ordering of a and b by *Bayes* average rank for fixed p, i, j and varying $m-k$, $m-l$.

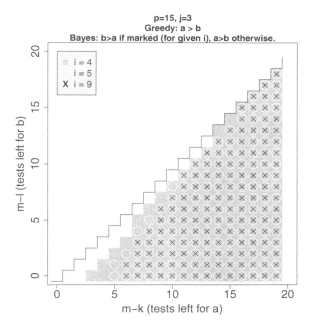

Figure 2: Effects of a's current rank, i, on the ordering of a and b by *Bayes* average rank.

To determine the *Bayes*-ordering of a and b, we implemented a computer program for computing $AR(\cdot)$, ran it for many different sets of values for m, p, k, l, i, j and show a few illustrative and typical results in figures 1, 2 and 3, as follows.

For the plot in figure 1, we fix $p = 15$, $i = 4$ and $j = 3$. We then make the axes of the plot vary $m - k$ and $m - l$ (which represent, respectively, the number of tests a and b have not seen yet). We can do this easily because the expression of $AR(\cdot)$ uses m and k (l) only via the quantity $m - k$ ($m - l$). Therefore this choice of axes has the benefit of not requiring a specific value for m, only a lower bound (e.g. for the shown plots it is implicitly assumed that $m \geq 20$). This kind of plot can be extended upwards and to the right if m is assumed larger.

For each pair $(m - k, m - l)$, the respective cell in the plot corresponds to a set of situations (defined by k, l, i, j) that may be encountered during the run of an algorithm on a problem (metric) from the class characterized by m and p. The cell is marked (colored gray) if $AR(b) > AR(a)$ (thus the *Bayes*-ordering disagrees with the *greedy*-ordering) for the respective combination of variable values. For easier interpretation, we also draw a separation between the areas $l > k$ and $l \leq k$. The results from [12] mean that there will never be anything marked on or above the diagonal ($l \leq k$).

Making such plots is essentially a way of empirically investigating the space of possible algorithm states on problems characterized by some value for p and a lower bound for m. We are not concerned with how the algorithm gets to a certain state or how it should proceed from there, merely what it should output if queried in that state. However, note that states encountered early during the run of an algorithm (when partially-evaluated potential solutions have seen very few tests) will correspond to cells in the upper right corner of the plot corresponding to the domain's m and p.

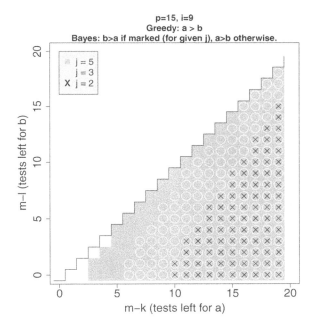

Figure 3: Effects of b's current rank, j on the ordering of a and b by *Bayes* average rank.

Figures 2 and 3 help us determine how the nature of this kind of plot changes depending on the relationship between the current ranks of a and b (i and j, respectively). In figure 2 we fix $j = 3$ and show the effects for three different values of i (4, 5 and 9) by overlaying different marking symbols (gray squares, white circles and black crosses, respectively). Thus if, for example, a cell is marked with a gray square and white circle but not a black cross, then *Bayes* considers

b better than a if $i = 4$ or $i = 5$, and a better than b if $i = 9$. Similarly, in figure 3 we fix $i = 9$ and vary j.

We observe a few things from the plots. Firstly, for fixed j (figure 2), as i decreases, the area where *Bayes* considers b better appears to increase. This is supported by the math, because $AR(a)$ is monotonically increasing as a function of i, so if $AR(a|k, i_1) < AR(b|l, j)$, then $\forall i_2, j < i_2 < i_1$, $AR(a|k, i_2) < AR(a|k, i_i) < AR(b|l, j)$. Similarly, for fixed i (figure 3), as j increases, the area where *Bayes* considers b better appears to increase as well. This too is supported by the math, because $AR(b)$ is monotonically increasing as a function of j, so if $AR(a|k, i) < AR(b|l, j_1)$, then $\forall j_2, j_1 < j_2 < i$, $AR(a|k, i) < AR(b|l, j_1) < AR(b|l, j_2)$. In other words, the closer the current ranks of two partially-evaluated potential solutions are, the more potential there is that *Bayes* will disagree with *greedy* about their relative ordering.[12]

Secondly, regardless of the values of i and j, the boundary of the area where *Bayes* considers b better appears to be converging towards the sub-diagonal[13] as $m - k$ increases. The proof that is indeed the case is presented in appendix A. As a corollary, also included in appendix A, we determine how fast the sub-diagonal is reached. Specifically, we find a bound $bd(p)$, such that $\forall k : m - k > bd(p)$, *Bayes* considers b better for all pairs $(m-k, m-l)$ with $0 \le m-l \le m-k-1$ ($\Leftrightarrow l > k$), regardless of the values of i and j ($2 \le j < i$). Note that for this to be possible, since $m - k \le m - 1$, we must have $m - 1 > bd(p)$.

The important consequence of this result is that, when the domain is such that $m - 1 > bd(p)$ and the algorithm is in a state where a's current rank is better than b's current rank ($i > j$) and k, the number of tests seen by a, is such that $m - k > bd(p)$, determining the *Bayes* ordering of potential solutions a and b does not require computing the average-rank summations; instead, simply consider a better if $l \le k$ and consider b better if $l > k$. Making use of symmetry and rearranging inequality terms, this can be restated more generally as follows: if the domain and, respectively, algorithm state are such that $m - bd(p)$ is strictly greater than 1 and also strictly greater than the number of tests seen by the potential solution that has a better current rank, then *Bayes* considers better the potential solution that has seen more tests.

Impact of completely-unevaluated potential solutions.

We now return to the matter of what *Bayes* average rank will actually output, since it considers not only the partially-evaluated potential solutions a and b, but also any completely-unevaluated potential solution c. We are particularly interested in whether *Bayes* would ever output c in the "simplicity regime" described above. The proof in appendix B shows that the answer is in fact "no". Specifically, it shows that if $m - bd(p) > 1$ and at least one of the partially-evaluated potential solutions has current rank ≥ 2, *Bayes* average rank will not output c, regardless of the values of k, l, i, j ($\max(i, j) \ge 2$). Therefore, in situations when $m - bd(p)$ is strictly greater than 1 and also strictly greater than the number of tests seen by the potential solution with a better current rank, implementing the *Bayes* average-rank output

[12] By "more potential" we mean a larger percentage out of all possible algorithmic state sets (denoted via plot cells).
[13] The sub-diagonal is given by $y = x - 1$.

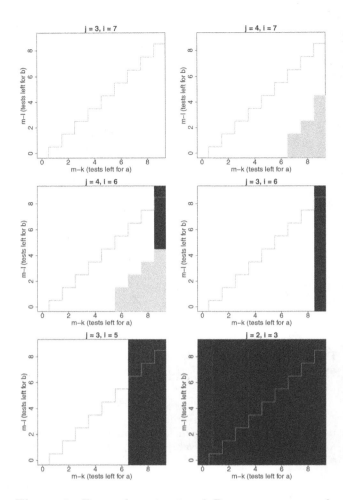

Figure 4: Example outputs of *Bayes* average rank when considering two partially-evaluated potential solutions a and b and a completely-unevaluated potential solution c. Fixed $m = 10$, $p = 30$ ($m - bd(p) < 1$) and various combinations of i and j. Output is c in black areas, b in gray areas and a in white areas.

mechanism for the case of only two partially-evaluated potential solutions remains as simple as described above. This is true for both Case II (one of i and j is equal to 1 and the other is ≥ 2) and Case III (both $i, j \ge 2$).

Complex situations.

For the case $m - bd(p) \le 1$, the above analysis does not suggest any means of ordering the average ranks of a, b and c without actually computing them. To get some sense for when each of these potential solutions is outputted by *Bayes*, we use the computer program for computing $AR(\cdot)$ and extend the visualization introduced in figure 1 to incorporate c (cells where it is outputted are colored black) and show a few examples in figure 4. Note that to be able to compute $AR(c)$ we now need a specific value for m, not just a lower bound. The plots do not immediately suggest a pattern and further research would be needed to determine if additional simplicity regimes may be isolated. Until then, implementing *Bayes* when $m - bd(p) \le 1$ has to rely on computing the $AR(\cdot)$ summations.

3.3.2 General Bayes Procedure

Real algorithms will generally sample and measure interactions corresponding to more than two potential solutions. Therefore, we next extend our analysis of the *Bayes* average-rank output mechanism to situations with more than two partially-evaluated potential solutions. We do this by reasoning about multiple pairwise comparisons and describe a procedure that minimizes the number of average-rank summations computed.

Firstly, note that *Bayes* will never output a partially-evaluated potential solution of current rank 1, regardless of how many tests it has seen. This is because the average rank of such potential solutions is also 1 and therefore worse than both the average rank of partially-evaluated potential solutions of current rank at least 2 and the average rank of completely-unevaluated potential solutions (as shown under cases I and II at the beginning of section 3.3).

Thus, if all partially-evaluated potential solutions have current rank 1, then *Bayes* will output a randomly-selected, completely-unevaluated potential solution (i.e. c).

Otherwise, *Bayes* disregards all partially-evaluated potential solutions of current rank 1 and needs to choose amongst all partially-evaluated potential solutions of current rank at least 2 and the completely-unevaluated potential solution representative c.

Denote the former by a list $a_1, a_2, ..., a_q$ of potential solutions that have been partially evaluated with, respectively, $k_1, k_2, ..., k_q$ tests and have current ranks $i_1, i_2, ..., i_q \geq 2$. Assume without loss of generality that the list has already been sorted in order of increasing current rank, specifically such that $2 \leq i_1 \leq i_2 \leq ... \leq i_q$ and $i_x = i_{x+1} \Rightarrow k_x \leq k_{x+1}$.

We know that when comparing two partially-evaluated potential solutions with the same current rank, *Bayes* considers better the one that has seen more tests. Additionally, out of two potential solutions of different current ranks, if the one with the better current rank has also seen more tests, then it will be consider better by *Bayes*. If multiple potential solutions have both the same current rank and the same number of tests seen, then they are equivalent from the perspective of *Bayes*, and the procedure we describe maintains only one from each such cluster.

Consequently, *Bayes* can further drop from consideration and thus avoid computing summations for any partially-evaluated potential solution a_x if $\exists y > x : k_y \geq k_x$. The following procedure can be used to prune all such cases:

```
L ← ()
for (x in 1..(q − 1)) {
    found ← false
    for (y in (x + 1)..q) {
        if (k_x ≤ k_y) {
            found ← true
            break
        }
    }
    if (!found) {
        L ← concat(L, a_x)
    }
}
L ← concat(L, a_q)
```

The resulting list $L = \{a_{x_1}, a_{x_2}, ..., a_{x_n}\}$ has the property that $2 \leq i_{x_1} < i_{x_2} < ... < i_{x_n}$ and $k_{x_1} > k_{x_2} > ... > k_{x_n} \geq 1$, $x_n = q$. The list will contain at least one element, $a_{x_n} = a_q$. Moreover k_{x_1} must be equal to $\max(k_1, k_2, ..., k_q) = k_*$.

At this point, further potential solutions may be dropped from consideration (and thus computing summations for them avoided) by determining how the quantity $m - bd(p)$ compares to 1 and to the $k_{x_1}...k_{x_n}$.

When $1 \geq m - bd(p)$ there is no known simplification, thus $n + 1$ average-rank summations must be computed (n for the a-s and one for c) and n comparisons performed to determine the maximum out of them and output the respective potential solution.

For the case $m - bd(p) > 1$ we recall two findings from the analysis. Firstly, the average rank of any partially-evaluated potential solution of current rank at least 2 is greater than that of c, thus we need not compute the average-rank summation for c, as it will not be outputted. Additionally, when comparing any two partially-evaluated potential solutions of current rank at least 2, if $m - bd(p)$ is strictly greater than the number of tests seen by the potential solution that has a better current rank, then *Bayes* considers better the potential solution that has seen more tests (thus the one that has seen fewer tests can be dropped from consideration and its average rank need not be computed). If we are not in this situation, then the only way we know of determining which of the two potential solutions has a better average rank is to compute and compare the respective summations. Using this information and the properties of the list L (increasing current ranks, decreasing numbers of tests seen), we conclude we can encounter the following three sub-cases.

If $k_{x_1} > k_{x_2} > ... > k_{x_n} \geq m - bd(p) > 1$, then n average-rank summations must be computed (for all remaining a-s) and $n - 1$ comparisons performed to determine the maximum out of them and output the respective potential solution.

If $k_{x_1} > k_{x_2} > ... > k_{x_r} \geq m - bd(p) > k_{x_{r+1}} > ... > k_{x_n} > 1$, $r \geq 2$, then we can drop from consideration (and not need to compute summations for) $a_{x_{r+1}}...a_{x_n}$, since the analysis findings summarized above tells us any of them will have a worse average rank than any of $a_{x_1}...a_{x_r}$ (the former have better current ranks than the latter and have seen less than $m - bd(p)$ tests, and the latter have seen more tests). Thus we only need to compute and compare the r summations for $a_{x_1}...a_{x_r}$.

Finally, if $m - bd(p) > k_{x_2}$ (either $k_{x_1} \geq m - bd(p) > k_{x_2} > ...k_{x_n} > 1$ or $m - bd(p) > k_{x_1} > ...k_{x_n} > 1$) then we do not need to compute any summations, *Bayes* will simply output a_{x_1}.

3.3.3 Discussion

Let us examine more closely the practicality of the general *Bayes* procedure described above. We start by discussing the knowledge needed to implement it.

Firstly, the procedure requires the ability to determine whether the current rank of a partially-evaluated potential solution is 1. This is equivalent to knowing what the domain's worst possible metric value is, which is not uncommon.

Next, the sorting and pruning of partially-evaluated potential solutions to obtain the list L simply requires comparing numbers of tests seen so far and current ranks. As already discussed in section 3.1, the former will typically require storing all measured interactions, while the latter is equivalent to comparing current quality (which can easily be tracked), actual ranks need not be known.

The following step requires assessing inequalities involving the quantity $m - bd(p)$ and numbers of tests seen so far. This is straightforward if the exact values of m (total number of tests) and p (number of possible metric values) are known. However, for certain domains m and especially p may not be easy to determine. In such cases, being able to put bounds on these values may still allow us to determine whether the inequalities hold or not.

For instance, for the ship design domain from [10] (described in section 2.1), the exact value of m was known to be 11480, whereas the exact value of p was not known, but the values of f were known to be bounded by 0 and 958. Therefore $p \leq 959$, but it is in fact rather obvious given the nature of f in that domain that it cannot take every value between 0 and 958, thus the bound on p is rather loose. We have $bd(959) = 13145.18 > 11479 = m - 1$. Conversely, solving for $bd(p) < 11479$ yields $p \leq 853$. Thus, whether or not this domain has potential for a simple *Bayes* implementation, and how much potential, depends on how much smaller p is compared to 853. For instance, if upon closer investigation of the domain we were able to show $p < 800$, then *Bayes* would be able to assess the required inequalities (and conclude summations need not be computed) as long as the algorithm maintained $k_{x_2} \leq \lfloor m - bd(p) \rfloor = \lfloor 11480 - bd(800) \rfloor = 807$.

Assuming the inequalities could be assessed, there are two possible outcomes. One is that *Bayes* simply outputs a_{x_1} (potential solution of highest rank greater than 1 amongst those that have seen the most tests) without any further consideration. The other is that some average-rank summations must be computed. In this latter case, since the number of terms in the summations corresponds to the current ranks, implementing *Bayes* further requires the ability to determine a partially-evaluated potential solution's current rank from its current quality. This a less common domain property than merely identifying current rank 1.

If we can determine current ranks, then we can implement *Bayes* by computing summations, but this adds some complexity. Consider first $AR(c) = \sum_{q=0}^{p-1} \left(1 - \frac{q}{p}\right)^m$. Computing this can be done in $O(\log(p) \cdot \log(m))$, where $log(p)$ reflects the time required to add the terms in the summation and $\log(m)$ the time required to compute the exponential in each term. While p may be small for some domains, m is typically very large, or else exhaustive evaluation of potential solutions could be performed and the problem mapped onto traditional optimization. Note however that $AR(c)$ needs to be computed only once (and only if $m - bd(p) \leq 1$), regardless of how many times the algorithm is asked to produce an output and regardless of how many potential solutions the algorithm has partially evaluated up to that point.

Summations for partially-evaluated potential solutions are given by $AR(\cdot | k, i) = \sum_{q=0}^{i-1} \left(1 - \frac{q}{p}\right)^{m-k}$. Thus, should they need to be computed, they have the same worst case O complexity as $AR(c)$, however they will typically have fewer terms (since $1 \leq i \leq p$) and smaller term exponents (since $m - k < m$). Note also that the average rank of a partially-evaluated potential solution need only be recomputed if the potential solution has seen additional tests since the last time its average rank was computed. This means that its k will have increased by at least 1, thus making $m - k$ smaller and consequently the computation of each exponential term less costly. Additionally, since the current rank i of a potential solution can only decrease (get worse) upon seeing

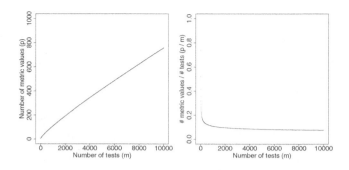

Figure 5: Impact of the relationship between p and m (left) and p/m and m (right) on *Bayes* average rank's implementation simplicity. For domains situated below the boundary curve there is potential for a simple implementation (i.e. not requiring computing summations).

additional tests, the number of terms in the summation will potentially decrease as well. In other words, reassessing the average rank of a partially-evaluated potential solution will be less costly each time it needs to be done again. Further speed-ups may be obtained by using caching techniques to store and reuse across summation terms with the same base and exponent.

An additional consideration when having to compute summations is that $1 - \frac{q}{p}$ is less than 1 and consequently the larger m is, the smaller $\left(1 - \frac{q}{p}\right)^m$ will be, approaching 0. Thus, for very large m, computing such terms may run into computer precision errors if using basic numeric data types. Appendix C details when basic implementations must be replaced with ones using arbitrary-precision data types.

Let us now take a closer look at the inequalities determining whether or not *Bayes* requires computing summations. Consider first $m - bd(p) > 1 \Leftrightarrow m > 1 + bd(p)$. On the left hand side of figure 5 we plot the curve $(1 + bd(p), p)$. The *Bayes* average rank has potential for being simple to implement (i.e. not require computing summations) for domains represented by pairs (m, p) situated below this curve. For the potential to be realized, during the run of the algorithm $(m - k_{x_2}, p)$ must also be below the curve, therefore the further away from the curve (m, p) is, the more potential there is. The shape of the curve implies that as the total number of tests (m) increases, if the number of metric values (p) remains fixed, the potential for a simple implementation increases. In fact, the potential is retained even if p increases, as long as the rate of increase of p is lower than that of m. To get a quantitative view of this, on the right hand side of figure 5 we plot the curve $(p/(1 + bd(p)), p/m)$. The potential for a simple implementation is for domains with $(m, p/m)$ below this curve, meaning that the larger the number of tests is, the smaller the ratio of number of metric values to number of tests must be.

The condition $k_{x_2} < m - bd(p)$ means that generally speaking the potential for a simple *Bayes* implementation is at the beginning of the algorithm, since the number of tests seen so far by any given potential solution increases as the algorithm's execution progresses. The larger m is compared to $bd(p)$, the longer an algorithm can run with a simple *Bayes* implementation.

Note that for many real domains the maximum number of tests seen by any potential solution during the entire course of the algorithm, and therefore k_{x_2}, is in fact much smaller than the total number of tests (m). Further, k_{x_2} can be arbitrarily smaller than $k_{x_1} = k_* = \max(k_1, k_2, ..., k_q)$, as it is not necessarily the second largest of the original list $k_1, k_2, ..., k_q$ (recall the pruning steps). Additionally, the value of k_{x_2} can be somewhat controlled via the search heuristic. This opens up the interesting prospect of designing search heuristics that try to help the *Bayes* output mechanism avoid having to compute summations, by keeping k_{x_2} small. However, in aiming for such designs, one must be mindful that there are free lunches with respect to search heuristics as well.

4. CONCLUSIONS

It is common in the field of algorithms to use greedy approaches known to be suboptimal when the optimal algorithm would be computationally prohibitive. This has been the case in co-optimization as well. Variants of the *greedy* output mechanism introduced in section 2.2.2 have been used in practice (see examples in appendix D). However, from the perspective of aggregated (expected) performance, *greedy* has been shown to be strictly worse than the theoretically-optimal *Bayes* output mechanism, yet the latter appeared prohibitive to implement.

The main contribution of this paper is to show that for certain domains and algorithm states *Bayes* is in fact practical and coincides with a simple and fast procedure, which we exhibited. We have provided quantitative characterizations of these situations and detailed what information needs to be known about the domain and what information needs to be maintained by the algorithm.

These results have been derived for a certain class of co-optimization problems (the best worst case solution concept) and a certain kind of of aggregated performance (average rank). In addition, certain assumptions have been made. In the following, we discuss the potential for further research by extending the work to other problem classes and other kinds of aggregated performance, and by relaxing some of the assumptions.

A first noteworthy assumption is that the number of metric values, p, and the number of tests, m, are finite. The original argument in support of these assumptions put forward by [22, 23] is that computers have finite precision and memory. However, a natural question to consider is whether the conclusions presented here change if, modulo computer limitations, there are an infinite number of metric values and/or tests. Even if there were still situations when *Bayes* was practical, its operation might look different from the procedure described in section 3.3.2. A full exploration of this question will likely require adjustments to the analysis techniques (e.g. replacing summations with integrals).

A second assumption is that, given the sets $\mathcal{B}_1$, $\mathcal{B}_2$ and V, all possible metrics f are equally likely. One way to view this assumption is as a uniform distribution over the set of possible metrics; in other words, the aggregation utilized in the *Bayes* output mechanism treats each possible metric consistent with observed information as equally likely. A natural question is whether this assumption could be relaxed by extending the present work to admit other distributions over

possible metrics. Distributions might be designed to model known structure of a set of problems of interest; extending the analysis to such distributions could permit the development of optimal algorithms for a given set of problems with known structure..

Average rank is not the only way aggregated performance may be judged. Other aggregation functions have been explored, such as average value [12] and actual solution count [19]. The question remains whether the results here generalize to the above and other aggregation mechanisms. The current analysis and that in [12] suggest that generic results may be easier to achieve when the dependence of aggregated performance on the actual metric values is indirect, for instance via rank or ordering. Investigating additional solution concepts is also of interest, especially in light of the mapping discussed at the end of section 3.2 between best worst case, maximum expected utility and simultaneous maximization of all outcomes for domains with binary metric outcomes.

Finally, while this work centered around the mechanism by which potential solutions are chosen for output, we feel the analysis presented should inform the design of an algorithm's search heuristic as well. This is another promising avenue for future work, since it is already known from [23, 19] that some search heuristics are better than others in the free-lunch sense discussed here.

5. ACKNOWLEDGMENTS

This work has been made possible through the support by ONR under contract number N00014-09-C-0393.

6. REFERENCES

[1] H. Barbosa. A coevolutionary genetic algorithm for constrained optimization. In *CEC-1999: Proceedings of the Congress on Evolutionary Computation*. IEEE Press, 1999.

[2] J. Branke and J. Rosenbusch. New approaches to coevolutionary worst-case optimization. In *PPSN-X: Parallel Problem Solving from Nature*. Springer-Verlag, 2008.

[3] E. D. De Jong. The MaxSolve algorithm for coevolution. In *GECCO-2005: Proceedings of the Genetic and Evolutionary Computation Conference*. ACM Press, 2005.

[4] S. G. Ficici. *Solutions concepts in Coevolutionary Algorithms*. PhD thesis, Brandeis University Department of Computer Science, USA, 2004.

[5] J. W. Hermann. A genetic algorithm for minimax optimization problems. In *CEC-1999: Proceedings of the Congress on Evolutionary Computation*. IEEE Press, 1999.

[6] M. T. Jensen. Finding worst-case flexible schedules using coevolution. In *GECCO-2001: Proceedings of the Genetic and Evolutionary Computation Conference*. Morgan Kaufmann, 2001.

[7] M. T. Jensen. *Robust and flexible scheduling with evolutionary computation*. PhD thesis, Department of Computer Science, University of Aarhus, Denmark, 2001.

[8] M. T. Jensen. *Metaheuristics*, chapter A new look at solving minimax problems with coevolutionary genetic algorithms. Kluwer Academic Publishers, 2004.

[9] E. Popovici. *An Analysis of Two-Population Coevolutionary Computation*. PhD thesis, George Mason University, USA, 2006.

[10] E. Popovici, O. Bandte, and P. Gaudiano. New approaches for the automated performance evaluation and design of control systems: A firemain example. In *Proceedings of the Automation and Controls Symposium*, 2007.

[11] E. Popovici, A. Bucci, R. P. Wiegand, and E. D. De Jong. *Handbook of Natural Computing*, chapter Coevolutionary Principles. Springer-Verlag, 2010.

[12] E. Popovici and K. A. De Jong. Monotonicity versus performance in co-optimization. In *Foundations of Genetic Algorithms X*. ACM Press, 2009.

[13] J. Rosenbusch. New methods for fitness evaluation in coevolutionary worst case optimization. Master Thesis, Karlsruhe University, Germany, 2008.

[14] C. D. Rosin. *Coevolutionary search among adversaries*. PhD thesis, University of California, USA, 1997.

[15] C. Schumacher, M. D. Vose, and L. D. Whitley. The no free lunch and problem description length. In *GECCO-2001: Proceedings of the Genetic and Evolutionary Computation Conference*. Morgan Kaufmann, 2001.

[16] T. C. Service. Free lunches in pareto coevolution. In *GECCO-2009: Proceedings of the Genetic and Evolutionary Computation Conference*. ACM Press, 2009.

[17] T. C. Service. Unbiased coevolutionary solution concepts. In *Foundations of Genetic Algorithms X*. ACM Press, 2009.

[18] T. C. Service and D. R. Tauritz. Co-optimization algorithms. In *GECCO-2008: Proceedings of the Genetic and Evolutionary Computation Conference*. ACM, 2008.

[19] T. C. Service and D. R. Tauritz. A no-free-lunch framework for coevolution. In *GECCO-2008: Proceedings of the Genetic and Evolutionary Computation Conference*. ACM, 2008.

[20] K. Sims. Evolving 3D morphology and behaviour by competition. In *Artificial Life IV Proceedings*. MIT Press, 1994.

[21] P. Stuermer, A. Bucci, J. Branke, P. Funes, and E. Popovici. Analysis of coevolution for worst-case optimization. In *GECCO-2009: Proceedings of the Genetic and Evolutionary Computation Conference*. ACM Press, 2009.

[22] D. Wolpert and W. Macready. No free lunch theorems for optimization. *IEEE Transactions on Evolutionary Computation*, 1(1):67–82, April 1997.

[23] D. Wolpert and W. Macready. Coevolutionary free lunches. *IEEE Transactions on Evolutionary Computation*, 9(6):721–735, December 2005.

APPENDIX

A. ORDERING TWO PARTIALLY-EVALUATED POTENTIAL SOLUTIONS

THEOREM 1. *Fix $2 \leq j < i \leq p$ (so $i \geq 3, p \geq 3$) and let $1 \leq k, l \leq m$. As $m - k$ increases, the boundary of the*

area where Bayes average rank considers b better converges to the sub-diagonal.

PROOF. For notational simplicity, let $\alpha = m - k$ and $\beta = m - l$, so $0 \leq \alpha, \beta \leq m - 1$. For the purpose of this appendix only, we use $AR(\cdot|\alpha, i)$ to mean the average rank of a potential solution that has α tests *left to see* and has current rank i. With this notation we have:

$$AR(a|\alpha, i) = \sum_{q=0}^{i-1} \left(1 - \frac{q}{p}\right)^{\alpha}, \; AR(b|\beta, j) = \sum_{q=0}^{j-1} \left(1 - \frac{q}{p}\right)^{\beta}.$$

We know that $l \leq k$ $(\alpha \leq \beta) \Rightarrow AR(b|\beta, j) < AR(a|\alpha, i)$. Note also that $AR(b|\beta, j)$ is monotonically decreasing as a function of β. Therefore, for a given α_0, either $AR(b|0, j) < AR(a|\alpha_0, i)$, or there must exist β_0, $0 \leq \beta_0 \leq \alpha_0 - 1$ such that we have $AR(b|\beta_0, j) > AR(a|\alpha_0, i)$ but $AR(b|\beta_0+1, j) \leq AR(a|\alpha_0, i)$. Moreover, if we extend $AR(b)$ from integers to real numbers, then there must exist x_0, $x_0 < \alpha_0$ such that $AR(b|x_0, j) = AR(a|\alpha_0, i)$. If $x_0 < 0$, then $AR(b|0, j) < AR(a|\alpha_0, i)$. If $x_0 \geq 0$ then β_0 exists and it is equal to $\lceil x_0 - 1 \rceil$. Since the values of x_0 and β_0 will be dependent on the given α_0, we can see them as functions of α and write them as $x_0(\alpha)$ and $\beta_0(\alpha)$. We show that $\lim_{\alpha \to +\infty} x_0(\alpha) = \alpha$ as follows.

$$\exists x_0(\alpha) < \alpha : AR(b|x_0(\alpha), i) = AR(a|\alpha, i)$$

$$\Leftrightarrow \exists x_0(\alpha) < \alpha : \sum_{q=0}^{j-1} \left(1 - \frac{q}{p}\right)^{x_0(\alpha)} = \sum_{q=0}^{i-1} \left(1 - \frac{q}{p}\right)^{\alpha}$$

Let $z = 1 - \frac{1}{p} = \frac{p-1}{p}$. Since $j \geq 2, i \geq 3, p \geq 3$, the above is further equivalent with:

$$1 + z^{x_0(\alpha)} + \delta(x_0(\alpha)) = 1 + z^{\alpha} + \epsilon(\alpha)$$

where

$$\delta(x_o(\alpha)) = \begin{cases} 0 & , \text{if } j = 2 \\ \sum_{q=2}^{j-1} (1 - \frac{q}{p})^{x_0(\alpha)} & , \text{if } j \geq 3 \end{cases}$$

and

$$\epsilon(\alpha) = \sum_{q=2}^{i-1} \left(1 - \frac{q}{p}\right)^{\alpha}.$$

Then our equality is further equivalent to:

$$z^{x_0(\alpha)} = z^{\alpha} + \epsilon(\alpha) - \delta(x_o(\alpha))$$

$$\Leftrightarrow z^{x_0(\alpha)-\alpha} = 1 + \frac{\epsilon(\alpha) - \delta(x_0(\alpha))}{z^{\alpha}}$$

$$\Leftrightarrow x_0(\alpha) - \alpha = \log_z \left(1 + \frac{\epsilon(\alpha) - \delta(x_0(\alpha))}{z^{\alpha}}\right).$$

Since $x_0(\alpha) < \alpha$, $z < 1$ and $\delta(x_0(\alpha)) \geq 0$ we have:

$$0 > x_0(\alpha) - \alpha \geq \log_z \left(1 + \frac{\epsilon(\alpha)}{z^{\alpha}}\right).$$

We show $\lim_{\alpha \to +\infty} \log_z \left(1 + \frac{\epsilon(\alpha)}{z^{\alpha}}\right) = 0$ as follows:

$$\lim_{\alpha \to +\infty} \log_z \left(1 + \frac{\epsilon(\alpha)}{z^{\alpha}}\right) = \log_z \left(1 + \lim_{\alpha \to +\infty} \frac{\epsilon(\alpha)}{z^{\alpha}}\right)$$

$$= \log_z \left(1 + \lim_{\alpha \to +\infty} \sum_{q=2}^{j-1} \left(\frac{1 - \frac{q}{p}}{1 - \frac{1}{p}} \right)^\alpha \right)$$

$$= \log_z \left(1 + \sum_{q=2}^{j-1} \lim_{\alpha \to +\infty} \left(\frac{p - q}{p - 1} \right)^\alpha \right)$$

$$= \log_z \left(1 + \sum_{q=2}^{j-1} 0 \right) = \log_z(1) = 0.$$

So $x_0(\alpha) - \alpha$ is bounded by 0 and a quantity whose limit is 0, therefore $\lim_{\alpha \to +\infty} (x_0(\alpha) - \alpha) = 0 \Leftrightarrow \lim_{\alpha \to +\infty} x_0(\alpha) = \alpha$.

As a consequence of $\lim_{\alpha \to +\infty} x_0(\alpha) = \alpha$ and $x_0(\alpha) < \alpha$, we have $\lim_{\alpha \to +\infty} \beta_0(\alpha) = \lim_{\alpha \to +\infty} \lceil x_0(\alpha) - 1 \rceil = \alpha - 1$. This concludes the proof that, as $\alpha = m - k$ increases, the boundary of the area where *Bayes* average rank considers b better converges to the sub-diagonal. $\square$

Next, we determine when the sub-diagonal is reached. Specifically, we find an α_0 such that $\forall \alpha > \alpha_0 : \beta_0(\alpha) = \alpha - 1$.

COROLLARY 2. *Let* $2 \leq j < i \leq p$ *(so $i \geq 3, p \geq 3$) and* $1 \leq k, l \leq m$. *Let* $bd(p) = \dfrac{\log(p - 1) + \log(p - 2)}{\log(p - 1) - \log(p - 2)}$. *Then* $\forall \alpha > bd(p) : \beta_0(\alpha) = \alpha - 1$.

PROOF. From the proof of the preceding theorem, note that if $\log_z \left(1 + \dfrac{\epsilon(\alpha)}{z^\alpha} \right) > -1$, then $0 > x_0(\alpha) - \alpha > -1$ and since α is an integer, it follows that $\beta_0(\alpha) = \lceil x_0(\alpha) - 1 \rceil = \alpha - 1$. Since $z < 1$, $\log_z \left(1 + \dfrac{\epsilon(\alpha)}{z^\alpha} \right) > -1$ is equivalent to:

$$\Leftrightarrow 1 + \frac{\epsilon(\alpha)}{z^\alpha} < z^{-1} = \frac{p}{p - 1}$$

$$\Leftrightarrow \sum_{q=2}^{j-1} \left(\frac{p - q}{p - 1} \right)^\alpha < \frac{p}{p - 1} - 1 = \frac{1}{p - 1}.$$

We have

$$\forall q \geq 2 : \frac{p - q}{p - 1} \leq \frac{p - 2}{p - 1},$$

therefore:

$$\sum_{q=2}^{j-1} \left(\frac{p - q}{p - 1} \right)^\alpha < (j - 2) \left(\frac{p - 2}{p - 1} \right)^\alpha < (p - 2) \left(\frac{p - 2}{p - 1} \right)^\alpha,$$

since $j \leq p$.

If α is such that:

$$(p - 2) \left(\frac{p - 2}{p - 1} \right)^\alpha < \frac{1}{p - 1},$$

then the original condition on the logarithm holds. This inequality is further equivalent to:

$$\alpha \cdot \log \frac{p - 2}{p - 1} < \log \frac{1}{(p - 1)(p - 2)}$$

$$\Leftrightarrow \alpha > \frac{-(\log(p - 1) + \log(p - 2))}{\log(p - 2) - \log(p - 1)}$$

$$\Leftrightarrow \alpha > \frac{\log(p - 1) + \log(p - 2)}{\log(p - 1) - \log(p - 2)} = bd(p).$$

In summary, if $\alpha > \alpha_0 = bd(p)$, then $\beta_0(\alpha) = \alpha - 1$. Note that for this to be possible, since $\alpha = m - k \leq m - 1$, we must have $m - 1 > bd(p)$. $\square$

B. IMPACT OF COMPLETELY-UNEVALU-ATED POTENTIAL SOLUTIONS

THEOREM 3. *Let* $p \geq 3, 1 \leq k, l \leq m, 1 \leq i, j \leq p$. *If* $\max(i, j) \geq 2$ *and* $m - 1 > bd(p)$, *then* $\max(AR(a), AR(b)) > AR(c)$.

PROOF. $AR(a) = AR(a|k, i) = \sum_{q=0}^{i-1} \left(1 - \dfrac{q}{p} \right)^{m-k}$ is monotonically increasing both as a function of i (there are more terms in the summation) and as a function of k (summation terms are larger). Therefore:

$$\forall k \geq 1, \forall i \geq 2 : AR(a|k, i) \geq AR(\cdot|1, 2).$$

Similarly:

$$\forall l \geq 1, \forall j \geq 2 : AR(b) = AR(b|l, j) \geq AR(\cdot|1, 2).$$

Thus:

$$\forall k, l \geq 1, \forall i, j \geq 2 : \max(AR(a), AR(b)) \geq AR(\cdot|1, 2).$$

When $i > j = 1$, as already seen in section 3.3.1, we have $AR(a) > AR(b) = 1$, and since this also means $i \geq 2$, we still have $AR(a|k, i) \geq AR(\cdot|1, 2)$. Similarly, if $j > i = 1$ then $AR(b) > AR(a) = 1$ and also $AR(b) \geq AR(\cdot|1, 2)$. Combining all inequalities, we get:

$$\forall k, l \geq 1, \forall i, j \geq 1, \max(i, j) \geq 2 :$$

$$\max(AR(a), AR(b)) \geq AR(\cdot|1, 2).$$

We prove $AR(c) < AR(\cdot|1, 2)$, from which will follow $AR(c) < \max(AR(a), AR(b))$. We have:

$$AR(c) < AR(\cdot|1, 2)$$

$$\Leftrightarrow \sum_{q=0}^{p-1} \left(1 - \frac{q}{p} \right)^m < \sum_{q=0}^{1} \left(1 - \frac{q}{p} \right)^{m-1} = 1 + \left(\frac{p - 1}{p} \right)^{m-1}$$

$$\Leftrightarrow \frac{p^m + (p - 1)^m + \dots + 2^m + 1^m}{p^m} < \frac{p^{m-1} + (p - 1)^{m-1}}{p^{m-1}}$$

$$\Leftrightarrow p^m + (p - 1)^m + \dots + 2^m + 1^m < p \cdot (p^{m-1} + (p - 1)^{m-1})$$

$$\Leftrightarrow (p - 1)^m + \dots + 2^m + 1^m < p \cdot (p - 1)^{m-1}.$$

Since $p \geq 3$, the above is further equivalent with:

$$(p - 2)^m + \dots + 1^m < (p - 1)^{m-1} \cdot ((p - 1) - p) = (p - 1)^{m-1}.$$

We have:

$$m > m - 1 > bd(p) = \frac{\log(p - 1) + \log(p - 2)}{\log(p - 1) - \log(p - 2)} \Rightarrow$$

$$m \cdot \log \frac{p - 1}{p - 2} > \log(p - 1)(p - 2) \Leftrightarrow \left(\frac{p - 1}{p - 2} \right)^m > (p - 1)(p - 2)$$

$$\Leftrightarrow (p - 1)^{m-1} > (p - 2)^{m+1} = (p - 2)(p - 2)^m$$

$$\Rightarrow (p - 1)^{m-1} > (p - 2)^m + (p - 3)^m + \dots 2^m + 1^m$$

$$\Leftrightarrow AR(c) < AR(\cdot|1, 2)$$

$$\Rightarrow AR(c) < \max(AR(a), AR(b)).$$

$\square$

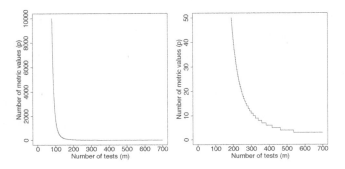

Figure 6: Bound above which the computation of $AR(c)$ hits computer precision limitations for Java type `double`. Right hand side plot is a zoom-in on $p \in 3..50$.

C. COMPUTER PRECISION

Consider as an example the Java programming language, in which the smallest positive nonzero value of type `double` is 2^{-1074}. In computing $AR(c) = \sum_{q=0}^{p-1} \left(1 - \dfrac{q}{p}\right)^m$, difficulties arise when m, p and q are such that

$$\left(1 - \frac{q}{p}\right)^m < 2^{-1074}$$

$$\Leftrightarrow m \cdot \log_2 \left(1 - \frac{q}{p}\right) < -1074$$

$$\Leftrightarrow m > -\frac{1074}{\log_2 \left(1 - \frac{q}{p}\right)} = \frac{1074}{\log_2 \frac{p}{p-q}} = \delta(p,q).$$

As q increases, $\delta(p,q)$ decreases, so this condition will be hit for smaller and smaller m. Since $AR(c)$ needs to compute terms for $q \in 1..(p-1)$, the issues will occur as soon as $m > \delta(p, p-1) = 1074/\log_2 p = \delta(p)$. The plots in figure 6 show the curve $(\delta(p), p)$. For domains represented by pairs (m, p) situated above this curve, precision error issues need to be dealt with by switching to more sophisticated, arbitrary-precision data types (e.g. BigDecimal in Java).

D. COEVOLUTIONARY ALGORITHMS

Though the co-search algorithm framework was presented in section 2.2.1 in an abstract way suitable for analysis, one particular application that inspired the current work is to co-evolutionary algorithms (CoEAs). Since it may not be clear how to map a commonly-used algorithm into this framework, we sketch here an example of such a mapping for a generational, two population CoEA applied to a two role test-based problem.

When expressed as a co-search algorithm, the majority of a CoEA's evolution-inspired logic is embedded in the search heuristic. Specifically, the search heuristic of such a CoEA will maintain two populations, one of potential solutions and one of tests, and a queue of interactions. Upon being called, the search heuristic will attempt to extract and return the interaction at the front of the queue. If the queue is empty, which would occur on generation boundaries, the search heuristic will first update its populations and push some set of interactions on to the queue.

Updating the populations will consist of applying some (typically stochastic) form of parent selection and offspring generation via genetic operators. Parent selection in particular will use some of the measurements in the history, possibly creating different biases in the two populations. For potential solutions, selection is typically based on current quality with respect to the history. For tests, the most common selection metaphors are difficulty (e.g. reward tests that give metric values seen as bad for potential solutions from the perspective of the solution concept at hand) and informativeness (reward tests that help differentiate potential solutions).

Once the new populations are generated, the set of interactions to be pushed onto the queue can be chosen in various ways, e.g. full mixing (pair every potential solution in one population with every test in the other population), shuffled one-to-one, etc.

The output selection mechanism most commonly used by such a CoEA would be a variation of *greedy*, where the potential solution of best current quality with respect to the history is chosen from the ones present in the population at the time output is required. Variations of this include using information from further back in the history by maintaining archives (separate from the respective populations) of potential solutions and/or tests, and computing current quality / selecting output based on them.

E. NOTATION TABLES

Notation	Description
$\mathcal{B}_i$ (for $i = 1, 2$)	Entity sets of an interactive domain. The domains considered have two roles $i = 1, 2$ and $\mathcal{B}_i$ is the entity set associated with role i.
$f : \mathcal{B}_1 \times \mathcal{B}_2 \to \mathbb{R}$	A metric.
$e = (b_1, b_2) \in \mathcal{B}_1 \times \mathcal{B}_2$	An interaction between b_1 and b_2. Also called an event.
$(e, f(e))$	A measured interaction.
$\mathcal{E} = \mathcal{B}_1 \times \mathcal{B}_2$	The set of all interactions (events).
$\mathcal{S}$	The set of potential solutions of a co-search problem.
$\mathcal{C} : \mathcal{S} \to \{true, false\}$	The solution concept of a co-search problem.
$g : \mathcal{S} \to \mathbb{R}$	A quality function, typically defined via a metric and a solution concept; it represents the quality of potential solutions in S.
$g : \mathcal{S} \times \mathcal{H} \to \mathbb{R}$	A quality function taking account of history; $g(ps, \mathrm{H}^t)$ denotes the quality of potential solution ps given the history H^t.

Table 1: Notation for interactive domains, as introduced in section 2.1.

Notation	Description
H^t	A history of measured interactions of length t.
$\mathcal{H}^t$	The set of all histories of distinct measured interactions of length t.
$\mathcal{H} = \bigcup\limits_{t=0}^{|\mathcal{E}|} \mathcal{H}^t$	The set of all possible histories.
A	A co-search algorithm, consisting of a search heuristic and an output selection function.
$h_A : \mathcal{H} \to \mathcal{E}$	A search heuristic.
$output_A : \mathcal{H} \to \mathcal{S}$	An output selection function.
$\phi_{A,t} \in \mathbb{R}$	Performance of a co-search algorithm A at time t.
$\phi : \mathcal{S} \to \mathbb{R}$	Alternate form of performance function where $\phi_{A,t} = \phi(output_A(H^t))$ for $H^t \in \mathcal{H}^t$. In this paper we choose $\phi = g$.
$p = |V|$	The number of values a metric can take.
$V = \{v_1, v_2, ..., v_p\}$	The ordered set of values a metric can take.
$rank_V$	A function giving the rank of a value in its value set; that is, $rank_V(v_i) = i$ for all $v_i \in V$.
$Agg_{H^t}(\phi_{A,t})$	The average-rank aggregated performance of algorithm A at time t after history H^t is observed. Equal to the average of $rank_V(\phi(output_A(H^t)))$ taken over all possible metrics f that are consistent with the history H^t.

Table 2: Notation for algorithms and algorithm performance, as introduced in section 2.2.

Notation	Description
$p = |V|$	The number of values a metric can take; equivalently, the possible ranks a potential solution may take.
$m = |\mathcal{B}_2|$	The number of tests; that is, $\mathcal{B}_2 = \{t_1, t_2, \ldots, t_m\}$
a	A partially-evaluated potential solution.
k	The number of tests with which a has interacted according to the current history.
i	The current rank of a according to the quality function; that is, $g(a, H^t) = v_i$.
b	A partially-evaluated potential solution.
l	The number of tests with which b has interacted according to the current history.
j	The current rank of b according to the quality function: $g(b, H^t) = v_j$.
c	A representative completely-unevaluated potential solution.
$AR(x)$	The average rank of a potential solution x taken over all metrics consistent with the history H, $avg_H(rank_V(\phi(x)))$.
$AR(x|k,i)$	Also the average rank of potential solution x, but with the parameters k and i made explicit.
$bd(p)$	The lower bound on $m-1$ determining whether a domain has a simple implementation of $Bayes$.

Table 3: Notation used in analysis, as introduced in section 3.

Handling Expensive Optimization with Large Noise

Rémi Coulom
Grappa, SequeL, Université
Charles-de-Gaulle,
Lille, France
Remi.Coulom@univ-
lille3.fr

Philippe Rolet
TAO-INRIA,LRI, UMR 8623
CNRS - Université Paris-Sud,
Orsay, France
rolet@lri.fr

Nataliya Sokolovska
TAO-INRIA,LRI, UMR 8623
CNRS - Université Paris-Sud,
Orsay, France
nataliya@lri.fr

Olivier Teytaud
TAO-INRIA,LRI, UMR 8623
CNRS - Université Paris-Sud,
Orsay, France
teytaud@lri.fr

ABSTRACT

We present lower and upper bounds on runtimes for expensive noisy optimization problems. Runtimes are expressed in terms of number of fitness evaluations. Fitnesses considered are monotonic transformations of the *sphere* function. The analysis focuses on the common case of fitness functions quadratic in the distance to the optimum in the neighbourhood of this optimum—it is nonetheless also valid for any monotonic polynomial of degree $p > 2$. Upper bounds are derived via a bandit-based estimation of distribution algorithm that relies on *Bernstein races* called R-EDA. It is an evolutionary algorithm in the sense that it is based on selection, random mutations, with a distribution (updated at each iteration) for generating new individuals. It is known that the algorithm is consistent (i.e. it converges to the optimum asymptotically in the number of examples) even in some non-differentiable cases. Here we show that: (i) if the variance of the noise decreases to 0 around the optimum, it can perform well for quadratic transformations of the norm to the optimum, (ii) otherwise, a convergence rate is slower than the one exhibited empirically by an algorithm called Quadratic Logistic Regression (QLR) based on surrogate models—although QLR requires a probabilistic prior on the fitness class.

Categories and Subject Descriptors

F.m [**Theory of Computation**]: Miscellaneous; I.2.8 [**Artificial Intelligence**]: Problem Solving, Search

General Terms

Theory

Keywords

Noisy optimization, Bernstein races, Runtime analysis.

1. INTRODUCTION

" Noisy optimization" means that the result of a fitness evaluation at a given point is a random variable, whose probability distribution depends only on the location of the point—this noise model will be detailed in Section 2, as well as the class of fitnesses that we address. Expensive means that each fitness call is considered costly: for example, evaluating the fitness of an individual might involve the building and testing of a prototype, or hours of simulations. Therefore, an expensive optimization algorithm's performance is measured by the number of fitness calls required to find the optimum with a given precision, rather than considering the computational time required by the algorithm to function.

State of the art

Using evolutionary algorithms and Estimation of Distribution algorithms (EDAs) to deal with noisy fitnesses is a topic that has been substantially discussed in the literature. Notably, many question the idea that repeatedly evaluating the same points in order to average values and decrease noise variance is effective, as compared to, for instance, simply increasing the population size [13, 7, 14, 1, 3]. A brief survey can be found in [24], where it has been shown that averaging can be efficient when used in the framework of *multi-armed bandits*, a statistical approach to model sequential dependencies (following ideas of [18]), and *races[22]*. Specifically, it is proved that an EDA using Bernstein races to choose the number of evaluations of a given point reaches an optimal convergence rate for certain noise models (see, for instance [25]).

When dealing with noisy optimization, it is important to distinguish cases in which the variance of the noise decreases to zero near the optimum—which we will refer to as the *small noise* assumption hereafter—and cases where it does not—*large noise* assumption (see Section 2 for more details on noisy settings). The small noise case, which is much easier and therefore more widely analyzed, has been tackled in [20] for a quite restricted noise model. [2] have then shown that in case of large noise, all usual step-size adaptation rules diverge or stop converging: the usual behavior of evolutionary algorithms for models with large noise is that they stop converging as they get too close to the optimum, and then keep a residual error, with a step-size which does not decrease to zero. The residual error remains large even w.r.t. computers' numerical accuracy of zero.

In [24] and [26] cases of large noise have been tackled, but only for fitness functions of the form $x \mapsto \lambda\|x - x^*\| + c$ excluding the quadratic (or higher-order polynomial) fitness functions. Furthermore, algorithms for noise handling such as Uncertainty Handling for Covariance Matrix Adaptation (UH-CMA), empirically quite efficient for small noise, are unfortunately not yet stable enough to deal with large noise cases. For the Scaled-Translated sphere (STS) model presented below, UH-CMA does not converge. Consistently with these results, [28] has shown that fast convergence involves a number of evaluations running to infinity with the number of iterations. This was further developed in [24, 26] with both lower bounds and algorithms reaching the bound in many cases. However, the natural case of fitnesses that are quadratic in the distance to the optimum was not covered. In the following, we show that:

- a version of Estimation of Distribution Algorithm dedicated to noisy optimization has been proposed in [26]; this version, termed R-EDA, is recalled in Algorithm 3, is based on a Race and has good theoretical guarantees, for both small noise and large noise scenarios;

- our R-EDA algorithm is not supposed to be a practical algorithm; we use it to derive complexity upper bounds, and to show that these complexity upper bounds can be reached by evolutionary algorithms based on races (races are discussed in section 2);

- R-EDA is empirically outperformed in large noise cases by surrogate models if $p = 2$ (an example of such a surrogate model is Quadratic Logistic Regression (QLR) which fits a quadratic model using a Bayesian prior);

- R-EDA also converges at a controlled rate for polynomial functions of the distance to the optimum.

Note that R-EDA has first been used in [26], and has not been modified for this work. All positive properties of R-EDA are preserved, in particular its consistency in many difficult cases, e.g. for fitnesses $f(x) = c + \Theta(\|x - x^*\|)$, i.e. for functions that behave similarly to a translated sphere function in the neighborhood of the optimum x^*.

2. FRAMEWORK

The optimization framework is described in Algorithm 1. This is a black-box optimization framework: the algorithm can request the fitness values at any chosen point, and no other information on the fitness function is available. We consider a fitness function f parameterized by the (unknown) location of its optimum, t. The noise is accounted for by a random variable $\theta \in [0,1]^{\mathbb{N}}$; each coordinate θ_i for $i \in \{1, 2, \dots\}$ is uniformly distributed in $[0,1]$. The goal is to find the optimum t of $f(., t)$, by observing noisy measurement of f at x_i. Measurements are random variables $F_t(x_i)$ on the interval $[0,1]$. They satisfy $\mathbb{E}[F_t(x_i)] = f(x_i, t)$. For the proof of the lower bound, the law of random variable $F_t(x_i)$ is Bernouilli, with parameter $f(x_i, t)$ as shown in Algorithm 1. This fits applications based on highly noisy optimization, such as games: let x be a parameter of a game

---

Algorithm 1 Noisy optimization framework. Opt is an optimization heuristic: it takes as input a sequence of visited points and their binary, noisy fitness values, and outputs a candidate optimum, that is a points of the domain such that $f(x, t)$ is as small as possible. This point is the point whose fitness is asked next. Opt is successful on target f parameterized by t and random noise θ if $Loss(t, \theta, Opt)$ is small.

Parameters: N, number of fitness evaluations; t, unknown element of X.
θ: random state of the nature $\in [0,1]^{\mathbb{N}}$; each coordinate θ_i for $i \in \{1, 2, \dots\}$ is uniformly distributed in $[0,1]$.

for $n \in [[0, N-1]]$ **do**
    $x_{n+1}^{t,\theta} = Opt(x_1^{t,\theta}, \dots, x_n^{t,\theta}, y_1^{t,\theta}, \dots, y_n^{t,\theta})$
    //Return noisy fitness $\sim \mathcal{B}(f(x_{n+1}^{t,\theta}, t))$
    $y_{n+1}^{t,\theta} = (f(x_{n+1}^{t,\theta}, t) < \theta_{n+1})?1 : 0$
end for
$Loss(t, \theta, Opt) = d(t, x_N^{t,\theta})$

---

strategy, that we wish to set at its best value; a noisy observation is a game against a baseline, resulting either in a win or in a loss; the aim is to find the value of x maximizing the probability of winning. Usual viability problems or binary control problems tackled by direct policy search also involve this kind of optimization.

We are interested in the number of requests needed for an optimization algorithm to find optimum t with precision ϵ and confidence $1 - \delta$; $\epsilon = \|x_n - t\|$ is the Euclidian distance between t and the output x_n of the algorithm after n fitness calls. The paper focuses on fitnesses of the form $(x, t) \mapsto c + \lambda\|x - t\|^p$, referred to as the Scaled-Translated sphere (STS) model. It is more general than the STS model of [26] which addresses only $p = 1$. In the following, t is not handled stochastically, i.e. the lower bounds are not computed in expectation w.r.t. all the possible fitness functions yielded by different values of t. Rather, we will consider the worst case on t. Therefore the only random variable in this framework is θ, accounting for noise in fitness measurements, and all probability / expectation operators are w.r.t. θ. For simplicity, we considered only deterministic optimization algorithms; the extension to stochastic algorithms is straightforward by including a random seed of the algorithm in θ.

In the following, $\tilde{O}$ means that logarithmic factors in ϵ are neglected. In all the paper, $[[a, b]] = \{a, a+1, a+2, \dots, b\}$.

Races

The algorithm used to prove upper bounds on convergence rates is based on Bernstein confidence bounds. It is a variation of the well-known Hoeffding bounds [19] (aimed at quantifying the discrepancy between an empirical mean and an expectation for bounded random variables), which takes variances into account [9, 5, 6]. It is therefore tighter in some settings. A detailed survey of Hoeffding, Chernoff and Bernstein bounds is beyond the scope of this paper; we will only present the Bernstein bound, within its application to *races*. A *race* between two or more random variables aims at distinguishing with high confidence random variables with better expectation from those with worse expectation. Algorithm 2 is a *Bernstein race* applied to distinct points x_i of a domain X—the 3 random variables are $F_t(x_i)$, the goal is to find a good point and a bad point such that we are confident that the good one is closer to the optimum than the bad one.

It is crucial in this situation to ensure that there exist i, j such that $f(x_i, t) \neq f(x_j, t)$, otherwise the race will last very long, and the output will be meaningless. At the end of the race, $3T$ evaluations have been performed, therefore T is called the halting time. Intuitively, the closer the points x_i are in terms of fitness value, the larger T will be. This is formalized below.

Algorithm 2 Bernstein race between 3 points. Eq. 1 is Bernstein's inequality to compute the precision for empirical estimates (see e.g. [11, p124]); $\hat{\sigma}_i$ is the empirical estimate of the standard deviation of point x_i's associated random variable $F_t(x_i)$ (it is 0 in the first iteration, which does not alter the algorithm's correctness); $\hat{f}(x)$ is the average of the fitness measurements at x.

$Bernstein(x_1, x_2, x_3, \delta')$
$T = 0$
repeat
$\quad T \leftarrow T + 1$
Evaluate the fitness of points x_1, x_2, x_3 once, *i.e.* evaluate the noisy fitness at each of these points.
Evaluate the precision:

$$\epsilon_{(T)} = 3 \log\left(\frac{3\pi^2 T^2}{6\delta'}\right) / T + \max_i \hat{\sigma}_i \sqrt{2 \log\left(\frac{3\pi^2 T^2}{6\delta'}\right) / T}.$$
(1)

until Two points $(good, bad)$ satisfy $\hat{f}(bad) - \hat{f}(good) \geq 2\epsilon$
— **return** $(good, bad)$

Let us define $\Delta = \sup\{\mathbb{E}F_t(x_1), \mathbb{E}F_t(x_2), \mathbb{E}F_t(x_3)\} - \inf\{\mathbb{E}F_t(x_1), \mathbb{E}F_t(x_2), \mathbb{E}F_t(x_3)\}$. It is known [23] that if $\Delta > 0$ and if we consider a fixed number of arms[1] (in the context of multi-armed bandits),

- with probability $1 - \delta'$, the Bernstein race is consistent: $\mathbb{E}F_t(good) < \mathbb{E}F_t(bad)$;

- the Bernstein race halts almost surely, and with probability at least $1 - \delta'$, the halting time T

$$T \leq K \log\left(\frac{1}{\delta'\Delta}\right) / \Delta^2,$$
(2)

where K is a universal constant;

- if, in addition,

$$\Delta \geq C \sup\{\mathbb{E}F_t(x_1), \mathbb{E}F_t(x_2), \mathbb{E}F_t(x_3)\},$$
(3)

then the Bernstein race halts almost surely, and with probability at least $1 - \delta'$, the halting time T

$$T \leq K' \log\left(\frac{1}{\delta'\Delta}\right) / \Delta,$$
(4)

where K' depends on C only.

The interested reader is referred to [23] and other references for more information.

---

[1] We here consider 3 arms only, but more general cases can be handled with a logarithmic dependency (see e.g. [23]).

3. LOWER BOUND

This section describes a general lower bound derived in [24], and concludes with the application of this bound to the scaled-translated sphere model.

Let us consider a domain X, a function $f : X \times X \to \mathbb{R}$, and define

$$d(t_1, t_2) = \sup_{x \in X} |f(x, t_1) - f(x, t_2)|$$

for t_1 and t_2 in X. $B(n, p)$ denotes a binomial random variable (sum of n independent Bernoulli variables of parameter p).

THEOREM 1. *For any optimization algorithm* Opt, *let* $N \in \mathbb{N}^*$ *(a number of points visited)*, $\epsilon_0 > 0$, $0 < \epsilon < \epsilon_0$, $D \in \mathbb{N}^*$, $\delta \in]0, 1[$. *We assume:*

- $H(\epsilon_0, D)$: $\forall \epsilon_1 < \epsilon_0 \ \exists (t_1, \ldots, t_D) \in X^D, \forall (i, j) \in [[1, D]]^2, i \neq j \Rightarrow d(t_i, t_j) = \epsilon_1$ *(generalized dimension)*

- $H_{PAC}(\epsilon, N, \delta)$: $\forall t, P(d(x_N^{t,\theta}, t) < \epsilon/2) \geq 1 - \delta$.

Then, if $\delta < 1/2D$,

$$P(B(N, \epsilon) \geq \lceil \log_2(D) \rceil) \geq 1 - D\delta.$$
(5)

The lower bound is related to a topological property of space X: a number D is taken such that for any distance $\epsilon < \epsilon_0$, D equidistant points of X can be found (assumption $H(\epsilon_0, D)$). This is closely related to the dimension of X: for instance, in $\mathbb{R}^d$, the maximum number of such equidistant points is $d + 1$.

The theorem states that if an optimization algorithm is able to find the optimum at precision ϵ with probability $1 - \delta$ in N fitness calls (i.e. the algorithm satisfies assumption $H_{PAC}(\epsilon, N, \delta)$), then N is necessarily large; the theorem explicitly gives a lower bound on N. Indeed, Eq. 5 implies a clearer expression of the lower bound (using Chebyshev inequality):

$$N = \Omega(\log_2(D)/\epsilon)$$
(6)

for fixed D, where N is the number of iterations required to reach precision ϵ with confidence $1 - \delta$ for $\delta < 1/2D$. The theorem holds for any monotonic transformation of the sphere function. However, the distance d is not the same for different classes of fitnesses. As mentioned earlier, we are interested in the Scaled-Translated sphere model $((x, t) \mapsto c + \lambda \|x - t\|^p$ with optimum $t)$.

COROLLARY 2. *Under the conditions of Theorem 1, for any optimization algorithm learning a fitness of the STS model, if ϵ_N is the quantile $1 - \delta$ of the Euclidean distance to the optimum after N fitness calls and if $p \geq 1$, then $\epsilon_N = \Omega(log(D)/N)$.*

As stated in [24], the lower bound for $p = 1$ is straightforward, since in this case it is clear that $d(t_1, t_2) = \|t_1 - t_2\|$. Moreover, in the general STS model, we can show that for any $p \geq 2$, $d(t_1, t_2) = \Theta(\|t_2 - t_1\|)$, which validates the above corollary. The lower bound of the corollary is tight for $p = 1$ (see [24]). We will see that it is also tight if $p = 2$ for $c = 0$—in this case, both QLR and R-EDA reach this dependency.

4. UPPER BOUNDS

Upper bounds on the convergence rate for the STS model will now be presented, using R-EDA (Algorithm 3 along with a Bernstein race). In the model restricted to $p = 1$, upper bounds for small noise (i.e. $c = 0$) have been derived in [24], and upper bounds for large noise (i.e. $c > 0$) have been derived in [26]. In both cases, the bounds match the lower bound. This is why we focus on $p \geq 2$, which includes the case $p = 2$ that often appears in practice. In this section, the optimum will be referred to as x^*, and $f(x, x^*)$ will be noted $f(x)$ for short.

R-EDA is a (3,3) evolution strategy: the parent population consists of 3 points, and 3 points are generated from this population and act as the new population. The difference with respect to "standard" EDAs is as follows:

- the algorithm is derandomized: population t is generated deterministically from population $t - 1$;

- since $\mu = \lambda$, there is no need for actually ranking all the points (the algorithm still orders two points among the three as will be seen below).

The algorithm is comparison-based (since fitness values only matter by how they order the population), and fits the general description of an EDA.

Algorithm 3 R-EDA: algorithm for optimizing noisy fitness functions. *Bernstein* denotes a Bernstein race, as defined in Algorithm 2. The initial domain is $[x_0^-, x_0^+] \in \mathbb{R}^D$, δ is the confidence parameter.

$n \leftarrow 0$
while True **do**
$\quad c_n = \arg\max_i (x_n^+)_i - (x_n^-)_i \quad$ // Pick the coordinate with highest uncertainty
$\quad \delta_n^{\max} = (x_n^+)_{c_n} - (x_n^-)_{c_n}$
$\quad$**for** $i \in [[1, 3]]$ **do**
$\quad\quad x'^i_n \leftarrow \frac{1}{2}(x_n^- + x_n^+) \quad$ // Consider the middle point
$\quad\quad (x'^i_n)_{c_n} \leftarrow (x_n^-)_{c_n} + \frac{i-1}{2}(x_n^+ - x_n^-)_{c_n} \quad$ //The c_n^{th} coordinate may take $3 \neq$ values
$\quad$**end for**
$\quad (good_n, bad_n) = Bernstein(x'^1_n, x'^2_n, x'^3_n, \frac{6\delta}{\pi^2(n+1)^2})$.
$\quad$// A good and a bad point
$\quad$Let H_n be the halfspace
$\quad \{x \in \mathbb{R}^D; ||x - good_n|| \leq ||x - bad_n||\}$
$\quad$Split the domain: $[x_{n+1}^-, x_{n+1}^+] = H_n \cap [x_n^-, x_n^+]$
$\quad n \leftarrow n + 1$
end while

Sketch of R-EDA (Algorithm 3). We will use R-EDA (Algorithm 3) for showing the upper bounds. It proceeds by iteratively splitting the domain in two (not necessarily equal) halves, and retaining the one that most probably contains the optimum. At iteration n, from the n_{th} domain $[x_n^-, x_n^+]$, the $(n+1)_{th}$ domain $[x_{n+1}^-, x_{n+1}^+]$ is obtained by:

- Finding the coordinate c_{n+1} such that $\delta_n^{max} = (x_n^+)_{c_n} - (x_n^-)_{c_n}$ is maximal;

- Selecting three regularly spaced points along this coordinate (see Figure 1);

- Repeatedly assessing those 3 points until we have confidence that the optimum is closer to one point x'^i_n than to another x'^j_n (by Bernstein race);

- Splitting the domain by the hyperplane in the middle of these points and normal to the line they define, and keeping only the side of the domain containing x'^i_n.

It is important to notice that three points selected at each iteration are necessarily distinct. A key element in proving upper bounds with this algorithm is that the fitness monotonic in the distance to the optimum ($||a - x^*|| > ||b - x^*|| \Rightarrow f(a) > f(b)$), and it also has spherical symmetry ($||a - x^*|| = ||b - x^*|| \Rightarrow f(a) = f(b)$). Consequently, it is guaranteed that when choosing three points as in Algorithm 3, at least one of them will have an expected fitness that is different from two others. That is why the race will output a consistent result with high probability.

For simplicity, it is assumed that the initial domain is a hyperrectangle. Consequently, at any iteration n, the halfspace H_n is a hyper-rectangle, whose largest axis' length δ_n^{max} (defined in Algorithm 3) satisfies $\delta_n^{max} \leq \frac{3}{4}^{\lfloor n/D \rfloor}$. The straightforward proof of this fact is given in [24], where R-EDA first appears.

The following lemma will be used for the upper bound. A similar lemma was published in [24], but it only applied to $p = 1$. Notations are those introduced in Algorithm 3.

LEMMA 3. (The conditions of the Bernstein race are met) *Assume that $x^* \in [x_n^-, x_n^+]$ and $p \geq 2$. Then*

$$\max_{(i,j) \in [[1,3]]^2} f(x'^j_n) - f(x'^i_n) \geq 2 \left(\frac{\delta_{max}^n}{2}\right)^p. \tag{7}$$

Proof of Lemma 3. Let $\bar{x}_n^*$ be the projection of x^* on the line on which x'^1_n, x'^2_n, x'^3_n lie. The result will now be proved for $(\bar{x}_n^*)_{c_n} \in [(x'^1_n)_{c_n}, (x'^2_n)_{c_n}]$. The proof for the case $(\bar{x}_n^*)_{c_n} \in [(x'^2_n)_{c_n}, (x'^3_n)_{c_n}]$ is symmetric (see Figure 1).

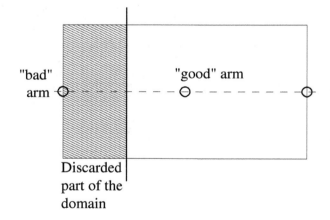

Figure 1: **The large rectangle is the domain $[x_n^-, x_n^+]$. The three circles are arms x'^1_n, x'^2_n, x'^3_n; the left arm is the "bad" arm, whereas the arm in the center is the "good" arm, i.e. the one which proved to be closer to the optimum than the left arm, with confidence $1 - 6\delta/(\pi^2 n^2)$; the point on the right is the third arm which is considered to be neither "good", nor "bad".**

First of all, we have

$$\Delta_n \doteq \max_{i,j \in [[1,3]]^2} f(x'^i_n) - f(x'^j_n) \geq f(x'^3_n) - f(x'^2_n).$$

By Pythagora's theorem, $\forall i \in [[1,3]], ||x'^i - x^*||^2 = ||x'^i_n - \bar{x}^*_n||^2 + ||\bar{x}^*_n - x^*||^2$. Thus,

$$\Delta_n \geq \left(\sqrt{||x'^3_n - \bar{x}^*_n||^2 + ||\bar{x}^*_n - x^*||^2} \right)^p$$
$$- \left(\sqrt{||x'^2_n - \bar{x}^*_n||^2 + ||\bar{x}^*_n - x^*||^2} \right)^p .$$

Note that $||x'^3 - \bar{x}^*_n|| = ||x'^2_n - \bar{x}^*_n|| + \delta^{\max}_n/2$. Define $d = ||\bar{x}^*_n - x^*||^2$ and $a = ||x'^3 - \bar{x}^*_n||$. Then, observing that $\delta^{\max}_n \geq a \geq \delta^{\max}_n/2$, we have

$$\Delta_n \geq \left(\sqrt{a^2 + d} \right)^p - \left(\sqrt{(a - \delta^{\max}_n/2)^2 + d} \right)^p$$

$$\geq a^p \left(\left(\sqrt{1 + d/a^2} \right)^p - \left(\sqrt{\left(1 - \frac{\delta^{\max}_n}{2a} \right)^2 + \frac{d}{a^2}} \right)^p \right)$$

$$\geq \left(\frac{\delta^{\max}_n}{2} \right)^p \left((\sqrt{1 + d/a^2})^p - (\sqrt{\frac{1}{4} + \frac{d}{a^2}})^p \right) . \qquad (8)$$

By setting $u = d/a^2$, it is clear that Δ_n is greater than the minimum of $u \mapsto (\sqrt{1+u})^p - (\sqrt{1/4 + u})^p$ on the interval $[0, D]$ (since $\sqrt{d} = ||\bar{x}^*_n - x^*|| \leq \sqrt{D}\delta^{\max}_n/2$). This function is non-decreasing for $p \geq 2$, and therefore its minimum is its value in 0, which is, for all $p \geq 2$, at least $\frac{1}{2}$; injecting in Equation 8 yields $\Delta_n \geq 2 \left(\frac{\delta^{\max}_n}{2} \right)^p$, as stated by Eq. 7. $\square$

THEOREM 4. (Upper bounds for the STS model) *Consider the STS model, and a fixed dimension D. The number of evaluations requested by R-EDA (Algorithm 3) to reach precision ϵ with probability at least $1 - \delta$ is $\tilde{O}(\frac{\log(1/\delta)}{\epsilon^{2p}})$.*

Proof of Theorem 4. First, note that at iteration n, ϵ is upper bounded by $||x^-_n - x^+_n||$. Eq. 7 (shown in Lemma 3) ensures that $\Delta_n = \Omega(||x^+_n - x^-_n||^p)$ (Δ_n is defined by Eq. 3). Therefore, applying the concentration inequality, presented as Eq. 2, the number of evaluations in the nth iteration is at most

$$\tilde{O} \left(\log \left(\frac{6\delta}{\pi^2 (n+1)^2} \right) / ||x^-_n - x^+_n||^{2p} \right) . \qquad (9)$$

Now, let us consider the number $N(\epsilon)$ of iterations before a precision ϵ is reached. Eq. 4 shows that there is a constant $k < 1$ such that $\epsilon \leq ||x^+_n - x^-_n|| \leq Ck^{N(\epsilon)}$. Injecting this in Eq. 9 shows that the cost (the number of evaluations) in the last call to the Bernstein race is

$$Bound_{last}(\epsilon) = \tilde{O} \left(-\log \left(\frac{6\delta}{\pi^2 (N(\epsilon) + 1)^2} \right) / \epsilon^{2p} \right) . \qquad (10)$$

Since $N(\epsilon) = O(\log(1/\epsilon))$, $Bound_{last} = O(\log(\log(1/\epsilon)/\delta))/\epsilon^{2p}$. For a fixed dimension D, the cost of the $(N(\epsilon) - i)^{th}$ iteration is $O(\lceil Bound_{last}/(k')^i \rceil)$ because the algorithm ensures that after D iterations, $||x^+_n - x^-_n||$ decreases by at least $3/4$ (see Eq. 4). The sum of the costs for $N(\epsilon)$ iterations is the sum of $O(Bound_{last}/(k')^i)$ for $i \in [[0, N(\epsilon) - 1]]$, that is $O(Bound_{last}/(1 - k')) = O(Bound_{last})$ (plus $O(N(\epsilon))$ for the rounding associated to the $\lceil ... \rceil$). The overall cost is therefore $O(Bound_{last} + \log(1/\epsilon))$, yielding the expected result. $\square$

Theorem 4 can be modified to use the small noise assumption, i.e. the case $c = 0$. We then get a Bernstein's type rate, as follows:

THEOREM 5. (Upper bounds for the STS model with small noise) *Consider the STS model, and a fixed dimension D. Assume additionally that $c = 0$, i.e. the scaled sphere model. The number of evaluations requested by R-EDA (Algorithm 3) to reach precision ϵ with probability at least $1 - \delta$ is $\tilde{O}(\frac{\log(1/\delta)}{\epsilon^p})$.*

Proof of Theorem 5. The variance of a Bernoulli random variable is always upper bounded by its expectation. The case $c = 0$ implies that the expectation is upper bounded by the square of the distance to the optimum. Therefore, Eq. 3 holds. Thanks to Eq. 3, we can then use Eq. 4 instead of Eq. 2 in the proof of Theorem 4. This yields the expected result. $\square$

Note that this analysis is not limited to fitnesses that are exactly described by $f(x) = c + ||x - x^*||^p$, but apply to any monotonic transformation of the sphere function that has a Taylor expansion of degree p around its optimum.

5. EXPERIMENTS

We illustrate results of our experiments with an algorithm without surrogate models, UH-CMA, introduced in [17], and an algorithm with surrogate models, QLR (based on Quadratic Logistic Regression, i.e. it is assumed that the function is locally quadratic).

UH-CMA is an uncertainty handling approach based on a state-of-the-art CMA-ES. QLR, in comparison to many alternative methods, has only one mega-parameter to adjust (a Bayesian prior) and keeps information on all observed data.

5.1 Experimental results for UH-CMA— optimization without surrogate models

UH-CMA has been developed with intensive testing on the BBOB challenge [4], which includes mild models of noise. See [16] for the source code used in these experiments. The optimization domain is $\mathbb{R}^2$. Let $\mathcal{B}(q)$ denote a Bernoulli distribution of parameter q, $\mathcal{N}(\mu, \sigma^2)$ denote a Gaussian distribution centered on μ with variance σ^2, and $\mathcal{U}(I)$ denote a uniform distribution on interval I. UH-CMA[2] was tested on four different noisy fitnesses: 1) $||x||^2(1 + \mathcal{N}(0, 0.1))$; 2) $||x||^2 + \mathcal{U}([0, 1])$; 3) $\mathcal{B}(||x||^2)$; 4) $\mathcal{B}(||x||^2 + 0.5)$.

The experiments with UH-CMA have been carried out using the following setting. The number of repeats equals 100, the population size $\lambda = 4 + \lfloor 3 \log N \rfloor$, where N is the problem dimension, and the parent number $\mu = \lfloor \lambda/2 \rfloor$.

The initial values required by UH-CMA to start the search were sampled from $\mathcal{U}([0,1]^2)$. The convergence (and divergence) of UH-CMA—illustrated on Figure 2—is known to be log-linear.

For $||x||^2(1 + \mathcal{N}(0, 0.1))$, the algorithm converges efficiently: the precision decreases exponentially as the number of iterations increases. For $||x||^2 + \mathcal{U}([0, 1])$, the precision stops improving after a few hundred iterations. For $\mathcal{B}(||x||^2)$ and $\mathcal{B}(||x||^2 + 0.5)$ we observed divergence.

Let us point out that by adding some specific rules for averaging multiple fitness evaluations depending on the step-size, specifically for each fitness function, it is possible to

---

[2]The version of UH-CMA used in our experiments is the one that was available at that time in http://www.lri.fr/~hansen/cmaesintro.html. The noise handling was activated and it was not modified in any manner.

obtain much better rates [15]. However, to the best of our knowledge, the rates remain worse than those reached by QLR.

5.2 Experiments with QLR—optimization with surrogate models

QLR is based on a Bayesian quadratic logistic regression. It samples regions of the search space with maximum variance of the posterior probability, i.e. regions with high variance conditionally to past observations. This is a key difference w.r.t. algorithms without surrogate models, which tend to sample points close to the optimum. QLR is fully described by [12, 8, 21] (design of experiments for quadratic logistic model), [27] (active learning for logistic regression). See [10] for the code we used here, specifically tailored to binary noisy fitnesses.

QLR was tested on fitnesses of the form $B(||x||^p+c)$, for p in $\{1, 2\}$ and c in $\{0, 1/2\}$. The search space is $\mathbb{R}^2$. Figure 3 shows the experimental results:

Top left (p=1, c=0): QLR converges on $x \mapsto B(||x - x^*||)$, but with a suboptimal exponent $\frac{1}{2}$ (the slope of the curve is $-\frac{1}{2}$ in log-scale), i.e. $\mathbb{E}f(x_n) - \mathbb{E}f(x^*) \simeq \Theta(1/\sqrt{n})$. R-EDA reaches a better $1/n$ in this case;

Top right (p=1, c=1/2): QLR converges with optimal exponent $1/\sqrt{n}$ also reached by R-EDA;

Bottom left (p=2, c=0): QLR reaches $\mathbb{E}f(x_n) - \mathbb{E}f(x^*) \simeq \Theta(1/n)$ as well as R-EDA;

Bottom right (p=2, c=1/2): QLR still reaches $\mathbb{E}f(x_n) - \mathbb{E}f(x^*) \simeq \Theta(1/n)$ whereas R-EDA only reaches $1/\sqrt{n}$.

6. CONCLUSION

The convergence rates for R-EDA (see [26]) and QLR are:

fitness	$||x_n - x^*||$ for R-EDA	Theoretical lower-bound	$||x_n - x^*||$ for QLR $(p = 2)$
$\lambda||x - x^*||$	$\tilde{O}(1/n)$	$\Omega(1/n)$	$\simeq 1/\sqrt{n}$
$\lambda||x - x^*|| + c$	$\tilde{O}(1/\sqrt{n})$	$\Omega(1/n)$	$\simeq 1/\sqrt{n}$
$g(||x - x^*||)$	$o(1)$	–	–
$\lambda||x - x^*||^p + c$	$\tilde{O}(1/n^{1/2p})$	$\Omega(1/n)$	$\simeq 1/\sqrt{n}$
$\lambda||x - x^*||^p$	$\tilde{O}(1/n^{1/p})$	$\Omega(1/n)$	$\simeq 1/\sqrt{n}$
$\lambda||x - x^*||^2$	$\tilde{O}(1/\sqrt{n})$	$\Omega(1/n)$	$\simeq 1/\sqrt{n}$

Convergence rates are given for minimization; the fitness at point x is the Bernoulli random variable $\mathcal{B}(f(x))$ with parameter $\min(1, \max(0, f(x)))$, x_n is the approximation of the optimum after n fitness evaluations, x^* is the optimum, $c > 0$, and g is some increasing mapping.

For the rightmost column, it is important to point out that we run experiments with QLR *without* knowledge of the parameter p, so that the comparison with other algorithms is fair. In particular, there is a single algorithm, R-EDA, which provably realizes the upper bounds above; a better algorithm should be better for all cases simultaneously without problem-specific parametrization.

The original results of our paper are presented by three last rows and the rightmost column; in particular we have shown:

- The upper and lower bounds for an exponent $p > 1$;

- For $p = 1$ and $c = 0$, QLR is not optimal; R-EDA reaches (provably) $\tilde{O}(1/n)$ whereas QLR has convergence $1/\sqrt{n}$. By construction, it is probably difficult for QLR to do better than $1/\sqrt{n}$;

- For $p = 1$ and $c > 0$, QLR and R-EDA perform equivalently $(1/\sqrt{n})$; the lower bound does not match the upper bound. For R-EDA we have a mathematical proof and for QLR empirical evidence.

- For $p = 2$ and $c = 0$, QLR and R-EDA perform equivalently $(1/\sqrt{n})$; the lower bound does not match the upper bound. For R-EDA we have a mathematical proof and for QLR empirical evidence.

- For $p = 2$ and $c > 0$, QLR (empirically) performs better than the proved upper bound and worse than the proved lower bound.

There is therefore still room for improvements.

Results for QLR and for UH-CMA are empirical, based on current versions of the algorithms. The available implementation of UH-CMA cope quite well with small noise situations, but as soon as the variance does not go to zero sufficiently fast it does not succeed.

R-EDA is efficient in many cases, yet its theoretical convergence rates are suboptimal in the case $B(c+||x - x^*||^2)$, more relevant from a practical point of view. However, R-EDA is not limited to Bernoulli-like fitness functions, whereas QLR is. This is why QLR is more efficient in the case $B(c+||x - x^*||^2)$ for $c > 0$. UH-CMA does not converge in such cases, what demonstrates that algorithms tailored for small noise models do not easily extend to models with large noise. However, UH-CMA is the only algorithm with log-linear precision as a function of the number of iterations in the easy case $||x - x^*||^2(1 + \mathcal{N})$.

R-EDA can be applied to any fitness of the form $x \mapsto g(||x - x^*||)$ with x^* the optimum and g an increasing mapping, and will converge to the optimum. If, in addition, if g is differentiable in 0 with non-zero derivative, then the convergence rate is guaranteed to meet the rates $p = 1$ presented above. More generally, if g is p times differentiable in 0, with the $p - 1$ first derivatives null, then the convergence rate is the general rate presented above for a given p. A relevant further work would be to extend the algorithm to non-spherical models (i.e. no spherical symmetry around the optimum), in order to have more general convergence bounds.

Given the convergence rate table above, one can see that lower bounds for $p > 1$ or $c > 0$ are not tight. A relevant further work would be either to find out how to reach these bounds, or to prove lower bounds achieving tightness—which seems more likely, given that the current lower bounds are quite optimistic.

7. ACKNOWLEDGEMENTS

This work was supported by the IST Programme of the European Community, under the PASCAL2 Network of Excellence, IST-2007-216886; by Ministry of Higher Education and Research, Nord-Pas de Calais Regional Council and FEDER through the "CPER 2007–2013".

8. REFERENCES

[1] D. V. Arnold and H.-G. Beyer. Efficiency and mutation strength adaptation of the (mu/muI,lambda)-es in a noisy environment. In *Parallel Problem Solving from Nature*, volume 1917 of *LNCS*, pages 39–48. Springer, 2000.

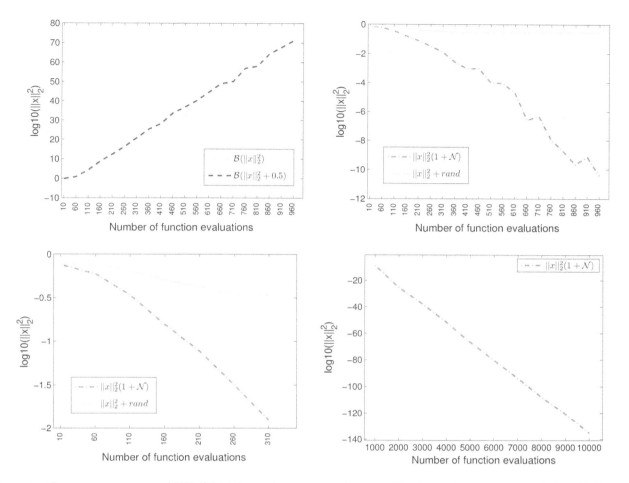

Figure 2: **Convergence rate of UH-CMA in various cases. Cases with Bernoulli noise are not handled properly by the optimization tool.**

[2] D. V. Arnold and H.-G. Beyer. A general noise model and its effects on evolution strategy performance. *IEEE Transactions on Evolutionary Computation*, 10(4):380–391, 2006.

[3] Dirk V. Arnold and Hans-Georg Beyer. Evolution strategies with cumulative step length adaptation on the noisy parabolic ridge. *Natural Computing: an international journal*, 7(4):555–587, 2008.

[4] Anne Auger, Steffen Finck, Nikolaus Hansen, and Raymond Ros. BBOB 2009: Comparison Tables of All Algorithms on All Noisy Functions. Technical Report RT-0384, INRIA, 04 2010.

[5] S.N. Bernstein. On a modification of chebyshev's inequality and of the error formula of laplace. *Original publication: Ann. Sci. Inst. Sav. Ukraine, Sect. Math. 1*, 3(1):38–49, 1924.

[6] S.N. Bernstein. *The Theory of Probabilities*. Gostehizdat Publishing House, Moscow, 1946.

[7] H.-G. Beyer. *The Theory of Evolutions Strategies*. Springer, Heidelberg, 2001.

[8] Kathryn Chaloner. Bayesian design for estimating the turning point of a quadratic regression. *Communications in Statistics—Theory and Methods*, 18(4):1385–1400, 1989.

[9] H. Chernoff. A measure of asymptotic efficiency for tests of a hypothesis based on the sum of observations. *Annals of Math. Stat.*, 23:493–509, 1952.

[10] R. Coulom. Source code for qlr, March 2010. http://remi.coulom.free.fr/QLR/.

[11] L. Devroye, L. Györfi, and G. Lugosi. *A probabilistic Theory of Pattern Recognition*. Springer, 1997.

[12] Ellinor Fackle Fornius. *Optimal Design of Experiments for the Quadratic Logistic Model*. PhD thesis, Department of Statistics, Stockholm University, 2008.

[13] J. M. Fitzpatrick and J. J. Grefenstette. Genetic algorithms in noisy environments. *Machine Learning*, 3:101–120, 1988.

[14] Ulrich Hammel and Thomas Bäck. Evolution strategies on noisy functions: How to improve convergence properties. In Yuval Davidor, Hans-Paul Schwefel, and Reinhard Männer, editors, *Parallel Problem Solving From Nature*, volume 866 of *LNCS*, pages 159–168, Jerusalem, 1994. Springer.

[15] N. Hansen. Personal communication.

[16] N. Hansen. Source code for UH-CMA, June 2008. Version 3, http://www.lri.fr/~hansen/cmaesintro.html.

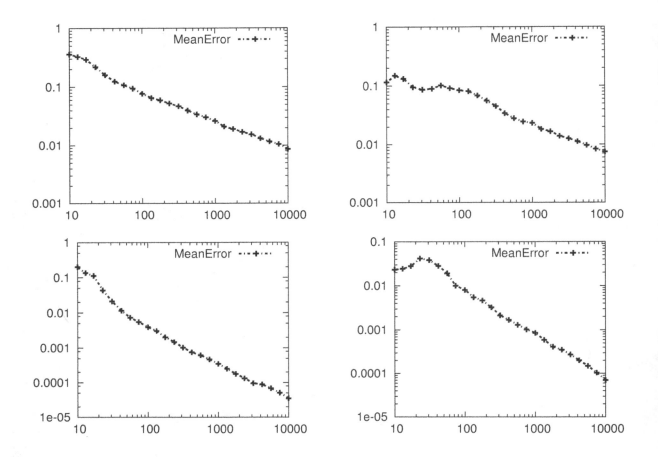

Figure 3: Convergence rate of QLR in various cases. On the X-axis: the number of evaluations; on the Y-axis: $\mathbb{E}f(x_n) - \mathbb{E}f(x^*)$. **Both are in log-scale to emphasize the exponent. The noisy fitnesses tested are of the form** $B(||x||^p + c)$ **(top:** $p = 1$, **bottom:** $p = 2$, **left:** $c = 0$, **right:** $c = 1/2$).

[17] Nikolaus Hansen, Andre Niederberger, Lino Guzzella, and Petros Koumoutsakos. A Method for Handling Uncertainty in Evolutionary Optimization with an Application to Feedback Control of Combustion. *IEEE Transactions on Evolutionary Computation*, 2009.

[18] Verena Heidrich-Meisner and Christian Igel. Hoeffding and Bernstein races for selecting policies in evolutionary direct policy search. In *ICML '09: Proceedings of the 26th Annual International Conference on Machine Learning*, pages 401–408, New York, NY, USA, 2009. ACM.

[19] W. Hoeffding. Probability inequalities for sums of bounded random variables. *Journal of the American Statistical Association*, 58:13–30, 1963.

[20] Mohamed Jebalia and Anne Auger. On multiplicative noise models for stochastic search. In *Parallel Problem Solving From Nature*, Dortmund, Germany, 2008.

[21] André I. Khuri, Bhramar Mukherjee, Bikas K. Sinha, and Malay Ghosh. Design issues for generalized linear models: A review. *Statistical Science*, 21(3):376–399, 2006.

[22] T.L. Lai and H. Robbins. Asymptotically efficient adaptive allocation rules. *Advances in Applied Mathematics*, 6:4–22, 1985.

[23] Volodymyr Mnih, Csaba Szepesvári, and Jean-Yves Audibert. Empirical Bernstein stopping. In *ICML '08: Proceedings of the 25th international conference on Machine learning*, pages 672–679, New York, NY, USA, 2008. ACM.

[24] P. Rolet and O. Teytaud. Bandit-based estimation of distribution algorithms for noisy optimization: Rigorous runtime analysis. In *Proceedings of International Conference on Learning and Intelligent Optimization (LION)*, 2009.

[25] Philippe Rolet. *Elements for Learning and Optimizing Expensive Fuctions*. PhD thesis, Université Paris Sud, 2010.

[26] Philippe Rolet and Olivier Teytaud. Adaptive Noisy Optimization. In *EvoStar 2010*, 2010.

[27] Andrew I. Schein and Lyle H. Hungar. Active learning for logistic regression: An evaluation. *Machine Learning*, 68(3):235–265, 2007.

[28] Olivier Teytaud and Anne Auger. On the adaptation of the noise level for stochastic optimization. In *IEEE Congress on Evolutionary Computation*, Singapore, 2007.

Computational Complexity Analysis of Simple Genetic Programming On Two Problems Modeling Isolated Program Semantics

Greg Durrett
MIT CSAIL
32 Vassar Street
Cambridge, MA 02139
gdurrett@mit.edu

Frank Neumann
School of Computer Science
University of Adelaide
Adelaide, SA 5005, Australia
frank@cs.adelaide.edu.au

Una-May O'Reilly
MIT CSAIL
32 Vassar Street
Cambridge, MA 02139
unamay@csail.mit.edu

ABSTRACT

Analyzing the computational complexity of evolutionary algorithms (EAs) for binary search spaces has significantly informed our understanding of EAs in general. With this paper, we start the computational complexity analysis of genetic programming (GP). We set up several simplified GP algorithms and analyze them on two separable model problems, ORDER and MAJORITY, each of which captures a relevant facet of typical GP problems. Both analyses give first rigorous insights into aspects of GP design, highlighting in particular the impact of accepting or rejecting neutral moves and the importance of a local mutation operator.

Categories and Subject Descriptors

F.2 [**Theory of Computation**]: Analysis of algorithms and problem complexity

General Terms

Algorithms, Theory

1. INTRODUCTION

Because of the complexity of genetic programming (GP) variants and the challenging nature of the problems they address, it is arguably impossible in most cases to make formal guarantees about the number of fitness evaluations needed for an algorithm to find an optimal solution. Current theoretical approaches investigate foundational aspects of GP tangential to this goal, such as schema theories, search spaces, bloat and problem difficulty [13]. However, in this work, we instead choose to follow the path taken for evolutionary algorithms working on fixed-length binary strings. Initial work on pseudo-Boolean functions illustrated the working principles of simple evolutionary algorithms (see e.g. [7, 15, 2]); subsequently, results have been derived for a wide range of classical combinatorial optimization problems such as shortest paths, maximum matchings or minimum spanning trees (see e.g. [9]). These studies have contributed substantially to our theoretical understanding of evolutionary algorithms for binary representations. Poli et al. [13] state, "we expect to see computational complexity techniques being used to model simpler GP systems, perhaps GP systems based on mutation and stochastic hill-climbing." This contribution is a fulfillment of this prediction: its goal is to show a GP variant that identifies optimal solutions in provably low numbers of fitness function evaluations for two much simplified, but still insightful, problems that exhibit a few simple aspects of program structure.

The simple parameterized GP algorithm we analyze can succinctly be described as both a hill climber and a randomized algorithm. It has four parametric instantiations we call (1+1) GP-single, (1+1) GP-multi, (1+1) GP*-single, and (1+1) GP*-multi that differ in the acceptance criterion and the size of the mutation proposed. Initially, a candidate solution is chosen at random. In each iteration, we produce by random mutation exactly one offspring of the current solution, and replace the current solution by this proposal as specified by the acceptance criterion. The algorithm iterates until it finds an optimal solution. This simple form of GP algorithm has historical precedent in very early comparisons between Koza-style genetic programming and GP stochastic iterated hill climbing [10, 11, 12], though it does not include a finite bound on fitness evaluations, random restarts or a limit on how many times mutation will be applied to the current solution. Another simplification of the algorithm is that it uses a genetic operator that is as similar to bit-wise mutation as possible. A single bit-wise mutation is the smallest step possible in an binary EA's search space. Our mutation operator makes the smallest alteration possible to the GP tree while respecting the key properties of the GP tree search space: variable length and hierarchical structure.

The two model problems we select for our analysis are OR-DER and MAJORITY, defined in section 2 exactly as in [3]. We have chosen ORDER and MAJORITY because more realistic problems are, at the moment, too difficult to analyze. They allow fitness function evaluation without explicitly executing the program defined by the GP tree. Also, they are minimally sufficient to capture several key properties of GP, including the existence of multiple optimal solutions but they are not real world application problems. Neither are they ad-hoc toy problems intended to demonstrate GP's strength (such as Boolean multiplexer for classical GP [5] or lawnmower for GP with automatically defined functions [6]). Each problem has a simple relation to more realistic GP problems: ORDER requires correct ordering as in conditional programs and MAJORITY requires the correct set of solution components.

We proceed as follows: in section 2, we formally describe the GP variants and the two problems, which includes describing program initialization from a primitive set and our mutation operator which is called HVL-Prime. We then proceed in sections 3 and 4 with our analyses of ORDER and MAJORITY in terms of the expected number of fitness evaluations until our algorithms have produced a globally optimal solution for the first time. This is called the expected optimization time of the algorithm. Our results are followed by a discussion in section 5 and conclusions and future work in section 6.

2. DEFINITIONS

2.1 Program Initialization

To use tree-based genetic programming [5], one must first choose a set of primitives A, which contains a set F of functions and a set L of terminals. Each primitive has explicitly defined semantics; for example, a primitive might represent a Boolean condition, a branching statement such as an IF-THEN-ELSE conditional, the value bound to an input variable, or an arithmetic operation. Functions are parameterized. Terminals are either functions with no parameters, i.e. arity equal to zero, or input variables to the program that serve as actual parameters to the formal parameters of functions.

In our derivations, we assume that a GP program is initialized by its parse tree construction. In general, we start with a root node randomly drawn from A and recursively populate the parameters of each function in the tree with subsequent random samples from A, until the leaves of the tree are all terminals. Functions constitute the internal nodes of the parse tree, and terminals occupy the leaf nodes. The exact properties of the tree generated by this procedure will not figure into the analysis of the algorithm, so we do not discuss them in depth.

2.2 HVL-Prime

The HVL-Prime operator is an update of O'Reilly's HVL mutation operator ([10, 11]) and motivated by minimality rather than inspired from a tree-edit distance metric. HVL first selects a node at random in a copy of the current parse tree. Let us term this the `currentNode`. It then, with equiprobability, applies one of three sub-operations: insertion, substitution, or deletion. Insertion takes place above `currentNode`: a randomly drawn function from F becomes the parent of `currentNode` and its additional parameters are set by drawing randomly from L. Substitution changes `currentNode` to a randomly drawn function of F with the same arity. Deletion replaces `currentNode` with its largest child subtree, which often admits large deletion sub-operations.

The operator we consider here, HVL-Prime, functions slightly differently, since we restrict it to operate on trees where all functions take two parameters. Rather than choosing a node followed by an operation, we first choose one of the three sub-operations to perform. The operations then proceed as shown in Figure 1. Insertion and substitution are exactly as in HVL; however, deletion only deletes a leaf and its parent to avoid the potentially macroscopic deletion change of HVL that is not in the spirit of bit-flip mutation. This change makes the algorithm more amenable to complexity analysis and specifies an operator that is only as general as our simplified problems require, contrasting with the generality of HVL, where all sub-operations handle primitives of any arity. Nevertheless, both operators respect the nature of GP's search among variable-length candidate solutions because each generates another candidate of potentially different size, structure, and composition.

In our analysis on these particular problems, we make one further simplification of HVL-Prime: substitution only takes place at the leaves. This is because our two problems only have one generic "join" function specified, so performing a substitution anywhere above the leaves is a vacuous mutation. Such operations only constitute one-sixth of all operations, so this change has no impact on any of the runtime bounds we derive.

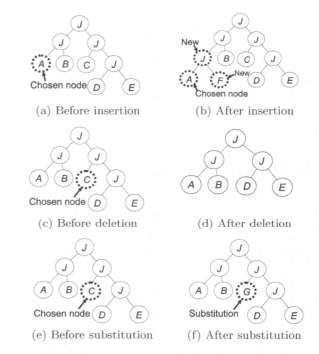

(a) Before insertion (b) After insertion

(c) Before deletion (d) After deletion

(e) Before substitution (f) After substitution

Figure 1: Example of the operators from HVL-Prime.

2.3 Algorithms

We define two genetic programming variants called (1+1) GP and (1+1) GP*. Both algorithms work with a population of size one and produce in each iteration one single offspring. (1+1) GP is defined in Algorithm 1 and accepts an offspring if it is as least as fit as its parent.

ALGORITHM 1   ((1+1) GP).

1. *Choose an initial solution X.*

2. *Set $X' := X$.*

3. *Mutate X' by applying HVL-Prime k times. For each application, randomly choose to either substitute, insert, or delete.*

- *If substitute, replace a randomly chosen leaf of X' with a new leaf $u \in L$ selected uniformly at random.*

- *If insert, randomly choose a node v in X' and select $u \in L$ uniformly at random. Replace v with a join node whose children are u and v, with the order of the children chosen randomly.*

- *If delete, randomly choose a leaf node v of X', with parent p and sibling u. Replace p with u and delete p and v.*

4. If $f(X') \geq f(X)$, set $X := X'$.

5. Go to 2.

(1+1) GP* differs from (1+1) GP by accepting only solution that are strict improvements (see Algorithm 2).

ALGORITHM 2 (ACCEPTANCE FOR (1+1) GP*).

4'. If $f(X') > f(X)$, set $X := X'$.

For each of (1+1) GP and (1+1) GP* we consider two further variants which differ in using one application of HVL-Prime ("single") or in using more than one ("multi"). For (1+1) GP-single and (1+1) GP*-single, we set $k = 1$, so that we perform one mutation at a time according to the HVL-Prime framework. For (1+1) GP-multi and (1+1) GP*-multi, we choose $k = 1 + \text{Pois}(1)$, so that the number of mutations at a time varies randomly according to the Poisson distribution.

We will analyze these four algorithms in terms of the expected number of fitness evaluations to produce an optimal solution for the first time. This is called the expected optimization time of the algorithm.

2.4 The ORDER problem

We consider two separable problems called ORDER and MAJORITY that have an independent, additive fitness structure. They both have multiple solutions, which we feel is a key property of a model GP problem because it holds generally for all real GP problems. They also both use the same primitive set, where $\bar{x}_i$ is the complement of x_i:

- $F := \{J\}$, J has arity 2.

- $L := \{x_1, \bar{x}_1, \ldots, x_n, \bar{x}_n\}$

ORDER represents problems where the primitive sets include conditional functions, which gives rise to conditional execution paths. GP classification problems, for example, often employ a numerical comparison function (e.g. greater than X, less than X, or equal to X). This sort of function has two arguments (subtrees), one branch which will be executed only when the comparison returns true, the other only when it returns false [5]. Thus, a conditional function results in a branching or conditional execution path, so the GP algorithm must identify and appropriately position the conditional functions to achieve the correct conditional execution behavior for all inputs.

ORDER is an abstracted simplification of this challenge: the conditional execution paths of a program are determined by tree inspection rather than execution. Instead of evaluating a condition test and then executing the appropriate

condition body explicitly, an ORDER program's conditional execution path is determined by simply inspecting whether a primitive or its complement occurs first in an in-order leaf parse. Correct programs for the ORDER problem must express each positive primitive x_i before its corresponding complement $\bar{x}_i$. This correctness requirement is intended to reflect a property commonly found in the GP solutions to problems where conditional functions are used: there exist multiple solutions, each with a set of different conditional paths.

ALGORITHM 3 ($f(X)$ FOR ORDER).

1. Derive conditional execution path P of X:

Init: l an empty leaf list, P an empty conditional execution path

1.1 Parse X inorder and insert each leaf at the rear of l as it is visited.

1.2 Generate P by parsing l front to rear and adding ("expressing") a leaf to P only if it or its complement are not yet in P (i.e. have not yet been expressed).

2. $f(X) = |\{x_i \in P\}|$.

For example, for a tree X, with (after the inorder parse) $l = (x_1, \bar{x}_4, x_2, \bar{x}_1, x_3, \bar{x}_6)$, $P = (x_1, \bar{x}_4, x_2, x_3, \bar{x}_6)$ and $f(X) = 3$ because $x_1, x_2, x_3 \in P$.

2.5 The MAJORITY problem

MAJORITY is a GP equivalent of the GA OneMax problem [3]. MAJORITY reflects a general (and thus weak) property required of GP solutions: a solution must have correct functionality and no incorrect functionality. Like ORDER, MAJORITY is a simplification that uses tree inspection rather than program execution. A correct program in MAJORITY must exhibit at least as many occurrences of a primitive as of its complement and it must exhibit all the positive primitives of its terminal (leaf) set. Both the independent sub-solution fitness structure and inspection property of MAJORITY are necessary to make our analysis tractable.

ALGORITHM 4 ($f(X)$ FOR MAJORITY).

1. Derive the combined execution statements S of X:

Init: l an empty leaf list, S is an empty statement list.

1.1 Parse X inorder and insert each leaf at the rear of l as it is visited.

1.2 For $i \leq n$: if $count(x_i \in l) \geq count(\bar{x}_i \in l)$ and $count(x_i \in l) \geq 1$, add x_i to S

2. $f(X) = |S|$.

For example, for a tree X, with (after the inorder parse) $l = (x_1, \bar{x}_4, x_2, \bar{x}_1, \bar{x}_3, \bar{x}_6, x_1, x_4)$, $S = (x_1, x_2, x_4)$ and $f(X) = 3$.

3. ANALYSIS FOR ORDER

Here we present bounds for ORDER on the number of runtime evaluations needed in the execution of (1+1) GP and (1+1) GP*.

We will analyze this GP problem using fitness-based partitions [2]. This requires us to compute the probability of improving the fitness from k to $k + 1$ for each value of k between 0 and $n - 1$, inclusive. Although our HVL-Prime operator is complex, we can obtain a lower bound on the probability of making an improvement by considering fitness improvements that arise from insertions. This is described in the following lemma.

LEMMA 1. *Define p_k to be the probability that we perform an insertion that improves the fitness value of the GP tree from k to $k + 1$. For the single- and multi-operation variants of (1+1) GP and (1+1) GP* applied to the ORDER problem,*

$$p_k = \Omega \left(\frac{(n - k)^2}{n \max(T, n)} \right)$$

where n is the number of variables and T is the number of leaves in the GP tree at the particular iteration.

PROOF. When the fitness value is k, it must be the case that k different x_i appear before their corresponding $\bar{x}_i$. To improve the fitness, we must insert one of the $n - k$ unexpressed x_i as a leaf that will be visited before a leaf containing the corresponding $\bar{x}_i$. Assume for notational ease that these unexpressed x_i are indexed by $\{x_1, ..., x_{n-k}\}$. Define A_i to be the event that we insert x_i into the tree with our mutation operation, and define B_i to be the event that x_i is inserted before the corresponding $\bar{x}_i$. Given this, we can write out p_k as follows:

$$p_k = \sum_{i=1}^{n-k} \Pr(A_i)\Pr(B_i|A_i).$$

With a single operation, the probability of choosing to insert a particular x_i is $\frac{1}{6n}$, since we choose to insert with probability $\frac{1}{3}$ and select the variable uniformly at random from the set of $2n$ possible terminals. We can cover the multi-operation case with this analysis as well because the number of operations is sampled according to $1 + \text{Pois}(1)$, so the probability of performing exactly one operation is $\frac{1}{e}$. The probability of A_i is therefore at least $\frac{1}{6en}$, so in both the single- and multi-operation cases, we have

$$p_k \geq \frac{1}{6en} \sum_{i=1}^{n-k} \Pr(B_i|A_i).$$

We need to analyze two cases in computing this sum. Preliminarily, we define S to be the total number of nodes in the GP tree. Note that $S = 2T - 1$, so $S = \Theta(T)$.

Case 1: $T \geq n - k$. We first note that the probability of inserting x_i such that it is visited between the $j - 1$st leaf and the jth leaf in the traversal is at least $\frac{1}{2S}$, since we choose to insert at the jth leaf with probability $\frac{1}{S}$ and then add x_i as a left child of the new join node with probability $\frac{1}{2}$.

Inserting any of the $n - k$ unexpressed x_i before the first leaf in the tree clearly improves the fitness. If we insert at the second position instead, there must still be at least $n - k - 1$ choices of x_i that yield an improvement: there is only one node that will be traversed before this position in the tree, so there is at most one $\bar{x}_i$ expressed before this position. We can iterate this argument to see that at the ith position, there are still $n - k - i + 1$ x_i that can be inserted for an improvement to the fitness. By reindexing the x_i, we then have that x_i can be inserted in at least the

first i positions in the tree. Using the fact that the number of leaves T is at least $n - k$, we have that

$$p_k \geq \frac{1}{6en} \sum_{i=1}^{n-k} \Pr(B_i|A_i)$$

$$\geq \frac{1}{6en} \sum_{i=1}^{n-k} \frac{n - k - i + 1}{2S} = \frac{1}{6en} \sum_{i=1}^{n-k} \frac{i}{2S}$$

$$= \frac{1}{6en} \frac{(n-k)(n-k+1)}{4S} \geq \frac{1}{6en} \frac{(n-k)^2}{\max(4S, n)}.$$

Noting that $S = \Theta(T)$, the asymptotic result follows.

Case 2: $T < n - k$: We can apply the argument of Case 1 up to the Tth position. After this, we have that for $n - k - T + 1$ of the unexpressed x_i, the corresponding $\bar{x}_i$ appears nowhere in the tree, so the probability of an insertion improving the fitness is 1. We also note that $S < 2n$ in this case, allowing us to simplify our expression for p_k as follows:

$$p_k \geq \frac{1}{6en} \sum_{i=1}^{n-k} \Pr(B_i|A_i)$$

$$\geq \frac{1}{6en} \left[\sum_{i=1}^{T} \frac{i}{2S} \right] + \frac{1}{6en} \sum_{i=T+1}^{n-k} 1$$

$$\geq \frac{1}{6en} \left[\sum_{i=1}^{T} \frac{i}{4n} \right] + \frac{n - k - T}{6en}$$

$$= \frac{T(T+1)}{24en^2} + \frac{(n - k - T)(n - k)}{6en(n - k)}.$$

If $T = \Omega(n - k)$, then we lower-bound p_k using only the first term, which behaves asymptotically in this case as $\Omega \left(\frac{(n-k)^2}{n^2} \right)$. Otherwise, if $T = o(n - k)$, then we use the second term, which then grows according to $\Omega \left(\frac{(n-k)^2}{n^2} \right)$. In either case, because T is less than n, we have the desired asymptotic behavior. $\square$

With this lemma, we can now state the general theorem about the number of fitness evaluations needed for our (1+1) GP variants.

THEOREM 1. *The expected optimization time of the single-operation and multi-operation cases of (1+1) GP and (1+1) GP* on ORDER is $O(nT_{\max})$ in the worst case, where n is the number of x_i and $T_{\max}$ denotes the maximal tree size at any stage during the evolution of the algorithm.*

PROOF. We can apply Lemma 1 to these algorithms, which implies an asymptotic lower bound on p_k, the probability of improving the fitness from k to $k + 1$ via an insertion. This also serves as an asymptotic lower bound on the probability of improving the fitness at all, and therefore provides an expected time necessary to improve the fitness, regardless of whether or not we accept neutral moves. In order to determine the total number of evaluations, we must sum the expected number of fitness function evaluations over all intermediate fitness values, from $k = 0$ to $k = n - 1$.

The expected optimization time is therefore upper

bounded by

$$\sum_{k=0}^{n-1} \frac{1}{p_k} = \sum_{k=0}^{n-1} O\left(\frac{n \max(T_k, n)}{(n-k)^2}\right)$$

$$= nT_{\max} \sum_{k=0}^{n-1} O\left(\frac{1}{(n-k)^2}\right)$$

$$= O\left(nT_{\max} \sum_{j=1}^{\infty} \frac{1}{j^2}\right)$$

$$= O(nT_{\max})$$

where the second equality follows from the fact that $T_{\max} \geq T_n \geq n$, and the last equality follows from the fact that $\sum_{j=1}^{\infty} \frac{1}{j^2} \leq 2$. $\square$

Note that most GP algorithms explicitly limit the maximum tree size that can be used in an algorithm. If we enforce a linear bound of $O(n)$ nodes in the tree, our algorithm solves the ORDER problem in expected time $O(n^2)$. However, it is also sometimes possible to show that, even in the absence of an imposed limit, the tree does not get too big during the optimization process. We examine this for (1+1) GP*-single and present an upper bound on the expected optimization time.

COROLLARY 1. *The expected optimization time of (1+1) GP*-single on ORDER is $O(n^2)$ if the tree is initialized with $O(n)$ terminals.*

PROOF. We note that the maximum value of the fitness is n, and the fitness is integer-valued, so if it is strictly increasing with each operation that is accepted, there must be no more than n operations accepted. In the single-operation framework, each operation adds at most two nodes to the tree (if it is an insertion), which means that $T_{\max} \leq O(n) + 2n = O(n)$ holds during the run of the algorithm. $\square$

The case of (1+1) GP*-multi is more difficult to analyze because the expected length of accepted moves may be very different from the expected length of proposed moves, as conditioning on accepting the move will skew the distribution. We conjecture that the bound from Corollary 1 holds in this case as well, but do not present a proof of this.

We also note that because of how our fitness-based partition argument is structured, invoking the average case does not enable us to find any better bounds. Although k will initially be somewhat greater than zero, we will generally still need to improve the fitness $\Theta(n)$ times, so we will have the same asymptotic result.

4. ANALYSIS FOR MAJORITY

We next consider the MAJORITY problem. We start with some preliminary definitions.

DEFINITION 1. *For a given GP tree, let $c(x_i)$ be the number of x_i variables and $c(\bar{x}_i)$ be the number of negated x_i variables present in the tree. For a GP tree representing a solution to the MAJORITY problem, we define the* deficit *in the ith variable by*

$$D_i = c(\bar{x}_i) - c(x_i).$$

DEFINITION 2. *In a GP tree for MAJORITY, we say that x_i is expressed when $D_i \leq 0$ and $c(x_i) > 0$.*

The fitness of a tree T is simply the number of variables that are expressed.

We note a property of HVL-Prime for this particular problem that we will make use of later.

DEFINITION 3. *The substitution decomposability property (SDP) for MAJORITY states that a substitution is exactly equivalent to a deletion followed by an insertion, which are accepted or rejected as a unit.*

This property follows from the fact that the order of the terminals has no bearing on the fitness of a solution for MAJORITY. The variable to be replaced by substitution is selected uniformly at random from the set of leaves of the tree. This is identical to how the variable to be deleted is chosen when using the deletion operator. Substitution then inserts a variable selected uniformly at random from the set of possible terminals, just as the insertion operator does.

We begin our analysis in section 4.1, with worst case bounds for all variants except (1+1) GP-multi. We find that (1+1) GP-single solves the problem quite efficiently, yielding polynomial-time worst-case complexity. However, not accepting neutral moves, as in (1+1) GP*, results in poor performance: (1+1) GP*-single fails to terminate in the worst case, and (1+1) GP*-multi requires a number of fitness evalutions exponential in the size of the initial tree. In section 4.2 we derive average case bounds that assume that the initial solution tree has $2n$ terminals each selected uniformly at random from L. This random tree initialization allows us to bound the maximum deficit in any variable. We show that (1+1) GP-single runs in time $O(nT_{\max} \log \log(n))$ in the average case. By contrast, (1+1) GP*-single still has a constant probability of failing to terminate, and so the expected runtime is infinite.

4.1 Worst Case Bounds

4.1.1 (1+1) GP-single

We will show here some properties of (1+1) GP-single on MAJORITY and give a polynomial-time worst-case bound on the performance. Our analysis considers the evolution of the deficits D_i over the course of the algorithm as n parallel random walks. We will show that each positive D_i reaches zero at least as quickly as a balanced random walk, which is the condition for the corresponding x_i to be expressed; this, then, gives us the expected number of operations that we are required to perform on a particular variable before it is expressed. Because these arguments do not easily extend to (1+1) GP-multi, we omit from this section any treatment of that case.

We begin by establishing the validity of modeling the temporal sequence of each of the D_i as a random walk.

LEMMA 2. *For (1+1) GP-single on MAJORITY:*
a) The probability of proposing an operation that changes either the number of x_i or the number of $\bar{x}_i$ is $\Omega\left(\frac{1}{n}\right)$.
b) If some x_i has a deficit $D_i = d > 0$, we require in expectation $O(dT_{\max})$ proposed operations involving that variable before it is successfully expressed, where $T_{\max}$ is the maximum number of nodes in our GP tree at any timestep of the algorithm.

PROOF. a) To see that a particular operation involves x_i or $\bar{x}_i$ with probability $\Omega\left(\frac{1}{n}\right)$, we simply note that the probability of inserting one of the two variables is $\frac{1}{3} \times \frac{2}{2n} = \Omega\left(\frac{1}{n}\right)$.

b) We address each of the three types of operations in turn and show that each is at least as favorable as a balanced random walk in terms of reducing D_i to zero.

Insertion: The probability of inserting x_i into the tree is $\frac{1}{6n}$, which is the same as the probability of inserting $\bar{x}_i$. Therefore, given that we change D_i with an insertion, we increase it or decrease it in a balanced manner, with probability $\frac{1}{2}$.

Deletion: The probability of a deletion changing D_i is

$$\frac{c(x_i) + c(\bar{x}_i)}{T}$$

where T is the size of the GP tree. Given that we do such a deletion, we increase D_i with probability $\frac{c(x_i)}{c(x_i)+c(\bar{x}_i)}$ and decrease it with probability $\frac{c(\bar{x}_i)}{c(x_i)+c(\bar{x}_i)}$, since we pick the variable to delete uniformly at random. However, note that because $D_i > 0$, we have that $c(x_i) < c(\bar{x}_i)$, so the probability of decreasing D_i is greater than the probability of increasing it, so this is actually slightly better than a balanced random walk for the purpose of reducing D_i.

Substitution: We now make use of the substitution decomposability property (SDP) defined previously to observe that substitution consists of a deletion followed by an insertion. Therefore, a substitution is simply equivalent to taking one or two steps that tend to reduce D_i with probability at least $\frac{1}{2}$ if D_i is greater than 0.

Consider the 1-dimensional random walk on the integers $0, 1, \ldots, n$, with n being a reflecting barrier and 0 being an absorbing barrier. The expected time to reach 0 when starting at k is $O(kn)$, following the analysis for random walks on undirected graphs carried out in [1]. This is precisely the setting we have for our random walk on the D_i if we set $k = d$ and $n = T_{\max}$, so we have that the random walk performed by the D_i reaches zero after at most $O(dT_{\max})$ accepted operations.

We now must address the question of how many operations on the variable must be proposed in order to accept $O(dT_{\max})$ of them. Note that if x_i is unexpressed, any insertion or deletion affecting D_i will be accepted, since it cannot possibly decrease the fitness value. The probability of a substitution affecting D_i is, by the SDP, less than or equal to the probability that an insertion affects D_i plus the probability that a deletion affects D_i. Therefore, even if every substitution is rejected, we still accept a constant fraction of proposed operations that affect D_i, so we only require $O(dT_{\max})$ proposed operations involving x_i and $\bar{x}_i$ in order to have $O(dT_{\max})$ accepted operations.

Once D_i reaches zero, we are done and x_i is expressed unless $c(x_i) = c(\bar{x}_i) = 0$. In this case, we clearly cannot do any more deletes, but will either add in an x_i or $\bar{x}_i$ via an insertion or a substitution. Through either operation, we add each variable with probability $\frac{1}{2}$, and therefore successfully express x_i with probability $\frac{1}{2}$. In the case where we insert an $\bar{x}_i$ and increase D_i to one, we again apply our one-dimensional random walk result with $k = 1$ and $n = T_{\max}$ to see that we will return to zero again after only $O(T_{\max})$ additional moves, whereupon either x_i is present in the tree and we are done or we can once again attempt to add it. Because we expect to do this procedure only twice before succeeding, it only adds $O(T_{\max})$ steps, and therefore does not change our bound of $O(dT_{\max})$. $\square$

This lemma allows us to establish an upper bound on the number of evaluations for (1+1) GP on MAJORITY given a bound on the largest deficit.

THEOREM 2. *Let $D = \max_i D_i$ for an instance of MA-JORITY initialized with T terminals drawn from a set of size $2n$ (i.e. terminals $x_1, \ldots, x_n, \bar{x}_1, \ldots, \bar{x}_n$). Then the expected optimization time of (1+1) GP-single is*

$$O(n \log n + DT_{\max} n \log \log n)$$

in the worst case.

PROOF. We draw upon a result from Myers and Wilf [8] about a generalized form of the coupon collector problem. If we have n coupons and wish to acquire at least k of each coupon, we need to draw, in expectation, $O(n \log n + kn \log \log n)$ coupons. When k is at least $\log n$, this is a slight improvement over the naive bound of $O(kn \log n)$ from simply iterating the basic coupon collector problem k times.

Lemma 2 tells us two things. Firstly, we have that a proposed operation involves x_i or $\bar{x}_i$ with probability $\Omega(\frac{1}{n})$, so we have a coupon collector problem with slightly perturbed coupon probabilities. Secondly, we find that we need to propose $O(DT_{\max})$ operations involving each terminal in order to express all of our variables. Plugging these into the bound described above yields an asymptotic requirement of $O(n \log n + DT_{\max} n \log \log n)$ fitness function evaluations, as desired.

The only wrinkle in this picture is that the coupon collector assumes that a variable is "complete" after a set number of coupons have been collected. While we do not accept moves that reduce the fitness value, an expressed variable x_i could become unexpressed if, during the course of a substitution operation, another variable x_j were simultaneously expressed. However, in this case, we must have had $D_i = 0$ and $D_j = 1$, and we have merely reversed the two, which amounts to a relabeling of the x_i and x_j. Because the D_i are the only state variables that we care about in this case, this move effectively does nothing except cause us to make a vacuous move. Because substitutions only make up $\frac{1}{3}$ of all of the proposed moves, such wasted moves can only make up a constant fraction of the total number of moves, and therefore do not change the asymptotics. $\square$

As a corollary of Theorem 2 we can bound the initial D by considering tree initialization.

COROLLARY 2. *When MAJORITY is initialized with $m = O(n)$ terminals drawn from a set of size $2n$, the expected optimization time of (1+1) GP-single is*

$$O(n^2 T_{\max} \log \log n).$$

PROOF. This follows from Theorem 2 with $D = m$, since the deficit cannot be greater than the number of terminals in the tree. $\square$

We can consider the outcome of the worst case tree initialization both intuitively and experimentally. We have $D = m$ when all of the leaves consist of instances of one bar variable, say $\bar{x}_1$. Since the $\bar{x}_1$ occupy such a large fraction of the tree, they will frequently be substituted out or deleted. This suggests that the balanced random walk argument is quite pessimistic given this circumstance. We thus expect that, in practice, this initial condition will be quickly erased. If we put $T_{\max} = O(n)$, we know, from the coupon collector problem, that after an initial phase of $O(n \log n)$ steps, we will have proposed a deletion on every leaf that was initialized in the GP tree. Because deletions are always accepted on negated variables, we will have deleted all of the initial $\bar{x}_1$ variables by the end of this "erasure" phase, and only expect to introduce at most $O(\log n)$ of any particular bar variable through insertions and substitutions. This implies that, after this relatively short phase, $D = O(\log n)$, giving an optimization time of $O(n^2 \log n \log \log n)$, a bound very close to the average-case optimization time we present in 4.2.1.

We experimented with this initialization to confirm our intuition. Figure 2 shows the results of solving MAJORITY using (1+1) GP-single with increasing problem size and trees initialized with $2n$ leaves, each occupied by $\bar{x}_1$. We tracked the number of fitness evaluations required and, even though we imposed no bound on the tree size, the order of growth relative to n appears to be just barely superlinear. This empirical evidence supports the intuition that the worst-case performance is much closer to the average-case than Corollary 2 would suggest.

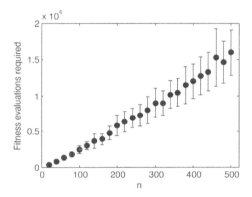

Figure 2: Plot of the average optimization time given a "bad" initialization of size $2n$ with $D_1 = 2n$ for x_1. Fifty trials were used to compute each point. Circles indicate the mean number of fitness function evaluations for each value of n, and error bars show the standard deviation of the 50 trials.

4.1.2 (1+1) GP*

Unlike in the case of the ORDER problem, where accepting or not accepting neutral moves makes no difference in the performance of the algorithm, for MAJORITY, such a distinction matters tremendously. Intuitively, this behavior arises because there is a notion of "working towards" a solution here that is absent from the ORDER problem. In ORDER, our analysis relied on our ability to express an x_i by simply inserting it as a terminal early enough in the tree, which required only one step. However, in MAJORITY, if there are k x_i and ℓ $\bar{x}_i$ present in the GP tree, at least $\lceil \frac{\ell-k}{2} \rceil$ mutation operations will be required to make up this deficit, all but the last of which will be neutral moves.

Because of the importance of neutral moves, we find that (1+1) GP*-single and (1+1) GP*-multi perform quite badly. Even when we initialize with a tree with size linear in n, the number of terminal symbols, we can demonstrate an initialization where (1+1) GP*-single never terminates and (1+1) GP*-multi takes an exponential amount of time to do

so. Consider the tree T_{bad} which has as leaves the variables

$$x_1, x_2, x_3, ..., x_{n-1}, \underbrace{\bar{x}_n, \bar{x}_n ..., \bar{x}_n}_{n+1 \text{ of these}}$$

THEOREM 3. *Let T_{bad} be the initial solution to MAJORITY. Then the expected optimization time of (1+1) GP*-single is infinite.*

PROOF. It is clear that, with one move, the deficit in x_n can only be changed by at most two. There is a deficit of $n+1$ to make up, which is impossible, therefore (1+1) GP*-single will never find its way out of this local optimum. □

THEOREM 4. *Let T_{bad} be the current solution to MAJORITY. Then the expected optimization time of (1+1) GP*-multi is at least exponential in n.*

PROOF. The fitness value of T_{bad} is $n-1$, with x_1 through x_{n-1} expressed, so the only way to improve the fitness is to make a move that expresses x_n. Therefore, the moves that achieve this are the only moves that will be accepted. We compute the probability of making such a move in this configuration in order to determine the expected time to make such a move.

Note that any mutation operation that successfully improves the fitness must make up for a deficit of $n+1$, which requires at least $\lceil \frac{n+1}{2} \rceil$ operations, assuming that we, in each case, substitute an $\bar{x}_n$ with an x_n. The number of moves per mutation is distributed as $1 + \text{Pois}(1)$, so the Poisson random variable must take a value of at least $\lceil \frac{n-1}{2} \rceil$. The probability of this when $\lambda = 1$ is given by

$$\sum_{i=\lceil \frac{n-1}{2} \rceil}^{\infty} \frac{e^{-1}}{i!} \leq \frac{1}{(\frac{n-1}{2})!} = O\left(\left(\frac{n}{2e}\right)^{-\frac{n}{2}}\right)$$

by Stirling's formula.

We can take this probability as a (very weak) upper bound on the probability of improving the fitness. Inverting it, we see that the expected number of moves required is $\Omega\left(\left(\frac{n}{2e}\right)^{\frac{n}{2}}\right)$. □

4.2 Average Case Bounds

To provide average case bounds we consider a GP tree which is initialized with what we term "unity expectation": it has $2n$ terminals (leaves) each selected uniformly at random from the set of possible terminals.

4.2.1 (1+1) GP

The average case bound follows more or less directly from Theorem 2 once a result from the literature is applied to give an expected bound on the maximum initial deficit.

COROLLARY 3. *For MAJORITY with a terminal set of size $2n$ under unity expectation initialization, the expected optimization time of (1+1) GP-single is $O(nT_{\max} \log n)$.*

PROOF. A result from Raab and Steger [14] tells us that, with probability at least $1 - O\left(\frac{1}{n^k}\right)$ for any integer k, no $\bar{x}_i$ appears more than $O\left(\frac{\log n}{\log \log n}\right)$ times in the GP tree, so $D = O\left(\frac{\log n}{\log \log n}\right)$. Set $k = 2$, so that the probability of having a larger deviation is $O\left(\frac{1}{n^2}\right)$. The worst-case bound of $O\left(n^2 T_{\max} \log \log n\right)$ from Corollary 2 ensures that these uncommon cases contribute only an $O(T_{\max} \log \log n)$ term to the expectation. Substituting $D = O\left(\frac{\log n}{\log \log n}\right)$ into the expression in Theorem 2 gives us the desired bound for the common case, which is also the overall runtime bound. $\square$

4.2.2 (1+1) GP*

Assuming unity expectation initialization, we can improve on our result from 4.1.2 and show (1+1) GP*-single has a constant probability of failing to terminate. Our general strategy will be to prove that there is a constant probability that, when starting with a deficit of size three in x_1, this deficit will be preserved until the fitness is $n - 1$. At this point, when all the other variables are expressed, there will remain a gap that cannot be closed in a single step. Such a deficit could disappear over the course of the algorithm because substitution has the ability to shrink the deficit (by removing $\bar{x}_1$ and replacing it with a x_i in order to express that variable), but this proof shows that there is nonetheless a constant probability of the deficit being preserved.

First, we establish a lemma about the prevalence of constant-size deficits arising based on our initialization.

LEMMA 3. *Suppose we have a $2n$-length instance of the MAJORITY problem with unity expectation initialization. Let A_k denote the event that $\bar{x}_1$ appears exactly k times without x_1 appearing at all, where k is any constant. Then $Pr(A_k) = \Omega(1)$.*

PROOF. To compute $\Pr(A_k)$, we count the number of $2n$-length sequences of terminals for which this is true and divide by the total number of possible sequences. Under A_k, we must have k instances of $\bar{x}_1$ and zero instances of x_1, so there are $\binom{2n}{k}$ positions that can be occupied by the $\bar{x}_1$ and the remaining $2n - k$ positions should each be occupied by one of the $2n - 2$ elements that are not x_1 or $\bar{x}_1$. In total, there are $(2n)^{2n}$ possible $2n$-length sequences of terminals. Combining these facts yields

$$
\begin{aligned}
\Pr(A_k) &= \frac{\binom{2n}{k}(2n-2)^{2n-k}}{(2n)^{2n}} \\
&= \frac{1}{k!} \frac{(2n)!}{(2n-k)!(2n-2)^k}\left(\frac{2n-2}{2n}\right)^{2n} \\
&\geq \frac{1}{k!}\left(\frac{2n-k}{2n-2}\right)^k\left(1 - \frac{1}{n}\right)^{2n} \\
&= \frac{1}{k!} \times \Omega(1) \times \Omega(1) \\
&= \Omega(1)
\end{aligned}
$$

assuming that k is a constant. $\square$

Next, we lower-bound the size of the GP tree when running (1+1) GP*-single on MAJORITY. The tree must be large enough so that we are not too likely to substitute out the $\bar{x}_1$ over the course of the algorithm.

LEMMA 4. *Using (1+1) GP-single on MAJORITY with any initialization of size $2n$, the size of the GP tree is always greater than $\frac{7n}{6}$ with probability one.*

PROOF. A deletion can only improve the fitness if we delete some $\bar{x}_i$ when $c(x_i) = n$ and $c(\bar{x}_i) = n + 1$, with n positive. Such a configuration requires at least three occurrences of x_i and $\bar{x}_i$ in the GP tree, so at most $\frac{2n}{3}$ variables can be present in this fashion initially. Of the at least

$\frac{n}{3}$ variables that remain, at most half can be expressed by a deletion, because they must be first put into this configuration during the course of a substitution that expresses some other variable x_j. Therefore, we are forced to accept at least $\frac{n}{6}$ insertions or substitutions over the course of the algorithm, giving us an upper bound of $\frac{5n}{6}$ on the number of deletions accepted. This in turn guarantees that our tree always remains larger than $2n - \frac{5n}{6} = \frac{7n}{6}$. $\square$

Finally, we can prove the claim directly.

THEOREM 5. *With probability $\Omega(1)$, the optimization time of (1+1) GP*-single with unity expectation initialization is infinite on MAJORITY.*

PROOF. Lemma 3 tells us that, with a constant probability, we initialize one of the variables, say x_1, with $c(x_1) = 0$ and $c(\bar{x}_1) = 3$. We now show that, also with a constant probability, such a deficit is preserved during the course of the expression of at most $n - 1$ of the other variables.

We make such an argument by induction. Define the jth step of the algorithm as the period after j variables have been expressed, at the end of which we propose the move that expresses the $j + 1$st move. Suppose that at the jth step, it is true that $c(x_1) = 0$ and $c(\bar{x}_1) = 3$. The $j + 1$st variable expressed cannot possibly be x_1, since there is no way to make up a deficit of three with a single move. If the move we accept to express the $j + 1$st variable is an insertion or a deletion, we preserve our deficit of three and do not change the state of the variable x_1 at all, since we must either insert some variable in the set $\{x_2, ..., x_n\}$ or delete some variable in the set $\{\bar{x}_2, ..., \bar{x}_n\}$.

If we express the $j + 1$st variable with a substitution, however, it is possible that we might insert an x_1 or delete one of the $\bar{x}_1$. An accepted substitution must either replace some variable with a variable in the set $\{x_2, ..., x_n\}$ or substitute out some $\{\bar{x}_2, ..., \bar{x}_n\}$. However, a substitution also involves an "extraneous" insertion or deletion, by the SDP. If this operation impacts a variable different than the $j + 1$st variable we are expressing, it must be an operation that, on its own, would keep the fitness constant. For an extraneous insertion, we note that it is always admissible to insert any of the n symbols in the set $\{x_1, x_2, ..., x_n\}$ without decreasing the fitness. Therefore, the probability of inserting neither x_1 nor $\bar{x}_1$ in a neutral or better move is at least $1 - \frac{2}{n}$.

If the extraneous operation is a deletion, we note that it is always possible to delete at least $\frac{T-n}{2}$ terminals, where T is the current tree size. Any variable expressed with $c(x_i) = 1$ and $c(\bar{x}_i) = 0$ cannot be removed, so there might be as many as n terminals forbidden for this reason. For any variable not in this configuration, we have one of two cases. If the variable is unexpressed or is expressed with a deficit less than or equal to -1, any occurrence of x_i or $\bar{x}_i$ can safely be deleted without decreasing the fitness. If the variable is expressed with a deficit of zero, there must be at least as many $\bar{x}_i$ as there are x_i, and any of these $\bar{x}_i$ can be safely deleted. Therefore, we set aside at most n "singleton" symbols that cannot be deleted, and of those remaining, it must always be acceptable to delete at least half, yielding $\frac{T-n}{2}$.

We therefore preserve our three $\bar{x}_1$ variables with probability at least

$$
\frac{\frac{T-n}{2} - 3}{\frac{T-n}{2}} = 1 - \frac{6}{T-n}.
$$

We now invoke the result from Lemma 4. Because the size of the tree is at least $\frac{7n}{6}$ at all times, we can lower-bound the probability of preserving the $\bar{x}_1$ as $1 - \frac{36}{n}$.

These situations (extraneous inserts and extraneous deletes) are mutually exclusive, and of the two, the deletes are the more probable to interfere with our x_1 setup. Nevertheless, the probability of preserving our deficit of three in x_1 from the jth step to the $j + 1$st step is at least $1 - \frac{O(1)}{n}$. Because there are at most $n - 1$ such steps of the algorithm, our overall probability of preserving the deficit is

$$\left(1 - \frac{O(1)}{n}\right)^{n-1} = \Omega(1).$$

We have constant probability of initializing with such a deficit, and a constant probability of preserving the deficit, in which case the algorithm never terminates. Therefore, with constant probability, (1+1) GP*-single never terminates on MAJORITY. □

COROLLARY 4. *Using unity expectation initialization, the expected optimization time of (1+1) GP*-single on MAJOR-ITY is infinite.*

PROOF. This follows directly from Theorem 5 □

While Theorem 5 does demonstrate that the probability of getting stuck in a local optimum is at least a constant, the actual constant yielded by the proof is rather small. However, our proof technique made several very conservative assumptions for simplicity. To investigate this further, we tried to solve MAJORITY with (1+1) GP*-single experimentally, observing when we would get stuck in a local minimum. Experimentally, the actual probability of (1+1) GP*-single failing to converge to the optimum is actually quite high, as demonstrated by Figure 3.

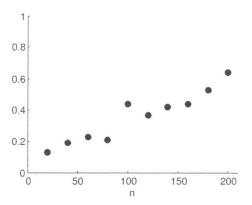

Figure 3: Plot showing the probability of (1+1) GP*-single failing to terminate on MAJOR-ITY when the initial solution tree has $2n$ terminals each selected uniformly at random, i.e. with unity expectation initialization. Each probability was determined empirically over the course of 100 simulations for each value of n.

However, we do not know how to show a similar result for (1+1) GP*-multi. We note that difficult MAJORITY instances, such as T_{bad} presented in section 4.1.2, are exponentially unlikely to occur when the initial solution tree has $2n$ terminals each selected uniformly at random. From Raab

and Steger [14], we know that deficits larger than logarithmic occur with exponentially small probability, and in any case large deficits should tend to equalize over the course of the algorithm execution, even if we only accept a linear number of moves. However, if the last unexpressed variable has a deficit of size k, we will require at least $\Omega\left(n^{-\frac{k}{2}}\right)$ steps to correctly substitute out enough instances of $\bar{x}_i$ for x_i even in the best case, so unless k can be bounded at a constant, we will have an expected runtime that is superpolynomial.

5. SUMMARY AND DISCUSSION

Table 1 aggregates our expected optimization time results for all algorithm variants and each problem.

	ORDER	
	(1+1) GP	(1+1) GP*
single	$O(nT_{\max})$ w.c. †	$O(n^2)$ w.c.
multi	$O(nT_{\max})$ w.c. †	$O(nT_{\max})$ w.c. †

	MAJORITY	
	(1+1) GP	(1+1) GP*
single	$O(n^2 T_{\max} \log\log n)$ w.c. † $O(nT_{\max} \log n)$ a.c.	$\Omega(\infty)$ a.c.
multi	?	$\Omega\left(\left(\frac{n}{2e}\right)^{\frac{n}{2}}\right)$ w.c.

Table 1: Results of the computational complexity analysis for our sample problems. We use w.c. to denote a worst-case bound and a.c. to denote an average-case bound. The daggers indicate where we conjecture that better bounds exist.

From the perspective of a GP practitioner, the insights provided by this rigorous analysis may be more valuable than the complexity results themselves. In section 5.1 we discuss how our treatment sheds light upon the important but subtle interactions between a problem, the acceptance criterion, and the genetic operator. Section 5.2 discusses the impact of the sub-operations on the mutation operator we considered. In section 5.3, we address the implications of our design and analysis methodology for practical GP algorithm design. Section 5.4 covers some of our analysis techniques, and finally section 6 presents future work avenues and concludes.

5.1 Accepting Neutral Moves in ORDER and MAJORITY

It might initially seem immaterial whether or not we accept neutral moves with our genetic operator for OR-DER and MAJORITY. However, our analysis provides rigorous evidence that the differences in performance between (1+1) GP and (1+1) GP* are substantial for both of these problems. Similar results have already been obtained in the context of evolutionary algorithms for binary representations [4].

ORDER's focus on condition semantics gives it the property that only the first occurrence of each terminal matters. A large tree makes the probability of improvements smaller because many of the mutations will change variables that have no effect on expression, being sequentially later than earlier occurrences of those same variables. Therefore, not accepting neutral moves helps prevent "bloat" and using (1+1) GP* is significantly advantageous. (1+1) GP's acceptance of neutral moves causes a feedback loop that stimulates growth of the tree: there is a slight bias towards accepting insertions as opposed to deletions, which makes the tree large, which increases the time to find an improvement and results in many neutral insertions, which increase the tree size even more. In general, to solve ORDER with runtime performance that respects the complexity analysis, the tree must not grow too large, and not accepting neutral moves assures this.

Solving MAJORITY, we see the opposite effect: (1+1) GP very handily beats (1+1) GP* in terms of expected optimization time. Neutral moves have the effect of balancing both the relative frequency of variables and the number of positive versus negative occurrences. This draws us toward a very favorable average case where every variable is either expressed or very close to being expressed. If neutral moves are not accepted, improvement can frequently stagnate, underscoring the fact that there are large flat regions in the search space. (1+1) GP is better equipped to escape these than (1+1) GP*, so one should, in fact, clearly choose (1+1) GP so that there is a guarantee of termination and to avoid the exponential-time worst-case associated with (1+1) GP*-multi.

Overall, these results highlight the fact that, in choosing whether or not to accept neutral moves, one should consider their general effect with respect to both the fitness landscape and growth in tree size. Tying this knowledge into expected optimization time also requires an understanding of the mechanisms by which the fitness increases. We recognize that for ORDER and MAJORITY, this is much easier to do rigorously than for more realistic problems. However, perhaps our exercise with ORDER and MAJORITY can provide intuitive insight to GP practitioners.

5.2 Mutation

Our results also tell us more about our HVL-Prime framework, and show that it has several interesting properties and behaves quite differently for the two problems.

Interestingly, the analysis for ORDER, which uses the fitness partition method, only relies on the use of insert. However, we could not run the algorithm with only insertion, because the tree would get very large and the expected time to termination would actually become infinite, in the absence of a strict bound on the tree size. Therefore, even if they are less effective in improving fitness, deletions are necessary to control the size of the tree. We could, however, envision designing an alternative operator without substitution, whose insertion and deletion probabilities are imbalanced. By choosing these probabilities appropriately, we could prevent the tree size from getting too large (without explicitly bounding it) while still doing as many insertions as possible, thus allowing the algorithm to reach the optimum with the lowest number of fitness evaluations.

For MAJORITY, the substitution decomposability property indicates that, for this particular problem, the substitution operation is more complex than insertion and deletion and is, in fact, a macro operator which is a combination of the two. A superficial glance at the operator does not necessarily reveal this; in fact, it is tempting to believe that substitution is generally the least complex of the operators, because it most closely resembles a bit-flip in a fixed-length

representation and does not change the size or structure of the GP tree at all. However, it could be beneficial to dispense with substitution altogether; this would simplify some of the analysis and achieve the goal of making our mutation operator as "local" as possible for the given problem.

Locality is a property that depends on fitness landscape and operator. Here we see the interaction explicitly and reflect upon the influence of the fitness landscape, which itself depends upon the genotype to phenotype mapping. A substitution makes the same genotypic change because MAJORITY and ORDER share the same primitive set. But in MAJORITY, to a first order approximation, the amortized average change in fitness is larger than in ORDER because ORDER's expression mechanism places emphasis on only the front of the parsed leaf list whereas MAJORITY's depends on the entire set of leaves.

Both problems also reveal a fundamental asymmetry between deletions and insertions. Insertions select uniformly from the set of possible terminals, so each terminal is affected with the same probability, but deletions select uniformly from the set of leaves, so the probability of the operation changing a particular terminal depends on the concentration of that terminal in the tree. In the case of ORDER, this has ramifications for the evolution of the tree size over time, because insertions end up being less likely to decrease the fitness than deletions, so the tree grows over time. For MAJORITY, this phenomenon has a positive effect, rather than a negative one: if there are more occurrences of a negated variable than its corresponding positive variable, we will tend to remove those negations with higher probability, and simultaneously balance the relative concentration of each variable.

5.3 Informing GP Practice

This analysis also prompts one to revisit and review assumptions about the necessity of a population and a crossover operator in GP. It does not imply that they are unnecessary but it explicitly shows, at least, simple circumstances when they are not. This may advise GP practitioners to assure themselves empirically that a population and a crossover operator are needed (alone or together) when they start their algorithm development. These algorithms and operators are simple and easy to code, yielding a quick solution to the problem while at the same time supporting parallelism and featuring similar efficiency to conventional GP. Even though the problem at hand is not likely to have the simple problem structure observed here and even though it may require a more sophisticated operator, starting from a provably correct algorithm provides a platform for rationally exploring how to address the separate challenges presented by a harder problem or designing an operator specifically for the problem.

Additionally, this analysis contrasts with conventional GP design practice. Conventionally, GP design proceeds in a very practical manner, but one which is antithetical to theoretical algorithm designers. Rather than derive an algorithm that is provably correct and of efficient complexity, practitioners use biological inspiration, empirical insight and current GP theory. This current theory tries to provide transparent explanations of how GP bloats, how it constructs solutions from schema and how it navigates a fitness landscape with its operators and selection. The resulting heuristic can be expected to generate initial mixed results and require subsequent trial and error to "perfect" its use on the problem of interest. There exist some best practices and rules of thumb for robust algorithms but little useful guidance on algorithm customization (via, e.g. genetic operators) for this subsequent design phase. The process finally yields a heuristic which, though a randomized algorithm, is intractable to analyze post-hoc for correctness or efficiency. One can offer to a user its computational expense, which is the product of population size, generations, and number of runs, as well as some empirical estimate of the likelihood of finding a sufficiently optimal solution on a future problem instance. An open question is whether the algorithm design methodology taken in this contribution, that of algorithmic theoreticians, could be blended with or complement the method of practice. Our methodology yields a fundamentally different new form of theoretical result for GP: a randomized algorithm of established computational efficiency (which is different from computational expense), that is guaranteed to find a solution. However, our analysis is tractable only because the fitness structure of the model problems is simple, and the algorithms use only a simple hierarchical variable length mutation operator. It is an open question as to whether the first pass application of the simple algorithms and operators on a realistic problem might prove useful for insight or well founded design choices. Forums such as the annual Genetic Programming: From Theory to Practice workshop which encourage explicit interactions among theoreticians and practitioners may encourage the investigation of this question and provide a means of collecting the experiences.

5.4 Analysis Techniques

We also comment briefly on our analysis techniques. The analysis of ORDER used the method of fitness partitions [2], a very general method that has found many applications in the complexity analysis of EAs for binary representation. The method was successful because, in ORDER, we are always only one move away from expressing a particular variable. However, MAJORITY required different analysis techniques because, unlike in ORDER, there is not an easily computable probability of improving the fitness given only the fitness value; there is also a crucial dependence on the neutral moves we make. The coupon collector and random walk method considered optimizing all of the variables jointly, and in doing so achieved a bound on performance very close to the theoretical lower bound. This indicates that perhaps more complex fitness functions that are not separable might be admissible to similar styles of analysis.

6. CONCLUSION

We see three main directions for future work in the computational complexity analysis of genetic programming. Obviously the goal of bridging a gap from what exists to practice is daunting. However, modest steps forward may be revealing. The first extension is to increase the complexity of the genetic operators that are acting on these two problems. Our $1+1$ operators are essentially just stochastic hill climbers, and while understanding of such an optimization technique is valuable in and of itself, real-world GP implementations clearly involve more individuals. From GA theory, there is a precedent of taking $1 + 1$ analysis of a problem and extending it to $\mu + 1$ analysis, where μ is the size of the population (see e.g. [16]). This would admit tree-based crossover operators (if they can be shown to be necessary for an efficient optimization time).

The other extension is to consider harder problems. While ORDER and MAJORITY each capture a couple very simple properties of a program, both rely upon inspection and neither problem's fitness function takes into account the hierarchical nature of a GP tree, which is of crucial importance for all practical applications of GP. We could extend these problems in several ways to address the latter issue. One could keep the same terminal set and join nodes, but make the fitness function take subtrees into account somehow. Alternatively, one could introduce a new type of join operation and use the fitness function to impose a constraint that forces us to optimize the higher levels of the tree as well, perhaps by giving higher fitness to individuals when this "join prime" has regular joins as its children and vice versa. Either of these changes would increase the interest of the problem and make the results more relevant to the way that GP is used in practice. However, any new problem in this form may require new or modified mutation operators to be admissible to analysis. We could also try to extend the difficulty of MAJORITY by designing a new objective that requires the correct terminals (and no incorrect terminals) to be in the right order, in addition to being present. A model problem which abstracts the semantics of iteration might also provide insights, if tractable. Whether the currently used proof techniques–fitness partitioning, random walks and use of the coupon collector–are sufficient to address more challenging setups is an open question.

7. REFERENCES

[1] R. Aleliunas, R. M. Karp, R. J. Lipton, L. Lovász, and C. Rackoff. Random walks, universal traversal sequences, and the complexity of maze problems. In *FOCS*, pages 218–223. IEEE, 1979.

[2] S. Droste, T. Jansen, and I. Wegener. On the analysis of the (1+1) evolutionary algorithm. *Theor. Comput. Sci.*, 276:51–81, 2002.

[3] D. E. Goldberg and U.-M. O'Reilly. Where does the good stuff go, and why? how contextual semantics influence program structure in simple genetic programming. In W. Banzhaf, R. Poli, M. Schoenauer, and T. C. Fogarty, editors, *Proceedings of the First European Workshop on Genetic Programming*, volume 1391 of *LNCS*, pages 16–36, Paris, 14-15 Apr. 1998. Springer-Verlag.

[4] T. Jansen and I. Wegener. Evolutionary algorithms - how to cope with plateaus of constant fitness and when to reject strings of the same fitness. *IEEE Trans. Evolutionary Computation*, 5(6):589–599, 2001.

[5] J. R. Koza. *Genetic Programming: On the Programming of Computers by Means of Natural Selection*. MIT Press, Cambridge, MA, USA, 1992.

[6] J. R. Koza. *Genetic Programming II: Automatic Discovery of Reusable Programs*. MIT Press, Cambridge Massachusetts, May 1994.

[7] H. Mühlenbein. How genetic algorithms really work: mutation and hillclimbing. In *Proc. of PPSN '92*, pages 15–26. Elsevier, 1992.

[8] A. N. Myers and H. S. Wilf. Some new aspects of the coupon collector's problem. *SIAM J. Discret. Math.*, 17(1):1–17, 2004.

[9] F. Neumann and C. Witt. *Bioinspired Computation in Combinatorial Optimization – Algorithms and Their Computational Complexity.* Springer, 2010.

[10] U.-M. O'Reilly. *An Analysis of Genetic Programming.* PhD thesis, Carleton University, Ottawa-Carleton Institute for Computer Science, Ottawa, Ontario, Canada, 22 Sept. 1995.

[11] U.-M. O'Reilly and F. Oppacher. Program search with a hierarchical variable length representation: Genetic programming, simulated annealing and hill climbing. In Y. Davidor, H.-P. Schwefel, and R. Manner, editors, *Parallel Problem Solving from Nature – PPSN III,* number 866 in Lecture Notes in Computer Science, pages 397–406, Jerusalem, 9-14 Oct. 1994. Springer-Verlag.

[12] U.-M. O'Reilly and F. Oppacher. A comparative analysis of GP. In P. J. Angeline and K. E. Kinnear, Jr., editors, *Advances in Genetic Programming 2,* chapter 2, pages 23–44. MIT Press, Cambridge, MA, USA, 1996.

[13] R. Poli, L. Vanneschi, W. Langdon, and N. McPhee. Theoretical results in genetic programming: the next ten years? *Genetic Programming and Evolvable Machines,* 11:285–320, 2010. 10.1007/s10710-010-9110-5.

[14] M. Raab and A. Steger. Balls into bins - a simple and tight analysis. In *RANDOM '98: Proceedings of the Second International Workshop on Randomization and Approximation Techniques in Computer Science,* pages 159–170, London, UK, 1998. Springer-Verlag.

[15] G. Rudolph. *Convergence properties of evolutionary algorithms.* Hamburg: Kovaï£¡c, 1997.

[16] C. Witt. Runtime analysis of the (mu + 1) EA on simple pseudo-boolean functions. *Evolutionary Computation,* 14(1):65–86, 2006.

The Logarithmic Hypervolume Indicator

Tobias Friedrich
Max-Planck-Institut für Informatik
66123 Saarbrücken, Germany

Karl Bringmann
Universität des Saarlandes
66041 Saarbrücken, Germany

Thomas Voß
Institut für Neuroinformatik
Ruhr-Universität Bochum
44780 Bochum, Germany

Christian Igel
Department of Computer Science
University of Copenhagen
2100 Copenhagen Ø, Denmark

ABSTRACT

It was recently proven that sets of points maximizing the hypervolume indicator do *not* give a good multiplicative approximation of the Pareto front. We introduce a new "logarithmic hypervolume indicator" and prove that it achieves a close-to-optimal multiplicative approximation ratio. This is experimentally verified on several benchmark functions by comparing the approximation quality of the multi-objective covariance matrix evolution strategy (MO-CMA-ES) with the classic hypervolume indicator and the MO-CMA-ES with the logarithmic hypervolume indicator.

Categories and Subject Descriptors

F.2 [**Theory of Computation**]:
Analysis of Algorithms and Problem Complexity

General Terms

Measurement, Hypervolume Indicator

Keywords

Multiobjective Optimization, Theory,
Performance Measures, Selection

1. INTRODUCTION

Most real-world optimization problems have to deal with multiple objectives (like time vs. cost) and cannot be easily described by some scalar objective function. The quality of solutions to such multi-criteria optimization problems are measured by vector-valued objective functions. This implies that there is in general no unique optimal value, but a possibly very large set of incomparable optimal values, which form the Pareto front. The corresponding solutions constitute the Pareto set and have the defining property that they cannot be improved in some objective without getting worse in another one.

Many different multi-objective evolutionary algorithms (MOEAs) have been developed to find a Pareto set of (small) size n which gives a *good approximation* of the Pareto front. A popular way to measure the quality of a Pareto set is the hypervolume indicator (HYP), which measures the volume of the dominated space [23]. For small numbers of objectives, MOEAs directly using the hypervolume indicator to guide the search have become the methods of choice. These include for example the generational MO-CMA-ES [10, 20], the SMS-EMOA [3, 8], and variants of IBEA [22, 25]. Despite its popularity, up to recently there was not much rigorously known about the distribution of solution sets that maximize the hypervolume. Such solution sets have been described empirically as "well distributed" in [8, 13, 14]. In contrast to this it was observed that "convex regions may be preferred to concave regions" [17, 23] as well as that HYP is "biased towards the boundary solutions" [7]. For the number of points $n \to \infty$, it is also known that the density of points only depends on the gradient of the function describing the front [2].

At first sight, it is not obvious why maximizing the hypervolume indicator should yield a good approximation of the Pareto front. If we are, for example, interested in a good multiplicative approximation, an "ideal" indicator would directly measure the approximation quality of a solution set P by returning the smallest $\alpha \in \mathbb{R}^+$ such that each element of the Pareto front is dominated by some vector resulting from dividing an element in P by α (we consider minimization and assume positive objective function values). This corresponds to the binary multiplicative ε-indicator [16, 24] applied to the solution set and the (possibly infinite) Pareto front. Unfortunately, such an indicator cannot be used in practice because the Pareto front is usually unknown. This leads to the important question of how close the approximations achieved by realistic indicators such as the hypervolume indicator come to those that could be obtained by an "ideal" indicator. This can be measured by the approximation ratio of a solution set maximizing the hypervolume [4, 5, 9]. Formal definitions of the multiplicative approximation ratio and the alternative additive approximation ratio are given in Definitions 3.1 and 3.4, respectively.

The approximation quality achieved by the hypervolume indicator has been analyzed rigorously for bi-criterion maximization problems by Bringmann and Friedrich [4, 5]. They prove in [5] that for all possible Pareto fronts the multiplicative approximation factor achieved by a set of n solutions maximizing the hypervolume indicator is $1 + \Theta(1/n)$

(cf. Theorem 4.1)[1]. This is *asymptotically equivalent* to the optimal multiplicative approximation factor (cf. Corollary 3.2) [5]. Thus, one can conclude that the hypervolume indicator is guiding the search in the correct direction for sufficiently large n. However, the constant factors hidden by the Θ's are larger for the set maximizing hypervolume compared to the set with best possible approximation factor. Bringmann and Friedrich [4] studied the multiplicative approximation factor relative to the ratio A/a between the largest and smallest coordinate[2]. Using this notation, the precise result of [5] is the computation of the optimal multiplicative approximation ratio as $1 + \log(A/a)/n$ (cf. Corollary 3.2). In [4] it is further shown that the multiplicative approximation ratio for a set maximizing the hypervolume is strictly larger, namely of the order of at least $1 + \sqrt{A/a}/n$ (cf. Theorem 4.2). This implies that the multiplicative approximation ratio achieved by a set maximizing the hypervolume can be *exponentially worse* in the order of the ratio A/a. Hence for numerically very wide spread fronts there are Pareto sets which give a much better multiplicative approximation than Pareto sets which maximize the hypervolume.

These results about the multiplicative approximation ratio were surprisingly bad news for the hypervolume indicator. On the other hand, Bringmann and Friedrich [4] also examined the additive approximation ratio and observed that while the multiplicative approximation factor is determined by the ratio A/a, the additive approximation factor is determined by the width of the domain $A - a$. They proved that the optimal additive approximation ratio is $(A - a)/n$ (cf. Theorem 3.3) and upper bound the additive approximation ratio achieved by a set maximizing the hypervolume by $(A-a)/(n-2)$ (cf. Theorem 4.3). This is a very strong statement, because, apart from a small factor of $n/(n-2)$, the additive approximation ratio achieved when maximizing the hypervolume is optimal. This shows that the hypervolume indicator yields a much better additive than multiplicative approximation for maximization problems.

Our Results

An obvious next question is to verify whether the same results hold for minimization problems. The first part of this paper accordingly confirms this and presents the results of Bringmann and Friedrich [4, 5] in a minimization setting. In the main part, we address the open question whether there are natural indicators which provably achieve a good multiplicative approximation ratio. Since it is known that the hypervolume gives a very good additive approximation, we hypothesize that an indicator achieving a good multiplicative approximation can be constructed by taking the logarithm of all axes before computing the classic hypervolume. We call this new indicator the *logarithmic hypervolume indicator* and analyze its properties in this study. Note that in the setting of weighted hypervolume indicators [25] this corresponds to a reciprocal weight function (cf. Section 4.3). We prove that the logarithmic hypervolume indicator achieves a multiplicative approximation ratio of less than $1 + \log(A/a)/(n-2)$ (cf. Corollary 4.6), which is again optimal apart from the factor $n/(n-2)$.

---

[1]The precise statements of this and the following results is slightly more technical. For details see the respective theorems.

[2]The approximation ratio depends on the ratios in both dimensions. To simplify the presentation in the introduction, we assume that the ratio A/a in the first dimension is equal to the ratio B/b in the second dimension.

These theoretical results indicate that one should get a much better multiplicative approximation of the Pareto-front if one uses the logarithmic instead of the classic hypervolume indicator as a subroutine of an indicator-based evolutionary algorithm. However, the results do not directly apply to solutions returned by such an algorithm: First, these algorithms might fail to return a solution maximizing the (logarithmic) hypervolume indicator, because they did not run long enough or got stuck in a local optimum. Second, in the theoretical part we measure the approximation quality in the worst-case over all possible fronts, which gives only upper, but no lower bounds for "typical" fronts. And third, the factor $n/(n-2)$ the logarithmic hypervolume is worse in the worst-case, goes to 1 for large n, but the number of non-dominated solutions n can be very small in a solution returned by an evolutionary algorithm. To examine whether the logarithmic hypervolume indicator yields indeed a better multiplicative approximation than the classic hypervolume indicator for a typical indicator-based evolutionary algorithm, we compare the $(\mu+1)$-MO-CMA-ES with the classic hypervolume indicator and the $(\mu+1)$-MO-CMA-ES with the logarithmic hypervolume indicator. This study is performed on the DTLZ benchmark functions [6]. We observe that the results for the theoretical worst-case bounds match well with the empirically measured approximation ratios for these benchmark functions. On all benchmark functions, the approximation achieved by the logarithmic hypervolume indicator compared to the classic hypervolume indicator is better by up to 31% (cf. Table 1). This implies that for multiplicative problems the logarithmic hypervolume indicator should be preferred over the classic hypervolume indicator.

The remainder of this paper is structured as follows. In Section 2 we define the used notation. The following two Sections 3.1 and 3.2 define the concepts of multiplicative and additive approximation ratios. Section 4 introduces the weighted, normal and logarithmic hypervolume indicator. The following Section 4.4 proves the bounds on the multiplicative approximation ratio of the logarithmic hypervolume indicator. Finally, Section 5 presents our experimental framework and results.

2. PRELIMINARIES

All three previous papers on the approximation ratio of the hypervolume indicator [4, 5, 9] only consider maximization problems. As benchmark functions such as DTLZ [6] usually consider minimization problems, the first part of this paper (till Section 3.2) deals with translating the results of Bringmann and Friedrich [4, 5] for the approximation ratios of maximization problems to minimization problems. This is straight-forward for the definitions, but not obvious for all of the theorems. All results still hold analogously if the handling of the boundary solutions is adapted. As these changes are easy to verify, all proofs of theorems which are translated from the maximization setting of [4, 5] are omitted.

As in [4, 5], we consider the case of two objectives where there is a mapping from an arbitrary search space to an objective space which is a subset of $\mathbb{R}^2$. Throughout this paper, we will only work on the objective space. For points from the objective space we define the following dominance relation:

$$(x_1, y_1) \preceq (x_2, y_2) \text{ iff } x_1 \leqslant x_2 \text{ and } y_1 \leqslant y_2,$$
$$(x_1, y_1) \prec (x_2, y_2) \text{ iff } (x_1, y_1) \preceq (x_2, y_2) \text{ and }$$
$$(x_1, y_1) \neq (x_2, y_2).$$

We restrict ourselves to Pareto fronts that can be written as $\{(x, f(x)) \mid x \in [a, A]\}$ where $f \colon [a, A] \to [b, B]$ is a (not necessarily strictly) monotonically decreasing, lower semi-continuous[3] function with $f(a) = B$, $f(A) = b$ for some $a < A$, $b < B$ with $a, A, b, B \in \mathbb{R}$. We write $\mathcal{F} = \mathcal{F}_{[a,A] \to [b,B]}$ for the set of all such functions f. We will use the term *front* for both, the set of points $\{(x, f(x)) \mid x \in [a, A]\}$, and the function f.

The condition of f being lower semi-continuous cannot be relaxed further as without it the front lacks a certain symmetry in the two objectives: This condition is necessary and sufficient for the existence of the inverse function $f^{-1} \colon [b, B] \to [a, A]$ defined by setting $f^{-1}(y) := \min\{x \in [a, A] \mid f(x) \leqslant y\}$. Without lower semi-continuity this minimum does not necessarily exist. Furthermore, this condition implies that there is a set maximizing the hypervolume indicator.

Note that the set $\mathcal{F}$ of fronts we consider is a very general one. Many papers that theoretically examine the hypervolume indicator assume that the front is continuous and differentiable (e.g. [1, 2, 9]), and are thus not able to give results about discrete fronts. Let $n \in \mathbb{N}$. For fixed $[a, A], [b, B] \subset \mathbb{R}$ we call a set $P = \{p_1, \ldots, p_n\} \subset [a, A] \times [b, B]$ a *solution set* (of size n) and write $\mathcal{P} = \mathcal{P}_n$ for the set of all such solution sets. A solution set P is said to be *feasible* for a front $f \in \mathcal{F}$, if $y \geqslant f(x)$ for all $p = (x, y) \in P$. We write $\mathcal{P}^f \subseteq \mathcal{P}$ for the set of all solution sets that are feasible for f.

A common approach to measure the quality of a solution set is to use unary indicator functions [26]. They assign to each solution set a real number that somehow reflects its quality, i.e., we have a function $\mathrm{ind} \colon \bigcup_{n=1}^{\infty} \mathcal{P}_n \to \mathbb{R}$. As throughout the paper $n \in \mathbb{N}$ is fixed, it is sufficient to define an indicator $\mathrm{ind} \colon \mathcal{P}_n \to \mathbb{R}$. Note that as we are only working on the objective space, we here slightly deviate from the usual definition of an indicator function where the domain is the search space, not the objective space.

A final remark regarding our notation: We will mark every variable with a $+$ or $*$ depending on whether it belongs to the additive or multiplicative approximation.

3. APPROXIMATING THE PARETO FRONT

When attempting to minimize an indicator function, we actually try to find a solution set $P \in \mathcal{P}$ that constitutes a good approximation of the front f. In the following, we introduce notions of multiplicative and additive approximtion quality.

3.1 Multiplicative Approximation

According to the custom of approximation algorithms, we measure the quality of a solution by its multiplicative approximation ratio. This can be transferred to the world of

multi-objective optimization. For this we use the following definition of Papadimitriou and Yannakakis [18], which was also used in [4, 5, 9, 15, 16]. Note that it is crucial to require $a, b > 0$ here, as it is unclear what multiplicatively approximating a negative number should mean. We will always assume this when talking about multiplicative approximation throughout the paper.

DEFINITION 3.1. *Let $f \in \mathcal{F}$ and $P \in \mathcal{P}^f$. The solution set P is a* multiplicative α-approximation *of f if for each $\hat{x} \in [a, A]$ there is a $p = (x, y) \in P$ with*

$$\hat{x} \geqslant x/\alpha \quad \text{and} \quad f(\hat{x}) \geqslant y/\alpha$$

where $\alpha \in \mathbb{R}$, $\alpha \geqslant 1$. The multiplicative approximation ratio of P with respect to f is defined as

$$\alpha^*(f, P) := \inf\{\alpha \in \mathbb{R} \mid P \text{ is a mult. } \alpha\text{-approximation of } f\}.$$

The quality of an algorithm which calculates a solution set of size n for each Pareto front in $\mathcal{F}$ has to be compared with the respective optimal approximation ratio defined as follows.

DEFINITION 3.2. *For fixed $[a, A]$, $[b, B]$, and n, let*

$$\alpha^*_{OPT} := \sup_{f \in \mathcal{F}} \inf_{P \in \mathcal{P}^f} \alpha^*(f, P).$$

The value α^*_{OPT} is chosen such that every front in $\mathcal{F}$ can be approximated by n points to a ratio of α^*_{OPT}, and there is a front which cannot be approximated better. In [5] the following results was shown.

THEOREM 3.1. $\alpha^*_{OPT} = \min\{A/a, B/b\}^{1/n}$.

As shown in [5], this implies the following corollary.

COROLLARY 3.2. *For all $n \geqslant \log(\min\{A/a, B/b\})/\varepsilon$ and $\varepsilon \in (0, 1)$,*

$$\alpha^*_{OPT} \geqslant 1 + \frac{\log(\min\{A/a, B/b\})}{n},$$
$$\alpha^*_{OPT} \leqslant 1 + (1 + \varepsilon) \frac{\log(\min\{A/a, B/b\})}{n}.$$

We further want to measure the approximation of the solution set of size n maximizing an indicator ind. As there might be several solution sets maximizing ind, we consider the worst case and use the following definition.

DEFINITION 3.3. *For a unary indicator* ind *and fixed $[a, A]$, $[b, B], n$, and $f \in \mathcal{F}$ let*

$$\mathcal{P}^f_{\mathrm{ind}} := \left\{ P \in \mathcal{P}^f \mid \mathrm{ind}(P) = \max_{Q \in \mathcal{P}^f} \mathrm{ind}(Q) \right\} \text{ and}$$
$$\alpha^*_{\mathrm{ind}} := \sup_{f \in \mathcal{F}} \sup_{P \in \mathcal{P}^f_{\mathrm{ind}}} \alpha^*(f, P).$$

The set $\mathcal{P}^f_{\mathrm{ind}}$ is the set of all feasible solution sets that maximize ind on f. The value α^*_{ind} is chosen such that for every front f in $\mathcal{F}$ every solution set maximizing ind approximates f by a ratio of at most α^*_{ind}.

3.2 Additive Approximation

Depending on the problem at hand, one can also consider an additive approximation ratio. Analogous to Definition 3.1 we use the following definition.

---

[3] Semi-continuity is a weaker property than normal continuity. A function f is said to be lower semi-continuous if for all points x of its domain, $\liminf_{y \to x} f(y) \geqslant f(x)$. Intuitively speaking this means that for all points x the function values for arguments near x are either close to $f(x)$ or greater than $f(x)$. For more details see e.g. Rudin [19].

DEFINITION 3.4. *Let $f \in \mathcal{F}$ and $P \in \mathcal{P}^f$. The solution set P is an* additive α-approximation *of f if for each $\hat{x} \in [a, A]$ there is a $p = (x, y) \in P$ with*

$$\hat{x} \geqslant x - \alpha \quad \text{and} \quad f(\hat{x}) \geqslant y - \alpha$$

where $\alpha \in \mathbb{R}$, $\alpha \geqslant 0$. The additive approximation ratio of P with respect to f is defined as

$$\alpha^+(f, P) := \inf\{\alpha \in \mathbb{R} \mid P \text{ is an add. } \alpha\text{-approximation of } f\}.$$

Again, we are interested in the optimal approximation ratio for Pareto fronts in $\mathcal{F}$. Analogous to Definition 3.2 we use the following definition.

DEFINITION 3.5. *For fixed $[a, A]$, $[b, B]$, and n, let*

$$\alpha^+_{OPT} := \sup_{f \in \mathcal{F}} \inf_{P \in \mathcal{P}^f} \alpha^+(f, P).$$

Bringmann and Friedrich [4] showed the following result which identifies α^+_{OPT} equivalently to Theorem 3.1 for α^*_{OPT}. It will be reproven in Section 4.4 to illustrate the relationship between additive and multiplicative approximation ratios.

THEOREM 3.3. $\alpha^+_{OPT} = \min\{A - a, B - b\}/n$.

Moreover, the analog for α^*_{ind} is defined similarly to Definition 3.3.

DEFINITION 3.6. *For a unary indicator* ind *and fixed $[a, A]$, $[b, B]$, n, and $f \in \mathcal{F}$ let*

$$\alpha^+_{\text{ind}} := \sup_{f \in \mathcal{F}} \sup_{P \in \mathcal{P}^f_{\text{ind}}} \alpha^+(f, P).$$

4. HYPERVOLUME INDICATORS

In this section we come to concrete indicators for which upper bounds for α^*_{ind} or α^+_{ind} are known. First, we recap the general framework of the weighted hypervolume indicator. Then we review the results for the classic hypervolume indicator. After that, a new indicator designed for multiplicative approximation—the logarithmic hypervolume indicator—is proposed. We then show how to carry over additive approximation results to multiplicative approximation. Further, we discuss the combination of classic and logarithmic indicator.

4.1 The Weighted Hypervolume

The classic definition of the hypervolume indicator is the volume of the dominated portion of the objective space relative to a fixed footpoint called the reference point $R = (R_x, R_y) \succeq (A, B)$. As a general framework for our two indicators we use the more general weighted hypervolume indicator of [25]. It weights points with a weight distribution $w \colon \mathbb{R}^2 \to \mathbb{R}$. The *hypervolume* $\text{HYP}_w(P, R)$ (or $\text{HYP}_w(P)$ for short) of a solution set $P \in \mathcal{P}$ is then defined as

$$\text{HYP}_w(P) := \text{HYP}_w(P, R) := \iint_{\mathbb{R}^2} A(x, y)\, w(x, y)\, dy\, dx$$

where the attainment function $A \colon \mathbb{R}^2 \to \mathbb{R}$ is an indicator function on the objective space which describes the space below the reference point which weakly dominates P. Formally, $A(x, y) = 1$ if $(R_x, R_y) \succeq (x, y)$ and there is a $p = (p_x, p_y) \in P$ such that $(x, y) \succeq (p_x, p_y)$, and $A(x, y) = 0$ otherwise.

The original purpose of the weighted hypervolume indicator was to allow the decision maker to stress certain regions of the objective space. In this paper we unleash one of its hidden powers by showing that one gets a better multiplicative approximation choosing the right weight distribution.

4.2 The Classic Hypervolume

If w is the all-ones functions $\mathbb{1}$ with $\mathbb{1}(x, y) = 1$ for all $x, y \in \mathbb{R}$, above definition matches to the classic definition of the hypervolume indicator. In this case we write $\text{HYP} = \text{HYP}_{\mathbb{1}}$ for short. Bounds for this indicator are of particular interest. Bringmann and Friedrich [5] examined α^*_{HYP} and showed the following upper bound that has the same asymptotic behavior as α^*_{OPT}, but a much larger constant factor

THEOREM 4.1. *Let $f \in \mathcal{F}$ and $n > 4$. If we have*

- $R_x \geqslant A + \frac{1}{n-2} \min\{\sqrt{Aa}\, B/b, A\sqrt{B/b}\}$ *and*

- $R_y \geqslant B + \frac{1}{n-2} \min\{\sqrt{Bb}\, A/a, B\sqrt{A/a}\}$

for the reference point $R = (R_x, R_y)$, then

$$\alpha^*_{HYP} \leqslant 1 + \frac{\sqrt{A/a} + \sqrt{B/b}}{n - 4}.$$

This shows that for sufficiently large n the hypervolume yields a good multiplicative approximation. However, this does not hold for small n as shown by the following lower bound of [5] for the case $A/a = B/b$.

THEOREM 4.2. *Let $n \geqslant 7$ and $\frac{A}{a} = \frac{B}{b} \geqslant 13$. Then*

$$\alpha^*_{HYP} \geqslant 1 + \frac{2\sqrt{A/a - 1}}{3(n + 1)}.$$

Hence the multiplicative approximation ratio of HYP is exponentially worse in the ratio A/a. On the other hand, the following theorem of [4] shows that HYP has a close to optimal additive approximation ratio.

THEOREM 4.3. *If $n > 2$ and*

$$(n - 2) \min\{R_x - A, R_y - B\} \geqslant \sqrt{(A - a)(B - b)}$$

we have

$$\alpha^+_{HYP} \leqslant \frac{\sqrt{(A - a)(B - b)}}{n - 2}.$$

Note that the precondition is fulfilled if n is large enough *or* if the reference point is sufficiently far away from (a, b). Compared to Theorem 3.3 it means that for $A - a \approx B - b$ and moderately sized n, α^+_{HYP} is very close to α^+_{OPT}. For $A - a \ll B - b$ (or the other way around) the constant is the geometric mean of $A - a$ and $B - b$ instead of the minimum of both.

4.3 The Logarithmic Hypervolume

Up to now we have mainly reviewed the results for the approximation ratios of the hypervolume indicator for maximization problems and have confirmed that the classic hypervolume indicator yields a good additive approximation also in the minimization setting. For getting a good multiplicative approximation HYP turned out to be inapplicable. We propose the *logarithmic hypervolume indicator* to address this problem. For a solution set $P \in \mathcal{P}$ and reference point $R = (R_x, R_y)$ with $(R_x, R_y) \succeq (A, B)$ we define

$$\text{LOGHYP}(P, R) := \text{HYP}_{\mathbb{1}}(\log P, \log R),$$

where $\log P := \{(\log x, \log y) \mid (x, y) \in P\}$ and $\log R := (\log R_x, \log R_y)$. Here, as in the classic case, the reference point is a parameter to be chosen by the user. Note, that we do not really change the axes of the problem to logarithmic scale: We only change the calculation of the hypervolume, not the problem itself.

Above definition is nice in that it allows to compute LOGHYP using existent implementations of algorithms for HYP, only wiring the input differently.

It is very illustrative, though, to observe that the logarithmic hypervolume indicator fits very well in the weighted hypervolume framework: An equivalent definition of LOGHYP is

$$\mathrm{LOGHYP}(P, R) := \mathrm{HYP}_{\hat{w}}(P, R),$$

where $\hat{w}(x, y) = 1/(xy)$ is the appropriate weight distribution.

LEMMA 4.4. $\mathrm{HYP}_1(\log P, \log R) = \mathrm{HYP}_{\hat{w}}(P, R)$.

Proof. Let $\{(x_1, y_1), \ldots, (x_k, y_k)\} \subseteq P$ be the set points in P not dominated by any other point in P with $x_1 < \ldots < x_k, y_1 > \ldots > y_k$. With $x_{k+1} := R_x$ we can then compute HYP as

$$\mathrm{HYP}_1(\log P, \log R) = \sum_{i=1}^{k} \int_{\log x_i}^{\log x_{i+1}} \int_{\log y_i}^{\log R_y} 1 \, dy \, dx$$

$$= \sum_{i=1}^{k} \int_{x_i}^{x_{i+1}} \int_{y_i}^{R_y} \frac{1}{xy} \, dy \, dx$$

$$= \mathrm{HYP}_{\hat{w}}(P, R). \qquad \square$$

The first main result of this paper is now that the logarithmic hypervolume indicator yields a good multiplicative approximation, just like the classic hypervolume indicator yields a good additive approximation. The following result will be shown in Section 4.4.

THEOREM 4.5. *If $n > 2$ and*

$$(n-2) \log \min\{R_x/A, R_y/B\} \geqslant \sqrt{\log(A/a) \log(B/b)}$$

we have

$$\alpha^*_{logHYP} \leqslant \exp\left(\frac{\sqrt{\log(A/a) \log(B/b)}}{n-2} \right).$$

Note that the precondition is fulfilled if n is large enough *or* we choose the reference point far enough away from (A, B).

This is a very good upper bound compared to $\alpha^*_{OPT} = \exp(\min\{\log(A/a), \log(B/b)\}/n)$. Also compare the next corollary to Corollary 3.2. Its proof is analogous to the one of Corollary 3.2 in [5].

COROLLARY 4.6. *For $\varepsilon \in (0, 1)$ and all*

$$n \geqslant 2 + \sqrt{\log(A/a) \log(B/b)} / \min\{\varepsilon, \log(R_x/A), \log(R_y/B)\}$$

we have

$$\alpha^*_{logHYP} \leqslant 1 + (1 + \varepsilon) \frac{\sqrt{\log(A/a) \log(B/b)}}{n-2}.$$

Hence we get a much better constant factor than in the bound of α^*_{HYP}.

4.4 Relationship Between Additive and Multiplicative Approximation

Now we describe a relationship that allows to transfer results on multiplicative approximation into results on additive approximation and the other way around. This proves Theorems 3.3 and 4.5 and gives the intuition behind the logarithmic hypervolume indicator, as it is the classic hypervolume indicator transferred into the world of multiplicative approximation.

Consider a front $f^* \in \mathcal{F}_{[a^*, A^*] \to [b^*, B^*]}$ and a solution set $P^* \in \mathcal{P}^{f^*}$ that is a multiplicative α^*-approximation of f^*. This means that we have for any $\hat{x}^* \in [a^*, A^*]$ a point $(x^*, y^*) \in P^*$ with

$$\hat{x}^* \geqslant x^*/\alpha^* \quad \text{and} \quad f^*(\hat{x}^*) \geqslant y^*/\alpha^*.$$

Logarithmizing both inequalities gives

$$\log \hat{x}^* \geqslant \log x^* - \log \alpha^* \quad \text{and} \quad \log f^*(\hat{x}^*) \geqslant \log y^* - \log \alpha^*.$$

This corresponds to an additive approximation. We set $x^+ := \log x^*$, $y^+ := \log y^*$, $\hat{x}^+ := \log \hat{x}^*$, $\alpha^+ := \log \alpha^*$ and $f^+ := \log \circ f^* \circ \exp$ and get

$$\hat{x}^+ \geqslant x^+ - \alpha^+ \quad \text{and} \quad f^+(\hat{x}^+) \geqslant y^+ - \alpha^+.$$

This means that $P^+ := \{(\log x, \log y) \mid (x, y) \in P^*\}$ is an additive α^+-approximation of the front $f^+ \in \mathcal{F}_{[a^+, A^+] \to [b^+, B^+]}$ with $a^+ = \log a^*$, $A^+ = \log A^*$, $b^+ = \log b^*$, $B^+ = \log B^*$. Observe that this corresponds to logarithmizing both axes.

All operations we used above are invertible, so that we can do the same thing the other way round: Having a solution set P^+ on a front f^+ achieving an additive α^+-approximation, we get a solution set $P^* = \{(\exp x, \exp y) \mid (x, y) \in P^+\}$ on a front $f^* = \exp \circ f^+ \circ \log$ achieving a multiplicative α^*-approximation, with $\alpha^* = \exp \alpha^+$. Thereby the interval bounds like a^+ are also exponentiated and we get $a^* = \exp a^+$.

Let $\mathcal{F}^* := \mathcal{F}_{[a^*, A^*] \to [b^*, B^*]}$ and $\mathcal{F}^+ := \mathcal{F}_{[a^+, A^+] \to [b^+, B^+]}$. Then we have a bijection $\mathcal{F}^* \to \mathcal{F}^+$, $f^* \mapsto f^+$ and for any $f^* \in \mathcal{F}^*$ a bijection $\mathcal{P}^{f^*} \to \mathcal{P}^{f^+}$, $P^* \mapsto P^+$ that satisfies $\alpha^+(f^+, P^+) = \log \alpha^*(f^*, P^*)$. Though Theorem 3.3 was already proven in [4] (for maximization problems), it is interesting to reprove it to illustrate above technique as follows.

Proof of Theorem 3.3. We want to prove $\alpha^+_{OPT} = \min\{A^+ - a^+, B^+ - b^+\}/n$. By definition and the above bijection (*) we know that

$$\alpha^+_{OPT} = \sup_{f^+ \in \mathcal{F}^+} \inf_{P^+ \in \mathcal{P}^{f^+}} \alpha^+(f^+, P^+)$$

$$\overset{(*)}{=} \sup_{f^+ \in \mathcal{F}^+} \inf_{P^+ \in \mathcal{P}^{f^+}} \log \alpha^*(f^*, P^*)$$

$$\overset{(*)}{=} \sup_{f^* \in \mathcal{F}^*} \inf_{P^* \in \mathcal{P}^{f^*}} \log \alpha^*(f^*, P^*)$$

$$= \log \sup_{f^* \in \mathcal{F}^*} \inf_{P^* \in \mathcal{P}^{f^*}} \alpha^*(f^*, P^*).$$

The last expression matches the definition of α^*_{OPT}. We replace α^*_{OPT} using Theorem 3.1 and a^* by $\exp a^+$ etc. and get

$$\alpha_{OPT}^+ = \log \alpha_{OPT}^*$$
$$= \log\left(\min\{A^*/a^*, B^*/b^*\}^{1/n}\right)$$
$$= \min\{\log A^* - \log a^*, \log B^* - \log b^*\}/n$$
$$= \min\{A^+ - a^+, B^+ - b^+\}/n. \qquad \square$$

With similar reasoning we can now also prove Theorem 4.5.

Proof of Theorem 4.5. We want to show that

$$\alpha_{logHYP}^* \leqslant \exp\left(\frac{\sqrt{\log(A^*/a^*)\log(B^*/b^*)}}{n-2}\right).$$

For a solution set $P^* \in \mathcal{P}^*$ and a reference point $R^* = (R_x^*, R_y^*)$ we defined LOGHYP by setting $\text{LOGHYP}(P^*, R^*) = \text{HYP}_1(\log P^*, \log R^*)$ with $\log P^* = \{(\log x, \log y) \mid (x, y) \in P^*\}$ and $\log R^* = (\log R_x^*, \log R_y^*)$. This $\log P^*$ is exactly P^+ as defined above. Writing $R^+ := \log R^*$ we thus have $\text{LOGHYP}(P^*, R^*) = \text{HYP}(P^+, R^+)$. Now, consider a solution set P^* maximizing $\text{LOGHYP}(P^*, R^*)$, thus, also maximizing $\text{HYP}(P^+, R^+)$. We know that P^+ is an α_{HYP}^+-approximation of the front f^+, so using Theorem 4.3 and above bijections we get

$$\alpha^*(f^*, P^*) = \exp \alpha^+(f^+, P^+)$$
$$\leqslant \exp\left(\sqrt{(A^+ - a^+)(B^+ - b^+)}/(n-2)\right)$$
$$= \exp\left(\sqrt{\log(A^*/a^*)\log(B^*/b^*)}/(n-2)\right).$$

The observation that the precondition of Theorem 4.3 transforms directly into the precondition of Theorem 4.5 concludes the proof. $\qquad \square$

Note that we could also have proceeded the other way round: Proving a bound for α_{logHYP}^* and transforming it into a result for α_{HYP}^+. Above proof also makes clear why we defined LOGHYP as it is: Maximizing $\text{HYP}(P^+, R^+)$ gives a very good additive approximation which transforms into a very good multiplicative approximation going back to P^*.

4.5 A Hybrid Indicator

The results of Bringmann and Friedrich [4, 5] imply that guiding the search with the hypervolume indicator is an appropriate choice if we want an additive approximation. On the other hand, guiding the search with the proposed logarithmic hypervolume indicator is preferable if we want a multiplicative approximation.

Of course, it may happen that one wants an additive approximation of some objectives and a multiplicative of others. We propose a simple rule of thumb for this case: Logarithmize all objectives of the second type, i.e., that should get multiplicatively approximated (and leave the objectives of the first type as they are) and then compute the hypervolume indicator. This hybrid indicator should work as intended, i.e., maximizing it should give a good additive approximation of the objectives of the first type and a good multiplicative approximation of the objectives of the second type.

For details, assume we have two objectives, x and y, and want to approximate x additively and y multiplicatively. Then we use the hybrid indicator $\text{ind}(P, R) := \text{HYP}(P', (R_x, \log R_y))$, where $P' = \{(x_i, \log y_i) \mid (x_i, y_i) \in$

$P\}$ and R is again a reference point. This indicator logarithmizes the y-axis and applies HYP afterwards. Along the lines of the proofs in this paper one can show that maximizing ind on a front f yields a solution set P with the following property: For any $\hat{x} \in [a, A]$ there is a $p = (x, y) \in P$ with

$$\hat{x} \geqslant x - \alpha^+ \quad \text{and} \quad f(\hat{x}) \geqslant y/\alpha^*,$$

where $\alpha^* = \exp \alpha^+$ and $\alpha^+ \leqslant \frac{\sqrt{(A-a)(\log(B) - \log(b))}}{n-2}$. This means that we get an additive approximation of x and a multiplicative approximation of y, as desired.

5. EXPERIMENTS

Above theoretical results indicate that for getting good multiplicative approximations one should maximize LOGHYP instead of HYP. This section substantiates this claim experimentally by taking a particular indicator-based selection scheme and running it with the indicator LOGHYP instead of HYP on typical test problems.

5.1 Experimental Setup

For the empirical evaluation, we implemented both the classic as well as the logarithmic hypervolume indicator in the indicator-based selection strategy of the $(\mu + 1)$-MO-CMA-ES (see [11, 21]) using the Shark software library [12]. We evaluate both algorithms on a set of benchmark functions taken from the literature, namely DTLZ1-7 (see [6]). Note that for all considered fitness functions, we lower bound the individual objectives to 10^{-6} as otherwise any multiplicative approximation ratio would be ∞ (if the solution set does not include exactly the leftmost point of the front). For each algorithm and each fitness function, we conducted 25 independent trials with 50,000 fitness function evaluations each. The parent population size μ has been chosen as 50. For both variants of the $(\mu + 1)$-MO-CMA-ES, we rely on the parameter setup presented in [21].

We evaluated the final fronts obtained by both variants of the $(\mu + 1)$-MO-CMA-ES with respect to the absolute hypervolume indicator and with respect to the multiplicative approximation ratio. In the latter case, we rely on a logarithmic sample of 10000 points of the true Pareto-optimal front as reference. For the statistical testing procedure, we refer again to [21].

5.2 Results

The results of the performance evaluation are presented in Figures 1, 2, and 3 and Table 1. For all fitness functions the $(\mu+1)$-MO-CMA-ES with the logarithmic hypervolume indicator outperformed its counterpart maximizing the original hypervolume indicator regarding the multiplicative approximation ratio (at a significance level of $p < 0.001$). For the functions DTLZ2, DTLZ4, DTLZ5, DTLZ6, and DTLZ7, both variants find solution sets very close to the optimal approximation ratio 1. However, the solutions found by guiding the search with the logarithmic hypervolume indicator still give a slightly better multiplicative approximation ratio. On DTLZ1 and DTLZ3, both variants are far from the optimal approximation ratio 1. Here the logarithmic hypervolume indicator has the largest improvement of more than 17% and 31%, respectively (cf. Table 1). Additionally, we also examined how both algorithms perform with respect to the classic hypervolume indicator. As expected, guiding the $(\mu + 1)$-MO-CMA-ES with the classic hypervolume indica-

Empirical multiplicative approximation ratio for		
$(\mu + 1)$-**MO-CMA-ES** **with HYP**	$(\mu + 1)$-**MO-CMA-ES** **with logHYP**	
DTLZ1 3.1581	**2.6864**	17.56% smaller
DTLZ2 1.0285	**1.0245**	0.4% smaller
DTLZ3 3.0734	**2.3398**	31.35% smaller
DTLZ4 1.0618	**1.0461**	1.51% smaller
DTLZ5 1.0285	**1.0245**	0.039% smaller
DTLZ6 1.0120	**1.0117**	0.029% smaller
DTLZ7 1.0133	**1.0131**	0.019% smaller

Table 1: Experimental results for the $(\mu+1)$-MO-CMA-ES with the classic and the logarithmic hypervolume indicator. Best values in each row are marked in bold if they are statistically significant at a significance level of $p < 0.001$.

Theoretical worst-case bound for multiplicative approximation ratio		
OPT	$1 + \dfrac{\log(\min\{A/a, B/b\})}{n}$	(cf. Corollary 3.2)
HYP	$1 + \dfrac{\sqrt{A/a} + \sqrt{B/b}}{n - 4}$	(cf. Theorem 4.1)
logHYP	$1 + \dfrac{\sqrt{\log(A/a)\,\log(B/b)}}{n - 2}$	(cf. Corollary 4.6)

Table 2: Theoretical results for the optimal approximation ratio and upper bounds for the approximation ratios of HYP and LOGHYP. See the cited theorems for the precise statements. The results for OPT and HYP are proven in [4, 5]. The result for LOGHYP is shown in Section 4.4 of this paper.

tor gives a larger (classic) hypervolume for DTLZ1, DTLZ2, DTLZ5, and DTLZ6 (see Figures 1, 2, and 3). In case of DTLZ4, both variants are on par w.r.t. the classic hypervolume. Surprisingly, this is not the case for DTLZ3 and DTLZ7. For these two fitness functions, the variant with the logarithmic hypervolume indicator achieves a large classic hypervolume after 50,000 fitness function evaluations. We expect that this results from the limited number of fitness function evaluations and that also for DTLZ3 and DTLZ7 the classic hypervolume indicator achieves a larger classic hypervolume for a larger number of fitness function evaluations.

On the set of DTLZ fitness functions our empirical evaluation matches with the theoretical results obtained beforehand. They further suggest to rely on the logarithmic hypervolume indicator if an optimal multiplicative approximation ratio is desired.

6. CONCLUSION

After it was shown in [4, 5] that the classic hypervolume indicator does not give an optimal multiplicative approximation factor, it was natural to ask what other indicator might have this desirable property. We defined a new indicator LOGHYP and proved that it yields a close-to-optimal multiplicative approximation ratio. This was confirmed empirically on a set of typical benchmark functions.

References

[1] A. Auger, J. Bader, D. Brockhoff, and E. Zitzler. Investigating and exploiting the bias of the weighted hypervolume to articulate user preferences. In *Proc. 11th annual Conference on Genetic and Evolutionary Computation (GECCO '09)*, pp. 563–570. ACM Press, 2009.

[2] A. Auger, J. Bader, D. Brockhoff, and E. Zitzler. Theory of the hypervolume indicator: optimal μ-distributions and the choice of the reference point. In *Proc. 10th International Workshop on Foundations of Genetic Algorithms (FOGA '09)*, pp. 87–102. ACM Press, 2009.

[3] N. Beume, B. Naujoks, and M. T. M. Emmerich. SMS-EMOA: Multiobjective selection based on dominated hypervolume. *European Journal of Operational Research*, 181:1653–1669, 2007.

[4] K. Bringmann and T. Friedrich. Tight bounds for the approximation ratio of the hypervolume indicator. In *Proc. 11th International Conference Parallel Problem Solving from Nature (PPSN XI)*, Vol. 6238 of *LNCS*, pp. 607–616. Springer, 2010.

[5] K. Bringmann and T. Friedrich. The maximum hypervolume set yields near-optimal approximation. In *Proc. 12th annual Conference on Genetic and Evolutionary*

Computation (GECCO '10), pp. 511–518. ACM Press, 2010.

[6] K. Deb, L. Thiele, M. Laumanns, and E. Zitzler. Scalable multi-objective optimization test problems. In *Proc. Congress on Evolutionary Computation (CEC '02)*, pp. 825–830. IEEE Press, 2002.

[7] K. Deb, M. Mohan, and S. Mishra. Evaluating the ε-domination based multi-objective evolutionary algorithm for a quick computation of Pareto-optimal solutions. *Evolutionary Computation*, 13:501–525, 2005.

[8] M. T. M. Emmerich, N. Beume, and B. Naujoks. An EMO algorithm using the hypervolume measure as selection criterion. In *Proc. Third International Conference on Evolutionary Multi-Criterion Optimization (EMO '05)*, pp. 62–76. Springer, 2005.

[9] T. Friedrich, C. Horoba, and F. Neumann. Multiplicative approximations and the hypervolume indicator. In *Proc. 11th annual Conference on Genetic and Evolutionary Computation (GECCO '09)*, pp. 571–578. ACM Press, 2009.

[10] C. Igel, N. Hansen, and S. Roth. Covariance matrix adaptation for multi-objective optimization. *Evolutionary Computation*, 15:1–28, 2007.

[11] C. Igel, T. Suttorp, and N. Hansen. Steady-state selection and efficient covariance matrix update in the multi-objective CMA-ES. In *Proc. 4th International Conference on Evolutionary Multi-Criterion Optimization (EMO '07)*, Vol. 4403 of *LNCS*, pp. 171–185. Springer, 2007.

[12] C. Igel, T. Glasmachers, and V. Heidrich-Meisner. Shark. *Journal of Machine Learning Research*, 9:993–996, 2008.

[13] J. D. Knowles and D. Corne. Properties of an adaptive archiving algorithm for storing nondominated vectors. *IEEE Trans. Evolutionary Computation*, 7:100–116, 2003.

[14] J. D. Knowles, D. W. Corne, and M. Fleischer. Bounded archiving using the Lebesgue measure. In *Proc. IEEE Congress on Evolutionary Computation (CEC '03)*, Vol. 4, pp. 2490–2497. IEEE Press, 2003.

[15] R. Kumar and N. Banerjee. Running time analysis of a multiobjective evolutionary algorithm on simple and hard problems. In *Proc. 8th International Workshop on Foundations of Genetic Algorithms (FOGA '05)*, Vol. 3469 of *LNCS*, pp. 112–131. Springer, 2005.

[16] M. Laumanns, L. Thiele, K. Deb, and E. Zitzler. Combining convergence and diversity in evolutionary multiobjective optimization. *Evolutionary Computation*, 10(3):263–282, 2002.

[17] G. Lizarraga-Lizarraga, A. Hernandez-Aguirre, and S. Botello-Rionda. G-metric: an m-ary quality indicator for the evaluation of non-dominated sets. In *Proc. 10th annual Conference on Genetic and Evolutionary Computation (GECCO '08)*, pp. 665–672. ACM Press, 2008.

[18] C. H. Papadimitriou and M. Yannakakis. On the approximability of trade-offs and optimal access of web sources. In *Proc. 41st annual Symposium on Foundations of Computer Science (FOCS '00)*, pp. 86–92. IEEE Press, 2000.

[19] W. Rudin. *Real and complex analysis*. McGraw-Hill Book Co., New York, 3rd edition, 1987.

[20] T. Suttorp, N. Hansen, and C. Igel. Efficient covariance matrix update for variable metric evolution strategies. *Machine Learning*, 75:167–197, 2009.

[21] T. Voß, N. Hansen, and C. Igel. Improved step size adaptation for the MO-CMA-ES. In *Proc. 12th Annual Conference on Genetic and Evolutionary Computation Conference (GECCO '10)*, pp. 487–494. ACM Press, 2010.

[22] E. Zitzler and S. Künzli. Indicator-based selection in multiobjective search. In *Proc. 8th International Conference Parallel Problem Solving from Nature (PPSN VIII)*, Vol. 3242 of *LNCS*, pp. 832–842. Springer, 2004.

[23] E. Zitzler and L. Thiele. Multiobjective evolutionary algorithms: a comparative case study and the strength Pareto approach. *IEEE Trans. Evolutionary Computation*, 3:257–271, 1999.

[24] E. Zitzler, L. Thiele, M. Laumanns, C. M. Fonseca, and V. Grunert da Fonseca. Performance assessment of multiobjective optimizers: an analysis and review. *IEEE Trans. Evolutionary Computation*, 7:117–132, 2003.

[25] E. Zitzler, D. Brockhoff, and L. Thiele. The hypervolume indicator revisited: On the design of Pareto-compliant indicators via weighted integration. In *Proc. Fourth International Conference on Evolutionary Multi-Criterion Optimization (EMO '07)*, Vol. 4403 of *LNCS*, pp. 862–876. Springer, 2007.

[26] E. Zitzler, L. Thiele, and J. Bader. On set-based multiobjective optimization. *IEEE Trans. Evolutionary Computation*, 14:58–79, 2010.

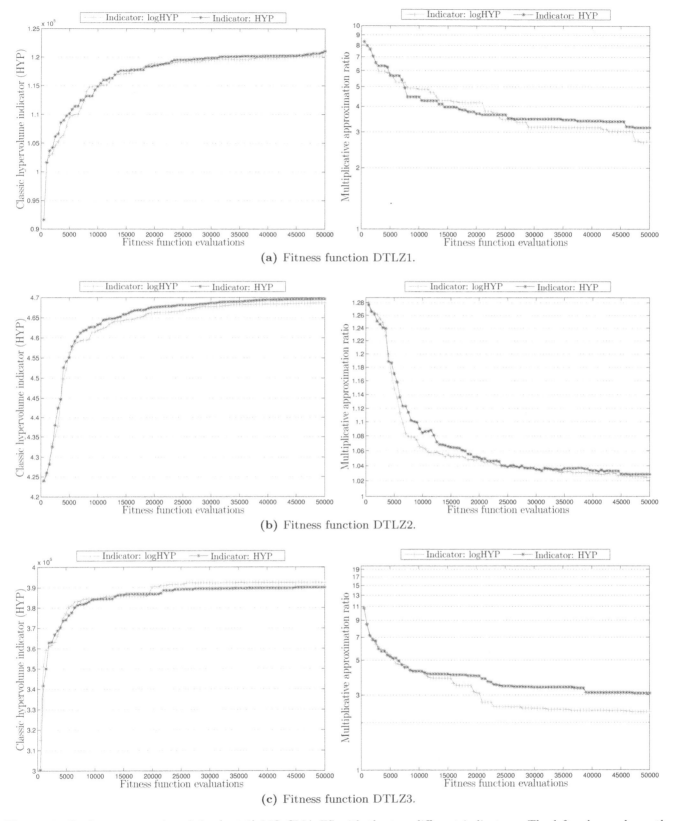

(a) Fitness function DTLZ1.

(b) Fitness function DTLZ2.

(c) Fitness function DTLZ3.

Figure 1: Performance results of the $(\mu + 1)$-MO-CMA-ES with the two different indicators. The left column shows the results for the classic hypervolume indicator. The right column shows the results for the multiplicative approximation ratio (scaled logarithmically).

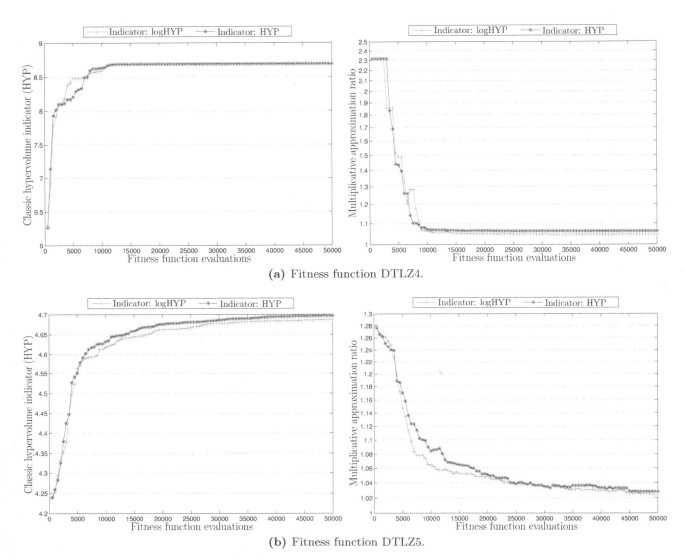

(a) Fitness function DTLZ4.

(b) Fitness function DTLZ5.

Figure 2: Performance results of the $(\mu + 1)$-MO-CMA-ES with the two different indicators. The left column shows the results for the classic hypervolume indicator. The right column shows the results for the multiplicative approximation ratio (scaled logarithmically).

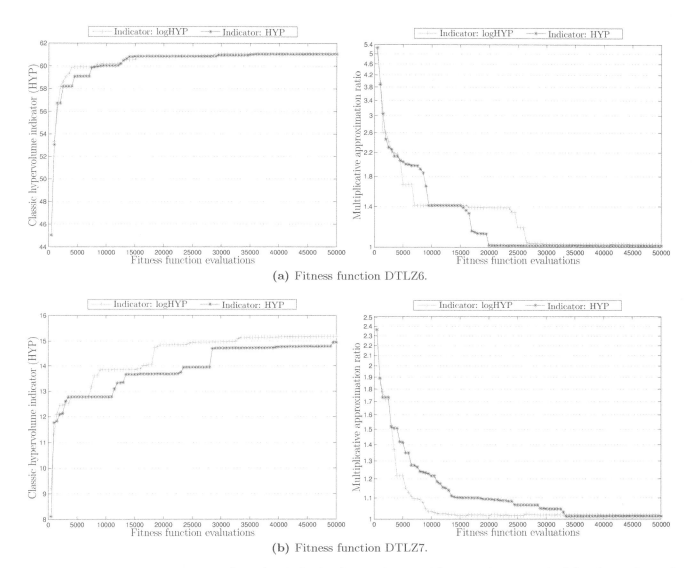

(a) Fitness function DTLZ6.

(b) Fitness function DTLZ7.

Figure 3: Performance results of the $(\mu + 1)$-MO-CMA-ES with the two different indicators. The left column shows the results for the classic hypervolume indicator. The right column shows the results for the multiplicative approximation ratio (scaled logarithmically).

Approximating the Distribution of Fitness over Hamming Regions

Andrew M. Sutton
L. Darrell Whitley
Adele E. Howe

Department of Computer Science
Colorado State University
Fort Collins, CO 80523
{sutton,whitley,howe}@cs.colostate.edu

ABSTRACT

The distribution of fitness values across a set of states sharply influences the dynamics of evolutionary processes and heuristic search in combinatorial optimization. In this paper we present a method for approximating the distribution of fitness values over Hamming regions by solving a linear programming problem that incorporates low order moments of the target function. These moments can be retrieved in polynomial time for select problems such as MAX-k-SAT using Walsh analysis. The method is applicable to any real function on binary strings that is epistatically bounded and discrete with asymptotic bounds on the cardinality of its codomain.

We perform several studies on the ONE-MAX and MAX-k-SAT domains to assess the accuracy of the approximation and its dependence on various factors. We show that the approximation can accurately predict the number of states within a Hamming region that have an improving fitness value.

Categories and Subject Descriptors

I.2.8 [**Artificial Intelligence**]: Problem Solving, Control Methods, and Search

General Terms

Theory, Algorithms

Keywords

Pseudo-Boolean functions, search space analysis

1. INTRODUCTION

Evolutionary processes and heuristic search algorithms operate by dynamically moving through a large set of states. The behavior of such algorithms strongly depends on the distribution of fitness values over this configuration space. In

general, it is intractable to characterize this distribution. It can be approximated for general fitness functions by direct sampling or by biased (e.g., Metropolis) sampling [8, 1, 2]. However, when the fitness function is *epistatically bounded*, i.e., has bounded nonlinearity, it has a sparse representation in an alternate (Walsh polynomial) basis which can be invoked for the efficient calculation of low order *moments* of the distribution without resorting to sampling. In this paper we will derive an analytical approximation of the distribution of certain epistatically bounded fitness functions over volumes of Hamming space by exploiting this fact.

Heckendorn et al. [4] first showed how low order moments of the distribution of fitness values over the entire configuration space can be computed in polynomial time for epistatically bounded functions (which they called *embedded landscapes*). Later, Heckendorn [3] extended this work to show that moments of the distribution of fitness values over hyperplanes can be computed in polynomial time for epistatically bounded fitness functions.

While hyperplane statistics are important from the perspective of hyperplane sampling for selection-based genetic algorithms, processes that explore the configuration space in a *localized* manner are also strongly influenced by the distribution of fitness values in volumes of the configuration space that are in some sense "nearby". Toward that end, Sutton et al. [9] further generalized the work of Heckendorn et al. to show how low order moments of the fitness distribution over local regions (Hamming balls and spheres) can be computed in polynomial time for epistatically bounded functions.

Though low *moments* of the fitness distribution over such functions can be efficiently computed, it is still an open question exactly how these moments relate to the fitness distribution function itself. We show how the moments over Hamming regions can be used to derive an approximation of the fitness distribution over these regions when the fitness function is epistatically bounded and discrete with asymptotic bounds on the cardinality of the codomain.

Rather than resorting to sampling, we take advantage of the fact that the moments over Hamming regions are related to the distribution over that region by a system of linear equations. Though it is intractable to compute arbitrarily high moments of this distribution, we use a linear programming approach to solve an underdetermined linear system. The solution of this system approximates the distribution of fitness over any Hamming region.

Discrete, epistatically bounded fitness functions are pervasive in many combinatorial optimization domains such as

MAX-k-SAT and MAX-CUT and appear in certain models of evolutionary systems such as the quantized model of NK-landscapes [7]. The distribution of fitness over a Hamming region is an important analytical characteristic of the fitness landscape. For instance, consider a Hamming region around a particular state x. The fitness distribution over that region determines quantities such as the count of elements in the region with higher fitness than x, or even the count of best values in the region. Approximations of this distribution are directly applicable to estimating such quantities.

Given all the fitness function moments over a region, our approach gives the exact distribution of values over that region. However, we show that if $P \neq NP$, it is intractable to compute all the moments over general Hamming regions. The linear programming formulation allows for the incorporation of bounds on higher moments into the approximation. We also show the approach allows us to compute an exact upper and lower bound on the fitness distribution function over any Hamming region. This bound provides an exact limit on the count of states at a particular fitness value lying in the region.

To demonstrate the accuracy of the approximation we first compare the approximated fitness distribution function in the ONE-MAX domain in which we can exactly calculate true fitness distribution functions analytically. We find the accuracy improves with region size and is better toward the extrema of the fitness function. We then apply the approach to an actual combinatorial optimization domain, the MAX-k-SAT problem, and find the approximation accurately predicts the number of states in a region with higher fitness than the point at the center of the region.

This approximation is useful to practitioners in several ways. In general, the approximated distribution estimates the number of states in a region of the configuration space that lie within any range of the fitness function. Thus it may be possible to estimate the probability of a global optimum lying within a certain Hamming distance of a given state. The approximated distribution can be also used to estimate the probability of a hill-climbing search or a mutation-only evolutionary algorithm reaching a state with a given fitness value. Furthermore, the approximation makes it possible to compare two arbitrary points in the search space by estimating the relative merits of exploration near each state.

2. HAMMING REGIONS

We study fitness landscapes over length-n binary sequences $\{0,1\}^n$ where the fitness function $f : \{0,1\}^n \to A$ has the following two properties.

1. f is epistatically bounded by a constant k.

2. The codomain $A \subset \mathbb{R}$ of f is discrete with cardinality $O(n)$.

Local search algorithms and some evolutionary processes make small changes to a given state (e.g., by inverting a small number of bits). The short-term dynamics of such algorithms are influenced by the statistical properties of the states that are mutually reachable by a small number of changes. Accordingly, we are interested in the distribution of fitness values over regions that are somehow "local" to a given state. We formalize this as follows. Consider two points $x, y \in \{0,1\}^n$. The Hamming distance $\mathcal{D}(x, y)$ is the number of positions in which the strings x and y differ.

The set $\{0,1\}^n$ together with the Hamming distance function form a metric space and, given a "centroid" x, we can partition $\{0,1\}^n$ into regions about x.

DEFINITION 1. *A sphere of radius r around a point $x \in \{0,1\}^n$ is defined as the set*

$$S^{(r)}(x) = \{y \in \{0,1\}^n : \mathcal{D}(x, y) = r\}.$$

Similarly, we define a union of concentric spheres as follows.

DEFINITION 2. *A ball of radius r around a point $x \in \{0,1\}^n$ is defined as the set*

$$B^{(r)}(x) = \{y \in \{0,1\}^n : \mathcal{D}(x, y) \leq r\}.$$

We will use the term *Hamming region* to denote either a sphere or ball of arbitrary radius around any arbitrary point.

2.1 The fitness statistics of Hamming regions

If $X \subseteq \{0,1\}^n$ is a Hamming region as defined above, then the cth moment of a function f over X is defined as

$$\mu_c(X) = \frac{1}{|X|} \sum_{y \in X} f(y)^c \tag{1}$$

For any k-bounded pseudo-Boolean function, as long as k and c are taken to be constants, Heckendorn et al. [4] showed that the cth moment of the fitness function over the entire landscape can be computed in polynomial time using Walsh analysis.

Sutton et al. [9] extended this result to Hamming regions and used a Walsh transform to construct an algorithm that computes $\mu_c(X)$ for any Hamming region X in time polynomial in n. This moment computing algorithm relies on the fact that k-bounded functions and their powers have a sparse representation in the Walsh basis and that moments of f over Hamming regions can be written as a bounded sum of weighted Walsh functions. When the epistasis of f is bounded by k, the moment algorithm of Sutton et al. has a time complexity of $O(rn^{ck})$ where r is the Hamming radius of the region. Moreover, if f can be expressed as a sum over $m \ll n^k$ subfunctions, the complexity results can be improved to $O(rm^c)$. Note that this bound holds even when $|X|$ is exponential in n (this includes the result of Heckendorn et al. [4] as a special case: when X is a Hamming ball of radius n).

Since we have constrained the codomain of the fitness function to a finite set with linearly bounded cardinality it must take the form

$$f : \{0,1\}^n \to A$$

where

$$A = \{a_0, a_1, \ldots, a_{q-1}\}$$

is a finite set of q elements where q is $O(n)$. This asymptotic bound on the codomain size is important to subsequent analysis since we later characterize the distribution of fitness values as the solution to q linear equations in q unknowns.

Without loss of generality, let us impose a total order on A so that $i < j \implies a_i < a_j$. Assuming maximization, let

$$a^* = \max_{x \in \{0,1\}^n} f(x)$$

Given a Hamming region X, we define the measure

$$p_X : A \to [0, 1]$$

where $p_X(a_i)$ is the probability that the element chosen *uniformly at random* from X has fitness a_i. In this case, p_X is a *probability mass function* with support A. For a given distribution, the set of q discrete values $\{p_X(a_i)\}$ are called the *impulses* of the probability mass function.

We can thus define the distribution of fitness values, or the *fitness distribution function*, over the region X as a function

$$N_X : A \to \mathbb{N}$$

where $N_X(a_i) = |X| p_X(a_i)$ is the number of states $y \in X$ such that $f(y) = a_i$.

The fitness distribution function thus exactly characterizes the allocation of fitness values to states in a region X. Under the assumption of maximization, $N_X(a^*)$ is the number of optimal solutions in X, and

$$\sum_{a_i > f(x)} N_X(a_i)$$

is the number of states in the Hamming region with improving fitness function value with respect to a point x. Thus, an approximation of this quantity can be used to estimate the number of optimal solutions in X and the number of states in in X with improving fitness.

When the fitness function has the constraints we have imposed, the moments of a region X appear in a system of equations that determine the fitness distribution N_X. We now show this.

2.2 Computing the exact fitness distribution

Consider a state drawn uniformly at random from the Hamming region X. Its fitness can be modeled as a random variable Z. Since each state $y \in X$ has a probability $\frac{1}{|X|}$ of being selected, we can write the expectation of Z raised to the cth power as

$$\mathbb{E}[Z^c] = \frac{1}{|X|} \sum_{y \in X} f(y)^c$$
$$= \mu_c(X) \qquad \text{by (1).} \qquad (2)$$

But $\mathbb{E}[Z^c]$ is, by definition, the cth moment of the distribution of the random variable Z. Note that the distribution of Z is the above defined probability mass function p_X. Hence we can write

$$\mathbb{E}[Z^c] = \sum_{i=0}^{q-1} a_i^c p_X(a_i). \qquad (3)$$

Putting together Equations (2) and (3) we have the following identity:

$$\mu_c(X) = \sum_{i=0}^{q-1} a_i^c p_X(a_i). \qquad (4)$$

In other words, the cth moment of f is equal to the cth moment of the probability mass function p_X.

Consider the lowest $|A| = q$ moments of X:

$$\{\mu_0(X), \mu_1(X), \dots, \mu_{q-1}(X)\}.$$

Using the identity in (4) we have the following system of q equations in q unknowns.

$$\sum_{i=0}^{q-1} a_i^j p_X(a_i) = \mu_j(X) \qquad (5)$$

for $j = \{0, 1, \dots, q-1\}$. Letting

$$\boldsymbol{p} = (p_X(a_0), p_X(a_1), \dots, p_X(a_{q-1}))^\top$$

and

$$\boldsymbol{\mu} = (\mu_0(X), \mu_1(X), \dots, \mu_{q-1}(X))^\top,$$

if the $q \times q$ matrix

$$\boldsymbol{M}_{i,j} = \left((a_i)^j \right)^\top$$

is nonsingular, there is a unique solution $\boldsymbol{p}$ to

$$\boldsymbol{M}\boldsymbol{p} = \boldsymbol{\mu}$$

which defines the probability mass function for the Hamming region since $p_X(a_i) = \boldsymbol{p}_i$. The fitness distribution is then given by $N_X(a_i) = |X| p_X(a_i)$.

$\boldsymbol{M}$ belongs to a well-known class of matrices known as Vandermonde matrices. The determinant is

$$\det(\boldsymbol{M}) = \prod_{i < j} (a_j - a_i).$$

The matrix is nonsingular if and only if all the values of a_i are distinct. In our case, since A is a set, all elements $a_i \in A$, by definition are distinct so $\boldsymbol{M}$ always has an inverse and the above system of equations always has a unique solution. Hence, if we have q moments of the Hamming region, we can obtain exactly the probability mass function over X by solving the system. Since q is $O(n)$, the size of the linear system is polynomial in n, even if $|X|$ is exponential in n.

3. DISTRIBUTION APPROXIMATION

In the foregoing, q moments of f over X are needed to characterize N_X. Thus we must be able to retrieve moments of *arbitrary order*. If $\mathsf{P} \neq \mathsf{NP}$, this is computationally difficult, as is captured by the following theorem.

THEOREM 1. *In general, the calculation of N_X is #P-hard.*

PROOF. Let $\mathcal{F}$ be a propositional 3-SAT formula with n variables and m clauses. Let $f : \{0,1\}^n \to \{0, 1, \dots, m\}$ give the number of clauses satisfied under an assignment. Note that f satisfies the conditions we have imposed.

Let X be a ball of radius n around an arbitrary assignment x. In other words, $X = \{0,1\}^n$ and $N_X(m)$ gives the number of satisfying assignments to $\mathcal{F}$, solving #3-SAT which is #P-complete [10]. □

Given all q moments, it is theoretically possible to solve the linear system in polynomial time. Thus the computational intractability must arise in the calculation of the moments themselves. Indeed, the calculation of $\mu_c(X)$ is exponential in c [4, 9]. Hence, we are interested in finding a way to approximate the distribution using only low moments of f over the region.

Given only $0 < c \ll q$ moments, we have the partial Vandermonde system where j in Equation (5) runs from 0 to $c - 1$. Algebraically, let $\boldsymbol{M}'$ be the $c \times q$ *partial* Vandermonde matrix that consists of the first c rows of $\boldsymbol{M}$ and a *truncated* moment vector $\boldsymbol{\mu}' = (\mu_0(X), \mu_1(X), \ldots, \mu_{c-1}(X))^\top$ consisting of the lowest c moments. We seek a solution $\hat{\boldsymbol{p}}$ to the linear system[1]

$$\boldsymbol{M}'\hat{\boldsymbol{p}} = \boldsymbol{\mu}'. \tag{6}$$

This system is underdetermined, so there are potentially infinite solutions. Furthermore, there is no guarantee that $\hat{\boldsymbol{p}}$ gives a valid probability mass function. A solution to (6) may contain elements that are meaningless as probabilities, i.e., lying outside of the unit interval.

However, we can encode this requirement as a set of fixed variables and bounding constraints by posing the formulation of a solution to the partial Vandermonde system in Equation (6) in terms of a linear programming problem.

$$
\begin{aligned}
\max \quad & \boldsymbol{b}^\top \hat{\boldsymbol{p}} \\
\text{s.t.} \quad & \boldsymbol{M}'\hat{\boldsymbol{p}} = \boldsymbol{\mu}'. \\
& 0 \le \hat{\boldsymbol{p}} \le 1.
\end{aligned} \tag{7}
$$

where $\boldsymbol{b}$ is a length q vector of coefficients.

A solution to this system has a number of desirable properties. First, it is a probability mass function in the sense that its elements lie between 0 and 1 because of the constraints imposed by the linear program. Moreover, the zeroth moment $\mu_0(X) = 1$ corresponding to the first row of $\boldsymbol{M}'$ ensures the elements sum to unity. Thus we can define the *approximated* probability mass over X in terms of $\hat{\boldsymbol{p}}$: $\hat{p}_X(a_i) = \hat{\boldsymbol{p}}_i$. Finally, the approximated probability mass function shares low moments with the exact solution to (5). This is captured by the following.

THEOREM 2. *Let $\hat{\boldsymbol{p}}$ be a solution to the above linear program. Taken as probability mass functions p_X has the same j^{th} moment as $\hat{p}_X$ for $0 \le j < c$.*

PROOF. Let $0 \le j < c$. The jth moment of $\hat{p}_X$ is

$$
\begin{aligned}
\sum_{i=0}^{q-1} a_i^j \hat{p}_X(a_i) &= \sum_{i=0}^{q-1} \boldsymbol{M}'_{j,i} \hat{\boldsymbol{p}}_i \\
&= \boldsymbol{\mu}'_j \qquad \text{by (7)} \\
&= \mu_j(X).
\end{aligned}
$$

By (4), $\mu_j(X)$ is equivalent to the jth moment of p_X: the true probability mass function over X. $\qquad\square$

In other words, since mean and variance depend only on the first and second moments, for $c > 2$, the approximated probability mass function given by solving the above linear program has the same mean and variance as the true probability mass function of the region. The fitness distribution over X is approximately

$$\hat{N}_X(a) = |X|\hat{p}_X(a). \tag{8}$$

3.1 Choosing the coefficient vector

It is not immediately clear what an appropriate choice for the coefficient vector $\boldsymbol{b}$ in the objective function for the linear program in (7) might be. One particular approach will be used in Section 3.3 to obtain an exact bound on the fitness distribution function.

We would expect impulse values occurring near the mean (that is, the values of a_i closest to $\mu_1(X)$) to be highest in

the probability mass function. Hence a heuristic might be to maximize impulses near $\mu_1(X)$. Let ω be a "window size" parameter. Define also the index of the element nearest to the mean as $\zeta = \arg\min_i |a_i - \mu_1(X)|$ (recall we have imposed a total order on A). We can then define the coefficient vector as

$$
b_i = \begin{cases} 1 & \text{if } |\zeta - i| \le \omega \\ 0 & \text{otherwise} \end{cases}
$$

Maximizing $\boldsymbol{b}^\top \hat{\boldsymbol{p}}$ is akin to finding the approximated probability mass function in which impulses lying near the mean value are maximal. Determining more principled values for $\boldsymbol{b}$ remains a direction for future research.

3.2 Limiting impulse values

Since the linear program is very underconstrained, the above approach tends to result in sparse probability mass functions in which a large amount of mass is allocated to few impulses. Empirical data suggests that the nonzero impulse values tend to be "clustered" around the mean, each with a limited mass. To further refine the accuracy of the approximation we introduce an upper limit to the mass contribution of each impulse.

If $A \subset \mathbb{N}$ and $\hat{p}_X$ is reasonably well-behaved, then a suitable continuity correction would allow us to model $\hat{p}_X$ with a continuous distribution. Neglecting higher moments, we note that a normal probability distribution with variance σ^2 has a maximum of $\frac{1}{\sqrt{2\pi\sigma^2}}$. Hence we might limit the maximum value of the impulses in $\hat{p}_X$ by

$$\left(2\pi(\mu_2(X) - \mu_1(X)^2)\right)^{-1/2}$$

to mitigate the sparse distribution of mass in the above approach.

Imposing this heuristic limit does not violate the constraints of the program and hence the resulting solution is still a probability mass function with the same c moments as p_X. We find in many cases that the limit improves the accuracy of the approximated fitness distribution function.

3.3 An exact bound

One consequence of the linear programming approach is that we can use it to provide an exact bound on the impulses of the distribution function. By choosing the appropriate coefficient vector, we can ensure the resulting solution bounds a particular impulse of N_X.

THEOREM 3. *Let X be a Hamming region. Let $\hat{p}_X^\star$ be the probability mass function obtained by solution to the linear program in (7) with $\boldsymbol{b}$ being the standard j^{th} basis vector:*

$$b_i = \delta_{ij}, \quad i = 0, 1, \ldots, q-1$$

where δ is the Kronecker delta function. Then

$$N_X(a_j) \le |X|\hat{p}_X^\star(a_j).$$

PROOF. By definition, $N_X(a_j) = |X|p_X(a_j)$ so it is enough to prove that $p_X(a_j) \le \hat{p}_X^\star(a_j)$.

Suppose for contradiction that $p_X(a_j) > \hat{p}_X^\star(a_j)$. In other words, we have $\boldsymbol{p}_j > \hat{\boldsymbol{p}}_j^\star$. By definition, $\hat{\boldsymbol{p}}^\star$ is the unique solution that maximizes

$$\boldsymbol{b}^\top \hat{\boldsymbol{p}}^\star = \hat{\boldsymbol{p}}_j^\star = \hat{p}_X^\star(a_j)$$

and satisfies the partial Vandermonde system $\boldsymbol{M}'\hat{\boldsymbol{p}}^\star = \boldsymbol{\mu}'$. Now, consider the full Vandermonde system $\boldsymbol{M}\boldsymbol{p} = \boldsymbol{\mu}$. Since

---

[1]As a notational convention we use the prime symbol ($'$) to denote truncation and the hat symbol ($\hat{\ }$) to denote approximation.

all equations in the partial system corresponding to M' are contained in the full system, it follows that $M'p = \mu'$ is also satisfied. But $p_j > \hat{p}_j^\star \implies b^\top p > b^\top \hat{p}^\star$, a contradiction that $\hat{p}^\star$ maximizes the linear program corresponding to the partial Vandermonde system. $\square$

Iteratively maximizing the linear program using the jth standard basis vector for $j = 0, 1, \ldots, q - 1$ thus generates an upper bound for each of the impulses of the distribution function N_X. A lower bound can be analogously found by solving the corresponding minimization problem using j^{th} standard basis vectors.[2]

3.4 Incorporating bounds on higher moments

Another advantage to the linear programming approach is that we can incorporate bounds on higher moments into the approximation. Let c be the maximum moment degree available and d be an arbitrary increment. Bounds on moments of higher degree can be added explicitly to the linear program as doubly bounded constraints:

$$LB(\mu_{c+d}(X)) \leq \sum_{i=0}^{q-1} a_i^j p_X(a_i) \leq UB(\mu_{c+d}(X)) \quad (9)$$

where $LB(\mu_{c+d}(X))$ and $UB(\mu_{c+d}(X))$ are lower and upper bounds (respectively) on the moment of order $c+d$. Obtaining the exact moments of higher degrees becomes computationally difficult (and is generally intractable by Theorem 1). However, if bounds on higher moments can be efficiently obtained, they may be incorporated into the approximation in this way.

We now impose some mild restrictions on the codomain A of f and calculate upper and lower bounds on higher moments. First, we will assume $\forall a_i \in A$, $a_i \geq 0$. Since A is a finite set with cardinality linear in the problem size, we can impose this condition without loss of generality since the evaluation of f can always be shifted by an appropriate constant. Before deriving upper and lower moment bounds, we prove the following preparatory lemma.

LEMMA 1. *Let X be a Hamming region. As long as there exist at least two states $x_1, x_2 \in X$ with $f(x_1) \geq 1$ and $f(x_2) \geq 1$, then, for $c, d \geq 1$,*

$$\frac{1}{|X|} \sum_{y \in X} f(y)^c \left(\sum_{z \in X \setminus \{y\}} f(z)^d \right) \geq \mu_c(X).$$

PROOF. Since either $x_1 \in X \setminus \{y\}$ or $x_2 \in X \setminus \{y\}$, we have $\sum_{z \in X \setminus \{y\}} f(z)^d \geq 1$. $\square$

The conditions for the lemma are relatively weak since, if necessary, we can shift f without altering the total order on A. We are now ready to give an upper bound on moments of degree $c + d$.

THEOREM 4. *Let X be a Hamming region with at least two states $x_1, x_2 \in X$ such that $f(x_1) \geq 1$ and $f(x_2) \geq 1$. Let $d \geq 1$. Then,*

$$\mu_{c+d}(X) \leq |X| \mu_c(X) \mu_d(X) - \mu_c(X).$$

PROOF.

$$\mu_c(X)\mu_d(X) = \left(\frac{1}{|X|} \sum_{y \in X} f(y)^c \right) \left(\frac{1}{|X|} \sum_{y \in X} f(y)^d \right)$$

$$= \frac{1}{|X|^2} \sum_{y \in X} f(y)^{c+d} + \frac{1}{|X|^2} \sum_{y \in X} f(y)^c \left(\sum_{z \in X \setminus \{y\}} f(z)^d \right)$$

$$= \frac{1}{|X|} \mu_{c+d}(X) + \frac{1}{|X|^2} \sum_{y \in X} f(y)^c \left(\sum_{z \in X \setminus \{y\}} f(z)^d \right)$$

Rearranging terms and multiplying by the cardinality of X we have

$$|X|\mu_c(X)\mu_d(X) - \frac{1}{|X|} \sum_{y \in X} f(y)^c \left(\sum_{z \in X \setminus \{y\}} f(z)^d \right)$$
$$= \mu_{c+d}(X)$$

and by Lemma 1, $|X|\mu_c(X)\mu_d(X) - \mu_c(X) \geq \mu_{c+d}$. $\square$

We can also derive the following trivial lower bound.

THEOREM 5. *Let X be a Hamming region such that for all $x \in X$, $f(x) = 0$ or $f(x) \geq 1$. Let $d \geq 1$. Then,*

$$\mu_{c+d}(X) \geq \mu_c(X).$$

PROOF. Since for all $x \in X$, $f(x)^{c+d} \geq f(x)^c$ we immediately have

$$\frac{1}{|X|} \sum_{y \in X} f(y)^{c+d} \geq \frac{1}{|X|} \sum_{y \in X} f(y)^c$$

which proves the claim. $\square$

Again, the conditions for the theorem are relatively weak since: (1) domains where $A \subset \mathbb{N}$ already satisfy them, and (2) the elements of A can be appropriately shifted without changing the total order. These bounds can be added to the linear program in the manner mentioned at the beginning of the section.

4. ACCURACY MEASUREMENTS

In order to demonstrate the proficiency of the approximation derived in the foregoing sections, we perform a number of numerical measurements to compare the approximated fitness distribution with the true fitness distribution. Since we are working with discrete values, it is easier to visualize and compare distribution functions using their cumulative forms. We define the *cumulative probability distribution function* as

$$c_X(a) = \sum_{a_i \leq a} p_x(a_i)$$

and the *cumulative fitness distribution function* as

$$C_X(a) = \sum_{a_i \leq a} N_x(a_i)$$

We define $\hat{c}_X$ and $\hat{C}_X$ analogously as the approximated cumulative distribution functions simply by replacing the probability and fitness distribution functions in the above definitions with their approximated form. In order to compare

---

[2]In practice we found this lower bound obtained with reasonable values of c to be degenerate, i.e., $N_X(a_j) \geq 0$.

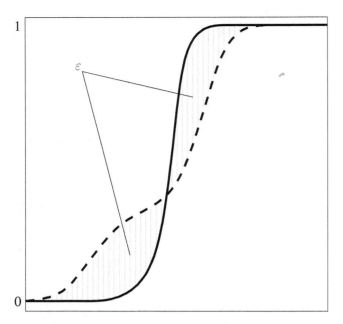

Figure 1: Illustration of the ε measure for two hypothetical cumulative distribution functions. ε measures the shaded area: the extent to which two distribution functions disagree.

how well an approximated distribution fits the true distribution, we define the (normalized) measure of absolute error as

$$\varepsilon = \frac{1}{q} \sum_{i=0}^{q-1} |c_X(a_i) - \hat{c}_X(a_i)|.$$

Note that $0 \leq \varepsilon \leq 1$ and measures the extent to which the two cumulative probability distribution functions disagree (see Figure 1). The ε metric has a loose similarity to the Kolmogorov-Smirnov statistic which measures the maximum deviation between two (continuous) cumulative distributions.

4.1 ONE-MAX

According to the result of Theorem 1, for the general class of epistatically bounded functions, it is #P-hard to compute the true fitness distribution function for all possible Hamming regions. However, if we restrict ourselves to a special class of functions, we can take advantage of its properties to compute the true distribution efficiently. It then becomes straightforward to test the accuracy of the approximation, even over intractably large regions of the space.

Given a binary sequence of length n, the ONE-MAX fitness function simply counts the number of elements in the sequence that are equal to one.

$$f : \{0,1\}^n \to \{0,1,\ldots,n\}; \quad f(x) = |\{i : x[i] = 1\}|, \quad (10)$$

where $x[i]$ denotes the ith element in the sequence. This class of functions satisfies the constraints laid out in Section 2 since f is bitwise additively separable (and thus has maximum epistasis $k = 1$) and the cardinality of its codomain is clearly linearly bounded in n.

The appeal of using the ONE-MAX fitness function is that

it becomes possible to derive an analytical expression for the true fitness distribution function.

4.1.1 Analytical formula

The distribution of ONE-MAX fitness values over a sphere of radius r can be written in closed form. We begin by defining the following quantity.

DEFINITION 3. *Let $x, y \in \{0,1\}^n$. We define the quantity*

$$\beta(x,y) = |\{j : x[j] = 1 \text{ and } y[j] = 0\}|$$

to be the number of 1-bits in x that are inverted to produce y (equivalently, the number of 1-bits in $x \wedge \bar{y}$ where $\wedge$ and $\bar{y}$ represent bitwise conjunction and complementation, respectively).

We claim a number of trivial constraints on $\beta(x,y)$ that will become useful in the proof of Theorem 6.

CLAIM 1. *For any $x, y \in \{0,1\}^n$, the following constraints hold for $\beta(x,y)$.*

1. *Since $\beta(x,y)$ is a count, $\beta(x,y) \in \mathbb{N}_0$.*

2. *Since there are $f(x)$ 1-bits in x, $\beta(x,y) \leq f(x)$.*

3. *Since there are $n - f(x)$ 0-bits in x, $0 \leq \mathcal{D}(x,y) - \beta(x,y) \leq n - f(x)$.*

The analytical form of the fitness distribution function for ONE-MAX is given by the following theorem.

THEOREM 6. *Let f be the ONE-MAX fitness function defined in (10). Let $x \in \{0,1\}^n$. The count of states y in a sphere of radius r around x with $f(y) = a$ can be written in the following closed form. Let $\xi = \frac{1}{2}(f(x) + r - a)$.*
Consider the following three conditions for ξ.

1. $\xi \in \mathbb{N}_0$

2. $\xi \leq f(x)$

3. $0 \leq r - \xi \leq n - f(x)$

then,

$$N_{S^{(r)}(x)}(a) = \begin{cases} \binom{f(x)}{\xi}\binom{n-f(x)}{r-\xi} & \text{if conditions on } \xi \text{ hold;} \\ 0 & \text{otherwise.} \end{cases}$$

$$(11)$$

PROOF. Consider any $y \in S^{(r)}(x)$. Since $\mathcal{D}(x,y) = r$, we must invert exactly r elements of x to transform it into y. According to Definition 3, there are $\beta(x,y)$ 1-bits in x that are inverted to produce y and $r - \beta(x,y)$ 0-bits in x are inverted to produce y. Since there are $f(x)$ 1-bits in x, the number of 1-bits in y is

$$f(y) = (f(x) - \beta(x,y)) + (r - \beta(x,y)). \quad (12)$$

We can write

$$N_{S^{(r)}(x)}(a) = |\{y \in S^{(r)}(x) : f(y) = a\}|$$

and by Equation (12),

$$= |\{y \in S^{(r)}(x) : a = f(x) + r - 2\beta(x,y)\}|$$

and, solving for $\beta(x,y)$ in terms of a,

$$= |\{y \in S^{(r)}(x) : \beta(x,y) = \tfrac{1}{2}\left(f(x) + r - a\right)\}|$$

Letting $\xi = \tfrac{1}{2}\left(f(x) + r - a\right)$,

$$= |\{y \in S^{(r)}(x) : \beta(x,y) = \xi)\}|$$

Thus we have equated the quantity $N_{S^{(r)}(x)}(a)$ to the number elements y in the sphere where $\beta(x,y) = \xi$. Intuitively, this is the number of ways of inverting exactly ξ 1-bits in x and exactly $r - \xi$ 0-bits in x.

If ξ satisfies the three constraints in Claim 1 above, then there are

$$\binom{f(x)}{\xi}\binom{n - f(x)}{r - \xi}$$

ways to choose ξ 1-bits in x and $r - \xi$ 0-bits in x.

On the other hand, if ξ does not satisfy the three constraints on $\beta(x,y)$ given in Claim 1, then it must be the case that for any $y \in S^{(r)}(x)$, $\xi \neq \beta(x,y)$. If so, then vacuously,

$$\{y \in S^{(r)}(x) : \beta(x,y) = \xi)\} = \emptyset$$

and $N_{S^{(r)}(x)}(a) = 0$. $\qquad\square$

Since the spheres around a state x are mutually disjoint we always have the following identity

$$N_{B^{(r)}(x)}(a) = \sum_{u=0}^{r} N_{S^{(u)}(x)}(a).$$

Substituting the terms on the r.h.s. with (11) gives the analytical expression for the true ONE-MAX fitness distribution over the ball of radius r around a state x.

These formulas permit the direct calculation of the true fitness distribution for ONE-MAX. We use this in our first approach to assessing the accuracy of the approximation.

4.1.2 ONE-MAX approximation accuracy

Figure 2 plots the actual and estimated cumulative distributions for the $n = 50$ ONE-MAX fitness function. The solid line gives the true cumulative distribution of fitness values obtained by the explicit formula in (11) over a Hamming ball X of radius $r = 10$ in the space of length-50 bitstrings. The centroid of the ball has a fitness of 5. The broken line shows the approximation obtained by solving Equation (7) with the truncated moment vector

$$\boldsymbol{\mu}' = (\mu_0(X), \dots, \mu_5(X))^\top$$

containing six moments obtained by the algorithm in [9]. To solve Equation (7) we used the GNU Linear Programming Kit (GLPK) using a simplex-based LP solver [5].

The window length used was $\omega = 10$. We used these settings for all ONE-MAX distribution approximations reported in this section.

The analytical formula in Equation (11) allows us to compute the true distribution function without explicitly enumerating the region. Thus we can measure the accuracy of the approximation over arbitrarily large regions of Hamming space. A close examination of the analytical formula reveals that the fitness distribution function over a Hamming ball is uniquely determined by the fitness of its centroid and the

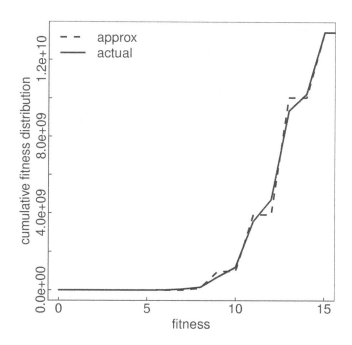

Figure 2: Cumulative fitness distribution on a single $n = 50$ ONE-MAX instance: actual vs. approximated over Hamming ball of radius 10 with centroid fitness 5.

radius of the ball. Hence there are exactly $(51)^2 = 2601$ uniquely determined ONE-MAX fitness distribution functions over $\{0,1\}^{50}$. We can calculate each of these explicitly along with the corresponding approximation and determine the dependence of the accuracy measure (ε) on radius or centroid fitness.

In Figure 3, the solid line shows the mean ε over all unique ONE-MAX fitness distribution functions over $\{0,1\}^{50}$ as a function of radius. The broken lines bracket the extremal values above and below the mean. At radius 0 (a Hamming ball containing only one point), the accuracy, of course, is always perfect since the true fitness distribution contains a single impulse whose location is entirely determined by the first two moments $\mu_0(X)$ and $\mu_1(X)$. A similar phenomenon occurs at radius 1. Subsequently, as radius increases, the accuracy diminishes until the radius reaches values in the interval $[3, 6]$. After this point, the accuracy begins to steadily improve as a function of radius.

Figure 4 plots the accuracy (ε) over all unique ONE-MAX fitness distribution functions over $\{0,1\}^{50}$ as a function of centroid fitness. The broken line shows the maximum values (the minimum value is always $\varepsilon = 0$, occurring at low radii, c.f., Figure 3). For ONE-MAX, the accuracy is highest when the fitness of the centroid lies at extremal boundaries of the fitness function and decays as the centroid fitness approaches $n/2$: the average fitness over $\{0,1\}^n$.

We remark that ε remains very low in all cases. This corresponds to a high approximation accuracy.

4.2 MAX-k-SAT

The results in the last section are somewhat academic since the approximation is unnecessary when an exact expression is available by Equation (11). In this section we apply the approximation to the maximum k-satisfiability

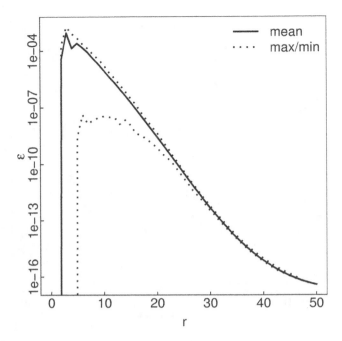

Figure 3: Dependence of approximation accuracy on ball radius for the ONE-MAX domain. The y-axis is on a logarithmic scale.

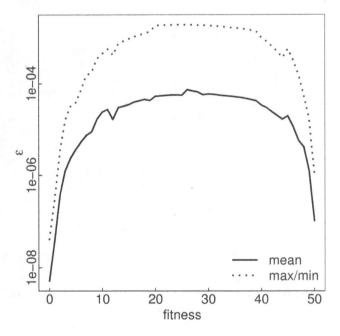

Figure 4: Dependence of approximation accuracy on centroid fitness for the ONE-MAX domain. The y-axis is on a logarithmic scale.

problem (MAX-k-SAT), an important NP-hard combinatorial problem. In this case, unless P = NP, it is intractable to generate the true fitness distribution over all Hamming regions since such a quantity yields a solution to the decision problem.

Therefore, given a Hamming region, we construct the true

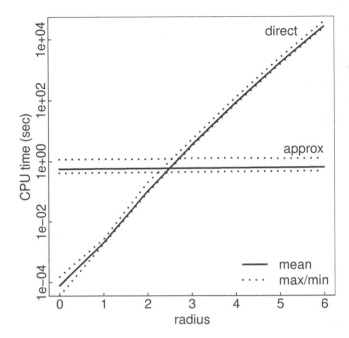

Figure 5: A comparison of time (in seconds) to exhaustively compute true distribution and time to perform LP approximation as a function of ball radius. The y-axis is on a logarithmic scale.

fitness distribution by a direct count of states at each fitness value in the region and compare it with the approximated distribution. Of course this limits the comparison to computationally manageable regions. Figure 5 illustrates this with a logarithmic plot of CPU time in seconds necessary to compute the true distribution as a function of Hamming ball radius on a 100 variable MAX-k-SAT instance. The required time is directly proportional to the cardinality of the Hamming ball which is exponential in the radius. As a comparison, we also plot in Figure 5 the time required to perform the LP approximation of the distribution. While the time to compute the true distribution increases to over 20 minutes for each Hamming region, the time to perform the LP approximation remains less than a second on average. This means it becomes intractable to compare the approximation accuracy for all radius values on nontrivial instances. However, we conjecture that the approximation accuracy remains stable with increasing radius, or possibly improves as it does in the case of ONE-MAX.

An instance of MAX-k-SAT consists of a Boolean formula with n variables and a set of m clauses. Each clause is composed of at most k literals in logical disjunction (a literal is an instance of a variable or its negation). The objective is to find a variable assignment that maximizes the number of satisfied clauses. The fitness function $f : \{0,1\}^n \to \{0, \ldots, m\}$ maps a variable assignment represented by a length-n binary string to the number of clauses satisfied under that assignment.

The function f is a sum over m subfunctions of length at most k, hence it is k-bounded. Furthermore, its codomain is the set $A = \{0, 1, \ldots, m\}$, so we have exactly the type of specialized function described in Section 2. For any Hamming

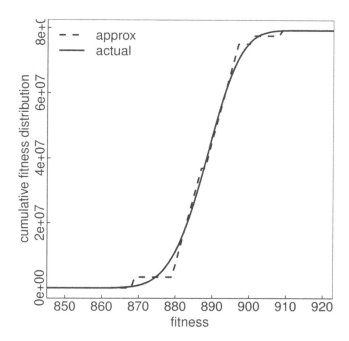

Figure 6: Cumulative fitness distribution on a single MAX-2-SAT instance: actual vs. approximated over region of radius 5.

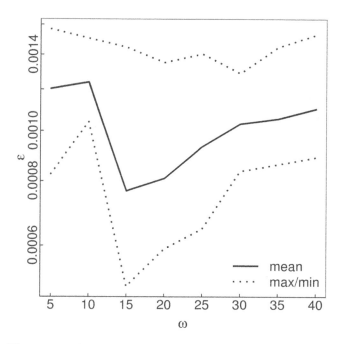

Figure 7: Dependence of approximation accuracy on window size for MAX-k-SAT benchmark set s2v100c1200. The y-axis is on a logarithmic scale.

region X, if we are given the $m + 1$ moments

$$\{\mu_0(X), \mu_1(X), \ldots, \mu_m(X)\}$$

we could solve the $(m+1) \times (m+1)$ linear system (e.g., using a specialized algorithm for pure Vandermonde systems [6]) to obtain N_X. Due to Theorem 1, it is NP-hard to construct all these moments in general. Since f is k-bounded, lower moments can be found in polynomial time, even when $|X|$ is superpolynomial [9].

4.2.1 MAX-k-SAT approximation accuracy

In this section we report accuracy results for the approximation on the MAX-k-SAT domain. As a test set, we use the 10 instance s2v100c1200 MAX-2-SAT benchmark set from the MAXSAT-2009 competition.[3] Each instance contains 100 variables and 1200 clauses. Each fitness distribution is evaluated over Hamming balls of fixed radius $r = 5$. Thus the calculations are over regions containing 79375496 states.

We plot the actual vs. approximated cumulative distribution function in Figure 6 for a radius 5 Hamming ball around a random point sampled from a particular instance from the benchmark set (the results are consistent across instances). The approximation is calculated using a truncated moment vector of the first four moments of the region

$$\boldsymbol{\mu}' = (\mu_0(X), \mu_1(X), \mu_2(X), \mu_3(X))^\top,$$

each generated using the algorithm in [9]. The approximation reported here also incorporates the upper and lower bounds on moments $\mu_4(X)$, $\mu_5(X)$, and $\mu_6(X)$, as in Section 3.4, and uses the heuristic impulse limit based on the second moment (Section 3.2). The window was set to $\omega = 20$. The measured ε value is approximately 7.47×10^{-5}.

[3]http://www.maxsat.udl.cat/09/

To determine the dependence of approximation accuracy on window size, we varied the window size from

$$\omega = 5, 10, \ldots, 40.$$

For each unique ω value, we sampled 10 states from each of the 10 instances. For each state we compute the ε for the approximation (using the current ω value) with respect to the actual fitness distribution (obtained exhaustively). Figure 7 shows that the accuracy as a function of window size appears to tend toward a minimum at $\omega = 15$.

To determine the dependence of approximation accuracy on the length of the moment vector, added bounds on higher moments (Section 3.4), and heuristic impulse limiting (Section 3.2), we repeat the experiment, holding the window size at 15 and varying the number of moments used (1 to 4), and the bounds on higher moments. We performed the experiments with and without heuristic impulse limiting. The results are given in Figure 8. As expected, the more moments, the more accurate the approximation. The higher moment bounds, however, do not appear to produce a strong effect. Clearly, the heuristic impulse limit improves the approximation accuracy in this case.

The results for ONE-MAX suggest that the approximation accuracy depends on the fitness of the centroid point (Figure 4). We also find this phenomenon occurs to some degree in the MAX-k-SAT domain. To show this, we select a representative instance (s2v100c1200-1) and measure the approximation accuracy for a number of different centroid states at varying fitness levels.

Since arbitrarily low fitness values are somewhat extraneous in the MAX-k-SAT domain (at least from the perspective of optimization), we limit our investigation to a range of fitness values that run from the average fitness of the instance to near-optimal fitness values. Consider a MAX-k-

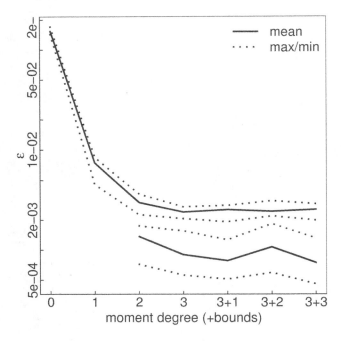

Figure 8: Dependence of approximation accuracy on moment degree (and bounds on higher moments) for MAX-k-SAT benchmark set s2v100c1200. Top lines are *without* heuristic impulse limit, bottom lines are *with* heuristic impulse limit (note the heuristic impulse limit requires the second moment). The y-axis is on a logarithmic scale.

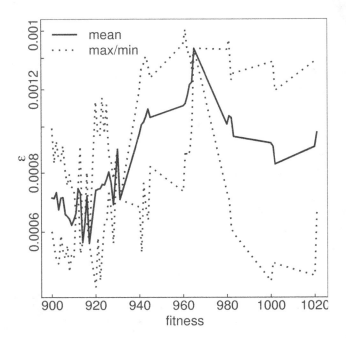

Figure 9: Dependence of approximation accuracy on centroid fitness for MAX-k-SAT instance s2v100c1200-1. Expected fitness of a random solution 900, best fitness 1031. The y-axis is on a logarithmic scale.

SAT formula with n variables and m clauses such that each clause contains exactly k literals. Given a particular literal, a random assignment satisfies that literal with probability $\frac{1}{2}$. Each clause is satisfied by $2^k - 1$ of the 2^k possible assignments of the literals they contain. Hence, each clause is satisfied under a random assignment with probability $\frac{2^k-1}{2^k}$. Depending on whether it is satisfied or not, a clause contributes a one or a zero to the fitness function. By linearity of expectation, the expected fitness under a random assignment is thus $\left(\frac{2^k-1}{2^k}\right) \times m$. For the 1200 clause MAX-2-SAT instance s2v100c1200-1, the expected fitness of a random state is $\frac{3}{4} \times 1200 = 900$. The optimal fitness level (found by a complete solver) of this particular instance is 1031.

In order to focus on pertinent levels of the fitness function for this instance, we considered a set of seven target fitness levels: 900, 920, 940, 960, 980, 1000, and 1020, which range from the random expectation value to near-optimal. For each target fitness level, we performed 100 episodes of a local hill-climbing search to generate solutions at or above the target level. Each resulting solution was then used as a centroid in a Hamming ball of radius 5, the true and approximated fitness distributions were subsequently calculated, and the resultant ε was computed (see Figure 9). Due to statistical noise, the MAX-k-SAT results are somewhat harder to interpret than the exact ONE-MAX results. However, we do note that accuracy has a stronger trend toward the boundary values of the target value range.

Again, in all cases, we note the very small ε values. We can thus conclude that the approximation is substantially accurate.

4.2.2 *Estimating the number of improving states*

To evaluate how well the model predicts the number of improving states in a region, we generated 100 random states on each of the 10 instances (1000 states total). For each generated state x, we counted the actual number of states with improving fitness that lie in the Hamming ball of radius $r = 5$ about x:

$$|\{y \in B^{(r)}(x) : f(y) > f(x)\}| = |B^{(r)}(x)| - C_{B^{(r)}(x)}(f(x)).$$

We then computed our approximation of this quantity using $\hat{N}_X$ defined in (8). We plot the actual number of improving states vs. the number predicted in Figure 10. Using the above settings, the approximation tends to slightly overpredict for lower values.

To evaluate the approximation for high-fitness states, we sampled, using hill-climbing local search, 700 states from instance s2v100s1200-1 whose fitness values lie in the interval $[900, 1020]$ (recall the global optimum is at 1031). Using each of these states as centroids, we enumerated a radius 5 Hamming ball and counted the number of states lying in the ball with fitness at least 90% of optimal. We compare this with the corresponding count predicted by the approximation in Figure 11. In both cases we find a tight correlation between the estimate and the true count.

5. CONCLUSION

In this paper we have introduced a method for approximating the distribution of fitness values over regions of the fitness landscape. Our method is applicable to epistatically bounded fitness functions that map binary strings into a set with bounded cardinality. Such fitness functions are often found in hard combinatorial optimization problems such as

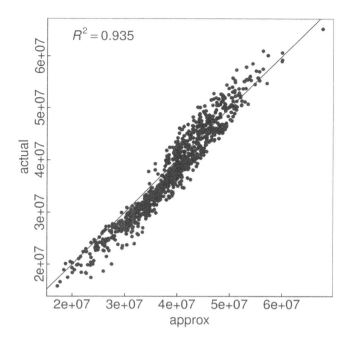

Figure 10: Number of actual improving states vs. number predicted in 1000 random regions of radius 5 over s2v100c1200 MAX-k-SAT benchmark set.

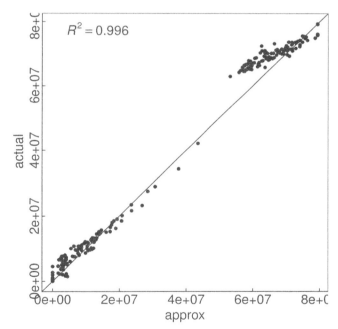

Figure 11: Number of states within 90% of optimal vs. number predicted in 700 high-fitness regions of radius 5 on the s2v100c1200-1 instance taken from the MAX-k-SAT benchmark set.

MAX-k-SAT, spin models, and MAX-CUT as well as certain models of evolution, e.g., quantized NK-landscapes.

In tests on two domains, we found our method to be highly accurate at approximating the distributions. The accuracy of the approximation depends on the size of the moment vector used, as well as the fitness of the centroid. Moreover,

the distribution in its cumulative form can be used to accurately predict the number of improving states in a large Hamming region.

Accurate predictions of the distribution of fitness values over states in local regions can impact both evolutionary and local search processes. These predictions can be used to estimate the number of states in a region that lie in a certain fitness range (such as closer to the optimal), or to compare two arbitrary states to select the one more likely to have improving states nearby (i.e., lying within a given Hamming radius). Moreover, this information can be obtained with reasonable computational effort and without resorting to sampling.

Acknowledgements

This research was sponsored by the Air Force Office of Scientific Research, Air Force Materiel Command, USAF, under grant number FA9550-08-1-0422. The U.S. Government is authorized to reproduce and distribute reprints for Governmental purposes notwithstanding any copyright notation thereon.

6. REFERENCES

[1] Torsten Asselmeyer, Werner Ebeling, and Helge Rose. Smoothing representation of fitness landscapes – the genotype-phenotype map of evolution. *BioSystems*, 39(1):63–76, 1996.

[2] Stefano Ermon, Carla Gomes, and Bart Selman. Computing the density of states of Boolean formulas. In *Proceedings of the 16th International Conference on Principles and Practice of Constraint Programming*, 2010.

[3] Robert B. Heckendorn. Embedded landscapes. *Evolutionary Computation*, 10(4):345–369, 2002.

[4] Robert B. Heckendorn, Soraya Rana, and Darrell Whitley. Polynomial time summary statistics for a generalization of MAXSAT. In *Proceedings of the Genetic and Evolutionary Computation Conference*, pages 281–288, 1999.

[5] Andrew O. Makhorin. GLPK: GNU Linear Programming Kit [computer software]. Available from http://www.gnu.org/software/glpk/, 2000–2008.

[6] Miroslav Morháč. An iterative error-free algorithm to solve Vandermonde systems. *Applied Mathematics and Computation*, 117(1):45 – 54, 2001.

[7] Mark E. J. Newman and Robin Engelhardt. Effect of neutral selection on the evolution of molecular species. In *Proc. R. Soc. London B.*, volume 256, pages 1333–1338, 1998.

[8] Helge Rose, Werner Ebeling, and Torsten Asselmeyer. The density of states-a measure of the difficulty of optimisation problems. In *Proceedings of the 4th International Conference on Parallel Problem Solving from Nature*, pages 208–217. Springer Verlag, 1996.

[9] Andrew M. Sutton, L. Darrell Whitley, and Adele E. Howe. Computing the moments of k-bounded pseudo-Boolean functions over Hamming spheres of arbitrary radius in polynomial time. *Theoretical Computer Science*, 2011, doi:10.1016/j.tcs.2011.02.006

[10] Leslie G. Valiant. The complexity of computing the permanent. *Theoretical Computer Science*, 8(2):189 – 201, 1979.

The Role of Selective Pressure When Solving Symmetric Functions In Polynomial Time

Lars Kaden
Daimler AG
lars.kaden@daimler.com

Nicole Weicker
nicole@weicker.info

Karsten Weicker
HTWK Leipzig
Gustav-Freytag-Str. 42a
04277 Leipzig, Germany
weicker@imn.htwk-
leipzig.de

ABSTRACT

This paper is concerned with the question to which extent a change in the selective pressure might improve the runtime of an optimization algorithm considerably. The subject of this examination is the class of symmetric functions, i.e. OneMax with a subsequent application of a real valued function. We consider an improvement in runtime as considerable if an exponential runtime becomes polynomial. The basis for this examination is a Markov chain analysis. An exact criterion for static selective pressure, telling which functions are solvable in polynomial time, is extended to a sufficient (but not necessary) criterion for changing selection pressure.

General Terms

Algorithms, Theory

Categories and Subject Descriptors

F.2.2 [**Analysis of Algorithms and Problem Complexity**]: Nonnumerical algorithms and problems; G.1.6 [**Numerical Analysis**]: Optimization

1. INTRODUCTION

Genetic algorithms consist of several components, like mutation, recombination, and selection. Strong dependencies between parameters of these different components [2] challenge both the understanding of the dynamics within an optimization run as well as the prediction of "good" parameter settings.

The most important concepts within the genetic algorithm are the population, encoding of a problem space, recombination of (at least) two individuals, mutation and (parental) selection. In this work we focus on two concepts, mutation and selection, within a very simple setup. Our primary interest is the question to what extent the variation of the selection pressure contributes to the solvability of

a problem. The concrete algorithm consists of a population containing one individual, a one-bit flipping mutation and a local search "Metropolis" selection [10], that accepts the mutated individual if it is better or with the probability $\alpha^{|f(x)-f(mutate(x))|}$ otherwise ($\alpha \in (0,1)$). Smaller values of α correspond to a higher selective pressure. Note that the notation in this contribution differs from the literature. Usually, the probability to accept worsenings is formulated as $e^{-\frac{|f(mutate(x))-f(x)|}{k \cdot T}}$ with temperature T and Boltzmann constant k. In case of maximization this is equivalent to our notation with $\alpha = e^{-\frac{1}{k \cdot T}}$.

When we address "solvability" in this paper, we mean scalability actually, and distinguish two classes of problems for an (arbitrary) given algorithm. The first class contains all problems that can be "solved in polynomial time"—this means in the context of this paper that the expected hitting time $T(n)$ for the optimum is in $T(n) \in P := \cup_{k>0} \mathcal{O}(n^k)$. The second class encompasses all problems that are not solvable in polynomial time—a class that includes problems requiring exponential runtime in expectancy among others.

Where many other works tend to generalize the runtime analysis for a wider class of evolutionary algorithms [6], more complex algorithms (e.g. multi-objective methods in [5]), or special problems (e.g. minimum spanning tree in [11]), we consider a simple algorithm and a well-known, comprehensive class of problems and try to prove exact criteria that describe which function within the class is solvable in polynomial time using which selective pressure.

The framework for this examination are the all-ones symmetric functions that are based on bit counting. There is a wide range of well-examined instantiations of these functions: from OneMax to deceptive trap functions [1] or the valley function [3].

DEFINITION 1. *A function* $f : \{0,1\}^n \to \mathbb{R}$ *is called a* symmetric function *iff the function value depends only on the number of ones in the input string*

$$f(x) = f_k \in \mathbb{R}, \qquad k = \|x\|_1, x \in \{0,1\}^n.$$

In the case of all-ones symmetric functions, *the unique global maximum is located at the bit string* $(1, \ldots, 1)$.

We distinguish the terms

- *function* which is in our case always of the form

$$f^{(n)} : \{i \in \mathbb{N} \mid 0 \le i \le n\} \to \mathbb{R}$$

mapping the number of ones in a bit-string on the fitness value (for a given $n \in \mathbb{N}$),

- *family of functions* which is always a subset of

$$\{f \mid f \text{ is a function}\}$$

—for simplicity we pretend in the remainder of the paper that there is always exactly one function $f^{(n)}$ for each $n \in \mathbb{N}$—however the complete proof is valid even if there are various functions $f^{(n)}$ for any value of n; we determine asymptotic bounds for the hitting time when this family of functions is optimized using a given algorithm, and

- *problem class* is a set that contains families of functions and a common asymptotic time bound—for each of these families there exists an optimization algorithm that solves the function family within the time bound. Note, that the problem class differs from a complexity class since we do not require the problem class to be complete.

In [7] we have determined the concrete problem class containing the all-ones symmetric functions that are solvable in polynomial time by the Metropolis algorithm. The result is quickly reviewed in section 3. Droste et.al. [3] have shown that there are function families, e.g. the valley function, that are not solvable by Metropolis in polynomial time—except if the selective pressure is increased during optimization (which is equivalent to simulated annealing [9]). Also, Sorkin [12] has shown a fractal function with this property that is not a symmetric function.

The function families with this property is the primary objective of our paper. We want to know to what extent the polynomial solvable problem class increases when the selection pressure changes during optimization. Contrary to [3] we do not change the selective pressure continuously but rather simplify and change the selective parameter only once as is shown in algorithm 1. We will denote this algorithm as "modified Metropolis algorithm" in the remainder of the paper. Note, additionally, that the algorithm in [3] uses reciprocal value of α instead.

2. TECHNIQUES FOR THE ANALYSIS

This section briefly discusses the main techniques used in the runtime analysis and provides a short proof sketch.

Algorithm 1 Modified Metropolis algorithm with one-bit flipping mutation for maximization problems; parameters $\alpha, \beta \in (0, 1)$ control the selective pressure and t_{change} determines the time step when the change from α to β occurs.

METROPOLIS(fitness function $f : \{0, 1\}^n \to \mathbb{R}$)

```
1   t ← 0
2   γ ← α
3   x ← uniformly choose from {0,1}^n
4   while f(x) is not optimal
5   do ⌈ i ← uniformly choose from {1,...,n}
6        y ← flip the ith bit in x
7        p ← uniformly choose from (0,1)
8        if p ≤ min{γ^{f(x)−f(y)}, 1}
9        then ⌊ x ← y
10       t ← t + 1
11       if t = t_change
12       ⌊ then ⌊ γ ← β
13  return x
```

2.1 Markov model

Runtime or convergence analyzes are usually obtained using Markov chain models [4]. In case of all-ones symmetric functions the Markov chain M is rather simple (see e.g. [3]) where each state $0 \le i \le n$ corresponds to the number of ones in the current individual. The transitions are defined by probability p_i^+ to advance from state i to state $i + 1$ in one step $(0 \le i < n)$ and probability p_i^- for a step from state i to $i - 1$ $(0 < i \le n)$. Apparently the following equations hold:

$$p_i^+ = \frac{n - i}{n} \cdot \min\{\alpha^{f_i - f_{i+1}}, 1\}$$
$$p_i^- = \frac{i}{n} \cdot \min\{\alpha^{f_i - f_{i-1}}, 1\}.$$

The probability to stay in state i equals $1 - p_i^+ - p_i^-$ $(0 \le i \le n)$ where in addition $p_0^- = p_n^+ = 0$.

Now, the random variable T_M denotes the hitting time of the optimum using Markov chain M. The random variable $T_{M,i}$ $(0 \le i \le n)$ is the hitting time when starting in state i of the Markov chain. Using a uniformly random initial individual in the optimization, T_M can be expressed as

$$T_M = \sum_{0 \le i \le n} \frac{\binom{n}{i}}{2^n} \cdot T_{M,i}.$$

If we assume an initial distribution $\vec{a}$ of the probabilities to be in the different states of the Markov chain, $0 \le (\vec{a})_i \le 1$ for state $0 \le i \le n$ with $\sum_{0 \le i \le n} (\vec{a})_i = 1$, the random variable $T_{M,\vec{a}}$ denotes the hitting time when starting with $\vec{a}$. Clearly, $T_{M,\vec{a}}$ can be expressed as

$$T_{M,\vec{a}} = \sum_{0 \le i \le n} (\vec{a})_i \cdot T_{M,i}.$$

If the context is clear, we omit the subscript M and write only T, T_i, and $T_{\vec{a}}$.

2.2 Polynomial equivalence

Contrary to many other publications, we are merely interested in distinguishing between polynomial and superpolynomial asymptotic runtimes in this work. The latter include exponential runtime. In our search for families of functions that are solvable in polynomial time we derive a criterion to assess all possible functions. As a consequence all functions that are within a polynomial factor to any given polynomial function are considered equivalent. For this purpose we introduce the notion of polynomial equivalence to keep the mathematical conditions simple.

DEFINITION 2. *Two functions* $f : \mathbb{N} \to \mathbb{R}$ *and* $g : \mathbb{N} \to \mathbb{R}$ *are called* P-equivalent

$$f \sim_P g \quad :\Leftrightarrow \quad \exists \text{ polynomials } p(n), q(n) :$$
$$f(n) \le p(n)g(n) \wedge g(n) \le q(n)f(n).$$

Note that P-equivalence partitions the functions in the complement of P into an infinite number of classes—which is of no relevance in this paper since we distinguish between polynomial and super-polynomial functions only. As long as $f \in P$ and $f \sim_P g$ holds, it is true that $g \in P$. Also $f \notin P$ and $f \sim_P g$ imply $g \notin P$. To derive the polynomial time criteria the following lemma is used. For a proof we refer to [7].

LEMMA 1. *Let* $f : \mathbb{N} \to \mathbb{R}$ *be a sum of a polynomially bound number of terms* $s(i,n)$ *(with* $a(n) \leq i \leq b(n)$ *and* $b(n) - a(n) + 1 \in P$*). Then*

$$f(n) = \sum_{i=a(n)}^{b(n)} s(i,n) \quad \sim_P \quad \max_{a(n) \leq i \leq b(n)} s(i,n).$$

2.3 Comparing probability distributions

In the main result of this paper, the polynomial runtime criterion with changing selection pressure, the probability distribution along the Markov chain is characterized. In order to compare two distributions we use the relation of right- and left-orientedness.

DEFINITION 3. *The vector* $\vec{a} \in \mathbb{R}_+^{n+1}$ *is more right-oriented than* $\vec{b} \in \mathbb{R}_+^{n+1}$ *iff*

$$\forall 0 \leq i \leq n : \sum_{j=i}^{n} (\vec{a})_j \geq \sum_{j=i}^{n} (\vec{b})_j.$$

We write $\vec{a} \geq_R \vec{b}$. *Analogously* $\vec{a}$ *is more left-oriented* $\vec{a} \geq_L \vec{b}$ *iff*

$$\forall 0 \leq i \leq n : \sum_{j=0}^{i} (\vec{a})_j \geq \sum_{j=0}^{i} (\vec{b})_j.$$

This definition appears to be a special case of the partial ordering for probability measures as it was already examined e.g. in [8].

Usually $\vec{a}$ and $\vec{b}$ are probability distributions where $(\vec{x})_j$ denotes the probability to be in state i within distribution $\vec{x}$.

A set of simple properties can be shown for the relations:

(P1) They are transitive: $\vec{a} \geq_R \vec{b}$ and $\vec{b} \geq_R \vec{c} \Rightarrow \vec{a} \geq_R \vec{c}$.

(P2) They are invariant against addition:
$\vec{a} \geq_R \vec{b}$ and $\vec{c} \geq_R \vec{d} \Rightarrow \vec{a} + \vec{c} \geq_R \vec{b} + \vec{d}$.

(P3) $\geq_R$ and $\geq_L$ are complementary: $\vec{a} \geq_R \vec{b} \Leftrightarrow \vec{b} \geq_L \vec{a}$.

(P4) A sequence of distributions $\vec{s_i}$ $(i \in \mathbb{N})$ with $\vec{s_i} \geq_R \vec{s_{i+1}}$ converges at $\lim_{i \to \infty} \vec{s_i}$.

(P5) For a converging sequence of distributions $\vec{s_i}$ $(i \in \mathbb{N})$ with $\vec{s_i} \geq_R \vec{s_{i+1}}$ it holds that $\vec{s_i} \geq_R \lim_{i \to \infty} \vec{s_i}$ for all $i > 0$.

(P6) For two vectors with $\vec{a} \geq_R \vec{b}$ and $0 \leq p \leq q \leq 1$ it holds:

$$q \cdot \vec{a} + (1-q) \cdot \vec{b} \geq_R p \cdot \vec{a} + (1-p) \cdot \vec{b}.$$

Since we want to make statements on the expected runtime, the following lemma introduces an interesting connection between orientedness and expected runtime. We use this result to determine a lower bound for the distribution at the phase change.

LEMMA 2. *Given two initial distributions* $\vec{a}$ *and* $\vec{b}$ *with* $\vec{a} \geq_R \vec{b}$, *then* $E(T_{M,\vec{a}}) \leq E(T_{M,\vec{b}})$.

2.4 Overall approach

The optimization process is modeled using two different Markov chains for the phases with distinct selective parameters α and β. The Markov chain of the first phase is simplified in order to determine a limiting distribution which is used in the lower bound for the probability distribution when the selective parameter is changed from α to β. In this part of the analysis the right-orientedness of distributions is used. Because of the simplification of the first phase Markov chain we can only derive a sufficient criterion.

The second phase Markov chain uses the limiting distribution as starting point and can be modeled like the optimization with static selective pressure published in [7].

The expected hitting time of the optimum is computed quantitatively. By using the notion of P-equivalence a sufficient criterion for the polynomially solvable problem class (using the modified Metropolis algorithm in algorithm 1) is derived.

3. STATIC SELECTIVE PRESSURE

Concerning a static selective pressure during the search process, the following theorem has been shown which decides for any symmetric function whether it will be solved in polynomial runtime (in expectancy).

THEOREM 1 (STATIC POLYNOMIAL TIME CRITERION).
If and only if the following conditions hold for arbitrary but fixed values $c_1, c_2 \in \mathbb{R}_{>0}$:

$(S1)$ $n(\ln n - \ln 2) +$
$$\max_{0 \leq m \leq j \leq \lfloor \frac{n}{2} \rfloor} (g_\alpha(m) - f_j |\ln \alpha|) \leq c_1 \ln n$$

$(S2)$ $\displaystyle \max_{\substack{0 \leq m \leq j \\ \lfloor \frac{n}{2} \rfloor < j \leq n}} (g_\alpha(m) - g_\alpha(j)) \leq c_2 \ln n$

where $g_\alpha(x) = f_x |\ln \alpha| - (n-x) \widetilde{\ln}(n-x) - x \widetilde{\ln} x$

and $\widetilde{\ln} x = \begin{cases} 1, & \text{iff } x \leq 0 \\ \ln x, & \text{iff } x > 0 \end{cases}$

then it holds for the expected runtime $E(T)(n) \in P$.

The proof has been published in [7] and is based on the initial situation in [3]. Within the proof the exact number of steps (in expectancy) $E(T_i)$ has been derived—given that the optimization process starts in state i:

$$E(T_i) = \sum_{j=i}^{n-1} \sum_{k=0}^{j} n \cdot \frac{(n-j-1)!j!}{(n-k)!k!} \cdot \frac{\alpha^{f_j - f_k}}{\min\{\alpha^{f_j - f_{j+1}}, 1\}}. \quad (1)$$

This intermediate result will be used within the proof of the main result of this paper.

This theorem can be used in two different ways: First, we can determine the problem class containing those families of functions that are solvable in polynomial time depending on a (possibly given) selective pressure α. Second, we can examine a given family of functions to find out for which values of α it is solvable in polynomial time.

Before the new criterion for the modified Metropolis algorithm is discussed in the next section, we want to have a brief look at how the criterion for the static case is used—using the well-known function family $F^{(1)}$ with

$$f_k = k$$

which describes OneMax.

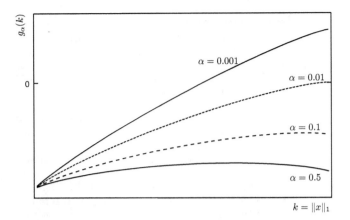

Figure 1: Function g_α for the OneMax function family $F^{(1)}$—exemplary shown for $n = 100$ and various values for α.

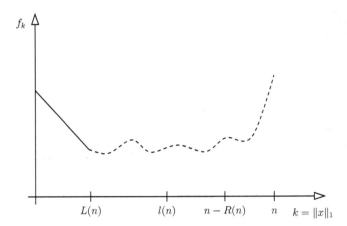

Figure 2: Condition (D2) in theorem 2 requires the left part of the fitness functions to be monotonically decreasing.

COROLLARY 1. *The Metropolis algorithm solves the One-Max function $F^{(1)}$ in polynomial time (in expectancy) if and only if $\alpha \leq \sqrt[n]{n^{c_2}} - 1$.*

PROOF. If we rearrange the first condition (S1)

$$\max_{0 \leq m \leq j \leq \lfloor \frac{n}{2} \rfloor} ((f_m - f_j)|\ln \alpha| - (n - m)\widetilde{\ln}(n - m) - m\widetilde{\ln}m)$$
$$+ n(\ln n - \ln 2) \leq c_1 \ln n$$

we see that the first part of the maximum term is never > 0 because of the increasing function values of OneMax; for $j = m$ the term equals 0. As a consequence the second term determines the maximum with $m = \frac{n}{2}$. The resulting condition

$$-2 \cdot \frac{n}{2} \ln \frac{n}{2} + n(\ln n - \ln 2) \leq c_1 \ln n$$

is fulfilled trivially since the left-hand side equals 0.

For condition (S2) we have a closer look at the function g_α which is displayed in figure 1. Apparently the maximum term can only be positive if $g_\alpha(j) < g_\alpha(m)$ where $j > m$. We find this maximum if we choose $j = n$ and $m = \frac{n}{\alpha+1}$ (where the function g_α is maximal). Now, we can analyze condition (S2).

$$\frac{n}{\alpha+1}|\ln \alpha| - (n - \frac{n}{\alpha+1})\ln(n - \frac{n}{\alpha+1}) - \frac{n}{\alpha+1}\ln\frac{n}{\alpha+1}$$
$$- n|\ln \alpha| + n\ln n \leq c_2 \ln n$$
$$\Leftrightarrow -(\frac{\alpha}{\alpha+1}n)\ln(\frac{n}{\alpha+1}) - \frac{n}{\alpha+1}\ln\frac{n}{\alpha+1} + n\ln n \leq c_2 \ln n$$
$$\Leftrightarrow n(\ln n - \ln\frac{n}{\alpha+1}) \leq c_2 \ln n$$
$$\Leftrightarrow (\alpha + 1)^n \leq n^{c_2}$$
$$\Leftrightarrow \alpha \leq \underbrace{\sqrt[n]{n^{c_2}} - 1}_{>0}.$$

And the polynomial runtime follows as stated in the corollary. □

4. INCREASING SELECTIVE PRESSURE

Now, we want to consider the case when the selective pressure changes during the optimization process. We restrict ourselves to a singular change. Since the goal is polynomial runtime we require that this change happens after $p(n)$ steps with polynomial p. Contrary to the results with static selective pressure, the following criterion is sufficient but not necessary.

THEOREM 2 (DYNAMIC POLYNOMIAL TIME CRITERION). *Let the selection pressure change from α to β during the optimization process. If the following conditions hold for arbitrary but fixed values $c_1, c_2, d \in \mathbb{R}_{>0}$, monotonically increasing functions $L(n)$ and $R(n)$ (not bound by a constant value) and a function $l(n) \leq n - R(n)$:*

$(D1)$ $|f_m^{(n)} - f_{m+1}^{(n)}| > d$ *for all* $0 \leq m \leq \min\{l(n), L(n)\}$

$(D2)$ $f_m^{(n)} > f_{m+1}^{(n)}$ *for all* $0 \leq m \leq \min\{l(n), L(n)\}$

$(D3)$ $\displaystyle\max_{0 \leq m \leq j \leq l(n)} (g_\alpha(m) - g_\alpha(j)) \leq c_1 \ln n,$

$(D4)$ $\displaystyle\max_{\substack{0 \leq m \leq j \leq n \\ 0 \leq i \leq l(n) \\ i \leq j}} (g_\beta(m) - g_\beta(j) + g_\alpha(i)) -$
$$\max_{0 \leq k \leq l(n)} g_\alpha(k) \leq c_2 \ln n$$

where $g_\gamma(x) = f_x|\ln \gamma| - (n - x)\widetilde{\ln}(n - x) - x\widetilde{\ln}x$

and $\widetilde{\ln}x = \begin{cases} 1, & \text{iff } x \leq 0 \\ \ln x, & \text{iff } x > 0. \end{cases}$

Then there exists a polynomial p such that a change from α to β after at least $p(n)$ steps guarantees a runtime $E(T)(n) \in P$.

The condition $(D1)$ is merely a technical one—we require at one point of the proof that there are no plateaus when one bit is flipped.

The condition $(D2)$ requires an uninterrupted monotonically decreasing function (starting at state 0) to an acceptable fraction of the search space. This condition is visualized in figure 2 and is again mere technical.

The condition $(D3)$ makes a statement on how the function values in the worse part of the search space should relate to each other.

The condition $(D4)$ is the main requirement since it connects the function values and the two selection parameters α and β.

As can be seen clearly the criterion loosens the conditions for polynomial runtime compared to theorem 1. Condition (D3) is the equivalent to (S1) using $l(n)$ instead of $\lfloor \frac{n}{2} \rfloor$. Condition (D4) is the equivalent to (S2) with β replacing α—

however the function values are related to the first selection parameter α which increases the possible differences of the function values. Still, the two terms with α can only contribute positively to the criterion if i is pushed to a position different from k or if m and j are moved because of i.

5. PROOF OF THEOREM 2

The proof is primarily organized in accordance with the course of an optimization run.

5.1 Initial situation

For an exact result on average, the initial distribution $\vec{m}_0$ is assumed to be defined by $(\vec{m}_0)_i = \frac{1}{2^n} \cdot \binom{n}{i}$ $(0 \leq i \leq n)$. However, we are deriving a sufficient criterion only. As a consequence we assume as a worst case that we will start in state 0 which leads to an upper bound for the exact result.

Since the modified Metropolis algorithm is divided into two phases with different selection pressure, we analyze first the optimization steps that are necessary to reach state $l(n)$ (in the subsequent section 5.2). In the remaining part of the proof we will derive a "lower bound" for the probability distribution when entering the second phase. To get a sensible runtime criterion we must be sure that the second phase focuses primarily on the states $> l(n)$.

5.2 Expectancy value of the first phase

First the number of steps are determined that are necessary to get from state 0 to state $l(n)$.

LEMMA 3. *Being in the phase with selective pressure α, state $l(n)$ is reached in the P-equivalent time*

$$E(T_{0 \to l(n)})(n) \quad \sim_P \quad e^{\max\limits_{0 \leq k \leq j \leq l(n)} g_\alpha(k) - g_\alpha(j)}$$

where $g_\gamma(x) = f_x |\ln \gamma| - (n-x)\widetilde{\ln}(n-x) - x \widetilde{\ln} x$. The random variable $T_{0 \to l(n)}$ denotes the optimization time to reach state $l(n)$ from starting state 0.

PROOF. Analogously to the approach in [3] the expectancy value is derived:

$$E(T_{0 \to l(n)})(n) =$$
$$\sum_{j=0}^{l(n)-1} \sum_{k=0}^{j} n \cdot \frac{(n-j-1)!j!}{(n-k)!k!} \cdot \frac{\alpha^{f_j - f_k}}{\min\{\alpha^{f_j - f_{j+1}}, 1\}}.$$

Using lemma 1 and transformations eliminating the factor $\min\{\alpha^{f_j - f_{j+1}}, 1\}$ lead to the following equation.

$$E(T_{0 \to l(n)})(n) \sim_P$$
$$\max_{0 \leq k \leq j \leq l(n)} \left(n \cdot \frac{(n-j-1)!j!}{(n-k)!k!} \cdot \alpha^{f_j - f_k} \right).$$

Replacing the faculty values by the Stirling formula and further technical simplifications lead to the formula in the lemma. □

Lemma 3 is equivalent to the condition (D3) of the theorem.

5.3 Minimum probability for reaching the second phase

Analogously to the proof in [3] we can derive the minimum probability $1 - \left(\frac{1}{2}\right)^{p(n)}$ that the state $l(n)$ was active at least once after $2 \cdot p(n) \cdot E(T_{0 \to l(n)})(n)$ steps—where $p(n)$ is an

arbitrary polynomial. This result will be an essential part of the analysis of the state distribution when the second phase starts. In fact, the number of steps before the phase change takes place should be at least $2 \cdot p(n) \cdot E(T_{0 \to l(n)})(n)$.

5.4 Monotony of the Markov chain

In order to get a very general elementary formula for the polynomial time criterion, an as precise as possible estimation of the behavior of the optimization process is necessary. For a broad class of Markov chains we can use the steady state to estimate the distribution after a minimum number of optimization steps. This estimation will lead to a simple set of linear equations that will be solved later.

For a Markov chain to fulfill the requirements of runtime comparison (lemma 2) and steady state, a single step in the Markov chain must preserve the right-orientedness—which we will denote as *monotony*. As the following lemma shows, the condition $p_a^+ + p_{a+1}^- \leq 1$ must hold for all neighboring states a and $a+1$ $(0 \leq a \leq n-1)$. This was defined and used similarly in [8]. In the lemma the distribution $\vec{m}$ is transformed to the distribution $S(\vec{m})$ by one optimization step.

LEMMA 4. *If $p_a^+ + p_{a+1}^- \leq 1$ holds for an $0 \leq a < n$ as well as $\sum_{i=0}^{b}(\vec{m})_i \leq \sum_{i=0}^{b}(\vec{m'})_i$ for distributions $\vec{m}$ and $\vec{m'}$ and $a - 1 \leq b \leq a + 1$, then*

$$\sum_{i=0}^{a}(S(\vec{m}))_i \leq \sum_{i=0}^{a}(S(\vec{m'}))_i.$$

PROOF. We omit the simple cases $a = 0$ and $a = n$ and show only the general case $1 \leq a < n$.

$$\sum_{i=0}^{a}(S(\vec{m}))_i = \sum_{i=0}^{a}(\vec{m})_i - p_a^+ \cdot (\vec{m})_a + p_{a+1}^- \cdot (\vec{m})_{a+1}$$

$$= p_{a+1}^- \cdot \sum_{i=0}^{a+1}(\vec{m})_i + (1 - p_{a+1}^-) \cdot \sum_{i=0}^{a-1}(\vec{m})_i$$
$$+ (1 - p_{a+1}^- - p_a^+) \cdot (\vec{m})_a$$

$$= p_{a+1}^- \cdot \underbrace{\sum_{i=0}^{a+1}(\vec{m})_i}_{\leq \sum_{i=0}^{a+1}(\vec{m'})_i} + \underbrace{(1 - p_{a+1}^- - p_a^+)}_{\geq 0} \cdot \underbrace{\sum_{i=0}^{a}(\vec{m})_i}_{\leq \sum_{i=0}^{a}(\vec{m'})_i}$$
$$+ p_a^+ \cdot \underbrace{\sum_{i=0}^{a-1}(\vec{m})_i}_{\leq \sum_{i=0}^{a-1}(\vec{m'})_i}$$

$$\leq p_{a+1}^- \cdot \sum_{i=0}^{a+1}(\vec{m'})_i + (1 - p_{a+1}^- - p_a^+) \cdot \sum_{i=0}^{a}(\vec{m'})_i$$
$$+ p_a^+ \cdot \sum_{i=0}^{a-1}(\vec{m'})_i$$

$$= \sum_{i=0}^{a}(S(\vec{m'}))_i. \quad \square$$

Now, the following corollary results immediately and extends the local left-orientedness to the global $\geq_L$.

COROLLARY 2. *If $p_a^+ + p_{a+1}^- \leq 1$ for $0 \leq a < n$ and $m' \geq_L m$, then*

$$S(\vec{m'}) \geq_L S(\vec{m}).$$

5.5 Family of functions with monotonous Markov chains

In this section, a family of functions with monotonous Markov chains is described by relating the function values f_i and f_{i+1} $(0 \le i < n)$ to the condition $p_i^+ + p_{i+1}^- \le 1$.

- If $f_i < f_{i+1}$ then $p_i^+ = \frac{n-i}{n}$ and $p_{i+1}^- = \frac{i+1}{n} \cdot \alpha^{f_{i+1}-f_i}$. By substitution we get

$$\frac{n-i}{n} + \frac{i+1}{n} \cdot \alpha^{f_{i+1}-f_i} \le 1$$

$$\alpha^{f_{i+1}-f_i} \le \frac{i}{i+1}$$

$$f_{i+1} - f_i \ge \frac{|\ln i - \ln(i+1)|}{|\ln \alpha|}.$$

- If $f_i \ge f_{i+1}$ then $p_i^+ = \frac{n-i}{n} \cdot \alpha^{f_i-f_{i+1}}$ and $p_{i+1}^- = \frac{i+1}{n}$. These values lead to the condition

$$f_i - f_{i+1} \ge \frac{|\ln(1 - \frac{1}{n-i})|}{|\ln \alpha|}$$

$$= \frac{|\ln(n-i-1) - \ln(n-i)|}{|\ln \alpha|}$$

which is symmetric to the first condition (with regard to $\frac{n}{2}$).

Since this requirement is rather unhandy in the further analysis we replace it by the following weaker condition.

- There are two monotonous increasing functions $L : \mathbb{N} \to \mathbb{N}$ and $R : \mathbb{N} \to \mathbb{N}$ (with $L(n), R(n) \in \{0, \dots, n\}$) that are not bound by a constant value, i.e.

$$\forall c \in \mathbb{N} \; \exists n_0 \in \mathbb{N} : L(n_0) > c$$

(and analogously for R). The boundaries L and R partition the assignment of fitness values to the number of ones $\|x\|_1$ into three ranges.

- The function is decreasing for the left range smaller than $L(n)$:

$$\forall i < L(n) : f_i > f_{i+1}.$$

- The function is increasing for the right range:

$$\forall i > n - R(n) : f_i < f_{i+1}.$$

- Neighboring values differ by a delta of $d > 0$:

$$\exists d > 0 \; \forall n \in \mathbb{N} \; \forall 0 \le i < n : |f_i - f_{i+1}| \ge d.$$

These requirements are visualized in figure 3.

LEMMA 5. *Given a set of functions F and the existence of functions L and R with the requirements described above, the Markov chains of all functions in F are asymptotically monotonous, that is: $\exists n_0 \in \mathbb{N}$ such that $\forall n \ge n_0 : f^{(n)} \in F$ is monotonous.*

PROOF. Since we are interested in asymptotic statements only, it suffices to show that there exists a value n_0 such that for all $n > n_0$ the Markov chain is monotonous. We choose n_0 big enough that $L(n_0) \ge \frac{1}{\alpha^{-d}-1}$ and $R(n_0) \ge \frac{1}{1-\alpha^d}$. We will show that

(a) if $f_i < f_{i+1}$ (which is only possible for $i \ge L(n)$):
$\alpha^{f_{i+1}-f_i} \le \frac{i}{i+1}$.

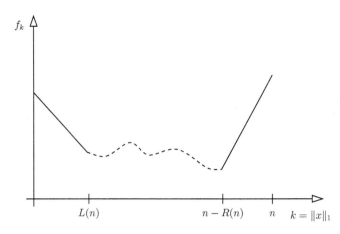

Figure 3: Condition for asymptotically monotonous Markov chains: The decreasing part on the left and the increasing part on the right are shown simplifying as linear function.

(b) if $f_i \ge f_{i+1}$ (which is only possible for $i < n - R(n)$):
$\alpha^{f_i-f_{i+1}} \le 1 - \frac{1}{n-i}$.

The proof of (a): First we show for $i = L(n_0)$

$$\alpha^{f_{i+1}-f_i} \le \alpha^d \stackrel{!}{\le} \frac{L(n_0)}{L(n_0)+1}.$$

The inequality follows directly from:

$$\frac{L(n_0)}{L(n_0)+1} = 1 - \frac{1}{L(n_0)+1} \ge 1 - \frac{1}{\frac{1}{\alpha^{-d}-1}+1} = \frac{1}{\alpha^{-d}} = \alpha^d.$$

Since $\frac{i}{i+1}$ and L are monotonous increasing, (a) follows for all $i \ge L(n)$ $(n \ge n_0)$.

Analogously the proof of (b) follows directly from the prerequisites (here, for $i = n_0 - R(n_0)$)

$$\alpha^{f_i-f_{i+1}} \le \alpha^d \le 1 - \frac{1}{R(n_0)}. \quad \square$$

5.6 Modified Markov chain for the α phase

In order to enable the further proof steps, a different Markov chain is considered that is analyzable easily. To do so, the exact Markov chain M must have a more right-oriented distribution than the new Markov chain. We consider the following Markov chain M' with the transition probabilities

$$p_i'^- = p_i^- \qquad p_i'^+ = \begin{cases} p_i^+, & \text{if } i \ne l(n) \\ 0, & \text{if } i = l(n). \end{cases}$$

Now the following lemma can be shown by an inductive proof. Subsequently we suppose both Markov chains M and M' to be monotonous.

LEMMA 6. *Let the initial distribution $\vec{m}_0'$ of M' be chosen in such a way that $\vec{m}_0 \ge_R \vec{m}_0'$ and $(\vec{m}_0')_i = 0$ for $l(n) < i \le n$. If the monotony $p_i^+ + p_{i+1}^- \le 1$ holds for $0 \le i < l(n)$ in the initial Markov chain, then for all iterations $i > 0$:*

$$S_M^i(\vec{m}_0) \ge_R S_{M'}^i(\vec{m}_0')$$

where S_M^i denotes the distribution after the i-th iteration.

That means that the Markov chain M has more right-oriented distributions—alas M' is actually doing worse than M. Therefore an analysis of M' will lead to an upper bound of the runtime (or the sufficient but not necessary condition).

PROOF. We prove the lemma by induction. The base case ($i = 0$) holds because

$$S_M^0(\vec{m}_0) = \vec{m}_0 \geq_R \vec{m}_0' = S_{M'}^0(\vec{m}_0').$$

We assume that $S_M^i(\vec{m}_0) \geq_R S_{M'}^i(\vec{m}_0')$ and—due to the modification at state $l(n)$—that

$$(S_{M'}^i(\vec{m}_0'))_j = 0 \text{ for } l(n) < j \leq n.$$

We show that $S_M^{i+1}(\vec{m}_0) \geq_R S_{M'}^{i+1}(\vec{m}_0')$.

Using property (P3), the first assumption is equivalent to $S_{M'}^i(\vec{m}_0') \geq_L S_M^i(\vec{m}_0)$ or by using the definition:

$$\forall 0 \leq a \leq n : \sum_{j=0}^{a} (S_{M'}^i(\vec{m}_0'))_j \geq \sum_{j=0}^{a} (S_M^i(\vec{m}_0))_j.$$

Given $p_j^+ = p_j'^+$ and $p_j^- = p_j'^-$ for $0 \leq j < l(n)$ the respective components of the successive distributions (at $i + 1$) can be computed using the same Markov chain M. Since the monotony condition holds for $0 \leq j < l(n)$ lemma 4 may be applied which leads to

$$\forall 0 \leq a \leq n : \sum_{j=0}^{a} (S_{M'}^{i+1}(\vec{m}_0'))_j \geq \sum_{j=0}^{a} (S_M^{i+1}(\vec{m}_0))_j.$$

The cases $a \geq l(n)$ hold trivially because the requirements $p_{l(n)}'^+ = 0$ and $(\vec{m}_0')_j = 0$ for $l(n) < j \leq n$ imply

$$(S_{M'}^i(\vec{m}_0'))_j = 0 \text{ for } l(n) < j \leq n$$

which is equivalent to

$$\sum_{j=0}^{l(n)} (S_{M'}^i(\vec{m}_0'))_j = 1. \quad \square$$

This lemma will be used in the following section where the limiting distribution is determined and again in the computation of the overall estimation of the expected hitting time.

5.7 Introducing the asymptotic distribution

In this section, we prepare the estimation of the process by a limiting distribution. First, we show that certain Markov processes are monotonous.

LEMMA 7. *Let $\vec{m}_0$ be the distribution with*

$$(\vec{m}_0)_j = \begin{cases} 0, & \text{if } j \neq l(n) \\ 1, & \text{if } j = l(n). \end{cases}$$

For a Markov chain M with $p_{l(n)}^+ = 0$ and $p_i^+ + p_{i+1}^- \leq 1$ ($i < l(n)$) it follows that

$$S_M^i(\vec{m}_0) \geq_R S_M^j(\vec{m}_0) \text{ for } i \leq j.$$

PROOF. It follows immediately from $p_{l(n)}^+ = 0$ and $(\vec{m}_0)_j = 0$ for $j > l(n)$ that the probabilities for states $> l(n)$ equal 0 for all succeeding distributions. In particular: $\vec{m}_0 \geq_R S(\vec{m}_0)$. Now we can apply lemma 6 by choosing $M' = M$ and the given initial distribution as $\vec{m}_0$ and $\vec{m}_0' = S(\vec{m}_0)$ which leads to

$$S_M^i(\vec{m}_0) \geq_R S_M^i(S(\vec{m}_0)) \quad (= S_M^{i+1}(\vec{m}_0)).$$

The proof is finished by using property (P1). $\quad \square$

The following corollary results from lemma 7 by applying the properties (P4) and (P5).

COROLLARY 3. *Let $\vec{m}_0$ be the distribution with*

$$(\vec{m}_0)_j = \begin{cases} 0, & \text{if } j \neq l(n) \\ 1, & \text{if } j = l(n). \end{cases}$$

For a Markov chain M with $p_{l(n)}^+ = 0$ and $p_i^+ + p_{i+1}^- \leq 1$ ($i < l(n)$) it follows that

$$S_M^i(\vec{m}_0) \geq_R \lim_{j \to \infty} S_M^j(\vec{m}_0) \text{ for } i \geq 0.$$

5.8 Estimation of the distribution at the phase change

The estimation of the distribution at the phase change requires a minimum probability for reaching state $l(n)$ and the monotonous convergence of the Markov process starting at state $l(n)$. We show the following lemma.

LEMMA 8. *For a Markov chain M' with the properties described above, an initial distribution $\vec{m}_0'$ with $(\vec{m}_0')_j = 0$ for $j > l(n)$, and minimum probability p for reaching state $l(n)$ after t_0 steps, it holds that for all $t \geq t_0$:*

$$S_{M'}^t(\vec{m}_0') \geq_R p \cdot \lim_{t \to \infty} S_{M'}^t(\vec{m}_R) + (1 - p) \cdot \vec{m}_L$$

where

$$(\vec{m}_R)_j = \begin{cases} 0, & \text{if } j \neq l(n) \\ 1, & \text{if } j = l(n) \end{cases} \qquad (\vec{m}_L)_j = \begin{cases} 0, & \text{if } j \geq 1 \\ 1, & \text{if } j = 0. \end{cases}$$

PROOF. Let p_t be the probability that the Markov process hits state $l(n)$ for the first time at time step t. We can describe the process by superposing two processes: (a) the process that reaches $l(n)$ within t_0 steps and (b) the process that needs more steps. Since the single steps are linear functions both processes may be added using an appropriate distribution $\vec{r}$ that denotes the distribution after t_0 steps not reaching $l(n)$.

$$\forall t \geq t_0 : S_{M'}^t(\vec{m}_0') = \left(\sum_{i=0}^{t_0} p_i \cdot S_{M'}^{t-i}(\vec{m}_R) \right) + \left(1 - \sum_{i=0}^{t_0} p_i \right) \cdot S_{M'}^{t-t_0}(\vec{r}).$$

If we apply corollary 3 to the first process and use the fact that any distribution is more right-oriented than $\vec{m}_L$ for the second process, it follows from property (P2) for all $t \geq t_0$:

$$S_{M'}^t(\vec{m}_0') \geq_R \left(\sum_{i=0}^{t_0} p_i \right) \cdot \lim_{t \to \infty} S_{M'}^t(\vec{m}_R) + \left(1 - \sum_{i=0}^{t_0} p_i \right) \cdot \vec{m}_L.$$

From the requirements we know that $\sum_{t=0}^{t_0} p_t \geq p$. As a consequence we can apply property (P6) and receive the claimed statement. $\quad \square$

5.9 Estimation of the overall hitting time

Now, we want to put the results together in order to compute the estimated overall hitting time.

Lemma 6 has shown that

$$S_M^t(\vec{m}_0) \geq_R S_{M'}^t(\vec{m}_0').$$

If we assume that the expected number of steps to reach $l(n)$ is bound by a polynomial $q(n)$: $E(T_{0 \to l(n)}) \leq q(n)$, we know from section 5.3 that the minimum probability is $1 - (\frac{1}{2})^{p(n)}$ for reaching state $l(n)$ at least once after $2 \cdot p(n) \cdot q(n)$ steps.

Using lemma 8 we can follow for all steps $t \geq 2p(n)q(n)$ that

$$S_{M'}^t(\vec{m}_0') \geq_R \vec{m}_g$$

where

$$\vec{m}_g = \left(1 - \left(\frac{1}{2}\right)^{p(n)}\right) \cdot \lim_{t \to \infty} S_{M'}^t(\vec{m}_R) + \left(\frac{1}{2}\right)^{p(n)} \cdot \vec{m}_L. \quad (2)$$

From the transitivity in (P1) it follows directly for all $t \geq 2p(n)q(n)$ that

$$S_M^t(\vec{m}_0) \geq_R \vec{m}_g.$$

From now on the Markov chain M'' denotes the optimization process with selective pressure β. We denote by $T_{M'',\vec{m}}$ the hitting time for the optimum when using Markov chain M'' for the initial distribution $\vec{m}$. Concretely, lemma 2 leads to the following lemma in which the hitting time for the initial distribution $S_M^{2p(n)q(n)}(\vec{m}_0)$ can be bound by the hitting time for the distribution $\vec{m}_g$.

LEMMA 9. Let $E(T_{M,0 \to l(n)}) \leq q(n)$. In addition, let $L(n)$ and $R(n)$ be monotone increasing functions, not bound by a constant value, for which $f_m^{(n)}$ is monotonically decreasing for $m \leq \min\{l(n), L(n)\}$ (with $l(n) \leq n - R(n)$). And neighboring values should differ by at least $d > 0$. Then

$$E(T_{M'',S_M^{2p(n)q(n)}(\vec{m}_0)}) \leq E(T_{M'',\vec{m}_g}).$$

5.10 Computing the limiting distribution

From now on, we want to derive concrete formulas for the quantities in the given equations. As a first step the limiting distribution $\vec{s}_{\lim} := \lim_{t \to \infty} S_{M'}^t(\vec{m}_R)$ is computed as the steady state of the Markov chain M'. The following condition must hold: $\vec{s}_{\lim} = S_{M'}(\vec{s}_{\lim})$.

For the individual components of the limiting distribution the three equations must hold ($1 \leq i < n$):

$$(\vec{s}_{\lim})_0 = (1 - p_0^+) \cdot (\vec{s}_{\lim})_0 + p_1^- \cdot (\vec{s}_{\lim})_1$$
$$(\vec{s}_{\lim})_i = p_{i-1}^+ \cdot (\vec{s}_{\lim})_{i-1} +$$
$$(1 - p_i^- - p_i^+) \cdot (\vec{s}_{\lim})_i + p_{i+1}^- \cdot (\vec{s}_{\lim})_{i+1}$$
$$(\vec{s}_{\lim})_n = p_{n-1}^+ \cdot (\vec{s}_{\lim})_{n-1} + (1 - p_n^-) \cdot (\vec{s}_{\lim})_n.$$

The following lemma can be shown.

LEMMA 10.

$$\forall 0 < i \leq n : (\vec{s}_{\lim})_i = \frac{\prod_{l=0}^{i-1} p_l^+}{\prod_{l=1}^{i} p_l^-} \cdot (\vec{s}_{\lim})_0.$$

PROOF. We show that the given formulas for $(\vec{s}_{\lim})_i$ hold in the conditions for the steady state.

First equation:

$$p_1^- \cdot \frac{\prod_{l=0}^{1-1} p_l^+}{\prod_{l=1}^{1} p_l^-} \cdot (\vec{s}_{\lim})_0 + (1 - p_0^+) \cdot (\vec{s}_{\lim})_0$$
$$= p_0^+ \cdot (\vec{s}_{\lim})_0 + (1 - p_0^+) \cdot (\vec{s}_{\lim})_0 = (\vec{s}_{\lim})_0.$$

Second equation:

$$p_{i-1}^+ \cdot \frac{\prod_{l=0}^{i-2} p_l^+}{\prod_{l=1}^{i-1} p_l^-} \cdot (\vec{s}_{\lim})_0$$
$$+ (1 - p_i^- - p_i^+) \cdot \frac{\prod_{l=0}^{i-1} p_l^+}{\prod_{l=1}^{i} p_l^-} \cdot (\vec{s}_{\lim})_0$$
$$+ p_{i+1}^- \cdot \frac{\prod_{l=0}^{i} p_l^+}{\prod_{l=1}^{i+1} p_l^-} \cdot (\vec{s}_{\lim})_0$$
$$= \frac{\prod_{l=0}^{i-2} p_l^+}{\prod_{l=1}^{i-1} p_l^-} \cdot (\vec{s}_{\lim})_0 \cdot (p_{i-1}^+$$
$$+ (1 - p_i^- - p_i^+) \cdot \frac{p_{i-1}^+}{p_i^-} + \frac{p_{i-1}^+ \cdot p_i^+}{p_i^-})$$
$$= \frac{\prod_{l=0}^{i-2} p_l^+}{\prod_{l=1}^{i-1} p_l^-} \cdot (\vec{s}_{\lim})_0 \cdot \frac{p_{i-1}^+}{p_i^-} = \frac{\prod_{l=0}^{i-1} p_l^+}{\prod_{l=1}^{i} p_l^-} \cdot (\vec{s}_{\lim})_0.$$

Third equation:

$$p_{n-1}^+ \cdot \frac{\prod_{l=0}^{n-2} p_l^+}{\prod_{l=1}^{n-1} p_l^-} \cdot (\vec{s}_{\lim})_0 + (1 - p_n^-) \cdot \frac{\prod_{l=0}^{n-1} p_l^+}{\prod_{l=1}^{n} p_l^-} \cdot (\vec{s}_{\lim})_0$$
$$= \frac{\prod_{l=0}^{n-2} p_l^+}{\prod_{l=1}^{n-1} p_l^-} \cdot (\vec{s}_{\lim})_0 \cdot (p_{n-1}^+ + (1 - p_n^-) \cdot \frac{p_{n-1}^+}{p_n^-})$$
$$= \frac{\prod_{l=0}^{n-1} p_l^+}{\prod_{l=1}^{n} p_l^-} \cdot (\vec{s}_{\lim})_0. \quad \square$$

As a consequence, we can state the limiting distribution explicitly.

LEMMA 11.

$$(\vec{s}_{\lim})_i = \begin{cases} \frac{\frac{n!}{(n-i)!i!} \cdot \alpha^{f_0 - f_i}}{\sum_{k=0}^{l(n)} \frac{n!}{(n-k)!k!} \cdot \alpha^{f_0 - f_k}}, & \text{if } i \leq l(n) \\ 0 & \text{otherwise.} \end{cases}$$

PROOF. If we replace the fraction in lemma 10 using the equation

$$\frac{\prod_{l=a+1}^{b+1} p_l^-}{\prod_{l=a}^{b} p_l^+} = \frac{(n-b-1)!(b+1)!}{(n-a)!a!} \cdot \alpha^{f_{b+1} - f_a}$$

which was shown within the proof of lemma 2 in [7] we get

$$(\vec{s}_{\lim})_i = \frac{\prod_{l=0}^{i-1} p_l^+}{\prod_{l=1}^{i} p_l^-} \cdot (\vec{s}_{\lim})_0 = \left(\frac{\prod_{l=1}^{i} p_l^-}{\prod_{l=0}^{i-1} p_l^+}\right)^{-1} \cdot (\vec{s}_{\lim})_0$$
$$= \left(\frac{(n-(i-1)-1)! \cdot (i-1+1)!}{(n-0)! \cdot 0!} \cdot \alpha^{f_{i-1+1} - f_0}\right)^{-1}$$
$$\cdot (\vec{s}_{\lim})_0$$
$$= \frac{n!}{(n-i)! \cdot i!} \cdot \alpha^{f_0 - f_i} \cdot (\vec{s}_{\lim})_0.$$

Because of $p_{l(n)}^+ = 0$ and the initial distribution $\vec{m}_R$ all distributions during optimization are 0 in the components with index $> l(n)$. That means that

$$\sum_{i=0}^{l(n)} (\vec{s}_{\lim})_i = 1.$$

It follows immediately that

$$(\vec{s}_{\lim})_0 = \frac{1}{\sum_{k=0}^{l(n)} \frac{n!}{(n-k)!k!} \cdot \alpha^{f_0 - f_k}}.$$

and the lemma results. $\square$

An estimation of the distribution at the phase change can be obtained immediately by substituting $\vec{s}_{\lim}$ in equation (2).

COROLLARY 4.

$$(\vec{m}_g)_j = \begin{cases} (1 - (\frac{1}{2})^{p(n)}) \cdot \frac{\frac{n!}{(n-i)!i!} \cdot \alpha^{f_0 - f_i}}{\sum_{k=0}^{l(n)} \frac{n!}{(n-k)!k!} \cdot \alpha^{f_0 - f_k}} + (\frac{1}{2})^{p(n)}, \\ \quad if \ j = 0 \\ (1 - (\frac{1}{2})^{p(n)}) \cdot \frac{\frac{n!}{(n-i)!i!} \cdot \alpha^{f_0 - f_i}}{\sum_{k=0}^{l(n)} \frac{n!}{(n-k)!k!} \cdot \alpha^{f_0 - f_k}}, \\ \quad if \ 1 \le j \le l(n) \\ 0, \quad if \ j > l(n). \end{cases}$$

5.11 Quantitatively estimated expected hitting time

Now the expected runtime of M'' can be computed using the steady state distribution $\vec{m}_g$ for initializing the process. As a consequence the expectancy value results as

$$E(T_{M'', \vec{m}_g}) = \sum_{i=0}^{n} (\vec{m}_g)_i \cdot E(T_i)$$

where $E(T_i)$ denotes the expected runtime when starting in state i.

We know from the proof of the static case that $E(T_i)$ is described by equation (1) (with β instead of α). If we put everything together we get the following exact expected hitting time.

THEOREM 3.

$$E(T_{M'', \vec{m}_g}) =$$

$$\sum_{i=0}^{l(n)} \left(1 - \left(\frac{1}{2}\right)^{p(n)}\right) \cdot \frac{\frac{n!}{(n-i)!i!} \cdot \alpha^{f_0 - f_i}}{\sum_{k=0}^{l(n)} \frac{n!}{(n-k)!k!} \cdot \alpha^{f_0 - f_k}} \cdot$$

$$\sum_{j=i}^{n-1} \sum_{k=0}^{j} n \cdot \frac{(n-j-1)!j!}{(n-k)!k!} \cdot \frac{\beta^{f_j - f_k}}{\min\{\beta^{f_j - f_{j+1}}, 1\}}$$

$$+ \left(\frac{1}{2}\right)^{p(n)} \sum_{j=0}^{n-1} \sum_{k=0}^{j} n \cdot \frac{(n-j-1)!j!}{(n-k)!k!} \cdot \frac{\beta^{f_j - f_k}}{\min\{\beta^{f_j - f_{j+1}}, 1\}}.$$

5.12 Deriving the polynomial runtime criterion

The transformation of the exact result in theorem 3 into the polynomial runtime criterion is outlined here.

First, we use lemma 1 and transform the result into the notion of P-equivalence by replacing the summations by maximum terms. Second, it holds that $1 - (\frac{1}{2})^{p(n)} \sim_P 1$ why we can eliminate the factor on the left-hand side. Third, the factors $\min\{\ldots\}$ may be eliminated for the same reason as in the proof of theorem 1. The intermediate result is the following formula:

$$E(T_{M'', \vec{m}_g}) \sim_P$$

$$\max \left\{ \frac{\max\limits_{\substack{0 \le k \le j \le n \\ 0 \le i \le j, l(n)}} \left(\frac{n!}{(n-i)!i!} \cdot \alpha^{f_0 - f_i} \cdot n \cdot \frac{(n-j-1)!j!}{(n-k)!k!} \cdot \beta^{f_j - f_k}\right)}{\max\limits_{0 \le k \le l(n)} \left(\frac{n!}{(n-k)!k!} \cdot \alpha^{f_0 - f_k}\right)}, \right.$$

$$\left. \left(\frac{1}{2}\right)^{p(n)} \cdot \max\limits_{0 \le k \le j \le n} \left(n \cdot \frac{(n-j-1)!j!}{(n-k)!k!} \cdot \beta^{f_j - f_k}\right) \right\}.$$

In the fourth step, we apply the Stirling formula to remove the faculties. Several factors are P-equivalent to 1 and can be omitted. By transforming the two terms within the outer maximum to an exponential representation we get the following expression.

$$E(T_{M'', \vec{m}_g}) \sim_P$$

$$\max \left\{ e^{\max\limits_{\substack{0 \le k \le j \le n \\ 0 \le i \le j, l(n)}} (g_\beta(k) - g_\beta(j) + g_\alpha(i)) - \max\limits_{0 \le k \le l(n)} g_\alpha(k)}, \right.$$

$$\left. \left(\frac{1}{2}\right)^{p(n)} \cdot e^{\max\limits_{0 \le k \le j \le n} (g_\beta(k) - g_\beta(j))} \right\}.$$

Because we are interested in function classes that are solvable in polynomial time, we can introduce the prerequisite that state $l(n)$ is reached within polynomial runtime (using the selective parameter α in the first phase). Now the following lemma can be used to simplify the polynomial runtime criterion.

LEMMA 12. Supposed $E(T_{M, 0 \to l(n)}) \le q(n)$ with polynomial $q(n)$, then there exists a polynomial $p(n)$ for which it holds:

$$\max \left\{ e^{\max\limits_{\substack{0 \le k \le j \le n \\ 0 \le i \le j, l(n)}} (g_\beta(k) - g_\beta(j) + g_\alpha(i)) - \max\limits_{0 \le k \le l(n)} g_\alpha(k)}, \right.$$

$$\left. \left(\frac{1}{2}\right)^{p(n)} \cdot e^{\max\limits_{0 \le k \le j \le n} (g_\beta(k) - g_\beta(j))} \right\} \in P$$

$$\Longleftrightarrow e^{\max\limits_{\substack{0 \le k \le j \le n \\ 0 \le i \le j, l(n)}} (g_\beta(k) - g_\beta(j) + g_\alpha(i)) - \max\limits_{0 \le k \le l(n)} g_\alpha(k)} \in P.$$

PROOF. We assume k_0 and j_0 are those indices for which

$$e^{\max\limits_{0 \le k \le j \le n} (g_\beta(k) - g_\beta(j))} = e^{g_\beta(k_0) - g_\beta(j_0)}.$$

We consider the case $j_0 \le l(n)$ first. If we substitute the function g_β by its definition we get

$$e^{g_\beta(k_0) - g_\beta(j_0)} \le e^{|\ln \beta| \cdot (f_{k_0} - f_{j_0}) + 2n \widetilde{\ln} n}.$$

Furthermore we can conclude from the prerequisite

$$E(T_{M, 0 \to l(n)}) \le q(n)$$

and $j_0 \le l(n)$ and lemma 3 for the first phase of the algorithm that there exists a polynomial $q'(n)$ for which

$$e^{\max\limits_{0 \le k \le j \le l(n)} (g_\alpha(k) - g_\alpha(j))} \le q'(n).$$

This leads to the following inequation:

$$e^{|\ln \alpha| \cdot (f_{k_0} - f_{j_0}) + 2n \widetilde{\ln} n} \le q'(n)$$

$$|\ln \alpha| \cdot (f_{k_0} - f_{j_0}) + 2n \widetilde{\ln} n \le \ln q'(n)$$

and for $k_0 \le j_0 \le l(n)$

$$f_{k_0} - f_{j_0} \le \frac{\ln q'(n) - 2n \widetilde{\ln} n}{|\ln \alpha|}.$$

Now we can put everything together and get

$$e^{\max\limits_{0 \le k \le j \le n} (g_\beta(k) - g_\beta(j))} \le e^{|\ln \beta| \left(\frac{\ln q'(n) - 2n \widetilde{\ln} n}{|\ln \alpha|}\right) + 2n \ln n}$$

$$\le e^{q''(n)}$$

for a polynomial $q''(n)$. Furthermore, if we choose $p(n) = \frac{q''(n) + n}{\ln 2}$ the term

$$\left(\frac{1}{2}\right)^{p(n)} \cdot e^{\max\limits_{0 \le k \le j \le n} (g_\beta(k) - g_\beta(j))} \le e^{-n}$$

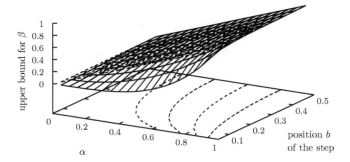

Figure 4: The upper bound for β is shown (with solid lines) as well as the value of α (with dashed lines).

which does not affect the fact whether the whole expression is in P.

For the case that $j_0 > l(n)$, we consider the index $k'_0 \leq l(n)$ with

$$g_\alpha(k'_0) = \max_{0 \leq k \leq l(n)} g_\alpha(k).$$

Then we can replace the maximum term by $g_\alpha(k'_0)$ at two positions in the following expression:

$$e^{\displaystyle \max_{\substack{0 \leq k \leq j \leq n \\ 0 \leq i \leq j, l(n)}} (g_\beta(k)-g_\beta(j)+g_\alpha(i))- \max_{0 \leq k \leq l(n)} g_\alpha(k)}$$

$$\geq e^{\displaystyle \max_{\substack{0 \leq k \leq j \leq n \\ l(n) \leq j}} (g_\beta(k)-g_\beta(j))+g_\alpha(k'_0)-g_\alpha(k'_0)}$$

$$\geq e^{g_\beta(k_0)-g_\beta(j_0)} = e^{\displaystyle \max_{0 \leq k \leq j \leq n} (g_\beta(k)-g_\beta(j))}.$$

Again the second maximum term does not influence the criterion. □

This lemma concludes the proof of theorem 2. Note, that certain prerequisites of the lemmata show up in modified form within the theorem. For example, the restrictions for the functions are more strict in section 5.5. Since we only need these properties in the worse part of the search space, we have formulated the prerequisites for the affected function values only.

6. IMPACT OF THE THEOREM

In this section we give an example for a function that is not solvable in polynomial runtime by the standard Metropolis algorithm, but falls into the polynomial class of functions for the modified Metropolis algorithm where the selection parameter changes from a given value α to a given value β.

Since the values of f_k are decreasing in the worse part of the search space we (i.e. $0 \leq k \leq L(n)$) can choose an arbitrary $0 < b < \frac{1}{2}$ which determines $L(n) = b \cdot n - 1$.

Furthermore we restrict the possible values of β as follows

$$\ln \beta < \frac{|\ln \alpha| \cdot \ln 2}{(1-b) \cdot \ln(1-b) + b \cdot \ln b}. \tag{3}$$

This upper bound for β is shown in figure 4. As can be seen clearly there is a bigger necessary gap between α and β the closer the step ($L(n)$) in the function moves towards the left side.

Now, we define the function $F^{(2)}_{\alpha \to \beta}$ as follows

$$f_k = \begin{cases} \frac{1}{|\ln \alpha|} \cdot h(k), & \text{if } 0 \leq k \leq b \cdot n \\ step_n + h''_{b,n}, & \text{if } k = b \cdot n + 1 \\ \frac{1}{|\ln \beta|} \cdot h(k) + h'_{b,n} + h''_{b,n}, & \text{otherwise} \end{cases}$$

with

$$h(k) = k \cdot \widetilde{\ln} k + (n-k) \cdot \widetilde{\ln}(n-k)$$

$$step_n = \frac{1}{|\ln \alpha|} \cdot (g_\beta(0) - g_\beta(b \cdot n) + h(k))$$

$$h'_{b,n} = -\frac{1}{|\ln \beta|} \cdot h(b \cdot n + 1) + step_n$$

$$h''_{b,n} = \max\{0, \ (\frac{1}{|\ln \alpha|} - \frac{1}{|\ln \beta|}) \cdot n \ln n - h'_{b,n}\}$$

$$g_\gamma(k) = f_k \cdot |\ln \gamma| - h(k).$$

The function values are shown for a few exemplary values in figure 5. The course of the function is invariant to changes in n but the height of the step changes depending on α, β, and b.

It is fairly easy to see that this function is not solvable with the original Metropolis algorithm with selection parameter α'. For values $\alpha' > \beta$ it can be shown that (S2) is not fulfilled for $m = b \cdot n + 2$ and $j = n$. For values $\alpha' \leq \beta$ the condition (S1) is not fulfilled for $m = 0$ and $j = b \cdot n$—here we need the restriction of equation (3). The details of the proof are left to the reader.

THEOREM 4. *Function $F^{(2)}_{\alpha \to \beta}$ is solvable in polynomial time by the modified Metropolis algorithm (algorithm 1) where the selection parameter changes from α to β.*

PROOF. We have to show that the four conditions (D1)–(D4) hold. Concerning (D1), it is possible to show that fitness values of neighboring f_k and f_{k+1} hold

$$|f_k - f_{k+1}| \geq \left| \frac{\ln(1-b) - \ln b}{\ln \alpha} \right|$$

for $0 \leq k < b \cdot n - 1 = L(n)$. It is also easy to see that (D2) holds for the same range of values for k.

Now, we choose the function $R(n)$ in such a way that $l(n) = b \cdot n + 1$ results. Since the conditions (D3) and (D4) depend heavily on the functions g_α and g_β, it is helpful to have a closer look on how these functions behave. To illustrate our points we have also included an exemplary plot of the functions in figure 6.

The function is constructed such that $g_\alpha(k) = 0$ for $0 \leq k \leq b \cdot n$ and $g_\beta(k)$ is constant for $b \cdot n + 1 \leq k \leq n$.

As a consequence the left-hand side of condition $(D3)$ equals 0 since for $j < l(n)$ always $g_\alpha(m) - g_\alpha(j) = 0 - 0 = 0$ and for $j = l(n)$ the term $g_\alpha(m) - g_\alpha(j)$ is either negative with $m < l(n)$ or 0 with $m = l(n)$. All these values can be bound by $\ln n$ and condition $(D3)$ follows.

For condition (D4), the second maximum term is maximal at $k = l(n)$ (since the function is 0 for smaller values of k); this leads to

$$\max_{0 \leq k \leq l(n)} g_\alpha(k) = g_\beta(0) - g_\beta(b \cdot n) + |\ln \alpha| \cdot h''_{b,n}.$$

For the first maximum term we need to consider three different cases.

Case $l(n) \leq m, j$: Since g_β is constant for this range, it holds that $g_\beta(m) - g_\beta(j) = 0$. As a consequence, the index

114

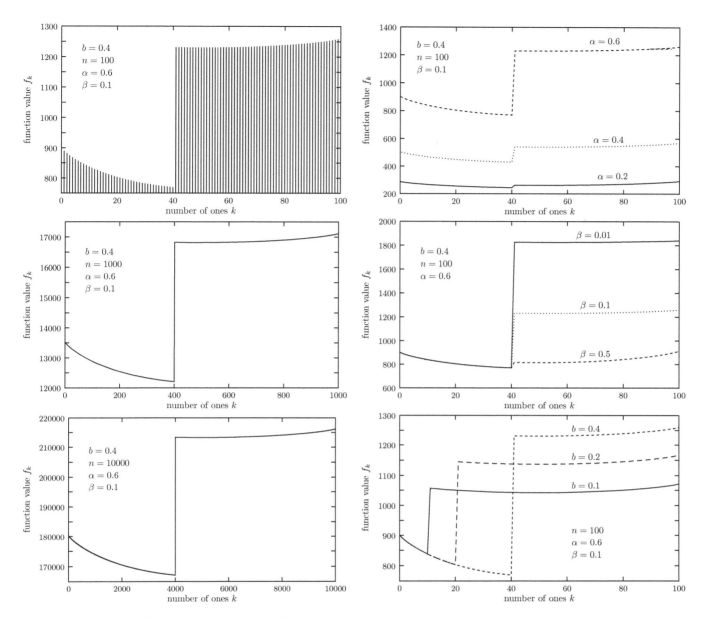

Figure 5: Function $F_{\alpha \to \beta}^{(2)}$ is shown exemplary for increasing n (left column) and changes in α, β, and b (right column from top down).

$i = l(n)$ maximizes the first term and the left-hand side (with both maximum terms) evaluates to 0.

Case $m < l(n) \leq j$: Since $g_\beta(j)$ is constant for values bigger than $l(n)$, it is sufficient to consider $j = l(n)$. Furthermore, we omit the term $h''_{b,n}$ in the first instance.

$$g_\beta(m) - g_\beta(j) = \left(\frac{|\ln \beta|}{|\ln \alpha|} - 1 \right) \cdot h(m) - h'_{b,n} \cdot |\ln \beta|.$$

Because of $h(m)$ being maximal at $m = 0$ and $\frac{|\ln \beta|}{|\ln \alpha|} - 1 > 0$, we can reformulate the equation:

$$g_\beta(m) - g_\beta(j) \leq \left(\frac{|\ln \beta|}{|\ln \alpha|} - 1 \right) \cdot n \ln n - h'_{b,n} \cdot |\ln \beta|.$$

As long as

$$h'_{b,n} \geq \left(\frac{|\ln \beta|}{|\ln \alpha|} - 1 \right) \cdot n \ln n$$

it holds that $g_\beta(m) - g_\beta(j) \leq 0$. This condition is true as soon as we re-insert the term $h''_{b,n}$. Again $i = l(n)$ completes the maximum term and the left-hand side of (D4) results in 0.

Case $m, j < l(n)$: It holds

$$g_\beta(m) - g_\beta(j) = \left(\frac{|\ln \beta|}{|\ln \alpha|} - 1 \right) \cdot (h(m) - h(j)).$$

Since $h(x)$ is decreasing in the considered range of values the whole term is maximal with $m = 0$ and $j = b \cdot n$. The

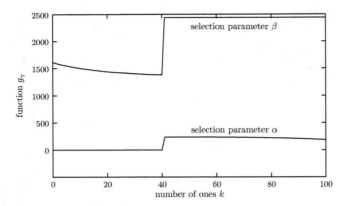

Figure 6: Functions g_α and g_β for $F^{(2)}$ exemplary shown for $\alpha = 0.6$, $\beta = 0.1$, $b = 0.4$, and $n = 100$.

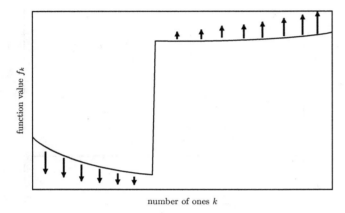

Figure 7: Possible simple modifications of $F^{(2)}$ that leave the function in polynomial runtime.

third summand $g_\alpha(i)$ in the first maximum term is 0. The second term is again maximal for $k = b \cdot n + 1$. If we omit the $h''_{b,n}$, the left-hand side of (D4) results in

$$g_\beta(0) - g_\beta(b \cdot n) - g_\alpha(b \cdot n + 1) = 0.$$

If we re-insert $h''_{b,n}$ the summand $g_\alpha(b \cdot n + 1)$ will become bigger and the whole term is negative.

For all cases the condition is fulfilled which means that the left-hand side of (D4) is bound logarithmically. $\quad\square$

Eventually, we want to discuss three modifications we can apply to $F^{(2)}$ and still expect polynomial runtime.

The first kind of possible changes is shown in figure 7. We will certainly make the function easier if we lower the function values in the range $0 \leq k \leq b \cdot n$ concertedly. And in an analogous way, we can raise the function values for $l(n) \leq k \leq n$. Still we have to make sure not to introduce a more than logarithmic difference between function values (falling from left to right). In addition, we do not know whether theorem 2 is still applicable and probably the new function is even solvable in polynomial runtime by the original Metropolis algorithm.

A second modification concerns the step in the function to the higher fitness level. Theorem 2 does not require that this step is realized when $\|x\|_1$ increases by 1. This is shown

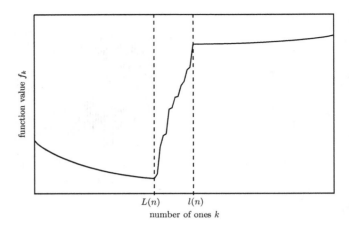

Figure 8: Polynomial modification of $F^{(2)}$ where the step to the higher fitness level is stretched.

in figure 8. In the proof of the runtime the functions $L(n)$ and $l(n)$ have to be chosen appropriately.

And eventually, we can supply all these functions with logarithmic noise in the better part of the search space:

$$f_k^* = \begin{cases} f_k, & \text{for } k \leq l(n) \\ f_k + (\ln n) \cdot X, & \text{otherwise} \end{cases}$$

where X is a random variable with uniform distribution in $[-1, 1]$. This kind of ruggedness will not disturb the polynomial runtime.

So far we have only considered selection parameters that are constant. To conclude this section we want to have a short look at how functions change when we allow the selection parameter β to change with increasing problem size n. We examine the function $F^{(3)}$ defined by

$$f_k = \begin{cases} \frac{1}{\lceil \ln 0.6 \rceil} \cdot h(k), & \text{for } 0 \leq k < \frac{1}{4} \cdot n \\ k + 5 \cdot n \cdot \ln n, & \text{otherwise.} \end{cases}$$

This function family is a combination of $F_2^{(n)}$ in the left part of the function and $F_1^{(n)}$ in the right part. It is not solvable by the original Metropolis algorithm in polynomial time since the condition (S2) of theorem 1 requires again $\alpha \leq \sqrt[n]{n} - 1$. However, the left-hand side of condition (S1) is not bound by a logarithm for $\alpha < 0.6$.

COROLLARY 5. *The function $F^{(3)}$ with $h(k) = k \cdot \widetilde{\ln} k + (n - k) \cdot \widetilde{\ln}(n - k)$ is solved by the modified Metropolis algorithm (algorithm 1) with $\alpha = 0.6$ and $\beta = \frac{1}{n}$ in polynomial time (in expectancy).*

PROOF. We choose $l(n) = \frac{1}{4} \cdot n$. (D1), (D2) and (D3) are again fulfilled analogously to $F_2^{(n)}$. In (D4) there are again three possible cases.

For $l(n) \leq m, j$, it holds $i = k$ and the respective terms equalize each other. Moreover $g_\beta(m) - g_\beta(j) \leq c_2 \cdot \ln n$ is true because $\beta = \frac{1}{n} < n^{\frac{1}{n}} - 1$.

For $m < l(n) \leq j$, there are no positive values possible since both $g_{\frac{1}{n}}(0) < g_{\frac{1}{n}}\left(\frac{n}{4}\right)$ as well as $g_{\frac{1}{n}}(0) < g_{\frac{1}{n}}(n)$.

For $m, j < l(n)$, the maximum is met at $m = i = 0$, $j = \frac{n}{4} - 1$, and $k = \frac{n}{4} = l(n)$. It follows

$$g_{\frac{1}{n}}(0) - g_{\frac{1}{n}}\left(\frac{n}{4} - 1\right) + \underbrace{g_{0.6}(0)}_{=0} - g_{0.6}\left(\frac{n}{4}\right)$$

$$= \left(\frac{|\ln n|}{|\ln 0.6|} - 1\right) \cdot h(0) - \underbrace{\left(\frac{|\ln n|}{|\ln 0.6|} - 1\right)}_{>0} \cdot \underbrace{h\left(\frac{n}{4} - 1\right)}_{>h(\frac{n}{4})}$$

$$\qquad - |\ln 0.6| \cdot \left(\frac{n}{4} + 5 \cdot n \cdot \ln n\right) + h\left(\frac{n}{4}\right)$$

$$\leq \left(\frac{|\ln n|}{|\ln 0.6|} - 1\right) \cdot h(0) - \left(\frac{|\ln n|}{|\ln 0.6|} - 1\right) \cdot h\left(\frac{n}{4}\right)$$

$$\qquad - |\ln 0.6| \cdot \left(\frac{n}{4} + 5 \cdot n \cdot \ln n\right) + h\left(\frac{n}{4}\right)$$

$$= \left(2 - \frac{|\ln n|}{|\ln 0.6|}\right) \cdot \underbrace{\left(\frac{n}{4} \ln \frac{n}{4} + \frac{3n}{4} \ln \frac{3n}{4}\right)}_{=n \ln n - n \ln 4 + \frac{3n}{4} \ln 3}$$

$$\qquad + \left(\frac{|\ln n|}{|\ln 0.6|} - 1\right) \cdot h(0) - |\ln 0.6| \cdot \left(\frac{n}{4} + 5 \cdot n \cdot \ln n\right)$$

$$= n \ln n + \left(\frac{|\ln n|}{|\ln 0.6|} - 2\right) \cdot n \cdot \left(\ln 4 - \frac{3}{4} \ln 3\right)$$

$$\qquad - |\ln 0.6| \cdot \left(\frac{n}{4} + 5 \cdot n \cdot \ln n\right)$$

$$= n \ln n \underbrace{\left(1 + \frac{\ln 4 - \frac{3}{4} \ln 3}{|\ln 0.6|} - |\ln 0.6| \cdot 5\right)}_{<0}$$

$$\qquad - n \cdot \underbrace{\left(2 \cdot \left(\ln 4 - \frac{3}{4} \ln 3\right) + \frac{|\ln 0.6|}{4}\right)}_{>0} \leq 0. \quad \square$$

When comparing $F_2^{(n)}$ and $F_3^{(n)}$, it is interesting to see that the step in the function at $l(n)$ depends in both cases on $n \ln n$ only. The increasing selection pressure $\beta = \frac{1}{n}$ actually does not lead to an (asymptotically) higher step in the function.

7. CONCLUSION

We have extended the polynomial runtime criterion for the Metropolis algorithm to a variant of the algorithm where the selection pressure changes once. Within the proof a number of technical assumptions have been used which led to a sufficient runtime criterion that is not necessary anymore. We have constructed a function class that is only solvable in polynomial runtime when the selection parameter changes. A closer investigation of this function class gives a deep insight on how the selection parameters need to relate to each other and how this choice affects the shape of the function. An easier comprehensible function family that falls into the problem class of interest is the OneMax variant $F_3^{(n)}$ with a deceptive tail at the left.

Concerning the practical application of the theorem, it is of interest how to choose the iteration for changing the selection pressure. We did not investigate this topic so far but point to section 5.3 and the proof of lemma 12.

In this combination, the P-equivalence and the orientedness of distributions have not been used before. Whether these techniques can be extended to more complicated algorithms like simulated annealing or different problems is an open question.

8. REFERENCES

[1] D. H. Ackley. *A Connectionist Machine for Genetic Hillclimbing*. Kluwer, Boston, MA, 1987.

[2] K. Deb and S. Agrawal. Understanding interactions among genetic algorithm parameters. In W. Banzhaf and C. Reeves, editors, *Foundations of Genetic Algorithms 5*, pages 265–286. Morgan Kaufmann, San Francisco, CA, 1999.

[3] S. Droste, T. Jansen, and I. Wegener. Dynamic parameter control in simple evolutionary algorithms. In W. N. Martin and W. M. Spears, editors, *Foundations of Genetic Algorithms 6*, pages 275–294. Morgan Kaufmann, San Francisco, 2001.

[4] A. E. Eiben and G. Rudolph. Theory of evolutionary algorithms: A bird's eye view. *Theoretical Computer Science*, 229(1):3–9, 1999.

[5] T. Friedrich, J. He, N. Hebbinghaus, F. Neumann, and C. Witt. Approximation covering problems by randomized search heuristics using multi-objective models. In *Proc. of the 9th annual conference on Genetic and evolutionary computation*, pages 797–804, New York, 2007. ACM.

[6] J. He and Y. Yao. Towards an analytic framework for analysing the computation time of evolutionary algorithms. *Artificial Intelligence*, 145(1–2):59–97, 2003.

[7] L. Kaden, N. Weicker, and K. Weicker. Metropolis and symmetric functions: A swan song. In C. Cotta and P. Cowling, editors, *Evolutionary Computation in Combinatorial Optimization, 9th European Conference EvoCOP 2009*, pages 204–215, Berlin, 2009. Springer.

[8] T. Kamae, U. Krengel, and G. L. O'Brien. Stochastic inequalities on partially ordered spaces. *The Annals of Probability*, 5(6):899–912, 1977.

[9] S. Kirkpatrick, C. D. Gelatt Jr., and M. P. Vecchi. Optimization by simulated annealing. *Science*, 220(4598):671–680, 1983.

[10] N. Metropolis, A. W. Rosenbluth, M. N. Rosenbluth, A. H. Teller, and E. Teller. Equation of state calculations by fast computing machines. *Journal of Chemical Physics*, 21(6):1087–1092, 1953.

[11] F. Neumann and I. Wegener. Randomized local search, evolutionary algorithms, and the minimum spanning tree problem. *Theoretical Computer Science*, 378(1):32–40, 2007.

[12] G. B. Sorkin. Efficient simulated annealing on fractal energy landscapes. *Algorithmica*, 6:367–418, 1991.

Runtime Analysis of the (1+1) Evolutionary Algorithm on Strings over Finite Alphabets

Benjamin Doerr   Daniel Johannsen
Max-Planck-Institut für Informatik
Campus E1 4
66123 Saarbrücken, Germany

Martin Schmidt
Universität des Saarlandes
Campus E1 3
66123 Saarbrücken, Germany

ABSTRACT

In this work, we investigate a (1+1) Evolutionary Algorithm for optimizing functions over the space $\{0, \ldots, r\}^n$, where r is a positive integer. We show that for linear functions over $\{0, 1, 2\}^n$, the expected runtime time of this algorithm is $O(n \log n)$. This result generalizes an existing result on pseudo-Boolean functions and is derived using drift analysis. We also show that for large values of r, no upper bound for the runtime of the (1+1) Evolutionary Algorithm for linear function on $\{0, \ldots, r\}^n$ can be obtained with this approach nor with any other approach based on drift analysis with weight-independent linear potential functions.

Categories and Subject Descriptors

F.2 [**Theory of Computation**]: Analysis of Algorithms and Problem Complexity

General Terms

Theory, algorithms, performance

Keywords

Evolutionary algorithm, runtime analysis, drift analysis

1. INTRODUCTION

In their seminal work [8], Droste, Jansen, and Wegener analyzed the runtime of the (1+1) Evolutionary Algorithm ((1+1) EA) for several classes of pseudo-Boolean functions, including the class of linear pseudo-Boolean functions. Their results motivated a number of further studies of randomized search heuristics on basic pseudo-Boolean functions (e.g., [5, 11, 14]) and later on combinatorial optimization problems (e.g., [15, 17, 19]); see [16, 1] for an overview.

In the last decade, particular interest was given to the study of the (1+1) EA optimizing linear pseudo-Boolean functions of the form

$$f \colon \{0,1\}^n \to \mathbb{R}, \quad x \mapsto w_0 + \sum_{i=1}^{n} w_i x_i, \quad w_0, w_1, \ldots, w_n \in \mathbb{R}.$$

For this class of functions, Droste, Jansen, and Wegener showed that the (expected) runtime of the (1+1) EA is in $\Theta(n \log n)$ for non-zero weights, and Doerr, Johannsen, and Winzen [5] showed that the leading constants in this bound are between 1 and 1.39.

One reason for our interest in the class of linear functions is the analytic challenge of its runtime analysis. For example, all known proofs that obtain asymptotically sharp runtime bounds of $O(n \log n)$ do not study the progress of the (1+1) EA with respect to the actual function value, but instead with respect to a structure-related potential function.

For example, in [8] and [6] the progress of the (1+1) EA minimizing linear functions is measured with respect to the potential function

$$g_0 \colon \{0,1\}^n \to \mathbb{R}, \quad x \mapsto \sum_{i=1}^{\lfloor n/2 \rfloor} 2x_i + \sum_{i=\lfloor n/2 \rfloor+1}^{n} x_i,$$

in [11, 12] with respect to the potential function

$$g_1 \colon \{0,1\}^n \to \mathbb{R}, \quad x \mapsto \log\left(1 + \sum_{i=1}^{n} x_i\right),$$

and in [14] and [5] with respect to the potential function

$$g_2 \colon \{0,1\}^n \to \mathbb{R}, \quad x \mapsto |x|_1 := \sum_{i=1}^{n} x_i.$$

The study of the progress of an algorithm with respect to a potential function is called *drift analysis* (the *drift* is the expected change in potential) and is briefly introduced in Section 3, see He and Yao [11, 13], Doerr, Johannsen, Winzen [5, 6] and Hajek [10] for details on this technique.

An important progress in the understanding of the optimization behavior of the (1+1) EA on linear functions was made by Jägersküpper [14]. By studying the underlying Markov chain, he showed a basic but important invariance property on its distribution: For any search point $x \in \{0,1\}^n$ generated by the (1+1) EA minimizing a linear function, we have that

$$\Pr[x_i = 0 \wedge x_j = 1] \leq \Pr[x_i = 1 \wedge x_j = 0]$$

whenever $w_i \leq w_j$.

In fact, it is this invariance property that enabled him to use the simple (and intuitive) potential function g_2 to analyze the optimization behavior of the (1+1) EA on linear pseudo-Boolean functions.

In contrast to linear pseudo-Boolean functions, the optimization behavior of the (1+1) EA on combinatorial problems like the minimum spanning tree problems [15, 17, 18] or the shortest path tree problem [2, 3, 4, 19] are still poorly understood with respect to structural insights.

For example, consider the minimum spanning tree problem. As an optimal subgraph problem, search points can be represented by bitstrings indicating which edges appear in the respective subgraph. For this problem, we have a linear fitness function given by the sum of the edge weights in the subgraph (which we assume to be positive integers). However, in contrast to linear pseudo-Boolean functions, not all search points are feasible. More precisely, the (1+1) EA starts with an arbitrary spanning subgraph of the input graph and rejects all search points that represent disconnect subgraphs.

For the minimum spanning tree problem [15, 18], the best known upper bounds on the runtime are a general bound of $O(m^3 \log m)$ and a bound of $O(m^2(\log m + \log w_{\max}))$ depending on the maximum edge weight $w_{\max}$. Note that the latter bound is worse than the former if $w_{\max}$ is much larger than m^m. However, [15] also gives the lower bound $O(m^2 \log m)$. We conjecture that this is the right order of magnitude, i.e., that the logarithmic factor in the maximal weight is unnecessary.

This conjecture is motivated by the observation that the equally difficult problem of finding a maximum spanning forest generalizes the problem of maximizing a linear pseudo-Boolean function (represented by the problem of finding a maximum spanning forest on a path). Now, in the (equivalent) analysis of the minimum spanning tree problem, the progress of the (1+1) EA is simply measured by the current fitness distance to the optimum. If we apply the same analysis to linear pseudo-Boolean functions, we only obtain a weight-dependent runtime bound of $O(m(\log m + \log w_{\max}))$.

With this in mind, one might hope that the technique of measuring the progress of the (1+1) EA for the minimum spanning tree problem by a weight-independent potential function like in the case of linear pseudo-Boolean functions will remove the logarithmic factor in the maximal weight from the upper bound of the runtime.

In this work, we approach this question by analyzing the optimization behavior of the (1+1) EA for linear functions over the space $\{0, \ldots, r\}^n$, i.e., function of the form

$$f : \{0, \ldots, r\}^n \to \mathbb{R}, \quad x \mapsto w_0 + \sum_{i=1}^n w_i x_i$$

where n and r are positive integers and $w_0, \ldots, w_n$ are real-valued weights. One might expect that the known methods by Droste, Jansen, and Wegener [8], He and Yao [13], and Jägersküpper [14] generalize to this setting. Indeed, in Section 3 we introduce a potential function that allows us to bound the runtime of the (1+1) EA for the case $r = 2$, i.e., for the search space $\{0, 1, 2\}^n$.

THEOREM 1. *The expected runtime of the (1+1) Evolutionary Algorithm (Algorithm 1) minimizing a linear function over $\{0, 1, 2\}^n$ is in $O(n \log n)$.*

Surprisingly, it turns out that the proof of the invariance

property in the approach of Jägersküpper does not immediately generalize to this setting. In fact, in line with the results in [5], we show in Section 4 that this approach and also more general approaches using arbitrary weight-independent linear potential functions fail for values of r larger than 43 (the actual value of this constant is of minor importance and we expect it to be much smaller than 43).

Similar restrictions on the current techniques of analysis have been encounter in [5, 6] for the study of the (1+1) EA with mutation rates larger than $1/n$.

2. A (1+1) EVOLUTIONARY ALGORITHM FOR STRINGS OVER FINITE ALPHABETS

In this section, we present the (1+1) Evolutionary Algorithm ((1+1) EA) for minimizing functions over the search space $\{0, 1, \ldots, r\}^n$ with positive integers n and r. This algorithm is a generalization of the classical (1+1) EA for pseudo-Boolean functions (see, e.g., [8]).

In the classical (1+1) EA, the mutation operator flips each bit of the current search point with probability $1/n$. Accordingly, we define a mutation operator on $\{0, 1, \ldots, r\}^n$ that still "flips" each position with probability $1/n$, where "flipping" means that the respective entry is changed to a different value chosen uniformly at random.

DEFINITION 2 (**mut**(x)). *Let n and r be positive integers. Let $x \in \{0, 1, \ldots, r\}^n$. The mutation operator* mut(x) *generates a random search point y in $\{0, 1, \ldots, r\}^n$. Independently for each $i \in \{1, \ldots, n\}$, the probability that $y_i \neq x_i$ is $1/n$. In this case, y_i is chosen uniformly at random from $\{0, 1, \ldots, r\} \setminus \{x_i\}$.*

Using this mutation operator, we generalize the search space of the classical (1+1) EA optimizing pseudo-Boolean functions to $\{0, 1, \ldots, r\}^n$. This (1+1) Evolutionary Algorithm on $\{0, 1, \ldots, r\}^n$ is given by Algorithm 1. It was studied before by Gunia [9] to analyze the minimum make-span scheduling problem with $r + 1$ machines.

Algorithm 1: The (1+1) EA on $\{0, 1, \ldots, r\}^n$.

---

input function $f : \{0, 1, \ldots, r\}^n \to \mathbb{R}$;	1
initialization Choose $x \in \{0, 1, \ldots, r\}^n$ uniformly at random;	2
repeat	3
$\quad y := \text{mut}(x)$;	4
$\quad$ **if** $f(y) \leq f(x)$ **then** $x := y$;	5
until *forever*;	6

Note that, as common in theoretical runtime analysis, we do not specify a stopping criterion (see [8] for a discussion of this). Our focus is determining the *runtime* of the algorithm, which we define to be the random variable T that denotes the number of fitness evaluations (Step 4) until a global optimum (i.e., minimum) of f is found.

In the remainder of this work we focus on linear functions over $\{0, 1, \ldots, r\}^n$. A *linear function* f over $\{0, 1, \ldots, r\}^n$ is a function

$$f : \{0, 1, \ldots, r\}^n \to \mathbb{R}, \quad x \mapsto w_0 + \sum_{i=1}^n w_i x_i$$

with $w_i \in \mathbb{R}$ for $0 \le i \le n$. Note that for $r = 1$ this definition specializes to linear pseudo-Boolean functions. Like for linear pseudo-Boolean functions, we may assume that $w_0 = 0$ and all other weights are positive and non-increasing, i.e.,

$$0 = w_0 < w_1 \le w_2 \le \ldots \le w_n$$

This is not a real restriction. First, the size of the weight w_0 does not influence the behavior of the $(1+1)$ EA. Second, since Algorithm 1 ensures that every position flips independently, reordering the weights is not a restriction and in case a weight w_i is negative we may replace w_i and x_i by $-w_i$ and $1 - x_i$ respectively, without changing the optimization behavior.

3. THE RUNTIME OF THE (1+1) EVOLUTIONARY ALGORITHM OPTIMIZING LINEAR FUNCTIONS OVER $\{0,1,2\}^N$

The aim of this section is to prove Theorem 1, i.e., that the expected runtime of the $(1+1)$ EA for linear functions on $\{0,1,2\}^n$ is $O(n \log n)$. For this, we apply drift analysis, more precisely, the multiplicative drift theorem from [7].

THEOREM 3. *Let $\{x^{[t]}\}_{t \in \mathbb{N}}$ be a sequence of random variables in a finite space $\mathcal{S}$. Furthermore, let $g \colon \mathcal{S} \to \mathbb{R}$ be a potential function on $\mathcal{S}$ such that $\min_{x \in \mathcal{S} \colon g(x) > 0}\{g(x)\} \ge 1$. Let T be the random variable that denotes the first point in time $t \in \mathbb{N}$ such that $g(x^{[t]}) = 0$.*

Suppose that

$$\mathrm{E}\left[g(x^{[t]}) - g(x^{[t+1]}) \mid g(x^{[t]})\right] \ge \delta g(x^{[t]}). \quad (1)$$

holds for all $t \in \mathbb{N}$. Then,

$$\mathrm{E}\left[T \mid g(x^{[0]})\right] \le \frac{1 + \ln g(x^{[0]})}{\delta}.$$

We apply this theorem to the search points $\{x^{[t]}\}_{t \in \mathbb{N}}$ generated by the $(1+1)$ EA (Algorithm 1) minimizing a linear function

$$f \colon \{0,1,2\}^n \to \mathbb{R}, \quad x \mapsto \sum_{i=1}^{n} w_i x_i$$

with

$$0 < w_1 \le \cdots \le w_n.$$

Let $x^{[0]}$ be the random search point represented by x after Step 2 in a run of the $(1+1)$ EA. For $t \ge 1$, let $x^{[t]}$ be the search points represented by x after the t-th iteration of Step 5 in a run of the $(1+1)$ EA.

In order to apply Theorem 3 and prove Theorem 1, we define the potential function

$$g \colon \{0,1,2\}^n \to \mathbb{R}, \quad x \mapsto \sum_{i=1}^{n} g_i x_i := \sum_{i=1}^{n} \left(1 + \tfrac{1}{n}\right)^{i-1} x_i.$$

For this potential function, we have for $g_{n+1} := (1 + 1/n)^n$ that

$$1 = g_1 \le \cdots \le g_n \le g_{n+1} \le \mathrm{e}. \quad (2)$$

Furthermore, by the formula for geometric sums, it holds that

$$\sum_{i=1}^{k} g_i = \sum_{i=0}^{k-1} \left(1 + \tfrac{1}{n}\right)^i = \frac{\left(1 + \tfrac{1}{n}\right)^k - 1}{\left(1 + \tfrac{1}{n}\right) - 1} = n(g_{k+1} - 1) \quad (3)$$

for all $k \in \{1, \ldots, n\}$ and therefore, for all $x \in \{0,1,2\}^n$,

$$g(x) \le \sum_{i=1}^{n} 2g_i = 2n(g_{n+1} - 1) = O(n).$$

Let $x \in \{0,1,2\}^n$ be a fixed point and let $y \in \{0,1,2\}^n$ be the random search point generated by $\mathrm{mut}(x)$. Furthermore, let $z \in \{-2,-1,0,1,2\}^n$ be the vector given by

$$z := x - y,$$

and let its positive and negative parts $z^+, z^- \in \{0,1,2\}^n$ be given by

$$z_i^+ := \max\{x_i - y_i, 0\} \quad \text{and} \quad z_i^- := \max\{y_i - x_i, 0\}$$

for all $i \in \{1, \ldots, n\}$, such that

$$z = z^+ - z^-.$$

Let $t \in \mathbb{N}$. Suppose that $x^{[t]} = x$ and y is the search point generated by mutation of x in Step 4 of the $(1+1)$ EA. By the selection performed in Step 5, we have $x^{[t+1]} = y$ if $f(z) \ge 0$ and $x^{[t+1]} = x$ otherwise. Thus,

$$g(x^{[t]}) - g(x^{[t+1]}) = g(z)\chi(f(z) \ge 0)$$

where g and f are extended to $\{-2,-1,0,1,2\}^n$ in the obvious way and $\chi(\mathcal{A}) \in \{0,1\}$ is the random variable that denotes the indicator function of the event $\mathcal{A}$ such that

$$\Pr[\chi(\mathcal{A}) = 1] = \Pr[\mathcal{A}].$$

Therefore,

$$\mathrm{E}\left[g(x^{[t]}) - g(x^{[t+1]}) \mid x^{[t]} = x\right] = \mathrm{E}\left[g(z)\chi(f(z) \ge 0)\right].$$

If we show the following statement then Theorem 1 directly follows from the previous equation and from Theorem 3.

LEMMA 4. *Independently of the choice of $x \in \{0,1,2\}^n$, we have that*

$$\mathrm{E}\left[g(z)\chi(f(z) \ge 0)\right] = \Omega\big(g(x)/n\big).$$

The remainder of this section is devoted to the proof of this lemma (which immediately concludes the proof of Theorem 1). We distinguish four main cases, namely whether the value of $|z^+| := \sum_{i+1}^{n} z_i^+$ is zero, one, two, or at least three.

$$\begin{aligned}
\mathrm{E}\left[g(z)\chi(f(z) \ge 0)\right] = {} & \mathrm{E}\left[g(z)\chi(|z^+| = 0 \wedge f(z) \ge 0)\right] \\
& + \mathrm{E}\left[g(z)\chi(|z^+| = 1 \wedge f(z) \ge 0)\right] \quad (4) \\
& + \mathrm{E}\left[g(z)\chi(|z^+| = 2 \wedge f(z) \ge 0)\right] \\
& + \mathrm{E}\left[g(z)\chi(|z^+| \ge 3 \wedge f(z) \ge 0)\right].
\end{aligned}$$

The first term in the sum of (4) is easily seen to be zero.

PROPOSITION 5. *It holds that*

$$\mathrm{E}\left[g(z)\chi(|z^+| = 0 \wedge f(z) \ge 0)\right] = 0.$$

PROOF. Together, the conditions $|z^+| = 0$ and $f(z) \ge 0$ imply $x = y$ and therefore $g(z) = 0$. □

Since $\mathrm{E}[g(z^+)]$ is reasonably bounded, we see that the fourth (and last) term in the sum of (4) is at least zero.

PROPOSITION 6. *It holds that*

$$\mathrm{E}\left[g(z)\chi(|z^+| \ge 3 \wedge f(z) \ge 0)\right] \ge 0.$$

PROOF. Let $\mathcal{A}$ be the event that we have $|z^+| \geq 3$ and $f(z) \geq 0$. We consider the (conditional) expected values of $g(z^+)$ and $g(z^-)$ independently.

On the one hand,

$$\mathrm{E}\left[g(z^+)\chi(\mathcal{A})\right] = \mathrm{E}\left[g(z^+) \mid \mathcal{A}\right]\Pr\left[\mathcal{A}\right] \geq 3\Pr\left[\mathcal{A}\right],$$

since $|z^+| \geq 3$ implies $|g(z^+)| \geq 3$.

On the other hand,

$$\mathrm{E}\left[g(z^-)\chi(\mathcal{A})\right] = \sum_{j=1}^n g_j\,\mathrm{E}\left[z_j^- \mid \mathcal{A}\right]\Pr\left[\mathcal{A}\right].$$

For all $j \in \{1,\dots,n\}$, the condition $\mathcal{A}$ does not increase the expected value of z_j^-. Therefore,

$$\mathrm{E}\left[z_j^- \mid \mathcal{A}\right] \leq \mathrm{E}\left[z_j^-\right] \leq \tfrac{1}{2n}\cdot 1 + \tfrac{1}{2n}\cdot 2 = \tfrac{3}{2n},$$

where for the last inequality we pessimistically assume that we have $x_j = 0$. Together, this gives us

$$\mathrm{E}\left[g(z^-)\chi(\mathcal{A})\right] \leq \sum_{j=1}^n \tfrac{3}{2n}g_j \Pr\left[\mathcal{A}\right]$$

and by applying (3) we get

$$\mathrm{E}\left[g(z^-)\chi(\mathcal{A})\right] \leq \tfrac{3(\mathrm{e}-1)}{2}\Pr\left[\mathcal{A}\right] \leq 3\Pr\left[\mathcal{A}\right].$$

The proposition follows from

$$\mathrm{E}\left[g(z)\chi(\mathcal{A}_i)\right] = \mathrm{E}\left[g(z^+)\chi(\mathcal{A}_i)\right] - \mathrm{E}\left[g(z^-)\chi(\mathcal{A}_i)\right].$$

In the proof of Proposition 8 we will review this argument. For this, note that we did not actually needed the condition $|z^+| \geq 3$ and that the weaker condition $g(z^+) \geq 3(\mathrm{e}-1)/2$ is sufficient to prove non-negative drift. $\square$

The substantial contribution to the sum in (4) comes from the second term which is of order $\Omega(g(x)/n)$.

PROPOSITION 7. *It holds that*

$$\mathrm{E}\left[g(z)\chi(|z^+| = 1 \,\wedge\, f(z) \geq 0)\right] \geq \tfrac{3-\mathrm{e}}{8\mathrm{e}^2}\cdot\tfrac{g(x)}{n}.$$

PROOF. For all $i \in \{1,\dots,n\}$ let $\mathcal{A}_i$ be the event that z_i^+ is the i-th vector of unity and that $f(z) \geq 0$.

Then the conditions $|z^+| = 1$ and $f(z) \geq 0$ imply that $\mathcal{A}_i$ holds for exactly one position $i \in \{1,\dots,n\}$ and

$$\mathrm{E}\left[g(z)\chi(|z^+| = 1 \,\wedge\, f(z) \geq 0)\right] = \sum_{i=1}^n \mathrm{E}\left[g(z)\chi(\mathcal{A}_i)\right].$$

Like in the proof of Proposition 7, we consider the (conditional) expected values of $g(z^+)$ and $g(z^-)$ independently. Let $i \in \{1,\dots,n\}$ with $\Pr[\mathcal{A}_i] > 0$. Then on the one hand,

$$\mathrm{E}\left[g(z^+)\chi(\mathcal{A}_i)\right] = \mathrm{E}\left[g(z^+) \mid \mathcal{A}_i\right]\Pr\left[\mathcal{A}_i\right] \geq g_i \Pr\left[\mathcal{A}_i\right].$$

On the other hand,

$$\mathrm{E}\left[g(z^-)\chi(\mathcal{A}_i)\right] = \sum_{j=1}^n g_j\,\mathrm{E}\left[z_j^- \mid \mathcal{A}_i\right]\Pr\left[\mathcal{A}_i\right].$$

For all $j \in \{1,\dots,i-1\}$, the condition $\mathcal{A}_i$ does not increase the expected value of z_j^-. Therefore,

$$\mathrm{E}\left[z_j^- \mid \mathcal{A}_i\right] \leq \mathrm{E}\left[z_j^-\right] \leq \tfrac{1}{2n}\cdot 1 + \tfrac{1}{2n}\cdot 2 = \tfrac{3}{2n},$$

where we pessimistically assume that $x_i = 0$ in the last inequality. However, for all $j \in \{i+1,\dots,n\}$, condition $\mathcal{A}_i$

implies $f(z^-) \leq w_i$ and therefore $z_j^- \leq 1$. Hence, in this case

$$\mathrm{E}\left[z_j^- \mid \mathcal{A}_i\right] \leq \mathrm{E}\left[z_j^-\right] \leq \tfrac{1}{2n}\cdot 1 = \tfrac{1}{2n},$$

where again we pessimistically assume that $x_i \neq 2$ in the last inequality. Together, this gives us

$$\mathrm{E}\left[g(z^-)\chi(\mathcal{A}_i)\right] \leq \sum_{j=1}^{i-1} \tfrac{3}{2n}g_j \Pr\left[\mathcal{A}_i\right] + \sum_{j=i+1}^{n} \tfrac{1}{2n}g_j \Pr\left[\mathcal{A}_i\right]$$

and by using (3) we get

$$\sum_{j=1}^{i-1} \tfrac{3}{2n}g_j = \tfrac{3}{2}(g_i - 1)$$

and

$$\sum_{j=i+1}^{n} \tfrac{1}{2n}g_j = \tfrac{1}{2n}\Big(\sum_{j=1}^{n} g_j - \sum_{j=1}^{i} g_j\Big) = \tfrac{1}{2}(g_{n+1} - g_{i+1}).$$

Therefore, with $g_{n+1} \leq \mathrm{e}$ and $g_{i+1} \geq g_i$, we have

$$\mathrm{E}\left[g(z^-)\chi(\mathcal{A}_i)\right] \leq \left(g_i - \tfrac{3-\mathrm{e}}{2}\right)\Pr\left[\mathcal{A}_i\right].$$

Since

$$\mathrm{E}\left[g(z)\chi(\mathcal{A}_i)\right] = \mathrm{E}\left[g(z^+)\chi(\mathcal{A}_i)\right] - \mathrm{E}\left[g(z^-)\chi(\mathcal{A}_i)\right]$$

and

$$\Pr\left[\mathcal{A}_i\right] \geq \tfrac{1}{2n}\left(1 - \tfrac{1}{1n}\right)^{n-1} \geq \tfrac{1}{2\mathrm{e}n},$$

and $g_i x_i \leq 2\mathrm{e}$ we have

$$\mathrm{E}\left[g(z)\chi(\mathcal{A}_i)\right] \geq \tfrac{3-\mathrm{e}}{8\mathrm{e}^2 n}g_i x_i$$

for all $i \in \{1,\dots,n\}$ with $x_i > 0$. Hence,

$$\mathrm{E}\left[g(z)\chi(\mathcal{A})\right] \geq \sum_{i\,:\,x_i>0} \tfrac{3-\mathrm{e}}{8\mathrm{e}^2 n}g_i x_i = \tfrac{3-\mathrm{e}}{8\mathrm{e}^2}\cdot\tfrac{g(x)}{n}$$

and the proposition follows. $\square$

In order to complete the proof of Lemma 4 and thus of Theorem 1, we still need to show that the third term in the sum of (4) is non-negative.

PROPOSITION 8. *Let $n \geq 200$. Then it holds that*

$$\mathrm{E}\left[g(z)\chi(|z^+| = 2 \,\wedge\, f(z) \geq 0)\right] \geq 0.$$

PROOF. For all $i \in \{1,\dots,n\}$ and $j \in \{i,\dots,n\}$ let $\mathcal{A}_{i,j}$ be the event that $z_j^+ = e_i + e_j$ (where e_i and e_j are the i-th and, respectively, j-th vector of unity), and that $f(z) \geq 0$. Furthermore, let

$$p_{i,j} := \begin{cases} \left(1 - \tfrac{1}{n}\right)^{n-1}\tfrac{1}{2n} & \text{if } i = j, \\ \left(1 - \tfrac{1}{n}\right)^{n-2}\tfrac{1}{4n^2} & \text{otherwise.} \end{cases}$$

Then either $\Pr[\mathcal{A}_{i,j}] = 0$ (which happens if $x_i = 0$, or $x_j = 0$, or $x_j = 1$ and $i = j$), or $\Pr[\mathcal{A}_{i,j}] \geq p_{i,j}$.

Then the conditions $|z^+| = 2$ and $f(z) \geq 0$ imply that $\mathcal{A}_{i,j}$ holds for exactly one such pair (i,j) and therefore

$$\mathrm{E}\left[g(z)\chi(|z^+| = 2 \,\wedge\, f(z) \geq 0)\right] = \sum_{i=1}^{n}\sum_{j=i+1}^{n} \mathrm{E}\left[g(z)\chi(\mathcal{A}_{i,j})\right].$$

Let $i \in \{1,\dots,n\}$ and $j \in \{i+1,\dots,n\}$ be two indices such that $\Pr[\mathcal{A}_{i,j}] \geq p_{i,j}$.

We may assume that $g_i + g_j \leq 3(\mathrm{e}-1)/2$. The reason for this is given at the end of the proof of Proposition 6. Let

$\mathcal{B}$ be the event that $z_\ell^- = 0$ for all $\ell \in \{j+1, \ldots, n\}$.

For all $k \in \{j+1, \ldots, n\}$ let

$\mathcal{C}_k$ be the event that $z_k^- = 1$ and that $z_\ell^- = 0$ for all $\ell \in \{j+1, \ldots, n\} \setminus \{k\}$, and let

$\mathcal{D}_k$ be the event that $z^- = 2e_k$.

For all $k \in \{j+1, \ldots, n\}$ and $\ell \in \{k+1, \ldots, n\}$ let

$\mathcal{E}_{k,\ell}$ be the event that $z^- = e_k + e_\ell$.

Then all of these events are pairwise disjoint.

Conditioned on $\mathcal{A}_{i,j}$ we have $f(z^-) \leq w_i + w_j$. Since $w_k \geq w_j$ for all $k > j$, this implies

$$\sum_{m=j+1}^{n} z_m^- \leq 2.$$

That is, there is either no position $k > j$ such that $z_k^- > 0$ (event $\mathcal{B}$), or exactly one position $k > j$ such that $z_k^- = 1$ (event $\mathcal{C}_k$), or exactly one position $k > j$ such that $z_k^- = 2$ (event $\mathcal{D}_k$), or exactly two distinct positions $\ell > k > j$ such that $z_k^- = 1$ and $z_\ell^- = 1$ (event $\mathcal{E}_{k,\ell}$). Note that for the events $\mathcal{D}_k$ and $\mathcal{E}_{k,\ell}$ we have

$$\sum_{m=j+1}^{n} z_m^- = 2.$$

In this case, we necessarily have

$$w_i = w_j = w_k \, (= w_\ell)$$

and hence also

$$\sum_{m=1}^{j-1} z_m^- = 0,$$

that is, $z_m^- = 0$ unless $m = k$ or $m = \ell$.

Therefore, conditioned on $\mathcal{A}_{i,j}$, one of the events $\mathcal{B}$, $\mathcal{C}_k$, $\mathcal{D}_k$, or $\mathcal{E}_{k,\ell}$ holds with $k \in \{j+1, \ldots, n\}$ and $\ell \in \{k+1, \ldots, n\}$. Thus,

$$\begin{aligned} \mathrm{E}\left[g(z)\chi(\mathcal{A}_{i,j})\right] = {} & \mathrm{E}\left[g(z)\chi(\mathcal{B} \wedge \mathcal{A}_{i,j})\right] \\ & + \sum_{k=j+1}^{n} \mathrm{E}\left[g(z)\chi(\mathcal{C}_k \wedge \mathcal{A}_{i,j})\right] \\ & + \sum_{k=j+1}^{n} \mathrm{E}\left[g(z)\chi(\mathcal{D}_k \wedge \mathcal{A}_{i,j})\right] \\ & + \sum_{k=j+1}^{n} \sum_{\ell=k+1}^{n} \mathrm{E}\left[g(z)\chi(\mathcal{E}_{k,\ell} \wedge \mathcal{A}_{i,j})\right]. \end{aligned}$$

Since $\Pr[\mathcal{A}_{i,j}] \geq p_{i,j}$, we know that $x_i \geq 1$ and $x_j \geq 1$ if $i \neq j$ and $x_i = x_j = 2$ if $i = j$ (otherwise this probability would be zero). In this case we have $\Pr[z = e_i + e_j] = p_{i,j}$. Now, the event "$z = e_i + e_j$" is a sub-event of the event $\mathcal{B} \wedge \mathcal{A}_{i,j}$. Therefore, we also have $\Pr[\mathcal{B} \wedge \mathcal{A}_{i,j}] \geq p_{i,j}$. Hence

$$\mathrm{E}\left[g(z)\chi(\mathcal{B} \wedge \mathcal{A}_{i,j})\right] = \mathrm{E}\left[g(z) \,\middle|\, \mathcal{B} \wedge \mathcal{A}_{i,j}\right] \Pr\left[\mathcal{B} \wedge \mathcal{A}_{i,j}\right].$$

To condition on $\mathcal{B}$ and $\mathcal{A}_{i,j}$ implies that $z_\ell^- = 0$ for all $\ell > j$ and does not increase the expected value of z_ℓ^- for $\ell < j$. Therefore, similar to Proposition 7 and Proposition 6

$$\mathrm{E}\left[g(z) \,\middle|\, \mathcal{B} \wedge \mathcal{A}_{i,j}\right] \geq g_i + g_j - \frac{3}{2n}\sum_{\ell=1}^{j-1} g_i \geq \frac{5}{2} - \frac{1}{2}g_j$$

by (3) and $g_i \geq 1$. Thus,

$$\mathrm{E}\left[g(z)\chi(\mathcal{B} \wedge \mathcal{A}_{i,j})\right] \geq \left(\tfrac{5}{2} - \tfrac{1}{2}g_j\right)\Pr[\mathcal{B} \wedge \mathcal{A}_{i,j}] \qquad (5)$$

Next, let $k \in \{j+1, \ldots, n\}$ such that $\Pr[\mathcal{C}_k \wedge \mathcal{A}_{i,j}] > 0$. Then

$$\mathrm{E}\left[g(z)\chi(\mathcal{C}_k \wedge \mathcal{A}_{i,j})\right] = \mathrm{E}\left[g(z) \,\middle|\, \mathcal{C}_k \wedge \mathcal{A}_{i,j}\right] \Pr\left[\mathcal{C}_k \wedge \mathcal{A}_{i,j}\right].$$

To condition on $\mathcal{C}_k$ and $\mathcal{A}_{i,j}$ does imply $z_k = 1$, $z_\ell^- = 0$ for all $\ell > j$ with $\ell \neq k$ and does not increase the expected value of z_ℓ^- for $\ell < j$. Therefore,

$$\mathrm{E}\left[g(z) \,\middle|\, \mathcal{C}_k \wedge \mathcal{A}_{i,j}\right] \geq g_i + g_j - g_k - \frac{3}{2n}\sum_{\ell=1}^{j-1} g_i \geq g_j + g_k$$

where we use (3) and the facts that $3/2 \geq (g_i + g_j)/(\mathrm{e}-1)$ and $g_i \geq g_j/(3(\mathrm{e}-1)/2-1)$.

Furthermore, if z satisfies $\mathcal{C}_k$ and $\mathcal{A}_{i,j}$ then $z' = z + e_k$ satisfies $\mathcal{B}$ and $\mathcal{A}_{i,j}$. Since the k-th entry flips in z but not in z' these two probabilities differ by a factor of $(1/2n)/(1 + 1/n)$ and we have

$$\Pr\left[\mathcal{C}_k \wedge \mathcal{A}_{i,j}\right] \leq \tfrac{1}{2(n-1)} \Pr\left[\mathcal{B} \wedge \mathcal{A}_{i,j}\right]$$

Thus,

$$\mathrm{E}\left[g(z)\chi(\mathcal{C}_k \wedge \mathcal{A}_{i,j})\right] \geq (g_j - g_k)\tfrac{1}{2(n-1)} \Pr\left[\mathcal{B} \wedge \mathcal{A}_{i,j}\right]$$

and, since for $n \geq 200$ we have $n\mathrm{e}/(n-1) \leq 11/4$, we get

$$\sum_{k=j+1}^{n} \mathrm{E}\left[g(z)\chi(\mathcal{C}_k \wedge \mathcal{A}_{i,j})\right] \geq \left((1-\tfrac{j}{2n})g_j - \tfrac{11}{8}\right)\Pr\left[\mathcal{B} \wedge \mathcal{A}_{i,j}\right]$$

Hence, together with (5), we have

$$\begin{aligned} & \mathrm{E}\left[g(z)\chi(\mathcal{B} \wedge \mathcal{A}_{i,j})\right] + \sum_{k=j+1}^{n} \mathrm{E}\left[g(z)\chi(\mathcal{C}_k \wedge \mathcal{A}_{i,j})\right] \\ & \geq \left(\tfrac{9}{8} + (\tfrac{1}{2} - \tfrac{j}{2n})g_j\right)\Pr\left[\mathcal{B} \wedge \mathcal{A}_{i,j}\right] \\ & \geq \left((4 - 4\tfrac{j}{n})g_j + 9\right)\tfrac{p_{i,j}}{8} \end{aligned}$$

Next, let $k \in \{j+1, \ldots, n\}$ such that $\Pr[\mathcal{D}_k \wedge \mathcal{A}_{i,j}] > 0$. This implies that $z_k = e_i + e_j - 2e_k$ and in particular that $w_i = w_j = w_k$. In this case,

$$\mathrm{E}[g(z) \,|\, \mathcal{D}_k \wedge \mathcal{A}_{i,j}] = g_i + g_j - 2g_k \geq 1 + g_j - 2g_k$$

and

$$\Pr[\mathcal{D}_k \wedge \mathcal{A}_{i,j}] \leq \tfrac{1}{2(n-1)}p_{i,j}.$$

Hence,

$$\mathrm{E}[g(z)\chi(\mathcal{D}_k \wedge \mathcal{A}_{i,j})] \geq \left(1 + g_j - 2g_k\right)\tfrac{1}{2(n-1)}p_{i,j}$$

and (again using $n\mathrm{e}/(n-1) \leq 11/4$) we have

$$\sum_{k=j+1}^{n} \mathrm{E}[g(z)\chi(\mathcal{D}_k \wedge \mathcal{A}_{i,j})] \geq \left((12 - 4\tfrac{j}{n})g_j - 18 - 4\tfrac{j}{n}\right)\tfrac{p_{i,j}}{8}$$

Finally, let $k \in \{j+1, \ldots, n\}$ and $\ell \in \{k+1, \ldots, n\}$ such that $\Pr[\mathcal{D}_k \wedge \mathcal{A}_{i,j}] > 0$. This implies that $z_k = e_i + e_j - e_k - e_\ell$ and in particular that $w_i = w_j = w_k = w_\ell$. In this case,

$$\mathrm{E}[g(z) \,|\, \mathcal{D}_k \wedge \mathcal{A}_{i,j}] \geq 1 + g_j - g_k - g_\ell$$

and

$$\Pr[\mathcal{D}_k \wedge \mathcal{A}_{i,j}] \leq \left(1 - \tfrac{1}{n}\right)^{-2} 4n^2 p_{i,j}.$$

Hence,

$$\mathrm{E}[g(z)\chi(\mathcal{D}_k \wedge \mathcal{A}_{i,j})] \geq \left(1 + g_j - g_k - g_\ell\right)\left(1 - \tfrac{1}{n}\right)^{-2}\tfrac{1}{4n^2}p_{i,j}$$

and with $e/(1 - 1/n)^2 \leq 11/4$ we get

$$\sum_{k=j+1}^{n}\sum_{\ell=k+1}^{n}\mathrm{E}[g(z)\chi(\mathcal{D}_k \wedge \mathcal{A}_{i,j})]$$
$$\geq \left((3 - 4\tfrac{j}{n})g_j - 5 + 4\tfrac{j}{n}\right)\tfrac{p_{i,j}}{8}.$$

Summing up, we get

$$\mathrm{E}\left[g(z)\chi(\mathcal{A}_{i,j})\right] \geq \left((9 - 6\tfrac{j}{n})g_j - 7\right)\tfrac{p_{i,j}}{4}.$$

To do so, we apply

$$g_j = \left(1 + \tfrac{1}{n}\right)^{j-1} \geq 0.99e^{j/n},$$

where the last inequality follows from $1 + a \geq e^{a-a^2}$ for all $a \in [0,1]$ and from $n \geq 200$. Now, we substitute $\alpha := j/n$ and verify that the function

$$h(\alpha) := 0.99(9 - 6\alpha)e^\alpha - 7$$

is positive on the interval $[0,1]$. This holds since we have

$$h'(\alpha) = 0.99(3 - 6\alpha)e^\alpha$$

and

$$h''(\alpha) = -0.99(3 + 6\alpha)e^\alpha,$$

that is on the interval $[0,1]$ the function h has a maximum at $\alpha = 1/2$ and two minima

$$h(0) = 1.91 \quad \text{and} \quad h(1) = 2.97e - 7 > 0$$

at $\alpha = 0$ and $\alpha = 1$ which are both positive. $\quad\square$

4. LIMITATIONS OF FIXED POTENTIAL FUNCTIONS

In the previous section we have seen how to use a single linear potential function to analyze all linear functions over $\{0,1,2\}^n$. One may ask whether this is possible also for linear function over $\{0,\ldots,r\}^n$ with larger r, potentially even growing in n.

In this section, we show that this is not the case. Already for $r = 3$, the proof in Section 3 does not generalize immediately. More importantly, we show that for $r \geq 43$, there exists no single ("universal") linear potential function over $\{0,1,\ldots,r\}^n$ that allows us to bound the expected runtime of the $(1+1)$ EA on all linear functions over the space $\{0,1,\ldots,r\}^n$. In this, we do not try to optimize the constant, that is, we do not know exactly up to which constant r the proof method of the previous section can be applied and from which point on the non-existence results for universal drift functions presented in this section holds.

In the previous section, we showed that our potential function g has a positive drift of $\Omega(g(x)/n)$ in every single point $x \in \{0,1,2\}^n$. In [14], Jägersküpper shows that this assumption is not necessary. Instead, he shows that for the search space $\{0,1\}^n$ it is sufficient to assume that x is chosen according to a semi-balanced distribution.

DEFINITION 9 (SEMI-BALANCED). *Let n and r be two positive integers. Let $\mathcal{D}$ be a distribution over $\{0,1\ldots,r\}^n$. Then, $\mathcal{D}$ is semi-balanced if for $x \in \{0,\ldots,r\}^n$ drawn according to $\mathcal{D}$ it holds that*

$$\Pr(x_i = a \wedge x_j = b) \leq \Pr(x_i = b \wedge x_j = a)$$

for all $i,j \in \{1\ldots n\}$ and $a,b \in \{0,\ldots,r\}$ with $i < j$ and $a < b$.

It turns out that it is difficult to extend Jägersküpper's result and show that in each iteration of the $(1+1)$ EA optimizing a linear function over $\{0,1,\ldots,r\}^n$ the search point is semi-balanced. However, even under the assumption that this is possible, we see that ultimately this alone will not yield a proof of a $O(n\log n)$ runtime bound for $r \geq 43$.

THEOREM 10. *Let $r \geq 43$ and let*

$$g\colon \{0,1,\ldots,r\}^n \to \mathbb{R} \quad g\colon x \mapsto \sum_{i=1}^{n}g_i x_i$$

be a linear potential function with real-valued weights

$$0 < g_1 \leq \cdots \leq g_n.$$

Then there exists a linear fitness function

$$f\colon \{0,1,\ldots,r\}^n \to \mathbb{R} \quad f\colon x \mapsto \sum_{i=1}^{n}w_i x_i$$

with real-valued weights

$$0 < w_1 \leq \cdots \leq w_n$$

and a semi-balanced distribution $\mathcal{D}$ on $\{0,1,\ldots,r\}^n$ such that if x is drawn according to $\mathcal{D}$ and $y = \mathrm{mut}(x)$, then

$$\mathrm{E}_{x,y}\left[(g(x) - g(y))\chi(f(y) \leq f(x))\right] \leq 0.$$

where again $\chi(\mathcal{A}) \in \{0,1\}$ is the random variable that denotes the indicator function of the event $\mathcal{A}$.

Note that this theorem does not imply that the runtime of the $(1+1)$ EA on linear functions over $\{0,1,\ldots,r\}^n$ is not in $O(n\log n)$ (which we actually conjecture to be true). Nor does it say that this result cannot be obtained using (multiplicative) drift analysis. Instead, it states that if such a proof is possible, the used potential function has to include more information on the weights $w_1,\ldots,w_n$ than just their order.

To prove the previous theorem, we first show two propositions. Without loss of generality, we may assume that $g_0 = 1$ since Theorem 3 is invariant under scaling. The first proposition tells us that the sum of weights in a suitable potential function may not be to large.

PROPOSITION 11. *Let n and r be two positive integers. Let*

$$g\colon \{0,1,\ldots,r\}^n \to \mathbb{R} \quad g\colon x \mapsto \sum_{i=1}^{n}g_i x_i$$

be a linear potential function with real-valued weights

$$1 = g_1 \leq \cdots \leq g_n$$

such that

$$\sum_{i=1}^{n}g_i > (r+1)n. \tag{6}$$

Let

$$f\colon \{0,1,\ldots,r\}^n \to \mathbb{R} \quad f\colon x \mapsto \sum_{i=1}^{n}x_i$$

and let $\mathcal{D}$ be the semi-balanced distribution on $\{0,1,\ldots,r\}^n$ that chooses e_1, i.e., the first unit vector, with certainty.

Suppose x is drawn according to $\mathcal{D}$ and $y = \mathrm{mut}(x)$, then

$$\mathrm{E}_{x,y}\left[(g(x) - g(y))\chi(f(y) \leq f(x))\right] < 0.$$

PROOF. We know that $x = e_1$ with $f(x) = w_1 = 1$ and $g(x) = g_1 = 1$. Hence, the only random variable we have to consider is $y = \mathrm{mut}(e_1)$. Let

$$\Delta := (g(x) - g(y))\chi(f(y) \leq f(x)) = (1 - g(y))\chi(f(y) \leq 1).$$

There are three cases such that $f(y) \leq 1$.

The first case is that $y = x = e_1$. The probability of this event is $(1 - 1/n)^n$ and conditioned on this event we have $\Delta = 0$.

The second case is that $y = (0, \ldots, 0)$. The probability of this event is $(1/rn)(1 - 1/n)^{n-1}$ and conditioned on this event we have $\Delta = 1$.

The third case is that $y = e_i$ with $i \geq 2$. For all $i \geq 2$, the probability that $y = e_i$ is $(1/rn)^2(1 - 1/n)^{n-2}$ and in this case we have $\Delta = 1 - g_i$. Thus,

$$\mathrm{E}_{x,y}[\Delta] = \tfrac{1}{rn}\left(1 - \tfrac{1}{n}\right)^{n-1} + \sum_{i=2}^{n}(\tfrac{1}{rn})^2\left(1 - \tfrac{1}{n}\right)^{n-2}(1 - g_i)$$

$$= \tfrac{1}{rn}\left(1 - \tfrac{1}{n}\right)^{n-2}\left(\tfrac{(r+1)n-1}{rn} - \tfrac{1}{rn}\sum_{i=1}^{n} g_i\right).$$

The proposition follows from (6) $\square$

The second proposition tells us that the sum of the first k weights in a suitable potential function may not grow too slowly.

PROPOSITION 12. *Let n and r be two positive integers. Let*

$$g: \{0, 1, \ldots, r\}^n \to \mathbb{R} \quad g: x \mapsto \sum_{i=1}^{n} g_i x_i$$

be a linear potential function with real-valued weights

$$1 = g_1 \leq \cdots \leq g_n$$

such that

$$\sum_{i=1}^{k} g_i > \tfrac{r+3}{r+1}\sum_{i=1}^{k}\left(1 - \tfrac{1}{n}\right)^{k-i} g_i \qquad (7)$$

Let $k \in \{1, \ldots, n\}$. Let

$$f: \{0, 1, \ldots, r\}^n \to \mathbb{R} \quad f: x \mapsto \sum_{i=1}^{n}(r+1)^i x_i$$

and let $\mathcal{D}_k$ be the (semi-balanced) uniform distribution over $\{e_1, \ldots, e_k\}$.

Suppose x is drawn according to $\mathcal{D}$ and $y = \mathrm{mut}(x)$, then

$$\mathrm{E}_{x,y}\left[(g(x) - g(y))\chi(f(y) \leq f(x))\right] < 0.$$

PROOF. Let $\Delta := (g(x) - g(y))\chi(f(y) \leq f(x))$. Then

$$\mathrm{E}_{x,y}[\Delta] = \tfrac{1}{k}\sum_{i=1}^{k} \mathrm{E}_{x,y}[\Delta \mid x = e_i].$$

Suppose that $x = e_i$ with $i \in \{1, \ldots, k\}$. Then we have that $\Delta \neq 0$ if and only if $y_i = \cdots = y_n = 0$ and this event happens with probability $\tfrac{1}{rn}\left(1 - \tfrac{1}{n}\right)^{n-i}$. Furthermore, we have

$$\mathrm{E}_{x,y}[\Delta \mid x = e_i \wedge y_i = \cdots = y_n = 0] = g_i - \sum_{j=1}^{i-1} g_j \, \mathrm{E}[y_j].$$

Therefore, since $\mathrm{E}[y_j] = \tfrac{r+1}{2n}$, we get

$$\mathrm{E}_{x,y}[\Delta \mid x = e_i \wedge y_i = \cdots = y_n = 0] = g_i - \tfrac{r+1}{2n}\sum_{j=1}^{i-1} g_j.$$

It follows that

$$\mathrm{E}_{x,y}[\Delta \mid x = e_i] = \tfrac{1}{rn}\left(1 - \tfrac{1}{n}\right)^{n-i}\left(g_i - \tfrac{r+1}{2n}\sum_{j=1}^{i-1} g_j\right)$$

and thus

$$\mathrm{E}_{x,y}[\Delta] = \tfrac{1}{krn}\sum_{i=1}^{k}\left(1 - \tfrac{1}{n}\right)^{n-i}\left(g_i - \tfrac{r+1}{2n}\sum_{j=1}^{i-1} g_j\right)$$

Furthermore, we see that

$$\sum_{i=1}^{k}\sum_{j=1}^{i-1}\left(1 - \tfrac{1}{n}\right)^{k-i} g_j = n\sum_{i=1}^{k}\left(1 - \left(1 - \tfrac{1}{n}\right)^{k-i}\right)g_i$$

and therefore

$$\mathrm{E}_{x,y}[\Delta] = \frac{\left(1 - \tfrac{1}{n}\right)^{n-k}}{2krn}\sum_{i=1}^{k}\left((r+3)\left(1 - \tfrac{1}{n}\right)^{k-i} - (r+1)\right)g_i.$$

The proposition follows from (7). $\square$

To prove Theorem 10, we now need to show that at least one of the two inequalities (6) or (7) holds for $r \geq 43$.

PROOF OF THEOREM 10. Let $\ell := \lceil \tfrac{2n}{r+1} \rceil$. Aiming at a contradiction, suppose that neither (6) nor (7) holds. Then we have by (7) that

$$\sum_{i=1}^{k} g_i \leq \left(1 + \tfrac{2}{r+1}\right)\sum_{i=1}^{k}\left(1 - \tfrac{1}{n}\right)^{k-i} g_i$$

for all $k \in \{\ell + 1, \ldots, n\}$ simultaneously.

For all $i \in \{1, \ldots, k\}$ let $a_i := \left(1 + \tfrac{2}{r+1}\right)\left(1 - \tfrac{1}{n}\right)^{k-i}$. Then

$$\sum_{i=1}^{k} g_i = \sum_{i=1}^{k-\ell} a_i g_i + \sum_{i=k-\ell+1}^{k} a_i g_i.$$

Since $a_i \leq 1 + \tfrac{2}{r+1}$ for all $i \leq k$, we have

$$\sum_{i=1}^{k} g_i \leq \sum_{i=1}^{k-\ell} a_i g_i + \sum_{i=k-\ell+1}^{k}\left(1 + \tfrac{2}{r+1}\right)g_i$$

and hence

$$\sum_{i=1}^{k-\ell}(1 - a_i)g_i \leq \frac{2}{r+1}\sum_{i=k-\ell+1}^{k} g_i. \qquad (8)$$

Since it holds for all $z \in \mathbb{R}$ that $1 + z \leq e^z$, we have

$$a_i \leq e^{\frac{2}{r+1} - \frac{k-i}{n}} \leq 1$$

for all $1 \leq i \leq k - \ell$. Thus, the coefficients on the left-hand side of (8) are all positive. Since $1 = g_1 \leq \cdots \leq g_k$, we obtain

$$\sum_{i=1}^{k-\ell}(1 - a_i) \leq \frac{2}{r+1}\sum_{i=k-\ell+1}^{k} g_i = \frac{2\ell}{r+1} g_k.$$

125

Now,

$$\sum_{i=1}^{k-\ell} a_i = \left(1 + \tfrac{2}{r+1}\right) \sum_{i=1}^{k-\ell} \left(1 - \tfrac{1}{n}\right)^{k-i}$$

$$= a_{k-\ell} \sum_{i=1}^{k-\ell} \left(1 - \tfrac{1}{n}\right)^{k-\ell-i}$$

$$= a_{k-\ell} \sum_{i=0}^{k-\ell-1} \left(1 - \tfrac{1}{n}\right)^{i}$$

$$= a_{k-\ell} n \left(1 - \left(1 - \tfrac{1}{n}\right)^{k-\ell}\right)$$

$$\leq n - \left(1 - \tfrac{1}{n}\right)^{k-\ell} n.$$

Thus,

$$g_k \geq \tfrac{r+1}{2\ell} \left(k - \ell - n + \left(1 - \tfrac{1}{n}\right)^{k-\ell} n\right)$$

and

$$\sum_{k=\ell+1}^{n} g_k \geq \tfrac{r+1}{2\ell} \sum_{k=\ell+1}^{n} \left(k - \ell - n + \left(1 - \tfrac{1}{n}\right)^{k-\ell} n\right)$$

$$= \tfrac{r+1}{2\ell} \sum_{k=1}^{n-\ell} \left(k - n + \left(1 - \tfrac{1}{n}\right)^{k} n\right)$$

$$= \tfrac{r+1}{2\ell} \left(\sum_{k=1}^{n-\ell} k - (n-\ell)n + n \sum_{k=1}^{n-\ell} \left(1 - \tfrac{1}{n}\right)^{k}\right)$$

$$\geq \tfrac{r+1}{4\ell} \left((1 - 2e^{-(n-\ell)/n}) n (n-1) + \ell(\ell-1)\right)$$

$$\geq \tfrac{(1 - 2e^{-(r-2)/(r+1)})(r+1)^2}{9} n$$

$$> (r+1)n$$

for $r \geq 43$. This is a contradiction to (6). $\square$

5. CONCLUSION

We have seen that drift analysis can be applied to analyze the $(1+1)$ EA on linear functions over $\{0, 1, 2\}^n$. However, for larger values of r, the approach to model the behavior of the $(1+1)$ EA for all linear functions over $\{0, 1, \ldots, r\}^n$ with a single linear potential function fails, even if we invoke a balance argument as in [14].

Observing such difficulties already for relatively simple optimization problems as the one regarded here, we feel that it is still a long way to go until drift analysis is sufficiently well-understood to solve problems like proving a runtime of $\Theta(m^2 \log m)$ for the $(1+1)$ EA on the minimum spanning tree problem (which we conjecture to be true).

We still believe that (multiplicative) drift analysis is an adequate way to approach this problem. Most likely, one needs a more problem-specific potential function that reveals (or needs?) more insight into the structure of the minimum spanning tree problem.

6. REFERENCES

[1] A. Auger and B. Doerr, editors. *Theory of Randomized Seach Heuristics*. World Scientific, 2011.

[2] S. Baswana, S. Biswas, B. Doerr, T. Friedrich, P. P. Kurur, and F. Neumann. Computing single source shortest paths using single-objective fitness. In *FOGA '09*, pages 59–66. ACM, 2009.

[3] B. Doerr, E. Happ, and C. Klein. A tight analysis of the $(1+1)$-EA for the single source shortest path problem. In *CEC '07*, pages 1890–1895. IEEE, 2007.

[4] B. Doerr and D. Johannsen. Edge-based representation beats vertex-based representation in shortest path problems. In *GECCO '10*, pages 759–766. ACM, 2010.

[5] B. Doerr, D. Johannsen, and C. Winzen. Drift analysis and linear functions revisited. In *CEC '10*, pages 1–8. ACM, 2010.

[6] B. Doerr, D. Johannsen, and C. Winzen. Multiplicative drift analysis. In *GECCO '10*, pages 1449–1456. ACM, 2010.

[7] B. Doerr, D. Johannsen, and C. Winzen. Multiplicative drift analysis. In *GECCO '10*, pages 1449–1456. ACM, 2010.

[8] S. Droste, T. Jansen, and I. Wegener. On the analysis of the $(1+1)$ evolutionary algorithm. *Theoretical Computer Science*, 276(1–2):51–81, 2002.

[9] C. Gunia. On the analysis of the approximation capability of simple evolutionary algorithms for scheduling problems. In *GECCO '05*, pages 571–578. ACM, 2005.

[10] B. Hajek. Hitting-time and occupation-time bounds implied by drift analysis with applications. *Advances in Applied Probability*, 14(3):502–525, 1982.

[11] J. He and X. Yao. Drift analysis and average time complexity of evolutionary algorithms. *Artificial Intelligence*, 127(1):57–85, 2001.

[12] J. He and X. Yao. Erratum to: drift analysis and average time complexity of evolutionary algorithms [Artificial Intelligence 127 (2001) 57–85]. *Artificial Intelligence*, 140(1–2):245–248, 2002.

[13] J. He and X. Yao. A study of drift analysis for estimating computation time of evolutionary algorithms. *Natural Computing*, 3(1):21–35, 2004.

[14] J. Jägersküpper. A blend of Markov-chain and drift analysis. In *PPSN '08*, pages 41–51. Springer, 2008.

[15] F. Neumann and I. Wegener. Randomized local search, evolutionary algorithms, and the minimum spanning tree problem. *Theoretical Computer Science*, 378(1):32–40, 2007.

[16] F. Neumann and C. Witt. *Bioinspired Computation in Combinatorial Optimization*. Springer, 2010.

[17] J. Reichel and M. Skutella. Evolutionary algorithms and matroid optimization problems. In *GECCO '07*, pages 947–954. ACM, 2007.

[18] J. Reichel and M. Skutella. On the size of weights in randomized search heuristics. In *FOGA '09*, pages 21–28. ACM, 2009.

[19] J. Scharnow, K. Tinnefeld, and I. Wegener. The analysis of evolutionary algorithms on sorting and shortest paths problems. *Journal of Mathematical Modelling and Algorithms*, 3(4):349–366, 2004.

Analyzing the Impact of Mirrored Sampling and Sequential Selection in Elitist Evolution Strategies

Anne Auger
TAO Team, INRIA
Saclay–Ile-de-France
LRI Paris Sud University
91405 Orsay Cedex, France
firstname.lastname@inria.fr

Dimo Brockhoff
System Modeling and
Optimization Team
Laboratoire d'Informatique
École Polytechnique
91128 Palaiseau Cedex, France
brockho@lix.polytechnique.fr

Nikolaus Hansen
TAO Team, INRIA
Saclay–Ile-de-France
LRI Paris Sud University
91405 Orsay Cedex, France
firstname.lastname@inria.fr

ABSTRACT

This paper presents a refined single parent evolution strategy that is derandomized with mirrored sampling and/or uses sequential selection. The paper analyzes some of the elitist variants of this algorithm. We prove, on spherical functions with finite dimension, linear convergence of different strategies with scale-invariant step-size and provide expressions for the convergence rates as the expectation of some known random variables. In addition, we derive explicit asymptotic formulae for the convergence rate when the dimension of the search space goes to infinity. Convergence rates on the sphere reveal lower bounds for the convergence rate of the respective step-size adaptive strategies. We prove the surprising result that the $(1+2)$-ES with mirrored sampling converges at the same rate as the $(1+1)$-ES without and show that the tight lower bound for the $(1+\lambda)$-ES with mirrored sampling and sequential selection improves by 16% over the $(1+1)$-ES reaching an asymptotic value of about -0.235.

Categories and Subject Descriptors

G.1.6 [**Numerical Analysis**]: Optimization—*global optimization, unconstrained optimization*; F.2.1 [**Analysis of Algorithms and Problem Complexity**]: Numerical Algorithms and Problems

General Terms

Algorithms, Theory

Keywords

Evolution Strategies, Mirroring, Sequential Selection, Plus-Selection

1. INTRODUCTION

Evolution Strategies (ESs) are robust search algorithms designed to minimize objective functions f that map a continuous search space $\mathbb{R}^d$ into $\mathbb{R}$. In a $(1 \overset{+}{,} \lambda)$-ES, λ candidate solutions, the offspring, are created from a single parent, $\boldsymbol{X}_k \in \mathbb{R}^d$. The λ offspring are generated by adding λ *independent* random vectors $(\boldsymbol{\mathcal{N}}_k^i)_{1 \leq i \leq \lambda}$ to $\boldsymbol{X}_k$. Then, the *best* of the λ offspring $\boldsymbol{X}_k + \boldsymbol{\mathcal{N}}_k^i$ in case of comma selection or of the λ offspring plus parent in case of plus selection is *selected* to become the next parent $\boldsymbol{X}_{k+1}$. The $(1+1)$-ES is arguably the most local, and the locally fastest, variant of an evolution strategy.

Derandomization of random numbers is a general technique where the independent samples are replaced by dependent ones with the objective of accelerating algorithm convergence. Derandomization by means of antithetic variables for isotropic samples was first introduced within general ESs in [27]. Mirrored samples, as used in this paper, are a special case, where the number of independent events is reduced by a factor of two only. In [26], the sequence of uniform random numbers used for sampling a multivariate normal distribution was replaced by scrambling-Halton and Sobol sequences. These sequences achieved consistent improvements of CMA-ES (covariance matrix adaptation evolution strategy) mainly on unimodal test functions, typically with $\leq 30\%$ speed-up and most pronounced in dimension 2. The improvements are however difficult to attribute to a cause for at least two reasons. First, in CMA-ES with $\mu > 1$, quasi-random numbers possibly introduce a (strong) bias on the step-size. For mirrored samples and Sobol sequences, we have verified this bias empirically (shown for mirrored sampling in [17]). The bias can improve convergence rates,[1] but violates the demand on a stochastic search algorithm to be unbiased [19, 22]. Second, random rotations of the quasi-random vector sets in [26] lead to a significant loss of the advantage. The investigated functions were however unrotated. This makes the identity as initial covariance matrix, represented in the given coordinate system and in connection with the quasi-random numbers, presumably a choice that is unintentionally biased towards the function testbed.

Consequently, it remains to be investigated to what extend the improvements can be attributed to a bias on the variance of the sum of selected vectors (leading to the bias

---

[1] For mirrored sampling this most probably happens if random vectors with different lengths are realized, which is the case in particular in small dimensions.

on the step-size), to a coordinate system dependency, or to the quasi-random structure itself.

Our own experiments with derandomizations beyond mirroring, similar to those in [27], revealed the most pronounced effects (unsurprisingly) by mirroring and in small populations. We have not considered algorithms that are—by themselves or in combination with CMA-ES—biased or not rotationally invariant.

Mirrored sampling is a derandomization technique similar to antithetic variables that was recently introduced within $(1+\lambda)$ and $(1,\lambda)$-ESs [17]. In addition, mirrored sampling has been coupled with *sequential selection*, a modification of the $(1,\lambda)$ and $(1+\lambda)$ selection schemes where the offspring are evaluated sequentially and the iteration is concluded as soon as one offspring is better than its current parent [17].

Sequential selection and mirrored sampling have been implemented within the CMA-ES and extensively empirically studied on 54 noiseless [20] and noisy [21] functions in a series of papers [4–10, 12–15]. In summary, the variants with mirrored mutation and sequential selection improved their baseline algorithms (without these two ideas) on almost all functions for almost all target values where the combination of the two concepts was never statistically significantly worse than the standard algorithms. In particular for the elitist $(1+1)$-CMA-ES, additional mirrored mutation and sequential selection improved the performance by about 17% on the non-separable ellipsoid function, by about 20% on the ellipsoid, the discus, and the sum of different powers functions, and by 12% on the sphere function while no statistically significant worsening of the performance was reported [6].

So far, theoretical investigations of mirrored sampling and sequential selection is restricted to comma selection [17]. Convergence rates of the scale-invariant step-size $(1,\lambda)$-ES with mirrored sampling and sequential selection on spherical functions have been derived and lower bounds for the convergence of the different strategies were compared. Those results hold for finite dimensions of the search space. In this paper, we aim at generalizing those theoretical results to plus selection: we extend finite dimension convergence proofs to plus selection and complement those results with asymptotic estimates of the convergence rates when the dimension goes to infinity.

The paper is structured as follows. In Section 2, we describe the $(1 \overset{+}{,} \lambda)$-ES with mirrored sampling and sequential selection and derive general properties. In Section 3, we derive the linear convergence of the $(1+\lambda)$-ES with mirrored sampling and sequential selection with scale-invariant step-size on spherical functions. We express the convergence rate in terms of the expectation of a random variable. In addition, we establish that the $(1+1)$-ES and the $(1+2_m)$-ES with mirrored sampling exhibit the same convergence rate. In Section 5, we derive some simple expressions for the asymptotic normalized convergence rate of the different algorithms, where asymptotic refers to the dimension tending to infinity. In Section 6, we numerically simulate the convergence rates for different dimensions and appraise quantitatively the improvements brought by mirrored sampling and sequential selection.

Notations: In this paper, a multivariate normal distribution with mean vector zero and covariance matrix identity will be called *standard* multivariate normal distribution. The first vector $(1, 0, \ldots, 0)$ of the canonical basis will be denoted $\boldsymbol{e}_1$.

Algorithm 1 Pseudocode for the $(1+\lambda)$-ES and the $(1,\lambda)$-ES with all combinations with/without mirrored sampling and/or sequential selection. $\boldsymbol{X}_k \in \mathbb{R}^d$ denotes the current search point and σ_k the current step-size at iteration k. $(\mathcal{N}_m)_{m\in\mathbb{N}}$ is a sequence of random vectors. In this paper, *skip mirror* is true whenever sequential selection is true.

---

given: $f : \mathbb{R}^d \to \mathbb{R}$, $\boldsymbol{X}_0 \in \mathbb{R}^d$, $\sigma_0 > 0$, $\lambda \in \mathbb{N}^+$, $(\mathcal{N}_m)_{m\in\mathbb{N}}$

$m \leftarrow 0$ number of random samples used
$j \leftarrow 0$ use previous sample if j is even
$k \leftarrow 0$ iteration counter for notational consistency
while stopping criterion not fulfilled **do**
    $i \leftarrow 0$ offspring counter
    while $i < \lambda$ **do**
       $i \leftarrow i + 1$, $j \leftarrow j + 1$
       if *mirrored sampling* and $j \equiv 0 \pmod 2$ **then**
          $\boldsymbol{X}_k^i = \boldsymbol{X}_k - \sigma_k \mathcal{N}_m$ use previous sample
       else
          $m \leftarrow m + 1$
          $\boldsymbol{X}_k^i = \boldsymbol{X}_k + \sigma_k \mathcal{N}_m$
       if $f(\boldsymbol{X}_k^i) \leq f(\boldsymbol{X}_k)$ **then**
          if *skip mirror* **then**
             $j \leftarrow 0$ continue with a fresh sample
          if *sequential selection* **then**
             break
    end while
    if *plus selection* **then**
       $\boldsymbol{X}_{k+1} = \arg\min\{f(\boldsymbol{X}_k), f(\boldsymbol{X}_k^1), \ldots, f(\boldsymbol{X}_k^i)\}$
    else
       $\boldsymbol{X}_{k+1} = \arg\min\{f(\boldsymbol{X}_k^1), \ldots, f(\boldsymbol{X}_k^i)\}$
    $\sigma_{k+1} = \text{update}(\sigma_k)$
    $k \leftarrow k + 1$ iteration counter
end while

---

2. $(1 \overset{+}{,} \lambda)$-ES WITH MIRRORED SAMPLING AND SEQUENTIAL SELECTION

In this section, we introduce the $(1 \overset{+}{,} \lambda)$-ES with mirrored sampling and sequential selection and derive general theoretical results on those algorithms.

2.1 Algorithm Description

Mirrored mutations and sequential selection have been introduced in [17] and are two independent ideas for improving simple local search strategies such as $(1 \overset{+}{,} \lambda)$-ESs. Algorithm 1 shows the pseudocode of a combination of both concepts within the $(1+\lambda)$-ES and the $(1,\lambda)$-ES. Note that we describe the algorithms without specifying which sampling distribution is used—though most of the time, for Evolution Strategies, multivariate normal distributions are used. However, since we will derive some results that are independent of the choice of the sampling distribution, we keep the description general and indicate when a standard multivariate normal distribution is required.

Mirrored sampling: The idea behind mirrored sampling is to derandomize the generation of new sample points. Instead of using two independent random vectors to create two offspring, with mirrored sampling only a single random vector instantiation is used to create two offspring: one by adding and the other by subtracting the vector from the current search point. The two instantiations are called *mirrored* or *symmetric* with respect to the parent $\boldsymbol{X}_k$ at itera-

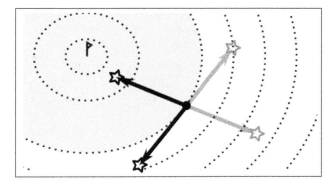

Figure 1: Mirrored sampling on an objective function with convex sub-level sets. The shaded region represents the set of solutions with a better objective function value than the parent solution (black dot). *Not both mirrored offspring can be better than the parent solution at the same time*: shown are two examples of an offspring (black) and its mirrored version (gray) where either one or both offspring are worse than the parent.

tion k if they take place in the same iteration. For odd λ, every other iteration, the first offspring uses the mirrored last vector from the previous iteration, see j in Algorithm 1. Consequently, in the $(1+1_m)$-ES, a mirrored sample is used if and only if the iteration index is even (given *skip mirror* in Algorithm 1 is false).

When evaluating a sampled solution and its mirrored counterpart, sometimes unnecessary function evaluations are performed: for example, on unimodal objective functions with convex sub-level sets, $\{x \mid f(x) \leq c\}$ for $c \in \mathbb{R}$, such as the sphere function, $f(x) = \|x\|^2$, the mirrored solution $\boldsymbol{X}_k - \mathcal{N}$ is always worse than the parent $\boldsymbol{X}_k$ if $\boldsymbol{X}_k + \mathcal{N}$ was better than $\boldsymbol{X}_k$, see Fig. 1 and Proposition 2 below. Setting *skip mirror* to true in Algorithm 1 prevents these mirrored samples from being realized.[2]

Note that in the $(1+\lambda_m)$-ES, two mirrored offspring are entirely dependent and, in a sense, complementary, similar to antithetic variables for Monte-Carlo numerical integration [18]. Mirrored sampling is also similar to using a symmetric difference quotient instead of the standard one-sided difference quotient. The technique has been applied to Evolutionary Gradient Search (EGS) with good success [1].

Sequential selection: In sequential selection, the offspring are evaluated one by one, compared to their parent, and the iteration is concluded immediately if one offspring is better than its parent. Sequential selection has been introduced in the context of comma selection, where it aims to combine the robustness advantage of comma selection with the speed advantage of elitist plus selection [17]. Sequential selection and mirrored sampling are independent of each other and can be employed separately within ESs, see Algorithm 1. We will see that sequential selection, in the elitist context, essentially comes down to the $(1+1)$-ES. The $(1+\lambda)$-ES variant employing sequential selection is denoted by $(1+\lambda^s)$-ES.

Combining mirrored sampling and sequential selection: Sequential selection has been combined with mirrored sampling in the $(1, \lambda)$-ES and, although not explicitly mentioned, *skip mirror* was in this case always applied [17]. Both concepts complement each other well for the $(1, \lambda)$-ES. Sequential selection tends to reduce the realized population size to a minimum and mirrored sampling improves the performance in particular for very small population sizes. In this paper as well, *skip mirror* is set to true when sequential selection and mirrored sampling are combined. With sequential selection, it is important that independent and mirrored offspring are evaluated alternately in order to profit immediately from the increased probability of the mirrored offspring being better after the independently drawn offspring was worse than the parent [17].

The $(1+\lambda)$-ES with mirrored sampling and sequential selection is denoted as $(1+\lambda^s_{ms})$-ES where the superscript refers to sequential selection and the subscript to mirrored sampling with *skip mirror* set to true. All results in this paper refer to strategies where *skip mirror* is true when sequential selection is applied.

2.2 General Properties of Mirrored Sampling and Sequential Selection

In this section, we derive general results on evolution strategies using mirrored sampling and sequential selection. Let us first recognize that the $(1+\lambda^s)$-ES is essentially a $(1+1)$-ES with smaller iteration counter. In both strategies, the parent is updated if and only if the currently sampled offspring is better (but see also Remark 1). Now, we also establish for mirrored sampling that $(1+1_{ms})$-ES and $(1+\lambda^s_{ms})$-ES all evaluate the same points, provided they use the same (constant or scale-invariant) step-size and the same random instance for generating the offspring.

PROPOSITION 1. *The $(1+\lambda^s_{ms})$-ES is for any $\lambda \geq 1$ the same algorithm—with possibly different iteration counter, given the same random vectors and the same step-sizes are used (for example the step-size σ_k is either constant or scale-invariant, i.e., $\sigma_k = \sigma\|X_k\|$ with σ constant).*

PROOF. We prove that the state of the algorithm (apart from the iteration counter) does not depend on λ. Independently of λ, because of sequential selection applied in combination with plus selection, any new evaluated offspring is sampled from the *best ever* evaluated point so far. Since step-size only depends on the parent or is constant, the same offspring will be sampled provided the random samples used are also independent of λ. However, the samples used are taken one by one from $(\mathcal{N}_m, -\mathcal{N}_m)_{m \in \mathbb{N}}$ where because *skip mirror* is true, some mirrored vectors $-\mathcal{N}$ are skipped. But the decision of whether or not to skip the mirroring of a sample is also independent of λ since it only depends on a comparison between the single last offspring and the parent. $\square$

Due to this result, the notations $(1+1_{ms})$-ES, $(1+2^s_{ms})$-ES and $(1+\lambda^s_{ms})$-ES refer, in this paper, all to the same strategy. However, this might not be the case in practice.

REMARK 1. *In practice, the behavior of ESs with sequential selection depends on λ, because the step-size is typically updated at the end of each iteration and therefore more often with small λ.*

REMARK 2. *For $\mu = 1$, sequential selection and/or mirroring have been combined with CMA-ES and extensively studied with plus and comma selection and different step-size rules [4–10, 12–15].*

---

[2] In the $(1+1_m)$-ES, these unnecessary mirrored solutions fall closely together with the previous parental solution.

We derive now some results on objective functions with convex sub-level sets. We first establish that on objective functions with convex sub-level sets two mirrored offspring cannot be both better than their parent (see also Fig. 1).

PROPOSITION 2. *Let f be an objective function with convex sub-level sets, then two mirrored offspring cannot be simultaneously strictly better than their parent.*

PROOF. Considering the convex sub-level set, given by the parent solution, and the tangent hyperplane in this solution, the two mirrored offspring can never lie on the same side of the tangent hyperplane, see Fig. 1. At the same time, due to the convexity of the sub-level set and the definition of the tangent hyperplane, all solutions that are better than the parent solution lie on the same side of the tangent hyperplane such that not both mirrored offspring can have better objective function values at the same time. $\square$

A consequence of Proposition 2 is that on objective functions with convex sub-level sets, sequential selection applied with two mirrored offspring has no effect on the sequence of *accepted* solutions. In this case, sequential selection combined with skip mirror only reduces the number of evaluated solutions.

COROLLARY 3 (IDENTICAL TRACE FOR $\lambda = 2$). *On objective functions with convex sub-level sets, the $(1+2_m)$-ES and the $(1+2_{ms}^s)$-ES deliver the same sequence of parental solutions (given they use the same random vectors and step-sizes). The same holds for the $(1, 2_m)$-ES and the $(1, 2_{ms}^s)$-ES.*

PROOF. We consider the iteration step k and assume that $m = k$ at the beginning of the inner while loop. According to Proposition 2, it can never happen that both offspring are better than the parent and only two remaining cases need to be investigated. (i) In case of both offspring being worse than the parent, both plus-selection algorithms will keep the parent whereas the better of the two offspring is taken as the new parent by both comma-strategy algorithms. (ii) In case that one of the two offspring is not worse than the parent, the other must be worse and all algorithms will take the better offspring as their new parent solution—there is only a difference between the algorithms if the first offspring is not worse than the parent. Only in this case, the algorithms with sequential selection will directly accept the first offspring as next parent while the other variants evaluate unnecessarily the second (worse) offspring as well. Since either both offspring are evaluated or the sample associated to the non-evaluated offspring is skipped, in the next iteration, a fresh sample $\mathcal{N}_{m+1}$ will be used for the first offspring thus $m = k+1$ at the beginning of the next inner while loop. $\square$

Because sequential selection evaluates sometimes only one solution per iteration, the corollary implies that on functions with convex sub-level sets, the $(1+2_{ms}^s)$-ES (or $(1, 2_{ms}^s)$-ES) will converge faster than the $(1+2_m)$-ES (or $(1, 2_m)$-ES) in case of convergence and diverge faster in case of divergence.

We can additionally establish that for all strategies with two offspring and sequential selection, the number of offspring evaluated per iteration is the same, independent of mirroring and elitism:

LEMMA 4. *Assume the $(1+2^s)$, $(1, 2^s)$, $(1+2_{ms}^s)$, $(1, 2_{ms}^s)$-ESs start at iteration k from the same parent $\boldsymbol{X}_k$, sample*

the same first offspring $\boldsymbol{X}_k + \mathcal{N}$, and optimize the same objective function. Then the number of evaluated offspring at iteration k will be the same for all strategies.

PROOF. In all the cases, the number of evaluated offspring will be 1 if $\boldsymbol{X}_k + \mathcal{N}$ is not worse than $\boldsymbol{X}_k$ and 2 otherwise. $\square$

Finally, we find that for λ to infinity, comma strategies using sequential selection without or with mirroring converge to the $(1+1)$-ES or the $(1+1_{ms})$-ES, respectively:

LEMMA 5 (EQUIVALENCE OF $(1, \infty^s)$-ES AND $(1+1)$-ES). *Using scale-invariant or constant step-size, the $(1, \infty^s)$-ES is equivalent to the $(1+1)$-ES and the $(1, \infty_{ms}^s)$-ES is equivalent with the $(1+1_{ms})$-ES.*

PROOF. The proof follows directly from the algorithm descriptions, similar to the proof of Proposition 1. $\square$

3. LINEAR CONVERGENCE AND LOWER BOUNDS

Evolution Strategies are rank-based search algorithms and as such cannot exhibit a faster convergence than linear [25]. We here define linear convergence as the logarithm of the distance to the optimum decreasing linearly with the increasing number of function evaluations. An example of linear convergence is illustrated in Fig. 2 for three different instances of the $(1+1)$-ES with scale-invariant step-size. Formally, for the $(1+1)$-ES, let $\boldsymbol{X}_k$ be the estimate of the solution at iteration k. Almost sure (a.s.) linear convergence takes place if there exists a constant $c \neq 0$, such that

$$\frac{1}{k} \ln \frac{\|\boldsymbol{X}_k\|}{\|\boldsymbol{X}_0\|} \to c \ a.s. \tag{1}$$

Literally, *convergence* of $\boldsymbol{X}_k$ takes place only if $c < 0$ and for $c > 0$ the term *divergence* is more appropriate. If the above expression goes to zero, the strategy might still converge sub-linearly [16]. In this paper, we analyze algorithms that do not have a constant number of function evaluations per iteration and we will use the following generalization of (1) that accounts for the actual number of function evaluations: let T_k be the number of function evaluations performed until iteration k. Almost sure linear convergence takes place if there exists a constant $c \neq 0$, such that

$$\frac{1}{T_k} \ln \frac{\|\boldsymbol{X}_k\|}{\|\boldsymbol{X}_0\|} \to c \ a.s. \tag{2}$$

For the $(1+1)$-ES both equations are equivalent and for the $(1 \dotplus \lambda)$-ES we have $T_k = k\lambda$. The constant c is called the *convergence rate* and it corresponds to the slope of the curves in Fig. 2. The dynamics and thus the convergence rate of a step-size adaptive ES obviously depends on the step-size rule. The fastest convergence rates for adaptive step-size ESs are in general reached for a specific step-size rule in the so-called *scale-invariant step-size* ES where the step-size σ_k at time k is proportional to the distance to the optimum. Assuming the optimum w.l.o.g. in 0, the scale-invariant step-size is $\sigma_k = \sigma \|\boldsymbol{X}_k\|$ for $\sigma > 0$ on spherical functions $g(\|x\|)$ for $g \in \mathcal{M}$ where $\mathcal{M}$ denotes the set of functions $g : \mathbb{R} \mapsto \mathbb{R}$ that are strictly increasing [23]. ESs with scale-invariant step-sizes are artificial algorithms as they use the distance to the optimum to adapt the step-size. However, they are interesting to study as (1) they are a realistic approximation of step-size adaptive isotropic ESs where $\|\boldsymbol{X}_k\|/\sigma_k$ is

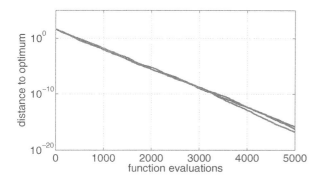

Figure 2: Distance to optimum versus number of function evaluations for three different instances of a (1+1)-ES minimizing the sphere function $g(\|x\|), g \in \mathcal{M}$ and with scale-invariant step-size $\sigma_k = \sigma\|X_k\|$ for $d = 20$ and $\sigma = 0.6/d$. Linear decrease is observed, the convergence rate corresponds to the slope of the curves.

usually a stable Markov Chain, here modeled as a constant, and (2) they achieve, for the right choice of the constant, optimal convergence rates. In addition, the simplification of $\|X_k\|/\sigma_k$ being a constant induces in general much simpler theoretical analysis. We now state formally the linear convergence of a (1+1)-ES with scale-invariant step-size and give an implicit expression for the convergence rate:

THEOREM 1 (LINEAR CONVERGENCE OF (1+1)-ES [23]). *The (1+1)-ES with scale-invariant step-size ($\sigma_k = \sigma\|X_k\|$) converges linearly on the class of spherical functions $g(\|x\|)$, $g \in \mathcal{M}$, and*

$$\lim_{k \to \infty} \frac{1}{k} \ln \frac{\|X_k\|}{\|X_0\|} = \mathrm{CR}_{(1+1)}(\sigma), \qquad (3)$$

with

$$\mathrm{CR}_{(1+1)}(\sigma) = -\frac{1}{2} E\big[\ln^{-}\big(1 + \underbrace{2\sigma[\mathcal{N}]_1}_{\text{gain if negative}} + \underbrace{\sigma^2\|\mathcal{N}\|^2}_{\text{loss}}\big)\big] \ ,$$

where $\ln^{-}$ is the negative part of the function $\ln$, i.e., $\ln^{-}(x) = -\min(\ln(x), 0)$, $\mathcal{N}$ is a standard multivariate normal distribution and $[\mathcal{N}]_1$ is the projection of $\mathcal{N}$ onto the first coordinate e_1.

The function $\sigma \mapsto \mathrm{CR}_{(1+1)}(\sigma)$ gives for each $\sigma > 0$ the convergence rate of the (1+1)-ES with step-size $\sigma_k = \sigma\|X_k\|$. The function has been studied in [23] and is plotted in Fig 4 (left) for different dimensions. The minimum of $\sigma \mapsto \mathrm{CR}_{(1+1)}(\sigma)$ gives for a given dimension the lower bound for the convergence rate of (1+1)-ES with offspring sampled with a standard multivariate normal distribution and *any step-size adaptation mechanism* on *any objective function* as formally stated now:

THEOREM 2 (LOWER BOUND FOR (1+1)-ES [23]). *Let $f : \mathbb{R}^d \mapsto \mathbb{R}$ be a measurable objective function and $x^* \in \mathbb{R}^d$. Assume that at each iteration k, the standard multivariate normal distribution used to sample the offspring is independent of σ_k and X_k and that $E[|\ln\|X_0 - x^*\||] < \infty$, then the convergence of the step-size adaptive (1+1)-ES is at most linear and*

$$\inf_{k \in \mathbb{N}} E[\ln\|X_k - x^*\|/\|X_0 - x^*\|] \geq \inf_{\sigma} \mathrm{CR}_{(1+1)}(\sigma) \ .$$

Objective for the rest of the paper: In the rest of the paper, we investigate the linear convergence of mirrored and sequential variants of the (1+λ)-ES with scale-invariant step-size. As for the (1+1)-ES, the minimum of the convergence rate in σ will represent lower bounds for the convergence rate of step-size adaptive methods with a standard multivariate normal sampling on any objective function. Before tackling the linear convergence of the different variants, we explain the main proof idea behind the linear convergence proofs.

How to prove linear convergence of scale-invariant step-size ESs? We sketch the proof idea in the case of the (1+1)-ES and we will explain in the core of the paper how to generalize this proof in particular for the case of a non-constant number of evaluation per iteration. The first step of the proof expresses the left-hand side (LHS) of (1) as a sum of k terms exploiting standard properties of the logarithm function:

$$\frac{1}{k} \ln \frac{\|X_k\|}{\|X_0\|} = \frac{1}{k} \sum_{i=0}^{k-1} \ln \frac{\|X_{i+1}\|}{\|X_i\|} \ . \qquad (4)$$

We then exploit the isotropy of the sphere function, the isotropy of the standard multivariate normal distribution and the scale-invariant step-size rule to prove that all terms $\ln(\|X_{i+1}\|/\|X_i\|)$ are independent identically distributed (i.i.d.). A law of large numbers[3] (LLN) therefore implies that the right-hand side (RHS) of (4) converges when k goes to infinity to $E[\ln(\|X_{i+1}\|/\|X_i\|)]$ almost surely.

4. CONVERGENCE RATE ON SPHERICAL FUNCTIONS IN FINITE DIMENSION

In this section, we analyze the linear convergence of the (1+2$_{\mathrm{m}}$)-ES and the (1+$\lambda^{\mathrm{s}}_{\mathrm{ms}}$)-ES for a fixed dimension d of the search space. Before to establish the main results, we derive some technical results and introduce some useful definitions.

4.1 Preliminary Results and Definitions

We establish first a lemma that simplifies the writing of the acceptance event of mirrored offspring.

LEMMA 6. *Let $X_{e_1} = e_1 + \sigma\mathcal{N}$ and $X^{\mathrm{m}}_{e_1} = e_1 - \sigma\mathcal{N}$ be two mirrored offspring sampled from the parent $e_1 = (1, 0, \ldots, 0)$. On spherical functions, the acceptance event $\{\|e_1 + \sigma\mathcal{N}\| \leq 1\}$ can be written as $\{2[\mathcal{N}]_1 + \sigma\|\mathcal{N}\|^2 \leq 0\}$. Similarly, the acceptance event of $X^{\mathrm{m}}_{e_1}$ satisfies $\{\|e_1 - \sigma\mathcal{N}\| \leq 1\} = \{-2[\mathcal{N}]_1 + \sigma\|\mathcal{N}\|^2 \leq 0\}$.*

PROOF. We remark first that $\|e_1 + \sigma\mathcal{N}\| \leq 1$ is equivalent to $\|e_1 + \sigma\mathcal{N}\|^2 \leq 1$. We now develop $\|e_1 + \sigma\mathcal{N}\|^2$ as $1 + 2\sigma[\mathcal{N}]_1 + \sigma^2\|\mathcal{N}\|^2$ and we immediately obtain that $1 + 2\sigma[\mathcal{N}]_1 + \sigma^2\|\mathcal{N}\|^2 \leq 1$ is equivalent to $2\sigma[\mathcal{N}]_1 + \sigma^2\|\mathcal{N}\|^2 \leq 0$. We proceed similarly for the acceptance event of $X^{\mathrm{m}}_{e_1}$. □

In the sequel, we will need to use the indicator function of the acceptance events of mirrored offspring sampled from e_1. For that reason we define the random variables W_1 and W^{m}_1 in the following way:

DEFINITION 1. *Let $W_1 = 2[\mathcal{N}]_1 + \sigma\|\mathcal{N}\|^2$ and $W^{\mathrm{m}}_1 = -2[\mathcal{N}]_1 + \sigma\|\mathcal{N}\|^2$.*

---

[3]Verifying some technical conditions such that the expectation and the variance of $\ln(\|X_{i+1}\|/\|X_i\|)$ are finite.

We can now express the indicator of the acceptance event of X_{e_1} as

$$1_{\{X_{e_1} \text{ is better than } e_1\}} = 1_{\{W_1 \leq 0\}} \ , \tag{5}$$

and the indicator of the acceptance of $X_{e_1}^m$ as

$$1_{\{X_{e_1}^m \text{ is better than } e_1\}} = 1_{\{W_1^m \leq 0\}} \ . \tag{6}$$

Using the expression of W_1 and a straightforward derivation, we find the following alternative expression for the convergence rate of the (1+1)-ES:

$$\mathrm{CR}_{(1+1)}(\sigma) = \frac{1}{2} E \left[\ln(1 + \sigma W_1 1_{\{W_1 \leq 0\}}) \right] \ . \tag{7}$$

We now establish two technical lemmas that will be useful to prove the equality of the convergence rate of the (1+1)-ES and the $(1+2_m)$-ES.

LEMMA 7. *Let $\mathcal{N}$ be a standard multivariate normal distribution, the following equality holds*

$$E \left[\ln(1 + (2\sigma[\mathcal{N}]_1 + \sigma^2\|\mathcal{N}\|^2) 1_{\{2[\mathcal{N}]_1 + \sigma\|\mathcal{N}\|^2 \leq 0\}} \right] =$$
$$E \left[\ln(1 + (-2\sigma[\mathcal{N}]_1 + \sigma^2\|\mathcal{N}\|^2) 1_{\{-2[\mathcal{N}]_1 + \sigma\|\mathcal{N}\|^2 \leq 0\}} \right] \tag{8}$$

or, using the notations W_1 and W_1^m

$$E \left[\ln(1 + \sigma W_1 1_{\{W_1 \leq 0\}}) \right] = E \left[\ln(1 + \sigma W_1^m 1_{\{W_1^m \leq 0\}}) \right] \tag{9}$$

PROOF. Since $\mathcal{N}$ is a standard multivariate normal distribution, $-\mathcal{N}$ follows the same distribution as $\mathcal{N}$ and thus (8) follows. $\square$

LEMMA 8. *The following equation holds*

$$E \left[\ln \left(1 + \sigma W_1 1_{\{W_1 \leq 0\}} + \sigma W_1^m 1_{\{W_1^m \leq 0\}} \right) \right]$$
$$= 2E \left[\ln \left(1 + \sigma W_1 1_{\{W_1 \leq 0\}} \right) \right] \tag{10}$$

where $W_1 = 2[\mathcal{N}]_1 + \sigma\|\mathcal{N}\|^2$ and $W_1^m = -2[\mathcal{N}]_1 + \sigma\|\mathcal{N}\|^2$ with $\mathcal{N}$ a random vector following a standard multivariate normal distribution.

PROOF. According to Proposition 2, two mirrored offspring cannot be simultaneously better than their parent on the sphere function. Since $\{W_1 \leq 0\}$ and $\{W_1^m \leq 0\}$ are the acceptance events of mirrored offspring started from e_1 on the sphere function ((5) and (6)), we know that they are incompatible such that $1_{\{W_1 \leq 0\}}$ and $1_{\{W_1^m \leq 0\}}$ are not simultaneously equal to 1. Consequently

$$\ln \left(1 + \sigma W_1 1_{\{W_1 \leq 0\}} + \sigma W_1^m 1_{\{W_1^m \leq 0\}} \right) =$$
$$\ln(1 + \sigma W_1 1_{\{W_1 \leq 0\}}) + \ln(1 + \sigma W_1^m 1_{\{W_1^m \leq 0\}}) \ .$$

Using the linearity of the expectation, we obtain that

$$E \left[\ln \left(1 + \sigma W_1 1_{\{W_1 \leq 0\}} + \sigma W_1^m 1_{\{W_1^m \leq 0\}} \right) \right] =$$
$$E \left[\ln(1 + \sigma W_1 1_{\{W_1 \leq 0\}}) \right] + E \left[\ln(1 + \sigma W_1^m 1_{\{W_1^m \leq 0\}}) \right] \ .$$

We now use Lemma 7 and obtain that the RHS of the last equation equals $2E \left[\ln(1 + \sigma W_1 1_{\{W_1 \leq 0\}}) \right]$. Hence the result. $\square$

4.2 Convergence Rate for the $(1 + 2_m)$-ES

In this section, we prove the linear convergence of the $(1+2_m)$-ES with scale-invariant step-size and prove the surprising result that the convergence rate of the $(1+2_m)$-ES equals the convergence rate of the (1+1)-ES. In a $(1+2_m)$-ES

with scale-invariant step-size, two mirrored offspring $X_k + \sigma\|X_k\|\mathcal{N}$ and $X_k - \sigma\|X_k\|\mathcal{N}$ are sampled from the parent X_k where $\mathcal{N}$ is a standard multivariate normal distribution independent of X_k and of the past (we omit the dependence in k for the sampled vectors for the sake of readability). Since on the sphere function, the offspring cannot be simultaneously better than their parent (see Proposition 2), the update equation for $\|X_k\|$ reads:

$$\|X_{k+1}\| = \|X_k + \sigma\|X_k\|\mathcal{N}\| \times 1_{\{\|X_k + \sigma\|X_k\|\mathcal{N}\| \leq \|X_k\|\}} +$$
$$\|X_k - \sigma\|X_k\|\mathcal{N}\| \times 1_{\{\|X_k - \sigma\|X_k\|\mathcal{N}\| \leq \|X_k\|\}} +$$
$$\|X_k\| \times 1_{\{\|X_k + \sigma\|X_k\|\mathcal{N}\| > \|X_k\|, \|X_k - \sigma\|X_k\|\mathcal{N}\| > \|X_k\|\}} \ . \tag{11}$$

Before to prove the linear convergence of the $(1+2_m)$-ES with scale-invariant step-size, we need to establish the following lemma:

LEMMA 9. *Let Z_k be the sequence of random variables*

$$Z_k = \frac{1}{2} \ln \left[\|Y_k + \sigma\mathcal{N}\|^2 1_{\{\|Y_k + \sigma\mathcal{N}\| \leq 1\}} + \right.$$
$$\left. \|Y_k - \sigma\mathcal{N}\|^2 1_{\{\|Y_k - \sigma\mathcal{N}\| \leq 1\}} + 1_{\{\|Y_k + \sigma\mathcal{N}\| > 1, \|Y_k - \sigma\mathcal{N}\| > 1\}} \right]$$

where $Y_k = X_k / \|X_k\|$ with X_k defined with (11). Then Z_k are independent identically distributed as

$$Z^{(1+2_m)} = \frac{1}{2} \ln \left[1 + \sigma W_1 1_{\{W_1 \leq 0\}} + \sigma W_1^m 1_{\{W_1^m \leq 0\}} \right] \ .$$

Moreover $E[|Z^{(1+2_m)}|] < \infty$.

PROOF. Because of the isotropy of the distribution of $\mathcal{N}$ and of the sphere function, in distribution Z_k equals

$$Z_k \overset{d}{=} \frac{1}{2} \ln \left[\|e_1 + \sigma\mathcal{N}\|^2 1_{\{\|e_1 + \sigma\mathcal{N}\| \leq 1\}} + \right.$$
$$\left. \|e_1 - \sigma\mathcal{N}\|^2 1_{\{\|e_1 - \sigma\mathcal{N}\| > 1\}} + 1_{\{\|e_1 + \sigma\mathcal{N}\| > 1, \|e_1 - \sigma\mathcal{N}\| > 1\}} \right] \tag{12}$$

where we have replaced Y_k by e_1. The independence of Z_k comes from the fact that $\mathcal{N}$ is independent of Y_k and from the isotropy of the sphere. The detailed proof of those two points is rather technical and we refer to [11, Lemma 1 and Lemma 2] to see how to have a fully formal proof. We are now going to simplify the following term

$$\|e_1 + \sigma\mathcal{N}\|^2 1_{\{W_1 \leq 0\}} + \|e_1 - \sigma\mathcal{N}\|^2 1_{\{W_1^m \leq 0\}} + 1_{\{W_1 > 0, W_1^m > 0\}}$$

that comes into play in the RHS of (12). Developing $\|e_1 + \sigma\mathcal{N}\|^2$ as $1 + 2\sigma[\mathcal{N}]_1 + \sigma^2\|\mathcal{N}\|^2$ and $\|e_1 - \sigma\mathcal{N}\|^2$ as $1 - 2\sigma[\mathcal{N}]_1 + \sigma^2\|\mathcal{N}\|^2$, we can simplify the previous equation into

$$1_{\{W_1 \leq 0\}} + \sigma W_1 1_{\{W_1 \leq 0\}} + 1_{\{W_1^m \leq 0\}} + \sigma W_1^m 1_{\{W_1^m \leq 0\}}$$
$$+ 1_{\{W_1 > 0, W_1^m > 0\}} \ .$$

Since $1_{\{W_1 \leq 0\}} + 1_{\{W_1^m \leq 0\}} + 1_{\{W_1 > 0, W_1^m > 0\}} = 1$ we can simplify the previous equation into

$$1 + \sigma W_1 1_{\{W_1 \leq 0\}} + \sigma W_1^m 1_{\{W_1^m \leq 0\}} \ .$$

Injecting this in (12), we obtain the result. The proof of the fact that $E[|Z^{(1+2_m)}|] < \infty$ comes from the proof of the integrability of $\ln[1 + W_1 1_{\{W_1 \leq 0\}}]$ that has been shown in detail in [23]. $\square$

We are now ready to prove the linear convergence of the $(1+2_m)$-ES and express its convergence rate as the expectation of the random variable $Z^{(1+2\mathrm{m})}$ introduced in the previous lemma divided by 2.

THEOREM 3. *For the $(1+2_\mathrm{m})$-ES with scale-invariant step-size on the class of spherical functions $g(\|x\|)$, $g \in \mathcal{M}$, linear convergence holds and*

$$\lim_{k\to\infty} \frac{1}{T_k} \ln \frac{\|\boldsymbol{X}_k\|}{\|\boldsymbol{X}_0\|} = \mathrm{CR}_{(1+2\mathrm{m})}(\sigma) \tag{13}$$

where

$$\mathrm{CR}_{(1+2_\mathrm{m})}(\sigma) = \frac{1}{2} E[Z^{(1+2_\mathrm{m})}]$$
$$= \frac{1}{4} E\left[\ln\left(1 + \sigma W_1 1_{\{W_1 \le 0\}} + \sigma W_1^\mathrm{m} 1_{\{W_1^\mathrm{m} \le 0\}}\right)\right] \tag{14}$$

where $W_1 = 2[\mathcal{N}]_1 + \sigma\|\mathcal{N}\|^2$ and $W_1^\mathrm{m} = -2[\mathcal{N}]_1 + \sigma\|\mathcal{N}\|^2$ with $\mathcal{N}$ a random vector following a standard multivariate normal distribution.

PROOF. We start from (11), square it, normalize the equation by $\|\boldsymbol{X}_k\|$ and take the logarithm. We obtain

$$\frac{1}{2} \ln \frac{\|\boldsymbol{X}_{k+1}\|^2}{\|\boldsymbol{X}_k\|^2} = \frac{1}{2} \ln \left[\|\boldsymbol{Y}_k + \sigma\mathcal{N}\|^2 1_{\{\|\boldsymbol{Y}_k + \sigma\mathcal{N}\| \le 1\}} + \right.$$
$$\left. \|\boldsymbol{Y}_k - \sigma\mathcal{N}\|^2 1_{\{\|\boldsymbol{Y}_k - \sigma\mathcal{N}\| \le 1\}} + 1_{\{\|\boldsymbol{Y}_k + \sigma\mathcal{N}\| > 1, \|\boldsymbol{Y}_k - \sigma\mathcal{N}\| > 1\}}\right]$$

where $\boldsymbol{Y}_k = \boldsymbol{X}_k/\|\boldsymbol{X}_k\|$. According to Lemma 9, by isotropy of the standard multivariate normal distribution, the random variables in the RHS of the previous equation are independent and identically distributed as

$$Z^{(1+2\mathrm{m})} = \frac{1}{2} \ln\left[1 + \sigma W_1 1_{\{W_1 \le 0\}} + \sigma W_1^\mathrm{m} 1_{\{W_1^\mathrm{m} \le 0\}}\right]$$

In addition, by Lemma 9, $E[|Z^{(1+2\mathrm{m})}|] < \infty$, and we can thus apply the LLN for independent random variables to

$$\frac{1}{T_k} \ln \frac{\|\boldsymbol{X}_k\|}{\|\boldsymbol{X}_0\|} = \frac{1}{2k} \ln \frac{\|\boldsymbol{X}_k\|}{\|\boldsymbol{X}_0\|} = \frac{1}{4k} \sum_{i=0}^{k-1} \ln \frac{\|\boldsymbol{X}_{i+1}\|^2}{\|\boldsymbol{X}_i\|^2}$$

and we obtain (14). □

Putting together (7), Lemma 8 and the expression of the convergence rate of the $(1+2_\mathrm{m})$-ES found in the previous theorem, we immediately obtain that the $(1+1)$-ES and the $(1+2_\mathrm{m})$-ES converge at the same rate. This result is stated in the following corollary.

COROLLARY 10. *On the class of spherical functions, the $(1+1)$-ES and $(1+2_\mathrm{m})$-ES with scale-invariant step-size converge at the same convergence rate, i.e.*

$$\mathrm{CR}_{(1+1)}(\sigma) = \mathrm{CR}_{(1+2_\mathrm{m})}(\sigma) \text{ for all } \sigma .$$

We close this section with a geometrically based argumentation for the corollary. Consider the tangent hyperplane at the parent location that divides the space into two half spaces and only one of the half spaces contains better solutions. The $(1+1)$-ES samples isotropically into both half spaces integrating over the entire space. The $(1+2_\mathrm{m})$-ES samples one offspring into one half space and the second one into the other. Together, the offspring integrate over exactly the same region as the single offspring in the $(1+1)$-ES. The worse offspring is never successful, while the better offspring realizes twice the expected improvement of the offspring in the $(1+1)$-ES.

4.3 Convergence Rate for the $(1 + \lambda_\mathrm{ms}^\mathrm{s})$-ES

In this section, we analyze the convergence rate of the $(1 + \lambda_\mathrm{ms}^\mathrm{s})$-ES. According to Proposition 1, for all λ, the $(1+\lambda_\mathrm{ms}^\mathrm{s})$-ES with scale-invariant step-size evaluate the same points in the search space provided they use the same independent random sequence $(\mathcal{N}_m)_{m\in\mathbb{N}}$. Therefore, also the convergence rate of the $(1+\lambda_\mathrm{ms}^\mathrm{s})$-ES is independent of λ. Note that this is true because we investigate the convergence rate defined as log-progress *per function evaluation* and not per iteration. Though we could think that the easiest algorithm to analyze is the $(1+1_\mathrm{ms})$-ES, we investigate the $(1+2_\mathrm{ms}^\mathrm{s})$ for which iterations are independent—contrary to the $(1+1_\mathrm{ms})$—allowing thus to apply *directly* the LLN for *independent* random variables.

THEOREM 4. *For the $(1 + \lambda_\mathrm{ms}^\mathrm{s})$-ES with scale-invariant step-size on the class of spherical functions $g(\|x\|)$, $g \in \mathcal{M}$, linear convergence holds and for all λ*

$$\lim_{k\to\infty} \frac{1}{T_k} \ln \frac{\|\boldsymbol{X}_k\|}{\|\boldsymbol{X}_0\|} = \frac{2}{2 - p_s(\sigma)} \mathrm{CR}_{(1+1)}(\sigma) \tag{15}$$

where $p_s(\sigma) = \Pr(2[\mathcal{N}]_1 + \sigma\|\mathcal{N}\|^2 \le 0)$ is the probability that the offspring $\boldsymbol{X}_{e_1} = e_1 + \sigma\mathcal{N}$ is better than its parent e_1 where $\mathcal{N}$ is a standard multivariate normal distribution.

PROOF. We have seen in Proposition 1 that the $(1+\lambda_\mathrm{ms}^\mathrm{s})$-ES with scale-invariant step-size evaluates the same points for all λ. Therefore for all λ, the $(1+\lambda_\mathrm{ms}^\mathrm{s})$-ESs with scale-invariant step-size have the same convergence rate. Let us analyze the $(1+2_\mathrm{ms}^\mathrm{s})$-ES. Let us write $\frac{1}{T_k} \ln \frac{\|\boldsymbol{X}_k\|}{\|\boldsymbol{X}_0\|}$ as $A_k B_k$ with $A_k = k/T_k$ and $B_k = \frac{1}{k} \ln(\|\boldsymbol{X}_k\|/\|\boldsymbol{X}_0\|)$. We are going to handle both terms separately. For B_k, we exploit Corollary 3 where we have seen that, starting from the same parent, the $(1+2_\mathrm{m})$-ES and $(1+2_\mathrm{ms}^\mathrm{s})$-ES have the same parent for the next iteration for objective functions with convex sub-level sets. Thus the sequence of parents $\boldsymbol{X}_k$ is the same for a $(1+2_\mathrm{m})$-ES and a $(1+2_\mathrm{ms}^\mathrm{s})$-ES and thus the expected relative improvement *per iteration* will be the same for both algorithms. By Corollary 10, we have that B_k goes to $2\,\mathrm{CR}_{(1+1)}(\sigma)$ (the factor 2 comes from the normalization by evaluations for the convergence rate of the $(1+2_\mathrm{m})$-ES). For the term A_k, we denote by Λ_i the number of offspring evaluated at iteration i. Then, $T_k = \Lambda_1 + \ldots + \Lambda_k$ and $1/A_k = \frac{1}{k} \sum_{i=1}^k \Lambda_i$. Similarly to [11, Lemma 8], the Λ_k are independent and identically distributed. In addition, according to Lemma 4, the number of evaluated offspring for the $(1+2_\mathrm{ms}^\mathrm{s})$ is the same as for the $(1, 2^\mathrm{s})$, we can therefore use the result shown in [6, Lemma 8] and obtain that $1/A_k$ converges almost surely to $2 - p_s(\sigma)$.

Therefore A_k times B_k converges to

$$\frac{2}{2 - p_s(\sigma)} \mathrm{CR}_{(1+1)}(\sigma) . \quad \square$$

We see in (15) that the convergence rate of the $(1+\lambda_\mathrm{ms}^\mathrm{s})$-ES is expressed as the product of the convergence rate of the $(1+1)$-ES times $2/(2 - p_s(\sigma))$. The term $2/(2 - p_s(\sigma))$—which is always larger or equal one—is the gain brought by sequential selection. Indeed, as sketched in the proof of the theorem, the gain brought by sequential selection in strategies with two offspring (with mirrored or non-mirrored sampling) always equals $2/(2 - p_s(\sigma))$.

We give a useful expression for the success probability $p_s(\sigma)$ for a single offspring on the sphere function.

LEMMA 11. *For all $\sigma > 0$, we have*

$$p_s(\sigma) = \Pr\left([\mathcal{N}]_1 \le -\frac{d}{2}\sigma \underbrace{\frac{\|\mathcal{N}\|^2}{d}}_{close\ to\ 1}\right) \qquad (16)$$

PROOF. The lemma follows from the definition of $p_s(\sigma) = \Pr\left(2[\mathcal{N}]_1 + \sigma\|\mathcal{N}\|^2 \le 0\right)$ □

The expression suggests that $\sigma \propto 1/d$ achieves a fairly d-independent success probability. A typical, close to optimal value is $\sigma \approx 1.2/d$ with $p_s \approx 1/4$ and $2/(2 - p_s) \approx 1.16$.

Finally, we can give the upper bound for the speed-up brought by sequential selection, when $\lambda = 2$.

COROLLARY 12 (SPEED-UP FOR $\lambda = 2$). *The upper bound for the speed-up brought by sequential selection for $\lambda = 2$ is given by*

$$\frac{2}{2 - p_s} < \frac{4}{3} = 1.333\ldots \qquad (17)$$

PROOF. From Lemma 11 we find for $\sigma > 0$ that $p_s < \Pr([\mathcal{N}]_1 \le 0) = 1/2$ which implies (17). For $\sigma = 0$ we have no speed-up. □

This upper bound holds equally well for savings by sequential selection whether or not *skip mirror* is applied.

5. ASYMPTOTIC CONVERGENCE RATES

So far, we have proven the linear convergence of some scale-invariant step-size ESs *for a fixed dimension of the search space*. In this section, we want to study how the finite dimension convergence rates derived previously behave when the dimension goes to infinity. We have observed that the convergence rate of the $(1+1_{ms})$-ES is a function of the convergence rate of the $(1+1)$-ES and of the probability of success p_s. We therefore study those two quantities asymptotically in order to obtain the asymptotic behavior of $CR_{(1+1_{ms})}$. Both asymptotic estimates were already (less rigorously) derived in [24].

5.1 Asymptotic Probability of Success

We first derive the limit of the probability of success $p_s(\sigma/d)$ when d goes to infinity.

LEMMA 13. *For all $\sigma > 0$*

$$\lim_{d \to \infty} p_s\left(\frac{\sigma}{d}\right) = \Pr([\mathcal{N}]_1 \le -\sigma/2)$$
$$= \Phi\left(-\frac{\sigma}{2}\right) \qquad (18)$$

where Φ is the cumulative distribution of a standard normal distribution, i.e. $\Phi(x) = \frac{1}{\sqrt{2\pi}}\int_{-\infty}^{x} e^{-t^2/2}\,dt$ or, with the error function erf, $\Phi(x) = \frac{1}{2}\left[1 + \mathrm{erf}\left(\frac{x}{\sqrt{2}}\right)\right]$.

PROOF. We start from the expression of $p_s(\sigma/d)$:

$$p_s(\sigma/d) = \Pr\left(2[\mathcal{N}]_1 + \frac{\sigma}{d}\|\mathcal{N}\|^2 \le 0\right) \qquad (19)$$

$$= E\left[1_{\{2[\mathcal{N}]_1 + \frac{\sigma}{d}\|\mathcal{N}\|^2 \le 0\}}\right] \qquad (20)$$

From the LLN, we know that

$$\lim_{d \to \infty}\frac{1}{d}\|\mathcal{N}\|^2 = \lim_{d \to \infty}\frac{1}{d}\sum_{i=1}^{d}\mathcal{N}_i^2 = 1$$

almost surely, where $\mathcal{N}_i$ are i.i.d. standard normal distributions that are the coordinates of the vector $\mathcal{N}$. Thus

$$2[\mathcal{N}]_1 + \frac{\sigma}{d}\|\mathcal{N}\|^2 \xrightarrow[d \to \infty]{} 2[\mathcal{N}]_1 + \sigma$$

and therefore we have that

$$1_{\{2[\mathcal{N}]_1 + \frac{\sigma}{d}\|\mathcal{N}\|^2 \le 0\}} \xrightarrow[d \to \infty]{} 1_{\{2[\mathcal{N}]_1 + \sigma \le 0\}}\ a.s.$$

Since $1_{\{2[\mathcal{N}]_1 + \frac{\sigma}{d}\|\mathcal{N}\|^2\}} \le 1$, we can apply the Lebesgue dominated convergence theorem that implies that

$$E\left[1_{\{2[\mathcal{N}]_1 + \frac{\sigma}{d}\|\mathcal{N}\|^2 \le 0\}}\right] \xrightarrow[d \to \infty]{} E\left[1_{\{2[\mathcal{N}]_1 + \sigma \le 0\}}\right]\ .$$

We can rewrite the RHS of the last equation as

$$E\left[1_{\{2[\mathcal{N}]_1 + \sigma \le 0\}}\right] = \Pr(2[\mathcal{N}]_1 + \sigma \le 0) = \Pr([\mathcal{N}]_1 \le -\sigma/2)\ .$$

Moreover, $\Pr([\mathcal{N}]_1 \le -\sigma/2) = \Phi(-\sigma/2)$. □

5.2 Asymptotic Convergence Rate of the $(1+1)$-ES

We will derive now the asymptotic convergence rate of the $(1+1)$-ES with scale-invariant step-size and find that it coincides with the negative of the well-known progress rate of the $(1+1)$-ES [24]. We first need to derive the following technical lemma:

LEMMA 14. *Let $\mathcal{N}$ be a standard normal distribution, the following equation holds*

$$E[\mathcal{N}1_{\{\mathcal{N} \le -\sigma/2\}}] = -\frac{1}{\sqrt{2\pi}}\exp(-\frac{\sigma^2}{8})\ , \qquad (21)$$

for all $\sigma > 0$.

PROOF. In a first step we write the LHS of (21) using the density of a normal distribution

$$E[\mathcal{N}1_{\{\mathcal{N} \le -\sigma/2\}}] = \frac{1}{\sqrt{2\pi}}\int_{-\infty}^{-\sigma/2} x\exp(-\frac{x^2}{2})dx\ . \qquad (22)$$

By integrating the RHS of (22) we obtain the result. □

We are now ready to derive the limit of the convergence rate of the $(1+1)$-ES.

THEOREM 5. *Let $\sigma > 0$, the convergence rate of the $(1+1)$-ES with scale-invariant step-size on spherical functions satisfies at the limit*

$$\lim_{d \to \infty} d \times CR_{(1+1)}\left(\frac{\sigma}{d}\right) = \frac{-\sigma}{\sqrt{2\pi}}\exp\left(-\frac{\sigma^2}{8}\right) + \frac{\sigma^2}{2}\Phi\left(-\frac{\sigma}{2}\right) \qquad (23)$$

where Φ is the cumulative distribution of a normal distribution.

PROOF. We are going to investigate the almost sure limit of the random variable inside the RHS of

$$CR_{(1+1)}(\sigma/d) = \frac{1}{2}E\left[\ln(1 + \frac{\sigma}{d}\min(2[\mathcal{N}]_1 + \frac{\sigma}{d}\|\mathcal{N}\|^2, 0))\right]\ . \qquad (24)$$

The following equation holds almost surely

$$\lim_{d \to \infty} d \times \frac{1}{2}\ln(1 + \sigma/d\min(2[\mathcal{N}]_1 + \frac{\sigma}{d}\|\mathcal{N}\|^2, 0))$$
$$\xrightarrow[d \to \infty]{} \frac{1}{2}\sigma\min(2[\mathcal{N}]_1 + \sigma, 0)\ . \qquad (25)$$

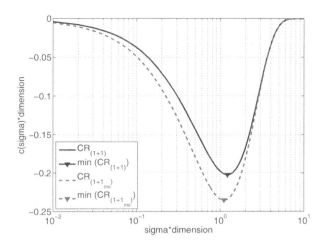 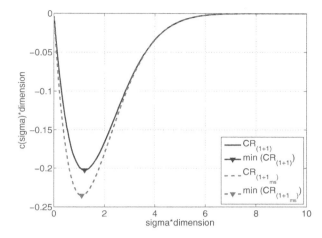

Figure 3: Theoretical limit results of the convergence rate for the $(1+1)$-ES (solid line) and for the $(1+\lambda_{ms}^s)$-ES (any $\lambda \geq 1$, dashed line) if d goes to infinity. Left: versus $\sigma \cdot d$ in log scale; right: versus $\sigma \cdot d$ in linear scale.

Assuming the uniform integrability of

$$d \times \frac{1}{2} \ln(1 + \sigma/d \min(2[\mathcal{N}]_1 + \frac{\sigma}{d}\|\mathcal{N}\|^2, 0)) \ ,$$

we deduce that

$$\lim_{d \to \infty} d \times \mathrm{CR}_{(1+1)}(\sigma/d) = \frac{\sigma}{2} E[\min(2[\mathcal{N}]_1 + \sigma, 0)] \ .$$

Moreover,

$$
\begin{aligned}
E[\min(2[\mathcal{N}]_1 + \sigma, 0)] &= E[(2[\mathcal{N}]_1 + \sigma)1_{\{2[\mathcal{N}]_1+\sigma \leq 0\}}] \\
&= 2E[([\mathcal{N}]_1)1_{\{2[\mathcal{N}]_1+\sigma \leq 0\}}] \\
&\quad + \sigma \Pr(2[\mathcal{N}]_1 + \sigma \leq 0) \\
&= 2E[([\mathcal{N}]_1)1_{\{[\mathcal{N}]_1 \leq -\sigma/2\}}] \\
&\quad + \sigma \Pr([\mathcal{N}]_1 \leq -\sigma/2) \ .
\end{aligned}
$$

Thus,

$$\lim_{d \to \infty} d \times \mathrm{CR}_{(1+1)}\left(\frac{\sigma}{d}\right) = \sigma E[[\mathcal{N}]_1 1_{\{[\mathcal{N}]_1 \leq -\frac{\sigma}{2}\}}] + \frac{\sigma^2}{2}\Phi\left(\frac{-\sigma}{2}\right) \ .$$

Using now Lemma 14, we obtain the result. □

This limit of the normalized convergence rate of the $(1+1)$-ES found in the previous theorem equals to the negated progress rate of the $(1+1)$-ES on the sphere function [24].

5.3 Deriving the Asymptotic Convergence Rate of the $(1 + \lambda_{ms}^s)$-ES

We can now combine Lemma 13 and Theorem 5 to derive the asymptotic convergence rate of the $(1+\lambda_{ms}^s)$-ES with scale-invariant step-size. Note again that the $(1+\lambda_{ms}^s)$-ES is here the same as the $(1+1_{ms})$-ES.

THEOREM 6. *Let $\sigma > 0$, the convergence rate of the $(1+1_{ms})$-ES with scale-invariant step-size on spherical functions satisfies*

$$\lim_{d \to \infty} d \times \mathrm{CR}_{(1+1_{ms})}\left(\frac{\sigma}{d}\right) = \frac{2}{2 - \Phi(-\sigma/2)} \times$$
$$\left(\frac{-\sigma}{\sqrt{2\pi}}\exp\left(-\frac{\sigma^2}{8}\right) + \frac{\sigma^2}{2}\Phi\left(-\frac{\sigma}{2}\right)\right) \ . \quad (26)$$

PROOF. Since the convergence rate of the $(1+1_{ms})$-ES equals the convergence rate of the $(1+1)$-ES times $2/(2-p_s)$ we have that the limit for d to infinity satisfies

$$\lim_{d \to \infty} d \times \mathrm{CR}_{(1+1_{ms})}\left(\frac{\sigma}{d}\right)$$
$$= \lim_{d \to \infty}\left(\frac{2}{2 - p_s}\right) \times \lim_{d \to \infty}\left(d \times \mathrm{CR}_{(1+1)}\left(\frac{\sigma}{d}\right)\right) \ .$$

Using Lemma 13 for the limit of $2/(2-p_s)$ and Proposition 5, we obtain the result. □

Figure 3 represents the limit of the normalized convergence rates of the $(1+1)$-ES and the $(1+1_{ms})$-ES. The minimal value of the convergence rate of the $(1+1)$-ES and $(1+1_{ms})$-ES respectively equal approximately -0.202 and -0.235. Mirrored sampling and sequential selection speed up the fastest single-parent evolution strategy asymptotically by a factor of about 1.16.

6. NUMERICAL SIMULATION OF CONVERGENCE RATES

To conclude on the improvements that can be brought by mirrored samples and sequential selection, we now compare the different convergence rates. However, those convergence rates are expressed only implicitly as the expectation of some random variables. We therefore simulate the convergence rate with a Monte-Carlo technique. For each convergence rate expression, we have simulated 10^7 times the random variables inside the expectation and averaged to obtain an estimate of the expectation and therefore of the convergence rate for different σ. Here, σ has been chosen such that $0.01 \leq \sigma \cdot d \leq 10$ and with steps of 0.01 in $\sigma \cdot d$. The minimum of the measured convergence rates over $\sigma \cdot d$ is used as estimate of the *best* convergence rate for each algorithm and dimension—resulting in a slightly (systematically) smaller value than the true one, due to taking the minimal value from several random estimates.

The plots of **Fig. 4** show the resulting convergence rate estimates versus σ in several dimensions. Overall, mirroring and/or sequential selection do not essentially change the

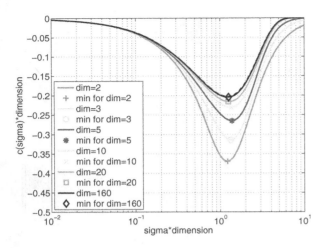
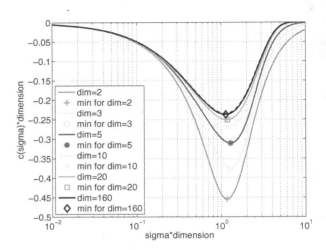

Figure 4: Convergence rate $c(\sigma)$ for different dimensions d and the (1+1)-ES and $(1+2_m)$-ES (both have the same convergence rate, left figure), and the $(1+\lambda_{ms}^s)$-ES (the same for all $\lambda \geq 1$, right figure), all with scale-invariant step-size. The dashed (uppermost) line shows the limit result for d to infinity.

picture. The (1+1)-ES realizes the largest optimal step-size of all variants, also compared with comma selection (not shown). **Figure 5** shows the relative improvement. For small step-sizes the $(1+\lambda_{ms}^s)$-ES is up to about 33% faster (compare (17)). For large step-sizes, both, $(1 + 1)$- and $(1+\lambda_{ms}^s)$-ES, show very similar convergence rates. For close to optimal step-sizes (somewhat above one), the $(1+\lambda_{ms}^s)$-ES is about 15% to 20% faster.

Figure 6 presents the estimated best convergence rates for several algorithms versus dimension. Here, the $(1, 4_{ms}^s)$-ES is shown additionally.[4] The convergence rate of the $(1, \lambda_{ms}^s)$-ES is monotonically increasing in λ (not shown) and in the limit for $\lambda \to \infty$, the $(1, \lambda_{ms}^s)$-ES coincides with the $(1+1_{ms})$-ES. In small dimension, already for $\lambda = 4$ the convergence rate is very close to the convergence rate of the $(1+1_{ms})$-ES. In all cases, the convergence rate of the $(1, 4_{ms}^s)$-ES is closer to the $(1+1_{ms})$-ES than to the (1+1)-ES. The difference between the original (1+1)-ES and the $(1+1_{ms})$-ES is roughly between 15 and 20%. In dimension 320, the values are very close to the limit value.

7. DISCUSSION

In this paper we have analyzed the $(1+\lambda)$-ES with mirrored sampling and/or sequential selection. With sequential (plus) selection, the parameter λ loses most of its meaning. Given that the step-size (and all other variation parameters) are updated in an identical way, the $(1+\lambda^s)$-ES, where ^{s} denotes sequential selection, and also the $(1, \infty^s)$-ES depict the same strategy for all $\lambda \geq 1$. The same holds analogously for the $(1+\lambda_{ms}^s)$-ESs, where the subscript $_{ms}$ denotes *m*irrored sampling with *s*kip mirror applied (on success).

We have obtained tight lower bounds for the convergence rate of the $(1+2_m)$-ES and of the $(1+1_{ms})$-ES that coincides with the $(1+\lambda_{ms}^s)$-ESs for any $\lambda \geq 1$. These bounds are also the convergence rate with scale-invariant optimal step-size on the sphere function. The $(1+2_m)$-ES has the same convergence rate as the (1+1)-ES, asymptotically with the

---

[4]Note that in previous publications such as [4, 5, 17], the slightly different notation $(1, 4_m^s)$-ES was used for the same algorithm.

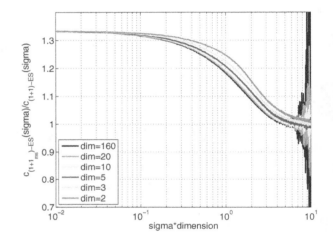

Figure 5: Relative improvement in the convergence rates $c(\sigma)$ of the $(1+1_{ms})$-ES over the (1+1)-ES plotted versus σ times dimension for scale-invariant step sizes. Smaller dimensions show the (slightly) larger improvements. The huge fluctuations to the right are due to the small success probability for large step-sizes and therefore a large variance when measuring a few events.

dimension to ∞ being $\geq -0.202 \ldots$ The asymptotic convergence rate of the $(1+1_{ms})$-ES is $\geq -0.235 \ldots$ and the relation

$$\mathrm{CR}_{(1+\lambda_{ms}^s)}(\sigma) = \mathrm{CR}_{(1+1_{ms})}(\sigma) \tag{27}$$

$$= \frac{2}{2 - p_s(\sigma)} \mathrm{CR}_{(1+2_m)}(\sigma) \tag{28}$$

$$= \frac{2}{2 - p_s(\sigma)} \mathrm{CR}_{(1+1)}(\sigma) \tag{29}$$

holds, where $p_s(\sigma)$ is the probability that an offspring, sampled isotropically with step-size σ, is better than its parent.

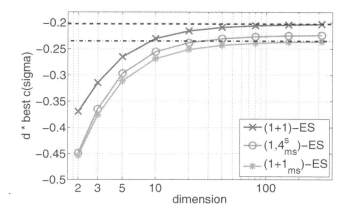

Figure 6: Estimated optimal convergence rates, in parts extracted from Fig. 4, multiplied by the dimension and plotted versus dimension for the algorithms $(1+1)$-ES (equivalent to $(1+2_m)$-ES), $(1+1_{ms})$-ES, and $(1, 4^s_{ms})$-ES with scale-invariant step-size. In addition, the theoretical limit results for d to infinity are shown for the $(1+1)$-ES (dashed) and for the $(1+1_{ms})$-ES (dotted-dashed).

The factor $2/(2 - p_s(\sigma)) < 4/3$ is the improvement brought by sequential selection for $\lambda = 2$, with plus as well as comma selection.

As to our knowledge, the $(1 + \lambda^s_{ms})$-ES is now the single-parent evolution strategy with the fastest known convergence rate, more than 15% faster than the $(1+1)$-ES, but no more than 5% faster than the $(1, 4^s_{ms})$-ES. Only strategies with weighted recombination can exhibit even faster convergence rates (also denoted as serial efficiencies), namely ≥ -0.25 when positive recombination weights are used [2].

The convergence rates derived assume that the step-size equals a constant times the distance to the optimum. This assumption simplifies the linear convergence derivation as the law of large numbers for independent random variables can then be used. For real adaptation schemes however, the analysis on spherical functions is in general more complicated, as $\sigma_k / \|\boldsymbol{X}_k\|$ is not a constant but a Markov chain. Law of large numbers for Markov chains can be used to prove linear convergence, the difficult task being to prove that $\sigma_k / \|\boldsymbol{X}_k\|$ is stable enough to satisfy a LLN [3, 16].

References

[1] D. V. Arnold and R. Salomon. Evolutionary gradient search revisited. *IEEE Transactions on Evolutionary Computation*, 11(4):480–495, 2007.

[2] D.V. Arnold. Optimal weighted recombination. *Foundations of Genetic Algorithms*, pages 215–237, 2005.

[3] A. Auger. Convergence results for the $(1, \lambda)$-SA-ES using the theory of φ-irreducible Markov chains. *Theoretical Computer Science*, 334(1–3):35–69, 2005.

[4] A. Auger, D. Brockhoff, and N. Hansen. Benchmarking the (1,4)-CMA-ES With Mirrored Sampling and Sequential Selection on the Noiseless BBOB-2010 Testbed. In *GECCO workshop on Black-Box Optimiza-*

tion Benchmarking (BBOB'2010), pages 1617–1624. ACM, 2010.

[5] A. Auger, D. Brockhoff, and N. Hansen. Benchmarking the (1,4)-CMA-ES With Mirrored Sampling and Sequential Selection on the Noisy BBOB-2010 Testbed. In *GECCO workshop on Black-Box Optimization Benchmarking (BBOB'2010)*, pages 1625–1632. ACM, 2010.

[6] A. Auger, D. Brockhoff, and N. Hansen. Comparing the (1+1)-CMA-ES with a Mirrored (1+2)-CMA-ES with Sequential Selection on the Noiseless BBOB-2010 Testbed. In *GECCO workshop on Black-Box Optimization Benchmarking (BBOB'2010)*, pages 1543–1550. ACM, 2010.

[7] A. Auger, D. Brockhoff, and N. Hansen. Investigating the Impact of Sequential Selection in the (1,2)-CMA-ES on the Noiseless BBOB-2010 Testbed. In *GECCO workshop on Black-Box Optimization Benchmarking (BBOB'2010)*, pages 1591–1596. ACM, 2010.

[8] A. Auger, D. Brockhoff, and N. Hansen. Investigating the Impact of Sequential Selection in the (1,2)-CMA-ES on the Noisy BBOB-2010 Testbed. In *GECCO workshop on Black-Box Optimization Benchmarking (BBOB'2010)*, pages 1605–1610. ACM, 2010.

[9] A. Auger, D. Brockhoff, and N. Hansen. Investigating the Impact of Sequential Selection in the (1,4)-CMA-ES on the Noiseless BBOB-2010 Testbed. In *GECCO workshop on Black-Box Optimization Benchmarking (BBOB'2010)*, pages 1597–1604. ACM, 2010.

[10] A. Auger, D. Brockhoff, and N. Hansen. Investigating the Impact of Sequential Selection in the (1,4)-CMA-ES on the Noisy BBOB-2010 Testbed. In *GECCO workshop on Black-Box Optimization Benchmarking (BBOB'2010)*, pages 1611–1616. ACM, 2010.

[11] A. Auger, D. Brockhoff, and N. Hansen. Mirrored Sampling and Sequential Selection for Evolution Strategies. Rapport de Recherche RR-7249, INRIA Saclay—Île-de-France, June 2010.

[12] A. Auger, D. Brockhoff, and N. Hansen. Mirrored Variants of the (1,2)-CMA-ES Compared on the Noiseless BBOB-2010 Testbed. In *GECCO workshop on Black-Box Optimization Benchmarking (BBOB'2010)*, pages 1551–1558. ACM, 2010.

[13] A. Auger, D. Brockhoff, and N. Hansen. Mirrored Variants of the (1,2)-CMA-ES Compared on the Noisy BBOB-2010 Testbed. In *GECCO workshop on Black-Box Optimization Benchmarking (BBOB'2010)*, pages 1575–1582. ACM, 2010.

[14] A. Auger, D. Brockhoff, and N. Hansen. Mirrored Variants of the (1,4)-CMA-ES Compared on the Noiseless BBOB-2010 Testbed. In *GECCO workshop on Black-Box Optimization Benchmarking (BBOB'2010)*, pages 1559–1566. ACM, 2010.

[15] A. Auger, D. Brockhoff, and N. Hansen. Mirrored Variants of the (1,4)-CMA-ES Compared on the Noisy BBOB-2010 Testbed. In *GECCO workshop on Black-Box Optimization Benchmarking (BBOB'2010)*, pages 1583–1590. ACM, 2010.

[16] A. Auger and N. Hansen. Theory of evolution strategies: a new perspective. In A. Auger and B. Doerr, editors, *Theory of Randomized Search Heuristics: Foundations and Recent Developments*. World Scientific Publishing, 2010. In press.

[17] D. Brockhoff, A. Auger, N. Hansen, D. V. Arnold, and T. Hohm. Mirrored Sampling and Sequential Selection for Evolution Strategies. In R. Schaefer et al., editors, *Conference on Parallel Problem Solving from Nature (PPSN XI)*, pages 11–21. Springer, 2010.

[18] J. M. Hammersley and D.C. Handscomb. *Monte Carlo methods*. Methuen's monographs on applied probability and statistics. Methuen, 1967.

[19] N. Hansen. An analysis of mutative σ-self-adaptation on linear fitness functions. *Evolutionary Computation*, 14(3):255–275, 2006.

[20] N. Hansen, S. Finck, R. Ros, and A. Auger. Real-parameter black-box optimization benchmarking 2009: Noiseless functions definitions. Technical Report RR-6829, INRIA, 2009. Updated February 2010.

[21] N. Hansen, S. Finck, R. Ros, and A. Auger. Real-parameter black-box optimization benchmarking 2009: Noisy functions definitions. Technical Report RR-6869, INRIA, 2009. Updated February 2010.

[22] N. Hansen and A. Ostermeier. Completely Derandomized Self-Adaptation in Evolution Strategies. *Evolutionary Computation*, 9(2):159–195, 2001.

[23] M. Jebalia, A. Auger, and P. Liardet. Log-linear convergence and optimal bounds for the (1+1)-ES. In N. Monmarché and al., editors, *Proceedings of Evolution Artificielle (EA'07)*, volume 4926 of *LNCS*, pages 207–218. Springer, 2008.

[24] I. Rechenberg. Optimierung technischer Systeme nach Prinzipien der biologischen Evolution Dr.-Ing. Dissertation. Technical report, Verlag Frommann-Holzboog, Stuttgart-Bad Cannstatt, 1973.

[25] O. Teytaud and S. Gelly. General lower bounds for evolutionary algorithms. In *Conference on Parallel Problem Solving from Nature (PPSN 2006)*, volume 4193, pages 21–31. Springer, 2006.

[26] O. Teytaud and S. Gelly. DCMA, yet another derandomization in covariance-matrix-adaptation. In D. Thierens et al., editors, *Genetic and Evolutionary Computation Conference (GECCO)*, pages 955–922. ACM Press, 2007.

[27] O. Teytaud, S. Gelly, and J. Mary. On the Ultimate Convergence Rates for Isotropic Algorithms and the Best Choices Among Various Forms of Isotropy . In T. P. Runarsson et al., editors, *Conference on Parallel Problem Solving from Nature (PPSN IX)*, volume 4193 of *LNCS*, pages 32–41. Springer, 2006.

Using Markov-Chain Mixing Time Estimates for the Analysis of Ant Colony Optimization

Dirk Sudholt
CERCIA, University of Birmingham
Birmingham, B15 2TT, UK

ABSTRACT

The Markov chain Monte Carlo paradigm has developed powerful and elegant techniques for estimating the time until a Markov chain approaches a stationary distribution. This time is known as mixing time. We introduce the reader into mixing time estimations via coupling arguments and use the mixing of pheromone models for analyzing the expected optimization time of ant colony optimization. We demonstrate the approach for plateaus in pseudo-Boolean optimization and derive upper bounds for the time until a target set is found. We also describe how mixing times can be estimated for MMAS ant systems on shortest path problems.

Categories and Subject Descriptors

F.2.2 [**Analysis of Algorithms and Problem Complexity**]: Nonnumerical Algorithms and Problems

General Terms

Algorithms, Performance, Theory

Keywords

Ant colony optimization, Markov chain Monte Carlo, mixing time, coupling, pseudo-Boolean optimization, shortest path problems

1. INTRODUCTION

Ant colonies in nature are capable of solving complex optimization problems, such as finding shortest paths between their nest and a food source. Certain ant species achieve this goal by a simple communication mechanism. These ants deposit pheromones on the ground while searching for food. These chemicals attract other ants, which then tend to follow pheromone trails. The more promising the food source, the more pheromone is deposited. Also, the shorter the path, the quicker it is invested with pheromones as more and more ants are attracted to following the path. Although the cognitive capabilities of a single ant are very limited, a whole ant colony exhibits intelligent behavior known as *swarm intelligence*.

This kind of swarm intelligence has been transferred to an optimization paradigm known as *ant colony optimization* (ACO). ACO algorithms have been successfully applied to the traveling salesman problem (TSP), the Quadratic Assignment Problem, network routing problems, and many other combinatorial problems [7]. The search of an ant is modeled by a random walk on a graph. An ant starts from a source node in search for a target node that represents food. On each edge a certain amount of artificial pheromone is deposited. At each node each ant chooses which edge to take next. This choice is made probabilistically and according to the amount of pheromone placed on the edges. Pheromones can thus be seen as a collective memory of an ant colony.

As in real ant colonies, the pheromones evaporate over time. The amount of evaporation is determined by the so-called *evaporation factor* ρ, $0 < \rho < 1$. In every pheromone update on every edge a ρ-fraction of the pheromone evaporates, i. e., if the edge contains pheromone τ, the remaining amount of pheromone is $(1 - \rho) \cdot \tau$ and then eventually new pheromone is added. Intuitively, a large evaporation factor implies that the impact of previously laid pheromones diminishes quickly and new pheromones have a large impact on the system. Small evaporation factors, on the other hand, imply that the system only adapts slowly to new pheromones.

The current state of an ACO algorithm depends crucially on the pheromone values. As pheromones depend on a long history of past solutions, ACO algorithms are, in general, harder to analyze than other search heuristics such as evolutionary algorithms (cf. the survey by Witt [39]). The current population in an evolutionary algorithm typically is Markovian. Contrarily, the set of the most recent solutions of an ACO algorithm generally is not Markovian as new solutions crucially depend on pheromone values. However, if we consider a stochastic process where the current pheromones are included as part of the current state then we can obtain a Markovian model of an ACO algorithm. In contrast to Markov-chain models of evolutionary algorithms, such a Markov chain contains continuous components as pheromones are real valued.

We contribute to the methods used for the analysis of ACO and other randomized search heuristics using ideas from the powerful Markov chain Monte Carlo (MCMC) paradigm [17]. This paradigm has been widely used to design efficient sampling algorithms via simulations of simple Markov

FOGA'11, January 5–9, 2011, A-6867 Schwarzenberg, Austria.
Copyright 2011 ACM 978-1-4503-0633-1/11/01 ...$10.00.

chains. The most famous applications include approximating the permanent of a matrix [18], sampling proper colorings of a graph [14] and computing the volume of convex bodies [26].

As common in MCMC, we regard an ACO algorithm as a Markov chain that—under some conditions—converges to a stationary distribution that represents an equilibrium state of the system. Properties of the system, such as the optimization time or other performance measures, can then be assessed using knowledge on the stationary distribution and the time until the system has come close to the stationary distribution. The latter time is known as *mixing time*.

The task of estimating mixing times for ACO is non-trivial as a Markov chain model of ACO must reflect the pheromone model—a probabilistic model with continuous components. In particular, the number of states attained by an ACO system may be (countably) infinite. A second difficulty is that, unlike for Markov chains for the Metropolis algorithm or the (1+1) EA on a plateau the Markov chain of an ACO algorithm is not time-reversible: while it may be possible to move from state x to state y, the reverse operation is, in general, impossible. Decreasing a pheromone of τ yields a value of $(1 - \rho)\tau$. But a reinforcement of the latter value yields pheromone $(1 - \rho)^2 \tau + \rho$, which in general is not equal to τ.

Nevertheless, we show in the following that it is possible to apply mixing time estimations and MCMC techniques to ACO and that this can be used for bounding the expected optimization time. We are confident that the presented techniques will find further applications for other probabilistic model-building algorithms and non-elitist search heuristics. This in particular includes evolutionary algorithms using more sophisticated selection mechanisms as cut selection for the environmental selection. This topic is highly relevant as there is a trend towards theoretical analyses of non-elitist evolutionary algorithms [13, 19, 23, 35].

After surveying previous work in Section 2, Section 3 introduces techniques for estimating the mixing time. This part can serve as a reference for researchers working on theory of randomized search heuristics. Section 4 then discusses possible implications that can be drawn from mixing times and stationary distributions. Section 5 demonstrates these techniques in an application to pseudo-Boolean optimization and Section 6 explains how the mixing time can be estimated for MMAS-type algorithms for shortest path problems in directed acyclic graphs. We finish with concluding remarks in Section 7.

2. PREVIOUS WORK

This work does not claim to be the first one using Markov chain Monte Carlo techniques in the context of randomized search heuristics. Markov chain techniques including arguments on stationary distributions have already been used for the analysis of evolutionary algorithms (see, e.g., Mitavskiy, Rowe, Wright, and Schmitt [27] and the references therein). In terms of running time analysis, for instance, Garnier, Kallel, and Schoenauer [9] used recurrence arguments based on stationarity for the analysis of the simple (1+1) EA on a needle function. Due to the lack of time-reversibility, this approach cannot be transferred to non-trivial ACO algorithms.

Also ad hoc mixing time approaches have been presented before in the context of evolutionary algorithms, where the

"distance" between the current distribution and the stationary distribution was bounded by ad hoc arguments, see the proof of Theorem 10 in Doerr, Gnewuch, Hebbinghaus, and Neumann [4] or Lemma 3 in Lässig and Sudholt [22]. Markov chain Monte Carlo techniques have recently also been used to establish conditions for the success of the Metropolis algorithm in the context of optimization by Sanyal, S, and Biswas [38]. The Metropolis algorithm is a very convenient algorithm for MCMC techniques as for this algorithm it is very easy to compute the stationary distribution.

The first running time analyses of ACO were presented independently by Gutjahr [10] (a technical report appeared in 2006) and Neumann and Witt [30, 32]. These studies focused on simple pseudo-Boolean functions, after this kind of work was explicitly demanded in a survey by Dorigo and Blum [6].

Neumann and Witt [30], Doerr, Neumann, Sudholt, and Witt [5], and Doerr and Johannsen [3] studied a simple algorithm 1-ANT that constructs a pseudo-Boolean solution according to a straightforward construction graph where an ant makes independent choices for each bit. The 1-ANT records the best solution found so far. In case a new solution is found which is not worse, the new solution replaces the old one and pheromones are updated with respect to the new solution. This mechanism implies that each new best-so-far solution leads to only one pheromone update. The mentioned studies have shown that in case ρ is too small this leads to a stagnation behavior as the knowledge gained through improvements cannot be adequately stored in the pheromones. There is a phase transition from polynomial to exponential optimization times for decreasing ρ.

In a different line of research, Gutjahr and Sebastiani [11] and Neumann, Sudholt, and Witt [36] studied an algorithm called MMAS, where the current best-so-far solution is reinforced in every generation. This holds regardless of whether the best-so-far solution has been changed or not. This means that the algorithm might reinforce the same solution over and over again, until the best-so-far solution is replaced. In stark contrast to the 1-ANT, the increased greediness of MMAS leads to polynomial upper bounds on simple pseudo-Boolean functions.

Recently, Neumann, Sudholt, and Witt [37] investigated a variant of MMAS with so-called *iteration-best update*. Instead of recording the current best-so-far solution, the algorithm creates λ ant solutions in each iteration and it reinforces the best one. This is similar to comma strategies in evolutionary computation. A surprising result is that $\lambda = 2$ ants are sufficient for optimizing ONEMAX in $O(n \log n)$ expected iterations. This result only holds if ρ is chosen appropriately. In particular, the authors prove that if ρ is too large (with respect to a trade-off between ρ and λ) then the expected optimization time is exponential, for every function with a unique global optimum. This phase transition is surprising as the effect is opposite to the phase transition for the 1-ANT; for iteration-best it is essential to choose small values of ρ.

Besides these results also analyses for hybridization with local search [34] and for ACO in combinatorial optimization have appeared. Neumann and Witt [31] investigated ACO algorithms for finding minimum spanning trees. They considered two different construction procedures and proved that for one procedure the use of heuristic information leads to a performance that is better than the performance of a simple evolutionary algorithm [29], in terms of the number of function evaluations.

Zhou [40] considered ACO for very simple instances of the TSP. This study was significantly extended by Kötzing, Neumann, Röglin, and Witt [21] who considered two different construction procedures and presented an average-case result for the performance of ACO. Kötzing, Lehre, Oliveto, and Neumann [20] investigated the performance of ACO for the minimum cut problem, but they only presented negative results for pheromone-based construction procedures.

Finally, Attiratanasunthron and Fakcharoenphol [2] and Horoba and Sudholt [15] considered ACO for the classical problem of finding shortest paths in graphs. The former authors presented an ant system n-ANT and proved that it can solve the single-destination shortest paths problem on directed acyclic graphs in $O((m\Delta\ell\log(\Delta\ell))/\rho)$ expected iterations. Here m is the number of edges, Δ is the maximum degree in the graph and ℓ is, loosely speaking, the maximum number of edges on any shortest path in the graph. This bound was later improved to $O(\Delta\ell^2 + (\ell\log(\Delta\ell))/\rho)$ iterations by Horoba and Sudholt [15] for a modified ant system MMAS$_{SDSP}$, when all shortest paths are unique. This algorithm is faster than n-ANT (when comparing upper bounds) and it overcomes the limitation to acyclic graphs. For the all-pairs shortest path problem a simple interaction mechanism between ants searching for different destinations leads to a remarkable speed-up, if ρ is not too large. This is another example where a slow adaptation of pheromones leads to the best known performance guarantees.

The last authors also presented an extension for stochastic shortest paths [16]. In this setting all edge weights are subject to noise that reflects possible delays and the task is to discover the real shortest paths despite the noise. They proved that in some settings the noise can mislead the search so that the system needs exponential time for finding decent approximate shortest paths.

3. MARKOV CHAINS AND MIXING TIMES

After having described previous work on the analysis of ACO, we start off with an introduction into mixing time techniques from Markov chain Monte Carlo. The basics described in this section can also be found in various book chapters and text books [1, 17, 24].

Mixing time estimations have deep roots in the Markov chain Monte Carlo paradigm. MCMC is a simple yet powerful technique for sampling that has found many applications (see Liu [25] for a detailed coverage of applications). Assume we have a space Ω and a positive weight function $w \colon \Omega \to \mathbb{R}^+$. The goal is to sample $x \in \Omega$ with a probability that is proportional to its weight, i.e., with probability $\pi(x) = w(x)/Z$ where Z is the sum of all weights, $Z := \sum_{x \in \Omega} w(x)$. The problem is that often Z is unknown.

The idea of Markov chain Monte Carlo is to construct a Markov chain (X_t) on the space Ω that converges to the desired distribution π. More precisely, we require that the probability of the current state being x at time t converges to $\pi(x)$ as $t \to \infty$, regardless of the initial state: for all $x_0 \in \Omega$ $\mathrm{Prob}\,(X_t = x \mid X_0 = x_0) \to \pi(x)$. In such a setting one can simulate the Markov chain for a sufficiently long time and then take the current state of the chain as an approximate sample. A crucial question is how long we need to simulate the Markov chain in order to get close to π. This time is called the *mixing time* of the Markov chain.

The mixing time is directly related to the efficiency of a sampling algorithm. Therefore, MCMC has developed powerful and interesting techniques for bounding the mixing time.

A sequence $(X_t) = X_0, X_1, \ldots$ of elements from Ω is a Markov chain if for all $x_0, \ldots, x_t$

$$\mathrm{Prob}\,(X_t = x_t \mid X_0 = x_0, \ldots, X_{t-1} = x_{t-1})$$
$$= \mathrm{Prob}\,(X_t = x_t \mid X_{t-1} = x_{t-1}).$$

In words, the current state depends only on the previous state. The Markov chain can therefore be described by transition probabilities: let $P(x, y)$ denote the probability of moving to state y given that the current state is in x. Then $P^t(x, y)$ denotes the probability of moving from x to y in exactly t steps.

Note that we can describe the Markov chain solely via its transition probabilities. A convenient way to do so is to take a matrix P of all transition probabilities. Given a current distribution x_t at time t then $x_{t+1} = x_t P$ describes the distribution at time $t + 1$.

Under certain conditions a Markov chain converges to a fixed distribution, known as *stationary distribution*.

DEFINITION 1. *A probability distribution π is a stationary distribution for P if $\pi = \pi P$.*

Once the chain has reached the stationary distribution, the current state will always be distributed according to π. We also say that the chain is at stationarity.

DEFINITION 2. *A Markov chain is called* irreducible *if there is a positive probability of reaching any target state from each state in finite time. Formally: for all states x, y there exists some $t \in \mathbb{N}_0$ such that $P^t(x, y) > 0$.*

For irreducible chains it might be the case that certain states may only be reachable periodically. For instance, we might have a Markov chain where with an initial state x_0 some state x only has positive probability if t is odd. In this case we would not expect the Markov chain to converge to a stationary distribution. The opposite term is *aperiodicity*.

DEFINITION 3. *A Markov chain P is aperiodic if for all states x, y we have $\gcd\{t \colon P^t(x, y) > 0\} = 1$.*

A Markov chain is aperiodic if it is irreducible and if there is at least one state $z \in \Omega$ with a positive self-loop probability, i.e., $P(z, z) > 0$. The reason is that from any state x there is a positive probability of reaching z in finite time, spending an arbitrary finite number of steps in the self-loop, and then moving on to y. This excludes the existence of periods.

For finite Markov chains it is known that irreducibility and aperiodicity implies that the Markov chain has a unique stationary distribution. In this case the Markov chain is called *ergodic*. As we will have to deal with countably infinite state spaces, we need one further condition. We have to know that some states can be revisited in finite time, formalized by the term *positive recurrence*.

DEFINITION 4. *State x is recurrent if $\sum_{t \geq 1} P^t(x, x) = 1$. A recurrent state x is positive recurrent if its expected time to return to x from x is finite: $\sum_{t \geq 1} t \cdot P^t(x, x) < \infty$.*

The following theorem is known as the fundamental theorem of Markov chains. The precise formulation is taken from

Mitzenmacher and Upfal [28, Theorem 7.11]; it states under which conditions a Markov chain with a finite or countably infinite state space converges to a stationary distribution.

THEOREM 1 (FUNDAMENTAL THEOREM). *Any irreducible aperiodic Markov chain belongs to one of the following two categories:*

1. *the chain is ergodic—for any pair of states i and j the limit $\lim_{t\to\infty} P^t(j, i)$ exists and is independent of j, and the chain has a unique stationary distribution $\pi_i = \lim_{t\to\infty} P^t(j, i)$ or*

2. *no state is positive recurrent—for all states i and j, $\lim_{t\to\infty} P^t(j, i) = 0$, and the chain has no stationary distribution.*

The distance between the current distribution and the stationary distribution is measured as follows.

DEFINITION 5 (TOTAL VARIATION DISTANCE). *For two probability distributions μ and ν on Ω the total variation distance is defined as*

$$||\mu - \nu|| = \frac{1}{2} \sum_{x \in \Omega} |\mu(x) - \nu(x)| = \max_{A \subseteq \Omega} |\mu(A) - \nu(A)|.$$

The total variation distance is thus the maximum difference in probability for any set $A \subseteq \Omega$.

DEFINITION 6 (MIXING TIME). *Consider an ergodic Markov chain starting in x with stationary distribution π. Let $p_x^{(t)}$ denote the distribution of the Markov chain after t steps. Let $t_x(\varepsilon)$ be the time until the total variation distance between the current distribution and the stationary distribution has decreased to ε: $t_x(\varepsilon) = \min\{t: ||p_x^{(t)} - \pi|| \leq \varepsilon\}$. Let $t(\varepsilon) := \max_{x \in \Omega} t_x(\varepsilon)$ be the worst-case time until this happens.*

The mixing time t_{mix} of the Markov chain is then defined as $t_{\mathrm{mix}} := t(1/(2e))$.

The constant $1/(2e)$ is chosen somewhat arbitrarily; any other constant strictly smaller than $1/2$ would lead to essentially the same results. In fact, when considering a time of αt_{mix} for some $\alpha > 1$ then the total variation distance decreases exponentially with α. This shows that an arbitrary precision can be achieved by letting the Markov chain run sufficiently long. The following statement is well known; a proof is given, e. g., in Levin et al. [24, page 55].

LEMMA 2. $t(\varepsilon) \leq t_{\mathrm{mix}} \lceil \log(1/\varepsilon) \rceil$.

One way to derive upper bounds on the mixing time of a Markov chain is by means of couplings. Given a Markov chain P a *coupling* is a pair process of two random processes (X_t, Y_t). Each process represents a copy of the original Markov chain, i. e., the transition probabilities for both X_t and Y_t are specified by P. However, X_t and Y_t can follow a joint distribution, so that X_t and Y_t need not be independent. For instance, we can let X_t and Y_t make the same random decisions, thus sharing the same source of randomness, as long as we do not change the transition probabilities. In fact, the goal of a coupling is to couple both Markov chains such that both chains at some point of time attain the same state. Whenever this happens, the two processes will always have the same state—we say that then X_t and Y_t have coupled.

DEFINITION 7 (COUPLING). *A coupling of a Markov chain P is a pair process (X_t, Y_t) where both X_t and Y_t, viewed in isolation, are copies of the Markov chain P and for all t it holds that if $X_t = Y_t$ then $X_{t+1} = Y_{t+1}$.*

The random time until the two processes have coupled is called the *coupling time*: $T_{xy} = \min\{t: X_t = Y_t \mid X_0 = x, Y_0 = y\}$. The worst-case coupling time for all x and y is related to the total variation distance between the current distribution and the stationary distribution as follows.

LEMMA 3.

$$\max_{x \in \Omega} ||p_x^{(t)} - \pi|| \leq \max_{x,y \in \Omega} \mathrm{Prob}\,(T_{xy} > t)$$

This immediately implies that the worst-case coupling time gives an upper bound on the mixing time.

COROLLARY 4.

$$t(\varepsilon) \leq \min\{t: \max_{x,y \in \Omega} \mathrm{Prob}\,(T_{xy} > t) \leq \varepsilon\}.$$

Intuitively, the reason why the worst-case coupling time is an upper bound for the mixing time is that it gives an upper bound for the time until a Markov chain X with an arbitrary initialization has coupled with another Markov chain Y that is at stationarity. The reason for this is that the stationary distribution is a convex combination of point distributions (i. e. the initial state has some fixed value with probability 1).

4. HOW TO USE MIXING TIME ESTIMATIONS

Let us discuss how estimations of the mixing time can be used for the analysis of randomized search heuristics. The goal of MCMC is the design of efficient sampling algorithms. A randomized search heuristic can be regarded as an algorithm trying to sample the set OPT of global optima.

THEOREM 5. *Consider a randomized search heuristic that can be represented by an ergodic Markov chain with stationary distribution π. Let OPT be the set of global optima and let t_{mix} denote the mixing time on the considered problem. Then the expected optimization time is at most $t_{\mathrm{mix}} \cdot O(\log(1/\pi(\mathrm{OPT})))/\pi(\mathrm{OPT})$.*

PROOF. For any initial state we have that after $t := t(\pi(\mathrm{OPT})/2)$ steps the total variation distance between the current distribution $p_x^{(t)}$ and the stationary distribution π has decreased to at most $||p_x^{(t)} - \pi|| \leq \pi(\mathrm{OPT})/2$. By the definition of total variation distance this means that $|p_x^{(t)}(\mathrm{OPT}) - \pi(\mathrm{OPT})| \leq \pi(\mathrm{OPT})/2$ and hence $p_x^{(t)}(\mathrm{OPT}) \geq \pi(\mathrm{OPT})/2$. So, after t steps the probability of being in a global optimum is at least $\pi(\mathrm{OPT})/2$. If this is not the case we wait for another t steps and repeat the arguments. Along with Lemma 2, the expected optimization time is at most

$$2t(\pi(\mathrm{OPT})/2)/\pi(\mathrm{OPT}) \leq 2t_{\mathrm{mix}} \cdot \lceil \log(2/\pi(\mathrm{OPT})) \rceil /\pi(\mathrm{OPT}).$$

$\square$

Note that we have to wait for the mixing time every time we are unsuccessful in sampling OPT. This is because the condition of not having found OPT implies a bias for the distribution of states in the next step. Hence, we have to wait for another mixing time steps to "reset" the current distribution towards a distribution that is close to stationarity.

Another use of mixing time arguments is the following. Assume we are interested in maximizing some performance criterion g that only depends on the current state of the algorithm. (An adaptation towards minimization is straightforward.) In the case of population-based algorithms one might think of, for instance, g describing the average, best, or worst fitness in the current population, or the closeness of the current population to some target point. After mixing, this performance measure will be close to the performance at stationarity.

THEOREM 6. *Let $g\colon \Omega \to \mathbb{R}$ be an arbitrary performance measure for the current state of the algorithm. Let $g_{\min}$ and $g_{\max}$ be its minimal and maximal values, respectively, and $\alpha \geq 1$. After $t_{\mathrm{mix}} \cdot 2\alpha$ iterations we have $\mathrm{E}\,(g) \geq \mathrm{E}_\pi(g) - 2^{-\alpha} \cdot (g_{\max} - g_{\min})$ where $\mathrm{E}_\pi(\cdot)$ denote the expectation of a random variable drawn according to π.*

PROOF. Note that $t(2^{-\alpha}) \leq t_{\mathrm{mix}} \lceil \log(2^\alpha) \rceil \leq t_{\mathrm{mix}} \cdot 2\alpha$, hence after $t_{\mathrm{mix}} \cdot 2\alpha$ steps the total variation distance between the current distribution and π is no more than $2^{-\alpha}$. Pessimistically estimating that the g-value is at $g_{\min}$ with the remaining probability $2^{-\alpha}$,

$$
\begin{aligned}
\mathrm{E}\,(g) &= \sum_{z \in \Omega} \mathrm{Prob}\,(g = z) \cdot z \\
&\geq \sum_{z \in \Omega} (1 - 2^{-\alpha}) \cdot \mathrm{Prob}\,(\pi = z) \cdot z + 2^{-\alpha} g_{\min} \\
&= (1 - 2^{-\alpha}) \cdot \mathrm{E}_\pi(g) + 2^{-\alpha} g_{\min} \\
&\geq \mathrm{E}_\pi(g) - 2^{-\alpha} g_{\max} + 2^{-\alpha} g_{\min}.
\end{aligned}
$$

$\square$

We see that mixing time estimates can be useful in various ways. In the next sections we show some concrete applications to ACO algorithms.

5. PLATEAUS IN PSEUDO-BOOLEAN OPTIMIZATION

5.1 ACO for Pseudo-Boolean Optimization

As a first application we consider MMAS for pseudo-Boolean optimization, i. e., the maximization of a pseudo-Boolean function $f\colon \{0,1\}^n \to \mathbb{R}$. Many classical combinatorial problems can be modeled as a pseudo-Boolean function. Examples are MAXSAT or selection problems like Knapsack, Vertex Cover, Minimum Spanning Trees or Maximum Matchings, where a bit indicates whether an object, vertex, or edge is selected or not.

A solution, i. e., a bit string of length n, can be obtained by letting an artificial ant traverse a so-called *construction graph* and mapping the path chosen by the ant to binary values. We use the following natural construction graph. In addition to a start node v_0, there is a node v_i for every bit i, $1 \leq i \leq n$. This node can be reached from v_{i-1} by two edges. The edge $e_{i,1}$ corresponds to setting bit i to 1, while $e_{i,0}$ corresponds to setting bit i to 0. The former edge is also called a *1-edge*, the latter is called *0-edge*. An example of a construction graph for $n = 5$ is shown in Figure 1.

In a solution construction process an artificial ant sequentially traverses the nodes $v_0, v_1, \ldots, v_n$. The decision which edge to take is made according to pheromones on the edges. Formally, we denote pheromones by a function $\tau\colon E \to \mathbb{R}_0^+$. From v_{i-1} the edge $e_{i,1}$ is then taken with probability $\tau(e_{i,1})/(\tau(e_{i,0}) + \tau(e_{i,1}))$.

MMAS (see Algorithm 1) starts with an equal amount of pheromone on all edges: $\tau(e_{i,0}) = \tau(e_{i,1}) = 1/2$. Moreover, we ensure that $\tau(e_{i,0}) + \tau(e_{i,1}) = 1$ holds, i. e., pheromones for one bit always sum up to 1. This implies that the probability of taking a specific edge equals its pheromone value; in other words, pheromones and traversal probabilities coincide. The algorithm also keeps track of the current best-so-far solution x^*. In every iteration, first a new solution x is constructed and it replaces x^* if its objective function value is not worse. Finally, the pheromones are updated with respected to the new best-so-far solution.

Algorithm 1 MMAS

1: Set $\tau(e) := 1/2$ for all $e \in E$.
2: Construct a solution x^*.
3: Update pheromones w. r. t. x^*.
4: **loop**
5:     Construct a solution x.
6:     **if** $f(x) \geq f(x^*)$ **then** $x^* := x$.
7:     Update pheromones w. r. t. x^*.
8: **end loop**

The pheromone update works as follows. Let $\mathrm{P}(x^*)$ denote the path of edges that have been chosen in the creation of x^*. First, a ρ-fraction of all pheromones evaporates and a $(1-\rho)$-fraction remains. Next, some pheromone is added to edges that are part of $\mathrm{P}(x^*)$. To prevent pheromones from dropping to arbitrarily small values, it is common practice to restrict all pheromones to a bounded interval. The precise interval is chosen as $[\tau_{\min}, 1 - \tau_{\min}]$ for some parameter $0 < \tau_{\min} \leq 1/2$. Pheromone bounds are essential to prevent the pheromones from diverging to values arbitrarily close to 0 or 1. The following analysis of the mixing time hinges on these pheromones bounds as a diverging system does not necessarily mix.

In previous work $\tau_{\min}$ was set to $1/n$, inspired by standard mutations in evolutionary computation where for every bit an evolutionary algorithm has a probability of $1/n$ of reverting a wrong decision. Our results will be more general to highlight the impact the choice of $\tau_{\min}$ has on performance.

Depending on whether an edge e is contained in $\mathrm{P}(x^*)$, the pheromone values τ are updated to τ' as follows:

$$
\begin{aligned}
\tau'(e) &= \min\left\{(1-\rho) \cdot \tau(e) + \rho,\ 1 - \tau_{\min}\right\} && \text{if } e \in \mathrm{P}(x^*), \\
\tau'(e) &= \max\left\{(1-\rho) \cdot \tau(e),\ \tau_{\min}\right\} && \text{if } e \notin \mathrm{P}(x^*).
\end{aligned}
\tag{1}
$$

Note that the pheromones on all 1-edges suffices to describe all pheromones as pheromones for the two edges for each bit sum up to 1.

5.2 An Upper Bound for MMAS on Needle

Randomized search heuristics are frequently confronted with *plateaus* in the search space. Plateaus are regions of equal fitness. As the fitness does not give any useful hints as to where to find better solutions, the best strategy is typically to perform a kind of random walk to explore the plateau. The largest possible plateau in a non-trivial setting

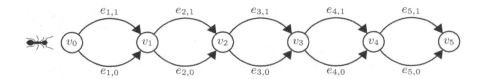

Figure 1: **Construction graph for pseudo-Boolean optimization with** $n = 5$ **bits.**

is encountered in the function

$$\textsc{Needle}(x) := \begin{cases} 1 & \text{if } x = x_{\text{OPT}}, \\ 0 & \text{otherwise,} \end{cases}$$

where x_{OPT} is the unique global optimum. It is known that every black-box algorithm needs on average at least $\Omega(2^n)$ function evaluations, where the average is taken over all possible x_{OPT} [8]. Neumann et al. [36] have shown the following upper bound for MMAS on Needle.

THEOREM 7 (NEUMANN ET AL. [36]). *The expected optimization time of MMAS with $\tau_{\min} = 1/n$ on Needle is bounded from above by $O((n/\rho)^2 (\log n) \cdot 2^n)$.*

The proof of Theorem 7 in [36] is tailored towards finding a single search point. W. l. o. g. assume that 1^n is the needle. Neumann et al. [36] then argue that, for every initial pheromone value, once a pheromone for a specific bit reaches a value of at least $1/2$ at some point of time t then the probability of creating a bit value 1 at this bit at any fixed point of time $t' \geq t$ is at least $1/2$. Intuitively, the probability of creating a 1 converges to $1/2$ from above. The expected time until all bits have reached a value of $1/2$ at least once is bounded by $O((n/\rho)^2 \log n)$ and then the probability of constructing the needle in the next iteration is 2^{-n}. In case the needle has not been found, the arguments have to be repeated from scratch as the event of not finding the needle introduces a bias towards low pheromones.

It should be remarked that in [33], a preliminary version of [36], a coupling argument was used. However, the coupling was trivial as two independent Markov chains were considered. The result was limited to constant values of ρ as the estimation of the coupling time breaks down for smaller ρ.

In the following we use coupling arguments with a more thorough coupling and mixing time estimates to re-prove Theorem 7 and to prove a more general result that overcomes the limitation of the needle being a single search point. Despite the larger generality, we emphasize that the focus is on the new proof method and not so much on the result itself.

Consider a generalized Needle function where the needle is an arbitrary target set S.

$$\textsc{Needle}_S(x) := \begin{cases} 1 & \text{if } x \in S, \\ 0 & \text{otherwise,} \end{cases}$$

hence S reflects all global optima.

In the remainder of this section we will prove the following result.

THEOREM 8. *The expected number of iterations until MMAS finds the optimum on $\textsc{Needle}_S$ for non-empty S is bounded from above by $O((\rho \tau_{\min})^{-2} (\log n) \cdot 2^n / |S|)$.*

Note that until MMAS finds the needle, it behaves as if it was optimizing the constant function that attains value 0

everywhere. Instead of looking at the function Needle, we will consider this constant function. On the constant function, the algorithm behaves independently from the best-so-far search point. Therefore, we can model the current state of the algorithm by looking at the n pheromones on the 1-edges only. We also speak of a *pheromone vector* and refer to the pheromones on the 1-edges.

The following set describes our state space.

DEFINITION 8. *Let $\mathcal{V}$ denote the set of all pheromone vectors τ such that $P^t(\tau^*, \tau) > 0$ for some $t \in \mathbb{N}$ and some $\tau^* \in \{\tau_{\min}, 1 - \tau_{\min}\}^n$.*

The set $\mathcal{V}$ might be infinitely large for appropriate ρ in case there is always one decision—increasing or decreasing a pheromone value—leading to a pheromone value that has not been attained before. However, the size of $\mathcal{V}$ is at most countably infinite as for every bit at most two new pheromone values can be reached in one iteration.

We assume in the following that MMAS is initialized with a pheromone vector in $\mathcal{V}$. Note that this differs from the common initialization where all pheromones are set to $1/2$. We will first prove Theorem 8 with this modified initialization and at the end of this section we will argue how to prove the result for the original initialization.

The first step for applying mixing time arguments is to show that the Markov chain fulfills all necessary requirements.

LEMMA 9. *Assume MMAS starts with a pheromone vector in $\mathcal{V}$. The Markov chain representing the pheromone vector of MMAS on the constant function is ergodic.*

PROOF. Let τ_x, τ_y be two pheromone vectors in $\mathcal{V}$. By definition of $\mathcal{V}$, there is a vector in $\{\tau_{\min}, 1 - \tau_{\min}\}$, w. l. o. g. $\tau^* = (\tau_{\min}, \ldots, \tau_{\min})$, such that τ_y can be reached from τ^* in t steps with positive probability.

If MMAS is currently in state τ_x, there is a positive probability that MMAS first decreases all pheromones to arrive at $(\tau_{\min}, \ldots, \tau_{\min})$ in finite time by always creating the search point 0^n. And there is a positive probability of reaching τ_y in t further steps. Hence, the Markov chain is irreducible. It is also aperiodic as there is a positive self-loop probability for all states where all pheromones are at some pheromone border.

By Theorem 1 the chain belongs to either of the two stated categories. To prove that it is ergodic we need to show that there is at least one positive recurrent state. Consider the state $\tau^* = (\tau_{\min}, \ldots, \tau_{\min})$ again. The state is clearly recurrent because of the mentioned self-loop. It is also positive recurrent since for any state we arrive at τ^* after having reinforced the solution 0^n at least $\ln(1/\tau_{\min})/\rho$ times. The last term follows from the fact that after evaporating pheromones $\ln(1/\tau_{\min})/\rho$ times any pheromone value τ_i has decreased towards $\tau_{\min}$:

$$(1-\rho)^{\ln(1/\tau_{\min})/\rho} \cdot \tau_i \leq e^{-\ln(1/\tau_{\min})} \cdot \tau_i \leq \tau_{\min}.$$

The probability of always creating the solution 0^n in this time span is at least $\tau_{\min}^{n \cdot \ln(1/\tau_{\min})/\rho}$. As this holds for every state, the expected time until we return to τ^* is bounded by $\tau_{\min}^{-n \cdot \ln(1/\tau_{\min})/\rho} + \ln(1/\tau_{\min})/\rho < \infty$. $\quad\square$

Now we know by the fundamental theorem of Markov chains that there exists a stationary distribution π for the pheromone vectors of MMAS on the constant function. By symmetry of bits, we know that all entries of π must follow the same distribution. We do not know the probability density function for this distribution. Actually, it turns out that we do not need to know the probability density function. The following insight on the symmetry of bit values is sufficient for our purposes.

OBSERVATION 10. *Let π denote the stationary distribution for MMAS on the constant function. Then π is symmetric in the following sense: if τ_y results from τ_x by "inverting" pheromones on an arbitrary set of bits (inverting means replacing pheromone z by $1 - z$) then $\pi(\tau_x) = \pi(\tau_y)$.*

A simple yet essential conclusion from this observation is the following.

LEMMA 11. *If the Markov chain for MMAS on the constant function is at stationarity, the next ant solution is drawn uniform from $\{0, 1\}^n$.*

PROOF. By Observation 10 we have $E_\pi\left(\tau_i^t\right) = 1/2$, where τ_i^t denotes the random pheromone of the i-th bit at time t. The probability of creating bit value 1 for bit i in the next solution construction is

$$\sum_p p \cdot \text{Prob}_\pi\left(\tau_i^t = p\right) = E_\pi\left(\tau_i^t\right) = 1/2.$$

As this holds independently for all bits, the next constructed solution is uniform. $\quad\square$

Now we know what the stationary distribution looks like, we can focus on estimating the time until we get close to it. We will basically show that the mixing time of MMAS on the constant function is $O((\rho\tau_{\min})^{-2} \log n)$. In order to prove this, we design the following coupling of two Markov chains X and Y.

The idea is to let X and Y share random decisions for constructing ant solutions whenever possible, without changing the original Markov chains. In each iteration we choose a random vector $r = (r_1, \ldots, r_n)$ where all entries r_i are chosen from the uniform distribution $U[0, 1]$. This vector shall serve as a shared source of randomness for both X and Y. Let $\tau^X = (\tau_1^X, \ldots, \tau_n^X)$ be the pheromone vector corresponding to the current state of X. Construct an ant solution for X as follows. For all i, if $r_i < \tau_i^X$ the bit i is set to 1 and to 0 otherwise. Hence, the bit is set to 1 with probability τ_i^X. Then the pheromones τ^X are updated with respect to this ant solution. The same is done for Y with the same random vector r, but with respect to the pheromone vector τ^Y. Note that this way both X and Y are faithful copies of the original process, when viewed in isolation.

It is obvious that once X and Y attain the same pheromone value at some bit i, they will always have equal pheromone values for this bit. (This is not necessarily true in settings where some kind of selection is involved, but in our setting equal bit values imply that the same bit value will be reinforced.) This allows us to focus on the coupling time of a single bit, i. e., the time until the pheromone values become equal on one bit. Once all bits have been coupled, X and Y will always have the same pheromone vector.

What is the coupling time for a single bit? It turns out that the pheromone borders are essential for this estimation. Assume w. l. o. g. that $0 < \tau_i^X < \tau_i^Y < 1$ and let us assume for a moment that there were no pheromone borders. Consider the distance $d_i(X, Y) := \tau_i^Y - \tau_i^X$ between the pheromones. If $r_i > \tau_i^Y$ then both pheromones are multiplied by $(1 - \rho)$ and the distance also decreases by a factor of $(1 - \rho)$. Symmetrically, if $r_i < \tau_i^X$ then the distance is changed to $(1-\rho)\tau_i^Y + \rho - ((1-\rho)\tau_i^X + \rho) = (1-\rho)d_i(X,Y)$. In the last case, if $\tau_i^X < r_i < \tau_i^Y$ then the distance increases to $(1-\rho)\tau_i^Y + \rho - (1-\rho)\tau_i^X = (1-\rho)d_i(X,Y) + \rho$. The best case is therefore a compression of the distance by $(1 - \rho)$. But even then a positive distance can never become 0 as the state space is continuous.

A conclusion drawn from these insights is that the pheromones have to meet at some border in order to couple. Gladly, the following simple observation helps. The distance between X and Y on bit i can be compressed by $(1 - \rho)$, but it cannot become negative. In other words, τ_i^Y cannot become smaller than τ_i^X; it always holds that $\tau_i^Y \geq \tau_i^X$. So, when τ_i^X hits the upper pheromone border $1 - \tau_{\min}$, we must have $\tau_i^X = \tau_i^Y$. The same holds when τ_i^Y hits the lower pheromone border $\tau_{\min}$. The coupling time for a bit thus boils down to estimating the time until an arbitrary pheromone value first hits a specific border.

LEMMA 12. *The expected coupling time for a specific bit is bounded by $O((\rho\tau_{\min})^{-2})$.*

In order to prove Lemma 12 we apply second-moment arguments. The following lemma is a simplification of Lemma 7 in [36].

LEMMA 13 (NEUMANN, SUDHOLT, AND WITT [36]). *Consider a stochastic process $\{X_t\}_{t \geq 0}$ on a bounded subset of $\mathbb{R}_0^+$. Let $\mathfrak{F}_t$ denote $X_0, \ldots, X_t$, $E_{t+1} := E(X_{t+1} \mid \mathfrak{F}_t)$ and*

$$\Delta_{t+1} = E\left((X_{t+1} - E_{t+1})^2 \cdot \mathbb{I}_{X_{t+1} < E_{t+1}} \mid \mathfrak{F}_t\right)$$

with $\mathbb{I}_F$ being the indicator function of event F.

Given $\alpha \in \mathbb{R}$, define $T := \min\{t \colon |X_t - X_0| \geq \alpha \mid X_0\}$. If

1. *$\{X_t\}_{t \geq 0}$ is a supermartingale (i. e. $E_{t+1} \leq X_t$) and*

2. *there exists $\delta > 0$ such that $\Delta_t \geq \delta$ for all $1 \leq t < T$*

then $E(T) \leq 1 + (2X_0 + \alpha) \cdot \alpha/\delta$.

PROOF OF LEMMA 12. By the discussion preceding this lemma, it suffices to estimate the time until the smaller pheromone τ_i^X hits the upper border or the larger pheromone τ_i^Y hits the lower pheromone border. Note that in at least one of these cases the considered pheromone has distance at least $1/2 - \tau_{\min}$ from the considered border.

Now consider a single pheromone τ_i and assume w. l. o. g. that initially $\tau_i > 1/2$. Then the coupling time is bounded by the time until the pheromone first hits $\tau_{\min}$. If $\tau_i < 1/2$ the argument is symmetric; in case $\tau_i = 1/2$ we just wait one iteration and then continue with one of the above cases.

When waiting until the lower pheromone border is reached, we imagine a modified process where the pheromone is not capped at the lower pheromone border. Let τ_i^t denote the random pheromone at time t, then the pheromone is a super-martingale: if the upper pheromone border is not hit then $\tau_i^{t+1} = (1-\rho)\tau_i^t + \rho$ with probability τ_i^t and $\tau_i^{t+1} = (1-\rho)\tau_i^t$ with probability $1 - \tau_i^t$, hence

$$\mathrm{E}\left(\tau_i^{t+1} \mid \tau_i^t\right) = (1-\rho) \cdot \tau_i^t + \tau_i^t \cdot \rho = \tau_i^t.$$

Obviously, taking into account the upper pheromone border $1 - \tau_{\min}$, this can only decrease the expected next pheromone, hence

$$\mathrm{E}\left(\tau_i^{t+1} \mid \tau_i^t\right) \le \tau_i^t.$$

As initially $\tau_i^0 > 1/2$ applying Lemma 13 with $\alpha := \tau_i^0 - \tau_{\min}$ the random time T in this lemma describes the random time until τ_i first reaches a value of or below $\tau_{\min}$. The first condition of the lemma has already been verified, so it remains to prove a lower bound on the one-sided variance.

Observe that $\mathrm{Prob}\left(\tau_i^{t+1} \le (1-\rho)\tau_i^t \mid \tau_i^t\right) \ge 1 - \tau_i^t$ as the pheromone is decreased with probability $1 - \tau_i^t$. Hence, the one-sided variance (i.e. the variance when considering only decreasing pheromone) is at least

$$(1 - \tau_i^t) \cdot (\rho\tau_i^t)^2 \ge (1 - \tau_{\min}) \cdot (\rho\tau_{\min})^2.$$

Invoking Lemma 13 yields that the expected time until the lower pheromone border is reached is at most

$$1 + (2\tau_i^0 + \alpha) \cdot \alpha/((1 - \tau_{\min})(\rho\tau_{\min})^2) = O((\rho\tau_{\min})^{-2}).$$

$\square$

Now we can finally assemble all the pieces to prove Theorem 8.

PROOF OF THEOREM 8. We first estimate the worst-case coupling time T where the worst case is taken over all possible pheromone vectors from $\mathcal{V}$ for X and Y. By Lemma 12 the expected time for coupling a single bit is bounded by $c(\rho\tau_{\min})^{-2}$ for some constant $c > 0$. By Markov's inequality the probability that the bit will not have coupled within $2c(\rho\tau_{\min})^{-2}$ iterations is at most $1/2$. As Lemma 12 holds for arbitrary initial pheromones, we can repeat this argument for an arbitrary number of $k \in \mathbb{N}$ phases of $2c(\rho\tau_{\min})^{-2}$ iterations each. The probability that after all phases a bit has not coupled is then bounded by 2^{-k}.

The straightforward way to continue is to choose $k := \log(2^n/|S|) + \log n + 1$. Taking the union bound over all bits yields $\mathrm{Prob}\left(T > 2ck \cdot (\rho\tau_{\min})^{-2}\right) \le |S|/2^{n+1}$. By Lemma 3 this is also a bound on the total variation distance. A solution drawn uniformly at random hits S with probability $|S|/2^n$. Along with Lemma 11 the probability of sampling the set S in the next constructed solution is at least $|S|/2^n - |S|/2^{n+1} = |S|/2^{n+1}$. Hence after $2ck(\rho\tau_{\min})^{-2} = O((\log(2^n/|S|) + \log n)(\rho\tau_{\min})^{-2})$ iterations the next constructed ant solution hits S with probability $\Omega(|S|/2^n)$. Repeating this argument until the algorithm is successful yields an upper bound of $O((\log(2^n/|S|) + \log n)(\rho\tau_{\min})^{-2} \cdot 2^n/|S|)$.

If $\log(2^n/|S|) = \omega(\log n)$ this way of arguing does not give the claimed bound. In this situation it actually makes sense to exploit the independence of bits once more and to argue about single bits directly. We consider the pheromone process and the coupling for a single bit only. Let T_i be the random time until bit i has coupled. Setting $k := \log n$ yields $\mathrm{Prob}\left(T_i > 2c(\log n) \cdot (\rho\tau_{\min})^{-2}\right) \le 2^{-k} = 1/n$. By Lemma 3 the total variation distance between the pheromone distribution on bit i and the stationary distribution

on bit i then has decreased to at most $1/n$. This means that the probability for creating bit value 1 at this bit in the next constructed ant solution is at least $1/2 - 1/n$. As this holds for all bits independently, the probability of constructing any specific target point is at least

$$\left(\frac{1}{2} - \frac{1}{n}\right)^n = 2^{-n} \cdot \left(1 - \frac{2}{n}\right)^n = \Omega(2^{-n}).$$

Hence the probability of finding $|S|$ after $2c(\log n)(\rho\tau_{\min})^{-2}$ iterations is $\Omega(|S|/2^n)$. This proves the claim. $\square$

At this point we can also answer the question how we can deal with an initialization of pheromones outside $\mathcal{V}$. Our estimation of mixing times states that the expected time until the algorithm reaches some pheromone vector in $\mathcal{V}$ is bounded by $O((\rho\tau_{\min})^{-2} \cdot \log n)$ as we only have to wait until every bit has hit some pheromone border at least once to reach $\mathcal{V}$. This additional waiting time vanishes in the bound from Theorem 8, hence our analysis generalizes to arbitrary initial pheromone vectors.

5.3 Further Conclusions

The preceding theorem can be immediately applied to function where plateaus appear as subspaces of $\{0, 1\}^n$. One such example was presented by Gutjahr and Sebastiani [11]: the function NH-ONEMAX consists of the NEEDLE function on $k = \log n$ bits and the function ONEMAX on $n - k$ bits, which can only be optimized if the needle has been found on the needle part. The function is defined as

$$\text{NH-ONEMAX}(x) = \left(\prod_{i=1}^{k} x_i\right) \left(\sum_{i=k+1}^{n} x_i\right).$$

Theorem 8 then gives another proof of a result published in Neumann et al. [36]: replacing n by k, the expected time until MMAS finds the needle is $O((\rho\tau_{\min})^{-2}(\log k) \cdot 2^k) = O((\rho\tau_{\min})^{-2}(\log \log n) \cdot n)$. Including the expected time until the ONEMAX part is optimized gives an upper bound for NH-ONEMAX.

The analysis from the preceding subsection has also shown that bits quickly attain a "random" state where the probability of constructing bit value 1 is close to $1/2$. The following result may be useful in a more complex context.

LEMMA 14. *Call a bit relevant with respect to MMAS and the current generation if flipping the bit would result in a different solution becoming the next best-so-far solution.*

If there is a bit that has not been relevant for MMAS in the past $(\rho\tau_{\min})^2\alpha$ iterations then the probability of constructing bit value 1 in the next constructed solution is within $1/2 - 2^{-\Omega(\alpha)}$ and $1/2 + 2^{-\Omega(\alpha)}$.

Results of this kind have already found applications for evolutionary algorithms in pseudo-Boolean optimization, see the proof of Theorem 10 in [4] and Lemma 3 in [22].

6. MIXING OF MMAS ALGORITHMS FOR SHORTEST PATHS

We present another example where mixing time arguments can be used in a more complex setting: ACO for shortest path problems. Previous work focused on MMAS algorithms with best-so-far update. With such an update mechanism, the underlying pheromone model is, in general, not irreducible as the algorithm will never leave the set of global optima. We therefore focus on MMAS algorithms with iteration-best update, where the best ant solution in the current iteration is reinforced. This implies that the best solution found so far can be lost and the system may converge to a non-trivial stationary distribution. Note that the best-so-far MMAS algorithm from Section 5 is, in fact, an iteration-best algorithm on the considered needle functions.

The motivation for analyzing iteration-best MMAS algorithms is manifold. This update scheme is often used in practice. The recent study by Neumann et al. [37] has shown that iteration-best MMAS systems can be surprisingly effective in pseudo-Boolean optimization. For shortest paths the analyses by Horoba and Sudholt [16] have shown that sticking to the best-so-far path might not be a good choice when dealing with noise. In a stochastic setting, this might encourage a risk-seeking behavior that leads to exponential running times on certain instances [16] as the ants may stick to a sub-optimal path with a large variance. This effect might become even stronger when, unlike in [16], negative noise is allowed. In this sense iteration-best ant systems might be more robust than best-so-far ant systems. Finally, iteration-best is closer to natural ants; it is interesting to see whether less powerful ants can perform as well as ants with a memory.

6.1 MMAS for Shortest Paths

We consider the single-destination shortest path problem on directed acyclic graphs. The task is to find shortest paths from every vertex to a single destination. For simplicity, we assume that the destination can be reached from every vertex as otherwise we can simply add edges with very large weights to obtain this property, without changing the shortest paths.

Assume an n-vertex weighted directed acyclic graph $G = (V, E, w)$ where $w(e)$ denotes the weight of edge e. We define a *path* of length ℓ from u to v as a sequence of vertices $(v_0, \ldots, v_\ell)$ where $v_0 = u$, $v_\ell = v$, and $(v_{i-1}, v_i) \in E$ for all i with $1 \leq i \leq \ell$. As the graph is acyclic, a path cannot contain the same vertex twice. For convenience, we also refer to the corresponding sequence of edges as path. Let $\deg(u)$ denote the out-degree of a vertex u and $\Delta(G)$ or simply Δ denote the maximum out-degree of any vertex $u \in V$. Let $\operatorname{diam}(G)$ denote the diameter of G, that is, the maximum number of edges on any path in G.

We describe the considered iteration-best MMAS algorithm and thereby remark that many of the following arguments transfer to other MMAS algorithms that use the same path construction procedure and the same pheromone update mechanism. The selection of the new paths to be reinforced can be different.

In each iteration from every vertex λ ants start heading for the destination. Each ant chooses a path by performing a random walk through the graph according to pheromones on the edges; the probability of taking an edge is proportional to the amount of pheromone. Algorithm 2 gives a formal description of this procedure.

Afterwards, for each vertex a best path among the λ constructed paths is chosen for an update of the pheromones. As in previous ant systems for shortest paths a local update rule is used: an ant at vertex u is responsible for updating the edges leaving its start vertex u. In the beginning, phero-

---

Algorithm 2 Path Construction from u to v

1: Initialize $i \leftarrow 0$, $p_0 \leftarrow u$, and $V_1 \leftarrow \{p \in V \setminus \{p_0\} \mid (p_0, p) \in E\}$
2: **while** $p_i \neq v$ and $V_{i+1} \neq \emptyset$ **do**
3:      $i \leftarrow i + 1$
4:      Choose a vertex $p_i \in V_i$ according to probabilities $\tau((p_{i-1}, p_i)) / \sum_{p \in V_i} \tau((p_{i-1}, p))$
5:      $V_{i+1} \leftarrow \{p \in V \setminus \{p_0, \ldots, p_i\} \mid (p_i, p) \in E\}$
6: **end while**
7: **return** $(p_0, \ldots, p_i)$

---

mones $\tau \colon E \to \mathbb{R}_0^+$ are initialized such that all edges leaving some vertex u receive the same amount of pheromone: if $e = (u, \cdot)$ then $\tau(e) = 1/\deg(u)$. Afterwards, in each iteration the pheromones are updated exactly as in Equation (1), where $P(x^*)$ is redefined to the set of edges that are chosen to be reinforced (i. e. the first edges on any path to be reinforced).

Note that in this setting for a vertex with a large degree it may happen that the sum of pheromones on the outgoing edges exceeds 1. This happens if many low pheromones τ_i for which $(1 - \rho)\tau_i < \tau_{\min}$ holds are set to $\tau_{\min}$ in the pheromone update (1), instead of being set to $(1 - \rho)\tau_i$. However, Horoba and Sudholt [15] have shown that when $\tau_{\min} \leq 1/\Delta$ holds—we assume that this condition always holds since it is required for the initialization to work properly—then probabilities and pheromones only differ by a factor of at most 2.

6.2 The Mixing Time of MMAS Algorithms

We explain how the mixing time of MMAS algorithms can be bounded. Consider a coupling of two Markov chains X, Y with pheromone vectors τ_X, τ_Y of arbitrary initial entries. In the coupling in each iteration λ ants are sent whose random walks are coupled as follows. Consider a setting where an ant has reached the same vertex in X and Y. Let p_i^X and p_i^Y be the probabilities of taking the i-th edge from the current vertex for X and Y, respectively. Then the j-th ants in X and Y with probability $\min\{p_i^X, p_i^Y\}$ both take the i-th edge. With the remaining probability $1 - \sum_i \min\{p_i^X, p_i^Y\}$ the ants make choices so that each ant makes random decisions according to the original path construction. This generalizes the coupling from Section 5. Note that whenever all pheromones at some vertex u are the same, all ants in X and Y make the same decisions at u.

We now consider an incremental coupling for the graph. W. l. o. g. let $V = \{1, \ldots, n\}$ and assume that the vertices are topologically ordered with respect to the destination n. Let G_i denote the subgraph of vertices $\{i, \ldots, n\}$. Once all pheromones on outgoing edges for these vertices are the same in X and Y we say that X and Y have coupled in G_i. As the vertices are due to a topological ordering, X and Y will always make the same decisions for any ant traversing G_i. Also the pheromones on edges in G_i will be the same in X and Y forever since only ants that start in G_i will change pheromones on edges of G_i.

Assuming that X and Y have coupled in G_{i+1}, we then estimate the time until X and Y have coupled in G_i. As in the previous analysis, we rely on pheromone borders for pheromones to attain equal values in X and Y. We call an edge e *saturated* if $\tau(e) = 1 - \tau_{\min}$. The idea is that once X and Y have both saturated the same edge at i, they will have the same pheromone values on all outgoing edges. This is verified in the following lemma.

LEMMA 15. *Consider a vertex u with a saturated outgoing edge e. Then for all other outgoing edges e' incident to u it holds that $\tau(e') = \tau_{\min}$.*

PROOF. Assume $\deg(u) > 1$ as otherwise there is nothing to prove. We prove the lemma by showing that

$$\sum_{e=(u,\cdot)\in E} \tau(e) \leq 1 + (\deg(u) - 2)\tau_{\min}.$$

This implies the claim since all $\deg(u) - 1$ non-saturated edges must have pheromone at most $\tau_{\min}$ for the upper bound to hold. Note that this upper bound improves upon Lemma 1 in Horoba and Sudholt [15] where only an upper bound of $1 + \deg(u)\tau_{\min}$ was proven.

We first show the following. Consider two pheromones τ_1, τ_2 and let τ_1', τ_2' denote their respective values after one pheromone update. If $\tau_1 + \tau_2 = 1$ and exactly one of these pheromones is reinforced then we claim that $\tau_1' + \tau_2' = 1$. In case τ_1' and τ_2' are not capped by pheromone borders, we have $\tau_1' + \tau_2' = (1 - \rho)(\tau_1 + \tau_2) + \rho = 1 - \rho + \rho = 1$. Otherwise, it is easy to verify that both pheromones hit pheromone borders: $\tau_1' = 1 - \tau_{\min} \Leftrightarrow \tau_2' = \tau_{\min}$ and the same holds when τ_1' and τ_2' are swapped. In this case we clearly have $\tau_1' + \tau_2' = 1 - \tau_{\min} + \tau_{\min} = 1$.

This argument proves the claim for $\deg(u) = 2$. For $\deg(u) > 2$ let $\tau_1, \ldots, \tau_{\deg(u)}$ denote all pheromones on outgoing edges of u in order of decreasing pheromones. Assume inductively that the sum of pheromones is bounded by $1 + (\deg(u) - 2)\tau_{\min}$; note that this property is true at initialization as there the sum equals 1. The sum of next pheromones is maximized if as many non-reinforced pheromones are at the lower border $\tau_{\min}$ as possible. This corresponds to $\tau_3 = \cdots = \tau_{\deg(u)} = \tau_{\min}$ and either τ_1 or τ_2 being reinforced. Due to our assumption, $\tau_1 + \tau_2 \leq 1$, hence by our previous arguments $\tau_1' + \tau_2' \leq 1$. The sum of new pheromones is hence at most $1 + (\deg(u) - 2)\tau_{\min}$. $\square$

Using this lemma, we arrive at the following result.

THEOREM 16. *Consider an iterative coupling of two Markov chains X and Y representing an MMAS algorithm on G. Let T_i be the random time (or a random variable that stochastically dominates it) until X and Y have saturated the same edge outgoing from i, given that X and Y have coupled in G_{i+1}. Then the mixing time of the algorithm is bounded by $O(\sum_{i=1}^{n-1} \mathrm{E}(T_i))$ and $O(\max\{\mathrm{E}(T_i)\} \cdot \mathrm{diam}(G) \log n)$.*

PROOF. By Lemma 15, $\mathrm{E}(T_i)$ is an upper bound on the expected coupling time for G_i under the given circumstances. Therefore, $\sum_{i=1}^{n-1} \mathrm{E}(T_i)$ is an upper bound on the expected coupling time for G. Using Corollary 4, along with Markov's inequality, the first upper bound on the mixing time follows.

The second bound follows from a layering argument: consider the set L_j of all vertices having a maximum number of j edges on their paths to the destination. Observe that when all vertices in $L_1, \ldots, L_{j-1}$ have coupled we can use the previous arguments to estimate the time until a fixed vertex in L_j becomes coupled. The expected time for this is at most $\max\{\mathrm{E}(T_i)\}$ and by Markov's inequality the probability of not having coupled in $2\max\{\mathrm{E}(T_i)\}$ iterations is at most $1/2$. Considering $(\log n) + 1$ periods of this length each, the probability of not having coupled is at most $1/(2n)$

for any fixed vertex in L_j. By the union bound, the probability that any vertex in L_j is not coupled is at most $1/2$. As the expected number of trials is at most 2, the bound $2((\log n) + 1) \cdot 2 \max\{\mathrm{E}(T_i)\}$ follows. Adding these times for all $\mathrm{diam}(G)$ layers proves the second bound. $\square$

A complete analysis of iteration-best MMAS algorithms is beyond the scope of this work. The purpose here is to illustrate how couplings can be used for bounding the mixing time in a setting where not all components are independent. The ansatz presented here may be used as a basis for future analyses. So we only sketch how one could continue to bound the coupling time of single vertices and arrive at a complete analysis.

If the ant system is parametrized so that it shows a rather chaotic behavior, which occurs for large ρ, one might hope to saturate a specific edge simply because the ant system might by chance only construct ant solutions that start with this edge, until the edge becomes saturated. This resembles the notion of a *landslide sequence* for pheromones used in [37]. Indeed, it is not difficult to prove a polynomial bound for the mixing time of an iteration-best MMAS system with λ ants if $\lambda/\rho = O(\log n)$.

On the other hand, in a setting where there is good guidance towards finding shortest paths and shortest paths are unique, we might experience a drift towards increasing pheromones on the unique first edge of a shortest path. This, in turn, might be transformed into an upper bound for the time until the edge becomes saturated.

Drift analysis can also be key for analyzing the stationary distribution. Already the famous work by Hajek [12] has established occupation time bounds for all considered states. Simply speaking, in the presence of a drift the probability of being in a specific state decreases exponentially with the distance from the state the drift is pointing to. This can then in turn be used to lower-bound the probability of being at a large distance and to show that the closest states (i. e., high pheromones on the edges of a shortest path) have a large probability mass in the stationary distribution. With this argument, an upper bound on the expected time until shortest paths are found can be shown.

This way of reasoning might also prove useful for iteration-best MMAS in pseudo-Boolean optimization as the upper bound in Neumann et al. [37] is based on a positive drift for all bits.

7. CONCLUSIONS

Mixing time estimations and coupling techniques can be applied to the analysis of randomized search heuristics. We have demonstrated this for ant colony optimization where the Markov chain reflects a pheromone model with continuous components. We have seen how MMAS deals with plateaus in pseudo-Boolean spaces and subspaces and discussed how to estimate the mixing time of MMAS systems for shortest paths in directed acyclic graphs.

We expect the presented techniques to find further applications for the analysis of bio-inspired search heuristics. This includes further probabilistic model-building algorithms such as estimation-of-distribution algorithms as well as particle swarm optimization and evolutionary algorithms. The latter class of algorithms is particularly relevant in the light of recent considerations of non-elitist environmental selection schemes [13, 19, 23, 36]. As these algorithms naturally converge to a non-trivial stationary distribution (in a sense that stationarity is not equivalent to being in a global optimum), Markov chain Monte Carlo techniques may lead to running time estimations where common techniques for elitist algorithms break down.

Acknowledgments

The author was partially supported by a postdoctoral fellowship from the German Academic Exchange Service while visiting the International Computer Science Institute in Berkeley, CA, USA and EPSRC grant EP/D052785/1. The author thanks Alistair Sinclair for an exciting lecture on Markov chain Monte Carlo techniques and Thomas Sauerwald for references and insightful discussions on whether the results in Section 5 can be improved. Thanks also go to Benjamin Doerr for advice on Markov chains with countably infinite states and to Christine Zarges and Daniel Johannsen for many useful comments on the presentation.

References

[1] D. Aldous and J. Fill. *Reversible Markov Chains and Random Walks on Graphs*. Monograph in preparation, `http://stat-www.berkeley.edu/users/aldous/RWG/book.html`, 2010.

[2] N. Attiratanasunthron and J. Fakcharoenphol. A running time analysis of an ant colony optimization algorithm for shortest paths in directed acyclic graphs. *Information Processing Letters*, 105(3):88–92, 2008.

[3] B. Doerr and D. Johannsen. Refined runtime analysis of a basic ant colony optimization algorithm. In *Proceedings of the Congress of Evolutionary Computation (CEC '07)*, pages 501–507. IEEE Press, 2007.

[4] B. Doerr, M. Gnewuch, N. Hebbinghaus, and F. Neumann. A rigorous view on neutrality. In *Proceedings of the Congress of Evolutionary Computation (CEC '07)*, pages 2591–2597. IEEE Press, 2007.

[5] B. Doerr, F. Neumann, D. Sudholt, and C. Witt. On the runtime analysis of the 1-ANT ACO algorithm. In *Proceedings of the Genetic and Evolutionary Computation Conference (GECCO '07)*, pages 33–40. ACM, 2007.

[6] M. Dorigo and C. Blum. Ant colony optimization theory: A survey. *Theoretical Computer Science*, 344:243–278, 2005.

[7] M. Dorigo and T. Stützle. *Ant Colony Optimization*. MIT Press, 2004.

[8] S. Droste, T. Jansen, and I. Wegener. Upper and lower bounds for randomized search heuristics in black-box optimization. *Theory of Computing Systems*, 39(4):525–544, 2006.

[9] J. Garnier, L. Kallel, and M. Schoenauer. Rigorous hitting times for binary mutations. *Evolutionary Computation*, 7(2):173–203, 1999.

[10] W. J. Gutjahr. First steps to the runtime complexity analysis of ant colony optimization. *Computers and Operations Research*, 35(9):2711–2727, 2008.

[11] W. J. Gutjahr and G. Sebastiani. Runtime analysis of ant colony optimization with best-so-far reinforcement. *Methodology and Computing in Applied Probability*, 10:409–433, 2008.

[12] B. Hajek. Hitting-time and occupation-time bounds implied by drift analysis with applications. *Advances in Applied Probability*, 14:502–525, 1982.

[13] E. Happ, D. Johannsen, C. Klein, and F. Neumann. Rigorous analyses of fitness-proportional selection for optimizing linear functions. In *Proceedings of the Genetic and Evolutionary Computation Conference (GECCO '08)*, pages 953–960. ACM, 2008.

[14] T. P. Hayes, J. C. Vera, and E. Vigoda. Randomly coloring planar graphs with fewer colors than the maximum degree. In *STOC '07: Proceedings of the thirty-ninth annual ACM symposium on Theory of computing*, pages 450–458. ACM, 2007.

[15] C. Horoba and D. Sudholt. Running time analysis of ACO systems for shortest path problems. In *Proceedings of Engineering Stochastic Local Search Algorithms (SLS '09)*, volume 5752 of *LNCS*, pages 76–91. Springer, 2009.

[16] C. Horoba and D. Sudholt. Ant colony optimization for stochastic shortest path problems. In *Proceedings of the Genetic and Evolutionary Computation Conference (GECCO '10)*, pages 1465–1472, 2010.

[17] M. Jerrum and A. Sinclair. The Markov chain Monte Carlo method: an approach to approximate counting and integration. In *Approximation Algorithms for NP-hard Problems*, pages 482–520. PWS Publishing, 1996.

[18] M. Jerrum, A. Sinclair, and E. Vigoda. A polynomial-time approximation algorithm for the permanent of a matrix with nonnegative entries. *Journal of the ACM*, 51(4):671–697, 2004.

[19] J. Jägersküpper and T. Storch. When the plus strategy outperforms the comma strategy – and when not. In *Proceedings of the 2007 IEEE Symposium on Foundations of Computational Intelligence (FOCI '07)*, pages 25–32. IEEE, 2007.

[20] T. Kötzing, P. K. Lehre, P. S. Oliveto, and F. Neumann. Ant colony optimization and the minimum cut problem. In *Proceedings of the Genetic and Evolutionary Computation Conference (GECCO '10)*, pages 1393–1400. ACM, 2010.

[21] T. Kötzing, F. Neumann, H. Röglin, and C. Witt. Theoretical properties of two ACO approaches for the traveling salesman problem. In *Seventh International Conference on Ant Colony Optimization and Swarm Intelligence (ANTS '10)*, volume 6234 of *LNCS*, pages 324–335. Springer, 2010.

[22] J. Lässig and D. Sudholt. The benefit of migration in parallel evolutionary algorithms. In *Proceedings of the Genetic and Evolutionary Computation Conference (GECCO '10)*, pages 1105–1112, 2010.

[23] P. K. Lehre and X. Yao. On the impact of the mutation-selection balance on the runtime of evolutionary algorithms. In *FOGA '09: Proceedings of the tenth ACM SIGEVO workshop on Foundations of genetic algorithms*, pages 47–58. ACM, 2009.

[24] D. A. Levin, Y. Peres, and E. L. Wilmer. *Markov Chains and Mixing Times*. American Mathematical Society, 2008.

[25] J. Liu. *Monte Carlo Strategies in Scientific Computing*. Springer, 2002.

[26] L. Lovász and S. Vempala. Simulated annealing in convex bodies and an $O^*(n^4)$ volume algorithm. *Journal of Computer and System Sciences*, 72(2):392–417, 2006.

[27] B. Mitavskiy, J. E. Rowe, A. H. Wright, and L. M. Schmitt. Quotients of Markov chains and asymptotic properties of the stationary distribution of the Markov chain associated to an evolutionary algorithm. *Genetic Programming and Evolvable Machines*, 9(2):109–123, 2008.

[28] M. Mitzenmacher and E. Upfal. *Probability and Computing*. Cambridge University Press, 2005.

[29] F. Neumann and I. Wegener. Randomized local search, evolutionary algorithms, and the minimum spanning tree problem. *Theoretical Computer Science*, 378(1):32–40, 2007.

[30] F. Neumann and C. Witt. Runtime analysis of a simple ant colony optimization algorithm. In *Proceedings of the 17th International Symposium on Algorithms and Computation (ISAAC '06)*, volume 4288 of *LNCS*, pages 618–627. Springer, 2006.

[31] F. Neumann and C. Witt. Ant Colony Optimization and the minimum spanning tree problem. In *Proceedings of Learning and Intelligent Optimization (LION '07)*, volume 5313 of *LNCS*, pages 153–166. Springer, 2008.

[32] F. Neumann and C. Witt. Runtime analysis of a simple ant colony optimization algorithm. *Algorithmica*, 54(2):243–255, 2009.

[33] F. Neumann, D. Sudholt, and C. Witt. Comparing variants of MMAS ACO algorithms on pseudo-Boolean functions. In *Proceedings of Engineering Stochastic Local Search Algorithms (SLS '07)*, volume 4638 of *LNCS*, pages 61–75. Springer, 2007.

[34] F. Neumann, D. Sudholt, and C. Witt. Rigorous analyses for the combination of ant colony optimization and local search. In *Proceedings of the Sixth International Conference on Ant Colony Optimization and Swarm Intelligence (ANTS '08)*, volume 5217 of *LNCS*, pages 132–143. Springer, 2008.

[35] F. Neumann, P. S. Oliveto, and C. Witt. Theoretical analysis of fitness-proportional selection: landscapes and efficiency. In *GECCO '09: Proceedings of the 11th Annual conference on Genetic and evolutionary computation*, pages 835–842. ACM, 2009.

[36] F. Neumann, D. Sudholt, and C. Witt. Analysis of different MMAS ACO algorithms on unimodal functions and plateaus. *Swarm Intelligence*, 3(1):35–68, 2009.

[37] F. Neumann, D. Sudholt, and C. Witt. A few ants are enough: ACO with iteration-best update. In *Proceedings of the Genetic and Evolutionary Computation Conference (GECCO '10)*, pages 63–70. ACM, 2010.

[38] S. Sanyal, R. S, and S. Biswas. Necessary and sufficient conditions for success of the metropolis algorithm for optimization. In *Proceedings of the Genetic and Evolutionary Computation Conference (GECCO '10)*, pages 1417–1424. ACM, 2010.

[39] C. Witt. Rigorous runtime analysis of swarm intelligence algorithms – an overview. In *Swarm Intelligence for Multi-objective Problems in Data Mining*, volume 242/2009 of *Studies in Computational Intelligence*, pages 157–177. Springer, 2009.

[40] Y. Zhou. Runtime analysis of an ant colony optimization algorithm for TSP instances. *IEEE Transactions on Evolutionary Computation*, 13(5):1083–1092, 2009.

Abstract Convex Evolutionary Search

Alberto Moraglio
School of Computing and Centre for Reasoning
University of Kent, Canterbury, UK
A.Moraglio@kent.ac.uk

ABSTRACT

Geometric crossover is a formal class of crossovers which
includes many well-known recombination operators across
representations. In this paper, we present a general result
showing that all evolutionary algorithms using geometric
crossover with no mutation perform the same form of convex
search regardless of the underlying representation, the specific selection mechanism, the specific offspring distribution,
the specific search space, and the problem at hand. We then
start investigating a few representation/space-independent
geometric conditions on the fitness landscape – various forms
of generalized concavity – that when matched with the convex evolutionary search guarantee, to different extents, improvement of offspring over parents for any choice of parents.
This is a first step towards showing that the convexity relation between search and landscape may play an important
role towards explaining the performance of evolutionary algorithms in a general setting across representations.

Categories and Subject Descriptors

I.2.8 [**Artificial Intelligence**]: Problem Solving, Control
Methods, and Search; G.1.6 [**Numerical Analysis**]: Op-
timization; F.2 [**Analysis of Algorithms and Problem
Complexity**]

General Terms

Theory

1. INTRODUCTION

In the research community there is a strong feeling that
the Evolutionary Computation (EC) field needs unification
and systematization in a rational framework to survive its
own success (De Jong [4]).

The various flavors of evolutionary algorithms (EAs) look
very similar when cleared of algorithmically irrelevant differences such as domain of application, phenotype interpretation and representation-independent algorithmic character-

istics that, in effect, can be freely exchanged between algorithms, such as the selection scheme. Ultimately, the origin
of the differences of the various flavors of evolutionary algorithms is rooted in the solution representation and relative
genetic operators.

Are these differences only superficial? Is there a deeper
unity encompassing all evolutionary algorithms beyond the
specific representation? Formally, is a general mathematical framework that unifies search operators for all solution
representations possible at all? Would such a general framework be able to capture essential properties encompassing
all EAs or would it be too abstract to say anything useful?
These are important, difficult open research questions which
the present paper attempts to start attacking.

A number of researchers have been pursuing EC unification across representations. Although, so far, no one has
been able to build a fully-fledged theory of representations.
For example, Radcliffe pioneered a unified theory of representations [12], although he never used the word "unification"; Poli unified the schema theorem for traditional genetic
algorithms and genetic programming [6]; Stephens suggested
that all evolutionary algorithms can be unified using the language of dynamical systems and coarse graining [18]; while
Rothlauf initiated a less formal theory of representations
[14]; Rowe et al., building upon Radcliffe's work, have de-
vised a theory of representation based on group theory [15];
Stadler et al. built a theory of fitness landscapes that connects with representations and search operators [13].

In the last decade, EC theory has experienced important
progress. However, the lack of a unified formal framework
encompassing different solution representations is at the origin of the fragmentation of evolutionary computation theory,
which has led to the development of significantly different
theories for different representations and for different problems. This fragmentation is symptomatic of the fact that
the very fundamental working principles underlying all evolutionary algorithms are not yet well understood. More fundamentally, the lack of a uniform formal language encompassing all representations prevents us from investigating
whether such common principles exist at all.

Recent research [9] has shown that a common geometric
framework is possible and that most of mutation and recombination operators across representations admit surprisingly simple common geometric characterizations, termed
geometric mutation and geometric crossover, based on an
axiomatic notion of distance. The geometric view of search
operators formalizes and simplifies the relationship between
representations, search operators and associated distance,

and it equates their induced search space and fitness landscape to the traditional notions of neighbourhood space and fitness landscape.

In this paper, we start building a representation-independent theory of evolutionary algorithms starting from the definition of geometric crossover [1]. The methodology used is based on *mathematical abstraction* (see for example [8][1]): it voluntarily ignores representation/search space specific properties of geometric crossover, and uses only those properties of geometric crossover which derive from the distance axioms, which are therefore common to all geometric crossovers across representations. Abstraction results in unification as a theory is obtained that applies to any representation and search space.

Abstraction is the key to showing that all evolutionary algorithms present a common behavioral core. In this paper, we will show that they all do the same type of convex search [2]. Naturally, those properties that a geometric crossover has by virtue of the nature of the specific class of underlying representation and search space are not within the scope of a theory of abstract search. Those properties are reserved for special investigation. To investigate such specific properties systematically within a general framework, a possible scenario consists of creating a hierarchy of less and less abstract spaces (a taxonomy of metric spaces) organized according to those characteristics that allow us to prove stronger and stronger statements on the performance of an evolutionary algorithm when specified to them. As convexity will appear to be a key element in evolutionary search, fundamental properties to consider may be the so called convexity numbers [20](e.g., Radon number and Helly number) that characterize at a more finely-grained scale the specific convexity of the underlying spaces. These numbers then would appear as parameters of a general relation characterizing the performance of an evolutionary algorithm as a function of the characteristics of the underlying space. This approach to a general theory of evolutionary algorithms follows, in spirit, the philosophy proposed by Stephens and Zamora [18] based on the notions of universality and taxonomy but it operates at a higher level of abstraction.

The convex search result is significant as it shows that indeed there is a common behavioral identity of all evolutionary algorithms that goes beyond the underlying representation. However, this result *per se* does not show that a meaningful general theory of evolutionary algorithms may be possible. Indeed, the NFL theorem [21] implies that a search algorithm must be well-matched with a certain class of fitness landscapes respecting some conditions to perform on average better than random search. As a consequence, any non-futile theory which aims at proving performance better than random search of a class of search algorithms needs to indicate with respect to what class of fitness landscapes. Therefore, an important question is: are there general conditions on the fitness landscape that guarantee good performances of the convex search for any space/representation?

Interestingly, the abstract convex search of an evolutionary algorithm suggests representation/space independent geometric conditions on the fitness landscape – various forms of generalized concavity – that guarantee to various extents that offspring improve over parents for any choice of the parents. This is an important property that links the topography of the fitness landscape with the parent/offspring fitness heritability throughout the evolutionary process. This shows that the underlying convexity relation between search and landscape *per se* may play a key role towards explaining the performance of evolutionary algorithms in a representation-independent fashion. In this paper, we consider a number of generalizations of the notion of concave function and approximately concave function to general metric spaces and start investigating their suitability as classes of fitness landscapes to employ as a basis for a theory of abstract convex evolutionary search.

In the long term, this theoretical framework may have interesting links with the theory of convex optimization [3], in which the notion of convexity of sets and functions is central. Most of the results in convex optimization pertain to continuous optimization, but there is ongoing research aimed at generalizing the results for continuous spaces to discrete spaces [11]. There are, however, at least two important differences between the generalized notion of convexity in convex optimization and that of the present paper: (i) in convex optimization, the discrete spaces considered for the generalization are restricted to spaces of integer vectors, rather than being general metric spaces encompassing, as important special case, combinatorial spaces based on structured representations (e.g., trees) as, instead, it is intended in the present work; (ii) in convex optimization, the generalization of convex function focuses on preserving and exploiting the property of traditional convex function of being unimodal, so that local and global optima always coincide. Instead the emphasis of the present work is on generalizing the notion of convex trend in the attempt to provide a formalization of the well-known notion of global convexity of the fitness landscape [2] that is known experimentally to be beneficial for the performance of evolutionary algorithms. This would make a theory based on the framework started in this paper of practical relevance because fitness landscapes normally associated with many important combinatorial problems have been shown to be globally convex [7].

It is worth mentioning that the results presented in this paper may look deceptively simple at first. On one hand, they are perfectly aligned with the geometric intuition everyone has about the Euclidean space. On the other hand, they are very general as they apply to general metric spaces and across representations. The latter aspect is non-trivial as only very few properties of the Euclidean space hold for general metric spaces. Many other properties break down, often in unexpected ways, in the transition from specific to more general spaces. An important contribution of this paper is to present results that derive only from those intuitive properties of the Euclidean space that hold for general metric spaces, so that their geometric intuition can be retained in the general context. This is insightful and allows us, for example, to apply the same geometric reasoning on continuous spaces and combinatorial spaces, even if in many respects they are very different types of spaces. The chal-

---

[1] In this paper, we do not consider mutation, not because we consider it an unimportant operator, but rather because the dynamics of the resulting search cannot be described purely in geometric terms. Mutation requires a more complex theoretical framework which combines abstract geometry with measure-theoretic elements. We leave this as future work.

[2] This property might be the only one all evolutionary algorithms with geometric crossover have in common. Nonetheless, this is an important property as it may be central to explain their performance in a unified way.

lenge in this line of theory is choosing appropriate general definitions that shape the framework and that allow us to generalize theorems holding for the Euclidean space in a natural and straightforward way.

2. ABSTRACT CONVEXITY

In this section we introduce two notions of abstract convexity, which are obtained by generalising the traditional notion of convex set in different directions, and show how they are related. Both notions of convexity and their relations are necessary to prove the results in the subsequent sections.

2.1 Preliminaries: Balls and Segments

A metric is a generalization of the notion of distance. A metric space is a set X with a distance function d (the metric) that, for every two points x and y in X, gives the distance between them as a nonnegative real number $d(x, y)$. A metric space must also satisfy:

1. $d(x, y) = 0$ iff $x = y$

2. $d(x, y) = d(y, x)$

3. $d(x, z) + d(z, y) \geq d(x, y)$ for all z in X

Given a metric space $M = (X, d)$ the *line segment* between x and y, termed extremes, is the set $[x, y]_d = \{z \in X | d(x, z) + d(z, y) = d(x, y)\}$, and the *closed ball* is the set $B_d(x; r) = \{y \in S | d(x, y) \leq r\}$ where r is a positive real number called the *radius* of the ball. Examples of balls and segments for different spaces are shown in Figure 1. Note how the same set can have different geometries (see Euclidean and Manhattan spaces) and how segments can have more than one pair of extremes. For instance, in the Hamming space, a segment coincides with a hypercube and the number of extremes varies with the length of the segment, while in the Manhattan space, a segment is a rectangle and it has two pairs of extremes. Also, a segment is not necessarily "slim", that is, it may include points that are not on the boundaries. Furthermore, a segment does not coincide with a shortest path connecting its extremes (*geodesic*). In general, there may be more than one geodesic connecting two extremes.

2.2 Definition of Abstract Convexity

In the Euclidean space, a set is convex iff the line segment connecting any two points in the set lies entirely in the set. A natural way of generalizing the notion of convex set to more general spaces is to generalize the notion of line segment and define convex sets using the relation above as its defining property, as follows.

The *abstract geodetic convexity* [20] $\mathcal{C}$ on X induced by M is the collection of geodetically-convex subsets of X, where a subset C of X is geodetically-convex provided $[x, y]_d \subseteq C$ for all x, y in C.

Using the definition above together with a specific distance d, one can, therefore, tell whether a set of points in the metric space endowed with the distance d is geodetically convex (with respect to that specific distance d). For example, in the Euclidean space, one can apply the definition of geodetic convexity with the Euclidean distance to see that the Euclidean ball is geodetically convex (with respect to the Euclidean distance, i.e., using the Euclidean segment).

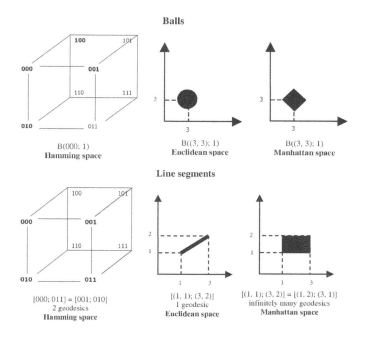

Figure 1: Examples of balls and segments

However, one can regard the notion of convex set from an abstract point of view by which a set of points in some *fixed but unspecified* metric space is geodetically convex with respect to the underlying (fixed but unspecified) distance associated with the metric space. An axiomatic approach to geodetically convex sets focuses on those properties of the collection of geodetically-convex sets that are independent on the specific distance considered and follow solely from the metric axioms and from the definition of abstract geodetic convexity *per se*. These properties are therefore valid for all metric spaces and associated space-specific geodetic convexities.

An alternative approach to generalizing the notion of convex set focuses on the property that the intersection of convex sets is a convex set, as follows. A family $\mathcal{X}$ of subsets of a set X is called *convexity on X* [20] if:

(C1) the empty set $\emptyset$ and the universal set X are in $\mathcal{X}$

(C2) if $\mathcal{D} \subseteq \mathcal{X}$ is non-empty, then $\bigcap \mathcal{D} \in \mathcal{X}$

(C3) $\mathcal{D} \subseteq \mathcal{X}$ is non-empty and totally ordered by inclusion, then $\bigcup \mathcal{D} \in \mathcal{X}$.

The pair $(X, \mathcal{X})$ is called *convex structure*. The members of $\mathcal{X}$ are called *convex sets*. By the axiom (C1) a subset A of X of the convex structure is included in at least one convex set, namely X. From axiom (C2), A is included in a smallest convex set, the *convex hull* of A: $co(A) = \bigcap\{C | A \subseteq C \in \mathcal{X}\}$. The convex hull of a finite set is called a *polytope*. The axiom (C3) requires *domain finiteness* of the convex hull operator: a set C is convex iff it includes $co(F)$ for each finite subset F of C. The following properties of the convex hull operator [20] will be useful:

(P1) $\forall A \subseteq X, co(co(A)) = co(A)$

(P2) $\forall A, B \subseteq X$, if $A \subseteq B$ then $co(A) \subseteq co(B)$

(P3) $\forall A, B \subseteq X$, if $A \subseteq co(B)$ then $co(A) \subseteq co(B)$

The two notions of convexity above are related as the collection $\mathcal{C}$ of geodetically convex sets under any metric d meet the convexity axioms. Notice, however, that if co denotes the convex hull operator of $\mathcal{C}$, then $\forall a, b \in X : [a, b]_d \subseteq co\{a, b\}$. So, there are metric spaces in which metric segments are not geodetically convex (i.e., in some spaces segments do not equal their convex hulls). In other words, an abstract metric segment is not necessarily geodetically convex. Also, there are metric spaces in which balls are not geodetically convex (e.g., in the Manhattan space, the Manhattan ball is not geodetically convex as the Manhattan segment between some pairs of points of the Manhattan ball is not completely included in the Manhattan ball). This exemplifies an important point: whereas the notion of abstract convexity appeals to the geometric intuition we all have for the Euclidean space, many familiar properties of the convexity in the Euclidean space do not hold across all metric spaces, hence do not hold for the abstract analogue of familiar shapes.

2.3 Euclidean and Hamming Convexities

When we specify the Euclidean distance in the definition of abstract geodesic convexity we obtain the traditional convexity for the Euclidean space [20]. However, the convexity for this space is not normally cast in terms of relations on distances between points (which we term *geometric characterization*) as the one obtained directly from the definition of geodesic convexity. Rather, it is expressed equivalently in algebraic terms using algebraic operations – sums of vectors and scalar products – which are well-defined on the Euclidean space but not on general metric spaces (which we term *algebraic characterization*). Naturally, this two-fold characterization is made possible for the case of the Euclidean space as there is a natural one-to-one correspondence between points in space and real vectors (i.e., their cartesian coordinates). The algebraic characterization of convex sets and related notions for the Euclidean space is as follows. A point p is in the convex hull of a set of points S iff the coordinates of p can be obtained by a convex combination of the coordinates of the points in S. The segment between two points is the convex hull of its extremes (i.e., segments in the Euclidean space are convex).

Analogously to the Euclidean case, when we specify the Hamming distance on binary strings in the definition of abstract geodesic convexity we obtain the specific convexity for this space. Also in this case, we can characterize the convexity equivalently in algebraic terms using operations and notations which are well-defined on the underlying representation of points in space, which is, on binary strings. The algebraic characterization of convex sets and related notions for the Hamming space is as follows. Let $H(a, b)$ be the schema obtained from the binary strings a and b by position-wise inserting a '*' symbol where they mismatch and inserting the common bit otherwise (e.g., $H(0101, 1001) = **01$). By abuse of notation, we consider a schema as being both a template and the set of strings matching the template. The binary string c is in the Hamming segment between the binary strings a and b iff c matches the schema $H(a, b)$ (e.g., 0001 is in the segment $[0101, 1001]$ as it matches the

schema $**01$ which can be verified using the definition of segment $d(0101, 0001) + d(0001, 1001) = d(0101, 1001)$). Every segment in the Hamming space is convex, because for $c, d \in H(a, b)$ the schema $H(c, d)$ can be obtained by changing some of the '*' symbols in $H(a, b)$ to 0 or 1, hence it is more specific than $H(a, b)$ (i.e., $H(c, d) \subseteq H(a, b)$). Every schema is a convex set as it corresponds to a segment between some pair of binary strings belonging to it. Every convex set is a schema because the set of all Hamming segments form the convexity structure on the Hamming space, as it is the product convexity of the trivial metric space [20]. Consequently, the intersection of two schemata is a schema or the empty set (e.g., $**101 \cap 1**01 = 1*101$) and the convex hull of a set of binary strings is the smallest schema (the schema matching the minimum number of strings) matching all of them (e.g., $co(0101, 1001, 0000) = **0*$). In summary, in the Hamming space, the notions of segment, convex set and schema essentially coincide.

3. CONVEX EVOLUTIONARY SEARCH

3.1 Geometric operators

Geometric operators are search operators defined using geometric shapes to characterize the spatial relation between parents and offspring in the search space. Importantly, the shapes considered are defined in terms of distances between points in space. The geometric view of search operators formalizes and simplifies the relationship between representations, search operators and associated distance, and it equates their induced search space and fitness landscape to the traditional notions of neighbourhood space and fitness landscape.

DEFINITION 1. *(Geometric crossover [10]) A recombination operator is a geometric crossover under the metric d if all offspring are in the d-metric segment between its parents.*

In a similar vein, geometric mutation is defined geometrically requiring that offspring are in a d-ball of a certain radius centered in the parent.

Notice that the definition is *representation-independent*, hence well-defined for any representation, as it depends on the underlying specific representation only indirectly via the metric d which is defined on the representation. This class of operators is really broad [3] [9]. For vectors of reals, various types of blend or line crossovers are geometric crossovers under Euclidean distance, and box recombinations and discrete recombinations are geometric crossovers under Manhattan distance. For binary and multary strings, all mask-based crossovers are geometric under Hamming distance. For permutations, PMX and Cycle crossover are geometric under swap distance and merge crossover is geometric under adjacent swap distance; other crossovers for permutations are also geometric. For genetic program trees, the family of homologous crossovers is geometric under structural Hamming distance. For biological sequences, various homologous recombinations that resemble more closely biological recombination at molecular level (as they align variable-length sequences on their contents, rather than position-wise, before

---

[3]The class of geometric crossover does not fully exhaust the range of crossover operators in common use. For example, sub-tree swap crossover for genetic program trees is provably not a geometric crossover under any metric.

swapping genetic material) are geometric under Levenshtein distance. Recombinations for several more complex representations are also geometric.

A more fine-grained definition of geometric crossover is possible by specifying a specific probability distribution of the offspring on the segment. For example, the uniform geometric crossover is defined as returning offspring sampled uniformly at random in the segment between parents. Uniform crossover on binary strings is known to be uniform geometric crossover for the Hamming distance [10]. The blend crossover on real vectors that samples offspring vectors uniformly at random in the line segment between parents is uniform geometric crossover for the Euclidean distance. Defining well-behaved probability distributions on general metric spaces needs a digression into measure theory and it is out of the scope of this framework. Pragmatically, uniform geometric crossover is well-defined on those metric spaces that admit a well-behaved notion of uniform distribution on segments, otherwise it is not definable. For most of the search spaces of interest uniform geometric crossover is well-defined.

A special class of probability distributions over the segment is that in which the probability of sampling an offspring z is a function of the distance $d(x, z)$ and $d(y, z)$ from its parents x and y. In this case, the points in the segment at the same distance from x are grouped into level sets according to the distance to x. This forms a partitioning on the points in the segment. Notice that any level set contains at least a point of the segment. So, if there are no points in the segment for a certain distance from the parent x, then there is no corresponding level set. Then the probability distribution specifies the probability of selecting a level set and then an offspring is sampled uniformly at random from the selected level set. For example, we could have a probability distribution that assigns the same probability of being selected to any level set i.e., one over the number of existing level sets in the segment. Note that this distribution equals the uniform geometric crossover in the Euclidean space (by appropriately considering limits and probability densities) as there is a single point at each distance level. However, it does not coincide to the uniform geometric crossover in the Hamming space as distance sets have different sizes (binomially distributed in the distance to the end-points of the segment).

Another special class of probability distributions over the segment is that of symmetric distribution probability in which the probability of obtaining the offspring z from the (ordered pair of) parents x and y is the same as when the role of the parents is reversed, i.e., $Pr(z|(x, y)) = Pr(z|(y, x))$. In practice, as the role of the parents as first or second parent is assigned at random with the same probability, the crossover operator can be always considered symmetric with probability distribution $f(z|x, y) = f(z|(x, y)) = f(z|(y, x)) = (Pr(z|(x, y)) + Pr(z|(y, x)))/2$.

3.2 Formal evolutionary algorithm and abstract evolutionary search

Geometric crossover and geometric mutation can be understood as functional forms taking the distance function d as a parameter. Therefore, we can see an evolutionary algorithm using these geometric operators as a function of the metric d too. That is, d can be considered as a parameter of the algorithm like any others, such as the mutation

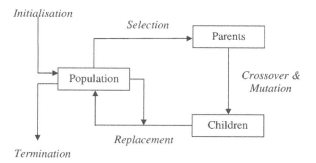

Figure 2: Evolutionary algorithm at a population level.

rate. However, notice the difference in the complexity of the objects passed as parameter: the mutation rate parameter takes values in the interval $[0, 1]$, that is, it is a simple real number, whereas the metric parameter takes values in the set of metrics, that is, it is a whole space.

We can now look at an evolutionary algorithm as a function of the distance d from an abstract point of view. To do this, we do not consider any metric in particular and we treat an evolutionary algorithm using geometric operators as a formal specification of a representation/space independent algorithm with a well-defined formal semantic arising from the metric axioms only. The transition to this more general point of view is analogous to the transition from geodesic convexity with respect to a specific metric space to the notion of abstract geodesic convexity. We refer to an evolutionary algorithm seen according to the latter interpretation as a *formal evolutionary algorithm*. A different notion of formal search algorithm based on equivalence classes was introduced by Radcliffe and Surry [19].

Normally, an algorithm can actually be run only when all its parameters have been assigned a value. We call an algorithm with all its parameters specified, a fully-specified algorithm. However, a formal model of the algorithm can be used to infer the behavior of a partially specified algorithm in which some parameters are left unspecified. In other words, using a formal model one can "run" a partially specified algorithm and infer its abstract behavior, i.e., those behavioral properties common to all specific behaviors obtained by assigning all possible specific values to the parameter left unspecified. We term *abstract evolutionary search* the behavior of a formal evolutionary algorithm in which the underlying metric d is unspecified. As this behavior is inferred from the formal evolutionary algorithm and the metric axioms only, *it is the behavior of the formal evolutionary algorithm on all possible search spaces and associated representations.*

The abstract behavior of a formal evolutionary algorithm is an axiomatic object itself based on the metric axioms. In the following sections, we will show that the behavior of a formal evolutionary algorithm can be profitably described axiomatically using the language of abstract convexity.

3.3 Genetic operators at a population level

An evolutionary algorithm can be seen as repeating a loop of operations at the population level (see Figure 2). The cycle selection-crossover-mutation-replacement can be seen as the sequential functional application of these operators to a population returning another population.

Let S be the search space and N be the set of natural numbers. A population is a multi-set in which each candidate solution can have multiple occurrences. The following population operators are presented very generally and probably could virtually cover any conceivable variant of evolutionary algorithm structure. The fitness function f and distance function d, which are parameters of the population operators, are fixed but unknown functions:

selection $OP_{SEL} : N^S \to N^S$: the selection operator is a possibly stochastic operator that takes in input a population and returns a population in which some of the elements have been reduced or increased in frequency and other have been eliminated according to some criteria, possibly fitness-based.

crossover $OP_{XO} : N^S \times N^S \to N^S$: the crossover operator at a population level is an operator that takes in input a population and returns a population of offspring obtained by applying any geometric crossover operator under d (with any probability distribution) to pairs of elements in the input population any number of times.

mutation $OP_{MUT} : N^S \to N^S$: the mutation operator at a population level is an operator that takes in input a population and returns a population of offspring obtained by applying any geometric mutation operator under d (with any probability distribution) to any element in the input population any number of times. The mutation is non-degenerate when it has non-zero probability of producing offspring different from parents.

replacement $OP_{REP} : N^S \times N^S \to 2^N$: the replacement operator is the sequential application of a merge operation, which merges the two population in input (union of multi-sets) followed by a selection operation.

3.4 Abstract convex search theorem

DEFINITION 2. *(Convex operator): let S be the solution set, an operator $OP : 2^S \to 2^S$ that takes a subset $P \subseteq S$ as input and returns a subset $OP(P) \subseteq S$ is a convex operator iff $\forall P \subseteq S : OP(P) \subseteq co(P)$*

The notions of abstract convexity and convex operators naturally extend to multisets and stochastic operators. The definition of convex operator extends to multisets substituting multisets with their underlying sets. The definition of convex operator extends to stochastic operators by substituting $OP(P)$, that is a random variable, with its support set $Im(OP(P))$ that is the set of elements that have probability non-zero to be returned by $OP(P)$.

THEOREM 1. *The composition of convex operators is a convex operator.*

PROOF. Let OP and OP' be two convex population operators and $OP'' = OP' \circ OP$. To prove that the composition of two convex operators is a convex operator we need to prove that $\forall P : OP(P) \subseteq co(P) \wedge OP'(P) \subseteq co(P) \longrightarrow OP''(P) = OP'(OP(P)) \subseteq co(P)$. By definition of convex population operator, it follows $OP(P) \subseteq co(P)$ and $OP'(OP(P)) \subseteq co(OP(P))$. From the property of convex hull $OP(P) \subseteq co(P)$ implies $co(OP(P)) \subseteq co(P)$. Hence, $OP'(OP(P)) \subseteq co(P)$. $\square$

THEOREM 2. *(Convexity of genetic operators at a population level) Selection, Crossover (as in Section 3.3) and Replacement (with the offspring population in the convex hull of the parent population) are convex population operators. Non-degenerate Mutation is not a convex operator.*

PROOF. *Selection*: let $P' = OP_{SEL}(P)$. As $P' \subseteq P$ by selection and $P \subseteq co(P)$ by a property of the convex hull then $OP_{SEL}(P) \subseteq co(P)$. Selection is a convex operator. *Crossover*: let $C = OP_{XO}(P)$. Every offspring in C is in the segment between two parents in P. For the geodesic convexity, for any $x, y \in P$ we have $[x, y] \subseteq co\{x, y\} \subseteq co(P)$, hence $OP_{XO}(P) = C \subseteq co(P)$. The crossover operator is a convex operator. *Replacement*: let $P' = OP_{REP}(P, C)$. We say that OP_{REP} is convex if when $C \subseteq co(P)$ then $OP_{REP}(P, C) \subseteq co(P)$. Since $C \subseteq co(P)$ then $co(P \cup C) \subseteq co(P \cup co(P)) = co(co(P)) = co(P)$, hence $P' = OP_{REP}(P, C) \subseteq co(P)$. The replacement operator is a convex operator. *Mutation*: every convex operator returns points within the convex hull of the input set. The convex hull of a single point is the single point itself. So, when the input set includes a single point, the output set of any convex operator must be the point itself. Mutation applied to a single point p may produce points different from p, hence it is not a convex operator. $\square$

THEOREM 3. *(Abstract convex evolutionary search) Let P_n be the population at time n. For any evolutionary algorithm repeating the cycle selection, crossover, replacement we have $co(P_{n+1}) \subseteq co(P_n) \subseteq \cdots \subseteq co(P_1) \subseteq co(P_0)$*

PROOF. The compound operator $OP = OP_{REP} \circ (OP_{ID}, OP_{XO} \circ OP_{SEL})$ that is equivalent to the sequential application of selection, crossover and replacement is a convex operator (OP_{ID} is the identity operator that outputs its own input). This is because OP_{SEL} and OP_{XO} are convex operators hence $OP_{XO} \circ OP_{SEL}$ is a convex operator for the composition of convex operators theorem. Hence OP_{REP} is also a convex operator because its second argument $OP_{XO} \circ OP_{SEL}$ is in the convex hull of its first argument OP_{ID}. Hence, for the composition of convex operators theorem, OP is a convex operator. Since $P_{n+1} = OP(P_n)$ then $P_{n+1} \subseteq co(P_n)$ and consequently $co(P_{n+1}) \subseteq co(P_n)$. Then the chain of nested inclusions is true by induction. $\square$

Theorem 3 is very general. *An evolutionary algorithm using geometric crossover with any probability distribution, any representation, any problem, any selection and replacement mechanism, does the same form of convex search.* Population size can vary over time and evolutionary search is still convex.

3.5 Convex evolutionary search in Euclidean and Hamming spaces

Theorem 3 applies to all metric spaces. It gives an abstract geometric description of the search that does not depend on any specific distance. In the following, we visualize the abstract convex search for the specific case of the 2-dimensional Euclidean space. This leads to a very simple and useful description of it which illustrates geometrically why the theorem 3 holds. Indeed, the geometric reason this theorem holds for the 2-dimensional Euclidean case is the same as the reason it holds in general metric spaces.

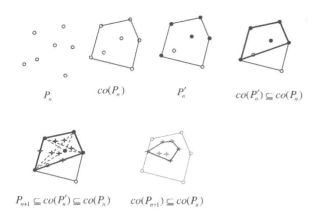

$$P_n \qquad co(P_n) \qquad P_n' \qquad co(P_n') \subseteq co(P_n)$$

$$P_{n+1} \subseteq co(P_n') \subseteq co(P_n) \qquad co(P_{n+1}) \subseteq co(P_n)$$

Figure 3: Convex Evolutionary Search.

Figure 3 illustrates the convex search. The hollow circles represent individuals in the population at time n, solid circles represent selected individuals (parents), while crosses represent individuals in the populations at time $n + 1$. The thin solid lines connecting hollow circles represent the boundaries of the convex hull formed by individuals in the population at time n. The thick solid lines connecting solid circles represent the boundaries of the convex hull formed by selected individuals from the population at time n. The solid lines connecting crosses represent the boundaries of the convex hull formed by individuals in the population at time $n + 1$. The broken lines connecting solid circles include all possible offspring of the selected individuals from the population at time n by applying geometric crossover (offspring are in the segment).

An evolutionary algorithm with mutation does not do convex search. It is the non-convexity of mutation that can cause the evolutionary search not to be convex as this allows for the possibility that an offspring can be produced outside the convex hull of the previous population.

The convex evolutionary search theorem shows that the convex hulls of the populations at successive iterations form a nested chain of inclusions. So, the search never diverges. Since the inclusions in the nested chain are not strict, the search either (i) converges to a fixed-point, or (ii) stops its convergence to a single set of points, e.g., for deterministic degenerate forms of selection, crossover and replacement that do not change the current population; or (iii) stops its convergence to a (possibly infinite) orbit of sets of points that have the same convex hull, e.g., when the individuals at the corners of the convex hull of the current population are always passed on to the next population, while the other individuals in the population are changed.

It is interesting to look at an example of the instantiation of the abstract convex search to the case of Hamming space on binary strings. Set $P_n = \{00010, 01100, 01110, 10000\}$. Then $co(P_n) = $ ****0. Selection is applied and say that only the last string is discarded, so the set of parents is $P_n' = \{00010, 01100, 01110\}$. Then $co(P_n') = $ 0***0 which gives 0***0 $\subseteq$ ****0. Recombination is then applied using the geometric crossover specified to the Hamming space (e.g., uniform crossover) and say we have the following recombinations: $CX(00010, 01100) \to 01110, 01000$, $CX(00010, 01110) \to 01010$ and $CX(01100, 01110) \to 01100$. Let us say we have a generational replacement scheme so

that the population of offspring replaces the population of parents, so $P_{n+1} = \{01110, 01000, 01010, 01100\}$. Then $P_{n+1} \subseteq co(P_n')$ as all offspring in P_{n+1} match the schema 0***0. Then $co(P_{n+1}) = $ 01**0 which gives $co(P_{n+1}) \subseteq co(P_n)$ as the schema 01**0 is more specific than the schema ****0.

4. CONVEX SEARCH AND CONCAVE FITNESS LANDSCAPE

4.1 Matching abstract search and abstract fitness landscape

The NFL theorem [21] implies that a search algorithm must be well-matched with a certain class of fitness landscapes respecting some conditions to perform on average better than random search. As a consequence, any non-futile theory which aims at proving performance better than random search of a class of search algorithms needs to indicate with respect to what class of fitness landscapes. Therefore, an important question is: are there general conditions on the fitness landscape that guarantee good performances of the convex search for any space/representation?

Since, at an abstract level, all evolutionary algorithms encompassed by the abstract evolutionary search theorem presents a unique behavior, it is reasonable to put forward the hypothesis that there should exist a general class of fitness landscapes that is well-matched to the evolutionary search as a whole. Otherwise stated, as evolutionary algorithms at heart present a common behavior, they should produce good performance on the same type of fitness landscape *for essentially the same underlying reason*. To make sense, the level of abstraction of the condition on the fitness landscape characterizing this class of fitness landscapes, whatever this class could be, must match the level of abstraction of the evolutionary search. So, the definition of the condition must be based on the distance of the search space, but, like the abstract convex search, it must be meaningful *per se* without referring to any specific distance. In other words, it must be a condition that matches convex search and fitness landscape at an abstract level. Figure 4 illustrates the envisioned functional relationship between search algorithm (SA), fitness landscape (FL), search behavior (SB) and search performance (SP) and their abstract counter-parts, formal search algorithm (FSA), abstract fitness landscape (AFL), abstract search behavior (ABS) and abstract search performance (ASP). The horizontal arrows in the bottom means that the algorithm SA is fed with the parameter fitness landscape FL which when run together give rise to the search behavior SB that produces the search performance SP. The horizontal arrows in the top mirror those in the bottom and depict analogous relations at an abstract level in which the underlying distance d is left unspecified. The vertical arrows relate abstract and concrete levels by functional application of the functional forms in the top with a specific distance d.

In the following sections, we will start investigating how to define classes of abstract fitness landscapes and how they affect abstract performance when matched with the abstract convex search. Abstract performance can be constant with the parameter d and hold across all metric spaces unchanged, or can be a general expression in which specific character-

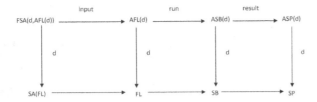

Figure 4: Functional relations between search algorithm, fitness landscape, search behavior, search performance and their abstract counter-parts.

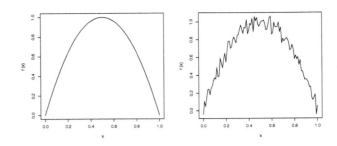

Figure 5: Examples of concave function (left) and function with a concave trend (right).

istics of the underlying metric d (e.g., dimensionality) are used as parameters.

4.2 Concave fitness landscapes

In this and in the following sections, we will explore several notions of concave fitness landscape progressively improving the scope of application.

The convex search of an evolutionary algorithm suggests a class of functions, which *suitably generalized*, could give rise to a class of abstract fitness landscapes well-matched with the abstract convex search for which we may obtain good performance: concave functions and approximately concave functions[4] (see Figure 5. In this section, we consider concave functions and in section 4.4 we will consider approximately convex functions). Note, however, that this intuition arises from the notion of convexity in the Euclidean space, and may easily not hold true across all metric spaces i.e., may not hold at an abstract level. Furthermore, even when the generalization to general metric spaces is possible, a great deal of caution is required, as a generalized notion of concave function which is meaningful when specified to continuous spaces may lead to only degenerate cases of little interest, when specified to combinatorial spaces. In this section, we will start considering candidate generalizations of the notion of concave functions to general metric spaces and show how the (abstract) performance of (abstract) convex search is bounded on these classes of (abstract) fitness landscapes. In the introduction, we have mentioned that we are interested in generalizing the "concave trend" character of a concave function, rather than its "unimodal" character. This is because it is known experimentally that, assuming minimization, global convexity of the fitness landscape [2] (i.e., a globally convex trend) is beneficial for the performance of evolutionary algorithms (also known as the "big valley" hypothesis) and many important combinatorial problems have been shown to be globally convex [7]. In the next section, we will extend the generalized notion of concave functions to generalized notion of functions with a concave trend in the attempt to characterize formally the notion of global concavity (and convexity).

For the following definitions see e.g. [3]. A real-valued function f defined on any convex subset C of some vector space is called concave iff the Jensen's inequality holds for any two points $x, y \in C$, i.e., for any $t \in [0, 1]$, $f(tx + (1 - t)y) \geq tf(x) + (1-t)f(y)$, which is, the chord connecting any two points of a concave function lies below or on the graph of the function. A function f is convex iff $-f$ is concave.

---

[4]We assume maximization. For minimization problems, the classes of functions to consider are convex functions and approximately convex functions.

If a function is convex and concave at the same time it is an affine function (e.g., any linear function in some vector space is affine).

There are a number of ways to generalize convex and concave functions to more general spaces than vector spaces to discrete spaces and to general metric spaces (see e.g., the monograph [16] on this topic with focus on generalizing results of convex optimization). We will consider generalizations which can be used as basis for the generalization of convex and concave trends. A concave function can be generalized to a metric space [17] (i.e., a concave fitness landscape) as follows. Let C be a geodetically convex set on a metric space endowed with distance d, then $f : C \to R$ is concave if for any two points $x, y \in C, d(x, y) \neq 0$ and bounded, and for any $z \in [x, y]_d$, $f(z) \geq \frac{d(y,z)}{d(x,y)} f(x) + \frac{d(x,z)}{d(x,y)} f(y)$. Analogously, the function is convex if the inequality obtained by changing $\geq$ to $\leq$ holds. This is a proper generalization of concave function, as when the space considered is a vector space endowed with the Euclidean distance, the generalized notion of concavity reduces to the classical notion [17]. Later in this section, we will illustrate with an example how this definition applies to combinatorial spaces. However, first we present a result that makes this definition potentially interesting for our framework.

We first need a condition of regularity of the underlying space. We say that a metric space (S, d) has symmetric segments if for any $x, y \in S$ the sizes of the distance level partitions on the segment from x i.e., the collection of sets $[x, y]_t = \{z : z \in [x, y] \land d(x, z) = t\}$ indexed by t (the admissible values of t are those which do not return an empty partition), correspond to the sizes of the distance level partitions from y, i.e., for all admissible t $[x, y]_t = [y, x]_t$.

THEOREM 4. *On a concave fitness landscape f endowed with any distance d with symmetric segments, the expected fitness of the offspring z obtained by recombining any two parents x and y using the geometric crossover associated with the distance d with any symmetric offspring probability distribution is not less than the average fitness of its parents, i.e., $E[f(z)|x, y] \geq \frac{f(x)+f(y)}{2}$.*

PROOF. We prove the theorem for the case of discrete spaces. The proof for continuous spaces is analogous and can be obtained by replacing probability mass functions with probability density functions and summations with integrals. A geometric crossover, given parents x and y, returns an offspring $z \in [x, y]$ according to a certain probability distribution over the segment $Pr(z|d(x, z) = t)$ of sampling a point z at a given distance t from x (first argument of the crossover). Hence, given the parents x and y the expected

fitness of the offspring is $E[f(z)|x,y] \geq$
$\sum_{t=0...d(x,y)} Pr(z|d(x,z)=t)\cdot((1-\frac{t}{d(x,y)})f(x)+\frac{t}{d(x,y)}f(y))$.
Exchanging the parents (x as second argument of the crossover and y as first argument) the probability distribution over the segment has origin in y and the expected offspring of the offspring becomes

$$\begin{aligned}
E[f(z)|x,y]' &\geq \sum_{t=0...d(x,y)} Pr(z|d(x,z)=t)' \cdot \\
& ((1-\frac{t}{d(x,y)})f(x)+\frac{t}{d(x,y)}f(y)) \\
&= \sum_{t=0...d(x,y)} Pr(z|d(x,z)=d(x,y)-t) \cdot \\
& ((1-\frac{t}{d(x,y)})f(x)+\frac{t}{d(x,y)}f(y)) \\
&= \sum_{t'=0...d(x,y)} Pr(z|d(x,z)=t') \cdot \\
& ((1-\frac{d(x,y)-t'}{d(x,y)})f(x)+\frac{d(x,y)-t'}{d(x,y)}f(y)) \\
&= \sum_{t'=0...d(x,y)} Pr(z|d(x,z)=t') \cdot \\
& (\frac{t'}{d(x,y)}f(x)+(1-\frac{t'}{d(x,y)})f(y)).
\end{aligned}$$

$E[f(z)|x,y]+E[f(z)|x,y]' \geq \sum_{t=0...d(x,y)} Pr(z|d(x,z)=t)\cdot$
$((1-\frac{t}{d(x,y)}+\frac{t}{d(x,y)})f(x)+(\frac{t}{d(x,y)}+1-\frac{t}{d(x,y)})f(y))$
$= \sum_{t=0...d(x,y)} Pr(z|d(x,z)=t)\cdot(f(x)+f(y))$
$= f(x)+f(y)$.
For symmetry of the probability distribution
$E[f(z)|x,y]' = E[f(z)|x,y]$ then $E[f(z)|x,y] \geq \frac{f(x)+f(y)}{2}$. $\square$

When the symmetry condition on the segment does not hold, the average of the fitness of the parents may be skewed toward one or the other parent. However, we always have $E[f(z)|x,y] \geq \min\{f(x),f(y)\}$. The theorem above can be easily extended to populations.

COROLLARY 1. *On a concave landscape, by applying geometric crossover on pairs of parents sampled uniformly at random (with replacement) from any population of parents, the expected average fitness of the offspring population is not less than the average fitness of the parent population.*

PROOF. The expected average fitness of the offspring population obtained by sampling at random the parent population Pop of size n is

$$\begin{aligned}
E[f(z)] &= \sum_{x,y \in Pop} \frac{1}{n^2} E[f(z)|x,y] \\
&\geq \frac{1}{2n^2} \sum_{x,y \in Pop} (f(x)+f(y)) \\
&= \frac{1}{2n^2}(\sum_{x,y \in Pop} f(x)+\sum_{x,y \in Pop} f(y)) \\
&= \frac{1}{2n^2}(2n \sum_{x \in Pop} f(x)) \\
&= \frac{\sum_{x \in Pop} f(x)}{n}.
\end{aligned}$$

$\square$

It is noticeable that the theorem above is a statement about the one-step performance of the formal evolutionary algorithm that holds in a very general setting. Notice also that the formal evolutionary algorithm on concave landscapes, on average, makes steady progress or, in the worst-case, does not get worse, *even in lack of selection*[5] at any stage of the search process, i.e., $\forall n : E[f(P_{n+1})] \geq E[f(P_n)]$. This is a rather strong statement about the one-step performance because, as a norm, the mean fitness of the offspring is less than the average fitness of their parents, and selection (or selective replacement) is a necessary ingredient to obtain progress [6].

We now illustrate with an example how the definition of convex function introduced earlier applies to combinatorial spaces by showing how it can be used to check whether a fitness landscape with any underlying metric d is convex, concave, affine or none of them. Let us consider the fitness landscape obtained by the One-Max function f on the space of binary strings endowed with the Hamming distance. Let $x = 000111$ and $y = 001100$. So we have $f(x) = 3$ and $f(y) = 2$ and $d(x,y) = 3$. The points in the segment $[x,y]$ are those matching the schema $H(x,y) = 00*1**$. Then, if f is concave, from the definition of generalized concavity, for each string z matching the schema we must have $f(z) \geq \frac{d(y,z)}{d(x,y)}f(x)+\frac{d(x,z)}{d(x,y)}f(y)$. Let us consider the point in the segment $z = 000100$ we have $f(z) = 1$, $d(x,z) = 2$ and $d(y,z) = 1$. By substituting these values in the inequality defining concave function, we obtain that it does not hold true. So, One-Max is not a concave function in the above sense. It is also possible to show that One-Max is not a convex function either as for the point in the segment $z = 001111$ the defining inequality for convex function does not hold. Unfortunately, the above scenario recurs over and over. It turns out that the only fitness landscapes based on binary strings endowed with the Hamming distance which are concave (and convex) in the above sense are constant landscapes. So, this makes the above definition of concavity unsuitable for our framework as it does not encompass interesting functions on the Hamming space.

So, are there alternative definitions of generalized concave function which encompass interesting fitness landscapes on the Hamming space? One possibility is to relax suitably the definition of concave function retaining the results of theorem 4 and its corollary. Interestingly, the theorem 4 holds when the average fitness of each distance level partition of the segment – rather than the fitness of any point in each distance level partition – is greater than the corresponding

---

[5]When parents are selected independently and with the same distribution increasing the selection pressure can lead to an increase of the average population fitness. In case of adversary selection schemes, in which worse individuals are preferred to better individuals, the one-step performance can decrease due to selection. Naturally, adversary selection is never used.

[6]On the general class of concave landscapes, this is the strongest lower bound one can obtain. Clearly, such a result does not lead to interesting lower-bounds for the n-step performance. However, one could consider restricted classes of concave landscapes with given curvature (e.g., concave landscapes which are also bi-Lipschitz with constant k), and derive stronger bounds for the one-step performance as a function of the degree of curvature that could lead to interesting bounds for the n-step performance. We will consider this possibility in future work.

linear combination of the fitness of the endpoints for that distance level. Therefore this weaker condition can be used to characterize a larger class of generalized concave functions for which theorem 4 and its corollary hold. In this weaker sense, the One-Max landscape turns out to be affine. So, the theorem 4 and its corollary apply to it with an equality sign rather than a greater and equal. In the next section, we consider a weaker form of concave functions – quasi-concave functions – which can be generalized to general metric spaces more naturally than concave functions.

4.3 Quasi-concave fitness landscapes

For the following definitions see e.g. [3]. A real-valued function f defined on any convex subset C of some vector space is called quasi-concave iff for any real number a the inverse image of the set of the form $(a, +\infty)$ is a convex set (notice that this implies that sets corresponding to larger values of a are included in the sets corresponding to smaller values of a), and quasi-convex iff the inverse image of any set of the form $(-\infty, a)$ is a convex set. A function that is both quasi-convex and quasi-concave is quasi-linear. All convex functions are also quasi-convex, but not all quasi-convex functions are convex, so quasi-convexity is a weak form of convexity. An analogous relation between concave and quasi-concave functions hold. Quasi-concave and quasi-convex functions can be equivalently characterized using inequalities. A real-valued function f defined on any convex subset C of some vector space is quasi-concave iff for any two points $x, y \in C$ for any $t \in [0, 1]$, $f(tx + (1-t)y) \geq \min(f(x), f(y))$, and quasi-convex iff for any two points $x, y \in C$ for any $t \in [0, 1]$, $f(tx + (1-t)y) \leq \max(f(x), f(y))$.

We can readily generalize quasi-concave functions to metric spaces by requiring that the inverse image of any set of the form $(a, +\infty)$ is a $geodetically$ convex set. As geodetically convex sets for the Euclidean distance reduce to traditional convex sets, the one above is a proper generalization of quasi-concave function. As the level sets are geodetically convex and form a nested chain of inclusions for increasing values of a, the function value at any point of a segment cannot be lower than the minimum of the function value of its endpoints. So, analogously to the traditional case we have that for generalized quasi-concave functions hold: $f(z) \geq \min(f(x), f(y))$ for any $z \in [x, y]$. Quasi-convex and quasi-linear functions can be generalized to metric spaces analogously.

As for the case of the generalization of concave functions, also for the generalization of quasi-concave functions we can bound the expected fitness of the offspring population on the average fitness of the parent population. From the definition of quasi-concave landscape, it is clear that the fitness of any offspring cannot be less than the the minimum fitness in the parent population. However, it is possible to have a stronger result considering order statistics, which involve the distribution of the min, second-to-last, ..., median, ... max in a fixed set of samples. The line of reasoning is as follows. As parents that undergo geometric crossover can be thought as of being selected independently from the mating-pool, the fitnesses of the two parents are i.i.d. random variables with distribution equalling the fitness distribution of the mating-pool. The expected fitness of the offspring is then larger than the expected fitness of the first order statistics of the two random variables. To form an understanding of how the lower bound of the expected fitness offspring population

is less than the average fitness of the parent population, we can linearly rank the parents in the mating-pool in the interval $[0, 1]$ so that rank 1 is the best, rank 0 is the worst, and rank 0.5 is the median. Then the expected rank of the offspring population is lower-bounded by the expected value of the first order statistic of the uniform distribution on $[0, 1]$, which is $1/3$. An analogous result holds for the generalization of quasi-convex function. Notice also that on quasi-linear functions the maximum fitness of the offspring population is upper-bounded by the maximum fitness of the parent population, so in this case, evolution will not take place because there is no chance for offspring to improve over the parents. So, assuming maximization, for improvement to be possible we need to have a quasi-concave landscape which is not quasi-linear.

Quasi-concave landscapes are interesting when considered together with combinatorial spaces because they give rise to discrete sets of fitness values, in other words, fitness functions on combinatorial spaces are quantized functions. This property allows us to check quasi-concavity of a landscape by checking directly one by one the convexity of all level sets. Also, we can use this property to easily construct quasi-concave functions for any representation and metric space once we have determined the specific form of geodetically convex sets. In the following, we illustrate this for the case of the Hamming space on binary strings. The idea for the construction procedure of a quasi-convex landscape is to build directly a nested chain of convex level sets starting from the largest level set with the minimum fitness value which is then recursively partitioned in two parts: (i) a convex set containing the next fitness level or fitness levels with higher values, and (ii) the complement of that set with respect to the convex set at the current level containing points whose fitness values are matching the current fitness level. Let us assign fitness equal or greater than zero to all points in space. So, for any x_0 matching the schema ******, which is the current level set, we have $f(x_0) >= 0$. Let us consider the convex subset 0***** of ****** and let us assign to any x_1 matching this schema fitness values of one or greater, i.e., $f(x_1) >= 1$. The complement set of 0***** with respect to ****** is 1***** for which all matching strings keep the fitness of the current level set, which is zero. So, the quasi-concave function we will obtain has fitness zero for any string starting with 1 and fitness strictly larger than 1 for any string starting with 0. Let us now consider 0***** which is the current level set which we need to partition. We chose the convex subset 01**** of 0***** to have fitness values equal or larger than 1, and its complement set in 0*****, which is 00****, to have fitness values at the current level, which is 1. So, the quasi-convex function will return fitness 1 for all strings starting with 00. Then the procedure continues so forth and so on partitioning the current sets until a convex set is reached which contains a single element, or at any time if one decides to assign the current fitness level also to the chosen convex set, so obtaining a landscape with a plateau. For example, continuing the procedure above we could construct the following function: $f(1*****) = 0$, $f(00****) = 1$, $f(011***) = 2$, $f(0101**) = 3$, $f(01000*) = 4$, $f(010010) = 5$, $f(010011) = 6$. As the Leading-One landscape can be built in this way, it is a quasi-concave landscape. It is possible to show that One-Max is not a quasi-concave landscape because its level sets are Hamming balls, which unlike Euclidean balls, are not geodetically convex.

Analogously to traditional quasi-concave functions, also for quasi-concave landscapes a number of combinations and transformations on quasi-concave landscapes produce quasi-concave landscapes. For example, if f, g are quasi-convex defined on the same domain, the following landscapes are quasi-convex: $\alpha f + \beta$ with α, β real numbers, $\min[f, g]$, and $h(f)$ with h monotonic increasing.

4.4 Fitness landscapes with concave trend

As we mentioned in the introduction, there is a well-known notion of global convexity of the fitness landscape [2] that is known experimentally to be beneficial for the performance of evolutionary algorithms. Interestingly, fitness landscapes normally associated with many important combinatorial problems have been shown to be globally convex [7]. Therefore, a theory which characterizes the performance of evolutionary search on this class of fitness landscapes would be very relevant to practice. In this section, we will start characterizing the notion of globally convex landscape formally and in a general way, by suitably extending the notions of convex and quasi-convex landscapes presented earlier. Naturally, the practical utility of the formalization proposed is bound to the extent to which fitness landscapes arising in practice fit nicely these formal notions. In future work, we will investigate this issue thoroughly and, if necessary, propose a refined definition of concave trend which suits better these landscapes.

In the literature, there are a number of ways of weakening the concavity/convexity requirement of a function to approximate concavity/convexity. A simple approach to defining approximately concave functions [5] (see Figure 5 (right)) is as follows. Let $\epsilon \geq 0$. A real-valued function f defined on any convex subset C of some vector space is called ϵ-concave if for any two points $x, y \in C$, for any $t \in [0, 1]$, $f(tx + (1-t)y) \geq tf(x) + (1-t)f(y) - \epsilon$. This is a well-studied and interesting class of functions whose concavity approximation is controlled by the parameter ϵ, the smaller the better the approximation. Interestingly, a function $f = g + h$ obtained from a concave function g and a bounded perturbing function h such that $\forall x : |h(x)| \leq \epsilon$ is 2ϵ-concave [5].

A ϵ-concave function can be generalized to a metric space analogously to the case of concave functions, as follows. Let C be a convex set on a metric space endowed with distance d, then $f : C \to R$ is ϵ-concave if for any two points $x, y \in C, x \neq y$ and for any $z \in [x, y]$, $f(z) \geq \frac{d(y,z)}{d(x,y)}f(x) + \frac{d(x,z)}{d(x,y)}f(y) - \epsilon$. As for the Euclidean case, an analogous result on the sum of a concave landscape with a bounded perturbing landscape is a 2ϵ approximately concave landscape. Also, the following result which extends theorem 4 to ϵ-concave landscape holds (as the constant ϵ can be pulled out from all summations).

THEOREM 5. *On a ϵ-concave fitness landscape, the expected fitness of the offspring $E[f(z)]$ obtained by recombining randomly selected parents using geometric crossover from a population with average fitness $\bar{f}$ is $E[f(z)] \geq \bar{f} - \epsilon$.*

It is noticeable that the parameter controlling the concavity of the landscape has a straightforward impact on the one-step performance and, inductively, on the overall performance of the formal evolutionary algorithm: the less the concavity approximation, the lower the performance can become.

Whereas the above class of approximately concave landscapes may not be interesting for combinatorial spaces, as it is based on a class which is not interesting on the Hamming space, weaker versions on this class may encompass interesting classes of fitness landscapes. For example, theorem 5 may well hold for the average version of concave landscapes, so that the theorem would give a lower-bound on the fitness of the offspring for perturbed One-Max landscapes.

We can also define a class of approximately quasi-concave fitness landscapes, as follows. Let C be a convex set on a metric space endowed with distance d, then $f : C \to R$ is ϵ-quasi-concave if for any two points $x, y \in C : f(z) \geq \min(f(x), f(y)) - \epsilon$ for any $z \in [x, y]$. The level sets of this class of functions are not convex, however they form a nested chain of inclusions, as level sets do so for any function. For $a \leq b$, denoting the corresponding level sets $ls(a)$ and $ls(b)$, in general we have $ls(a) \supseteq ls(b)$ but the relation $ls(a) \supseteq co(ls(b))$ does not necessarily hold in general, but it always holds for quasi-concave landscapes. However, this holds also for ϵ-quasi-concave landscapes when $b - a \geq \epsilon$. Analogously to the case of quasi-concave landscapes, this characterization in terms of level sets can be used to construct ϵ-quasi-concave landscapes based on combinatorial spaces or to check for what ϵ a landscape is ϵ-quasi-concave. Also, notice that a result relating the expected fitness of the offspring population with the fitness of the parent population as a function of ϵ holds on this class of landscapes.

Interestingly, the classes of ϵ-concave landscapes and ϵ-quasi-concave landscapes are flexible classes as any fitness landscape is ϵ-concave and ϵ-quasi-concave for ϵ large enough. The practical relevance of these classes is therefore bound to the extent to which fitness landscapes arising in practice fit these classes for small values of ϵ.

Another interesting consequence of the flexibility of these classes of fitness landscapes is that to some extent any fitness landscape is both approximately concave and approximately convex, with in general different degrees for concavity and convexity. Since for the case of convexity one can determine an upper-bound of the expected fitness of the offspring population with respect to of the average fitness of the parent population, from the knowledge of the degrees of convexity and concavity of a landscape, one can obtain a range for the expected fitness of the offspring population. This may allow us to characterize the performance for n-steps rather than for a single-step of the evolution, perhaps in the average case.

Finally, it would be interesting to consider approximated concave landscapes with ϵ being a random variable rather than a constant. This would define a statistical model of fitness landscapes which may be more suitable to study average-case performance rather than worst-case.

5. CONCLUSIONS

It is not at all clear that a unified theory of evolutionary algorithms across representations is possible. This is an important open research question. The main contribution of this paper is to start shaping the foundational concepts of a possible approach towards such a theory.

We have started developing the theory by making use of mathematical abstraction in the form of an axiomatic geometric language, based on the notion of geometric search operators, that encompasses all representations. We have defined the notion of abstract search behavior and used it to prove that all evolutionary algorithms with geometric crossover across representations do a form of abstract convex search. This is a significant result as it elicits a common behavioral identity of all evolutionary algorithms (without mutation) across representations.

The unity in behavior of evolutionary algorithms calls for the existence of a unique abstract underlying condition on the fitness landscape for which all evolutionary algorithms perform well. Convex search naturally suggests that the concavity of the fitness landscape may be the key condition for obtaining good performance of evolutionary algorithms. We have generalized to general metric spaces a number of notions of concave functions and considered their suitability for the framework. We have shown that quasi-concave functions may be a natural choice for fitness landscapes based on combinatorial spaces. However, further study is required to confirm the suitability of this notion.

We have proved a general result showing a direct relationship between the degree of concavity of a fitness landscape and its impact on the one-step performance of evolutionary algorithms. This may be of direct relevance to combinatorial problems as many are known to be associated with fitness landscapes which are globally convex. However, it remains to be seen if the formalized notion of concavity aligns well with the empirical notion of global convexity. Investigating this and refining the formal definitions is an important piece of future work.

At the moment is still unclear how far the theory can be brought forward at this level of abstraction. In future work, we will investigate to what extent results about convergence to the optimum, convergence rate and run-time analysis can be obtained at this level of abstraction. Finally, as an important piece of future work, we will study the effect of mutation on convex search and how to accommodate it within this general framework.

6. REFERENCES

[1] Blumental and Menger. *Studies in geometry*. Freeman and Company, 1970.
[2] K. D. Boese, A. B. Kahng, and S. Muddu. A new adaptive multi-start technique for combinatorial global optimizations. *Operations Research Letters*, 15:101–113, 1994.
[3] S. Boyd and L. Vandenberghe. *Convex Optimization*. Cambridge University Press, 2004.
[4] K. DeJong. *Evolutionary computation: a unified approach*. The MIT Press, 2006.
[5] J. W. Green. Approximately convex functions. *Duke Mathematical Journal*, 19:499–504, 1952.
[6] W. Langdon and R. Poli. *Foundations of Genetic Programming*. Springer-Verlag, 2002.
[7] P. Merz and B. Freisleben. Fitness landscapes and memetic algorithms. In D. Corne, M. Dorigo, and F. Glover, editors, *New ideas in optimization*. McGraw-Hill, 1999.
[8] E. H. Moore. Definition of limit in general integral analysis. In *Proceedings of the National Academy of Sciences of the United States of America*, volume 1, pages 628–632, 1915.
[9] A. Moraglio. *Towards a geometric unification of evolutionary algorithms*. PhD thesis, University of Essex, 2007.
[10] A. Moraglio and R. Poli. Topological interpretation of crossover. In *Proceedings of the Genetic and Evolutionary Computation Conference*, pages 1377–1388, 2004.
[11] K. Murota. Discrete convex analysis. *Mathematical Programming*, 83(1-3):313–371, 1998.
[12] N. Radcliffe. Equivalence class analysis of genetic algorithms. *Complex Systems*, 5:183–205, 1991.
[13] C. M. Reidys and P. F. Stadler. Combinatorial landscapes. *SIAM Review*, 44:3–54, 2002.
[14] F. Rothlauf. *Representations for Genetic and Evolutionary Algorithms*. Springer, 2002.
[15] J. E. Rowe, M. D. Vose, and A. H. Wright. Group properties of crossover and mutation. *Evolutionary Computation Journal*, 10(2):151–184, 2002.
[16] I. Singer. *Abstract Convex Analysis*. Wiley, 1997.
[17] V. P. Soltan. *Introduction to the Axiomatic Theory of Convexity*. Shtinitsa, 1984.
[18] C. R. Stephens and A. Zamora. EC theory: A unified viewpoint. In *Proceedings of the Genetic and Evolutionary Computation Conference*, pages 1394–1405, 2003.
[19] P. D. Surry and N. J. Radcliffe. Formal algorithms + formal representations = search strategies. In *Proceedings of Parallel Problem Solving from Nature Conference*, pages 366–375, 1996.
[20] M. van de Vel. *Theory of Convex Structures*. Elsevier, Amsterdam, 1993.
[21] D. H. Wolpert and W. G. Macready. No free lunch theorems for optimization. *IEEE Transaction on Evolutionary Computation*, 1(1):67–82, 1996.

Faster Black-Box Algorithms Through Higher Arity Operators

Benjamin Doerr[1]   Daniel Johannsen[1]   Timo Kötzing[1†]

Per Kristian Lehre[2*]   Markus Wagner[1]   Carola Winzen[1‡]

[1] Max-Planck-Institut für Informatik
Campus E1 4
66123 Saarbrücken, Germany

[2] DTU Informatics
Technical University of
Denmark
2800 Lyngby, Denmark

ABSTRACT

We extend the work of Lehre and Witt (GECCO 2010) on the unbiased black-box model by considering higher arity variation operators. In particular, we show that already for binary operators the black-box complexity of LEADINGONES drops from $\Theta(n^2)$ for unary operators to $O(n \log n)$. For ONEMAX, the $\Omega(n \log n)$ unary black-box complexity drops to $O(n)$ in the binary case. For k-ary operators, $k \leq n$, the ONEMAX-complexity further decreases to $O(n/\log k)$.

Categories and Subject Descriptors

F.2.2 [**Analysis of Algorithms and Problem Complexity**]: Nonnumerical Algorithms and Problems

General Terms

Algorithms, Performance, Theory

Keywords

Black-box complexity, runtime analysis, pseudo-Boolean optimization, theory

1. INTRODUCTION

When we analyze the optimization time of randomized search heuristics, we typically assume that the heuristic does not know anything about the objective function apart from its membership in a large class of functions, e.g., linear or monotone functions. Thus, the function is typically considered to be given as a black-box, i.e., in order to optimize the function, the algorithm needs to query the function values of various search points. The algorithm may then use the information on the function values to create new search points. We call the minimum number of function evaluations needed for a randomized search heuristic to optimize any function f of a given function class $\mathcal{F}$ the *black-box complexity* of $\mathcal{F}$. We may restrict the algorithm class with respect to how algorithms create new search points from the information collected in previous steps. Intuitively, the stronger restrictions that are imposed on the search points which the algorithms can query next, the larger the black-box complexity of the function class.

Black-box complexity for search heuristics was introduced in 2006 by Droste, Jansen, and Wegener [DJW06]. We call their model the *unrestricted* black-box model as it imposes few restrictions on how the algorithm may create new search points from the information at hand. This model was the first attempt towards creating a complexity theory for randomized search heuristics. However, the authors prove bounds that deviate from those known for well-studied search heuristics, such as random local search and evolutionary algorithms. For example, the well-studied function class ONEMAX has an unrestricted black-box complexity of $\Theta(n/\log n)$ whereas standard search heuristics only achieve a $\Omega(n \log n)$ runtime. Similarly, the class LEADINGONES has a linear unrestricted black-box complexity but we typically observe a $\Omega(n^2)$ behavior for standard heuristics.

These gaps, among other reasons, motivated Lehre and Witt [LW10] to propose an alternative model. In their *unbiased* black-box model the algorithm may only invoke a so-called unbiased variation operator to create new search points. A variation operator returns a new search point given one or more previous search points. Now, intuitively, the unbiasedness condition implies that the variation operator is symmetric with respect to the bit values and bit positions. Or, to be more precise, it must be invariant under Hamming-automorphisms. We give a formal definition of the two black-box models in Section 2.

Among other problem instances, Lehre and Witt analyze the unbiased black-box complexity of the two function classes ONEMAX and LEADINGONES. They can show that the complexity of ONEMAX and LEADINGONES match the above mentioned $\Theta(n \log n)$ and, respectively, $\Theta(n^2)$ bounds, if we only allow *unary* operators. I.e., if the varia-

---

*Supported by Deutsche Forschungsgemeinschaft (DFG) under grant no. WI 3552/1-1.

†Timo Kötzing was supported by the Deutsche Forschungsgemeinschaft (DFG) under grant NE 1182/5-1.

‡Carola Winzen is a recipient of the Google Europe Fellowship in Randomized Algorithms, and this research is supported in part by this Google Fellowship.

Model	Arity	OneMax		LeadingOnes	
unbiased	1	$\Theta(n \log n)$	[LW10]	$\Theta(n^2)$	[LW10]
unbiased	$1 < k \leq n$	$O(n/\log k)$	(here)	$O(n \log n)$	(here)
unrestricted	n/a	$\Omega(n/\log n)$	[DJW06]	$\Omega(n)$	[DJW06]
		$O(n/\log n)$	[AW09]		

Table 1: **Black-Box Complexity of OneMax and LeadingOnes. Note that upper bounds for the unbiased unary black-box complexity immediately carry over to higher arities. Similarly, lower bounds for the unrestricted black-box model also hold for the unbiased model.**

tion operator may only use the information from at most one previously queried search point (1-ary or unary operator), the unbiased black-box complexity matches the runtime of the well-known $(1 + 1)$ Evolutionary Algorithm.

In their first work, Lehre and Witt give no results on the black-box complexity of *higher arity* models. A variation operator is said to be of arity k if it creates new search points by recombining up to k previously queried search points. We are interested in higher arity black-box models because they include commonly used search heuristics which are not covered by the unary operators. Among such heuristics are evolutionary algorithms that employ uniform crossover, particle swarm optimization [KE01], ant colony optimization [DS04] and estimation of distribution algorithms [LL02].

Although search heuristics that employ higher arity operators are poorly understood from a theoretical point of view, there are some results proving that situations exist where higher arity is helpful. For example, Doerr, Klein, and Happ [DHK08] show that a concatenation operator reduces the runtime on the all-pairs shortest path problem. Refer to the same paper for further references.

Extending the work from Lehre and Witt, we analyze higher arity black-box complexities of OneMax and LeadingOnes. In particular, we show that, surprisingly, the unbiased black-box complexity drops from $\Theta(n^2)$ in the unary case to $O(n \log n)$ for LeadingOnes and from $\Theta(n \log n)$ to an at most linear complexity for OneMax. As the bounds for unbiased unary black-box complexities immediately carry over to all higher arity unbiased black-box complexities, we see that increasing the arity of the variation operators provably helps to decrease the complexity. We are optimistic that the ideas developed to prove the bounds can be further exploited to achieve reduced black-box complexities also for other function classes.

In this work, we also prove that increasing the arity further does again help. In particular, we show that for every $k \leq n$, the unbiased k-ary black-box complexity of OneMax can be bounded by $O(n/\log k)$. This bound is optimal for $k = n$, because the unbiased black-box complexity can always be bounded below by the unrestricted black-box complexity, which is known to be $\Omega(n/\log n)$ for OneMax [DJW06].

Note that a comparison between the unrestricted black-box complexity and the unbiased black-box complexity of LeadingOnes cannot be derived that easily. The asymptotic linear unrestricted black-box complexity mentioned above is only known to hold for a subclass of the class LeadingOnes considered in this work.

Table 1 summarizes the results obtained in this paper, and provides a comparison with known results on black-box complexity of OneMax and LeadingOnes.

2. UNRESTRICTED AND UNBIASED BLACK-BOX COMPLEXITIES

In this section, we formally define the two black-box models by Droste, Jansen, and Wegener [DJW06], and Lehre and Witt [LW10]. We call the first model the *unrestricted black-box model*, and the second model the *unbiased black-box model*. Each model specifies a class of algorithms. The black-box complexity of a function class is then defined with respect to the algorithms specified by the corresponding model. We start by describing the two models, then provide the corresponding definitions of black-box complexity.

In both models, one is faced with a class of pseudo-Boolean functions $\mathcal{F}$ that is known to the algorithm. An adversary chooses a function f from this class. The function f itself remains unknown to the algorithm. The algorithm can only gain knowledge about the function f by querying an oracle for the function value of search points. The goal of the algorithm is to find a globally optimal search point for the function. Without loss of generality, we consider maximization as objective. The two models differ in the information available to the algorithm, and the search points that can be queried.

Let us begin with some notation. Throughout this paper, we consider the maximization of pseudo-Boolean functions $f : \{0,1\}^n \to \mathbb{R}$. In particular, n will always denote the length of the bitstring to be optimized. For a bitstring $x \in \{0,1\}^n$, we write $x = x_1 \cdots x_n$. For convenience, we denote the positive integers by $\mathbb{N}$. For $k \in \mathbb{N}$, we use the notion $[k]$ as a shorthand for the set $\{1, \ldots, k\}$. Analogously, we define $[0..k] := [k] \cup \{0\}$. Furthermore, let S_k denote the set of all permutations of $[k]$. With slight abuse of notation, we write $\sigma(x) := x_{\sigma(1)} \cdots x_{\sigma(n)}$ for $\sigma \in S_n$. Furthermore, the bitwise exclusive-or is denoted by $\oplus$. For any bitstring x we denote its complement by $\overline{x}$. Finally, we use standard notation for asymptotic growth of functions (see, e.g., [CLRS01]). In particular, we denote by $o_n(g(n))$ the set of all functions f that satisfy $\lim_{n \to \infty} f(n)/g(n) = 0$.

The *unrestricted black-box model* contains all algorithms which can be formalized as in Algorithm 1. A basic feature is that this scheme does not force any relationship between the search points of subsequent queries. Thus, this model contains a broad class of algorithms.

To exclude some algorithms whose behavior does not resemble those of typical search-heuristics, one can impose further restrictions. The *unbiased black-box model* (see Algorithm 2) introduced in [LW10] restricts Algorithm 1 in two ways. First, the decisions made by the algorithm only depends on the observed fitness values, and not the actual search points. Second, the algorithm can only query search points obtained by variation operators that are unbiased in

Algorithm 1: Unrestricted Black-Box Algorithm

1 Choose a probability distribution p_0 on $\{0,1\}^n$.
2 Sample x^0 according to p_0 and query $f(x^0)$.
3 for $t = 1, 2, 3, \ldots$ *until termination condition met* **do**
4   Depending on $((x^0, f(x^0)), \ldots, (x^{t-1}, f(x^{t-1})))$, choose
5   a probability distribution p^t on $\{0,1\}^n$.
6   Sample x^t according to p^t, and query $f(x^t)$.

the following sense. By imposing these two restrictions, the black-box complexity matches the runtime of popular search heuristics on example functions.

DEFINITION 1. (UNBIASED k-ARY VARIATION OPERA-TOR [LW10]) *Let* $k \in \mathbb{N}$. *An* unbiased k-ary distribution $D(\cdot \mid x^1, \ldots, x^k)$ *is a conditional probability distribution over* $\{0,1\}^n$, *such that for all bitstrings* $y, z \in \{0,1\}^n$, *and each permutation* $\sigma \in S_n$, *the following two conditions hold.*

(i) $D(y \mid x^1, \ldots, x^k) = D(y \oplus z \mid x^1 \oplus z, \ldots, x^k \oplus z)$,

(ii) $D(y \mid x^1, \ldots, x^k) = D(\sigma(y) \mid \sigma(x^1), \ldots, \sigma(x^k))$.

An unbiased k-ary variation operator p *is a* k-ary opera-tor which samples its output according to an unbiased k-ary distribution.

The first condition in Definition 1 is referred to as $\oplus$-*invariance*, and the second condition is referred to as *per-mutation invariance*. Note that the combination of these two conditions can be characterized as invariance under Hamming-automorphisms: $D(\cdot \mid x^1, \ldots, x^k)$ is unbiased if and only if, for all $\alpha : \{0,1\}^n \to \{0,1\}^n$ preserving the Hamming distance and all bitstrings y, $D(y \mid x^1, \ldots, x^k) = D(\alpha(y) \mid \alpha(x^1), \ldots, \alpha(x^k))$. We refer to 1-ary and 2-ary variation operators as *unary* and *binary* variation opera-tors, respectively. E.g., the standard bitwise mutation op-erator is a unary operator, and the uniform crossover oper-ator is a binary operator. Note however that the one-point crossover operator is not permutation-invariant, and there-fore not an unbiased operator. The unbiased k-ary black-box model contains all algorithms which follow the scheme of Algorithm 2. While being a restriction of the old model, the unbiased model still captures the most widely studied search heuristics, including most evolutionary algorithms, simulated annealing and random local search.

Note that in line 5 of Algorithm 2, $y^1, \ldots, y^k$ don't neces-sarily have to be the k *immediately previously* queried ones. That is, the algorithm is allowed to choose any k previously sampled search points.

We now define black-box complexity formally. We will use query complexity as the cost model, where the algorithm is only charged for queries to the oracle, and all other compu-tation is free. The runtime $T_{A,f}$ of a randomized algorithm A on a function $f \in \mathcal{F}$ is hence the expected number of oracle queries until the optimal search point is queried for the first time. The expectation is taken with respect to the random choices made by the algorithm.

DEFINITION 2 (BLACK-BOX COMPLEXITY). *The complexity of a class of pseudo-Boolean functions* $\mathcal{F}$ *with respect to a class of algorithms* $\mathcal{A}$, *is defined as* $T_{\mathcal{A}}(\mathcal{F}) := \min_{A \in \mathcal{A}} \max_{f \in \mathcal{F}} T_{A,f}$.

The *unrestricted black-box complexity* is the complexity with respect to the algorithms covered by Algorithm 1. For any given $k \in \mathbb{N}$, the *unbiased k-ary black-box complexity* is the complexity with respect to the algorithms covered by Algorithm 2. Furthermore, the *unbiased $*$-ary black-box complexity* is the complexity with respect to the algorithms covered by Algorithm 2, without limitation on the arity of the operators used.

It is easy to see that every unbiased k-ary operator p can be simulated by an unbiased $(k+1)$-ary operator p' de-fined as $p'(z \mid x^1, \ldots, x^k, x^{k+1}) := p(z \mid x^1, \ldots, x^k)$. Hence, the unbiased k-ary black-box complexity is an upper bound for the unbiased $(k+1)$-ary black-box complexity. Similarly, the set of unbiased black-box algorithms for any arity is contained in the set of unrestricted black-box algorithms. Therefore, the unrestricted black-box complexity is a lower bound for the unbiased k-ary black-box complexity (for all $k \in \mathbb{N}$).

Algorithm 2: Unbiased k-ary Black-Box Algorithm

1 Sample x^0 uniformly at random from $\{0,1\}^n$ and query $f(x^0)$.
2 for $t = 1, 2, 3, \ldots$ *until termination condition met* **do**
3   Depending on $(f(x^0), \ldots, f(x^{t-1}))$, choose
4   an unbiased k-ary variation operator p^t, and
5 k previously queried search points $y^1, \ldots, y^k$.
6   Sample x^t according to $p^t(y^1, \ldots, y^k)$, and query $f(x^t)$.

3. THE UNBIASED $*$-ARY BLACK-BOX COMPLEXITY OF ONEMAX

In this section, we show that the unbiased black-box com-plexity of ONEMAX is $\Theta(n/\log n)$ with a leading constant between one and two. We begin with the formal definition of the function class ONEMAX$_n$. We will omit the subscript "n" if the size of the input is clear from the context.

DEFINITION 3 (ONEMAX). *For all* $n \in \mathbb{N}$ *and each* $z \in \{0,1\}^n$ *we define* $\mathrm{OM}_z : \{0,1\}^n \to \mathbb{N}, x \mapsto |\{j \in [n] \mid x_j = z_j\}|$.[1] *The class* ONEMAX$_n$ *is defined as* ONEMAX$_n := \{\mathrm{OM}_z \mid z \in \{0,1\}^n\}$.

To motivate the definitions, let us briefly mention that we do not further consider the optimization of specific functions such as $\mathrm{OM}_{(1,\ldots,1)}$, since they would have an unrestricted black-box complexity of 1: The algorithm asking for the bit-string $(1, \ldots, 1)$ in the first step easily optimizes the function in just one step. Thus, we need to consider some general-izations of these functions. For the unrestricted black-box model, we already have a lower bound by Droste Jansen, and Wegener [DJW06]. For the same model, an algorithm which matches this bound in order of magnitude is given by Anil and Wiegand in [AW09].

THEOREM 4. *The unrestricted black-box complexity of* ONEMAX$_n$ *is* $\Theta(n/\log n)$. *Moreover, the leading constant is at least 1.*

---

[1] Intuitively, OM_z is the function of n minus the Hamming distance to z.

As already mentioned, the lower bound on the complexity of $\textsc{OneMax}_n$ in the unrestricted black-box model from Theorem 4 directly carries over to the stricter unbiased black-box model.

COROLLARY 5. *The unbiased $*$-ary black-box complexity of $\textsc{OneMax}_n$ is at least $n/\log n$.*

Moreover, an upper bound on the complexity of $\textsc{OneMax}$ in the unbiased black-box model can be derived using the same algorithmic approach as given for the unrestricted black-box model (compare [AW09] and Theorem 4).

THEOREM 6. *The unbiased $*$-ary black-box complexity of $\textsc{OneMax}_n$ is at most $(1 + o_n(1))\frac{2n}{\log n}$.*

In return, this theorem also applies to the unrestricted black-box model and refines Theorem 4 by explicitly bounding the leading constant of the *unrestricted* black-box complexity for $\textsc{OneMax}$ by a factor of two of the lower bound. The result in Theorem 6 is based on Algorithm 3. This algorithm makes use of the operator `uniformSample` that samples a bitstring uniformly at random, which clearly is an unbiased (0-ary) variation operator. Further, it makes use of another family of operators: $\texttt{chooseConsistent}_{u^1,\dots,u^t}(x^1,\dots,x^t)$ chooses a bitstring $z \in \{0,1\}^n$ uniformly at random such that, for all $i \in [t]$, $\textsc{OM}_z(x^i) = u^i$ (if there exists one, and any bitstring uniformly at random otherwise). In other words, bitstring z is chosen such that the function values of $\textsc{OM}_z$ on the search points $x^1,\dots,x^t$ are consistent with the observed values $u^1,\dots,u^t$. It is easy to see that this is a family of unbiased variation operators.

Algorithm 3: Optimizing $\textsc{OneMax}$ with unbiased variation operators.

---
1 input Integer $n \in \mathbb{N}$ and function $f \in \textsc{OneMax}_n$;
2 initialization $t \leftarrow \left\lceil \left(1 + \frac{4\log\log n}{\log n}\right)\frac{2n}{\log n} \right\rceil$;
3 repeat
4   **foreach** $i \in [t]$ **do**
5 $x^i \leftarrow \texttt{uniformSample}()$;
6 $w \leftarrow \texttt{chooseConsistent}_{f(x^1),\dots,f(x^t)}(x^1,\dots,x^t)$;
7 until $f(w) = n$;
8 output w;

An upper bound of $(1 + o_n(1))2n/\log n$ for the expected runtime of Algorithm 3 follows directly from the following theorem which implies that the number of repetitions of steps 4 to 6 follows a geometric distribution with success probability $1 - o_n(1)$. This proves Theorem 6.

LEMMA 7. *Let n be sufficiently large (i.e., let $n \geq N_0$ for some fixed constant $N_0 \in \mathbb{N}$). Let $z \in \{0,1\}^n$ and let X be a set of $t \geq \left(1 + \frac{4\log\log n}{\log n}\right)\frac{2n}{\log n}$ samples chosen from $\{0,1\}^n$ uniformly at random and mutually independent. Then the probability that there exists an element $y \in \{0,1\}^n$ such that $y \neq z$ and $\textsc{OM}_y(x) = \textsc{OM}_z(x)$ for all $x \in X$ is bounded from above by $2^{-t/2}$.*

The previous lemma is a refinement of Theorem 1 in [AW09], and its proof follows the proof of Theorem 1

in [AW09], clarifying some inconsistencies[2] in that proof. To show Lemma 7, we first give a bound on a combinatorial quantity used later in its proof (compare Lemma 1 in [AW09]).

PROPOSITION 8. *For sufficiently large n,*

$$t \geq \left(1 + \frac{4\log\log n}{\log n}\right)\frac{2n}{\log n},$$

and even $d \in \{2,\dots,n\}$, it holds that

$$\binom{n}{d}\left(\binom{d}{d/2}2^{-d}\right)^t \leq 2^{-3t/4}. \qquad (1)$$

PROOF. By Stirling's formula, we have $\binom{d}{d/2} \leq \left(\frac{\pi d}{2}\right)^{-1/2}2^d$. Therefore,

$$\binom{n}{d}\left(\binom{d}{d/2}2^{-d}\right)^t \leq \binom{n}{d}\left(\frac{\pi d}{2}\right)^{-t/2}. \qquad (2)$$

We distinguish two cases. First, we consider the case $2 \leq d < n/(\log n)^3$. By Stirling's formula, it holds that $\binom{n}{d} \leq \left(\frac{en}{d}\right)^d$. Thus, we get from (2) that

$$\binom{n}{d}\left(\binom{d}{d/2}2^{-d}\right)^t \leq \left(\frac{en}{d}\right)^d\left(\frac{\pi d}{2}\right)^{-t/2}$$
$$= 2^{\left(\frac{2d}{t}\log\left(\frac{en}{d}\right) - \log\left(\frac{\pi d}{2}\right)\right)\frac{t}{2}}. \qquad (3)$$

We bound d by its minimal value 2 and maximal value $n/(\log n)^3$, and t by $2n/\log n$ to obtain

$$\frac{2d}{t}\log\frac{en}{d} - \log\frac{\pi d}{2} \leq \frac{1}{(\log n)^2}\log\frac{en}{2} - \log\pi.$$

Since the first term on the right hand side converges to 0 and since $\log\pi > 3/2$, the exponent in (3) can be bounded from above by $-3t/4$, if n is sufficiently large. Thus, we obtain inequality (1) for $2 \leq d < n/(\log n)^3$.

Next, we consider the case $n/(\log n)^3 \leq d \leq n$. By the binomial formula, it holds that $\binom{n}{d} \leq 2^n$. Thus,

$$\binom{n}{d}\left(\frac{\pi d}{2}\right)^{-t/2} \leq 2^n\left(\frac{\pi d}{2}\right)^{-t/2} = 2^{\left(\frac{2n}{t} - \log\frac{\pi d}{2}\right)\frac{t}{2}}. \qquad (4)$$

We bound $\pi d/2$ by $n/(\log n)^3$ and t by $\left(1 + \frac{4\log\log n}{\log n}\right)\frac{2n}{\log n}$ to obtain

$$\frac{2n}{t} - \log\frac{\pi d}{2} \leq \frac{\log n}{1 + \frac{4\log\log n}{\log n}} - \log(n/(\log n)^3)$$
$$= \frac{\log n}{1 + \frac{4\log\log n}{\log n}} - \log n + 3\log\log n$$
$$= \frac{3\log\log n + \frac{4\log\log n}{\log n}(-\log n + 3\log\log n)}{1 + \frac{4\log\log n}{\log n}}$$
$$= -\frac{\log n - 12\log\log n}{\log n + 4\log\log n}\log\log n.$$

---
[2] For example, in the proof of Lemma 1 in [AW09] the following claim is made. Let $d(n)$ be a monotone increasing sequence that tends to infinity. Then for sufficient large n the sequence $h_d(n) = \left(\frac{\pi d(n)}{8}\right)^{1/(2\ln n)}$ is bounded away from 1 by a constant $b > 1$. Clearly, this is not the case. For example, for $d(n) = \log n$, the sequence $h_{\log}(n)$ converges to 1.

Again, for sufficiently large n the right hand side becomes smaller than $-3/2$. We combine the previous inequality with inequalities (2) and (4) to show inequality (1) for $n/(\log n)^3 \leq d \leq n$. $\square$

With the previous proposition at hand, we finally prove Lemma 7.

PROOF OF LEMMA 7. Let n be sufficiently large, $z \in \{0,1\}^n$, and X a set of $t \geq \left(1 + \frac{4 \log \log n}{\log n}\right)\frac{2n}{\log n}$ samples chosen from $\{0,1\}^n$ uniformly at random and mutually independent.

For $d \in [n]$, let $A_d := \{y \in \{0,1\}^n \mid n - \text{OM}_z(y) = d\}$ be the set of all points with Hamming distance d from z. Let $d \in [n]$ and $y \in A_d$. We say the point y is *consistent* with x if $\text{OM}_y(x) = \text{OM}_z(x)$ holds. Intuitively, this means that OM_y is a possible target function, given the fitness of x. It is easy to see that y is consistent with x if and only if x and y (and therefore x and z) differ in exactly half of the d bits that differ between y and z. Therefore, y is never consistent with x if d is odd and the probability that y is consistent with x is $\binom{d}{d/2}2^{-d}$ if d is even.

Let p be the probability that there exists a point $y \in \{0,1\}^n \setminus \{z\}$ such that y is consistent with all $x \in X$. Then,

$$p = \Pr\left(\bigcup_{y \in \{0,1\}^n \setminus \{z\}} \bigcap_{x \in X} \text{"}y \text{ is consistent with } x\text{"}\right).$$

Thus, by the union bound, we have

$$p \leq \sum_{y \in \{0,1\}^n \setminus \{z\}} \Pr\left(\bigcap_{x \in X} \text{"}y \text{ is consistent with } x\text{"}\right).$$

Since, for a fixed y, the events "y is consistent with x" are mutually independent for all $x \in X$, it holds that

$$p \leq \sum_{d=1}^{n} \sum_{y \in A_d} \prod_{x \in X} \Pr(\text{"}y \text{ is consistent with } x\text{"}).$$

We substitute the probability that a fixed $y \in \{0,1\}^n$ is consistent with a randomly chosen $x \in \{0,1\}^n$ as given above. Using $|A_d| = \binom{n}{d}$, we obtain

$$p \leq \sum_{d \in \{1,\dots,n\}:\, d \text{ even}} \binom{n}{d}\left(\binom{d}{d/2}2^{-d}\right)^t.$$

Finally, we apply Proposition 8 and have $p \leq n2^{-3t/4}$ which concludes the proof since $n \leq 2^{t/4}$ for sufficiently large n (as t in $\Omega(n/\log n)$). $\square$

4. THE UNBIASED κ-ARY BLACK-BOX COMPLEXITY OF ONEMAX

In this section, we show that higher arity indeed enables the construction of faster black-box algorithms. In particular, we show the following result.

THEOREM 9. *For every $k \in [n]$ with $k \geq 2$, the unbiased k-ary black-box complexity of ONEMAX_n is at most linear in n. Moreover, it is at most $(1 + o_k(1))2n/\log k$.*

This result is surprising, since in [LW10], Lehre and Witt prove that the unbiased unary black-box complexity of the class of all functions f with a unique global optimum is $\Omega(n \log n)$. Thus, we gain a factor of $\log n$ when switching from unary to binary variation operators.

To prove Theorem 9, we introduce two different algorithms interesting on their own. Both algorithms share the idea to track which bits have already been optimized. That way we can avoid flipping them again in future iterations of the algorithm.

The first algorithm proves that the unbiased binary black-box complexity of ONEMAX_n is at most linear in n if the arity is at least two. For the general case, with $k \geq 3$, we give a different algorithm that provides asymptotically better bounds for k growing in n. We use the idea that the whole bitstring can be divided into smaller substrings, and subsequently those can be independently optimized. We show that this is possible, and together with Theorem 6, this yields the above bound for ONEMAX_n in the k-ary case for $k \geq 3$.

4.1 The Binary Case

We begin with the binary case. We use the three unbiased variation operators `uniformSample` (as described in Section 3), `complement` and `flipOneWhereDifferent` defined as follows. The unary operator `complement(x)` returns the bitwise complement of x. The binary operator `flipOneWhereDifferent(x, y)` returns a copy of x, where one of the bits that differ in x and y is chosen uniformly at random and then flipped. It is easy to see that `complement` and `flipOneWhereDifferent` are unbiased variation operators.

Algorithm 4: Optimizing ONEMAX with unbiased binary variation operators.

1 input Integer $n \in \mathbb{N}$ and function $f \in \text{ONEMAX}_n$;
2 initialization $x \leftarrow$ `uniformSample()`;
3 $y \leftarrow$ `complement(x)`;
4 repeat
5   Choose $b \in \{0,1\}$ uniformly at random;
6   **if** $b = 1$ **then**
7 $x' \leftarrow$ `flipOneWhereDifferent(x, y)`;
8   **if** $f(x') > f(x)$ **then** $x \leftarrow x'$;
9   **else**
10 $y' \leftarrow$ `flipOneWhereDifferent(y, x)`;
11   **if** $f(y') > f(y)$ **then** $y \leftarrow y'$;
12 until $f(x) = n$;
13 output x;

LEMMA 10. *With exponentially small probability of failure, the optimization time of Algorithm 4 on the class ONEMAX_n is at most $(1 + \varepsilon)2n$, for all $\varepsilon > 0$. The algorithm only involves binary operators.*

PROOF. We first prove that the algorithm is correct. Assume that the instance has optimum z, for some $z \in \{0,1\}^n$. We show that the following invariant is satisfied in the beginning of every iteration of the main loop (steps 4-12): for all $i \in [n]$, if $x_i = y_i$, then $x_i = z_i$. In other words, the positions where x and y have the same bit value are optimized. The invariant clearly holds in the first iteration, as x and y differ in all bit positions. A bit flip is only accepted if the fitness value is strictly higher, an event which occurs with positive probability. Hence, if the invariant holds in the current iteration, then it also holds in the following iteration. By induction, the invariant property now holds in every iteration of the main loop.

We then analyze the runtime of the algorithm. Let T be the number of iterations needed until n bit positions have been optimized. Due to the invariant property, this is the same as the time needed to reduce the Hamming distance between x and y from n to 0. An iteration is successful, i.e., the Hamming distance is reduced by 1, with probability $1/2$ independently of previous trials. The random variable T is therefore negative binomially distributed with parameters n and $1/2$. It can be related to a binomially distributed random variable X with parameters $2n(1+\varepsilon)$ and $1/2$ by $\Pr(T \geq 2n(1+\varepsilon)) = \Pr(X \leq n)$. Finally, by applying a Chernoff bound with respect to X, we obtain $\Pr(T \geq 2n(1+\varepsilon)) \leq \exp(-\varepsilon^2 n/2(1+\varepsilon))$. $\square$

It is easy to see that Algorithm 4 yields the same bounds on the class of monotone functions, which is defined as follows.

DEFINITION 11 (MONOTONE FUNCTIONS). *Let* $n \in \mathbb{N}$ *and let* $z \in \{0,1\}^n$. *A function* $f : \{0,1\}^n \to \mathbb{R}$ *is said to be monotone with respect to* z *if for all* $y, y' \in \{0,1\}^n$ *with* $\{i \in [n] \mid y_i = z_i\} \subsetneq \{i \in [n] \mid y'_i = z_i\}$ *it holds that* $f(y) < f(y')$. *The class* MONOTONE$_n$ *contains all such functions that are monotone with respect to some* $z \in \{0,1\}^n$.

Now, let f be a monotone function with respect to z and let y and y' be two bitstrings which differ only in the i-th position. Assume that $y_i \neq z_i$ and $y'_i = z_i$. It follows from the monotonicity of f that $f(y) < f(y')$. Consequently, Algorithm 4 optimizes f as fast as any function in ONEMAX$_n$.

COROLLARY 12. *The unbiased binary black-box complexity of* MONOTONE$_n$ *is* $O(n)$.

Note that MONOTONE$_n$ strictly includes the class of linear functions with non-zero weights.

4.2 Proof of Theorem 9 for Arity $k \geq 3$

For the case of arity $k \geq 3$ we analyze the following Algorithm 5 and show that its optimization time on ONEMAX$_n$ is at most $(1 + o_k(1))2n/\log k$. Informally, the algorithm splits the bitstring into blocks of length k. The n/k blocks are then optimized separately using a variant of Algorithm 3, each in expected time $(1 - o_k(1))2k/\log k$.

In detail, Algorithm 5 maintains its state using three bitstrings x, y and z. Bitstring x represents the preliminary solution. The positions in which bitstrings x and y differ represent the remaining blocks to be optimized, and the positions in which bitstrings y and z differ represent the current block to be optimized. Due to permutation invariance, it can be assumed without loss of generality that the bitstrings can be expressed by $x = \alpha\overline{\beta}\gamma$, $y = \overline{\alpha}\beta\gamma$, and $z = \alpha\beta\gamma$, see Step 6 of Algorithm 5. The algorithm uses an operator called flipKWhereDifferent$_\ell$ to select a new block of size ℓ to optimize. The selected block is optimized by calling the subroutine optimizeSelected$_{n,\ell}$, and the optimized block is inserted into the preliminary solution using the operator update.

The operators in Algorithm 5 are defined as follows. The operator flipKWhereDifferent$_k(x,y)$ generates the bitstring z. This is done by making a copy of y, choosing $\ell := \min\{k, H(x,y)\}$ bit positions for which x and y differ uniformly at random, and flipping them. The operator update(a,b,c) returns a bitstring a' which in each position

$i \in [n]$ independently, takes the value $a'_i = b_i$ if $a_i = c_i$, and $a'_i = a_i$ otherwise. Clearly, both these operators are unbiased. The operators uniformSample and complement have been defined in previous sections.

Algorithm 5: Optimizing ONEMAX with unbiased k-ary variation operators, for $k \geq 3$.

1 **input** Integers $n, k \in \mathbb{N}$, and function $f \in$ ONEMAX$_n$;
2 **initialization** $x^1 \leftarrow$ uniformSample(),
  $y^1 \leftarrow$ complement(x), and $\tau \leftarrow \lceil \frac{n}{k} \rceil$;
3 **foreach** $t \in [\tau]$ **do**
4 $\quad$ $\ell(t) \leftarrow \min\{k, n - k(t-1)\}$;
5 $\quad$ $z \leftarrow$ flipKWhereDifferent$_{\ell(t)}(x^t, y^t)$;
6 $\quad$ Assume that $x^t = \alpha\overline{\beta}\gamma$, $y^t = \overline{\alpha}\beta\gamma$, and $z = \alpha\beta\gamma$;
7 $\quad$ $w^t\beta\gamma \leftarrow$ optimizeSelected$_{n,\ell(t)}(\overline{\alpha}\beta\gamma, \alpha\beta\gamma)$;
8 $\quad$ $w^t\overline{\beta}\gamma \leftarrow$ update$(\alpha\overline{\beta}\gamma, w^t\beta\gamma, \alpha\beta\gamma)$;
9 $\quad$ $x^{t+1} \leftarrow w^t\overline{\beta}\gamma$ and $y^{t+1} \leftarrow w^t\beta\gamma$;
10 **output** $x^{\tau+1}$;

It remains to define the subroutine optimizeSelected$_{n,k}$. This subroutine is a variant of Algorithm 3 that only optimizes a selected block of bit positions, and leaves the other blocks unchanged. The block is represented by the bit positions in which bitstrings y and z differ. Due to permutation-invariance, we assume that they are of the form $y = \overline{\alpha}\sigma$ and $z = \alpha\sigma$, for some bitstrings $\alpha \in \{0,1\}^k$, and $\sigma \in \{0,1\}^{n-k}$. The operator uniformSample in Algorithm 3 is replaced by a 2-ary operator defined by: randomWhereDifferent(x, y) chooses z, where for each $i \in [n]$, the value of bit z_i is x_i or y_i with equal probability. Note that this operator is the same as the standard uniform crossover operator. The operator family chooseConsistent in Algorithm 3 is replaced by a family of $(r+2)$-ary operators defined by: chsConsSel$_{u^1,\ldots,u^r}(x^1,\ldots,x^r,\overline{\alpha}\sigma,\alpha\sigma)$ chooses $z\sigma$, where the prefix z is sampled uniformly at random from the set $Z_{u,x} = \{z \in \{0,1\}^k \mid \forall i \in [t]\ \text{OM}_z(x_1^i x_2^i \cdots x_k^i) = u^i\}$. If the set $Z_{u,x}$ is empty, then z is sampled uniformly at random among all bitstrings of length k. Informally, the set $Z_{u,x}$ corresponds to the subset of functions in ONEMAX$_n$ that are consistent with the function values $u^1, u^2, \ldots, u^r$ on the inputs $x^1, x^2, \ldots, x^r$. It is easy to see that this operator is unbiased.

Algorithm 6: optimizeSelected used in Algorithm 5.

1 **input** Integers $n, k \in \mathbb{N}$, and bitstrings $\overline{\alpha}\sigma$ and $\alpha\sigma$, where $\alpha \in \{0,1\}^k$ and $\sigma \in \{0,1\}^{n-k}$;
2 **initialization** $r \leftarrow \min\left\{k-2, \left\lceil \left(1 + \frac{4\log\log k}{\log k}\right)\frac{2k}{\log k}\right\rceil\right\}$,
  $f_\sigma \leftarrow \frac{f(\alpha\sigma) + f(\overline{\alpha}\sigma) - k}{2}$;
3 **repeat**
4 $\quad$ **foreach** $i \in [r]$ **do**
5 $\quad\quad$ $x^i\sigma \leftarrow$ randomWhereDifferent$(\alpha\sigma, \overline{\alpha}\sigma)$;
6 $\quad$ $w\sigma \leftarrow$
  chsConsSel$_{f(x^1\sigma)-f_\sigma,\ldots,f(x^r\sigma)-f_\sigma}(x^1\sigma,\ldots,x^r\sigma,\overline{\alpha}\sigma,\alpha\sigma)$;
7 **until** $f(w\sigma) = k + f_\sigma$;
8 **output** $w\sigma$;

PROOF OF THEOREM 9 FOR ARITY $k \geq 3$. To prove the

correctness of the algorithm, assume without loss of generality the input $f = $ ONEMAX for which the correct output is 1^n.

We first claim that a call to $\texttt{optimizeSelected}_{n,k}(\overline{\alpha}\sigma, \alpha\sigma)$ will terminate after a finite number of iterations with output $1^k\sigma$ almost surely. The variable f_σ is assigned in line 2 of Algorithm 6, and it is easy to see that it takes the value $f_\sigma = f(0^k\sigma)$. It follows from linearity of f and from $f(\alpha 0^{n-k}) + f(\overline{\alpha}0^{n-k}) = k$, that $f(w0^{n-k}) = f(w\sigma) - f(0^k\sigma) = f(w\sigma) - f_\sigma$. The termination condition $f(w\sigma) = k + f_\sigma$ is therefore equivalent to the condition $w\sigma = 1^k\sigma$. For all $x \in \{0,1\}^k$, it holds that $\text{OM}_{(1,\dots,1)}(x) = f(x)$, so 1^k is member of the set $Z_{u,x}$. Hence, every invocation of $\texttt{chsConsSel}$ returns $1^k\sigma$ with non-zero probability. Therefore, the algorithm terminates after every iteration with non-zero probability, and the claim holds.

We then prove by induction the invariant property that for all $t \in [\tau + 1]$, and $i \in [n]$, if $x_i^t = y_i^t$ then $x_i^t = y_i^t = 1$. The invariant clearly holds for $t = 1$, so assume that the invariant also holds for $t = j \leq \tau$. Without loss of generality, $x^j = \alpha\overline{\beta}\gamma$, $y^j = \overline{\alpha}\beta\gamma$, $x^{j+1} = w^{j}\overline{\beta}\gamma$, and $y^{j+1} = w^j\beta\gamma$. By the claim above and the induction hypothesis, both the common prefix w^j and the common suffix γ consist of only 1-bits. So the invariant holds for $t = j+1$, and by induction also for all $t \in [\tau + 1]$.

It is easy to see that for all $t \leq \tau$, the Hamming distance between $x^{t+1} = w^t\overline{\beta}\gamma$ and $y^{t+1} = w^t\beta\gamma$ is $H(x^{t+1}, y^{t+1}) = H(\alpha\overline{\beta}\gamma, \overline{\alpha}\beta\gamma) - \ell(t) = H(x^t, y^t) - \ell(t)$. By induction, it therefore holds that

$$H(x^{\tau+1}, y^{\tau+1}) = H(x^1, y^1) - \sum_{t=1}^{\tau} \ell(t)$$

$$= n - \sum_{t=1}^{\tau} \min\{k, n - k(t-1)\} = 0.$$

Hence, by the invariant above, the algorithm returns the correct output $x^{\tau+1} = y^{\tau+1} = 1^n$.

The *runtime* of the algorithm in each iteration is dominated by the subroutine $\texttt{optimizeSelected}$. Note that by definition, the probability that $\texttt{chsConsSel}_{f(x^1\sigma)-f_\sigma,\dots,f(x^r\sigma)-f_\sigma}(x^1\sigma, \dots, x^r\sigma, \overline{\alpha}\sigma, \alpha\sigma)$ chooses $z\sigma$ in $\{0,1\}^n$, is the same as the probability that $\texttt{chooseConsistent}_{f(x^1),\dots,f(x^r)}(x^1, \dots, x^r)$ chooses z in $\{0,1\}^k$. To finish the proof, we distinguish between two cases.

Case 1: $k \leq 53$. In this case, it suffices[3] to prove that the runtime is $O(n)$. For the case $k = 2$, this follows from Lemma 10. For $2 < k \leq 53$, it holds that $r = k - 2$. Each iteration in $\texttt{optimizeSelected}$ uses $r + 1 = k - 1 = O(1)$ function evaluations, and the probability that $\texttt{chsConsSel}$ optimizes a block of k bits is at least $1 - (1 - 2^{-k})^r = \Omega(1)$ (when $w = 1^k$). Thus, the expected optimization time for a block is $O(1)$, and for the entire bitstring it is at most $(n/k) \cdot O(1)$.

Case 2: $k \geq 54$. In this case, $r = \left\lceil \left(1 + \frac{4 \log \log k}{\log k}\right) \frac{2k}{\log k} \right\rceil$ holds. Hence, with an analysis analogous to that in the proof of Theorem 6, we can show that the expected runtime of $\texttt{optimizeSelected}$ is at most $(1 + o_k(1))2(k-2)/\log(k-2)$.

---

[3] Assume that the expected runtime is less than cn for some constant $c > 0$ when $k \leq 53$. It is necessary to show that $cn \leq 2n/\log k + h(k)2n/\log k$, for some function h, where $\lim_{k\to\infty} h(k) \to 0$. This can easily be shown by choosing any such function h, where $h(k) \geq c \log k/2$ for $k \leq 53$.

Thus, the expected runtime is at most $n/k \cdot (1 + o_k(1))2(k - 2)/\log(k - 2) = (1 + o_k(1))2n/\log k$. $\square$

5. THE COMPLEXITY OF LEADING-ONES

In this section, we show that allowing k-ary variation operators, for $k > 1$, greatly reduces the black-box complexity of the LEADINGONES functions class, namely from $\Theta(n^2)$ down to $O(n \log n)$. We define the class LEADINGONES as follows.

DEFINITION 13 (LEADINGONES). *Let $n \in \mathbb{N}$. Let $\sigma \in S_n$ be a permutation of the set $[n]$ and let $z \in \{0,1\}^n$. The function $\text{LO}_{z,\sigma}$ is defined via $\text{LO}_{z,\sigma}(x) := \max\{i \in [0..n] \mid z_{\sigma(i)} = x_{\sigma(i)}\}$. We set $\text{LEADINGONES}_n := \{\text{LO}_{z,\sigma} \mid z \in \{0,1\}^n, \sigma \in S_n\}$.*

The class LEADINGONES is well-studied. Already in 2002, Droste, Jansen and Wegener [DJW02] proved that the classical $(1 + 1)$ EA has an expected optimization time of $\Theta(n^2)$ on LEADINGONES. This bound seems to be optimal among the commonly studied versions of evolutionary algorithms. In [LW10], the authors prove that the unbiased unary black-box complexity of LEADINGONES is $\Theta(n^2)$.

Droste, Jansen and Wegener [DJW06] consider a subclass of LEADINGONES_n, namely $\text{LEADINGONES}_n^0 := \{\text{LO}_{z,\text{id}} \mid z \in \{0,1\}^n\}$, where id denotes the identity mapping on $[n]$. Hence their function class is not permutation invariant. In this restricted setting, they prove a black-box complexity of $\Theta(n)$. Of course, their lower bound of $\Omega(n)$ is a lower bound for the unrestricted black-box complexity of the general LEADINGONES_n class, and consequently, a lower bound also for the unbiased black-box complexities of this class.

The following theorem is the main result in this section.

THEOREM 14. *The unbiased binary black-box complexity of LEADINGONES_n is $O(n \log n)$.*

The key ingredient of the two black-box algorithm which yields the upper bound is an emulation of a binary search which determines the (unique) bit that increases the fitness *and* does flip this bit. Surprisingly, this can be done already with a binary operator. This works in spite of the fact that we also follow the general approach of the previous section of keeping two individuals x and y such that for all bit positions in which x and y agree, the corresponding bit value equals the one of the optimal solution.

We will use the two unbiased binary variation operators $\texttt{randomWhereDifferent}$ (as described in Section 4.2) and $\texttt{switchIfDistanceOne}$. The operator $\texttt{switchIfDistanceOne}(y, y')$ returns y' if y and y' differ in exactly one bit, and returns y otherwise. It is easy to see that $\texttt{switchIfDistanceOne}$ is an unbiased variation operators.

We call a pair (x, y) of search points *critical*, if the following two conditions are satisfied. (i) $f(x) \geq f(y)$. (ii) There are exactly $f(y)$ bit-positions $i \in [n]$ such that $x_i = y_i$. The following is a simple observation.

LEMMA 15. *Let $f \in \text{LEADINGONES}_n$. If (x,y) is a critical pair, then either $f(x) = n = f(y)$ or $f(x) > f(y)$.*

If $f(x) > f(y)$, then the unique bit-position k such that flipping the k-th bit in x reduces its fitness to $f(y)$ – or equivalently, the unique bit-position such that flipping this bit in y increases y's fitness – shall be called the *critical bit-position*. We also call $f(y)$ the value of the pair (x, y).

Note that the above definition does only use some function values of f, but not the particular definition of f. If $f = \text{LO}_{\sigma, z}$, then the above implies that x and y are equal on the bit-positions $\sigma(1), \ldots, \sigma(f(y))$ and are different on all other bit-positions. Also, the critical bit-position is $\sigma(f(y) + 1)$, and the only way to improve the fitness of y is flipping this particular bit-position (and keeping the positions $\sigma(1), \ldots, \sigma(f(y))$ unchanged). The central part of Algorithm 7, which is contained in lines 3 to 9, manages to transform a critical pair of value $v < n$ into one of value $v+1$ in $O(\log n)$ time. This is analyzed in the following lemma.

LEMMA 16. *Assume that the execution of Algorithm 7 is before line 4, and that the current value of (x, y) is a critical pair of value $v < n$. Then after an expected number of $O(\log n)$ iterations, the loop in lines 5-9 is left and (x, y) or (y, x) is a critical pair of value $v + 1$.*

PROOF. Let k be the critical bit-position of the pair (x, y). Let $y' = x$ be a copy of x. Let $J := \{i \in [n] \mid y_i \neq y_i'\}$. Our aim is to flip all bits of y' with index in $J \setminus \{k\}$.

We define y'' by flipping each bit of y' with index in J with probability $1/2$. Equivalently, we can say that y_i'' equals y_i' for all i such that $y_i' = y_i$, and is random for all other i (thus, we obtain such y'' by applying `randomWhereDifferent`(y, y')).

With probability exactly $1/2$, the critical bit was not flipped ("success"), and consequently, $f(y'') > f(y)$. In this case (due to independence), each other bit with index in J has a chance of $1/2$ of being flipped. So with constant probability at least $1/2$, $\{i \in [n] \mid y_i \neq y_i''\} \setminus \{k\}$ is at most half the size of $J \setminus \{k\}$. In this success case, we take y'' as new value for y'.

In consequence, the cardinality of $J \setminus \{k\}$ does never increase, and with probability at least $1/4$, it decreases by at least 50%. Consequently, after an expected number of $O(\log n)$ iterations, we have $|J| = 1$, namely $J = \{k\}$. We check this via an application of `switchIfDistanceOne`. □

We are now ready to prove the main result of this section.

PROOF OF THEOREM 14. We regard the following invariant: (x, y) or (y, x) is a critical pair. This is clearly satisfied after execution of line 1. From Lemma 16, we see that a single execution of the outer loop does not dissatisfy our invariant. Hence by Lemma 15, our algorithm is correct (provided it terminates). The algorithm does indeed terminate, namely in $O(n \log n)$ time, because, again by Lemma 16, each iteration of the outer loop increases the value of the critical pair by one. □

6. CONCLUSION AND FUTURE WORK

We continue the study of the unbiased black-box model introduced in [LW10]. For the first time, we analyze variation operators with arity higher than one. Our results show that already two-ary operators can allow significantly faster algorithms.

The problem ONEMAX cannot be solved in shorter time than $\Omega(n \log n)$ with unary variation operators [LW10]. However, the runtime can be reduced to $O(n)$ with binary operators. The runtime can be decreased even further

---

Algorithm 7: Optimizing LEADINGONES with unbiased binary variation operators.

```
1  initialization x ← uniformSample();
      y ← complement(x);
2  repeat
3  |  if f(y) > f(x) then (x, y) ← (y, x);
4  |  y' ← x;
5  |  repeat
6  |  |  y'' ← randomWhereDifferent(y, y');
7  |  |  if f(y'') > f(y) then y' ← y'';
8  |  |  y ← switchIfDistanceOne(y, y');
9  |  until f(y) = f(y');
10 until f(x) = f(y);
11 output x;
```

with higher arities than two. For k-ary variation operators, $2 \leq k \leq n$, the runtime can be reduced to $O(n / \log k)$, which for $k = n^{\Theta(1)}$ matches the lower bound in the classical black-box model. A similar positive effect of higher arity variation operators can be observed for the function class LEADING-ONES. While this function class cannot be optimized faster than $\Omega(n^2)$ with unary variation operators [LW10], we show that the runtime can be reduced to $O(n \log n)$ with binary, or higher arity variation operators.

Despite the restrictions imposed by the unbiasedness conditions, our analysis demonstrates that black-box algorithms can employ new and more efficient search heuristics with higher arity variation operators. In particular, binary variation operators allow a memory mechanism that can be used to implement binary search on the positions in the bitstring. The algorithm can thereby focus on parts of the bitstring that has not previously been investigated.

An important open problem arising from this work is to provide lower bounds in the unbiased black-box model for higher arities than one. Due to the greatly enlarged computational power of black-box algorithms using higher arity operators (as seen in this paper), proving lower bounds in this model seems significantly harder than in the unary model.

7. REFERENCES

[AW09]   G. Anil and R. P. Wiegand, *Black-box search by elimination of fitness functions*, Proc. of Foundations of Genetic Algorithms (FOGA'09), ACM, 2009, pp. 67–78.

[CLRS01] T. H. Cormen, C. E. Leiserson, R. L. Rivest, and C. Stein, *Introduction to Algorithms*, 2nd ed., McGraw Hill, 2001.

[DHK08] B. Doerr, E. Happ, and C. Klein, *Crossover can provably be useful in evolutionary computation*, Proc. of Genetic and Evolutionary Computation Conference (GECCO '08), ACM, 2008, pp. 539–546.

[DJW02] S. Droste, T. Jansen, and I. Wegener, *On the analysis of the (1+1) evolutionary algorithm*, Theoretical Computer Science **276** (2002), 51–81.

[DJW06] ———, *Upper and lower bounds for randomized search heuristics in black-box optimization*, Theoretical Computer Science **39** (2006), 525–544.

[DS04]   M. Dorigo and T. Stützle, *Ant colony optimization*, MIT Press, 2004.

[KE01]   J. Kennedy and R. C. Eberhart, *Swarm intelligence*, Morgan Kaufmann Publishers Inc., 2001.

[LL02]   P. Larrañaga and J. A. Lozano, *Estimation of distribution algorithms: a new tool for evolutionary computation*, Kluwer Academic Publishers, 2002.

[LW10]   P. K. Lehre and C. Witt, *Black-box search by unbiased variation*, Proc. of Genetic and Evolutionary Computation Conference (GECCO '10), ACM, 2010, pp. 1441–1448.

Non-uniform Mutation Rates for Problems with Unknown Solution Lengths

Stephan Cathabard
CIRRELT
University of Montreal
Montreal, Canada
cathabas@iro.umontreal.ca

Per Kristian Lehre
DTU Informatics
2800 Lyngby, Denmark
pkle@imm.dtu.dk

Xin Yao
University of Birmingham
Birmingham B15 2TT, UK
x.yao@cs.bham.ac.uk

ABSTRACT

Many practical optimisation problems allow candidate solutions of varying lengths, and where the length of the optimal solution is thereby *a priori* unknown. We suggest that non-uniform mutation rates can be beneficial when solving such problems. In particular, we consider a mutation operator that flips each bit with a probability that is inversely proportional to the bit position, rather than the bitstring length. The runtime of the (1+1) EA using this mutation operator is analysed rigorously on standard example functions. Furthermore, the behaviour of the new mutation operator is investigated empirically on a real world software engineering problem that has variable, and unknown solution lengths. The results show how the speedup that can be achieved with the new operator depends on the distribution of the solution lengths in the solution space. We consider a truncated geometric distribution, and show that the new operator can yield exponentially faster runtimes for some parameters of this distribution. The experimental results show that the new mutation operator leads to dramatically shorter runtimes on a class of instances of the software engineering problem that is conjectured to have short solutions on average.

Categories and Subject Descriptors

G.3 [**Probability and Statistics**]: Probabilistic Algorithms; F.2.2 [**Analysis of Algorithms and Problem Complexity**]: Nonnumerical Algorithms and Problems—*Computations on discrete structures*; D.2.5 [**Software Engineering**]: [Testing tools (e.g., data generators, coverage testing)]

General Terms

Algorithms, Theory

Keywords

runtime analysis, mutation operator, variable-length solutions, search-based software testing, FSM testing, unique input-output sequences

1. INTRODUCTION

Effective use of evolutionary algorithms (EAs) often requires the user to find parameter settings for the EA that are appropriate for the problem instance at hand. Experimental studies have suggested that EAs with some kind of adaptation can outperform standard ones. Empirical studies of the advantages of using adaptive parameter values as opposed to fixed values raised an interest in this field [16, 15]. Among others, such as the selective pressure and crossover rate, one of the most important parameter settings in EAs that use the bitwise mutation operator is the mutation rate. Adapting the mutation rate to the problem specifics will, when carefully chosen, produce better and robust results. The benefits in solving real-world problems would be of having a speedup of the search process, and to free the end user from the task of selecting suitable parameter values using a time-consuming trial and error process [7]. In particular, when the candidate solutions are represented by bitstrings of length n, a mutation rate of $1/n$ seems effective for some problems. Intuitively, this choice seems appropriate, since the operator will flip one bit in expectation, while still having a good probability of flipping more bits.

Theoretical investigations of the (1+1) EA show that a mutation rate of $\Theta(1/n)$ is asymptotically optimal for this EA on some simple functions. Droste et al [4] proved that if the mutation rate is decreased to $1/\alpha(n)n$, or increased to $\alpha(n)/n$, for any function $\alpha(n) = \omega(1)$, then the expected runtime of the (1+1) EA increases from $O(n \log n)$ to $\Omega(\alpha(n)n \log n)$ on ONEMAX. Deviating the mutation rate from $1/n$ by smaller, i.e. constant, factors has a weaker impact on the asymptotic expected runtime. Doerr and Goldberg recently proved that the (1+1) EA with mutation rate c/n, for any constant $c > 0$, can optimise any linear function in expected time $O(n \log n)$ [2]. It is important to point out that these results do not necessarily hold for more complex fitness functions and EAs. Jansen and Wegener presented functions where the (1+1) EA with a fixed mutation rate $1/n$ has super-polynomial runtime, whereas the runtime decreases to a polynomial when the mutation rate is increased to $\Theta(\log n/n)$ [8]. Doerr et al [3] showed that the mutation rate can be essential on strictly monotone functions, a class of functions that contains the linear functions. Considering the (1+1) EA with mutation rate c/n for a constant c, the expected runtime is $\Theta(n \log n)$ when $c < 1$. However, for higher mutation rates where $c > 33$, the runtime is $2^{\Omega(n)}$ with an overwhelmingly high probability [3]. For non-elitistic, population-based EAs, the mutation rate can be particularly critical, and must in general be set in accordance with the selective pressure in the EA [12, 11]. Keeping in mind these restrictions, a mutation rate of $1/n$ is often a simple choice in the absence of problem-specific knowledge.

However, setting the mutation rate to $1/n$ is only possible when the solution length n is known *a priori*. While this assumption is implicitly made in most theoretical studies, it does not hold for many practical optimisation problems. These problems often allow candidate solutions of different lengths, and the length of an optimal solution is typically not known. An example of such a problem, which we will discuss in Section 5, is the construction of testing sequences for finite state machines.

The purpose of this paper is to propose and analyse a mutation operator for optimisation problems where the solution lengths are *a priori* unknown. The paper is organised as follows. Section 2 formalises problems with variable-length solutions within the black-box scenario, and discusses how to quantify the runtime of algorithms working on such problems. Section 3 describes the mutation operator. The theoretical feasibility of the new mutation operator is then justified by runtime analysis on classical example functions in Section 4. Finally, in Section 5, we report experimental results on instances of a software engineering problem. A standard (1+1) EA is used as a baseline in both theoretical and experimental studies. Both strengths and limitations of the proposed approach are discussed in the conclusion.

2. VARIABLE-LENGTH PROBLEMS

We now formalise variable solution length problems within the black-box scenario [5]. In the classical black-box scenario, one considers an algorithm A and a class $\mathcal{F}$ of pseudo-Boolean functions $\{f_n : \{0,1\}^n \to \mathbb{R}\}$. An adversary selects a function f from this class. The algorithm knows the problem class $\mathcal{F}$, and in particular the solution length n, but has no information about the function chosen by the adversary. The goal of the algorithm is to find the optimum of function f by querying function values. The expected runtime of algorithm A on function f is the expected number of times the algorithm queries for a function value, before the optimum is evaluated for the first time. The expected runtime of algorithm A on the class $\mathcal{F}$ is the maximal expected runtime of A on any function in the class.

A variable-length problem consists of a function class $\mathcal{F}_n$ and a solution length distribution $K(n)$ over the integers from 1 to n. The class of functions is partitioned into subclasses $\mathcal{F}_n = \mathcal{G}_1 \cup \mathcal{G}_2 \cup \cdots \cup \mathcal{G}_n$, where each sub-class $\mathcal{G}_k, 1 \leq k \leq n$, contains a set of pseudo-Boolean functions $f : \{0,1\}^k \to \mathbb{R}$, corresponding to solution length k.

This time, the solution length k is sampled according to distribution $K(n)$, and k is unknown to the algorithm. Then, the adversary selects one of the functions f_k in the corresponding sub-class $\mathcal{G}_k$. To not reveal the number of input variables to the algorithm, the function is presented to the algorithm as a padded black-box function $\bar{f}_k$ that takes n input variables, defined as

$$\bar{f}_k(x_1 x_2 \cdots x_k x_{k+1} \cdots x_n) := f_k(x_1 x_2 \cdots x_k). \quad (1)$$

Hence, the function value of $\bar{f}_k$ is only determined by the first k bits in x. The algorithm knows the problem class $\mathcal{F}$, the maximal solution length n, and the solution length distribution $K(n)$. However, the algorithm has no information about the function f_k chosen by the adversary, or the sampled solution length k. The runtime of the search heuristic A on function $\bar{f}_k$ is the number of times search heuristic A evaluates function $\bar{f}_k$ until an optimal search point is evaluated for the first time. The expected runtime on the sub-class $\mathcal{G}_k$ is the worst case expected runtime of all functions in the class. Finally, the expected runtime on the entire class, denoted $T_{A,\mathcal{F},K}$ is the expected runtime on $\mathcal{G}_K$, where K is sampled according to distribution $K(n)$. In short, this will be referred to as the K-length runtime. Notice that this runtime is a random variable, and a function of random variable K specifying the underlying problem dimension. Clearly, the variable length runtime depends on the distribution K.

The runtime will be expressed as a function of two variables, the maximal solution length n, and a parameter ε that will control the distribution of K, i.e. the solution lengths. We will consider the case where K follows a variant of the geometrical distribution which is truncated to the set of integers $\{1, 2, \ldots, n\}$. We call this distribution pseudo-geometric. Several of the results obtained in this paper can easily be generalised to other distributions.

Definition 1 (PSEUDO-GEOMETRIC DISTRIBUTION). *A random variable X is said to follow a pseudo-geometric distribution with respect to the parameters $n \geq 1$ and $p \in (0, \frac{1}{n}]$ if*

$$\mathbf{Pr}\,[X = k] := \begin{cases} (1-p)^{k-1}p & \text{if } k \in \{1, 2, \ldots, n-1\}, \\ (1-p)^{n-1} & \text{if } k = n, \text{ and} \\ 0 & \text{otherwise.} \end{cases}$$

For notational convenience, we will use the parameter setting $p := n^{-\varepsilon}$, where $\varepsilon \in (0, 1)$, and consider ε as the parameter of the pseudo-geometric distribution. It is easy to see that the expectation of a pseudo-geometric random variable is asymptotically the same as the expectation of a geometric random variable.

Proposition 1. *If K is a pseudo-geometrically distributed random variable with parameter $p \geq n^{-\varepsilon}$ for $0 < \varepsilon < 1 - \delta$, where $\delta > 0$ is an arbitrarily small constant, then $\mathbf{E}\,[K] = \Theta(1/p)$.*

PROOF. For the lower bound, we have

$$\mathbf{E}\,[K] \geq (1/p)\mathbf{Pr}\,[K \geq 1/p]$$
$$\geq (1/p)(1-p)^{1/p-1}$$
$$\geq 1/ep.$$

For the upper bound, Eq. (2) in the appendix gives

$$\mathbf{E}\,[K] \leq n(1-p)^{n-1} + \frac{p}{1-p}\sum_{k=1}^{\infty} k(1-p)^k$$
$$= e^{-\Omega(n^\delta)} + \frac{p}{(1-p)}\frac{(1-p)}{p^2}$$
$$= O(1/p).$$

$\square$

3. POSITION-DEPENDENT MUTATION

The (1+1) EA using the new mutation operator can be described as follows.

Algorithm 1 (1+1) EA $_i$.

1: Choose x uniformly at random from $\{0, 1\}^n$.
2: **while** termination criterion is not met **do**
3:   Set $x' := x$.
4:   Flip each bit $i, 1 \leq i \leq n$, in x' with probability $\chi(i)$.
5:   **if** $f(x') \geq f(x)$ **then**
6:     $x := x'$.
7:   **end if**
8: **end while**

The only difference with the standard (1+1) EA is that we generalise the mutation rate in step 4 to $\chi(i)$. The classical (1+1) EA is obtained by setting the mutation rate function to $\chi(i) := 1/n$. In the following, we will compare this algorithm to the variant called (1+1) EA$_i$ where the mutation rate is defined as $\chi(i) := 1/(i+1)$. This algorithm flips early bit positions more often than later bit positions. In particular, bit position 1 is flipped in expectation every second iteration, whereas bit position n is flipped in expectation only once every $n + 1$ iterations.

The intuitive argument behind setting $\chi(i) = 1/(i + 1)$ is that for any solution length k, the majority of the bit positions will have the "right" asymptotic mutation rate of $\Theta(1/k)$. More precisely, for an arbitrarily small constant $\alpha > 0$, all the bit positions between αk and k have mutation rate $\Theta(1/k)$, where the asymptotic notation is with respect to variable k. A counterargument is that there is still a constant fraction of the bit positions where the mutation rate is too high, namely the positions from 1 to αk. In particular, the leading bit positions will be flipped very often. In the next section, we prove that the negative effects of having too high mutation rate in the first αk positions is out-weighted by the benefit of having the "right" mutation rate on the last $(1 - \alpha)k$ positions.

4. THEORETICAL RUNTIME ANALYSIS

The goal of this section is to analyse the runtime of the (1+1) EA with the position-dependant mutation operator on problems with unknown solution lengths. To this aim, we select the example functions ONEMAX and LEADINGONES, which are commonly considered in runtime analysis of new search heuristics. In the next experimental section, we will consider the UIO problem, which is a software testing problem. Note that there exist instances of the UIO problem that correspond exactly to the ONEMAX and LEADINGONES problems.

Before presenting the runtime analysis, we restate Jensen's inequality, which turns out to be a very useful tool in our scenario.

Lemma 1 (JENSEN'S INEQUALITY [14]). *Let X be a random variable with values in the interval (a, b). If f is a convex function over the interval (a, b), then*

$$f(\mathbf{E}[X]) \leq \mathbf{E}[f(x)].$$

If f is a concave function over the interval (a, b), then

$$f(\mathbf{E}[X]) \geq \mathbf{E}[f(x)].$$

The direct consequence of Jensen's inequality is that if the expectation of the random variable $T_{A,f,K}$ conditional on the event $K = k$ can be expressed as a convex function $g(k)$, then $g(\mathbf{E}[K])$ is a lower bound on the unconditional expectation of $T_{A,f,K}$. On the other hand if the expectation of $T_{A,f,K}$ conditional on the event $K = k$ can be expressed as a concave function $h(k)$, then $h(\mathbf{E}[K])$ is an upper bound on the unconditional expectation of $T_{A,f,K}$.

4.1 Simple Pseudo-Boolean Functions

We will first consider the function

$$\text{LEADINGONES}(x) = \sum_{i=1}^{n} \prod_{j=1}^{i} x_j.$$

Our goal is to describe how the expected runtime depends on the distribution of the solution lengths, i.e. on the distribution parameter ε.

Theorem 1. *If K is a pseudo-geometrically distributed random variable with parameter $p = 1/n^\varepsilon$, where $\varepsilon \in (0, 1 - \delta)$ for any constant $\delta \in (0, 1)$, then the expected K-length runtime of (1+1) EA$_i$ on LEADINGONES$_K$ is $\Theta(n^{3\varepsilon})$.*

PROOF. We start with the lower bound, and condition on the event $K = k$, for some $k, 1 \leq k \leq n$. It simplifies the analysis if we only consider the optimisation process during the period in which the current search point has at least $2k/3$ leading 1-bits, and less than $k - 2$ leading 1-bits, and do not account for the other time steps. So, let us assume that the current search point has $i, 2k/3 \leq i < k-2$, leading 1-bits. If the EA flips none of the first i bits, and flips the 0-bit in position $i + 1$, then a search point with at least $i + 1$ leading 1-bits is obtained. However, such a search point may have more than $i + 1$ leading 1-bits, depending on the bit values in position $i + 2$ and onwards. For the lower bound, we need to account for such 1-bits that the algorithm gains for "free".

More precisely, a bit-position $i + 2$ in a given run is called a *free-rider* if the first accepted search point with at least $i + 1$ leading 1-bits has a 1-bit in position $i + 2$. Following arguments similar to those in [4], it can be shown that the bits after the first 0-bit in the current search point are uniformly distributed. Hence, the number of free-riding bit positions among the last $k/3$ bit positions corresponds to the number of 1-bits in a random bitstring of length $k/3$. By a Chernoff bound, the probability of the event that there are more than $k/4$ free-riders is $e^{-\Omega(k)}$. We call this event a *failure*. Hence, with overwhelmingly high probability in k, we must wait for the EA to flip the left-most 0-bit in the current search point at least $k/3 - k/4 = k/12$ times.

In order to increase the number of leading 1-bits, all the first $i \geq 2k/3$ bits must remain unchanged. The probability of this event is no more than

$$\prod_{j=1}^{2k/3} \left(1 - \frac{1}{j+1}\right) = \prod_{j=1}^{2k/3} \frac{j}{j+1} = \frac{1}{2k/3 + 1}.$$

In addition, bit position $i + 1 \geq 2k/3 + 1$ must be flipped. Hence, the probability of increasing the number of leading 1-bits from i is no more than $1/(2k/3 + 1)(2k/3 + 2) =: q$.

Taking into account that this event must happen at least $k/12$ times, the expected number of iterations to reach an optimum is therefore at least $(k/12)(1/q) = \Omega(k^3)$. The function $f(k) = k^3$ satisfies $f''(k) \geq 0$ on the interval $[1, n]$, hence Jensen's inequality can be applied with respect to the expectation of K given in Proposition 1. Also taking into account the failure probability $e^{-\Omega(k)}$, the unconditional K-length runtime is $\Omega(n^{3\varepsilon})$.

We now prove the upper bound. Improving a solution from a position with i leading 1-bits is achieved by flipping bit position $i{+}1$, and flipping none of the first i bit positions. The probability of this event is

$$q_i \geq \frac{1}{i+2} \prod_{j=1}^{i} \left(1 - \frac{1}{i+1}\right) = \frac{1}{(i+1)(i+2)} \geq \frac{1}{2i^2}.$$

Hence, the expected time to obtain the optimum is no more than $\sum_{i=1}^{k} 1/q_i \leq 2k^3$, and an upper bound on the unconditional K-length runtime is

$$\mathbf{E}[T] \leq \sum_{k=1}^{n-1} 2k^3 \mathbf{Pr}[K = k]$$

$$\leq \frac{2p}{(1-p)} \sum_{k=1}^{\infty} k^3 (1-p)^k$$

$$= \frac{2p}{(1-p)} \frac{(1-p)\left(1 + 4(1-p) + (1-p)^2\right)}{p^4}$$

$$= O(p^{-3})$$

$$= O(n^{3\varepsilon}),$$

where the third step follows from Eq. (4) in the appendix. $\square$

We then consider the (1+1) EA with the classical mutation operator. It is well known that this algorithm has expected optimisation time $\Theta(n^2)$ on the LEADINGONES problem with fixed solution length [4]. While the variable-length optimisation time reduces with shorter expected solution lengths, the following theorem shows that the expected optimisation time of the (1+1) EA is never sub-linear on this problem.

Theorem 2. *If K is a pseudo-geometrically distributed random variable with $p = 1/n^\varepsilon$, where $\varepsilon \in (0, 1-\delta)$ for any constant $\delta \in (0,1)$, then the expected K-length runtime of the (1+1) EA on LEADINGONES$_K$ is $\Theta(n^{1+\varepsilon})$.*

PROOF. We condition on the event $K = k$. Given a current search point with $i, 0 \leq i < k$, leading 1-bits, the probability of making an improving step is at least $(1 - 1/n)^k (1/n) \geq 1/en$ and at most $1/n$. The EA must make at most k improving steps, and by the same arguments as in the proof of Theorem 1, at least $k/12$ improving steps. Hence, the expected runtime is at least $nk/12$ and at most enk. Note that the function $f(k) = cnk$ is both convex and concave for any constant c. Jensen's inequality with respect to the expectation of K given in Proposition 1 therefore implies that the expected K-length runtime is $\Theta(n/p) = \Theta(n^{1+\varepsilon})$. $\square$

We are now interested in determining when the (1+1) EA$_i$ outperforms the standard (1+1) EA, and *vice versa*. For this purpose, we define the expected speedup as the ratio between the expected K-length runtimes of the algorithms.

Corollary 1. *If K is a pseudo-geometrically distributed random variable with $p = 1/n^\varepsilon$, where $\varepsilon \in (0, 1-\delta)$ for any constant $\delta \in (0,1)$, then the expected speedup of (1+1) EA$_i$ over (1+1) EA on LEADINGONES$_K$ is $\Theta(n^{1-2\varepsilon})$.*

This result means that the (1+1) EA outperforms the (1+1) EA$_i$ when $\varepsilon > 1/2$, i.e. when the average solution length is above $\sqrt{n}$. In the worst case, when the solution length is fixed to n, the (1+1) EA$_i$ is a factor of n slower than the (1+1) EA. On the other hand, (1+1) EA$_i$ outperforms the (1+1) EA when $\varepsilon < 1/2$, i.e. when the average solution length is below $\sqrt{n}$. In particular, for $\varepsilon = \log\log n / \log n$, the (1+1) EA$_i$ is exponentially faster than the (1+1) EA! In this case, the (1+1) EA$_i$ has expected runtime $O(\log n)$, whereas the (1+1) EA has expected runtime $\Omega(n)$. (Recall that the expected waiting time until (1+1) EA flips a specific bit is n.)

We now consider another well known fitness function,

$$\text{ONEMAX}(x) := \sum_{i=1}^{n} x_i.$$

Theorem 3. *The expected running time of the (1+1) EA$_i$ on ONEMAX$_K$ whose shortest optimal solution is of length K is $O(n^{2\varepsilon} \log n)$, K being a pseudo-geometrically distributed random variable with parameter $p = n^{-\varepsilon}$, for a constant $\varepsilon, 0 < \varepsilon < 1$.*

PROOF. We condition on the event $K = k$. Given that the current search point x has $i, 0 \leq i < k$, 0-bits, the probability of increasing the number of 1-bits is

$$p_i \geq \sum_{\substack{j=1 \\ x_j=0}}^{k} \frac{1}{j+1} \prod_{\substack{r=1 \\ r \neq j}}^{k} \left(1 - \frac{1}{r+1}\right)$$

$$\geq \frac{i}{k+1} \prod_{r=1}^{k} \frac{r}{r+1}$$

$$= \frac{i}{(k+1)^2}.$$

Hence, the expected time to obtain k 1-bits is no more than $\sum_{i=1}^{k-1} 1/p_i = O(k^2 \log k)$. The expected K-length runtime is thus

$$\mathbf{E}[T] = \sum_{k=1}^{n} \mathbf{E}[T \mid K = k]\, \mathbf{Pr}[K = k]$$

$$= O(n^2 \log n)(1-p)^{n-1} + \sum_{k=1}^{n} O(k^2 \log k) p(1-p)^{k-1}$$

$$\leq O(\log n) \frac{p}{(1-p)} \sum_{k=1}^{\infty} k^2 (1-p)^k = O(n^{2\varepsilon} \log n),$$

where the last step follows from Eq. (3) in the appendix. $\square$

To prove a lower bound for (1+1) EA$_i$ on ONEMAX$_K$, it is necessary to take into account the positions of the 0-bits in the bitstring. In the most favourable case for the algorithm, all the 0-bits are located in the beginning of the bitstring, and the algorithm can easily flip many 0-bits. However, we think the 0-bits are unlikely to be positioned in such a way. We conjecture that the bound in Theorem 3 is tight when the distribution parameter ε is constant. On the other hand, for the classical (1+1) EA, we are able to prove a tight bound on the expected runtime.

Theorem 4. *Let K be pseudo-geometrically distributed with parameter $p = 1/n^\varepsilon$ where $\epsilon \in (0,1)$. Then the expected K-length running time of the (1+1) EA on ONEMAX$_K$ is $\Theta(\varepsilon n \log n)$.*

PROOF. For the lower bound, we first calculate the expected runtime conditional on a fixed solution length k. By Chernoff bounds, the probability that there are more than $2k/3$ 1-bits in the initial search point is bounded from above by $e^{-\Omega(k)}$. The probability that one of the remaining $k/3$ 0-bits has not been mutated within $n \ln k$ steps is

$$1 - \left(1 - \left(1 - \frac{1}{n}\right)^{n \ln k}\right)^{k/3} \geq 1 - \left(1 - \frac{1}{k}\right)^{k/3}$$
$$= \Omega(1).$$

Therefore we have $\mathbf{E}[T \mid K = k] = \Omega(n \log k)$. In particular, the expected runtime for $K = n^{\varepsilon} - 1$, i.e. slightly below the expectation of K is $\Omega(\varepsilon n \log n)$. The probability that K takes at least value $n^{\varepsilon} - 1$ is

$$\mathbf{Pr}[K \geq n^{\varepsilon} - 1] \geq (1 - p)^{n^{\varepsilon} - 1} \geq 1/e.$$

So a lower bound on the unconditional expected K-length runtime is

$$\mathbf{E}[T \mid K \geq n^{\varepsilon} - 1] \mathbf{Pr}[K \geq n^{\varepsilon} - 1] = \Omega(\varepsilon n \log n).$$

Following the same ideas as in the proof of Theorem 3, one can show that the expected runtime conditional on the event $K = k$ is $O(n \log k)$. An upper bound of $O(\varepsilon n \log n)$ now follows from Jensen's inequality. $\square$

It is worth noting that assuming the parameter ε is constant, the $(1+1)$ EA has asymptotically no advantage of shorter solution lengths. The speedup of $(1+1)$ EA_i over $(1+1)$ EA on ONEMAX_K is similar to that on $\mathrm{LEADINGONES}_K$. We did not prove any lower bound on the runtime of $(1+1)$ EA_i on ONEMAX_K, hence we can only show a lower bound on the speedup for this fitness function.

Corollary 2. *If K is a pseudo-geometrically distributed random variable with $p = n^{-\varepsilon}$, for a constant $\varepsilon, 0 < \varepsilon < 1$, then the expected speedup of $(1+1)$ EA_i over $(1+1)$ EA on ONEMAX_K is $\Omega(n^{1-2\varepsilon})$.*

5. EXPERIMENTAL RUNTIME ANALYSIS

The previous section provided rigorous results on the expected runtime of the two algorithms on example problems having a clear and simple structure. In practical optimisation settings, the problem structure can often be less clear, or unknown. In this section, we will experimentally compare the performance of the two algorithms on the problem of constructing so-called unique input-output sequences, which is a problem with less clear structure. See [13] for a discussion of how experimental investigations can complement a theoretical runtime analysis.

5.1 Problem Definition

Definition 2 (FINITE STATE MACHINE [10]). *A finite state machine (FSM) M is a quintuple $M = (I, O, S, \delta, \lambda)$, where I is the set of input symbols, O is the set of output symbols, S is the set of states, $\delta : S \times I \to S$ is the state transition function and $\lambda : S \times I \to O$ is the output function.*

For notational convenience, we extend the domain of the state transition function δ and the output function λ to the set of non-empty strings over the input alphabet, i.e.

$$\delta(s, a_1 a_2 \cdots a_n) := \delta(\delta(s, a_1 a_2 \cdots a_{n-1}), a_n), \text{ and}$$
$$\lambda(s, a_1 a_2 \cdots a_n) := \lambda(s, a_1) \cdot \lambda(\delta(s, a_1), a_2 \cdots a_n).$$

Definition 3 (UNIQUE INPUT-OUTPUT SEQUENCE [9]). *A unique input-output sequence (UIO) for a state s in an FSM M is a string x over the input alphabet of M such that $\lambda(s, x) \neq \lambda(t, x)$ for all states t, $t \neq s$.*

The interesting aspect of the UIO problem in the context of this paper is that the length of the UIOs are *a priori* unknown, and depends greatly on the problem instance. The shortest UIO sequence can be exponentially long with respect to the number of states [9]. On the other hand, experiments show that UIO sequences are typically short [1]. Trakhtenbrot and Barzdin considered a random FSM model with n states and m output symbols, showing that with probability $1 - O(1/n)$, any pair of distinguishable states in a random FSM can be distinguished by a sequence of no longer than $c \ln n / \ln m$, for some constant c [17].

To construct UIOs using an evolutionary algorithm, we need to find a way of representing and evaluating the quality of candidate solutions. Several approaches have been proposed in the literature. Here, we will use the approach described in [13]. Candidate solutions are represented as strings of length n over the input alphabet I of the FSM. The length parameter n specifies the maximal length of sequences among which we want to search for a UIO. We treat the problems of generating UIOs for the various states in the FSM separately, and define one fitness function for each state. UIOs for all the states in the FSM can be obtained simply by re-running the EA, once for each of the fitness functions. In the experiments, we therefore only considered finding UIOs for a designated state s_1.

Definition 4. *Given an FSM M, define the fitness function $f_{M,s} : I^n \to \mathbb{R}$ for state s as*

$$f_{M,s}(x) := |\{t \in S \mid \lambda(s, x) \neq \lambda(t, x)\}|.$$

Note that if x is an optimal solution, then so is the concatenation xy, for any input sequence y. Therefore, in analogy with the padding function in Eq. (1), one can consider the fitness function $f_{M,s}$ as a padded version of the true fitness function f_k, corresponding to a solution of length k.

Before describing the details of our experiments, we note that the problem of constructing UIOs has been studied extensively within the field *search-based software engineering* [6], which intersects evolutionary computation and software engineering. All previous studies used EAs with fixed mutation-rates.

5.2 Experimental Setup

Experiments were conducted on two FSM models, called the Random FSM model, and the Counter FSM model. The details of these models will be described in the next subsections. The experiments consisted of a series of runs. A run consists of first generating an instance with $n = 100$ states, where the corresponding fitness function was defined with a maximal solution length n. The $(1+1)$ EA and the $(1+1)$ EA_i were then started on this instance. An algorithm was stopped after 20000 iterations, or when an optimal solution had been found. If the algorithm did not find a solution within 20000 iterations, then the run was deemed unsuccessful for the algorithm. 10000 runs were made for the Random FSM model, and 10000 runs were made for the Counter FSM model. The number of iterations used by each algorithm and their success rates were recorded. The number of iterations used by each algorithm on the instances was plotted using box-and-whisker plots, indicating the smallest observed iteration number, the lower quartile, the median, the upper quartile, and the largest observed iteration number. The y-scale for the Random FSM model was log-transformed.

5.3 A Random FSM Model

For the purpose of this paper, we define a random FSM model $R = (I, O, S, \delta_R, \lambda_R)$. It has n states $S := \{s_1, \ldots s_n\}$, and binary input and output alphabets $I = O = \{0, 1\}$. A random machine is produced by first selecting uniformly at random a permutation σ over the states S and a random vector v of n states $v \in S^n$. Furthermore, a random bitstring x of length n is sampled, where each bit is 0 with probability $1 - 10/n$, and 1 with probability $10/n$. The output function λ_R and transition function δ_R are then defined as

$$\delta_R(s_i, 0) := \sigma(s_i) \qquad \lambda_R(s_i, 0) := 0$$
$$\delta_R(s_i, 1) := v_i \qquad \lambda_R(s_i, 1) := x_i.$$

The permutation σ guarantees that all states in the machine are reachable; Starting in state s_1, the machine cycles through all the states on input sequence 0^n. The bias towards 0-bits in the output on 1-input, ensures that many states will have the same output on this input, and is intended to make the problem instance harder.

5.4 A Counter FSM Model

To contrast the unstructured random FSM, we will also consider the highly structured counter FSM model $C = (I, O, S, \delta_C, \lambda_C)$ [13]. The counting machine has n states $S := \{s_1, s_2, \ldots, s_n\}$ and binary input and output alphabets $I = O = \{0, 1\}$. For all states $s_i \in S$, the output function λ_C is defined as

$$\lambda_C(s_i, 0) := 0, \text{ and, } \lambda_C(s_i, 1) := \begin{cases} 1 & \text{if } i = n, \text{ and} \\ 0 & \text{otherwise,} \end{cases}$$

and the transition function δ_C is defined as

$$\delta_C(s_i, 0) := s_i, \text{ and, } \delta_C(s_i, 1) := \begin{cases} s_1 & \text{if } i = n, \text{ and} \\ s_{i+1} & \text{otherwise.} \end{cases}$$

The counter FSM counts the number of 1-symbols in the input, and outputs a 1-symbol if and only if it has received n such inputs. In all other cases, the machine outputs a 0-symbol. It is known that the shortest UIO for state s_1 in the counter machine has length $n - 1$ [13], and is of the form 1^{n-1}.

5.5 Results and Discussion

The experimental results are summarised in Table 1 and Figure 2. Both algorithms had high success rates on both FSM models. It is difficult to compare the performance of the algorithms based on their success rates. However, the box-and-whisker plots in Figure 2 show that the median runtime of the $(1+1)$ EA$_i$ on the Random FSM model is an order of magnitude lower than the median runtime of the $(1+1)$ EA. Note that the scale is logarithmic. The upper quartile of the runs of $(1+1)$ EA$_i$ had lower runtime than the median runtime of the $(1+1)$ EA on the Random FSM model. The results are different for the Counter FSM model. Here, the median runtime of $(1+1)$ EA$_i$ is higher than the upper quartile runtime of the $(1+1)$ EA.

The results for the Counter FSM is consistent with the theoretical results. The $(1+1)$ EA outperforms the $(1+1)$ EA$_i$ when the solution length is close to what has been selected as the maximal candidate solution length. Random FSM instances are known to have short UIOs, i.e. solutions, on average [17]. The experimental results show that the $(1+1)$ EA$_i$ significantly outperforms the $(1+1)$ EA for such instances.

6. CONCLUSION

We have considered optimisation problems where the solution length is *a priori* unknown. For such problems, we have proposed a parameter-less mutation operator where the mutation rate is non-uniform. The operator can be applied in most evolutionary algorithms, and for many problems that have variable, or unknown solution lengths.

The approach is evaluated theoretically and experimentally using the $(1+1)$ EAs on three different problems, including one real-world FSM testing problem. A rigorous runtime analysis on two example functions shows that the $(1+1)$ EA$_i$ with position-dependant mutation operator can be exponentially faster than the standard $(1+1)$ EA when the solution lengths are short on average. The expected waiting time until the $(1+1)$ EA$_i$ flips a given bit position k is $k + 1$, while it is n for the $(1+1)$ EA. Hence, if only the first few bit positions need to be flipped, then the $(1+1)$ EA$_i$ may do so within shorter time than the $(1+1)$ EA$_i$. However, when the solution lengths are long, the modified mutation operator can incur a linear overhead in the expected runtime. Experimental results on computing testing sequences for FSMs are consistent with the theoretical results, showing that the new mutation operator can reduce the runtime significantly on instances that are conjectured to have short solution lengths on average.

A fundamental assumption behind this work is that the value of the cost function only depends on the k *left-most* variables in the problem, where k is unknown to the algorithm. If this assumption does not hold, e.g. the variable positions are permuted, then the new mutation operator cannot in general be expected to be more efficient than the standard mutation. While this assumption may seem strong, we think it is valid for many practical optimisation problems. For example, the assumption is valid in the practical problem that motivated this work, i.e., the construction of testing sequences for finite state machines.

As future work, we suggest a more extensive runtime analysis, and investigation of the approach in other problem domains where the solution lengths are unknown, or variable.

Acknowledgements

The main part of this work was done while Stephan Cathabard was a visiting student in The School of Computer Science at The University of Birmingham, UK. This work was supported by Deutsche Forschungsgemeinschaft (DFG) under grant no. WI 3552/1-1, and by EPSRC under grant no. EP/D052785/1.

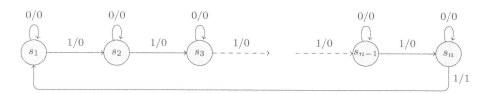

Figure 1: Counter FSM Model.

Algorithm	Random FSM Model	Counter FSM Model
(1+1) EA	9847 / 10000 (98.47 %)	10000 / 10000 (100 %)
(1+1) EA$_i$	9991 / 10000 (99.91 %)	10000 / 10000 (100 %)

Table 1: Success rates of runs of duration 20000 iterations.

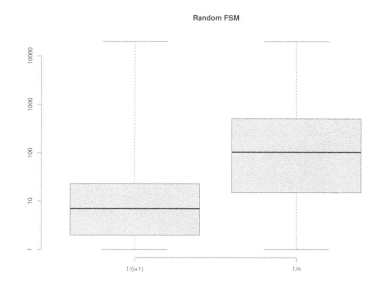

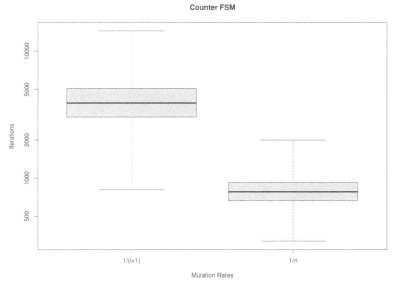

Figure 2: Results of experiments with position-dependant mutation (labelled $1/(i + 1)$, left) and normal mutation rates (labelled $1/n$, right).

7. REFERENCES

[1] Karnig Agop Derderian, Robert Mark Hierons, Mark Harman, and Qiang Guo. Automated unique input output sequence generation for conformance testing of FSMs. *The Computer Journal*, 49(3):331–344, 2006.

[2] Benjamin Doerr and Leslie Ann Goldberg. Adaptive drift analysis. In *Proceedings of Parallel Problem Solving from Nature - (PPSN XI)*, pages 32–41, 2010.

[3] Benjamin Doerr, Thomas Jansen, Dirk Sudholt, Carola Winzen, and Christine Zarges. Optimizing monotone functions can be difficult. In *Proceedings of the 11th international conference on Parallel problem solving from nature: Part I*, PPSN'10, pages 42–51, Berlin, Heidelberg, 2010. Springer-Verlag.

[4] Stefan Droste, Thomas Jansen, and Ingo Wegener. On the analysis of the (1+1) Evolutionary Algorithm. *Theoretical Computer Science*, 276:51–81, 2002.

[5] Stefan Droste, Thomas Jansen, and Ingo Wegener. Upper and lower bounds for randomized search heuristics in black-box optimization. *Theory of Computing Systems*, 39(4):525–544, 2006.

[6] Mark Harman, S. Afshin Mansouri, and Yuanyuan Zhang. Search based software engineering: A comprehensive analysis and review of trends techniques and applications. Technical Report TR-09-03, Department of Computer Science, King's College London, 2009.

[7] R. Hinterding, Z. Michalewicz, and A.E. Eiben. Adaptation in evolutionary computation: a survey. In *Evolutionary Computation, 1997., IEEE International Conference on*, pages 65 –69, April 1997.

[8] Thomas Jansen and Ingo Wegener. On the choice of the mutation probability for the (1+1) EA. In *PPSN VI: Proceedings of the 6th International Conference on Parallel Problem Solving from Nature*, pages 89–98, London, UK, 2000. Springer-Verlag.

[9] David Lee and Mihalis Yannakakis. Testing finite-state machines: state identification and verification. *IEEE Transactions on Computers*, 43(3):306–320, 1994.

[10] David Lee and Mihalis Yannakakis. Principles and methods of testing finite state machines-a survey. *Proceedings of the IEEE*, 84(8):1090–1123, 1996.

[11] Per Kristian Lehre. Negative drift in populations. In *Proceedings of Parallel Problem Solving from Nature - (PPSN XI)*, volume 6238 of *LNCS*, pages 244–253. Springer Berlin / Heidelberg, 2011.

[12] Per Kristian Lehre and Xin Yao. On the impact of the mutation-selection balance on the runtime of evolutionary algorithms. In *FOGA '09: Proceedings of the tenth ACM SIGEVO workshop on Foundations of genetic algorithms*, pages 47–58, New York, NY, USA, 2009. ACM.

[13] Per Kristian Lehre and Xin Yao. Runtime analysis of the (1+1) EA on computing unique input output sequences. *Information Sciences*, In Press., 2010.

[14] Michael Mitzenmacher and Eli Upfal. *Probability and Computing: Randomized Algorithms and Probabilistic Analysis*. Cambridge University Press, New York, NY, USA, 2005.

[15] Jim Smith and T.C. Fogarty. Self adaptation of mutation rates in a steady state genetic algorithm, 1996.

[16] Dirk Thierens. Adaptive mutation rate control schemes in genetic algorithms. In *Proceedings of the 2002 IEEE World Congress on Computational Intelligence: Congress on Evolutionary Computation*, pages 980–985. IEEE Press, 2002.

[17] B A Trakhtenbrot. *Finite automata; behavior and synthesis*. American Elsevier, 1973.

APPENDIX

For all x, where $|x| < 1$, it holds that

$$\sum_{i=1}^{\infty} ix^i = \frac{x}{(1-x)^2}, \tag{2}$$

$$\sum_{i=1}^{\infty} i^2 x^i = \frac{x(1+x)}{(1-x)^3}, \quad \text{and} \tag{3}$$

$$\sum_{i=1}^{\infty} i^3 x^i = \frac{x(1+4x+x^2)}{(1-x)^4}. \tag{4}$$

Adaptive Population Models for Offspring Populations and Parallel Evolutionary Algorithms

Jörg Lässig
ICS, University of Lugano
6906 Lugano, Switzerland

Dirk Sudholt
CERCIA, University of Birmingham
Birmingham B15 2TT, UK

ABSTRACT

We present two adaptive schemes for dynamically choosing the number of parallel instances in parallel evolutionary algorithms. This includes the choice of the offspring population size in a $(1+\lambda)$ EA as a special case. Our schemes are parameterless and they work in a black-box setting where no knowledge on the problem is available. Both schemes double the number of instances in case a generation ends without finding an improvement. In a successful generation, the first scheme resets the system to one instance, while the second scheme halves the number of instances. Both schemes provide near-optimal speed-ups in terms of the parallel time. We give upper bounds for the asymptotic sequential time (i. e., the total number of function evaluations) that are not larger than upper bounds for a corresponding non-parallel algorithm derived by the fitness-level method.

Categories and Subject Descriptors

F.2.2 [**Analysis of Algorithms and Problem Complexity**]: Nonnumerical Algorithms and Problems

General Terms

Algorithms, Design, Performance, Theory

Keywords

Parallel evolutionary algorithms, dynamic population size, island model, spatial structures, offspring populations, runtime analysis

1. INTRODUCTION

Parallelization is becoming a more and more important issue for solving difficult optimization problems [1]. Various implementations of parallel evolutionary algorithms (EAs) have been applied in the past decades [17]. An obvious way of using parallelization is to parallelize single operations of an EA such as executing fitness evaluations on different processors. This particularly applies to EAs using large offspring populations. So-called *island models* use parallelization on a higher level. The idea is to parallelize evolution itself, by having subpopulations, called islands, which evolve in parallel. Good solutions are exchanged between the islands in a *migration* process.

One of the most important questions when dealing with parallel EAs is how to choose the number of processors in order to decrease the *parallel optimization time*, defined as the number of generations until an EA has found a global optimum. Assume a setting where we can choose the number of processors to be allocated, but we have to pay costs for each processor in each generation it is being used. This situation is common in cloud computing or in large grids where processors are shared with other users. The total cost for all processors over time is called *sequential optimization time*. The task is now to choose the number of processors to be used such that the parallel optimization time is small, but at the same time the sequential time is reasonable. Allocating too many processors would waste computational effort and hence unnecessarily increase the sequential optimization time. Allocating too few processors implies a large parallel optimization time.

During the run of an EA, the "ideal" value for the number of processors is likely to change over time. One typical situation is that in the beginning of a run improvements are easy to obtain and only few processors are needed. The better the best fitness, the tougher it gets to find further improvements and then more processors are required. It therefore makes sense to look at adaptive mechanisms that can adjust the number of processors which are being used during the run of the EA. This obviously only makes sense in a setting where allocating and deallocating processors on-the-fly is possible and the cost for these operations and the cost for the communication between the processors are rather small. Hence we focus on balancing the parallel and sequential optimization times.

In the following we present adaptive schemes for choosing the number of processors that apply both to offspring populations as well as island models of EAs. We accompany our schemes by a rigorous theoretical analysis of their running time. Both schemes double the number of processors if the current generation fails to produce an offspring that has larger fitness than the current best fitness value. Otherwise, if the generation yields an improvement, the number of processors is decreased again. The difference between the two schemes lies in the way the number of processors is decreased.

FOGA'11, January 5–9, 2011, A-6867 Schwarzenberg, Austria.
Copyright 2011 ACM 978-1-4503-0633-1/11/01 ...$10.00.

The first scheme, called Scheme A, simply resets the number of processors to 1; only the best individual or island survives. This is to avoid an overly large number of processors when moving from a situation where improvements are hard to find to a situation where improvements are easy. This happens, for instance, if the EA escapes from a local optimum and then jumps to the basin of attraction of a better local optimum.

The second scheme, Scheme B, tries to maintain a fair number of processors over time; it also doubles the population size in unsuccessful generations and it halves the population size in successful generations. This strategy makes more sense in case the EA encounters similar probabilities for improvements over time. Both schemes are parameterless and oblivious with respect to the objective function. They can be applied in a black-box setting where no knowledge is available about the problem.

In terms of offspring populations we consider the $(1+\lambda)$ EA that maintains a single best individual and in each iteration creates λ offspring. A best offspring replaces its parent if its fitness is not worse. The λ offspring creations and function evaluations can be parallelized on λ processors. Concerning island models, we assume that migration sends copies of each island's best individual to each other island in every generation. So, whenever one island finds an improvement of the current best individual in the system, this is immediately communicated to all other islands. The island model then behaves similarly to offspring populations, but it is more general as the islands can work with populations of size larger than 1.

To unify the notation for island models and offspring populations, we simply speak of the *population size* in the following; this means the number of islands in the island model and the offspring population size for the $(1+\lambda)$ EA, respectively.

For EAs using either Scheme A or B we show that the expected parallel optimization time can be decreased drastically. In comparison to the well-known fitness-level method, in the parallel optimization time for every fitness value the expected waiting time for an improvement can be replaced by its logarithm. This can drastically reduce the parallel optimization time, in particular for problems where improvements are hard to find. The expected sequential time remains reasonable. We prove upper bounds on the expected sequential optimization time that are asymptotically no larger than upper bounds for a single instance obtained via the fitness-level method. For problems where the fitness-level method gives tight bounds, our results show that the two schemes automatically yield decreased expected parallel optimization times, without increasing the expected sequential time.

The mentioned bounds are general in the sense that they apply to islands running arbitrary elitist algorithms. Example applications are given that apply simultaneously to the $(1+\lambda)$ EA and to islands of population size 1. Various functions are considered: OneMax, LO, the class of unimodal functions and Jump_k.

Comparing the different schemes, our results indicate that Scheme B is more efficient than A, from an asymptotic perspective, as it quickly reduces the number of processors, if necessary. This adaptation automatically leads to optimal or near-optimal parallel optimization times on all considered examples. On one example Scheme B outper-

forms Scheme A. We also compare these results with tailored schemes that are allowed to use knowledge on the objective function.

Besides the main results this paper is also interesting because of the methods used. We introduce new techniques from the amortized analysis of algorithms, which represent natural and effective tools for analyzing adaptive mechanisms. These techniques may find further applications in the analysis of adaptive stochastic search algorithms.

The remainder of this work is structured as follows. In Section 2 we review previous work. Section 3 presents the algorithms and the considered population update schemes. In Section 4 we provide technical statements that will be used later on in our analyses and that may also help to understand the dynamics of the adaptive algorithms. Section 5 then presents general upper bounds for both schemes, while Section 6 deals with lower bounds on expected sequential times. Section 7 contains a brief discussion about tailored, that is, non-oblivious population update schemes. Our general theorems are applied to concrete example functions in Section 8. We finish with a discussion of possible extensions in Section 9 and conclusions in Section 10.

2. PREVIOUS WORK

2.1 Adaptive Population Models

Considering adaptive numbers of islands in the island model of EAs, previous work is very limited. However, there are numerous results for adaptive population sizes in EAs. Eiben, Marchiori, and Valko [5] describe EAs with on-the-fly population size adjustment. They compared the performance of the different strategies in terms of success rate, speed, and solution quality, measured on a variety of fitness landscapes. The best EAs with adaptive population resizing outperformed traditional approaches when considering the time to result, which is the parallel optimization time. Typical approaches are eliminating population size as an explicit parameter by introducing aging and maximum lifetime properties for individuals [12], the parameter-less GA (PLGA) which evolves a number of populations of different sizes simultaneously [7], random variation of the population size [3], and competition schemes [14].

Schwefel [15] first suggested the adaptation of the offspring population size during the optimization process. Herdy [8] proposed a mutative adaptation of λ in a two-level ES, where on the upper level, called population level, λ is treated as a variable to be optimized while on the lower level, called individual level, the object parameters are optimized.

In [6], a deterministic adaptation scheme for λ based on theoretical considerations on the relation between serial rates of progress for the actual number of offspring λ, for $\lambda - 1$ and for the optimal number of offspring is introduced. More specific, the local serial progress (i. e., progress per fitness function evaluation) is optimized in a $(1, \lambda)$ EA with respect to the number of offspring λ. The authors prove the following structural property: the serial progress-rate as a function of λ is either a function with exact one (local and global) maximum or a strictly monotonically increasing function.

Jansen, De Jong, and Wegener [9] further elaborate on the offspring population size, presenting a thorough runtime analysis of the effects of the offspring population size. They also suggest a simple way to dynamically adapt this parameter and present empirical results for this scheme, but no theoretical analysis of their scheme has been performed. The presented scheme doubles the offspring population size if the algorithm is unsuccessful to improve the currently best fitness value. Otherwise, it divides the current offspring population size by s, where s is the number of offspring with better fitness than the best fitness value so far. We will discuss in Section 9 how our schemes relate to their scheme and in how far our results can be transferred.

2.2 Theoretical Work on Parallel EAs

In [10], a first rigorous runtime analysis for island models has been performed by constructing a function where alternating phases of independent evolution and communication among the islands are essential. A simple island model with migration finds a global optimum in polynomial time, while panmictic populations as well as island models without migration need exponential time, with very high probability.

New methods for the running time analysis of parallel evolutionary algorithms with spatially structured populations have been presented in [11]. The authors generalized the well known fitness-level method, also called method of f-based partitions [18], from panmictic populations to spatially structured evolutionary algorithms with various migration topologies. These methods were applied to estimate the speed-up gained by parallelization in pseudo-Boolean optimization. It was shown that the possible speed-up for the parallel optimization time increases with the density of the topology. The expected sequential optimization time is asymptotically not larger than an upper bound for a corresponding non-parallel EA, derived via the fitness-level method.

More precisely, the classical fitness level method says that when s_i is a lower bound on the probability that one island leaves the current fitness level towards a better one, the expected time until this happens is at most $1/s_i$ for a panmictic population. In a parallel EA with a unidirectional ring, the expected parallel time decreases to $O(s^{1/2})$; in other words, the waiting time can be replaced by its square root. For a torus graph even the third root can be used and with a proper choice of the number μ of islands, a speed-up of order μ is possible in some settings.

Interestingly, the results from [11] can partially be interpreted in terms of adaptive population sizes. The analyses are based on the number of individuals on the current best fitness level. In our upper bounds, we pessimistically assume that only islands on the current best fitness level have a reasonable chance of finding better fitness levels. All worse individuals are ignored when estimating the waiting time for an improvement of the best fitness level. If a unidirectional ring topology is used, migration happens in every generation, and better individuals are guaranteed to win in the selection step, the number of individuals on the current best fitness level increases by 1 in each generation as always a new island is taken over. (We pessimistically ignore the fact that islands on worse fitness levels can improve their best fitness.) If any island finds an improvement, it is pessimistically assumed that then only one island has made it to a new, better fitness level.

This setting corresponds exactly to a parallel EA that in each unsuccessful generation acquires one new processor and to an adaptive $(1+\lambda)$ EA that increases λ by 1 in each unsuccessful generation. Once an improvement is found, the population size drops to 1 as in the case of our first scheme presented here. The upper bounds from [11] therefore directly transfer to additive population size adjustments.

In the following we show that multiplicative adjustments of the population size may admit better speed-ups than additive approaches as suggested in [11].

3. ALGORITHMS

In Sections 5 and 7 we present general upper bounds via the fitness-level method. These results are general in the following sense. If all islands in a parallel EA run elitist algorithms (i.e., algorithms where the best fitness in the population can never decrease) and if we have a lower bound on the probability of finding a better fitness level then this can be turned into an upper bound for the expected sequential and parallel running times of the parallel EA.

We present a scheme for algorithms where this argument applies. The goal is to maximize some fitness function f in an arbitrary search space. An adaptation towards minimization is trivial.

Algorithm 1 Elitist parallel EA with adaptive population

1: Let $\mu := 1$ and initialize a single island P_1^1 uniformly at random.
2: **for** $t := 1$ to ∞ **do**
3:   **for all** $1 \leq i \leq \mu$ in parallel **do**
4:     Select parents and create offspring by variation.
5:     Send a copy of a fittest offspring to all other islands.
6:     Create P_{t+1}^i such that it contains a best individual from the union of P_t^i, the new offspring, and the incoming migrants.
7:     $\mu_{t+1} :=$ updatePopulationSize(P_t^i, P_{i+1}^i)
8:     **if** $\mu_{t+1} > \mu_t$ **then** create $\mu_{t+1} - \mu_t$ new islands by copying existing islands.
9:     **if** $\mu_{t+1} < \mu_t$ **then** delete $\mu_t - \mu_{t+1}$ islands.

The selection of islands to be copied or removed, respectively, is left unspecified. Note that each island migrates individuals to all other islands. This corresponds to a complete migration topology. Due to this fact, all islands always contain an offspring with the current best fitness. This observation is sufficient for the upcoming analyses. With other topologies this selection would be based on the fitness values of the current elitists on all islands.

Note that we have neither specified a search space nor variation operators. However, in Section 6 we will discuss lower bounds that only hold in pseudo-Boolean optimization and for EAs that only use standard mutation (i.e., flipping each of n bits independently with probability $1/n$) for creating new offspring.

The $(1+\lambda)$ EA can be regarded a special case where we have λ islands and a single best individual takes over all λ islands. Setting $\lambda := 1$ yields the well-known $(1+1)$ EA.

Algorithm 2 $(1+\lambda)$ EA with adaptive population

1: Initialize a current search point x_1 uniformly at random.
2: **for** $t := 1$ to ∞ **do**
3:   Create λ offspring by mutation.
4:   Let x^* be an offspring with maximal fitness.
5:   **if** $f(x^*) \geq f(x_t)$ **then** $x_{t+1} := x^*$ **else** $x_{t+1} := x_t$.
6:   $\lambda :=$ updatePopulationSize$(\{x_t\}, \{x_{t+1}\})$

In Section 8 we will consider concrete example functions where the $(1+\lambda)$ EA with adaptive populations or, equivalently, an island model running $(1+1)$ EAs, with an adaptive number of islands are applied. The latter was called parallel $(1+1)$ EA in [10, 11].

We now define the population update schemes considered in this work. The function updatePopulationSize takes the old and the new population as inputs and it outputs a new population size.

In order to help finding improvements that take a long time to be found, we double the population size in each unsuccessful generation. As we might not need that many islands after a success, we reset the population size to 1.

Algorithm 3 updatePopulationSize(P_t, P_{t+1}) (Scheme A)

1: **if** $\max\{f(x) \mid x \in P_{t+1}\} \leq \max\{f(x) \mid x \in P_t\}$ **then**
2:     **return** $2\mu_t$
3: **else**
4:     **return** 1

On problems where finding improvements takes a similar amount of time, it might not make sense to throw away all islands at once. Especially if improvements have similar probabilities over time, it makes sense to stay close to the current number of islands. Therefore, in the following scheme we halve the population size with every successful generation. We will see that this does not worsen the asymptotic performance compared to Scheme A. For some problems this scheme will turn out to be superior.

Algorithm 4 updatePopulationSize(P_t, P_{t+1}) (Scheme B)

1: **if** $\max\{f(x) \mid x \in P_{t+1}\} \leq \max\{f(x) \mid x \in P_t\}$ **then**
2:     **return** $2\mu_t$
3: **else**
4:     **return** $\lfloor \mu_t/2 \rfloor$

The motivation for considering Scheme A is that we can assess the effect of gradually decreasing the population size, when comparing it to Scheme B. It also serves as a first step towards analyzing Scheme B, where the analysis turns out to be more involved.

Our schemes for parallel EAs are applicable in large clusters where the cost of allocating new processors is low, compared to the computational effort spent within the evolutionary algorithm. Many of our results can be easily adapted towards algorithms that do not use migration and population size updates in every generation, but only every τ generations, for a parameter $\tau \in \mathbb{N}$, called *migration interval*. This can significantly reduce the costs for allocating and deallocating new processors. Details can be found at the end of Section 5.

An algorithm using Scheme B can be implemented in a decentralized way as follows, where we assume that each island runs on a separate processor. Assume all processors are synchronized, i. e., they share a common timer. All processors have knowledge on the current best fitness level and they inform all other processors by sending messages in case they find a better fitness level. This message contains individuals that can be taken over by other processors so that all processors work on the current best fitness level.

In the adaptive scheme, if after one generation no message has been received, i. e., no processor has found a better

fitness level, each processor activates a new processor as follows. Each processor maintains a unique ID. The first processor has an ID that simply consists of an empty bit string. Each time a processor activates a new processor, it copies its current population and its current ID to the new processor. Then it appends a 0-bit to its ID while the new processor appends a 1-bit to its ID. At the end, all processors have enlarged their IDs by a single bit. When an improvement has been found, all processors first take over the genetic material in the messages that are passed. Then all processors whose ID ends with a 1-bit shut down. All other processors remove the last bit from their IDs.

It is easy to see that with this mechanism all processors will always have pairwise distinct IDs and no central control is needed to acquire and shut down processors.

As mentioned in the introduction, we define the *parallel optimization time* T^{par} as the number of generations until the first global optimum is evaluated. The *sequential optimization time* T^{seq} is defined as the number of function evaluations until the first global optimum is evaluated. The number of function evaluations is a common performance measure and it captures the total effort on all processors. Note that this includes all function evaluations in the generation of the algorithm in which the improvement is found. These definitions are consistent with the measures as suggested in the literature [9]. In both measures we allow ourselves to neglect the cost of the initialization as this only adds a fixed term to the running times.

4. TAIL BOUNDS AND EXPECTATIONS

In preparation for upcoming running time analyses we first prove tail bounds for the parallel optimization times in a setting where we are waiting for a specific event to happen. This, along with bounds on the expected parallel and sequential waiting times, will be useful to prove our main theorems. The tail bounds also indicate that the population will not grow too large.

In the remainder of this paper we abbreviate $\max\{x, 0\}$ by $(x)^+$.

LEMMA 1. *Assume starting with 2^k islands for some $k \in \mathbb{N}_0$ and doubling the number of islands in each generation. Let $T^{\mathrm{par}}(k, p)$ denote the random parallel time until the first island encounters an event that occurs independently on each island and in each generation with probability p. Let $T^{\mathrm{seq}}(k, p)$ be the corresponding sequential time. Then for every $\alpha \in \mathbb{N}_0$*

1. $\Pr\left[T^{\mathrm{par}}(k, p) > (\lceil \log(1/p) \rceil - k)^+ + \alpha + 1\right] \leq \exp(-2^\alpha)$,

2. $\Pr\left[T^{\mathrm{par}}(k, p) \leq \log(1/p) - k - \alpha\right] \leq 2 \cdot 2^{-\alpha}$,

3. $\log(1/p) - k - 3 < \mathrm{E}\left(T^{\mathrm{par}}(k, p)\right) < (\log(1/p) - k)^+ + 2$,

4. $\max\{1/p, 2^k\} \leq \mathrm{E}\left(T^{\mathrm{seq}}(k, p)\right) \leq 2/p + 2^k - 1$.

Each inequality remains valid if p is replaced by a pessimistic estimation of p (i. e., either an upper bound or a lower bound).

Proof. The condition $T^{\mathrm{par}}(k, p) > (\lceil \log(1/p) \rceil - k)^+ + \alpha + 1$ requires that the event does not happen on any island in this time period. The number of trials in the last generation is at least $2^{\lceil \log(1/p) \rceil + \alpha} \geq 1/p \cdot 2^\alpha$ for all $k \in \mathbb{N}_0$. Hence

$$\Pr\left[T^{\mathrm{par}}(k,p) > (\lceil \log(1/p) \rceil - k)^+ + \alpha + 1\right] \leq (1-p)^{1/p \cdot 2^\alpha}$$
$$\leq \exp(-2^\alpha) \,.$$

For the second statement we assume $k \leq \log(1/p) - \alpha$ as otherwise the claim is trivial. A necessary condition for $T^{\mathrm{par}}(k,p) \leq \log(1/p) - k - \alpha$ is that the event does happen at least once within in the first $\log(1/p) - k - \alpha$ generations. This corresponds to at most $\sum_{i=1}^{\log(1/p)-\alpha} 2^{i-1} \leq 2^{\log(1/p)-\alpha} = 1/p \cdot 2^{-\alpha}$ trials. If $p > 1/2$ the claim is trivial as either the probability bound on the right-hand side is at least 1 or the time bound is negative, hence we assume $p \leq 1/2$. Observing that then $1/p \cdot 2^{-\alpha} \leq 2(1/p - 1) \cdot 2^{-\alpha}$, the considered probability is bounded by

$$1 - (1-p)^{2(1/p-1) \cdot 2^{-\alpha}} \leq 1 - \exp(-2 \cdot 2^{-\alpha})$$
$$\leq 1 - (1 - 2 \cdot 2^{-\alpha}) = 2 \cdot 2^{-\alpha} \,.$$

To bound the expectation we observe that the first statement implies $\Pr\left[T^{\mathrm{par}}(k,p) \geq (\log(1/p) - k)^+ + \alpha + 2\right] \leq \exp(-2^\alpha)$. Since $T^{\mathrm{par}}(k,p)$ is non-negative, we have

$$\mathrm{E}\left(T^{\mathrm{par}}(k,p)\right) = \sum_{t=1}^\infty \Pr\left[T^{\mathrm{par}}(k,p) \geq t\right]$$
$$\leq (\log(1/p) - k)^+ + 1$$
$$+ \sum_{\alpha=0}^\infty \Pr\left[T^{\mathrm{par}}(k,p) \geq (\log(1/p) - k)^+ + \alpha + 2\right]$$
$$\leq (\log(1/p) - k)^+ + 1 + \sum_{\alpha=0}^\infty \exp(-2^\alpha)$$
$$< (\log(1/p) - k)^+ + 2$$

as the last sum is less than 1. For the lower bound we use that the second statement implies $\Pr\left[T \geq \log(1/p) - k - \alpha\right] \geq 1 - 2 \cdot 2^{-\alpha}$. Hence

$$\mathrm{E}\left(T^{\mathrm{par}}(k,p)\right) = \sum_{t=1}^\infty \Pr\left[T^{\mathrm{par}}(k,p) \geq t\right]$$
$$\geq \sum_{\alpha=2}^{\log(1/p)-k-1} \Pr\left[T^{\mathrm{par}}(k,p) \geq \log(1/p) - k - \alpha\right]$$
$$\geq \sum_{\alpha=2}^{\log(1/p)-k-1} (1 - 2 \cdot 2^{-\alpha})$$
$$= \log(1/p) - k - 2 - \sum_{\alpha=1}^{\log(1/p)-k-2} 2^{-\alpha}$$
$$> \log(1/p) - k - 3 \,.$$

For the fourth statement consider the islands one-by-one, according to some arbitrary ordering. Let $T(p)$ be the random number of sequential trials until an event with probability p happens. It is well known that $\mathrm{E}(T(p)) = 1/p$. Obviously $T^{\mathrm{seq}}(k,p) \geq T(p)$ since the sequential time has to account for all islands that are active in one generation. This proves $\mathrm{E}(T^{\mathrm{seq}}(k,p)) \geq \mathrm{E}(T(p)) \geq 1/p$. The second lower bound 2^k is obvious as at least one generation is needed for a success.

For the upper bound observe that $T^{\mathrm{seq}}(k,p) = 2^k$ in case $T(p) \leq 2^k$ and $T^{\mathrm{seq}}(k,p) = \sum_{i=k}^\ell 2^i$ in case $\sum_{i=k}^{\ell-1} 2^i < T(p) \leq \sum_{i=k}^\ell 2^i$. Together, we get that $T^{\mathrm{seq}}(k,p) \leq$

$\max\{2T(p), 2^k\} \leq 2T(p) + 2^k - 1$, hence $\mathrm{E}(T^{\mathrm{seq}}(k,p)) \leq 2/p + 2^k - 1$. $\qquad\square$

The presented tail bounds indicate that the population typically does not grow too large. The probability that the number of generations exceeds its expectation by an additive value of $\alpha+1$ is even an inverse doubly exponential function. The following provides a more handy statement in terms of the population size. It follows immediately from Lemma 1.

COROLLARY 1. *Consider the setting described in Lemma 1. For every $\beta \geq 1$, β a power of 2, the probability that while waiting for the event to happen the population size exceeds $\max\{2^{k+1}, 4/p\} \cdot \beta$ is at most $\exp(-\beta)$.*

One conclusion from these findings is that our schemes can be applied in practice without risking an overly large blowup of the population size. We now turn to performance guarantees in terms of expected parallel and sequential running times.

5. UPPER BOUNDS VIA FITNESS LEVELS

The following results are based on the fitness-level method, also known as method of f-based partitions (see, e.g., Wegener [18]). This method is well known for proving upper bounds for algorithms that do not accept worsenings of the population. Consider a partition of the search space into sets $A_1, \ldots, A_m$ where for all $1 \leq i \leq m-1$ all search points in A_i are strictly worse than all search points in A_{i+1} and A_m contains all global optima. If each set A_i contains only a single fitness value then the partition is called a *canonic* partition.

If s_i is a lower bound on the probability of creating a search point in $A_{i+1} \cup \cdots \cup A_m$, provided the current best search point is in A_i, then the expected optimization time is bounded from above by

$$\sum_{i=1}^{m-1} \Pr[A_i] \cdot \sum_{j=i}^{m-1} \frac{1}{s_j} \,,$$

where $\Pr[A_i]$ abbreviates the probability that the best search point after initialization is in A_i. The reason for this bound is that the expected time until A_i is left towards a higher fitness level is at most $1/s_i$ and each fitness level, starting from the initial one, has to be left at most once. Note that we can always simplify the above bound by pessimistically assuming that the population is initialized in A_1. This removes the term "$\sum_{i=1}^{m-1} \Pr[A_i] \cdot$" and only leaves $\sum_{j=1}^{m-1} 1/s_j$. This way of simplifying upper bounds can be used for all results presented hereinafter.

The fitness-level method yields good upper bounds in many cases. This includes situations where an evolutionary algorithm typically moves through increasing fitness levels, without skipping too many levels [16]. It only gives crude upper bounds in case values s_i are dominated by search points from which the probability of leaving A_i is much lower than for other search points in A_i or if there are levels with difficult local optima (i.e., large values $1/s_i$) that are only reached with a small probability.

Using the expectation bounds from Section 4 we now show in Theorem 1: For both schemes, A and B, in the upper bound for the expected parallel time the expected sequential waiting time can be replaced by its logarithm. In addition, the expected sequential time is asymptotically not larger than the upper bound for the serial algorithm, derived by f-based partitions.

In the remainder of the paper we denote with T_x^{par} and T_x^{seq}, $x \in \{A, B\}$ the parallel time and the sequential time for the schemes A and B, respectively.

THEOREM 1. *Given an f-based partition $A_1, \ldots, A_m$,*

$$\mathrm{E}\left(T_A^{\mathrm{seq}}\right) \leq 2 \sum_{i=1}^{m-1} \Pr\left[A_i\right] \cdot \sum_{j=i}^{m-1} \frac{1}{s_j} .$$

If the partition is canonic then also

$$\mathrm{E}\left(T_A^{\mathrm{par}}\right) \leq 2 \sum_{i=1}^{m-1} \Pr\left[A_i\right] \cdot \sum_{j=i}^{m-1} \log\left(\frac{2}{s_j}\right) .$$

The reason for the constant 2 in the $\log(2/s_j)$ term is to ensure that the term does not become smaller than 1; with a constant 1 the value $s_j = 1$ would even lead to a summand $\log(1/s_j) = 0$.

Proof. We only need to prove asymptotic bounds on the conditional expectations when starting in A_i, with a common constant hidden in all O-terms. The law of total expectation then implies the claim.

For Scheme A we apply Lemma 1 with $k = 0$. This yields that the expected sequential time for leaving the current fitness level A_j towards $A_{j+1} \cup \cdots \cup A_m$ is at most $2/s_j$ and the expected parallel time is at most $\log(1/s_j) + 2 \leq 2\log(2/s_j)$. The expected sequential time is hence bounded by $2 \sum_{j=i}^{m-1} 1/s_j$ and the expected parallel time is at most $2 \sum_{j=i}^{m-1} \log(2/s_j)$. □

We prove a similar upper bound for Scheme B using arguments from the amortized analysis of algorithms [2, Chapter 17]. Amortized analysis is used to derive statements on the average running time of an operation or to estimate the total costs of a sequence of operations. It is especially useful if some operations may be far more costly than others and if expensive operations imply that many other operations will be cheap. The basic idea of the so-called *accounting method* is to let all operations pay for the costs of their execution. Operations are allowed to pay excess amounts of money to fictional accounts. Other operations can then tap this pool of money to pay for their costs. As long as no account becomes overdrawn, the total costs of all operations is bounded by the total amount of money that has been paid or deposited.

THEOREM 2. *Given an f-based partition $A_1, \ldots, A_m$,*

$$\mathrm{E}\left(T_B^{\mathrm{seq}}\right) \leq 3 \sum_{i=1}^{m-1} \Pr\left[A_i\right] \cdot \sum_{j=i}^{m-1} \frac{1}{s_j} .$$

If the partition is canonic then also

$$\mathrm{E}\left(T_B^{\mathrm{par}}\right) \leq 4 \sum_{i=1}^{m-1} \Pr\left[A_i\right] \cdot \sum_{j=i}^{m-1} \log\left(\frac{2}{s_j}\right) .$$

Proof. We use the accounting method to bound the expected sequential optimization time of B as follows. Assume the algorithm being on level j with a population size of 2^k. If the current generation passes without leaving the current fitness level, we pay 2^k to cover the costs for the sequential time in this generation. In addition, we pay another 2^k to a fictional bank account. In case the generation is successful in leaving A_j and the previous generation was unsuccessful, we just pay 2^k and do not make a deposit. In case the current generation is successful and the last unsuccessful generation was on fitness level j, we withdraw 2^k from the bank account to pay for the current generation. In other words, the current generation is for free. This way, if there is a sequence of successful generations after an unsuccessful one on level j all but the first successful generations are for free.

Let us verify that the bank account cannot be overdrawn. The basic argument is that, whenever the population size is decreased from, say, 2^{k+1} to 2^k then there must be a previous generation where the population size was increased from 2^k to 2^{k+1}. It is easy to see that associating a decrease with the latest increase gives an injective mapping. In simpler terms, the latest generation that has increased the population size from 2^k to 2^{k+1} has already paid for the current decrease to 2^k.

When in the upper bound for A fitness level i takes sequential time $1 + 2 + \cdots + 2^k = 2^{k+1} - 1$ then for B the total costs paid are $2(1 + 2 + \cdots + 2^{k-1}) + 2^k$ as a successful generation does not make a deposit to the bank account. The total costs equal $2^{k+1} - 2 + 2^k \leq 3/2 \cdot (2^{k+1} - 1)$. In consequence, the total costs for Scheme B are at most $3/2$ the costs for A in A's upper bound. This proves the claimed upper bound for B.

By the very same argument an upper bound for the expected parallel time for B follows. Instead of paying 2^k and maybe making a deposit of 2^k, we always pay 1 and always make a deposit of 1. When withdrawing money, we always withdraw 1. This proves that also $\mathrm{E}\left(T_B^{\mathrm{par}}\right)$ is at most twice the corresponding upper bound for Scheme A. □

The argument in the above proof can also be used for proving a general upper bound for the expected parallel optimization time for B. When paying costs 2 for each fitness level, this pays for the successful generation with a population size of, say, 2^k and for one future generation where the population size might have to be doubled to reach 2^k again.

Imagine the sequence of population sizes over time and then delete all elements where the population size has decreased, including the associated generation where the population size was increased beforehand. In the remaining sequence the population size continually increases until, assuming a global optimum has not been found yet, after $n \log n$ generations a population size of at least n^n is reached. In this case the probability of creating a global optimum by mutation is at least $(1 - n^{-n})^{n^n} \approx 1/e$ as the probability of hitting any specific target point in one mutation is at least n^{-n}. The expected number of generations until this happens is clearly $O(1)$. We have thus shown the following.

COROLLARY 2. *For every function with m function values we have $\mathrm{E}\left(T_B^{\mathrm{par}}\right) \leq 2m + n \log n + O(1)$.*

This bound is asymptotically tight, for instance, for long path problems [4, 13]. So, the m-term, in general, cannot be avoided.

When comparing A and B with respect to the expected parallel time, we expect B to perform better if the fitness levels have a similar degree of difficulty. This implies that there is a certain target level for the population size. Note, however, that such a target level does not exist in case the

s_i-values are dissimilar. In the case of similar s_i-values A might be forced to spend time doubling the population size for each fitness level until the target level has been reached. This waiting time is reflected by the $\log(2/s_j)$-terms in Theorem 1. The following upper bound on B shows that these log-terms can be avoided to some extent. In the special yet rather common situation that improvements become harder with each fitness level, only the biggest such log-term is needed.

THEOREM 3. *Given a canonical f-based partition $A_1, \ldots, A_m$, $\mathrm{E}\left(T_{\mathrm{B}}^{\mathrm{par}}\right)$ is bounded by*

$$\sum_{i=1}^{m-1} \Pr\left[A_i\right] \cdot \left(3(m-i-1) + \log\left(\frac{1}{s_i}\right) \right.$$
$$\left. + \sum_{j=i+1}^{m-1} \left(\log\left(\frac{1}{s_j}\right) - \log\left(\frac{1}{s_{j-1}}\right) \right)^+ \right) .$$

If additionally $s_1 \geq s_2 \geq \cdots \geq s_{m-1}$ then the bound simplifies to

$$\sum_{i=1}^{m-1} \Pr\left[A_i\right] \cdot \left(3(m-i-1) + \log\left(\frac{1}{s_{m-1}}\right) \right) .$$

Proof. The second claim immediately follows from the first one as the log-terms form a telescoping sum.

For the first bound we again use arguments from amortized analysis. By Lemma 1 if the current population size is 2^k then the expected number of generations until an improvement from level i happens is at most $(\log(1/s_i) - k)^+ + 2$. This is a bound of 2 for $k \geq \log(1/s_i)$. We perform a so-called *aggregate analysis* to estimate the total cost on all fitness levels. These costs are attributed to different sources. Summing up the costs for all sources will yield a bound on the total costs and hence on $T_{\mathrm{B}}^{\mathrm{par}}$.

In the first generation the fitness level i^* the algorithm starts on pays $\log(1/s_{i^*})$ to the global bank account. Afterwards costs are assigned as follows. Consider a generation on fitness level i with a population size of 2^k.

- If the current generation is successful, we charge cost 2 to the fitness level; cost 1 pays for the effort in the generation and cost 1 is deposited on the bank account. In addition, each fitness level j that is skipped or reached during this improvement pays $(\log(1/s_j) - \log(1/s_{j-1}))^+$ as a deposit on the bank account. Note that this amount is non-negative and it may be non-integer.

- If $k \geq \log(1/s_i)$ and the current generation is unsuccessful we charge cost 1 to the fitness level.

- If $k < \log(1/s_i)$ and the current generation is unsuccessful we withdraw cost 1 from our bank account.

By Lemma 1 the expected cost charged to fitness level i in unsuccessful generations (i.e., not counting the last successful generation) is at most 1. Assuming for the moment that the bank account is never overdrawn, the overall expected cost for fitness level i is at most $1 + 2 + (\log(1/s_j) - \log(1/s_{j-1}))^+$. Adding the costs for the initial fitness level yields the claimed bound.

We use the so-called *potential method* [2, Chapter 17] to show that the bank account is never overdrawn. Our claim

is that at any point of time there is enough money on the bank account to cover the costs of increasing the current population size to at least $2^{\log(1/s_j)}$ where j is the current fitness level. We construct a potential function indicating the excess money on the bank account and show that the potential is always non-negative.

Let μ_t denote the population size in generation t and ℓ_t be the (random) fitness level in generation t. By b_t we denote the account balance on the bank account. We prove by induction that

$$b_t \geq (\log(1/s_{\ell_t}) - \log(\mu_t))^+ .$$

As this bound is always positive, this implies that the account is never overdrawn. After the initial fitness level has made its deposit we have $b_1 = \log(1/s_{\ell_1}) - 0$. Assume by induction that the bound holds for b_t.

If generation t is unsuccessful and $\log(\mu_t) \geq \log(1/s_{\ell_t})$ then the population size is doubled at no cost for the bank account. As by induction $b_t \geq 0$ we have $b_{t+1} = b_t \geq 0 = (\log(1/(s_{\ell_t})) - \log(\mu_{t+1}))^+$.

If generation t is unsuccessful and $\log(\mu_t) < \log(1/s_{\ell_t})$ then the algorithm doubles its population size and withdraws 1 from the bank account. As b_t is positive and $\log(\mu_{t+1}) = \log(\mu_t) + 1$, we have

$$b_{t+1} = b_t - 1 = \log(1/s_{\ell_t}) - \log(\mu_t) - 1 = \log(1/s_{\ell_t}) - \log(\mu_{t+1}).$$

If generation t is successful and the current fitness level increases from i to some $j > i$, the account balance is increased by

$$1 + \sum_{a=i+1}^{j} (\log(1/s_a) - \log(1/s_{a-1}))^+$$
$$\geq 1 + (\log(1/s_j) - \log(1/s_i))^+ .$$

This implies

$$b_{t+1} \geq b_t + 1 + (\log(1/s_j) - \log(1/s_i))^+$$
$$\geq (\log(1/s_i) - \log(\mu_t))^+ + 1 - \log(1/s_i) - \log(\mu_{t+1})$$
$$\geq (\log(1/s_j) - \log(\mu_t))^+ + 1$$
$$\geq (\log(1/s_j) - \log(\mu_{t+1}))^+ . \qquad \square$$

The upper bounds in this section can be easily adapted towards parallel EAs that do not perform migration and population size adaptation in every generation, but only every τ generations, for a migration interval $\tau \in \mathbb{N}$. Instead of considering the probability of leaving a fitness level in one generation, we simply consider the probability of leaving a fitness level in τ generations. This is done by considering $s_i' := 1 - (1 - s_i)^\tau$ instead of s_i. The resulting time bounds, based on $s_1', \ldots, s_{m-1}'$, are then with respect to the number of periods of τ generations. To get bounds on our original measures of time, we just multiply all bounds by a factor of τ.

6. LOWER BOUNDS FOR THE SEQUENTIAL TIME

In order to prove lower bounds for the expected sequential time we make use of recent results by Sudholt [16]. He presented a new lower-bound method based on fitness-level arguments. If it is unlikely that many fitness levels are skipped when leaving the current fitness-level set then good lower bounds can be shown.

The lower bound applies to every algorithm $\mathcal{A}$ in pseudo-Boolean optimization that only uses standard mutations (i. e., flipping each bit independently with probability $1/n$) to create new offspring. Such an EA is called a mutation-based EA. More precisely, every mutation-based EA $\mathcal{A}$ works as follows. First, $\mathcal{A}$ creates μ search points $x_1, \ldots, x_\mu$ uniformly at random. Then it repeats the following loop. A counter t counts the number of function evaluations; after initialization we have $t = \mu$. In one iteration of the loop the algorithm first selects one out of all search points $x_1, \ldots, x_t$ that have been created so far. This decision is based on the fitness values $f(x_1), \ldots, f(x_t)$ and, possibly, also the time index t. It performs a standard mutation of this search point, creating an offspring x_{t+1}.

To make this work self-contained, we cite (a slightly simplified version of) the result here. The performance measure considered is the number of function evaluations. This can be assumed to coincide with the number of offspring creations as every offspring needs to evaluated exactly once.

THEOREM 4 ([16]). *Consider a partition of the search space into non-empty sets $A_1, \ldots, A_m$ such that only A_m contains global optima. For a mutation-based EA $\mathcal{A}$ we say that $\mathcal{A}$ is in A_i or on level i if the best individual created so far is in A_i. Let the probability of traversing from level i to level j in one mutation be at most $u_i \cdot \gamma_{i,j}$ and $\sum_{j=i+1}^m \gamma_{i,j} = 1$. Assume that for all $j > i$ and some $0 < \chi \le 1$ it holds $\gamma_{i,j} \ge \chi \sum_{k=j}^m \gamma_{i,k}$. Then the expected number of function evaluations of $\mathcal{A}$ on f is at least*

$$\chi \sum_{i=1}^{m-1} \Pr[A_i] \cdot \sum_{j=i}^{m-1} \frac{1}{u_j} .$$

All population update schemes are compatible with this framework; every parallel mutation-based EA using an arbitrary population update scheme is still a mutation-based EA. Offspring creations are performed in parallel in our algorithms, but one can imagine these operations to be performed sequentially. We can cast a parallel EA with parallel offspring creations as a sequential mutation-based EA that simulates the population management of an island model in the background. Recall that the selection in the notion of a mutation-based EA can be based on the time index t. Hence, a sequential mutation-based EA can keep track of the times when individuals on a specific island have been created or when individuals have immigrated from a different island. The algorithm can then simulate offspring creations for an island by allowing only individuals on the island to become parents. There is one caveat: the parent selection mechanism in [16] does not account for possibly randomized decisions made during migration. However, the proof of Theorem 4 goes through in case additional knowledge is used.

We introduce the notion of *tight* fitness levels, where the success probabilities s_i from the classical fitness-level method are exact up to a constant factor.

DEFINITION 1. *Call an f-based partition $A_1, \ldots, A_m$ (asymptotically) tight for an algorithm $\mathcal{A}$ if there exist constants $c \ge 1 > \chi > 0$ and values $\gamma_{i,j}$ for $1 \le i, j \le m$ such that for each population in A_i the following holds.*

1. *The probability of generating a population in $A_{i+1} \cup \cdots \cup A_m$ in one mutation is at least s_i.*

2. *The probability of generating a population in A_j in one mutation, $j > i$, is at most $c \cdot s_i \cdot \gamma_{i,j}$.*

3. *For the $\gamma_{i,j}$-values it holds that $\sum_{j=i+1}^m \gamma_{i,j} = 1$ and $\gamma_{i,j} \ge \chi \sum_{k=j}^m \gamma_{i,k}$ for all $i < j$.*

Tight f-based partitions imply that the standard upper bound by f-based partitions [18] is asymptotically tight. This holds for all elitist mutation-based algorithms, that is, mutation-based algorithms where the best fitness value in the population can never decrease.

THEOREM 5. *Consider an algorithm $\mathcal{A}$ with an arbitrary population update strategy that only uses standard mutations for creating new offspring. Given a tight f-based partition $A_1, \ldots, A_m$ for a function f, we have*

$$\mathrm{E}(T^{\mathrm{seq}}) = \Omega\left(\sum_{i=1}^{m-1} \Pr[A_i] \cdot \sum_{j=i}^{m-1} \frac{1}{s_j} \right) .$$

Proof. The lower bound on $\mathrm{E}(T^{\mathrm{seq}})$ follows by a direct application of Theorem 4. We already discussed that this theorem applies to all algorithms considered in this work. Setting $u_j := cs_j$ for all $1 \le j \le m$, c and χ being as in Definition 1, Theorem 4 implies

$$\mathrm{E}(T^{\mathrm{seq}}) \ge \frac{\chi}{c} \sum_{i=1}^{m-1} \Pr[A_i] \cdot \sum_{j=i}^{m-1} \frac{1}{s_j} .$$

As both, χ and c, are constants, this implies the claim. $\square$

This lower bound shows that for tight f-based partitions both our population update schemes produce asymptotically optimal results in terms of the expected sequential optimization time, assuming no cost of communications.

7. NON-OBLIVIOUS UPDATE SCHEMES

We also briefly discuss update schemes that are tailored towards particular functions, in order to judge the performance of our oblivious update schemes.

Non-oblivious population update schemes may allow for smaller upper bounds for the expected parallel time than the ones seen so far. When the population update scheme has complete knowledge on the function f and the f-based partition, an upper bound can be shown where each fitness level contributes only a constant to the expected parallel time. By $T_{\mathrm{no}}^{\mathrm{seq}}$ and $T_{\mathrm{no}}^{\mathrm{par}}$ we denote the sequential and parallel times of the considered non-oblivious scheme.

THEOREM 6. *Given an arbitrary f-based partition $A_1, \ldots, A_m$, there is a tailored population update scheme for which*

$$\mathrm{E}(T_{\mathrm{no}}^{\mathrm{seq}}) = O\left(\sum_{i=1}^{m-1} \left(\Pr[A_i] \cdot \sum_{j=i}^{m-1} \frac{1}{s_j} \right) \right)$$

and

$$\mathrm{E}(T_{\mathrm{no}}^{\mathrm{par}}) = O\left(\sum_{i=1}^{m-1} \Pr[A_i] \cdot (m - i - 1) \right) .$$

In particular, $\mathrm{E}(T_{\mathrm{no}}^{\mathrm{par}}) = O(m)$.

Proof. The update scheme chooses to use $\lceil 1/s_i \rceil$ islands if the algorithm is in A_i. Then the probability of finding an improvement in one generation is at least $1 - (1 - s_i)^{1/s_i} \geq 1 - 1/e$. The expected parallel time until this happens is at most $e/(e-1)$ and so the expected sequential time is at most $e/(e-1) \cdot \lceil 1/s_i \rceil \leq 2e/(e-1) \cdot 1/s_i$. Summing up these expectations for all fitness levels from i to $m-1$ proves the two bounds. $\qquad\square$

In some situations it is possible to design schemes that perform even better than the above bound suggests. For instance, for trap functions the best strategy would be to use a very large population in the first generation so that the optimum is found with high probability, and before the algorithm is tricked to increasing the distance to the global optimum.

8. BOUNDS FOR EXAMPLE FUNCTIONS

The previous bounds are applicable in a very general context, with arbitrary fitness functions. We also give results for selected example functions to estimate possible speed-ups in more concrete settings.

We consider the same example functions and function classes that have been investigated in [11]. The goal is the maximization of a pseudo-Boolean function $f \colon \{0,1\}^n \to \mathbb{R}$. For a search point $x \in \{0,1\}^n$ write $x = x_1 \ldots x_n$, then $\mathrm{OneMax}(x) := \sum_{i=1}^{n} x_i$ counts the number of ones in x and $\mathrm{LO}(x) := \sum_{i=1}^{n} \prod_{j=1}^{i} x_j$ counts the number of leading ones in x. A function is called *unimodal* if every non-optimal search point has a Hamming neighbor (i. e., a point with Hamming distance 1 to it) with strictly larger fitness. For $1 \leq k \leq n$ we also consider

$$\mathrm{Jump}_k := \begin{cases} k + \sum_{i=1}^{n} x_i, & \text{if } \sum_{i=1}^{n} x_i \leq n - k \text{ or } x = 1^n, \\ \sum_{i=1}^{n} (1 - x_i) & \text{otherwise}. \end{cases}$$

This function has been introduced by Droste, Jansen, and Wegener [4] as a function with tunable difficulty. Evolutionary algorithms typically have to perform a jump to overcome a gap by flipping k specific bits.

For these functions we obtain bounds for T^{seq} and T^{par} as summarized in Table 1. The lower bounds for $\mathrm{E}(T^{\mathrm{seq}})$ on OneMax and LO follow directly from [16] for all schemes.

	Scheme	$\mathrm{E}(T^{\mathrm{seq}})$	$\mathrm{E}(T^{\mathrm{par}})$
OneMax	A	$\Theta(n \log n)$	$O(n \log n)$
	B	$\Theta(n \log n)$	$O(n)$
	non-oblivious	$\Theta(n \log n)$	$O(n)$
LO	A	$\Theta(n^2)$	$\Theta(n \log n)$
	B	$\Theta(n^2)$	$O(n)$
	non-oblivious	$\Theta(n^2)$	$O(n)$
unimodal f	A	$O(dn)$	$O(d \log n)$
with d f-values	B	$O(dn)$	$O(d + \log n)$
	non-oblivious	$O(dn)$	$O(d)$
Jump_k	A	$O(n^k)$	$O(n \log n)$
with $k \geq 2$	B	$O(n^k)$	$O(n + k \log n)$
	non-oblivious	$O(n^k)$	$O(n)$

Table 1: Asymptotic bounds for expected parallel running times $\mathrm{E}(T^{\mathrm{par}})$ and expected sequential running times $\mathrm{E}(T^{\mathrm{seq}})$ for the parallel (1+1) EA and the $(1+\lambda)$ EA with adaptive population models.

THEOREM 7. *For the parallel (1+1) EA and the $(1+\lambda)$ EA with adaptive population models the upper bounds for $E(T^{\mathrm{seq}})$ and $E(T^{\mathrm{par}})$ hold as given in Table 1.*

Proof. The upper bounds for Scheme A follow from Theorem 1, for Scheme B from Theorems 2 and 3 and for the non-oblivious scheme from Theorem 6. Starting pessimistically from the first fitness level, the following bounds hold:

- For OneMax we use the canonical f-based partition $A_i := \{x \mid \mathrm{OneMax}(x) = i\}$ and the corresponding success probabilities $s_i \geq (n - i)/n \cdot (1 - 1/n)^{n-1} \geq (n - i)/(en)$. Hence, $E(T_\mathrm{A}^{\mathrm{par}}) \leq 2 \sum_{i=1}^{n-1} \log(\frac{2en}{n-i}) \leq 2n \log(2en) = O(n \log n)$,

$$\begin{aligned} E(T_\mathrm{A}^{\mathrm{seq}}) &\leq 2 \sum_{i=0}^{n-1} \frac{1}{s_i} \leq 2 \sum_{i=0}^{n-1} \frac{en}{n-i} \\ &= 2en \sum_{i=1}^{n} \frac{1}{i} = 2en \cdot [(\ln n) + 1], \end{aligned}$$

$E(T_\mathrm{B}^{\mathrm{par}}) \leq (3(n-2) + \log(2en)) = O(n)$ and $E(T_\mathrm{B}^{\mathrm{seq}}) \leq 3en \cdot [(\ln n) + 1]$, $E(T_{\mathrm{no}}^{\mathrm{par}}) = O(n)$ and $E(T_{\mathrm{no}}^{\mathrm{seq}}) = O(n \log n)$.

- For LO we use the canonical f-based partition $A_i := \{x \mid \mathrm{LO}(x) = i\}$ and the corresponding success probabilities $s_i \geq 1/n \cdot (1 - 1/n)^{n-1} \geq 1/(en)$. Hence, $E(T_\mathrm{A}^{\mathrm{par}}) \leq 2 \sum_{i=0}^{n-1} \log(2en) = 2n \log(2en) = O(n \log n)$,

$$E(T_\mathrm{A}^{\mathrm{seq}}) \leq 2 \sum_{i=0}^{n-1} \frac{1}{s_i} \leq 2 \sum_{i=0}^{n-1} en = 2en^2,$$

$E(T_\mathrm{B}^{\mathrm{par}}) \leq (3(n - 2) + \log(en)) = O(n)$, $E(T_\mathrm{B}^{\mathrm{seq}}) \leq 3en^2$, $E(T_{\mathrm{no}}^{\mathrm{par}}) = O(n)$ and $E(T_{\mathrm{no}}^{\mathrm{seq}}) = O(n^2)$.

- For unimodal functions with d function values we use corresponding success probabilities $s_i \geq 1/(en)$. Hence, $E(T_\mathrm{A}^{\mathrm{par}}) \leq 2 \sum_{i=1}^{d-1} \log(2en) \leq 2d \log(2en) = O(dn)$,

$$E(T_\mathrm{A}^{\mathrm{seq}}) \leq 2 \sum_{i=1}^{d-1} \frac{1}{s_i} \leq 2 \sum_{i=1}^{d-1} en = 2edn,$$

$E(T_\mathrm{B}^{\mathrm{par}}) \leq 3(d-2) + \log(en) = O(d + \log n)$, $E(T_\mathrm{B}^{\mathrm{seq}}) = 3edn$, $E(T_{\mathrm{no}}^{\mathrm{par}}) = O(d)$ and $E(T_{\mathrm{no}}^{\mathrm{seq}}) = O(dn)$.

- For Jump_k functions with $k \geq 2$ and all individuals having neither $n - k$ nor n 1-bits, an improvement is found by either increasing or decreasing the number of 1-bits. This corresponds to optimizing OneMax. In order to improve a solution with $n - k$ 1-bits, a specific bit string with Hamming distance k has to be created, which has probability s_{n-k} at least

$$\left(\frac{1}{n}\right)^k \cdot \left(1 - \frac{1}{n}\right)^{n-k} \geq \left(\frac{1}{n}\right)^k \cdot \left(1 - \frac{1}{n}\right)^{n-1} \geq \frac{1}{en^k}.$$

Hence, $E(T_\mathrm{A}^{\mathrm{par}}) \leq O(n \log n) + 2 \log(en^k) \leq O(n \log n) + 2k \log(en) = O(n \log n)$, $E(T_\mathrm{A}^{\mathrm{seq}}) \leq O(n^k)$, $E(T_\mathrm{B}^{\mathrm{par}}) \leq O(n) + k \log(en) = O(n + k \log n)$, $E(T_\mathrm{B}^{\mathrm{seq}}) \leq O(n^k)$, $E(T_{\mathrm{no}}^{\mathrm{par}}) = O(n)$ and $E(T_{\mathrm{no}}^{\mathrm{seq}}) = O(n^k)$. $\qquad\square$

It can be seen from Table 1 that both our schemes lead to significant speed-ups in terms of the parallel time. The speed-ups increase with the difficulty of the function. This becomes obvious when comparing the results on OneMax and LO and it is even more visible for Jump$_k$.

The upper bounds for $\mathrm{E}\left(T_\mathrm{B}^\mathrm{par}\right)$ are always asymptotically lower than those for $\mathrm{E}\left(T_\mathrm{A}^\mathrm{par}\right)$, except for Jump$_k$ with $k = \Theta(n)$. However, without corresponding lower bounds we cannot say whether this is due to differences in the real running times or whether we simply proved tighter guarantees for B. We therefore consider the function LO in more detail and prove a lower bound for A. This demonstrates that Scheme B can be asymptotically better than Scheme A on a concrete problem.

THEOREM 8. *For the parallel (1+1) EA and the (1+λ) EA with adaptive population models on* LO *we have* $\mathrm{E}\left(T_\mathrm{A}^\mathrm{par}\right) = \Omega(n \log n)$.

Proof. We consider a pessimistic setting (pessimistic for proving a lower bound) where an improvement has probability exactly $1/n$. This ignores that all leading ones have to be conserved in order to increase the best LO-value. We show that with probability $\Omega(1)$ at least $n/30$ improvements are needed in this setting. As by Lemma 1 the expected waiting time for an improvement is at least $\max\{0, (\log n) - 3\}$, the conditional expected parallel time is $\Omega(n \log n)$. By the law of total expectation, also the unconditional expected parallel time is then $\Omega(n \log n)$.

Let us bound the expected increase in the number of leading ones on one fitness level. Let T_i^par denote the random number of generations until the best fitness increases when the algorithm is on fitness level i. By the law of total expectation the expected increase in the best fitness in this generation equals

$$\sum_{t=1}^\infty \Pr\left[T_i^\mathrm{par} = t\right] \cdot \mathrm{E}\left(\text{LO-increase} \mid T_i^\mathrm{par} = t\right) . \qquad (1)$$

The expected increase in the number of leading ones can be estimated as follows. With $T_i^\mathrm{par} = t$ the number of mutations in the successful generation is 2^{t-1}. Let I denote the number of mutations that increase the current best LO-value. A well-known property of LO is that when the current best fitness is i then the bits at positions $i+2, \ldots, n$ are uniform. Bits that form part of the leading ones after an improvement are called *free riders*. The probability of having k free riders is thus 2^{-k} (unless the end of the bit string is reached) and the expected number of free riders is at most $\sum_{k=0}^\infty 2^{-k} = 1$.

The uniformity of "random" bits at positions $i+2, \ldots, n$ holds after any specific number of mutations and in particular after the mutations in generation T_i^par have been performed. However, when looking at multiple improvements, the free-rider events are not necessarily independent as the "random" bits are very likely to be correlated. The following reasoning avoids these possible dependencies. We consider the improvements in generation T_i^par one-by-one. If F_1 denotes the random number of free riders gained in the first improvement, when considering the second improvement the bits at positions $i+3+F_1, \ldots, n$ are still uniform. In some sense, we give away the free riders from a fitness improvement for free for all following improvements. This leads to an estimation of $1 + F_1$ for the gain in the number of leading ones.

Iterating this argument, the expected total number of leading ones gained is thus bounded by $2I$, the expectation being taken for the randomness of free riders. Also considering the expectation for the random number of improvements yields the bound $2\mathrm{E}\left(I \mid I \geq 1\right)$ as I has been defined with respect to the last (i. e. successful) generation. We also observe $\mathrm{E}\left(I \mid I \geq 1\right) \leq 1 + \mathrm{E}(I) \leq 1 + 2^t/n$. Plugging this into Equation (1) yields

$$\sum_{t=1}^\infty \Pr\left[T_i^\mathrm{par} = t\right] \cdot (2 + 2^{t+1}/n)$$

$$= 2 + 2\sum_{t=0}^\infty \Pr\left[T_i^\mathrm{par} = t+1\right] \cdot 2^{t+1}/n$$

$$\leq 2 + 2\sum_{t=0}^\infty \Pr\left[T_i^\mathrm{par} > t\right] \cdot 2^{t+1}/n$$

$$\leq 2 + 2\sum_{t=0}^{\lceil \log n \rceil} 2^{t+1}/n + 2\sum_{t=\lceil \log n \rceil + 1}^\infty \Pr\left[T_i^\mathrm{par} > t\right] \cdot 2^{t+1}/n .$$

The first sum is at most 16. Using Lemma 1 to estimate the second sum, we arrive at the lower bound

$$18 + 2\sum_{\alpha=0}^\infty \Pr\left[T_i^\mathrm{par} > \lceil \log n \rceil + \alpha + 1\right] \cdot 2^{\lceil \log n \rceil + \alpha + 2}/n$$

$$\leq 18 + 2\sum_{\alpha=0}^\infty \exp(2^{-\alpha}) \cdot 2^{\lceil \log n \rceil + \alpha + 2}/n$$

$$\leq 18 + 16 \cdot \sum_{\alpha=0}^\infty \exp(2^{-\alpha}) \cdot 2^\alpha$$

$$< 29.8 .$$

With probability $1/2$ the algorithm starts with no leading ones, independently from all following events. The expected number of leading ones after $n/30$ improvements is at most $29.8/30 \cdot n$. By Markov's inequality the probability of having created n leading ones is thus at most $29.8/30$ and so with probability $1/2 \cdot 0.2/30 = \Omega(1)$ having $n/30$ improvements is not enough to find a global optimum. $\qquad \square$

9. GENERALIZATIONS & EXTENSIONS

We finally discuss generalizations and extensions of our results.

One interesting question is in how far our results change if the population is not doubled or halved, but instead multiplied or divided by some other value $b > 1$. Then the results would change as follows. With some potential adjustments to constant factors, the log-terms in the parallel optimization times in Theorems 1, 2 and 3 would have to be replaced by $\log_b$. For the sequential optimization times stated in these theorems one would need to multiply these bounds by $b/2$. This means that a larger b would further decrease the parallel optimization times at the expense of a larger sequential optimization time.

Our analyses can also be transferred towards the adaptive scheme presented by Jansen, De Jong, and Wegener [9]. Recall that in their scheme the population size is divided by the number of successes. In case of one success the population size remains unchanged. This only affects the constant factors in our upper bounds. When the number of successes is large, the population size might decrease quickly. In most cases, however, the number of successes will be rather small; for instance, the lower bound for LO, Theorem 8, has shown that the expected number of successes in a successful generation is constant. However, it might be possible that after a difficult fitness level an easier fitness level is reached and then the number of successes might be much higher. In an extreme case their scheme can decrease the population size like Scheme A. In some sense, their scheme is somewhat "in between" A and B. With a slight adaptation of the constants, the upper bound for Scheme A from Theorem 1 can be transferred to their scheme.

Another extension of the results above is towards maximum population sizes. Although we have argued in Section 4 that the population size does not blow up too much, in practice the maximum number of processors might be limited. The following theorem about $E(T_{\mathrm{A}}^{\mathrm{par}})$ for maximum population sizes can be proven by applying arguments from [11].

THEOREM 9. *The expected parallel optimization time of Scheme A for a maximum population size $\mu := \mu_{\max} > 1$ is bounded by*

$$E(T_{\mathrm{A}}^{\mathrm{par}}) \leq m \cdot [\log \mu_{\max} + 2] + \frac{2}{\mu_{\max}} \sum_{i=1}^{m-1} \frac{1}{s_i} .$$

Proof. We pessimistically estimate the expected parallel time by the time until the population consists of $\mu_{\max}$ islands plus the expected optimization time if $\mu_{\max}$ islands are available. The time until $\mu_{\max}$ islands are involved is $\log \mu_{\max}$ on one fitness level. Hence, summing up all levels pessimistically gives $m \log \mu_{\max}$. For $\mu_{\max}$ islands the success probability on fitness level i with success probability s_i for one island is given by $1 - (1 - s_i)^{\mu_{\max}}$. Hence, the expected time for leaving fitness level i if $\mu_{\max}$ islands are available is at most $1/[1 - (1 - s_i)^{\mu_{\max}}]$. Now we consider two cases.

If $s_i \cdot \mu_{\max} \leq 1$ we have $1 - (1 - s_i)^{\mu_{\max}} \geq 1 - (1 - s_i\mu_{\max}/2) = s_i\mu_{\max}/2$ because for all $0 \leq xy \leq 1$ it holds $(1-x)^y \leq 1-xy/2$ [11, Lemma 1]. Otherwise, if $s_i \cdot \mu_{\max} > 1$ we have $1 - (1 - s_i)^{\mu_{\max}} \geq 1 - e^{-s_i\mu_{\max}} \geq 1 - \frac{1}{e}$. Thus,

$$\sum_{i=1}^{m-1} \frac{1}{1 - (1 - s_i)^{\mu_{\max}}} \leq \sum_{i=1}^{m-1} \max\left\{ \frac{1}{1 - 1/e}, \frac{2}{\mu_{\max} \cdot s_i} \right\}$$
$$\leq m \cdot \frac{e}{e-1} + \frac{2}{\mu_{\max}} \sum_{i=1}^{m-1} \frac{1}{s_i} .$$

Adding the expected waiting times until $\mu_{\max}$ islands are involved yields the claimed bound. $\square$

In terms of our test functions OneMax, LO, unimodal functions, and Jump_k, this leads to the following result that can be proven like Theorem 7.

COROLLARY 3. *For the parallel (1+1) EA and the (1+λ) EA with Scheme A the following holds for a maximum population size $\mu := \mu_{\max} > 1$:*

- $E(T_{\mathrm{A}}^{\mathrm{par}}) = O(n \log \mu_{\max} + n \log(n)/\mu_{\max})$ *for* OneMax, *which gives* $O(n \log \log n)$ *for* $\mu_{\max} = \log n$,

- $E(T_{\mathrm{A}}^{\mathrm{par}}) = O(n \log \mu_{\max} + n^2/\mu_{\max})$ *for* LO, *which gives* $O(n \log n)$ *for* $\mu_{\max} = n$,

- $E(T_{\mathrm{A}}^{\mathrm{par}}) = O(d \log \mu_{\max} + dn/\mu_{\max})$ *for unimodal functions with d function values, which gives* $O(d \log n)$ *for* $\mu_{\max} = n$,

- $E(T_{\mathrm{A}}^{\mathrm{par}}) = O(n \log \mu_{\max} + n^k/\mu_{\max})$ *for* Jump_k, *which gives* $O(nk \log n)$ *for* $\mu_{\max} = n^{k-1}$.

Note that Corollary 3 has led to an improvement of $\mathrm{E}(T_{\mathrm{A}}^{\mathrm{par}})$ from $O(n \log n)$ to $O(n \log \log n)$ for $\mu_{\max} = \log n$. This obviously also holds in the setting of unrestricted population sizes.

10. CONCLUSIONS

We have presented two schemes for adapting the offspring population size in evolutionary algorithms and, more generally, the number of islands in parallel evolutionary algorithms. Both schemes double the population size in each generation that does not yield an improvement. Despite the exponential growth, the expected sequential optimization time is asymptotically optimal for tight f-based partitions. In general, we obtain bounds that are asymptotically equal to upper bounds via the fitness-level method.

In terms of the parallel computation time expected waiting times on a fitness level can be replaced by their logarithms for both schemes, compared to a serial EA. This yields a tremendous speed-up, in particular for functions where finding improvements is difficult. Scheme B, doubling or halving the population size in each generation, turned out to be more effective than resets to a single island as in Scheme A. This is because B can quickly decrease the population size if necessary. The effort spent while this happens does not affect the asymptotic bounds for expected parallel and sequential times.

Apart from our main results, we have introduced the notion of tight f-based partitions and new arguments from amortized analysis of algorithms to the theory of evolutionary algorithms.

An open question is how our schemes perform in situations where the fitness-level method does not provide good upper bounds. In this case our bounds may be off from the real expected running times. In particular, there may be examples where increasing the offspring population size by too much might be detrimental. One constructed function where large offspring populations perform badly was presented in [9]. Future work could characterize function classes for which our schemes are efficient in comparison to the real expected running times. The notion of tight f-based partitions is a first step in this direction.

Acknowledgments

The authors would like to thank the German Academic Exchange Service for funding their research. Part of this work was done while both authors were visiting the International Computer Science Institute in Berkeley, CA, USA. The second author was partially supported by EPSRC grant EP/D052785/1. The authors thank Carola Winzen for many useful suggestions that helped to improve the presentation.

11. REFERENCES

[1] E. Alba. Parallel metaheuristics: A new class of algorithms, 2005.

[2] T. H. Cormen, C. E. Leiserson, R. L. Rivest, and C. Stein. *Introduction to Algorithms*. The MIT Press, 2nd edition, 2001.

[3] J. Costa, R. Tavares, and A. Rosa. Experimental study on dynamic random variation of population size.

In *Proceedings of the IEEE International Conference on Systems, Man and Cybernetics*, 1999.

[4] S. Droste, T. Jansen, and I. Wegener. On the analysis of the (1+1) evolutionary algorithm. *Theoretical Computer Science*, 276:51–81, 2002.

[5] A. Eiben, E. Marchiori, and V. Valko. Evolutionary algorithms with on-the-fly population size adjustment. In *Parallel Problem Solving from Nature (PPSN 2004)*, pages 41–50. Springer, 2004.

[6] N. Hansen, A. Gawelczyk, and A. Ostermeier. Sizing the population with respect to the local progress in (1,λ)-evolution strategies–A theoretical analysis. In *1995 IEEE International Conference on Evolutionary Computation*, pages 80–85, 1995.

[7] G. Harik and F. Lobo. A parameter-less genetic algorithm. In *Proceedings of the Genetic and Evolutionary Computation Conference (GECCO 1999)*, pages 258–265, 1999.

[8] M. Herdy. The number of offspring as strategy parameter in hierarchically organized evolution strategies. *ACM SIGBIO Newsletter*, 13(2):9, 1993.

[9] T. Jansen, K. A. De Jong, and I. Wegener. On the choice of the offspring population size in evolutionary algorithms. *Evolutionary Computation*, 13:413–440, 2005.

[10] J. Lässig and D. Sudholt. The benefit of migration in parallel evolutionary algorithms. In *Proceedings of the Genetic and Evolutionary Computation Conference (GECCO 2010)*, pages 1105–1112, 2010.

[11] J. Lässig and D. Sudholt. General scheme for analyzing running times of parallel evolutionary algorithms. In *11th International Conference on Parallel Problem Solving from Nature (PPSN 2010)*, volume 6238 of *LNCS*, pages 234–243. Springer, 2010.

[12] Z. Michalewicz. *Genetic algorithms + data structures = evolution programs*. Springer, 1996.

[13] G. Rudolph. How mutation and selection solve long-path problems in polynomial expected time. *Evolutionary Computation*, 4(2):195–205, 1997.

[14] D. Schlierkamp-Voosen and H. Mühlenbein. Strategy adaptation by competing subpopulations. *Parallel Problem Solving from Nature (PPSN III)*, pages 199–208, 1994.

[15] H.-P. Schwefel. *Numerical optimization of computer models*. John Wiley & Sons, Inc. New York, NY, USA, 1981.

[16] D. Sudholt. General lower bounds for the running time of evolutionary algorithms. In *11th International Conference on Parallel Problem Solving from Nature (PPSN 2010)*, volume 6238 of *LNCS*, pages 124–133. Springer, 2010.

[17] M. Tomassini. *Spatially Structured Evolutionary Algorithms: Artificial Evolution in Space and Time*. Springer, 2005.

[18] I. Wegener. Methods for the analysis of evolutionary algorithms on pseudo-Boolean functions. In R. Sarker, X. Yao, and M. Mohammadian, editors, *Evolutionary Optimization*, pages 349–369. Kluwer, 2002.

On the Movement of Vertex Fixed Points in the Simple GA

Alden H. Wright
Computer Science
University of Montana
Missoula, MT 59812
alden.wright@umontana.edu

Tomáš Gedeon
Mathematical Sciences
Montana State University
Bozeman, MT 59714
gedeon@math.montana.edu

J. Neal Richter
Computer Science
Montana State University
Bozeman, MT 59714
richter@cs.montana.edu

ABSTRACT

The Vose dynamical system model of the simple genetic algorithm models the behavior of this algorithm for large population sizes and is the basis of the exact Markov chain model. Populations consisting of multiple copies of one individual correspond to vertices of the simplex. For zero mutation, these are fixed points of the dynamical system and absorbing states of the Markov chain. For proportional selection, the asymptotic stability of vertex fixed points is understood from previous work. We derive the eigenvalues of the differential at vertex fixed points of the dynamical system model for tournament selection. We show that as mutation increases from zero, hyperbolic asymptotically stable fixed points move into the simplex, and hyperbolic asymptotically unstable fixed points move outside of the simplex. We calculate the derivative of local path of the fixed point with respect to the mutation rate for proportional selection. Simulation analysis shows how fixed points bifurcate with larger changes in the mutation rate and changes in the crossover rate.

Categories and Subject Descriptors

I.2.8 [**Artificial Intelligence**]: Problem Solving, Control Methods, and Search—*Heuristic Methods*; G.1.m [**Mathematics of Computing**]: Miscelaneous—*Evolutionary Computation and Genetic Algorithms*

General Terms

Theory, Algorithms

Keywords

Genetic Algorithms, Theory, Crossover, Selection, Tournament Selection, Dynamical Systems, Fixed Points, Bifurcation

1. INTRODUCTION

As the name suggests, the infinite population model (IPM) of the simple genetic algorithm (SGA) is a deterministic dynamical systems model that describes the behavior of the SGA as the population size goes to infinity. It is also the basis for the exact mathematical description of the SGA, namely the exact Markov chain model. The infinite population model and the exact Markov chain model are primarily due to Michael Vose, but also to collaborators Gunar Liepins, Alden Wright, A. E. Nix, and others. See [12], [13], [14], [6].

Subsection 2.8 gives an example of the use of dynamical systems models to predict the behavior of a genetic algorithm.

The SGA is a generational genetic algorithm over bit strings of length ℓ. As developed by Vose in [12], it includes any mask-based crossover, a very general model of mutation, and proportional, ranking, or a special form of tournament selection. This paper extends the model to standard tournament selection. (The models for ranking and tournament selection assume that no two individuals have the same fitness.)

Vertices of the simplex (defined below) are fixed points of this dynamical system when there is zero mutation. Using the results of a paper of Vose and Wright [15], of section 11.3 of Vose's book [12], and section 2.7 of this paper, the asymptotic stability of these fixed points can be calculated when the fitness function can be calculated (such as when there is a formula for the fitness function). As the crossover rate increases, the number of stable vertex fixed points increases (or remains constant).

When a vertex fixed point is asymptotically stable, this means that when the infinite population model is started sufficiently close to the fixed point, it will converge to the the fixed point. Intuitively, it means that the when the SGA with a sufficiently large population size is started close to the fixed point, it is highly likely to converge to the uniform population corresponding to the fixed point. (When mutation is zero, the SGA Markov chain is absorbing, so the SGA actually converges.) Thus, one would expect that the infinite population model with a sufficiently low mutation rate when started at or sufficiently near the fixed point would converge to a point close to the fixed point. This paper proves this result. Thus, the SGA with a low mutation when started near to the fixed point is likely to stay close to the fixed point for a long time.

When a vertex fixed point is asymptotically unstable, this means that the infinite population model can be started arbitrarily close to the fixed point and diverge away from the

the fixed point. This paper shows that as positive mutation is introduced into the infinite population model in this case, the fixed point moves outside of the simplex. Thus, when the infinite population model with a low mutation rate is started at or sufficiently near the fixed point, it will diverge away from the fixed point. The behavior of the SGA in this case is discussed in subsection 4.4.

Populations are represented as vectors over the integers in half-open interval $[0, n)$ where these integers correspond to length ℓ bit strings through their binary representation and where $n = 2^\ell$. A population vector x has the properties $\sum_i x_i = 1$ and $x_i \geq 0$ for all $i \in [0, n)$. The relative frequency of the bit string i in the population is x_i. The space of all possible population vectors is the $(n-1)$-simplex Λ in $\mathbb{R}^n$. Thus, $\Lambda = \{x \in \mathbb{R}^n : \sum_i x_i = 1 \text{ and } x_i \geq 0\}$. The vertices of the simplex are the unit vectors in $\mathbb{R}^n$; the ith unit vector e_i corresponds to a uniform population consisting only of individuals whose string representation is the binary string representation of i.

Following [12], we use $\mathbf{1}$ as a notation for a column vector of all ones of length ℓ, which corresponds to a string of all ones. In particular, if $i \in [0, n)$, then $\mathbf{1}^T i$ denotes the number of ones in the binary representation of i. We also use $\mathbf{1}$ as a notation for a column vector of all ones of length $n = 2^\ell$. The meaning of the $\mathbf{1}$ symbol should be clear from the context.

The bitwise-AND of bit strings i and j is denoted by $i \otimes j$, and the bitwise-OR of i and j is denoted by $i \oplus j$. The ones-complement of i is denoted by $\bar{i}$.

Population vectors in the simplex can be viewed either as populations of indeterminate size, or as sampling distributions for the next generation of the finite-population GA. (The formula for the exact Markov chain model is simply the application of the multinomial theorem to this sampling distribution.)

The infinite population model is a discrete-time dynamical system where time steps correspond to generations of the SGA. The model is described by a continuously differentiable (C^1) map $\mathcal{G} : \Lambda \to \Lambda$ which will be defined below. If x is the current population of the SGA, then the next generation population is obtained by sampling from $\mathcal{G}(x)$.

The IPM is deterministic with trajectory $x, \mathcal{G}(x), \mathcal{G}^2(x), \ldots$. Vose [12] shows that the expected next finite population is $\mathcal{G}(x)$, he also has theorems that show that IPM is the limiting behavior of the SGA as the population size goes to infinity.

The $\mathcal{G}$ map extends naturally to a neighborhood of the simplex in $\mathbb{R}^n$, and we will use $\mathcal{G}$ to denote this extended map.

2. FIXED POINTS OF $\mathcal{G}$

The results of subsection 2.3, and of subsection 2.7 as applied to tournament selection, are new, while the other subsections relate previously published results.

The map $\mathcal{G}$ is the composition of a selection map $\mathcal{F}$ and a mixing map $\mathcal{M}$.

$$\mathcal{G} = \mathcal{M} \circ \mathcal{F}. \tag{1}$$

In this section, we describe the mixing map $\mathcal{M}$ and the selection map $\mathcal{F}$ for proportional and tournament selection.

2.1 The mixing map $\mathcal{M}$

We now define the mixing map. Following [12], we define

$$[expr] = \begin{cases} 1 & \text{if } expr \text{ is true} \\ 0 & \text{otherwise.} \end{cases}$$

For each integer $i \in [0, n)$, let the $n \times n$ permutation matrix σ_i be defined by

$$(\sigma_i)_{u,v} = [u \oplus v = i].$$

The matrix σ_i is symmetric and self-inverse. If $x \in \Lambda$, $(\sigma_i x)_j = x_{j \oplus i}$ and if M is an $n \times n$ matrix, $(\sigma_i M \sigma_i)_{u,v} = M_{u \oplus i, v \oplus i}$.

If mutation is given by a rate p, for each $i \in [0, n)$, define

$$\mu_i = p^{\mathbf{1}^T i}(1-p)^{\ell - \mathbf{1}^T i}.$$

In general (even when not defined by a rate), mutation is positive whenever $\mu_i > 0$ for all $i \in [0, n)$.

If we cross parent bit strings u and v using mask i, the children are $(u \otimes i) \oplus (v \otimes \bar{i})$ and $(u \otimes \bar{i}) \oplus (v \otimes i)$.

Define χ_i to be the probability that bit string i is used as a crossover mask. For example, for one-point crossover with crossover rate c, we have

$$\chi_i = \begin{cases} \frac{c}{\ell-1} & \text{if } i = 1, 3, 7, \ldots, 2^{\ell-1} - 1 \\ 1 - c & \text{if } i = 0 \\ 0 & \text{otherwise.} \end{cases}$$

Define the $n \times n$ mixing matrix M by

$$M_{u,v} = \sum_{i,j,k} \mu_i \mu_j \frac{\chi_k + \chi_{\bar{k}}}{2} [((u \oplus i) \otimes k) \oplus ((v \oplus j) \otimes \bar{k}) = 0].$$

Note that if mutation is zero, then

$$M_{u,v} = \sum_k \frac{\chi_k + \chi_{\bar{k}}}{2} [(u \otimes k) \oplus (v \otimes \bar{k}) = 0]. \tag{2}$$

Example. For string length 2, the mixing matrix for one-point crossover with rate c and no mutation is:

$$M(0) = \begin{pmatrix} 1 & 1/2 & 1/2 & 1/2 - 1/2\,c \\ 1/2 & 0 & 1/2\,c & 0 \\ 1/2 & 1/2\,c & 0 & 0 \\ 1/2 - 1/2\,c & 0 & 0 & 0 \end{pmatrix}.$$

Finally, define the mixing map $\mathcal{M}$ by

$$\mathcal{M}(x)_i = (\sigma_i x)^T M \sigma_i x = x^T (\sigma_i M \sigma_i) x.$$

The twist M^* of M is defined by

$$M^*_{i,j} = M_{i \oplus j, i}.$$

For example, the twist of the matrix $M(0)$ shown above is:

$$M(0)^* = \begin{pmatrix} 1 & 1/2 & 1/2 & 1/2 - 1/2\,c \\ 0 & 1/2 & 0 & 1/2\,c \\ 0 & 0 & 1/2 & 1/2\,c \\ 0 & 0 & 0 & 1/2 - 1/2\,c \end{pmatrix}.$$

For zero mutation, M^* is upper triangular. This can be derived directly from equation (2) and is stated on page 55 of [12].

For later reference, proposition 2.2 of [15] or theorem 6.13 of [12] show that the differential of $\mathcal{M}$ is given by

$$d\mathcal{M}_x = 2\sum_u \sigma_u^T M^* \sigma_u x_u.$$

For more explanation, see one of [15; 12; 13; 14; 6].

An important property of the mixing map is that $\mathcal{M}$ maps the simplex into itself, and when mutation is positive, $\mathcal{M}$ maps the simplex into its interior [12]. Thus, $\mathcal{G}$ also has this property. This is stated as theorem 4.7 of [12].

2.2 The selection map $\mathcal{F}$ for proportional selection

For proportional selection, let F denote the diagonal matrix whose diagonal entries are the elements of the fitness vector f. Then

$$\mathcal{F}(x) = \frac{Fx}{f^T x}. \tag{3}$$

For later reference, the differential of proportional selection is given by

$$d\mathcal{F}_x = \frac{f^T x F - Fx f^T}{(f^T x)^2}.$$

It is also not hard to see that

$$\mathbf{1}^T d\mathcal{F}_x = 0 \tag{4}$$

LEMMA 1.

$$\sigma_s d\mathcal{F}_{e_s} \sigma_s = \frac{1}{f_s}\left(\sigma_s F \sigma_s - e_0 f^T \sigma_s\right)$$

$$(\sigma_s d\mathcal{F}_{e_s}\sigma_s)_{i,v} = \begin{cases} \frac{f_{i\oplus s}}{f_s} & \text{if } i = v > 0 \\ -\frac{f_{i\oplus s}}{f_s} & \text{if } i = 0 \text{ and } v > 0 \\ 0 & \text{otherwise} \end{cases}$$

In particular, $\sigma_s d\mathcal{F}_{e_s}\sigma_s$ is upper triangular and only nonzero in the upper row and on the diagonal.

2.3 The selection map $\mathcal{F}$ for tournament selection

The selection of one individual by k-ary tournament selection is done by choosing with replacement a random sample of k individuals (which we will call a tournament) from the population and then selecting the best of these k.

To model k-ary tournament selection from a population $x \in \Lambda$, we consider the sample space of all unordered k-sequences (tournaments) weighted by their probability as determined by x. For example, if $k = 5$, one such tournament would be $0,0,1,1,1$ which would have probability $\binom{5}{2}x_0^2 x_1^3$.

In order for a tournament to correspond to the selection of element i, i must be the most fit element in the tournament. Thus, the probability of selecting element i by k-ary tournament selection is given by

$$\mathcal{F}(x)_i = \sum_{u=1}^{k}\binom{k}{u}x_i^u \left(\sum_j [f_j < f_i]x_j\right)^{k-u}. \tag{5}$$

This formula uses the assumption that fitness is injective, in other words, $u \neq v \Rightarrow f_u \neq f_v$.

Example: Tournament selection for $\ell = 2$ and $k = 3$ with fitness function $\langle 4, 1, 3, 2\rangle^T$ is given by:

$$\mathcal{F}(x) =$$

$$\begin{bmatrix} 3\,x0\,(x1 + x2 + x3)^2 + 3\,x0^2\,(x1 + x2 + x3) + x0^3 \\ x1^3 \\ 3\,x2\,(x1 + x3)^2 + 3\,x2^2\,(x1 + x3) + x2^3 \\ 3\,x3\,x1^2 + 3\,x3^2 x1 + x3^3 \end{bmatrix}$$

For completeness, here is a formula that does not assume injective fitness:

$$\mathcal{F}(x)_i =$$

$$\begin{cases} \sum_{u=1}^{k}\binom{k}{u}x_i^u \left(\sum_j[f_j < f_i]x_j\right)^{k-u} & \text{if } f_s = f_i \Rightarrow s = i \\ \sum_{u=1}^{k}\binom{k}{u}x_i^u \sum_{v=0}^{k-u}\frac{u}{u+v}\binom{k-u}{v} \\ \quad\left(\sum_{r\neq i}[f_r = f_i]x_r\right)^v \\ \quad\left(\sum_j[f_j < f_i]x_j\right)^{k-u-v} & \text{otherwise} \end{cases}$$

For the rest of this paper, we assume injective fitness in our analysis of tournament selection. A future paper will analyze non-injective fitness.

Vose [12] models a somewhat different version of tournament selection. Instead of choosing the best element of the tournament, he applies ranking selection to the tournament. His model of ranking selection follows that of Goldberg and Deb [4] in using the integral of a continuously increasing probability density function over the interval $[0,1]$. Goldberg and Deb call this an "assignment function". Ranking selection can be made to select only the best individual by using an assignment function that assigns unit mass to 1 (a translation of the Dirac delta function) as the assignment function. However, when ranking selection is used to select only the best individual, it is not continuous and thus not differentiable. Thus, Vose's results cannot be directly applied to tournament selection as we have defined it above (which we believe is the version most commonly used in practice). In addition, we feel that our model of tournament selection is much simpler and easier to work with.

LEMMA 2. For $i = 0, 1, \ldots, n - 1$,

$$\sum_{j=0}^{n-1}\mathcal{F}(x)_j = \left(\sum_{j=0}^{i}x_j\right)^k \tag{6}$$

Thus, if $x \in \Lambda$, $\sum_{j=0}^{n-1}\mathcal{F}(x)_j = 1$.

Proof Let π denote a permutation of $\{0, 1, \ldots, n-1\}$ such that $f_{\pi(0)} < f_{\pi(1)} < \cdots < f_{\pi(n-1)}$. Note that equation (5) can be written as

$$\mathcal{F}(x)_i = \sum_{u=1}^{k}\binom{k}{u}x_i^u \left(\sum_{j=0}^{i-1}x_{\pi(j)}\right)^{k-u}$$

For $i = 0, 1, \ldots, n - 1$ we prove by induction on i that

$$\sum_{j=0}^{i}\mathcal{F}(x)_j = \left(\sum_{j=0}^{i}x_{\pi(j)}\right)^k \tag{7}$$

For $i = 0$, we have $\mathcal{F}(x)_0 = x_{\pi(0)}^k$.

We assume equation (7) for $i - 1$ and prove it for i.

$$\left(\sum_{j=0}^{i} x_{\pi(j)} \right)^k = \left(x_{\pi(i)} + \sum_{j=0}^{i-1} x_{\pi(j)} \right)^k$$

$$= \sum_{u=0}^{k} \binom{k}{u} x_{\pi(i)}^u \left(\sum_{j=0}^{i-1} x_{\pi(j)} \right)^{k-u}$$

by the binomial theorem

$$= \left(\sum_{j=0}^{i-1} x_{\pi(j)} \right)^k + \sum_{u=1}^{k} \binom{k}{u} x_{\pi(i)}^u \left(\sum_{j=0}^{i-1} x_{\pi(j)} \right)^{k-u}$$

$$= \sum_{j=0}^{i-1} \mathcal{F}(x)_j + \mathcal{F}(x)_i = \sum_{j=0}^{i} \mathcal{F}(x)_j$$

This completes the induction proof.

Since we know that for $x \in \Lambda$, $\sum_{j=0}^{n-1} x_j = \sum_{j=0}^{n-1} x_{\pi(j)} = 1$, the second formula follows. $\square$

The following lemma is straightforward.

LEMMA 3.

$$\frac{\partial \mathcal{F}_i}{\partial x_v} = \tag{8}$$

$$\begin{cases} \displaystyle\sum_{u=1}^{k} \binom{k}{u} u x_i^{u-1} \left(\sum_j [f_j < f_i] x_j \right)^{k-u} & \text{if } v = i \\ \displaystyle\sum_{u=1}^{k-1} \binom{k}{u} x_i^u (k-u) \left(\sum_j [f_j < f_i] x_j \right)^{k-u-1} [f_v < f_i] & \text{if } v \neq i \end{cases} \tag{9}$$

LEMMA 4. For any x,

$$\mathbf{1}^T d\mathcal{F}_x = k\mathbf{1}^T \left(\sum_j x_j \right)^{k-1}$$

and for any $x \in \Lambda$,

$$\mathbf{1}^T d\mathcal{F}_x = k\mathbf{1}^T$$

Proof Lemma 2 showed that $\sum_j \mathcal{F}(x)_j = \left(\sum_j x_j \right)^k$. If we differentiate this equation with respect to x_i, we get:

$$\sum_j \frac{\partial \mathcal{F}_j}{\partial x_i} = k \left(\sum_j x_j \right)^{k-1}.$$

Since the right-hand expression is independent of i, the first statement of the lemma follows. The second statement is obvious. $\square$

Next we evaluate $d\mathcal{F}_{e_s}$ where e_s denotes the sth unit vector.

LEMMA 5.

$$(d\mathcal{F}_{e_s})_{i,v} = \begin{cases} k & \text{if } i = v \text{ and } f_s < f_v \\ k & \text{if } i = s \text{ and } f_s \geq f_v \\ 0 & \text{otherwise} \end{cases} \tag{10}$$

Proof Consider the first case where $i = v$ and $f_s < f_v$. The first case of formula (9) applies and is nonzero only

when $u = 1$. In this case, $u x_i^{u-1} = 1$ since the exponent $u - 1$ is zero. The factor $\left(\sum_j [f_j < f_i] x_j \right)^{k-u} = 1$ since for $j = s$, $f_s < f_i$.

Consider the second case where $i = s$ and $f_s \geq f_v$. The second case of formula (9) applies and is nonzero only when $u = k - 1$. In this case, $x_i^u = 1$ since $i = s$. The factor $\left(\sum_j [f_j < f_i] x_j \right)^{k-u-1} = 1$ since the exponent $k - u - 1$ is zero.

One can check that these are the only cases where $\frac{\partial \mathcal{F}_i}{\partial x_v}(e_s)$ is nonzero. $\square$

COROLLARY 6. For each $s = 0, 1, \ldots, n - 1$,

$$(\sigma_s d\mathcal{F}_{e_s} \sigma_s)_{i,v} = \begin{cases} k & \text{if } i = v \text{ and } f_s < f_{v \oplus s} \\ k & \text{if } i = 0 \text{ and } f_s \geq f_{v \oplus s} \\ 0 & \text{otherwise} \end{cases} \tag{11}$$

Thus, $\sigma_s d\mathcal{F}_{e_s} \sigma_s$ is upper triangular and has nonzero entries only in the upper row and on the diagonal. Furthermore, it has only a single nonzero entry k in each column.

Proof Recall that $(\sigma_s)_{x,y} = [x \oplus y = s]$, and that σ_s is symmetric and self-inverse. Further, if A is any $n \times n$ matrix,

$$(\sigma_s A \sigma_s)_{i,v} = A_{i \oplus s, v \oplus s}$$

Applying this formula to formula (10) gives (11). Upper triangularity is obvious, as is

$$\mathbf{1}^T \sigma_s d\mathcal{F}_{e_s} \sigma_s = k\mathbf{1}^T.$$

$\square$

2.4 A change of basis

In this subsection we show how to do an orthonormal change of basis so that we can work in the hyperplane containing the simplex. Recall that $\mathbf{1}$ is the vector of all ones. Note that $\{x \in \mathbb{R}^n : \mathbf{1}^T x = 1\}$ is the $(n-1)$-dimensional hyperplane that contains the simplex, and $\mathbf{1}^\perp = \{x \in \mathbb{R}^n : \mathbf{1}^T x = 0\}$ is the translate of this hyperplane to the origin.

LEMMA 7. Let A be an $n \times n$ real matrix. Suppose that $\mathbf{1}^T A = \lambda \mathbf{1}^T$ (so that $\mathbf{1}$ is an eigenvector of A^T). Then there is an orthonormal change of basis with basis change matrix B where the first column is $\mathbf{1}$ rescaled to have unit length, and where

$$B^T A B = \begin{pmatrix} \lambda & 0 \\ * & C \end{pmatrix}. \tag{12}$$

(Here $*$ denotes possibly nonzero entries.) Then C represents the action of A on the hyperplane $\mathbf{1}^\perp = \{x \in \mathbb{R}^n : \mathbf{1}^T x = 0\}$. The eigenvalues of A in addition to λ are the same as the eigenvalues of C.

PROOF. This proof is adapted from the proof of theorem 6.12 of [12].

Since $\mathbf{1}^T A = \lambda \mathbf{1}$, it follows that $A : \mathbf{1}^\perp \to \mathbf{1}^\perp$. Let $\{b_0, b_1, \ldots, b_{n-1}\}$ be an orthonormal basis with b_0 being $\mathbf{1}$ normalized to have unit length, and let B be the matrix whose columns are this basis. (The Walsh basis is such a basis.) Note that if $j > 0$, then

$$B^T A B e_j = B^{-1} A b_j \subseteq B^{-1}(\mathbf{1}^\perp) \subseteq e_0^\perp.$$

(Recall that e_j is the jth unit vector.) Thus, $B^T A B$ satisfies equation 12.

Observe that $e_0^T B^T AB = (B^T A\mathbf{1})^T = \lambda(B^{-1}b_0)^T = \lambda e_0^T$. Thus, the upper left entry of $B^T AB$ is λ.

With respect to the above basis the elements of $\mathbf{1}^\perp$ have the form $\begin{pmatrix} 0 \\ * \end{pmatrix}$. Thus, C represents A on $\mathbf{1}^\perp$. The eigenvalues of a matrix are invariant under a change of basis. $\square$

2.5   Dynamical system fixed points

Let g be a map that defines a discrete-time dynamical system. A fixed point v of g is *asymptotically stable* if there is a neighborhood U of the fixed point such that $\lim_{k\to\infty} g^k(y) = v$ for all $y \in U$. The fixed point v is *unstable* if there is a neighborhood U of v, such that for all $\delta > 0$ there exists a point y with $|y - v| < \delta$ such that $g^k(y)$ is not in U for some k.[1]

A fixed point v is *hyperbolic* if no eigenvalue of the differential dg_v has an eigenvalue with modulus 1. Vose and Eberlein have shown that for proportional selection, the fixed points of $\mathcal{G}$ are hyperbolic for a dense open set of fitness coefficients in the positive orthant [12]. Gedeon, et al. [3] show that for a "typical" mixing operator $\mathcal{G}$ has finitely many fixed points, and Hayes and Gedeon have shown that the fixed points of $\mathcal{G}$ are hyperbolic for a "typical" mixing operator [5].

For a hyperbolic fixed point v of g, the asymptotic stability of v is related to the differential dg_v at the fixed point. If all eigenvalues of dg_v have modulus less than 1, then v is *asymptotically stable*. And if any eigenvalue of dg_v has modulus greater than 1, then v is *asymptotically unstable*. We will define a hyperbolic fixed point to be a *saddle fixed point* if some eigenvalues have modulus less than 1 and some eigenvalues have modulus greater than 1. Clearly, a saddle fixed point is asymptotically unstable.

The stable manifold theorem (see theorem 10.1 of [9]) characterizes the behavior of g in a sufficiently small neighborhood of a hyperbolic fixed point. If there are s eigenvalues whose modulus is less than 1, then there is a stable manifold of dimension s, and if there are u eigenvalues whose modulus is greater than 1, then there is an unstable manifold of dimension u. The stable manifold consists of points x such that $\lim_{k\to\infty} g^k(x) = v$ and the unstable manifold consists of points x such that $\lim_{k\to\infty}(g^{-1})^k(x) = v$ where g^{-1} denotes the inverse of g when the inverse exists. When g is not locally invertible, the unstable manifold can be defined in terms of the past history of its points. See [9] or other books on dynamical systems for details.

Neighborhoods of saddle points can contain trajectories that are *eventually repelling*. In loose language, there exist initial conditions for which iterations move towards the fixed-point for a time, only to then eventually begin to move away from the fixed-point.

2.6   Fixed points of the SGA IPM

The Perron-Frobenius theorem states that there can exist only one fixed-point in the simplex for a linear system with positive irreducible transition matrix [2]. Further, this fixed point is asymptotically stable.

This is exactly the situation for the SGA IPM with proportional selection, positive mutation, and zero crossover since the normalization of proportional selection can be ignored in determining the long-term behavior of the IPM.

---
[1]This definition of unstable is the negation of Lyapunov stability, see [9] for details.

Thus, in this situation, $\mathcal{G}$ has one stable fixed point in the interior of the simplex.

Rowe [10] and Richter et al. [8; 7] are example analyses of the Perron-Frobenius situation and movement of the fixed-point under varying mutation rates.

When the mutation rate is 1/2, the mutation map takes all populations to the center of the simplex. Hence, $\mathcal{G}$ with crossover, any selection method, and any fitness function has the same property.

Vose [12] conjectures that when started at a point in the simplex Λ, the iterates of $\mathcal{G}$ converge to a fixed point. Wright and Bidwell [17] empirically tested this conjecture and found what appeared to be cyclic behavior. However, these examples used a non-standard mutation which is not bitwise mutation with a rate. Given the extensive experience with GAs, the conjecture seems very likely to be true for bitwise mutation by a rate where the rate is less than or equal to 1/2.

2.7   Vertex fixed points

Mask-based crossover is *pure* in that crossing an individual with itself results only in that individual. Thus, when mutation is zero, the mixing map $\mathcal{M}$ applied to a uniform population of identical individuals gives that population. Selection applied to a uniform population cannot produce any new individuals, and thus the selection map $\mathcal{F}$ applied to a uniform population also gives that population. Thus, we have shown the following:

LEMMA 8. *Assume no mutation. If v is a vertex of the simplex Λ, $\mathcal{G}(v) = v$. In other words, v is a fixed point of $\mathcal{G}$.*

The SGA Markov chain model is absorbing when mutation is zero, and the vertex populations are the absorbing states.

For vertex fixed points of $\mathcal{G}$, there are some special results on stability [15], section 11.3 of [12]. A suitable rearrangement of the rows and columns of the differential of $\mathcal{G}$ is upper triangular, so the eigenvalues are the diagonal elements. In this section we derive formulas for the eigenvalues for proportional and tournament selection. For proportional selection, these are from [15] and theorem 11.8 of [12]. For tournament selection as we have defined it, these results are new.

LEMMA 9. *For $x \in \Lambda$,*

$$\mathbf{1}^T d\mathcal{G}_x = 0 \text{ for proportional selection}$$

$$\mathbf{1}^T d\mathcal{G}_x = 2k\mathbf{1}^T \text{ for tournament selection}$$

Proof Theorem 6.13 of [12] shows $\mathbf{1}^T d\mathcal{M}_x = 2\left(\sum x_u\right)\mathbf{1}^T$. Thus, if $x \in \Lambda$, $\sum x_u = 1$, so $\mathbf{1}^T d\mathcal{M}_x = 2\mathbf{1}^T$. Applying the chain rule, $\mathbf{1}^T d\mathcal{G}_x = \mathbf{1}^T d\mathcal{M}_{\mathcal{F}(x)} d\mathcal{F}_x = 2\mathbf{1}^T d\mathcal{F}_x$. We now apply equation (4) for proportional selection and lemma 4 for tournament selection. $\square$

LEMMA 10. *Let $\mathcal{F}$ be the heuristic function for either proportional or tournament selection. For $s = 0, 1, \ldots, n-1$,*

$$\sigma_s d\mathcal{G}_{e_s}\sigma_s = 2M^*\sigma_s d\mathcal{F}_{e_s}\sigma_s$$

If mutation is zero, $\sigma_s d\mathcal{G}_{e_s}\sigma_s$ is upper triangular and the eigenvalues are the diagonal elements.

Proof First, note that $\mathcal{F}(e_s) = e_s$ since e_s is a population consisting only of individuals equal to s, and any such population is fixed under selection.

$$
\begin{aligned}
d\mathcal{G}_{e_s} &= d\mathcal{M}_{\mathcal{F}(e_s)} d\mathcal{F}_{e_s} \quad \text{by the chain rule} \\
&= d\mathcal{M}_{e_s} d\mathcal{F}_{e_s} \\
&= 2 \sum_u \sigma_u M^* \sigma_u(e_s)_u d\mathcal{F}_{e_s} \\
&= 2\sigma_s M^* \sigma_s d\mathcal{F}_{e_s}
\end{aligned}
$$

Thus, $\sigma_s d\mathcal{G}_{e_s} \sigma_s = 2M^* \sigma_s d\mathcal{F}_{e_s} \sigma_s$. Recall that zero mutation implies that M^* is upper triangular. Upper triangularity follows since both M^* and $\sigma_s d\mathcal{F}_{e_s} \sigma_s$ are upper triangular. $\square$

LEMMA 11. *Assume zero mutation and $s = 0, 1, \ldots, n-1$. If $\mathcal{F}$ is the heuristic function for tournament selection.*

$$
(\sigma_s d\mathcal{G}_{e_s} \sigma_s)_{i,v} = \begin{cases} 2kM_{i\oplus v,i} & \text{if } f_s < f_{v\oplus s} \\ 2kM_{0,v} & \text{if } f_s \geq f_{v\oplus s} \\ 0 & \text{otherwise} \end{cases} \tag{13}
$$

Proof

$$
\begin{aligned}
&(\sigma_s d\mathcal{G}_{e_s} \sigma_s)_{i,v} \\
&= 2 \sum_u M^*_{i,u} (\sigma_s d\mathcal{F}_{e_s} \sigma_s)_{u,v} \\
&= 2 \sum_u M^*_{i,u} k[((u=v) \wedge (f_s < f_{v\oplus s})) \vee ((u=0) \wedge (f_s \geq f_{v\oplus s}))] \\
&= \begin{cases} 2kM^*_{i,v} = 2kM_{i\oplus v,i} & \text{if } f_s < f_{v\oplus s} \\ 2kM^*_{i,0} = 2kM_{v,0} = 2kM_{0,v} & \text{if } f_s \geq f_{v\oplus s} \\ 0 & \text{otherwise} \end{cases}
\end{aligned}
$$

$\square$

THEOREM 12. *Assume tournament selection. If mutation is zero and $s = 0, 1, \ldots, n-1$, the eigenvalues of $d\mathcal{G}_{e_s}$ considered as a map from $\mathbf{1}^\perp$ to itself are*

$$
\{2kM_{0,v}[f_s < f_{v\oplus s}] : v = 1, 2, \ldots, n-1\}. \tag{14}
$$

Proof The eigenvalues of $d\mathcal{G}_{e_s}$ are the same as the eigenvalues of $\sigma_s d\mathcal{G}_{e_s} \sigma_s$. Thus, the eigenvalues of $d\mathcal{G}_{e_s}$ are given by the first case of equation (13) when $f_s < f_{v\oplus s}$ and $i = v$, and are zero when $f_s \geq f_{v\oplus s}$.

Lemma 9 shows that $\mathbf{1}$ is an eigenvector of $d\mathcal{G}_{e_s}^T$, so lemma 7 applies. Since the matrix B of lemma 7 (which can be the Walsh basis) is orthonormal, the eigenvalues of $d\mathcal{G}_{e_s}$ considered as a mapping from $\mathbf{1}^\perp$ to itself are the same as the eigenvalues of $d\mathcal{G}_{e_s}$ applied to $\mathbb{R}^n$ less the eigenvalue $2kM_{0,0} = 2k$. $\square$

THEOREM 13. *Assume proportional selection. If mutation is zero and $s = 0, 1, \ldots, n-1$, the eigenvalues of $d\mathcal{G}_{e_s}$ considered as a map from $\mathbf{1}^\perp$ to itself are*

$$
\left\{ \frac{f_{v\oplus s}}{f_s} M_{0,v} : v = 1, 2, \ldots, n-1 \right\}. \tag{15}
$$

Proof This theorem states the result of theorem 3.5 of [15] as extended by the results of section 4 of the same paper. It is also stated as one part of theorem 11.8 of [12]. It can be proved directly by combining lemma 1 with lemma 10, and then applying lemma 7. $\square$

If $i \in (0, n)$, let hi(i) and lo(i) be the smallest and largest k such that $i \otimes 2^k \neq 0$. In other words, lo(i) is the position of the leftmost one in the binary representation of i, and hi(i) is the position of the rightmost one in the binary representation of i. Let $\delta(i) = \text{hi}(i) - \text{lo}(i) + 1$; $\delta(i)$ is commonly called the defining length of i.

LEMMA 14. *For one-point crossover with crossover rate c and zero mutation,*

$$
M_{0,v} = \frac{1}{2} \left(1 - c + c\frac{\ell - \delta(v)}{\ell - 1} \right).
$$

For uniform crossover with crossover rate c and zero mutation,

$$
M_{0,v} = \frac{1}{2} \left(1 - c + c2^{1 - \mathbf{1}^T i} \right).
$$

PROOF. By equation (2) $M_{0,v} = \sum_u \frac{\chi_u + \chi_{\overline{u}}}{2}[u \otimes v = 0]$. The formulas follow by direct computation. More details for proof of the uniform crossover formula are given in the proof of lemma 5.2 of [15]. $\square$

COROLLARY 15. *Assume tournament selection. Let c denote the crossover rate for one-point or uniform crossover. For one-point crossover, the spectrum of $d\mathcal{G}_{e_k}$, considered as a map from $\mathbf{1}^\perp$ to itself, is given by*

$$
spec(d\mathcal{G}_{e_s}) = \\
\left\{ k\left(1 - c + c^\ell \frac{\ell - \delta(i)}{\ell - 1}[f_v < f_{v\oplus s}]\right) : i = 1, \ldots, n-1 \right\}.
$$

For uniform crossover, the spectrum of $d\mathcal{G}_{e_k}$ is given by

$$
spec(d\mathcal{G}_{e_s}) = \\
\left\{ k(1 - c + c2^{1 - \mathbf{1}^T i})[f_v < f_{v\oplus s}] : i = 1, \ldots, n-1 \right\}.
$$

COROLLARY 16. *Assume proportional selection. Let c denote the crossover rate for one-point or uniform crossover. For one-point crossover, the spectrum of $d\mathcal{G}_{e_k}$, considered as a map from $\mathbf{1}^\perp$ to itself, is given by*

$$
spec(d\mathcal{G}_{e_s}) = \left\{ \frac{f_{i\oplus s}}{f_s} \left(1 - c + c^\ell \frac{\ell - \delta(i)}{\ell - 1} \right) : i = 1, \ldots, n-1 \right\}.
$$

For uniform crossover, the spectrum of $d\mathcal{G}_{e_k}$ is given by

$$
spec(d\mathcal{G}_{e_s}) = \left\{ \frac{f_{i\oplus s}}{f_s}(1 - c + c2^{1 - \mathbf{1}^T i}) : i = 1, \ldots, n-1 \right\}.
$$

PROOF. This corollary is a restatement of theorem 3.4 and lemma 5.1 of [15]. It also follows directly from theorem 13 and lemma 14. $\square$

For an example of the application of this theorem, see subsection 5.1.

Note that corollary 16 shows that each eigenvalue of the differential of $\mathcal{G}$ at vertex fixed point e_k corresponds to the fitness of some other search space point $i \oplus k$. More precisely, it is the fitness ratio $\frac{f_{i\oplus k}}{f_k}$ times a factor that depends on i and on the crossover method.

For a crossover rate of zero (pure selection), only the vertices corresponding to global optima are stable fixed points. Global optima with no globally optimal neighbors are asymptotically stable. As the crossover rate increases, more vertices may become stable fixed points. But vertices corresponding to search space points with more fit neighbors can never be stable.

The following lemma shows that stability in $\mathbb{R}^n$ for vertex fixed points is the same as stability in the simplex.

LEMMA 17. *If v is a vertex fixed point with the spectral radius (modulus of largest eigenvalue) of $d\mathcal{G}_v$ greater than 1, then v is an asymptotically unstable fixed point of $\mathcal{G}$ considered as a map from the hyperplane containing the simplex to itself.*

PROOF. This is theorem 4.3 of [15]. Or lemma 7 can be used to prove this theorem. □

2.8 Bistability

In dynamical systems theory, bistability refers to a situation where there are two stable fixed points with distinct domains of attraction. The fixed point that the system converges to depends on the initial conditions.

It is easy to construct fitness functions with multiple peaks (local maxima) so that the SGA IPM with no mutation has stable fixed points which are the uniform populations consisting only of multiple copies of the fitness peaks. See theorems 15 and 16 for details. (Note, however, that a local maximum of the fitness function does not necessarily correspond to a stable fixed point.) It is one of the main results of this paper (see theorem 31) that with a sufficiently small increase in mutation, these fixed points move inside the simplex.

Thus, it is easy to construct examples where the SGA IPM has dynamical systems bistability, and these examples are not surprising. However, there is a more restricted form of bistability that can happen in infinite population models which is surprising.

When the mutation rate is $1/2$, then there is a single stable fixed point of the SGA IPM at the center of the simplex. One might guess that if there was a single fitness peak, then as the mutation rate decreased from $1/2$ to zero, this stable fixed point would migrate from the center of the simplex to the uniform population corresponding to the fitness peak. However, something more complex can happen [20]: at a critical mutation rate, the stable fixed point bifurcates into two stable fixed points and one unstable fixed point. As the mutation rate continues to decrease, one stable fixed point move toward the fitness peak, the other stays near the center of the simplex, with the unstable fixed point between them. At another smaller critical mutation rate, the unstable fixed point joins with the one of the stable fixed points, and both of these fixed points disappear. Thus, at a range of mutation rates between the two critical mutation rates, there are two stable fixed points which is bistability in the sense defined above. But it is surprising since the bistability is not caused by multiple fitness peaks, but is rather related to the disruptiveness of the combination of mutation and crossover. This situation with two stable fixed points and one fitness peak was called *bistability* in [20]; clearly this is a more restricted form of bistability than the dynamical system definition mentioned above.

The above description is based on the gene pool model given in [20]. Gene pool crossover takes the population directly to linkage equilibrium in one step. In this model, the fixed point equation reduces to an equation in a single variable for the NEEDLE (needle-in-the-haystack) and BINEEDLE fitness functions, experiments in running the SGA IPM with conventional two parent crossover show very similar bistability behavior on these fitness functions. Below are the formulations for NEEDLE and BINEEDLE.

$$NEEDLE(x) = \begin{cases} 1+a & \text{all ones string} \\ 1 & \text{otherwise} \end{cases} \quad (16)$$

$$BINEEDLE(x) = \begin{cases} 1+a & \text{all ones string} \\ 1 & \text{otherwise} \\ 1+a & \text{all zeros string} \end{cases} \quad (17)$$

In practical terms, when there is bistability, a GA initialized with a random population is likely to be trapped close to the center of the simplex stable fixed point which prevents it from accumulating points of the optimal population. This is illustrated by the results of Suzuki and Iwasa [11] on the NEEDLE fitness (which they called a "babel-like fitness landscape"). They found that crossover accelerated time to convergence if the crossover rate was not too high, but over a critical crossover rate, the time to find the needle diverged. The discovery of the bistability phenomenon explained their results.

Bistability (in the more restricted sense) is only known to occur in the presence of crossover, mutation, and selection. This more restricted bistability phenomenon was discovered by Boerjlist et al [1] in a quasi species model of virus reproduction, and was analyzed for the NEEDLE and the BINEEDLE fitness functions and proportional selection in [20]. These results were extended to truncation selection in [18] and to a "sloping plateau" fitness function in [19], all by using the gene pool model.

When bistability occurs, there is one fixed point "close" to the fitness peak, and one fixed point "close" to the center of the simplex. For the NEEDLE fitness functions, the fitness peak is at a vertex of the simplex. Thus, when the GA infinite population model is initialized with a population corresponding to the center of the simplex, the GA model will converge to the center of the simplex fixed point, and when the model is initialized with a population corresponding to the fitness peak, the model will converge to the fitness peak fixed point. A finite population GA with the same parameters and fitness function, when initialized with a random population will likely be "trapped" for a long time by the center of the simplex fixed point, and while when initialized at the fitness peak, will likely be "trapped" for a long time by the fitness peak fixed point. ("A long time" is the best that we can say since the GA with mutation is an ergodic Markov chain, and all populations will be visited infinitely often.)

3. QUESTIONS

The dichotomy of many fixed points for crossover-selection GAs and one fixed point for mutation-selection GAs and for mutation rate $1/2$ suggests some questions:

- What happens to the vertex fixed points when mutation is increased slightly from zero? We answer this question for hyperbolic fixed points in the next section.

- What happens to the vertex fixed points when the mutation rate is increased from 0 to 1/2? Recall that when the mutation rate is 1/2, there is a single stable fixed point at the center of the simplex.

- What happens to the Perron-Frobenius fixed point as the crossover rate is increased from zero? Presumably, the fixed point must bifurcate when there are multiple stable fixed points under crossover. What kinds of bifurcations are possible?

4. THE MOVEMENT OF VERTEX FIXED POINTS UNDER SMALL POSITIVE MUTATION

In this section we investigate the behavior of hyperbolic vertex fixed points of $\mathcal{G}$ as the mutation rate increases from zero. Let p denote the mutation rate, and let $\mathcal{G} : \Lambda \times (-1,1) \to \Lambda$ denote the SGA map parametrized by the mutation rate p. (While a negative mutation rate is not meaningful in terms of a GA, the formulas for $\mathcal{G}$ apply for a negative mutation rate, and this allows us to not consider one-sided derivatives.) Let $v = v_0$ be a hyperbolic vertex fixed point for $\mathcal{G}(x,0)$. We will use the notation $\mathcal{G}_p(x)$ for $\mathcal{G}(x,p)$ when it is convenient.

While we are stating our results in term of the mutation rate, in fact all we need is that $\mathcal{G}(x,p)$ is continuously (i. e. C^1) differentiable in both x and p, and $\mathcal{G}_p$ maps the simplex into its interior for $p > 0$.

In this section, we will be differentiating with respect to both x and p, so we will use a different notation for these derivatives. Let $\frac{\partial \mathcal{G}}{\partial x}(y,q)$ denote the derivative of $\mathcal{G}$ with respect to $x \in \mathbb{R}^n$ evaluated at $(y,q) \in \mathbb{R}^n \times (-1,1)$. (In the notation of the previous section, this was $d(\mathcal{G}_p)_{(y,q)}$.) Let $\frac{\partial \mathcal{G}}{\partial p}$ denote the derivative of $\mathcal{G}$ with respect to the mutation rate p.

Let $id : \mathbb{R}^n \to \mathbb{R}^n$ denote the identity map. Of course, the differential of id is the identity matrix.

LEMMA 18. *If $g : \mathbb{R}^n \to \mathbb{R}^n$ is differentiable at a point y with no eigenvalues equal to 1, then $g - id$ is differentiable with a nonsingular differential at y.*

PROOF. There is a similarity transformation P such that $P^{-1}\frac{dg}{dx}(y)P$ is in Jordan canonical form with the eigenvalues on the diagonal. Then $P^{-1}(\frac{dg}{dx}(y) - I)P$ is also in Jordan canonical form with eigenvalues on the diagonal. Thus, the eigenvalues of $\frac{dg}{dx}(y) - I$ are the eigenvalues of $\frac{dg}{dx}(y)$ minus 1, and by assumption these are nonzero. Thus, $\frac{dg}{dx}(y) - I$ is nonsingular. $\square$

Define $\mathcal{H} : \mathbb{R}^n \times (-1,1) \to \mathbb{R}^n$ by $\mathcal{H} = \mathcal{G} - id$. Recall that we have assumed that v is a hyperbolic vertex fixed point of $\mathcal{G}$ which means that $\frac{\partial \mathcal{G}}{\partial x}(p,0)$ has no eigenvalues on the unit circle. Thus, $\mathcal{H}(v,0) = 0$ and $\frac{\partial \mathcal{H}}{\partial x}(v,0) = \frac{\partial \mathcal{G}}{\partial x}(v,0) - I$ is non-singular by Lemma 18.

LEMMA 19. *There is a neighborhood V of v, an $\varepsilon > 0$, and a continuously differentiable function $h : [0,\varepsilon) \to V$ such that $\mathcal{H}(h(p),p) = 0$ and $h(0) = v$. If we define $v_p = h(p)$, then $\mathcal{G}(v_p,p) = v_p$, so v_p is a fixed point of $\mathcal{G}_p$. Furthermore, the derivative of h is given by*

$$\frac{\partial h}{\partial p}(p) = -\left(\frac{\partial \mathcal{H}}{\partial x}(h(p),p)\right)^{-1} \frac{\partial \mathcal{H}}{\partial p}(h(p),p). \quad (18)$$

PROOF. By the above argument our assumption of hyperbolicity of the vertex fixed point v implies that $\frac{\partial \mathcal{H}}{\partial x}(v,0)$ is nonsingular. There is a neighborhood U of v and a $\delta > 0$ such that $\frac{\partial \mathcal{H}}{\partial x}(x,p)$ is nonsingular for $x \in U$ and $p \in (-\delta,\delta)$. The implicit function theorem shows that there is a neighborhood $V \subseteq U$ of v, an $\varepsilon > 0$, and a function h with the required properties. $\square$

We have now shown that as p increases from 0, there is a path of fixed points v_p of $\mathcal{G}_p$. This path can intersect the boundary of the simplex only at $v = v_0$ since $\mathcal{G}_p$ maps the boundary of the simplex into the interior of the simplex for $p > 0$.

4.1 Asymptotically stable fixed vertex points

LEMMA 20. *Let v be a hyperbolic asymptotically stable vertex fixed point of $\mathcal{G}_0$. Then there is a neighborhood V of v in Λ and a $\delta > 0$ such that for all $p < \delta$, $\mathcal{G}_p$ has a unique fixed point in V, and this fixed point is asymptotically stable.*

PROOF. Taking standard matrix norm in the eigenvector basis $\|\cdot\|$ we have $\|\frac{\partial \mathcal{G}}{\partial x}(v,0)\| = \alpha < 1$. By continuity of the derivative, there exists a $\beta > \alpha$, a small neighborhood $U \subset \Lambda$ of v, and a $\delta > 0$ such that for all $(y,p) \in U \times [0,\delta)$ we have

$$\left\|\frac{\partial \mathcal{G}}{\partial x}(y,p)\right\| \leq \beta < 1.$$

By going to a smaller neighborhood $V \subseteq U$ if necessary, we have that for any $p \in [0,\delta)$ and any pair $y, z \in V$,

$$
\begin{aligned}
\|\mathcal{G}_p(y) - \mathcal{G}_p(z)\| &= \left\|\frac{\partial \mathcal{G}}{\partial x}(y)\right\| \|y - z\| + o(y - z) \\
&\leq \beta\|y - z\| + \frac{1-\beta}{2}\|y - z\| \\
&\leq \frac{1+\beta}{2}\|y - z\|.
\end{aligned}
$$

Thus, $\mathcal{G}_p$ is a contraction on V for all $p \in [0,\delta)$. By the contraction mapping theorem (theorem 2.5 of [9]), there is a unique fixed point $v_p \in V$ for all $p \in [0,\delta)$. $\square$

Our primary theorem on the movement of stable fixed points, theorem 31 is postponed to subsection 4.3

4.2 Unstable fixed vertex points

THEOREM 21. *Let $v = v_0$ be a hyperbolic unstable vertex fixed point of $\mathcal{G}_0$. Then for sufficiently small $p > 0$, $\mathcal{G}_p$ has no fixed point in Λ.*

PROOF. The domain of this proof is the $(n-1)$-dimensional hyperplane $H = \{x \in \mathbb{R}^n : \mathbf{1}^T x = 1\}$. We can apply lemma 7 to represent $\frac{\partial \mathcal{G}}{\partial x}(v_0,0)$ in the hyperplane $\mathbf{1}^\perp = \{x \in \mathbb{R}^n : \mathbf{1}^T x = 0\}$, and when we refer to differentials in this proof, we are referring to their representation in $\mathbf{1}^\perp$.

The implicit function theorem argument of lemma 19 shows that there is a $\xi > 0$ such that v_p is a hyperbolic fixed point of $\mathcal{G}(x,p)$ for $p \in (-\xi,\xi)$.

By applying the Center Manifold theorem [9] to the map $\mathcal{H} : H \times (-\xi,\xi) \to H \times (-\xi,\xi)$ defined by $\mathcal{H}(x,p) = (\mathcal{G}(x,p),p)$, we conclude that the stable manifold $W^s(v_p, \mathcal{G}(x,p))$ and the unstable manifold $W^u(v_p, \mathcal{G}(x,p))$ depend C^1 jointly on both x and p. In other words, there exists a $\delta > 0$ with $\delta < \xi$ such that for each such $p \in (-\delta, \delta)$ the unstable manifold can be represented as a graph of a C^1 function

$$\sigma : E^u_{(v_0,0)} \times (-\delta, \delta) \to E^s_{(v_0,0)}$$

where $E^u_{(v_0,0)}$ is a span of the eigenvectors that correspond to eigenvalues of $\frac{\partial \mathcal{G}}{\partial x}(v_0, 0)$ with modulus greater than 1 and where $E^s_{(v_0,0)}$ is a span of the eigenvectors that correspond to eigenvalues of $\frac{\partial \mathcal{G}}{\partial x}(v_0, 0)$ with modulus less than 1. The graph consists of triples $(x, p, \sigma(x,p))$ where $x \in E^u_{(x_0,0)}$, $p \in (-\delta, \delta)$ and $\sigma(x) \in E^s_{(x_0,0)}$.

Suppose that v_p for $p \in (0, \delta)$ lies in the interior of Λ. Since v_0 hyperbolic and unstable, $\frac{\partial \mathcal{G}}{\partial x}(v_0, 0)$ has at least one eigenvalue with modulus greater than 1. Thus, the unstable manifold $W^u(v_0, \mathcal{G}(x, 0))$ is nonempty. The graphs of $W^u(v_0, \mathcal{G}(x, 0)) = \sigma(0)$ and $W^u(v_0, \mathcal{G}(x, p)) = \sigma(p)$ are C^1 close to each other and have the same dimension.

Let $B^u_r(v_0)$ be a ball of radius r in $E^u_{(v_0,0)}$. For any $\varepsilon > 0$ (where ε will be chosen later), there exists an $r > 0$ and an η with $0 < \eta < \delta$ such that

$$\|\sigma(x, p) - \sigma(x, 0)\|_{C^1} < \varepsilon \quad \text{for all } x \in B^u_r(v_0), \ p \in (0, \eta). \tag{19}$$

Since v_0 is a vertex of Λ and $E^u_{(v_0,0)}$ is a linear space, we must have that

$$B^u_r(v_0) \cap \text{ext}(\Lambda) \neq \emptyset, \quad \text{for all } r$$

where $\text{ext}(\Lambda)$ is the exterior of Λ. Since $W^u_{(v_0,0)}$ is tangent to $E^u_{(v_0,0)}$ for sufficiently small r and $y \in B^u_r(v_0) \setminus \{v_0\}$, we must have

$$\text{graph}(\sigma(y, 0)) \cap \text{ext}(\Lambda) \neq \emptyset.$$

Let $y_0 \in \text{graph}(\sigma(y, 0)) \cap \text{ext}(\Lambda)$. Then there is a positive distance ϵ between the compact set $\text{graph}(\sigma(y_0, 0))$ and Λ. Therefore, by equation (19)

$$\text{graph}(\sigma(y_0, p)) \cap \text{ext}(\Lambda) \neq \emptyset$$

for all $p \in (0, \eta)$. Let y_p be in this set.

The reverse iterates of y_p under $\mathcal{G}_p$ must converge to v_p. Thus, there must be some reverse iterate of y_p that is in Λ but is mapped by $\mathcal{G}_p$ to $\text{ext}(\Lambda)$. But this contradicts that fact that $\mathcal{G}_p$ must map Λ to the interior of Λ. Thus, our assumption that $v_p \in \Lambda$ is not correct. $\square$

4.3 The direction of movement of fixed points as mutation increases from zero

Recall that the function h defined in lemma 19 defined the local path of fixed points as the mutation rate p increased from zero. In this section we calculate $\frac{dh}{dp}$ and discuss the implications of the result.

Throughout this section v will be a vertex fixed point of $\mathcal{G}_0$. Without loss of generality, we can rearrange the order of the coordinates of $\mathbb{R}^n$ so that $v = e_0$ which is the first unit vector in $\mathbb{R}^n$.

LEMMA 22. *Let v be a vertex fixed point and assume that mutation is bitwise mutation with mutation rate p. Then*

$$\frac{\partial \mathcal{G}}{\partial p}(v, 0) = \begin{cases} -\ell & \text{if } i = 0 \\ 1 & \text{if } \mathbf{1}^T i = 1 \\ 0 & \text{otherwise} \end{cases} \tag{20}$$

Furthermore, the vector $\frac{\partial \mathcal{G}}{\partial p}(v, 0) - v$ is in the direction of the simplex.

PROOF. The GA map g can be written as a composition of a selection map, a crossover map, and a mutation map. Thus,

$$\mathcal{G}(p, x) = \mathcal{U}(\mathcal{C}(\mathcal{F}(x, p))).$$

Since the crossover map $\mathcal{C}$ and the selection map $\mathcal{F}$ don't depend on the mutation rate p, and since v is a fixed point of $\mathcal{C}$ and $\mathcal{F}$, we have that $\frac{\partial \mathcal{G}}{\partial p}(v, 0) = \frac{d\mathcal{U}}{dp}(v, 0)$.

The definition of the mutation map is

$$\mathcal{U}(x, p) = Ax.$$

where A is the $n \times n$ matrix defined by

$$A_{i,j} = p^{\mathbf{1}^T(i \oplus j)}(1 - p)^{\ell - \mathbf{1}^T(i \oplus j)}.$$

Thus,

$$\mathcal{U}(p, x)_i = \sum_j p^{\mathbf{1}^T(i \oplus j)}(1 - p)^{\ell - \mathbf{1}^T(i \oplus j)} x_j.$$

Since v is the first unit vector in $\mathbb{R}^n$,

$$\mathcal{U}(p, v)_i = p^{\mathbf{1}^T i}(1 - p)^{\ell - \mathbf{1}^T i}.$$

Clearly, for $\mathbf{1}^T i \notin \{0, 1\}$, $\frac{\partial \mathcal{U}}{\partial p}(v, 0)_i = 0$, and it is easy to check that for $\mathbf{1}^T i = 1$, $\frac{\partial \mathcal{U}}{\partial p}(v, 0)_i = 1$ and $\frac{\partial \mathcal{U}}{\partial p}(v, 0)_0 = -\ell$. Thus, we have shown that equation (20) holds.

Define the change-of-basis matrix P to have columns $e_0, e_1 - e_0, e_2 - e_0, \ldots, e_{n-1} - e_0$. Note that the columns of P, except for the first, are the directions from $v = e_0$ to the other vertices of the simplex. Multiplying by P transforms the standard basis into a basis whose elements are the columns of P. A vector from v points into the simplex if it lies in the plane of the simplex (i. e., the sum of the coordinates are zero) and if its coordinates after the first in this basis are nonnegative. Clearly, $\frac{\partial g}{\partial p}(v, 0)$ satisfies these conditions. $\square$

Recall that in section 2 we defined the *twist* A^* of an $n \times n$ matrix A to have i, jth entry $A_{i \oplus j, i}$. A matrix A is called *separative* if $A_{i,j} \neq 0$ implies that $i^T j = 0$.

Mixing (crossover and mutation) is defined through a *mixing matrix* $M(p)$ which we parametrize by the mutation rate p. See subsection 2.1 for more details.

LEMMA 23. *The mixing matrix $M(0)$ (for zero mutation) is separative.*

PROOF. Theorems 6.5 and 6.6 of [12] show that $M(0)$ is separative. $\square$

If matrix A is separative, then its twist A^* satisfies the condition

$$A^*_{i,j} \neq 0 \implies i = i \otimes j.$$

We will call a matrix satisfying this condition *twist separative*. Clearly, $M(0)^*$ in the example above is twist separative.

For example, suppose that $i = 6 = 110$ and $j = 3 = 011$. Then $i \otimes j = 010 \neq 110 = i$, so if A is twist separative, $A_{6,3} = 0$. So whenever there is a locus of j which is zero while the corresponding locus of i is one, the pair i, j does not satisfy $i = i \otimes j$, and thus $A_{i,j} = 0$.

LEMMA 24. *A twist separative matrix is upper triangular.*

PROOF. $i = i \otimes j \Rightarrow i \leq j$. $\square$

LEMMA 25. *The inverse of a twist separative matrix is twist separative.*

PROOF. The following is a "back-substitution" algorithm to compute the inverse of an upper triangular matrix:

INVERSEUPPERTRIANGULAR(A)
1    $B \leftarrow$ a square zero matrix of the same dimensions as A
2   **for** $r \leftarrow 0$ **to** $n-1$ **do**
3      $B[r,r] \leftarrow 1/A[r,r]$
4   **for** $r \leftarrow 1$ **to** $n-1$ **do**
5   **for** $i \leftarrow 0$ **to** $n-r-1$ **do**
6        $j \leftarrow i+r$
7        $B[i,j] \leftarrow -\frac{1}{A[i,i]} \sum_{k=i+1}^{j} A[i,k]B[k,j]$
8   **return** B

Let i,j be such that $i \neq i \otimes j$. We need to show that $B[i,j] = 0$. As above, there must be a locus at which j has a zero bit while i has a one bit. Consider the possibilities for that locus of the summation index k in line 7 of the algorithm. If that locus of k is a one bit, then $k \neq k \otimes j$ which implies that $B[k,j] = 0$. If that locus of k is a zero bit, then $i \neq i \otimes k$ which implies that $A[i,k] = 0$. Thus, each term of the summation of line 7 is zero, which implies that $B[i,j] = 0$. $\square$

LEMMA 26. *If A is an $n \times n$ twist separative matrix and $B = A^{-1}$, then for j such that $\mathbf{1}^T j = 1$, $B_{0,j} = \frac{A_{0,j}}{A_{0,0}A_{j,j}}$.*

PROOF. Line 7 of the above algorithm applied to $B[0,i]$ is

$$B[0,j] \leftarrow -\frac{1}{A[0,0]} \sum_{k=1}^{j} A[0,k]B[k,j].$$

Since B is twist separative, $B[k,j] = 0$ for $k = 1, 2, \ldots, j-1$. Thus, the only nonzero term in the summation is $A[0,j]B[j,j] = A[0,j]/A[j,j]$. $\square$

LEMMA 27. *The product of twist separative matrices is twist separative.*

PROOF. The following is the algorithm to compute the product of upper triangular matrices:

PRODUCTUPPERTRIANGULAR(A, B)
1    $C \rightarrow$ a square matrix of the same dimensions as A and B
2   **for** $i \leftarrow 0$ **to** $n-1$ **do**
3   **for** $j \leftarrow i$ **to** $n-1$ **do**
4        $C[i,j] \leftarrow \sum_{k=i}^{j} A[i,k]B[k,j]$
5   **return** C

The argument of the proof of Lemma 25 applies to line 4 of this algorithm to show that $i \neq i \otimes j \Rightarrow C[i,j] = 0$. $\square$

LEMMA 28. *The differential of $\mathcal{G}$ at simplex vertex $v = e_0$ is given by*

$$\frac{\partial \mathcal{G}}{\partial x}(v,p) = \frac{\partial \mathcal{G}}{\partial x}(e_0,p) = 2M(p)^* \frac{d\mathcal{F}}{dx}(e_0).$$

where $\mathcal{F}$ denotes the selection map. For proportional, tournament, and ranking selection, $\frac{d\mathcal{F}}{dx}(e_0)$ is twist separative. The matrices $\frac{\partial \mathcal{H}}{\partial x}(v,0)$ and $\left(\frac{\partial \mathcal{H}}{\partial x}(v,0)\right)^{-1}$ are also twist separative (where $\mathcal{H}(x,p) = \mathcal{G}(x,p) - x$).

PROOF. Lemma 10 gives the formula for the differential. (Since we are taking the differential at e_0, the σ_0 permutation matrix is the identity.)

$M(0)^*$ is twist separative by lemma 23. Let the fitness vector be $\langle f_0, f_1, \ldots, f_{n-1}\rangle^T$. For proportional and tournament selection, lemmas 1 and corollary 6 show that $\frac{d\mathcal{F}}{dx}(e_0)$ is upper triangular with nonzero entries only on the diagonal and in the upper row. Theorem 7.3 of [12] can be used to prove the same for ranking selection. Thus, $\frac{d\mathcal{F}}{dx}(e_0)$ is twist separative. $\frac{\partial \mathcal{H}}{\partial x}(e_0,0) = \frac{\partial \mathcal{G}}{\partial x}(e_0,0) - I$ is clearly twist separative, and lemma 25 shows that $\left(\frac{\partial \mathcal{H}}{\partial x}(e_0,0)\right)^{-1}$ is twist separative. $\square$

The previous lemma depends on our rearrangement of coordinates so that $v = e_0$. Without this assumption, $\sigma_s \frac{d\mathcal{F}}{dx}(e_0)\sigma_s$ is twist separative.

LEMMA 29. *For proportional, ranking, and tournament selection, $\frac{\partial \mathcal{G}}{\partial x}(v,0) = \frac{\partial \mathcal{G}}{\partial x}(e_0,0)$ is upper triangular and its diagonal entries are its eigenvalues $\lambda_0, \lambda_1, \ldots, \lambda_{n-1}$. For proportional selection, $\lambda_0 = 0$ and for j such that $\mathbf{1}^T j = 1$, $\frac{\partial \mathcal{G}}{\partial x}(v,0)_{0,j} = -\lambda_j$.*

PROOF. The proof of lemma 28 shows that $\frac{d\mathcal{F}}{dx}(e_0)$ is upper triangular with nonzero elements only on the diagonal and in the upper row. For proportional selection, equation 4 shows that $\mathbf{1}^T \frac{d\mathcal{F}}{dx}(e_0) = 0$. Since $\frac{d\mathcal{F}}{dx}(e_0)$ is twist separative, the only nonzero entries in column j where $\mathbf{1}^T j = 1$ are the row 0 entry and the diagonal entry. Thus, the row 0 entry must be the negative of the diagonal entry λ_j. $\square$

Since $\frac{\partial \mathcal{G}}{\partial x}(v,0)$ is upper triangular, its diagonal entries are its eigenvalues $\lambda_0 = 0, \lambda_1, \ldots, \lambda_{n-1}$.

THEOREM 30. *Assume proportional selection. Let v be a hyperbolic fixed point of $\mathcal{G}_0$. Then*

$$\frac{dh}{dp}(0)_i = \begin{cases} -\sum_{j: \mathbf{1}^T j = 1} \dfrac{1}{1-\lambda_j} & \text{if } i = 0 \\ \dfrac{1}{1-\lambda_i} & \text{if } \mathbf{1}^T i = 1 \\ 0 & \text{otherwise} \end{cases}.$$

where λ_i is the ith diagonal entry and eigenvalue of $\frac{\partial \mathcal{G}}{\partial x}(v,0)$.

PROOF. Lemma 19 shows that

$$\frac{dh}{dp}(0) = -\left(\frac{\partial \mathcal{H}}{\partial x}(v,0)\right)^{-1} \frac{\partial \mathcal{H}}{\partial p}(v,0).$$

Since the identity map does not depend on p, $\frac{\partial \mathcal{H}}{\partial p}(v,0) = \frac{\partial \mathcal{G}}{\partial p}(v,0))$ which is given by equation (20). This shows that $\frac{dh}{dp}(0)_i = 0$ for i such that $i \neq 0$ and $\mathbf{1}^T i \neq 1$.

Let E denote the matrix $\left(\frac{\partial \mathcal{H}}{\partial x}(v,0)\right)^{-1}$. Note that the ith diagonal entry of the upper triangular matrix $\frac{\partial \mathcal{H}}{\partial x}(v,0)$ is $\lambda_i - 1$. and therefore the ith diagonal entry of E is $\frac{1}{1-\lambda_i}$.

Lemma 28 shows that E is twist separative. Then

$$\frac{dh}{dp}(0)_i = \sum_j E_{i,j} \frac{\partial \mathcal{H}}{\partial p}(v,0))_j. \qquad (21)$$

First, we consider $i > 0$ and the jth entry in this sum. By equation (20) $\frac{\partial \mathcal{H}}{\partial p}(v,0))_j$ is nonzero only when $j = 0$ or

$\mathbf{1}^T j = 1$, and in this latter case $\frac{\partial \mathcal{H}}{\partial p}(v,0))_j = 1$. Since E is twist separative, $E_{i,j}$ is nonzero only when $i = i \otimes j$. Thus, the only j for which the jth term in the summation of equation (21) is nonzero is when $i = j$. Thus, when $i > 0$, $\frac{dh}{dp}(0)_i = E_{i,i} = \frac{1}{1-\lambda_i}$.

Now we consider the jth entry in the sum of equation (21) when $i = 0$.

Since $\frac{\partial \mathcal{H}}{\partial p}(v,0))_j = 0$ except when $\mathbf{1}^T j = 1$ and $j = 0$, we only need to consider entries $E_{0,j}$ where $\mathbf{1}^T j = 1$ and $j = 0$.

Lemma 29 shows that $\frac{\partial \mathcal{G}}{\partial x}(v,0)_{0,0} = 0$. Thus, 29 shows that $\frac{\partial \mathcal{H}}{\partial x}(v,0)_{0,0} = E_{0,0} = -1$.

From lemma 26 and lemma 29 it follows that if $\mathbf{1}^T j = 1$, $E_{0,j} = \frac{\lambda_j}{-(\lambda_j - 1)} = \frac{\lambda_j}{1-\lambda_j}$. Thus,

$$\left(\frac{dh}{dp}\right)_0 = \ell + \sum_{j : \mathbf{1}^T j = 1} \frac{\lambda_j}{1-\lambda_j} = \sum_{j : \mathbf{1}^T j = 1} \frac{1}{1-\lambda_j}.$$

$\square$

Let $B_\varepsilon(v) = \{x \in \mathbb{R}^n : \|x - v\| < \varepsilon$ be the ball of radius ϵ around v. The next theorem shows that as mutation increases, a hyperbolic asymptotically stable fixed point moves into the interior of the simplex.

THEOREM 31. *Assume proportional selection, and assume that v is a hyperbolic asymptotically stable fixed point of $\mathcal{G}_0$, and h is the map defined in lemma 19. There is an $\varepsilon > 0$ and a $\gamma > 0$ such that for $p \in [0, \gamma)$, $h(p)$ is the unique fixed point of $\mathcal{G}_p$ in $B_\epsilon(v)$.*

PROOF. Lemma 22 shows that $\frac{\partial \mathcal{G}}{\partial p}(v,0) = \frac{\partial \mathcal{H}}{\partial p}(v,0) \neq 0$. Thus, $\frac{dh}{dp}(0) \neq 0$. By the continuity of the derivative, there is a $\eta > 0$ such that for $0 \le q \le \eta$, $\frac{dh}{dp}(q)^T \frac{dh}{dp}(0) > 0$. We can also assume that $\eta < \delta$ for the δ of lemma 20. Let $\gamma = \|v - h(q)\|$. Then for such q, $\|h(q) - v\|$ is strictly monotonically increasing as q increases. Let $\varepsilon > 0$ be such that $\varepsilon \le \|h(\eta) - v\|$ and $B_\varepsilon(v)$ gives the unique fixed point of lemma 20. Now choose $\gamma > 0$ to be sufficiently small that if $0 < p < \gamma < \delta$, then $h(p) \in B_\varepsilon$. Then $h(p)$ must be the unique fixed point of lemma 20. $\square$

4.4 Discussion

Let v be a hyperbolic vertex fixed point corresponding to a uniform population of k individuals, i. e., $v = e_k$. Theorem 16 shows that for proportional selection each eigenvalue of $\frac{\partial \mathcal{G}}{\partial x}(v,0)$ (other than 0) is determined by the fitness and the properties of some other point $i \oplus k$ of the search space. Theorem 30 shows that these fitnesses for the Hamming distance 1 neighbors of k determine the direction of $\frac{dh}{dp}(0)$. If all Hamming distance 1 neighbors have fitness less than the fitness of k, then the vector from v to $\frac{dh}{dp}(0)$ points in the direction of the interior of the face of Λ determined by v and its Hamming distance 1 neighbors. If some Hamming distance 1 neighbor has greater fitness, then the vector from v to $\frac{dh}{dp}(0)$ points outside of the simplex (providing an alternate proof of theorem 21 in this special case).

If $v = e_k$ is asymptotically unstable under zero mutation, this means that at least one eigenvalue of $\frac{\partial \mathcal{G}}{\partial x}(v,0)$ is greater than 1. Lemma 16 shows that each eigenvalue corresponds to some point in the search space other than k which has higher fitness than k. The instability of v means that when the SGA IPM is initialized a population which is both near to v, interior to the simplex, and not on the stable manifold

of v, it will diverge away from v due to the influence of the higher fitness points just mentioned..

Any population vector interior to the simplex must contain a nonzero representation of every point in the search space, including those higher fitness points that caused v to be unstable. But in a finite GA population in a situation where the string length is realistically long, this won't happen since the size of the search space grows exponentially with the string length. If the search space points that make v unstable have a large Hamming distance from v, they are unlikely to be included in a finite population near v. And if there is mutation with a mutation rate that is $\Theta(1/n)$, such points are unlikely to be discovered in a realistic time period. Thus, from the point of view of finite populations, v is stable in that when a with-mutation GA is at a population near v, it is likely to remain there for a long time (namely, until the higher-fitness points that make v unstable are discovered by mutation). In the case of no-mutation, we would conjecture that the GA would be likely to be absorbed into the population corresponding to v.

We can also conjecture that when the search space points that make v unstable at at least Hamming distance j from v, then as the mutation rate p increases from 0, the fixed point corresponding to v is order $O(p^j)$ close to the face of the simplex determined by v and its Hamming distance 1 neighbors. In other words, it would be very close to the simplex. When a saddle-point fixed point is very close to but not in the simplex, the IPM will move very slowly when close to this fixed point.

4.4.1 Examples

We give two examples of the situation just described. Both use proportional selection, 1-point crossover with crossover rate 7/8 and the following fitness function:

$$f(i) = \begin{cases} 20 & \text{if } \mathbf{1}^T i = 0 \\ 165 & \text{if } \mathbf{1}^T i = \ell \\ 1 & \text{otherwise} \end{cases}.$$

For any string length and 1-point crossover with rate 7/8, the uniform population consisting of the all zeros string is an unstable vertex fixed point because the eigenvalue corresponding to the all ones string is $\frac{33}{32}$ by theorem 16.

In the first example the SGA IPM (a model) is started at the all zeros string, which has fitness 20. The string length is 7 and the mutation rate is $\frac{1}{100}$. The all ones string, which has fitness 165, has a frequency of 10^{-14} after one time step. This frequency gradually increases. After one time step the fitness is 18.71, and this decreases to 18.641164 after 6 time steps. For the next 145 time steps, the fitness is very gradually decreasing, but to 8 significant digits, it remains at 18.641164. After 369 time steps, the fitness reaches a minimum of 18.272 and then it increases rapidly reaching 153.71 at time step 376. The IPM converges to within a tolerance of 10^{-12} after 382 time steps with a fitness of 153.79.

In the second example, the SGA (an actual GA) is run with the same fitness, string length 9, mutation rate $\frac{1}{10}$, and population size 1000. Initialization is with multiple copies of the all zeros string. The SGA was run until it found the optimum. With 100 runs, the average number of generations to find the optimum was 37,645 with a standard deviation of 34,767. The number of fitness evaluations was approximately 1000 times the number of generations. Clearly, while the all zeros uniform population is unstable as a fixed point, the GA takes a very long time to leave a neighborhood of this fixed point.

5. FIXED POINT MOVEMENT EXAMPLES

Next we will look in detail at gross movement of vertex fixed points for NEEDLE and BINEEDLE under varying mutation and crossover rates. The below is done via analysing and numerically iterating the $\mathcal{G}$-map, not with any running GA.

5.1 Stability of BINEEDLE Fixed Points

We assume that $\ell = 2$, $a = 1$, and no mutation. Interestingly, the center of the simplex $\langle 1/4, 1/4, 1/4, 1/4 \rangle$ is on the stable manifold of an unstable fixed point in the interior of the simplex. Thus, this fixed point can be found by iterating $\mathcal{G}$ starting at this point of the simplex.

The stability of the BINEEDLE fixed points can either be determined by directly computing the eigenvalues of the differential of $\mathcal{G}$ at the fixed point, or, in the case of vertex fixed points, by applying theorem 16. However, when directly computing the eigenvalues, there will be one eigenvalue that corresponds to a direction outside of the hyperplane of the simplex, and this eigenvalue is not relevant to the stability of $\mathcal{G}$ in the simplex. Theorem 16 says that this eigenvalue is 0 for proportional selection and for vertex fixed points.

Table 1 contains the results of doing this for these five fixed points of the $\mathcal{G}$-map with one-point crossover rate $c = 1.0$ and mutation rate $p = 0$ applied to the BINEEDLE fitness function. The eigenvalues not in the direction of the hyperplane of the simplex are not included.

Table 2 contains the same results for uniform crossover with crossover rate 1.

Table 1: BINEEDLE vertex fixed points, one-point crossover rate 1 and no mutation.

population	eigenvalues	type
$\langle 1, 0, 0, 0 \rangle$	$[1/2, 1/2, 0]$	*Stable*
$\langle 0, 1, 0, 0 \rangle$	$[2, 2, 0]$	Saddle
$\langle 0, 0, 1, 0 \rangle$	$[2, 2, 0]$	Saddle
$\langle 0, 0, 0, 1 \rangle$	$[1/2, 1/2, 0]$	*Stable*
$\langle 1/4, 1/4, 1/4, 1/4 \rangle$	$[4/3, 2/3, 0]$	Saddle

Table 2: BINEEDLE vertex fixed points, uniform crossover rate 1 and no mutation.

population	eigenvalues	type
$\langle 1, 0, 0, 0 \rangle$	$[1/2, 1/2, 1/2]$	*Stable*
$\langle 0, 1, 0, 0 \rangle$	$[2, 2, 1/2]$	Saddle
$\langle 0, 0, 1, 0 \rangle$	$[2, 2, 1/2]$	Saddle
$\langle 0, 0, 0, 1 \rangle$	$[1/2, 1/2, 1/2]$	*Stable*
$\langle 0.3202, 0.1798,$ $0.1798, 0.3202 \rangle$	$[1.219, 0.6906, 0.3716]$	Saddle

In both cases, simplex points of the form $\langle a, b, b, a \rangle$ with $a + b = 1/2$ are on the stable manifold of the fixed point which is interior to the fixed point, but as soon as the symmetry of points in this form is broken, then such points are in the domain of attraction of one of the stable fixed points.

It is interesting to note that one-point crossover with rate 1 for $\ell = 2$ takes any population to linkage equilibrium in one step. Thus, it is the same as gene pool crossover. This is not true for string lengths longer than 2.

5.2 Stability of points on the segment between vertices of maximum fitness

Define a variant of the NEEDLE for $\ell = 4$, $n = 2^4 = 16$ as follows:

$$CONCATNEEDLE : \langle 2, 2, 1, \ldots, 1 \rangle \qquad (22)$$

For a population of $x = \langle \alpha, \beta, 0, \ldots, 0 \rangle$ with $\alpha + \beta = 1$, it can be verified that $\mathcal{G}(x) = x$. Thus, there is a line segment of fixed points. At these fixed points, the differential of $\mathcal{G}$ has one eigenvalue of 1 and all other eigenvalues are less than 1. The eigenvector corresponding to the eigenvalue of 1 is in the direction of the line between the vertices corresponding to binary strings 0000 and 0001, the two points of higher fitness. This suggests that all points on this line segment are stable (but not asymptotically stable) fixed points.

5.3 Introducing Epsilon Mutation

For the BINEEDLE a computational study was done to attempt to determine where the vertex fixed points moved to under increasing mutation. Iteration experiments of the $\mathcal{G}$-map were done with initial populations set at either of the two stable vertex fixed point populations or the simplex-center population. String length $\ell = 4$ and one-point crossover were used with crossover rate 1. A range of mutation rates were chosen. Note that the experiment was explicitly done for both stable vertex-populations at all-ones and all-zeros. Note that the fitness function is symmetric under changing zeros to ones and ones to zeros, and the same is true of the $\mathcal{G}$ function when applied to such a fitness function. This symmetry of the fitness function means that fixed points are invariant under this symmetry, and for any fixed point that is not mapped to itself by this symmetry, there is another fixed point with the same stability properties which is the image of the original fixed point under the symmetry.

Three initial populations were used, one at the all-zeros needle, one at a center-of-simplex population, and one the midpoint population between the all-zeros and all-ones population.

Figures 1 and 2 both display an interpolated version of the bifurcation diagram. At each mutation rate the $\mathcal{G}$-map was initialized and iterated to convergence with each of the three initial populations. The fitness value of each converged map was recorded. The figures contain mutation rates on the x-axis and fitness values (or projections) on the y-axis.

The upper curve of Figure 1 displays *both* stable fixed points as the y-axis represents fitness and these points have the same fitness by symmetry. The lower curve displays the unstable saddle point's average fitness. The critical point of bifurcation is the mutation rate of $1/7.65$

This bifurcation is an instance of the pitchfork bifurcation, where a stable fixed point bifurcates into two stable fixed points and an unstable fixed point. The two stable fixed points are symmetric under changing zeros to ones and ones to zeros. In order to demonstrate this, we looked

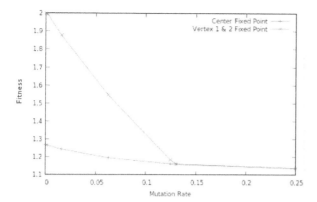

Figure 1: **Epsilon mutation bifurcation of the stable fixed points. The x-axis is the mutation rate p and the y-axis is fitness value of the f-p's population vector. The upper curve is actually two fixed-points with identical fitness values. At approximately $p = 1/7.65$ the three distinct fixed points merge into one.**

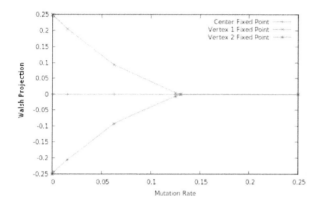

Figure 2: **Epsilon mutation bifurcation of stable fixed points in the Walsh basis. The x-axis is the mutation rate p and the y-axis is the Walsh projection. At approximately $p = 1/7.65$ the three distinct fixed points merge into one.**

for a projection of the fixed points that would demonstrate the pitchfork bifurcation. We found such a projection by representing the fixed points in the Walsh basis, which is described in [16].

Figure 2 shows the fixed points projected into coordinate 11 of their Walsh-basis representation as a function of the mutation rate. It shows a typical pitchfork bifurcation with a single stable fixed point splitting into two stable fixed points and an unstable fixed point which is "between" the stable fixed points.

As with the example with $\ell = 2$, points that are invariant under the symmetry are on the stable manifold of the unstable fixed point, and thus the unstable fixed point can be found by iteration. For more general problems, it would be difficult to find points on the stable manifold of unstable fixed points, and so this procedure would be unlikely to work.

The above results are by definition incomplete, they might

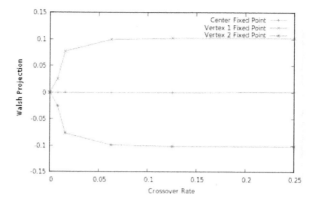

Figure 3: **Epsilon crossover bifurcation of stable fixed points. The x-axis is the crossover rate c and the y-axis is the Walsh projection. At approximately $c = 1/128$ the single fixed point splits into three.**

not contain all fixed points. Many more initial populations would need to be tried, and unstable (non-saddle) fixed points are not observable via iteration. With small mutation rates, the overall dynamics have not changed much from mutation rate 0. There still exist three observable fixed points, two stable and one saddle point. Yet it's clearly observable that at approximately mutation rate $1/7.65$ something interesting happens, a single stable fixed point splits into three fixed points.

5.4 Introducing Epsilon Crossover

A similar experiment was done examining the effects of adding epsilon one-point crossover to a fixed mutation rate $\mathcal{G}$-map. The mutation rate is set to a mutation rate of $1/n = 1/16$ (different than the classic $1/\ell$ rate), and the crossover rate is varied over a range. Note that with zero crossover the Perron-Frobenius theorem implies that there exists only a single stable fixed point in the interior of the simplex. Figure 3 displays an interpolated version of the bifurcation diagram. As in the last subsection, the figure displays the projection into coordinate 11 of the Walsh basis representation.

These results are very interesting in that they indicate an observable bifurcation of a single stable fixed into a two stable fixed points and a saddle point. This happens at approximately crossover rate $1/128$. Over $8,000$ iterations of the $\mathcal{G}$-map with this crossover rate were done starting from the uniform population consisting of the all-zeros strings. At this point that run was stopped, with the result seen in equation (23).

$$\langle 0.3, 0.05, 0.049, 0.016, 0.049, 0.016, 0.016, 0.032, \\ 0.05, 0.016, 0.016, 0.03, 0.016, 0.03, 0.032, 0.21 \rangle \quad (23)$$

The leading eigenvalue of the derivative at this stopping point was 0.99960, meaning that the trajectory of iteration is very likely close to the stable manifold of the saddle point. The leading eigenvalue of the derivative at the fixed-point in row 4 was exactly 1. Note that these numbers are approximate and at these types of critical points the numerics of computation in binary computers can result in some inaccuracies.

Once the crossover rate grew to $1/64$ and above a clear separation of iterative convergence was established between the different starting populations. At crossover rate 63/64 the interior saddle point's population approaches the center of the simplex population where all coordinates are equal to 1/16.

5.5 Revisiting Bistability

We now give an example of the movement of fixed points when there is bistability.

The fitness function used for this example is the sloping needle SNEEDLE which is defined below. This is a special case of the sloping plateau fitness functions from [19].

$$SNEEDLE_{a,b}(x) = \begin{cases} a + b + 1 & \text{if } \mathbf{1}^T x = 0 \\ b + (\ell - \mathbf{1}^T x)/\ell & \text{if } \mathbf{1}^T x > 0 \end{cases}$$

Figure 4 shows a plot of SNEEDLE for $\ell = 40$, $a = 39$, $b = 20$.

A key point of this fitness function is that the *floor* area of the function slopes directly to the needle. To a simple hill-climber $(1 + 1)EA$ this function is indistinguishable from a function like ZEROMAX (the inverse of ONEMAX). In addition it is easily solvable by an non-crossover EA/GA with an arbitrary population size. Just as with the sloping plateau, the function is designed to deceive proportional selection. In general, any EA with a large population will be slower to optimize this function than one with a small population where the effects of 'weak selection' are muted.

The infinite population model used for this example is a coarse graining of the SGA IPM to the equivalence classes defined by the equivalence $x \equiv y$ iff $\mathbf{1}^T x = \mathbf{1}^T y$. This unitation-based infinite population model (IPM) is described in more detail in [19]. When there is no crossover, the model accurately describes the behavior of the SGA IPM projected to unitation classes. However, with crossover, the model does not necessarily accurately described the behavior of the SGA IPM on the simplex when projected into unitation classes. But if we define the set $\Psi = \{x \in \Lambda : \mathbf{1}^T i = \mathbf{1}^T j \text{ implies } x_i = x_j\}$ of populations in the simplex where all elements with the same unitation have equal representation, then the unitation-based IPM does accurately describe the behavior of the SGA IPM on Ψ, and that is what the example of this section shows. However, the unitation-based IPM may not accurately represent the stability of fixed points, and "stable" below means stable relative to the unitation-based IPM.

The string length is $\ell = 40$. We hold the mutation rate fixed at $1/3\ell$ and the b parameter fixed at 20, and vary the a in a range in an effort to discover a bifurcation point. Uniform crossover with rate 1 was used. At each value of $a \in [1, 40]$ the $\mathcal{G}$-map was iterated to convergence starting from two initial populations. The first is the center of the simplex population with equal weights on all individuals, and the second consists entirely of members on the needle at the all-zeros string.

For values of $a < 21$ the IPM started from both initial populations converged to the same fixed point. At $a = 21$ a bifurcation point is reached. The stable fixed point splits into the two stable fixed points shown in figure 5. In dynamical systems, this does not happen without there also being an unstable fixed point which is not shown. For increasing values of a, the average population fitness of the higher-fitness fixed point climbs until it reaches approximately average fitness of 41 and then levels off. The fixed point converged to

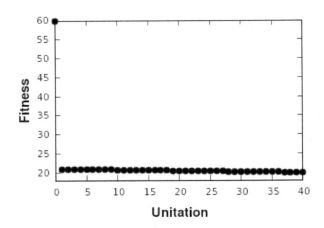

Figure 4: Sloping Needle Fitness, $\ell = 40$, $k = 1$, $a = 39$, $b = 20$

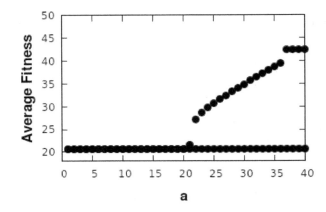

Figure 5: Sloping Needle fixed point bifurcation. The x-axis is the a parameter of SNEEDLE and the y-axis is the average fitness of the population vector. At approximately $a = 21$ the fixed point splits into two.

from the initial center of the simplex population remains at avg-fitness $= 20.5$ for all values of a tested.

The resulting bifurcation diagram is pictured in Figure 5. The y-axis represents the weighted average fitness of a fixed point. As stated above, we cannot be sure that these "stable" fixed points are stable for the SGA IPM.

6. CONCLUSIONS

Populations consisting of multiple copies of a single bit string are vertex fixed points for the infinite population model (IPM) for the simple genetic algorithm (SGA) under zero mutation. For proportional selection, when these fixed points are hyperbolic (no eigenvalue of the differential has modulus 1), the stability of these fixed points is understood from previous work—see corollary 16. We have derived formulas for the stability of vertex fixed points under standard tournament selection with the assumption that no two individuals have the same fitness—see corollary 15. However, the behavior of these fixed points as the mutation rate increases from zero was not known. We have shown that if a vertex fixed point is hyperbolic and asymptotically stable, then the fixed point moves into the interior of the simplex as the mutation rate increases from zero. If the vertex fixed point is hyperbolic and asymptotically unstable, then the simplex moves out of the simplex as the mutation rate increases from zero.

We have given examples of the behavior and bifurcation of fixed points as the mutation rate varies from 0 to $1/2$, and as the crossover rate varies when the mutation rate is held fixed.

In evolutionary computation, bistability is defined as two stable fixed points corresponding to one fitness peak. We have given an example of bistability for the sloping needle fitness function. This example shows how a stable fixed point bifurcates into two stable fixed points and an unstable fixed point as the height of the fitness function needle is increased. The example uses a unitation-based IPM which correctly describes the behavior of the SGA IPM on the subset of the simplex where populations have equal representations for all points in a unitation class.

Clearly, a direction for future work would be to rigorously describe the types of movement and bifurcation of fixed points under the variation of the parameters of mixing, especially the mutation and crossover rates. To make this task more tractable, there are two possible simplifying assumptions. The first is to use gene pool crossover as was done in [20] and [18]. The second is to assume a fitness function of unitation (where the fitness of a binary string depends only on the number of ones in the string), and then to use the unitation-based IPM described above and in section 5.5. With these two assumptions, it may be possible to reduce the fixed point equations to equations in a single variable as was done in [20].

7. ACKNOWLEDGMENTS

T. G. was partially supported by NSF grant DMS-0818785, NSF CMMI grant 0849433 and DARPA grant 00001741/HR0011-09-1-0055.

References

[1] M. C. Boerlijst, S. Bonhoeffer, and M. A. Nowak. Viral quasi-species and recombination. *Proc. Royal Society London B*, 263:1577–1584, 1996.

[2] M. Brin and G. Stuck. *Introduction to Dynamical Systems*. Cambridge University Press, Cambridge, 2002.

[3] T. Gedeon, C. Hayes, and R. Swanson. Genericity of the fixed point set for the infinite population genetic algorithm. In *Foundations of Genetic Algorithms (FOGA) 9*, pages 97–109, 2007.

[4] D. Goldberg and K. Deb. A comparative analysis of selection schemes used in genetic algorithms. In *Foundations of genetic algorithms 1*, volume 1, pages 69–93. Morgan Kaufmann, 1991.

[5] C. Hayes and T. Gedeon. Hyperbolicity of the fixed point set for the simple genetic algorithm. *Theoretical Computer Science*, 411(25):2368 – 2383, 2010.

[6] C. Reeves and J. Rowe. *Genetic algorithms: principles and perspectives: a guide to GA theory*. Kluwer Academic Pub, 2002.

[7] J. N. Richter, J. Paxton, and A. H. Wright. EA models and population fixed-points versus mutation rates for functions of unitation. In H.-G. Beyer and U.-M. O'Reilly, editors, *GECCO*, pages 1233–1240. ACM, 2005.

[8] J. N. Richter, A. Wright, and J. Paxton. Exploration of population fixed points versus mutation rates for functions of unitation. In K. D. et al., editor, *GECCO*, volume 3102 of *Lecture Notes in Computer Science*. Springer, 2004.

[9] C. Robinson. *Dynamical Systems: Stability, Symbolic Dynamics, and Chaos*. The CRC Press, 2nd edition, 199.

[10] J. E. Rowe. Population fixed-points for functions of unitation. In W. Banzhaf and C. R. Reeves, editors, *FOGA*, pages 69–84. Morgan Kaufmann, 1998.

[11] H. Suzuki and Y. Iwasa. Crossover accelerates evolution in gas with a babel-like fitness landscape: Mathematical analyses. *Evolutionary Computation*, 7(3):275–310, 1999.

[12] M. D. Vose. *The Simple Genetic Algorithm: Foundations and Theory*. MIT Press, Cambridge, MA, 1999.

[13] M. D. Vose and G. E. Liepins. Representational issues in genetic optimization. *Journal of Experimental and Theoretical Artificial Intelligence*, 2:101–115, 1989.

[14] M. D. Vose and A. H. Wright. Simple genetic algorithms with linear fitness. *Evolutionary Computation*, 4(2):347–368, 1994.

[15] M. D. Vose and A. H. Wright. Stability of vertex fixed points and applications. In L. D. Whitley and M. D. Vose, editors, *Foundations of genetic algorithms 3*, pages 103–113, San Mateo, 1995. Morgan Kaufmann.

[16] M. D. Vose and A. H. Wright. The simple genetic algorithm and the Walsh transform: Part I, theory. *Evolutionary Computation*, 6(3):253–273, 1998.

[17] A. H. Wright and G. L. Bidwell. A search for counterexamples to two conjectures on the simple genetic algorithm. In R. K. Belew and M. D. Vose, editors, *Foundations of Genetic Algorithms (FOGA-4)*, pages 73–84. Morgan Kaufmann, 1997.

[18] A. H. Wright and G. Cripe. Bistability of the needle function in the presence of truncation selection. In *GECCO 2004: Proceedings of the Genetic and Evolutionary Computation Conference*. Springer Verlag, 2004.

[19] A. H. Wright and J. N. Richter. Strong recombination, weak selection, and mutation. In M. Cattolico, editor, *GECCO*, pages 1369–1376. ACM, 2006.

[20] A. H. Wright, J. E. Rowe, R. Poli, and C. R. Stephens. Bistability in a gene pool GA with mutation. In J. E. Rowe, K. DeJong, and R. Poli, editors, *Foundations of Genetic Algorithms (FOGA-7)*, San Mateo, 2003. Morgan Kaufmann.

Simple Max-Min Ant Systems and the Optimization of Linear Pseudo-Boolean Functions

Timo Kötzing
Max-Planck-Institut für
Informatik
66123 Saarbrücken, Germany

Frank Neumann
School of Computer Science
University of Adelaide
Adelaide, SA 5005, Australia

Dirk Sudholt
CERCIA, University of
Birmingham
Birmingham, B15 2TT, UK

Markus Wagner
School of Computer Science
University of Adelaide
Adelaide, SA 5005, Australia

ABSTRACT

With this paper, we contribute to the understanding of ant colony optimization (ACO) algorithms by formally analyzing their runtime behavior. We study simple MAX-MIN ant systems on the class of linear pseudo-Boolean functions defined on binary strings of length n. Our investigations point out how the progress according to function values is stored in the pheromones. We provide a general upper bound of $O((n^3 \log n)/\rho)$ on the running time for two ACO variants on all linear functions, where ρ determines the pheromone update strength. Furthermore, we show improved bounds for two well-known linear pseudo-Boolean functions called ONEMAX and BINVAL and give additional insights using an experimental study.

Categories and Subject Descriptors

F.2.2 [**Analysis of Algorithms and Problem Complexity**]: Nonnumerical Algorithms and Problems

General Terms

Algorithms, Performance, Theory

Keywords

Ant colony optimization, MMAS, runtime analysis, pseudo-Boolean optimization, theory

1. INTRODUCTION

Ant colony optimization (ACO) is an important class of stochastic search algorithms that has found many applications in combinatorial optimization as well as for stochastic and dynamic problems [5]. The basic idea behind ACO is

that ants construct new solutions for a given problem by carrying out random walks on a so-called construction graph. These random walks are influenced by the pheromone values that are stored along the edges of the graph. During the optimization process the pheromone values are updated according to good solutions found during the optimization which should lead to better solutions in further steps of the algorithm.

Building up a theoretical foundation of this kind of algorithms is a challenging task as these algorithms heavily rely on random decisions. The construction of new solutions depends on the current pheromone situation in the used system which varies highly during the optimization run. Capturing the theoretical properties of the pheromone constellation is a hard task but very important to gain new theoretical insights into the optimization process of ACO algorithms.

With this paper, we contribute to the theoretical understanding of ACO algorithms. Our goal is to gain new insights into the optimization process of these algorithms by studying them on the class of linear pseudo-Boolean functions. There are investigations of different depths on the behavior of simple evolutionary algorithms for this class of functions. The main result shows that each linear pseudo-Boolean function is optimized in expected time $O(n \log n)$ by the well known (1+1) EA [7, 10, 11]. Furthermore, estimation-of-distribution algorithms have been analyzed and compared to evolutionary algorithms [6, 2, 1].

With respect to ACO algorithms, initial results on simplified versions of the MAX-MIN ant system [18] have been obtained. These studies deal with specific pseudo-Boolean functions defined on binary strings of length n. Such studies are primarily focused on well-known linear example functions called ONEMAX and BINVAL or the function LEADINGONES [16, 9, 4, 14, 15]. Recently, some results on the running time of ACO algorithms on combinatorial optimization problems such as minimum spanning trees [17] or the traveling salesman [13] have been obtained. These analyses assume that the pheromone bounds are attained in each iteration of the algorithms. This is the case if a MAX-MIN ant system uses an aggressive pheromone update which forces the pheromone only to take on the maximum and minimum value. The analyses presented in [17] and [13] do not carry over to less aggressive pheromone updates. In particular, there are no corresponding polynomial upper bounds if the number of different function values is exponential with respect to the given input size.

We provide new insights into the optimization of MAX-MIN ant systems for smaller pheromone updates on functions that may attain exponentially many functions values. Our study investigates simplified versions of the MAX-MIN ant system called MMAS* and MMAS [14] on linear pseudo-Boolean functions with non-zero weights. For these algorithms, general upper bounds of $O((n + (\log n)/\rho)D)$ and $O(((n^2 \log n)/\rho)D)$ respectively, have been provided for the running time on unimodal functions attaining D different function values [14]. As linear pseudo-Boolean function are unimodal, these bounds carry over to this class of functions. However, they only give weak bounds for linear pseudo-Boolean functions attaining many function values (e.g. for functions where the number of different function values is exponential in n).

We show an upper bound of $O((n^3 \log n)/\rho)$ for MMAS* and MMAS optimizing any linear pseudo-Boolean function. Furthermore, our studies show that the method of fitness-based partitions may also be used according to pheromone values as MAX-MIN ant systems quickly store knowledge about high-fitness solutions in the pheromone values. This is one of the key observations that we use for our more detailed analyses on ONEMAX and BINVAL in which we improve the results presented in [14].

To provide further insights that are not captured by our theoretical analyses, we carry out an experimental study. Our experimental investigations give comparisons to simple evolutionary algorithms, and consider the impact of the chosen weights of the linear functions and pheromone update strength with respect to the optimization time. One key observation of these studies is that ONEMAX is not the simplest linear function for the simple MAX-MIN ant systems under investigation. Additionally, the studies indicate that the runtime grows at most linearly with $1/\rho$ for a fixed value of n.

We proceed as follows. In Section 2, we introduce the simplified MAX-MIN ant systems that will be investigated in the following. In Section 3, we provide general runtime bounds for the class of linear pseudo-Boolean functions. We present specific results for ONEMAX and BINVAL in Section 4. Our experimental study which provides further insights is reported in Section 5. Finally, we discuss our results and finish with some concluding remarks.

2. SIMPLIFIED MAX-MIN ANT SYSTEMS

We first describe the simplified MAX-MIN ant systems that will be investigated in the sequel. The following construction graph is used to construct solutions for pseudo-Boolean optimization, i.e., bit strings of n bits. It is based on a directed multigraph $C = (V, E)$. In addition to a start node v_0, there is a node v_i for every bit i, $1 \leq i \leq n$. This node can be reached from v_{i-1} by two edges. The edge $e_{i,1}$ corresponds to setting bit i to 1, while $e_{i,0}$ corresponds to setting bit i to 0. The former edge is also called a *1-edge*, the latter is called *0-edge*. An example of a construction graph for $n = 5$ is shown in Figure 1.

In a solution construction process an artificial ant sequentially traverses the nodes $v_0, v_1, \ldots, v_n$. The decision which edge to take is made according to pheromones on the edges. Formally, we denote pheromones by a function $\tau: E \to \mathbb{R}_0^+$. From v_{i-1} the edge $e_{i,1}$ is then taken with probability $\tau(e_{i,1})/(\tau(e_{i,0}) + \tau(e_{i,1}))$. In the case of our construction graph, we identify the path taken by the ant with a corresponding binary solution x as described above and denote the path by $P(x)$.

All ACO algorithms considered here start with an equal amount of pheromone on all edges: $\tau(e_{i,0}) = \tau(e_{i,1}) = 1/2$. Moreover, we ensure that $\tau(e_{i,0}) + \tau(e_{i,1}) = 1$ holds, i.e., pheromones for one bit always sum up to 1. This implies that the probability of taking a specific edge equals its pheromone value; in other words, pheromones and traversal probabilities coincide.

Given a solution x and a path $P(x)$ of edges that have been chosen in the creation of x, a pheromone update with respect to x is performed as follows. First, a ρ-fraction of all pheromones evaporates and a $(1 - \rho)$-fraction remains. Next, some pheromone is added to edges that are part of the path $P(x)$ of x. To prevent pheromones from dropping to arbitrarily small values, we follow the MAX-MIN ant system by Stützle and Hoos [18] and restrict all pheromones to a bounded interval. The precise interval is chosen as $[1/n, 1 - 1/n]$. This choice is inspired by standard mutations in evolutionary computation where for every bit an evolutionary algorithm has a probability of $1/n$ of flipping a bit and hence potentially reverting a "wrong" decision made for a bit.

Depending on whether an edge e is contained in the path $P(x)$ of the solution x, the pheromone values τ are updated to τ' as follows:

$$\tau'(e) = \min \left\{ (1 - \rho) \cdot \tau(e) + \rho,\ 1 - \frac{1}{n} \right\} \quad \text{if } e \in P(x) \text{ and}$$
$$\tau'(e) = \max \left\{ (1 - \rho) \cdot \tau(e),\ \frac{1}{n} \right\} \quad \text{if } e \notin P(x).$$

The algorithm MMAS now works as follows. It records the best solution found so far, known as best-so-far solution. It repeatedly constructs a new solution. This solution is then compared against the current best-so-far and it replaces the previous best-so-far if the objective value of the new solution is not worse. Finally, the pheromones are updated with respect to the best-so-far solution. A formal description is given in Algorithm 1.

Note that when a worse solution is constructed then the old best-so-far solution is reinforced again. In case no improvement is found for some time, this means that the same solution x^* is reinforced over and over again and the pheromones move towards the respective borders in x^*. Previous studies [9] have shown that after $(\ln n)/\rho$ iterations of reinforcing the same solution all pheromones have reached their respective borders; this time is often called "freezing time" [14] (see also Lemma 1).

Algorithm 1 MMAS

1: Set $\tau_{(u,v)} = 1/2$ for all $(u, v) \in E$.
2: Construct a solution x^*.
3: Update pheromones w.r.t. x^*.
4: **repeat forever**
5:    Construct a solution x.
6:    **if** $f(x) \geq f(x^*)$ **then** $x^* := x$.
7:    Update pheromones w.r.t. x^*.

We also consider a variant of MMAS known as MMAS* [14] (see Algorithm 2). The only difference is that

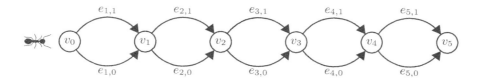

Figure 1: **Construction graph for pseudo-Boolean optimization with** $n = 5$ **bits.**

the best-so-far solution is only changed in case the new solution is strictly better. This kind of strategy is often used in applications of ACO. However, in [14] it was argued that MMAS works better on functions with plateaus as MMAS is able to perform a random walk on equally fit solutions.

Algorithm 2 MMAS*

1: Set $\tau_{(u,v)} = 1/2$ for all $(u, v) \in E$.
2: Construct a solution x^*.
3: Update pheromones w. r. t. x^*.
4: **repeat forever**
5:     Construct a solution x.
6:     **if** $f(x) > f(x^*)$ **then** $x^* := x$.
7:     Update pheromones w. r. t. x^*.

In the following we analyze the performance of MMAS and MMAS* on linear functions. We are interested in the number of iterations of the main loop of the algorithms until the first global optimum is found. This time is commonly called the optimization time. In our setting this time equals the number of function evaluations.

Note that the pheromones on the 1-edges $e_{i,1}$ suffice to describe all pheromones as $\tau(e_{i,0}) + \tau(e_{i,1}) = 1$. When speaking of pheromones, we therefore often focus on pheromones on 1-edges.

3. GENERAL RESULTS

We first derive general upper bounds on the expected optimization time of MMAS and MMAS* on linear pseudo-Boolean functions. A linear pseudo-Boolean function for an input vector $x = (x_1, \ldots, x_n)$ is a function $f \colon \{0,1\}^n \mapsto \mathbb{R}$, with $f(x) = \sum_{i=1}^{n} w_i x_i$ and *weights* $w_i \in \mathbb{R}$. We only consider positive weights since a function with a negative weight w_i may be transformed into a function with a positive weight $w_i' = -w_i$ by exchanging the meaning of bit values 0 and 1 for bit i. This results in a function whose value is by an additive term of w_i' larger. This and exchanging bit values does not impact the behavior of our algorithms. We also exclude weights of 0 as these bits do not contribute to the fitness. Finally, in this section we assume without loss of generality that the weights are ordered according to their values: $w_1 \geq w_2 \geq \ldots \geq w_n$.

Two well-known linear functions are the function ONE-MAX where $w_1 = w_2 = \cdots = w_n = 1$ and the function BINVAL where $w_i = 2^{n-i}$. These functions represent two extremes: for ONEMAX all bits are of equal importance, while in BINVAL a bit at position i can dominate all bits at positions $i + 1, \ldots, n$.

3.1 Analysis Using Fitness-based Partitions

We exploit a similarity between MMAS, MMAS* and evolutionary algorithms to obtain a first upper bound. We use the method of fitness-based partitions, also called fitness-level method, to estimate the expected optimization time. This method has originally been introduced for the analysis of elitist evolutionary algorithms (see, e. g., Wegener [20]) where the fitness of the current search point can never decrease. The idea is to partition the search space into sets $A_1, \ldots, A_m$ that are ordered with respect to fitness. Formally, we require that for all $1 \leq i \leq m - 1$ all search points in A_i have a strictly lower fitness than all search points in A_{i+1}. In addition, A_m must contain all global optima.

Now, if s_i is (a lower bound on) the probability of discovering a new search point in $A_{i+1} \cup \cdots \cup A_m$, given that the current best solution is in A_i, the expected optimization time is bounded by $\sum_{i=1}^{m-1} 1/s_i$ as $1/s_i$ is (an upper bound on) the expected time until fitness level i is left and each fitness level has to be left at most once.

Gutjahr and Sebastiani [9] as well as Neumann, Sudholt, and Witt [14] have adapted this method for MMAS*. If the algorithm does not find a better search point for some time, the same solution x^* is reinforced over and over again, until eventually all pheromones attain their borders corresponding to the bit values in x^*. This happens after at most $(\ln n)/\rho$ iterations (see [9, 14] or Lemma 1). We say that then all pheromones are saturated. In this setting the solution creation process of MMAS* equals a standard bit mutation of x^* in an evolutionary algorithm. If s_i is (a lower bound on) the probability that the a mutation of x^* creates a search point in $A_{i+1} \cup \cdots \cup A_m$, then the expected time until MMAS* leaves fitness level A_i is bounded by $(\ln n)/\rho + 1/s_i$ as either the algorithm manages to find an improvement before the pheromones saturate or the pheromones saturate and the probability of finding an improvement is at least s_i. This results in an upper bound of $m \cdot (\ln n)/\rho + \sum_{i=1}^{m-1} 1/s_i$ for MMAS*.

One restriction of this method is, however, that fitness levels are only allowed to contain a single fitness value; in the above bound m must equal the number of different fitness values. Without this condition—when a fitness level contains multiple fitness values—MMAS* may repeatedly exchange the current best-so-far solution within a fitness level. This can prevent the pheromones from saturating, so that the above argument breaks down. For this reason, all upper bounds in [14] grow at least linearly in the number of function values.

The following lemma gives an explanation for the time bound $(\ln n)/\rho$ for saturating pheromones (recall that this time is also called *freezing time*). We present a formulation that holds for arbitrary sets of bits. Though we do not make use of the larger generality, this lemma may be of independent interest.

LEMMA 1. *Given an index set $I \subseteq \{1, \ldots, n\}$ we say that a bit is in I if its index is in I. Let x^* be the current best-*

so-far solution of MMAS or MMAS* optimizing an arbitrary function. After $(\ln n)/\rho$ further iterations either all pheromones corresponding to bits in I have reached their respective bounds in $\{1/n, 1 - 1/n\}$ or x^* has been replaced by some search point x^{**} with $f(x^{**}) \geq f(x^*)$ for MMAS and $f(x^{**}) > f(x^*)$ for MMAS* such that x^{**} differs from x^* in at least one bit in I.

PROOF. Assume the bit values of the bits in I remain fixed in the current best-so-far solution for $(\ln n)/\rho$ iterations as otherwise there is nothing to prove. In this case for every bit x_i^* with $i \in I$ the same bit value x_i^* has been reinforced for $(\ln n)/\rho$ iterations. This implies that for the edge in the construction graph representing the opposite bit value the lower pheromone border $1/n$ has been reached, as for any initial pheromone $0 \leq \tau_i \leq 1$ on this edge we have $(1 - \rho)^{(\ln n)/\rho} \tau_i \leq e^{-\ln n} \tau_i \leq 1/n$. $\square$

So far, the best known general upper bounds for MMAS and MMAS* that apply to every linear function are $O((n^2 \log n)/\rho \cdot 2^n)$ and $O((\log n)/\rho \cdot 2^n)$, respectively, following from upper bounds for unimodal functions [14]. The term 2^n results from the fact that in the worst case a linear function has 2^n different function values. This is the case, for instance, for the function BINVAL. An exponential upper bound for linear functions is, of course, unsatisfactory. The following theorem establishes a polynomial upper bound (with respect to n and $1/\rho$) for both algorithms.

THEOREM 2. *The expected optimization time of MMAS and MMAS* on every linear function is in $O((n^3 \log n)/\rho)$.*

PROOF. The proof is an application of the above-described fitness-based partitions method. In the first step, we consider the time needed to sample a solution which is at least on the next higher fitness level. We analyze the two situations when the pheromones are either saturated or not. Our upper bound is the result of the repetition of such advancing steps between fitness levels.

Following Wegener [19], we define the fitness levels $A_0, \ldots, A_n$ with

$$A_i = \left\{ x \in \{0,1\}^n \;\middle|\; \sum_{j=1}^{i} w_j \leq f(x) < \sum_{j=1}^{i+1} w_j \right\}$$

for $0 \leq i \leq n - 1$ and $A_n := \{1^n\}$. Recall that $\sum_{j=1}^{i} w_j$ is the sum of the i largest weights. Since the weights are non-decreasing, a solution x is at least on fitness level A_i if the leftmost i bits have value 1.

The expected time spent sampling solutions on fitness level A_i (i.e., without sampling a solution of a higher fitness level) is the sum of the time spent in A_i with saturated pheromone values and the time spent in A_i with unsaturated pheromone values. In the following, we analyze for both situations the probabilities to sample a solution of a higher fitness level. In the end, as MMAS and MMAS* might not remain in one of both situations exclusively, but alternates between situations of saturated and unsaturated pheromone values, we take the sum of both run times as an upper bound.

First, when the pheromone values are saturated, the probability of setting the leftmost zero and keeping all other bits as in the best-so-far solution is $1/n \cdot (1 - 1/n)^{n-1} \geq 1/n \cdot 1/e$, as $(1 - 1/n)^{n-1} \geq 1/e \geq (1 - 1/n)^n$ holds for all $n \in \mathbb{N}$. This results in a probability of $\Omega(1/n)$ of advancing in such

a situation. Thus, after an expected number of $O(n)$ steps with saturated pheromone values, the algorithm will sample a solution on a higher fitness level.

For the second case, when the pheromone values are not saturated, let $i < n$, and suppose $x^* \in A_i$ is the current best solution. Our argument is intuitively as follows. If we don't find solutions with better fitness while unsaturated, then we will be saturated after at most $(\ln n)/\rho$ steps. Otherwise, we either make a *good* or a *bad* improvement: a good improvement gets the EA to a higher fitness level; a bad improvement is an improvement which does not go to a higher fitness level. This latter case is bad, since it prevents the pheromones from getting saturated, and we cannot quantify progress in this case. We will show that good improvements are at least $1/n^2$ times as likely as bad ones, which gives a limit on the number of bad improvements one can expect.

Then, let us denote by $G = \bigcup_{j > i} A_j$ all *good* solutions that are at least on the next higher fitness level, and by $B = \{x \in \{0,1\}^n \mid f(x) \geq f(x^*), x \notin G\}$ all *bad* solutions that are in A_i with an equal or a higher function value than x^*. Thus, every improving sampled solution belongs to $G \cup B$.

Let $h : \{0,1\}^n \mapsto \{0,1\}^n$ be the function that returns for a given solution $x \in G \cup B$ a solution $x' \in G$, where the leftmost 0 (if any) was flipped to 1. Let $P(x)$ be the probability of sampling a new solution x. Then the probability $q(x)$ of sampling any of x and $h(x)$ is greater than or equal to $P(x)$. The probability of sampling $h(x)$ is the probability of sampling any of x and $h(x)$, times the probability that the leftmost zero of x was sampled as a one. Thus, for all x, $P(h(x)) = q(x) \cdot 1/n \geq P(x)/n$, as the pheromone values are at least $1/n$.

Furthermore, each solution $h(x)$ has at most n preimages with respect to h. Note that, for all $x \in B$, $h(x) \in G$.

Thus, the probability of sampling the next solution $x \in G$ is

$$P(x \in G) = \sum_{x \in G} P(x) \geq \frac{\sum_{x \in B} P(h(x))}{n}$$
$$\geq \frac{\sum_{x \in B} P(x)}{n^2} = \frac{P(x \in B)}{n^2}.$$

So, sampling a good solution is at least $1/n^2$ times as likely as sampling a bad one.

Furthermore, while no bad solutions are sampled, at most $(\ln n)/\rho$ steps are spent before the pheromone values are saturated (based on Lemma 1).

Thus, up to $(\ln n)/\rho$ steps are spent with unsaturated pheromone values before sampling a new solution, and $O((n^2 \log n)/\rho)$ steps are spent in total sampling solutions in B before sampling a solution in G.

Consequently, the time spent on one fitness level is the sum of the times spent in either situation of the pheromone values, that is, $O(n) + O((n^2 \log n)/\rho) = O((n^2 \log n)/\rho)$.

Finally, as there are n fitness levels, the afore-described steps have to be performed at most n-times, which yields a total runtime of $O((n^3 \log n)/\rho)$. $\square$

3.2 Fitness-based Partitions for Pheromones

We describe an approach for extending the argument on f-based partitions to pheromones instead of the best-so-far solution. This alternate approach is based on *weighted pheromone sums*. Given a vector of pheromones τ and a linear function f, the *weighted pheromone sum (wps)* is $f(\tau)$.

The idea is that, during a run of the algorithm, the wps should rise until *value-saturated* with respect to the current best search point, and then a significant improvement should have a decent probability.

Define a function v on bit strings as follows.

$$v(x) = \sum_{i=1}^{n} \begin{cases} (1 - \frac{1}{n})w_i, & \text{if } x_i = 1; \\ \frac{1}{n}w_i, & \text{otherwise.} \end{cases}$$

A pheromone vector τ is called *value-saturated* with respect to a search point x^* iff

$$f(\tau) \geq v(x^*).$$

Note that this definition of value-saturation is very much different from previous notions of saturation.

Let, for all i, a_i be the bit string starting with i ones and then having only zeros.

We let

$$A_i = \{x \mid f(a_i) \leq f(x) < f(a_{i+1})\}$$

and

$$B_i = \{\tau \mid v(a_i) \leq f(\tau) < v(a_{i+1})\}.$$

While $(A_i)_i$ captures the progress of the search points towards the optimum, $(B_i)_i$ captures the progress of the pheromones.

LEMMA 3. *For all i, if the best-so-far solution was in $\bigcup_{j \geq i} A_j$ for at least $(\ln n)/\rho$ iterations, then $\tau \in \bigcup_{j \geq i} B_j$.*

PROOF. Let h be such that $\forall s : h(s) = \min(s(1-\rho) + \rho, 1 - 1/n)$. Let τ^0 be the vector of pheromones when the algorithm samples a solution in $\bigcup_{j \geq i} A_j$ for the first time, and let $(\tau^t)_t$ be the vectors of pheromones in the successive rounds. For all t we let h^t be the t-times composition of h with itself. Further, we define the sequence of *capped-out pheromones* $(\tau^{\mathrm{cap},t})_t$ such that, for all t, $\tau_j^{\mathrm{cap},t} = \min(h^t(1/n), \tau_j^t)$. For this capped-out version of pheromones we have, for all t,

$$f(\tau^{\mathrm{cap},t+1}) \geq \min((1-\rho)f(\tau^{\mathrm{cap},t}) + \rho f(a_i), (1-1/n)f(a_i)),$$

as pheromones will evaporate and at least an $f(a_i)$ weighted part of them will receive new pheromone ρ (note that the old capped-out pheromone raised by h cannot exceed the new cap). Thus, we get inductively

$$\forall t : f(\tau^{\mathrm{cap},t}) \geq h^t(1/n)f(a_i).$$

As we know from Lemma 1, for $t \geq (\ln n)/\rho$ we have $h^t(1/n) \geq 1 - 1/n$, and, thus, $\tau^t \in \bigcup_{j \geq i} B_j$. $\square$

This argument opens up new possibilities for analyses and we believe it to be of independent interest.

If it is possible to show, for all i, if $\tau \in B_i$, then the probability of sampling a new solution in $\bigcup_{j > i} A_j$ is $\Omega(1/n)$, then Lemma 3 would immediately improve the bound in Theorem 2 to $O\left(n^2 + (n \log n)/\rho\right)$. However, this claim is not easy to show.

It is possible to prove this for the special case of ONE-MAX using the following theorem by Gleser [8]. This theorem gives a very nice handle on estimating probabilities for sampling above-average solutions for ONEMAX.

THEOREM 4 (GLESER [8]). *Let τ, τ' be two pheromone vectors such that, for all $j \leq n$, the sum of the j least values*

of τ is at least the sum of the j least values of τ'. Let λ be the sum of the elements of τ'. Then it is at least as likely to sample $\lfloor \lambda + 1 \rfloor$ ones with τ as it is with τ'.

We can use this theorem to get a good bound for ONE-MAX: the worst case for the probability of an improvement is attained when all but at most one pheromones are at their respective borders. In this situation, when there are still i ones missing, the probability of an improvement is at least

$$i \cdot \frac{1}{n} \cdot \left(1 - \frac{1}{n}\right)^{n-1} \geq \frac{i}{en}.$$

Combining this with Lemma 3, we get the following result.

COROLLARY 5. *The expected optimization time of MMAS and MMAS* on ONEMAX is bounded by*

$$\sum_{i=1}^{n} \frac{en}{i} + n \cdot (\ln n)/\rho = O((n \log n)/\rho).$$

This re-proves the $O((n \log n)/\rho)$-bound for MMAS* in [14] and it improves the current best known bound for MMAS on ONEMAX by a factor of n^2. We will present an even improved bound for ONEMAX in Section 4.1.

However, with regard to general linear functions it is not clear how this argument can be generalized to arbitrary weights. In the following section we therefore turn to the investigation of concrete linear functions.

4. IMPROVED BOUNDS FOR SELECTED LINEAR FUNCTIONS

Using insights from Section 3.2 we next present improved upper bounds for the function ONEMAX (Section 4.1). Afterwards, we focus on the special function BINVAL (Section 4.2). These resulting bounds are much stronger than the general ones given in Section 3 above.

4.1 OneMax

Recall the bound $O((n \log n)/\rho)$ for MMAS and MMAS* from Corollary 5. In the following we prove a bound of $O(n \log n + n/\rho)$ for both MMAS and MMAS* by more detailed investigations on the pheromones and their dynamic growth over time. This shows in particular that the term $1/\rho$ has at most a linear impact on the total expected optimization time.

Let v and a_i be as in Section 3.2. For all $i \leq n$, we let $\alpha_i = i(1 - 1/n)$. Observe that $v(a_i) = \alpha_i + (n - i)/n$ and, in particular, $\alpha_i \leq v(a_i) \leq \alpha_i + 1$.

The following lemma gives a lower bound on the pheromone $f(\tau^+)$ after on iteration. Note that for ONE-MAX $f(\tau^+)$ corresponds to the sum of pheromones.

LEMMA 6. *Let $i < j$ and let τ be the current pheromones with $v(a_i) \leq f(\tau) < v(a_{i+1})$ and suppose that the best-so-far solution has at least j ones. We denote by τ^+ the pheromones after one iteration of MMAS or MMAS*. Then we have $f(\tau^+) \geq v(a_{i+1})$ or*

$$f(\tau^+) - \alpha_i \geq (f(\tau) - \alpha_i)(1 - \rho) + (j - i)\rho \geq v(a_i). \quad (1)$$

PROOF. Suppose that in rewarding bit positions from τ to get τ^+, exactly k positions cap out at the upper pheromone border $1 - 1/n$. From $f(\tau^+) < v(a_{i+1})$ (otherwise there is nothing left to show), we have $k \leq i$. We decompose $f(\tau^+)$

into the contribution of the capped-out bits (which is α_k, being k of the j rewarded positions) and the rest. Then we have

$$f(\tau^+) \geq \alpha_k + (f(\tau) - \alpha_k)(1 - \rho) + (j - k)\rho.$$

We now get

$$
\begin{aligned}
&\alpha_i + (f(\tau) - \alpha_i)(1 - \rho) + (j - i)\rho \\
&= \alpha_k + \alpha_{i-k} + (f(\tau) - \alpha_k - \alpha_{i-k})(1 - \rho) + (j - k)\rho + (k - i)\rho \\
&\leq f(\tau^+) + \alpha_{i-k} - \alpha_{i-k}(1 - \rho) + (k - i)\rho \\
&= f(\tau^+) + \rho(\alpha_{i-k} - (i - k)) \\
&\leq f(\tau^+).
\end{aligned}
$$

From $v(a_i) \leq f(\tau)$ we get

$$
\begin{aligned}
f(\tau^+) &\geq \alpha_i + (f(\tau) - \alpha_i)(1 - \rho) + (j - i)\rho \\
&\geq \alpha_i + (v(a_i) - \alpha_i)(1 - \rho) + (j - i)\rho \\
&= v(a_i) + \rho(j - i - v(a_i) + \alpha_i).
\end{aligned}
$$

From $v(a_i) - \alpha_i < 1$ and $j > i$ we get the desired conclusion. $\square$

One important conclusion from Lemma 6 is that once the sum of pheromones is above some value $v(a_i)$, it can never decrease below this term.

Now we extend Lemma 6 towards multiple iterations. The following lemma shows that, unless a value of $v(a_{i+1})$ is reached, the sum of pheromones quickly converges to α_j when j is the number of ones in the best-so-far solution.

LEMMA 7. *Let $i < j$ and let τ be the current pheromones with $v(a_i) \leq f(\tau) < v(a_{i+1})$ and suppose that the best-so-far solution has at least j ones. For all t, we denote by τ^t the pheromones after t iterations of MMAS or MMAS*. Then we have for all t $f(\tau^t) \geq v(a_{i+1})$ or*

$$f(\tau^t) - \alpha_i \geq (j - i)(1 - (1 - \rho)^t).$$

PROOF. Inductively for all t, we get from Lemma 6 $f(\tau^t) \geq v(a_{i+1})$ or

$$
\begin{aligned}
f(\tau^t) - \alpha_i &\geq (f(\tau^0) - \alpha_i)(1 - \rho)^t + (j - i)\rho \sum_{i=0}^{t-1}(1 - \rho)^i \\
&= (f(\tau^0) - \alpha_i)(1 - \rho)^t + (j - i)\rho \frac{1 - (1 - \rho)^t}{1 - (1 - \rho)} \\
&= (f(\tau^0) - \alpha_i)(1 - \rho)^t + (j - i)(1 - (1 - \rho)^t) \\
&\geq (j - i)(1 - (1 - \rho)^t).
\end{aligned}
$$

$\square$

THEOREM 8. *The expected optimization time of MMAS and MMAS* on ONEMAX is $O(n \log n + n/\rho)$.*

PROOF. Define $v(a_{-1}) = 0$. Let τ be the current pheromones and τ^t be the pheromones after t iterations of MMAS or MMAS*. We divide a run of MMAS or MMAS* into phases: the algorithm is in Phase j if $f(\tau) \geq f(a_{j-1})$, the current best-so-far solution contains at least j ones, and the conditions for Phase $j + 1$ are not yet fulfilled. We estimate the expected time until each phase is completed, resulting in an upper bound on the expected optimization time.

We first deal with the last $n/2$ phases and consider some Phase j with $j \geq n/2$. By Lemma 7 after t iterations we

either have $f(\tau^t) \geq v(a_{j+1})$ or $f(\tau^t) \geq \alpha_{j-1} + 1 - (1 - \rho)^t$. Setting $t := \lceil 1/\rho \rceil$, this implies $f(\tau^t) \geq \alpha_{j-1} + 1 - e^{-\rho t} \geq \alpha_{j-1} + 1 - 1/e$. We claim that then the probability of creating $j + 1$ ones is $\Omega((n - j)/n)$.

Using $j \geq n/2$, the total pheromone $\alpha_{j-1} + 1 - 1/e$ can be distributed on an artificially constructed pheromone vector τ' as follows. We assign value $1 - 1/n$ to $j - 1$ entries and value $1/n$ to $n - j$ entries. As $(n - j)/n \leq 1/2$, we have used pheromone of $\alpha_{j-1} + 1/2$ and so pheromone $1 - 1/2 - 1/e = \Omega(1)$ remains for the last entry. We now use Theorem 4 to see that it as least as likely to sample a solution with $j + 1$ ones with the real pheromone vector τ^t as it is with τ'. By construction of τ' this probability is at least $(1 - 1/n)^{j-1} \cdot (1/2 - 1/e) \cdot (n - j)/n \cdot (1 - 1/n)^{n-j-1} \geq (n - j)(1/2 - 1/e)/(en)$ as a sufficient condition is setting all bits with pheromone larger than $1/n$ in τ' to 1 and adding exactly one 1-bit out of the remaining $n - j$ bits.

Invoking Lemma 7 again for at least $j + 1$ ones in the best-so-far solution, we get $f(\tau^{t+t'}) \geq \alpha_{j-1} + 2(1 - (1 - \rho)^{t'})$, which for $t' := \lceil 2/\rho \rceil$ yields $f(\tau^{t+t'}) \geq \alpha_{j-1} + 3/2 \geq \alpha_j + 1/2 \geq v(a_j)$ as $j \geq n/2$.

For the phases with index $j < n/2$ we construct a pessimistic pheromone vector τ' in a similar fashion. We assign value $1 - 1/n$ to $j - 2$ entries, value $1/n$ to $n - j$ entries, and put the remaining pheromone on the two last bits such that either only one bit receives pheromone above $1/n$ or one bit receives pheromone $1 - 1/n$ and the other bit gets the rest. To show that the pheromones raise appropriately, we aim at a larger gain in the best number of ones. The probability of constructing at least $j + 2$ ones with any of the above-described vectors is at least $(1 - 1/n)^{j-2} \cdot \binom{n-j+2}{3} \cdot 1/n^3 \cdot (1 - 1/n)^{n-j} \geq 1/(48e) = \Omega((n - j)/n)$.

Using the same choice $t' := \lceil 2/\rho \rceil$ as above, Lemma 7 yields $f(\tau^{t+t'}) \geq \alpha_{j-1} + 3(1 - (1 - \rho)^{t'}) \geq \alpha_{j-1} + 2 \geq v(a_j)$.

Summing up the expected times for all phases yields a bound of

$$O\left(\sum_{i=0}^{n-1} \frac{n}{n - i} + n(t + t')\right) = O(n \log n + n/\rho).$$

$\square$

4.2 BinVal

The function BINVAL has similar properties as the well-known function LEADINGONES$(x) := \sum_{i=1}^{n} \prod_{j=1}^{i} x_j$ that counts the number of leading ones. For both MMAS and MMAS* the leading ones in x^* can never be lost as setting one of these bits to 0 will definitely result in a worse solution. This implies for both algorithms that the pheromones on the first LEADINGONES(x^*) bits will strictly increase over time, until the upper pheromone border is reached.

In [14] the following upper bound for LEADINGONES was shown.

THEOREM 9 ([14]). *The expected optimization time of MMAS and MMAS* on LEADINGONES is bounded by $O(n^2 + n/\rho)$ and $O\left(n^2 \cdot (1/\rho)^\varepsilon + \frac{n/\rho}{\log(1/\rho)}\right)$ for every constant $\varepsilon > 0$.*

The basic proof idea is that after an average waiting time of ℓ iterations the probability of rediscovering the leading ones in x^* is at least $\Omega(e^{-5/(\ell\rho)})$. Plugging in appropriate values for ℓ then gives the claimed bounds.

DEFINITION 10. *For $\ell \in \mathbb{N}$ and a sequence of bits $x_1, \ldots, x_i$ ordered with respect to increasing pheromones we say that these bits form an (i, ℓ)-layer if for all $1 \leq j \leq i$*

$$\tau_j \geq \min(1 - 1/n, 1 - (1 - \rho)^{j\ell}).$$

With such a layering the considered bits can be rediscovered easily, depending on the value of ℓ. The following lemma was implicitly shown in [14, proof of Theorem 6].

LEMMA 11. *The probability that in an (i, ℓ)-layer all i bits defining the layer are set to 1 in an ant solution is $\Omega(e^{-5/(\ell\rho)})$.*

Assume we have $k = \text{LEADINGONES}(x^*)$ and the pheromones form a (k, ℓ)-layer. Using Lemma 11 and the fact that a new leading one is added with probability at least $1/n$, the expected waiting time until we have $\text{LEADINGONES}(x^*) \geq k + 1$ and a $(k + 1, \ell)$-layer of pheromones is at most $O(n \cdot e^{5/(\ell\rho)} + \ell)$. As this is necessary at most n times, this gives us an upper bound on the expected optimization time. Plugging in $\ell = \lceil 5/\rho \rceil$ and $\ell = \lceil 5/(\varepsilon\rho\ln(1/\rho)) \rceil$ yields the same upper bounds for BIN-VAL as we had in Theorem 9 for LEADINGONES.

THEOREM 12. *The expected optimization time of MMAS and MMAS* on BINVAL is bounded by $O(n^2 + n/\rho)$ and $O\left(n^2 \cdot (1/\rho)^\varepsilon + \frac{n/\rho}{\log(1/\rho)}\right)$ for every constant $\varepsilon > 0$.*

These two bounds show that the second term "$+n/\rho$" in the first bound—that also appeared in the upper bound for ONEMAX—can be lowered, at the expense of an increase in the first term. It is an interesting open question whether for all linear functions when ρ is very small the runtime is $o(n/\rho)$, i.e., sublinear in $1/\rho$ for fixed n. The relation between the runtime and ρ is further discussed from an experimental perspective in the next section.

5. EXPERIMENTS

In this section, we investigate the behavior of our algorithms using experimental studies. Our goal is to examine the effect of the pheromone update strength as well as the impact of the weights of the linear function that should be optimized.

Our experiments are related to those in [3, 14]. The authors of the first article concentrate their analyses of 1-ANT and MMAS on ONEMAX, LEADINGONES, and random linear functions. A single problem size n for each function is used, and a number of theory-guided indicators monitors the algorithms' progress at every time step, in order to measure the algorithms' progress within individual runs. In the second article, the runtime of MMAS and MMAS* is investigated on ONEMAX and other functions, for two values of n and a wide range of values of ρ.

First, we investigate the runtime behavior of our algorithms for different settings of ρ (see Figure 2). We investigate ONEMAX, BINVAL, and random functions where the weights are chosen uniformly at random from the interval $]0, 1]$. For our investigations, we consider problems of size $n = 100, 150, \ldots, 1000$. Each fixed value of n is run for $\rho \in \{1.0, 0.5, 0.1, 0.05\}$ and the results are averaged over 1000 runs. Remember that, for $\rho = 1.0$, MMAS* is equivalent to the $(1+1)$ EA*, and MMAS is equivalent to the $(1+1)$ EA (see [12] for the definition of the evolutionary algorithms). As a result of the 1000 repetitions, the curves in

the plots of Figure 2 are fairly smooth, as the standard error of the mean of the average of 1000 identically distributed random variables is only $1/\sqrt{1000} \approx 3.2\%$ of the standard error of the mean of any single such variable.

One general observation is that the performance of MMAS* on random linear functions and BINVAL is practically identical to that of MMAS. This was expected, as several bit positions have to have the same associated weights in order for MMAS to benefit from its weakened acceptance condition. Furthermore, we notice that ONEMAX is not the simplest linear function for MMAS* to optimize. In fact, for certain values of ρ, ONEMAX is as difficult to optimize as BINVAL.

For all experiments, the performance of MMAS* with $\rho = 1.0$ is very close to that of MMAS with $\rho = 1.0$. However, with different values of ρ, several performance differences are observed. For example, MMAS* with $\rho = 0.5$ and $\rho = 0.1$ optimizes random linear functions faster than MMAS* with $\rho = 1.0$, which is on the other hand the fastest setup for ONEMAX. Furthermore, the performance of MMAS increased significantly with values of $\rho < 1.0$, e.g., MMAS with $\rho = 0.1$ is 30% faster than MMAS with $\rho = 1.0$. Another general observation is that MMAS* performs better on random linear functions, than on ONEMAX, e.g. for $n = 1000$ and $\rho = 0.1$ the runtime decreases by roughly 10%.

In the following, we give an explanation for this behavior. During the optimization process, it is possible to replace a lightweight 1 at bit i (i.e., a bit with a relatively small associated weight w_i) with a heavyweight 0 at bit j (i.e., a bit with a relatively large associated weight w_j). Afterwards, during the freezing process, the probability for sampling again the lightweight 1 at bit i (whose associated τ_i is in the process of being reduced to $\tau_{\min}$) is relatively high. Unlike in the case of ONEMAX, it is indeed possible for MMAS* to collect heavyweight 1-bits in between, and the "knowledge" of the lightweight 1-bits is available for a certain time, stored as a linear combination of the pheromones' values. This effect occurs in the phase of adjusting the pheromones, not when the pheromone values are saturated. Otherwise, the effect could be observed for the $(1+1)$ EA and the $(1+1)$ EA* as well.

We have already seen that the choice of ρ may have a high impact on the optimization time. The runtime bounds given in this paper increase with decreasing ρ. In the following, we want to investigate the impact of ρ closer by conducting experimental studies. We study the effect of ρ by fixing $n = 100$ and varying $\rho = 1/x$ with $x = 1, 11, 21, \ldots, 1001$. Note that these ρ-values are much smaller than the ones shown in Figure 2. The results are shown in Figure 3 and are averaged over 10.000 runs. As a result of the large number of repetitions, the standard error of the mean of the average is only $1/\sqrt{10000} = 1\%$ of the standard error of the mean of any run. The effect that small values of ρ can improve the performance on ONEMAX is observable again. The fitted linear regression lines, which are based on the mean iterations for $1/\rho \in (500, 1000]$, support our claim that the runtime grows at most linear with $1/\rho$ for a fixed value of n. In fact, the fitted lines indicate that the growth of the average runtime is very close to a linear function in $1/\rho$. The real curves appear to be slightly concave, which corresponds to a sublinear growth. However, the observable effects are too small to allow for general conclusions.

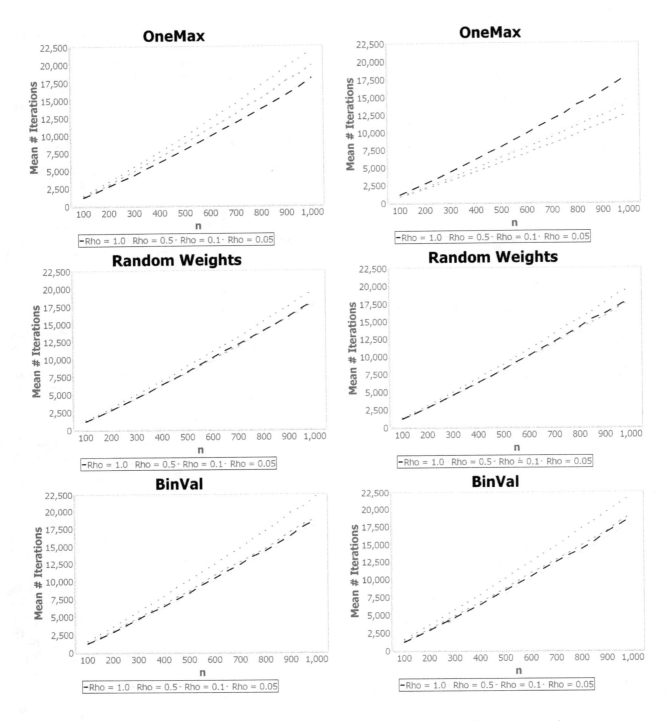

Figure 2: Runtime of MMAS* (left column) and MMAS (right column).

6. CONCLUSIONS AND FUTURE WORK

The rigorous analysis of ACO algorithms is a challenging task as these algorithms are of a high stochastic nature. Understanding the pheromone update process and the information that is stored in pheromone during the optimization run plays a key role in strengthening their theoretical foundations.

We have presented improved upper bounds for the performance of ACO on the class of linear pseudo-Boolean func-

tions. The general upper bound of $O((n^3 \log n)/\rho)$ from Theorem 2 applies to all linear functions, but in the light of the smaller upper bounds for ONEMAX and BINVAL we believe that this bound is still far from optimal. Stronger arguments are needed in order to arrive at a stronger result.

We also have developed novel methods for analyzing ACO algorithms without relying on pheromones freezing at pheromone borders. Fitness-level arguments on a pheromone level have revealed one possible way of reason-

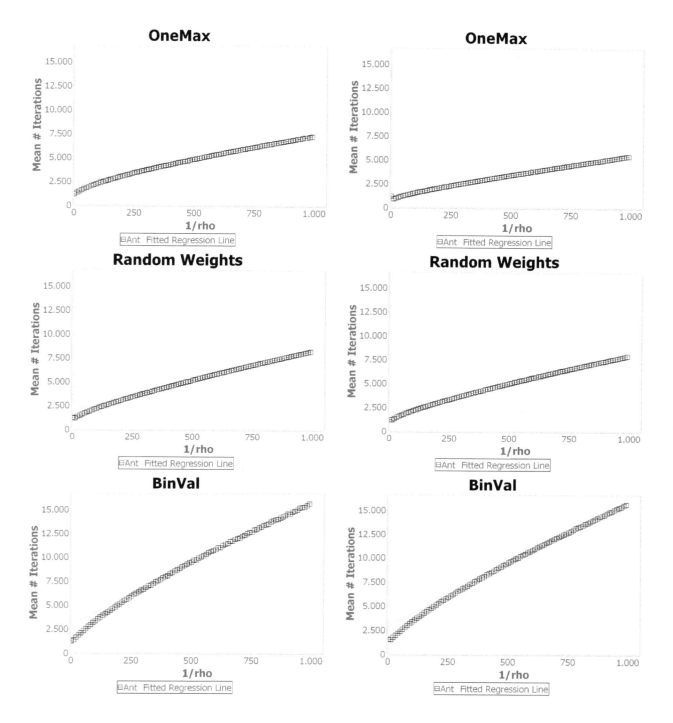

Figure 3: Impact of pheromone evaporation factor in MMAS* (left column) and MMAS (right column).

ing. For ONEMAX this approach, in combination with results from [8], has led to a bound of $O(n \log n + n/\rho)$, both for MMAS and MMAS*. This is a major improvement to the previous best known bounds $O((n^3 \log n)/\rho)$ for MMAS and $O((n \log n)/\rho)$ for MMAS* and it finally closes the gap of size n^2 between the upper bounds for MMAS and MMAS*. We conjecture that our improved bound holds for all linear functions, but this is still a challenging open problem.

Furthermore, our proof arguments have given more detailed insight into the precise dynamic growth of pheromones. For a fixed sum of pheromones, we have learned which distributions of pheromones among n bits are best and worst possible for increasing the best-so-far ONE-MAX value. We believe that this will prove useful for further theoretical studies of ACO.

The experimental results have revealed that a slow adaption of pheromone is beneficial for MMAS on ONEMAX as MMAS was faster than the (1+1) EA for all investigated ρ-

values not larger than 0.5. We also argued why MMAS* is faster on random-weight linear functions than on OneMax. The experiments also gave more detailed insights into the impact of the evaporation factor on the average runtime.

We conclude with the following two open questions and tasks for future work:

1. Do MMAS and MMAS* optimize all linear pseudo-Boolean functions in expected time $O(n \log n + n/\rho)$?

2. Analyze ACO for combinatorial problems like minimum spanning trees and the TSP in settings with slow pheromone adaptation.

Acknowledgments

Timo Kötzing and Frank Neumann were supported by the Deutsche Forschungsgemeinschaft (DFG) under grant NE 1182/5-1. Dirk Sudholt was partly supported by a postdoctoral fellowship from the German Academic Exchange Service while visiting the International Computer Science Institute in Berkeley, CA, USA and EPSRC grant EP/D052785/1.

The authors would like to thank Per Kristian Lehre and Daniel Johannsen for their comments on an earlier version of this paper.

7. REFERENCES

[1] T. Chen, P. K. Lehre, K. Tang, and X. Yao. When is an estimation of distribution algorithm better than an evolutionary algorithm? In *Proc. of CEC 2009*, pages 1470–1477. IEEE Press, 2009.

[2] T. Chen, K. Tang, G. Chen, and X. Yao. Analysis of computational time of simple estimation of distribution algorithms. *IEEE Transactions on Evolutionary Computation*, 14(1):1 –22, 2010.

[3] B. Doerr, D. Johannsen, and C. H. Tang. How single ant ACO systems optimize pseudo-Boolean functions. In *Proc. of PPSN 2008*, pages 378–388. Springer, 2008.

[4] B. Doerr, F. Neumann, D. Sudholt, and C. Witt. On the runtime analysis of the 1-ANT ACO algorithm. In *Proc. of GECCO 2007*, pages 33–40. ACM, 2007.

[5] M. Dorigo and T. Stützle. *Ant Colony Optimization*. MIT Press, 2004.

[6] S. Droste. A rigorous analysis of the compact genetic algorithm for linear functions. *Natural Computing*, 5(3):257–283, 2006.

[7] S. Droste, T. Jansen, and I. Wegener. On the analysis of the (1+1) evolutionary algorithm. *Theoretical Computer Science*, 276:51–81, 2002.

[8] L. Gleser. On the distribution of the number of successes in independent trials. *Annals of Probability*, 3(1):182–188, 1975.

[9] W. J. Gutjahr and G. Sebastiani. Runtime analysis of ant colony optimization with best-so-far reinforcement. *Methodology and Computing in Applied Probability*, 10:409–433, 2008.

[10] J. He and X. Yao. A study of drift analysis for estimating computation time of evolutionary algorithms. *Natural Computing*, 3(1):21–35, 2004.

[11] J. Jägersküpper. A blend of Markov-chain and drift analysis. In *Proc. of PPSN 2008*, pages 41–51. Springer, 2008.

[12] T. Jansen and I. Wegener. Evolutionary algorithms - how to cope with plateaus of constant fitness and when to reject strings of the same fitness. *IEEE Transactions on Evolutionary Computation*, 5(6):589–599, 2001.

[13] T. Kötzing, F. Neumann, H. Röglin, and C. Witt. Theoretical properties of two ACO approaches for the traveling salesman problem. In *Proc. of ANTS 2010*, pages 324–335. Springer, 2010.

[14] F. Neumann, D. Sudholt, and C. Witt. Analysis of different MMAS ACO algorithms on unimodal functions and plateaus. *Swarm Intelligence*, 3(1):35–68, 2009.

[15] F. Neumann, D. Sudholt, and C. Witt. A few ants are enough: ACO with iteration-best update. In *Proc. of GECCO 2010*, pages 63–70. ACM, 2010.

[16] F. Neumann and C. Witt. Runtime analysis of a simple ant colony optimization algorithm. *Algorithmica*, 54(2):243–255, 2009.

[17] F. Neumann and C. Witt. Ant colony optimization and the minimum spanning tree problem. *Theoretical Computer Science*, 411(25):2406–2413, 2010.

[18] T. Stützle and H. H. Hoos. MAX-MIN ant system. *Journal of Future Generation Computer Systems*, 16:889–914, 2000.

[19] I. Wegener. Theoretical aspects of evolutionary algorithms. In *Proceedings of the 28th International Colloquium on Automata, Languages and Programming (ICALP 2001)*, pages 64–78. Springer, 2001.

[20] I. Wegener. Methods for the analysis of evolutionary algorithms on pseudo-Boolean functions. In R. Sarker, X. Yao, and M. Mohammadian, editors, *Evolutionary Optimization*, pages 349–369. Kluwer, 2002.

Using Multivariate Quantitative Genetics Theory to Assist in EA Customization

Jeffrey K. Bassett
George Mason University
4400 University Dr, MS 4A1
Fairfax, Virginia
jbassett@cs.gmu.edu

Kenneth A. De Jong
George Mason University
4400 University Dr, MS 3A5
Fairfax, Virginia
kdejong@gmu.edu

ABSTRACT

Customizing and evolutionary algorithm (EA) for a new or unusual problem can seem relatively simple as long as one can devise an appropriate representation and reproductive operators to modify it. Unfortunately getting a customized EA to produce high quality results in a reasonable amount of time can be quite challenging. There is little guidance available to help practitioners deal with this issue. Most evolutionary computation (EC) theory is only applicable to specific representations, or assumes knowledge of the fitness function, such as the location of optima.

We are developing an approach based on theory from the biology community to address this problem. Multivariate quantitative genetics theory characterizes evolving populations as multivariate probability distributions of phenotypic traits. Some advantages it offers are a degree of independence from the underlying representation, and useful concepts such as phenotypic heritability. Re-working the quantitative genetics equations, we expose an additional term that we call "perturbation". We believe that perturbation and heritability provide quantitative measures of the exploration and exploitation, and that practitioners can use these to identify and diagnose imbalances in customized reproductive operators.

To illustrate, we use these tools to diagnose problems with a standard recombination operator for a Pittsburgh approach classifier system. With this knowledge we develop a new, more balanced, recombination operator, and show that its use leads to significantly better results.

Categories and Subject Descriptors

F.2 [**Theory of Computation**]: Analysis of Algorithms and Problem Complexity; G.3 [**Mathematics of Computing**]: Probability and Statistics—*Correlation and regression analysis, Multivariate statistics*

General Terms

Theory, Algorithms, Performance

Keywords

Evolutionary Computation, Quantitative Genetics, Heritability, Customization

1. INTRODUCTION

When using an EA to solve a new or unusual problem, two general strategies are available. The first is to encode the problem in a traditional linear representation and use the standard reproductive operators. Unfortunately this encoding process can often transform the fitness landscape to one that can be much more difficult to search. In some cases such an encoding may not even be possible, especially if potential solutions can differ in size.

The second approach is to customize the EA for the specific problem. This means using a representation that more naturally describes a potential solution to the problem, and then developing reproductive operators that can modify it. The problem with this approach is that it is not always obvious how to proceed, and sometimes it can be quite difficult to build operators that allow the EA to find high fitness solutions in a reasonable amount of time.

Ideally one would turn to theory for advice on performing customizations. Unfortunately EC theory tends not to be applicable in these situations. Most theory is either specific to certain representations, or requires detailed knowledge about the fitness landscape being searched. The practitioner is left to using an ad-hoc approach to perform their customizations. Our goal is to help provide a more principled approach.

We propose using multivariate quantitative genetics theory from the biology community to address this issue. This theory has the advantage of offering a degree of representation independence, which it achieves by dealing with individuals using only quantitative (e.g. real-valued) phenotypic traits. Populations are characterized as multivariate probability distributions of these traits, and a series of equations are used to model how these distributions change from one population to the next as a result of selection and reproduction. As part of these equations, the theory defines useful concepts like heritability that describe mathematically how well traits are retained during reproduction. We believe this provides a measure of a reproductive operator's contribution to an algorithm's ability to exploit good solutions.

Multivariate heritability also suggests a way of identifying where problems in a reproductive operator may lie. This can be determined by comparing the population's traits distributions before and after an operation is performed, to see how similar they are. When dissimilarities are found we can identify which sets of traits are most affected. If the traits have been carefully chosen, it will be possible trace the affected traits back to associated changes in the genome. Once we learn what is causing the distributions to differ, we can reason about how to improve the operators or representation in a way that will reduce or resolve the problem. Assuming one has chosen a set of traits that reasonably represent the search space, it should be possible to discover most problems with one's customized algorithm using this approach.

To illustrate the value of this theory, we will demonstrate its use in diagnosing a problem with a specific recombination operator. In previous work of ours using Pittsburgh approach classifiers systems, we noticed that the customized recombination operators often produced worse results than using standard EA operators on fixed length strings. This makes them a good candidate for attempts at improvement. We demonstrate that the two-point Pittsburgh recombination has lower heritability than the standard two-point recombination operator. We also show how problems with the operators can be identified by examining the way the operators transform the trait distributions of the populations. Using the knowledge we gain from this, we then develop a recombination operator that has much higher heritability, and correspondingly finds better solutions to a function approximation problem.

Multivariate quantitative genetics can act as the framework for a more principled approach to customizing EAs for new problems. As long as one can identify an appropriate set of traits to measure, the theory offers a representation independent way of modeling evolutionary processes and identifying problems within.

2. BACKGROUND

We offer a brief review of quantitative genetics, focusing particularly on those areas that pertain to our work. We will also review two areas of EC research that have, at least at times, applied quantitative genetics theory: evolvability theory and estimation of distribution algorithms (EDAs).

2.1 Quantitative Genetics

Quantitative genetics [6, 20] is concerned with measurable phenotypic traits that are statistically modeled at a population level. Statistical measures like mean, variance and covariance are used to characterize populations and the relationships between them. Several equations are then used to model the effects of selection, reproduction and genetic drift over time.

Quantitative genetics equations are often decomposed into meaningful terms and factors, each of which represents some important aspect of the evolutionary process. For example, Price's theorem [19] separates the average effects of selection and reproduction into two terms. Similarly, the equation for population variance includes terms for the effects of heritability, epistasis and variation due to the environment. Decompositions like these have the potential to offer insights into how and why certain operators and representations are not performing well.

Perhaps the most notable of these equations is the breeder's equation [6] which models the response to selection,

$$R = h^2 S \tag{1}$$

Here S represents the selection differential, h^2 is heritability and R is the response to selection. In very simplistic terms, S describes the change in the average value of a trait caused by selection culling low fitness individuals from the population. This description is not completely accurate though since high fitness individuals that are selected multiple times to be parents are counted as if multiple copies of them were in the population as well.

The response to selection (R) describes the change in the trait's average within the population from one generation to the next. Heritability (h^2) is a statistical measure of similarity between the *selected* parents and their offspring. It can also be thought of as indicating how well a trait is transmitted from a parent to its offspring during reproduction [2]. In this light, the breeder's equation can be read as follows: If selection causes an increase or decrease in the mean value of a trait, then the closer heritability is to 1, the more that change will also be manifested in the next generation.

Heritability is often estimated as a regression coefficient between parent and offspring trait values using the following equation,

$$h^2 = \tau \frac{\text{cov}(o_i, p_i)}{\text{var}(p_i)}, \tag{2}$$

where τ is the number of parents per offspring (1 for asexual reproduction and 2 for sexual reproduction), o_i is the value of the phenotypic trait for offspring i, and p_i is the trait values of the parents of i averaged together (also known as the midparent).

Values for h^2 tend to fall in the range 0 to 1, but are not limited to this. Note that, in the literature, the term for heritability is always h^2 and not h for historical reasons, even though h has little meaning by itself.

2.2 Evolvability

There are several cases where quantitative genetics theory has already been applied to EAs. One of the first was research done by Altenberg [1] in which he used Price's theorem [19] as the foundation for an infinite population dynamical systems model of EAs. His main result was to re-derive the schema theorem and show that recombination was essential for the schema theory to hold. His work also provided a theoretical justification for using the covariance between parent and offspring fitness as a predictor of EA performance, which up until then had been just a heuristic. Interestingly Altenberg might have found it easier to derive this result from the variance equations rather than Price's theorem, which measures changes in population means. Asoh and Mühlenbein [3] did just this when they examined heritability in EAs.

The importance of the relationship between parent and offspring fitness was known in the EA community before Altenberg's and Mühlenbein's work, and is one of the most effective tools for assisting the customization process. Using this measure, one can compare two operators to see which is more likely to improve an EAs performance [13]. Unfortunately it offers no indication of why an operator is performing poorly, and no suggestions for how to improve it.

Parent-offspring fitness covariance is also used as a measure of fitness landscape difficulty [23, 22, 9]. For example, consider a landscape where the fitness of neighboring points have no relationship to one-another. Without near–perfect knowledge of the landscape, no set of operators could perform well on this problem. On the other hand a poor choice of reproductive operators can have a similar effect by searching the landscape in an irregular and unpredictable way. Unfortunately, it is difficult to tell which case one is faced with.

Some have built tools based on quantitative genetics for evaluating the components of an EA either before or during a run. Langdon [12] used both Price's theorem and Fisher's fundamental theorem [18] to build his tools, but these make certain assumptions about the structure of the genome which make them somewhat representation dependent. Potter, Bassett and De Jong [17] also explored building tools with Price's theorem. Their results demonstrated the importance of reproductive variance in analyzing operators, leading them to explore approaches for measuring variance using Price's theorem as well [4] [5].

2.3 Estimation of Distribution Algorithms

Mühlenbein and Schlierkamp-Voosen [16] used the breeder's equation [6] to guide the design of their Breeder Genetic Algorithm (BGA). An analysis of crossover using this same equation led to the development of gene-pool crossover operators and then to the development of Estimation of Distribution Algorithms (EDAs) [15, 14]. EDAs differ from EAs in that they do not use standard reproductive operators. In each generation they estimate the probability distributions of the gene frequencies in the selected parents and use this information to generate a new population of offspring. Quantitative genetics played a continuing role in Mühlenbein's work, guiding the development of several new EDAs.

A newer branch of EDA research, called continuous EDAs [24, 25], takes an approach that is more like modeling phenotypic traits. As the name implies, an individual is represented by a set of real valued traits. This allows population distributions to be modeled using joint Gaussian distributions instead of just tracking genes values. The use of covariance matrices also allows epistatic relationships to be captured by orienting the distribution along a diagonal. The disadvantage to this approach is that it limits the types of genetic structures that can be modeled, only being applicable to real-valued optimization problems.

Statistical approaches such as quantitative genetics have played an important role in the process of customizing EAs. In particular measures similar to heritability of fitness have been some of the most effective tools to date for aiding ad-hoc design approaches. Next we will discuss Multivariate Quantitative Genetics and how it can assist in actually diagnosing problems.

3. MULTIVARIATE QUANTITATIVE GENETICS

So far, the quantitative genetics equations we have examined have dealt with only a single phenotypic trait. To observe how the population behaves in the search space as a whole, we need to consider multiple traits simultaneously. An extension to this theory called multivariate quantitative genetics [10, 11] was developed to address these kinds of issues. The equations essentially mirror the standard equations, but they use vectors and matrices to simultaneously manage several traits, and the interactions between them. For example, here is the multivariate version of equation 1, the breeder's equation:

$$\Delta \bar{z} = \mathbf{GP}^{-1}\mathbf{S} \qquad (3)$$

The individuals o_i and p_i are now described by a group of traits and are represented as vectors, as is the selection differential ($\mathbf{S}$) and the response to selection ($\Delta\bar{z}$). $\mathbf{G}$ is the cross-covariance matrix defined by $\tau\mathrm{cov}(o_i, p_i)$ and $\mathbf{P}$ is the covariance matrix describing the distribution of traits of the selected parents ($var(p_i)$). Heritability is now defined by the matrix $\mathbf{GP}^{-1}$, and high heritability values will be those near the identity matrix.

Biologists tend not to think in terms of heritability when using the multivariate form of the breeder's equation though. Instead they have worked under the assumption that the $\mathbf{G}$ and $\mathbf{P}$ matrices will remain stable over time, especially in the short term. If this is true, it is not difficult to see that heritability will remain constant, and therefore the breeder's equation could still be used to do prediction.

Our concerns are somewhat different from those of the biologists. Instead of predicting the algorithms behavior, we want to diagnose problems with the reproductive operators.

3.1 Modified Equations

We believe that heritability is an important metric to consider when developing a new operator, but it is clearly not the only important factor. For example, an operator that just produces clones of the parents is guaranteed to have the highest heritability possible, and yet we would not expect it to produce particularly good results.

We have examined the quantitative genetics equations again from first principles to see if we could identify other factors that could assist us during the design process. One common assumption we find is that all individuals will have the same number of parents. This makes it difficult to model many common EAs, where crossover and cloning are often performed in some proportion to one another in the same generation. We have developed a framework that can address these algorithms relatively easily.

Figure 1 provides a model of a single generation during an EA run. Some parents are selected and produce offspring, either through crossover or cloning, with the potential for mutation being applied at some point during the process as well. Note that every relationship between parent and offspring is represented. This means that midparent calculations (averaging parent traits) is not appropriate for this model. Also note that cases where an offspring is produced by a single parent, instead of two, are represented using two links. It is important that each link represent the same amount of "influence" that a parent has on it's offspring. Thus all offspring have two arrows leading to them, even if they come from the same parent. If other operators are used that require more than two parents, the appropriate number of arrows will be the least common multiple of parents-per-offspring of all the operators involved.

A vector of phenotypic traits ϕ_i is associated with each parent i. Similarly a vector of traits ϕ'_j is associated with each offspring j. The relationship between parents and offspring is defined by the by the set of links Γ, forming a directed graph. The two functions $\lambda(k)$ and $\lambda'(k)$ are defined such that they return the appropriate parent index and offspring index respectively, for a given link k. This allows

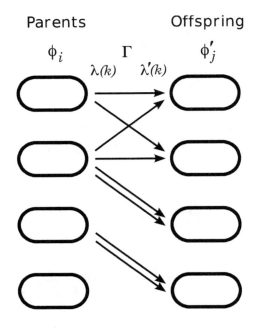

Parents ϕ_i $\qquad \Gamma \qquad$ **Offspring** ϕ'_j

$\lambda(k) \qquad \lambda'(k)$

Figure 1: A sample generation.

one to match up corresponding sets of parent and offspring traits, such as $\phi_{\lambda(k)}$ and $\phi'_{\lambda'(k)}$.

To abbreviate, we will sometimes refer to the traits of all parents as ϕ and all offspring as ϕ'. These actually indicate matrices where the row identifies an individual and the column identifies a specific trait. Similarly ϕ_λ refers to all traits of the *selected* parents, and $\phi'_{\lambda'}$ again refers to all the traits of the offspring, although in the case of figure 1 there are two copies of each child.

With the knowledge that $\text{var}(\phi') = \text{var}(\phi'_{\lambda'})$, and the identity $\text{var}(aX + bY) = a^2\text{var}(X) + b^2\text{var}(Y) + 2ab\,\text{cov}(X, Y)$, we can derive the following equation by setting $X = \phi_\lambda$, $Y = \phi'_{\lambda'}$, $a = -1$, and $b = 1$.

$$\text{var}(\phi') = \text{var}(\phi'_{\lambda'})$$
$$\text{var}(\phi') = 2\text{cov}(\phi'_{\lambda'}, \phi_\lambda) + \text{var}(\phi'_{\lambda'} - \phi_\lambda) - \text{var}(\phi_\lambda).$$

If we define the matrices $\mathbf{O} = \text{var}(\phi')$, $\mathbf{G}' = \text{cov}(\phi'_{\lambda'}, \phi_\lambda)$, $\mathbf{D} = \text{var}(\phi'_{\lambda'} - \phi_\lambda)$, and $\mathbf{P} = \text{var}(\phi_\lambda)$, we can rewrite the equation as follows:

$$\mathbf{O} = 2\mathbf{G}' + \mathbf{D} - \mathbf{P} \qquad (4)$$
$$\mathbf{O} = \mathbf{P}[2\mathbf{G}'\mathbf{P}^{-1} + \mathbf{D}\mathbf{P}^{-1} - \mathbf{I}], \qquad (5)$$

where $\mathbf{I}$ is the identity matrix.

In equation 5, everything within the brackets defines a transformation matrix that transforms the distribution of the traits of the selected parents ($\mathbf{P}$) into the distribution of the offspring population traits ($\mathbf{O}$). The factor $\mathbf{G}'\mathbf{P}^{-1}$ is very similar to the quantitative genetics notion of heritability. It is important to note that the $\mathbf{G}'$ in these equations is not quite the same as the $\mathbf{G}$ in equation 3. In fact, $\mathbf{G} = \tau\mathbf{G}'$, as long as τ (the number of parents per offspring) is constant for every operation performed. In other words, as long as there is no mixing of crossover and cloning. This means that in the case of crossover for example, $\mathbf{G}'\mathbf{P}^{-1}$ represents

the degree to which the traits of a *single* parent have been inherited, rather than both parents.

Equation 5 also exposes the term $\mathbf{D}\mathbf{P}^{-1}$, which is not commonly seen in quantitative genetics equations. We refer to this as perturbation, since it describes the amount of new variation that the operators are introducing into the population. It is our contention that perturbation measures an operator's capacity for exploration, while heritability measures it's potential for exploitation.

3.2 Covariance Matrices Metrics

When biologists consider the multivariate notion of heritability, they tend to think of it as the degree of similarity between the two probability distributions that $\mathbf{P}$ and $\mathbf{G}$ describe. These comparisons are often performed using statistical techniques like Common Principle Component Analysis [7, 8]. In our experiments with CPCA, we found its output to be too course grained to be useful to us as a diagnostic tool, and so we have developed our own approach.

For simplicity and ease of understanding, we would like to find a metric that expresses terms like heritability and perturbation as a single scalar value. We have chosen to use the following metric,

$$\text{m}(\mathbf{G}'\mathbf{P}^{-1}) = \sqrt[M]{\det(\mathbf{G}'\mathbf{P}^{-1})} \qquad (6)$$

where m is the metric function, and $\mathbf{G}'$ and $\mathbf{P}$ are M by M covariance matrices as described in the previous section. M, in other words, indicates the number of traits being measured.

The result of equation 6 is, of course, our scalar version of heritability from a single parent. Similarly, $\sqrt[M]{\det(\mathbf{D}\mathbf{P}^{-1})}$ would measure perturbation, and $\sqrt[M]{\det(\mathbf{O}\mathbf{P}^{-1})}$ gives us a measure of the overall similarity between the selected parent population and the resulting offspring population.

We chose to use determinants because they have an intuitive geometric interpretation. They are equal to the volume of a parallelogram that has its dimensions defined by the eigenvectors of the matrix. Thus the determinant gives us a rough measure of the volume under the curve of the distribution that the covariance matrix represents. Determinants do have one disadvantage though. They will evaluate to a zero if any of the traits in the populations becomes fixed (i.e. converged). This is why all the algorithms we will examine contain at least a small amount of mutation. We also use Schäfer and Strimmer's [21] shrinkage approach for estimating covariance matrices, that is guaranteed to produce semi-positive definite matrices.

We take the Mth root of each determinant in order to modify the units of the measure to be in line with those of a single trait. This makes interpretation more intuitive, much the way standard deviation values are often easier to interpret than variances.

We should note that this similarity metric could be potentially misleading in some situations. It is possible for two matrices that are fairly different to still have the same determinant. On the other hand, though, whenever the determinants are different, there is no way the matrices could be the same.

4. OBSERVING A SIMPLE EA

Before we begin looking at the Pittsburgh approach operators, we would like to set a baseline so that we know what we should expect to see, and thus what we would like to achieve with our customized operators. It also gives us a chance to compare the results of these measures against our existing understanding of how an EA works.

4.1 Standard Gaussian Mutation

We began by examining standard Gaussian mutation with a fixed σ (standard deviation) on a very simple function optimization problem. Specifically, we chose what is often referred to as the sphere function. The goal is to minimize the following fitness function,

$$f(x) = \sum x^2, \qquad (7)$$

where x is a vector of 10 real-valued genes. There are no explicit bounds placed on the gene values, but when the population is initialized, genes are randomly chosen in the range $[-5.12, 5.12)$. The Gaussian mutation is applied to every gene during reproduction, with $\sigma = 0.2$ remaining constant throughout the run.

Choosing quantitative traits for this problem is fairly straightforward. Each of the real-valued parameters to the fitness function make an ideal trait, especially since we tend to visualize the landscape in terms of this space. Since there is a direct relationship between the genes and the parameters, each gene value becomes one of our traits.

In figure 2, we plot the behavior of our EA on the sphere function, averaged over 30 runs. In all cases where we do this averaging, the averaged lines are reasonable representations of individual runs. We have plotted lines for $\sqrt[M]{\det(\mathbf{G'P^{-1}})}$, $\sqrt[M]{\det(\mathbf{DP^{-1}})}$ and $\sqrt[M]{\det(\mathbf{OP^{-1}})}$. These allow us to examine the heritability, perturbation, and overall change in the population respectively. We have also plotted the line $\sqrt[10]{\det(\mathbf{P})}$, signifying the overall size of the $\mathbf{P}$ matrix. This allows us to see how much the population has converged.

As we can see, the heritability of the mutation operator remains fairly high throughout the run, dipping only briefly just as the population is beginning to converge. This remained consistent over a wide range of values for σ. The perturbation, on the other hand, begins quite low, and then rapidly increases just as the population convergence begins to slow dramatically. This is exactly what we would expect to see when using a fixed Gaussian mutation with a fixed σ. As the population converges, it will eventually reach a point where the distribution of the population is similar in scale to the distribution generated by the Gaussian mutation. At that point it will become much more difficult, if not impossible, for the population to converge any further. The search process switches over to something much closer to random search, albeit in a very localized portion of the search space.

4.2 Standard 2-Point Crossover

Next we wanted to examine the behavior of a standard 2-point crossover operator. Ideally we might like to run an EA with crossover alone, but we found that these techniques do not function well if there is too little variance in the population. Consequently, we maintained a small amount of Gaussian mutation with $\sigma = 0.02$, which is applied after selection, but before crossover is applied. The probes that we use to measure the traits do not measure the effect of the mutation though. The traits of the individuals are examined directly before and after crossover is performed. In the following experiment, a crossover rate of 1.0 was used.

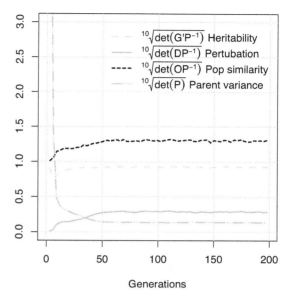

Figure 2: Gaussian mutation on the sphere function. A plot of $\mathbf{m(G'P^{-1})}$, $\mathbf{m(DP^{-1})}$, $\mathbf{m(OP^{-1})}$ and $\sqrt[10]{\det(\mathbf{P})}$, averaged over 30 runs.

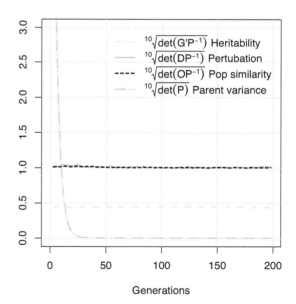

Figure 3: Standard 2-point crossover on the sphere function. A plot of $\mathbf{m(G'P^{-1})}$, $\mathbf{m(DP^{-1})}$, $\mathbf{m(OP^{-1})}$ and $\sqrt[10]{\det(\mathbf{P})}$, averaged over 30 runs. Gaussian mutation was also used, but it's effects are not measured here.

Figure 3 shows the effects of the 2-point crossover operator, averaged over 30 runs. The heritability from a single parent $(m(\mathbf{G'P}^{-1}))$ hovers close to 0.5 throughout the run, which is ideal for an operator that takes two parents. It may be somewhat hard to see on the plot, but both the perturbation $(m(\mathbf{DP}^{-1}))$ and the overall population similarity $(m(\mathbf{OP}^{-1}))$ hover close to 1.0 throughout the run. Compared to figure 2, the high values for perturbation are impressive, and they do not come at any cost to the overall population similarity. This is to be expected, of course. It is well understood that crossover is a much more aggressive search operator, and that it has an adaptive quality that allows it to maintain it's search even as the population converges. Of course, if we were to try this on a landscape that contained epistasis, we would expect lower values for $m(\mathbf{G'P}^{-1})$.

This gives us a sense for how the prototypical versions of these operators work. As we examine customized operators, any deviations from these patterns will give us a sense for what the problem is, and a more detailed examination of the traits should allow us to zero-in on the specific issues involved.

5. DIAGNOSING AN OPERATOR

Here we present a demonstration of how quantitative genetics theory can be used to diagnose problems with one of the standard recombination operators for Pittsburgh approach classifier systems.

5.1 Pittsburgh Approach

Learning classifier systems are a machine learning technique that use evolutionary algorithms to evolve sets of rules. The distinguishing characteristics of the Pittsburgh approach are that each individual defines an entire rule-set, and the number or rules can vary from individual to individual. Because of the way rule-sets are interpreted, the position of the genes (rules) on the genome does not affect the semantics. In most systems rules are defined to be fixed length, with a constant number of conditions on the left-hand-side and a constant number of actions on the right-hand-side of each rule.

To support inductive learning, some sort of generalization mechanism is required. A number of different approaches have been used, including wildcards (a.k.a. "don't care" symbols), ranges, and nearest neighbor matching mechanisms that fire the rule whose conditions are the shortest distance from the input in condition space. The experiments we perform here will use something akin to the nearest neighbor approach.

For a variable length genome to be useful, its size must be able to adapt to the problem. The standard reproductive operators will not modify the genome size, so a custom recombination operator was developed. Instead of choosing cut points that are in the same place in both genomes, the cut points on each genome are chosen independently of one another. The result is that one offspring may get more genes from its parents than the other does.

This recombination operator has never worked as well as hoped. Numerous attempts have been made to find better replacements. The most successful approach has been the development of a homologous recombination operator that compared genes on the two genomes, and only swapped

Table 1: Points defining the target function

X	Y	X	Y
-10.00	-7.0	3.62	-10.0
-3.80	-9.0	5.11	7.0
-2.22	-6.0	6.48	-5.0
-2.15	-1.0	8.61	2.0
2.75	8.0	10.00	9.0

genes that were similar. Unfortunately the matching process could become quite expensive for large genomes.

5.2 Function Approximation

We chose a problem domain that allowed us to create a test problem that is simple enough to demonstrate the diagnosis process, is well as creating a more complex problem to properly test our operators to see how they perform. The function approximation domain also made it fairly simple to define real-valued phenotypic traits using the sampling method described above.

5.2.1 Representation

The genome of an individual is a string of concatenated rules. All rules have the same length, but each genome can have a different number of rules. The rules consists of a single condition/input and a single action/output. Thus a rule identifies a single point on a function $g(x) = y$, where x is the input and y is the output.

The generalization mechanism is similar to nearest neighbor, but instead of returning the output of the the rule with the closest condition, an interpolation is returned between the two rules who's conditions bound it on either side. When an input value does not lie between two rules, the output value of the one closest rule is returned. The result is that each individual defines a piecewise-linear function, where the rules define each the vertices.

When individuals are randomly initialized in the first generation, all input and output values lie within the range $[-10, 10]$. There is nothing in place to enforce this range past initialization though.

5.2.2 Target Functions

While it is possible to approximate almost any function using this representation, we chose a function that could be represented exactly by an ideal individual. We were concerned that a smooth function might encourage the EA to learn very large rule-sets in order to get the best approximations possible. This might complicate our analysis.

Our target function was defined using the points shown in Table 1. The function that these points describe is plotted in Figure 4. A very simple function seemed appropriate for the diagnosis.

For performing rigorous tests of the operators, a more complex test function was developed. It consists of 50 randomly generated points within the same $[-10, 10]$ range.

5.2.3 Fitness

Fitness is calculated using a set of 30 training examples that are drawn randomly from the target function. A new training set is drawn each generation with the goal of reduc-

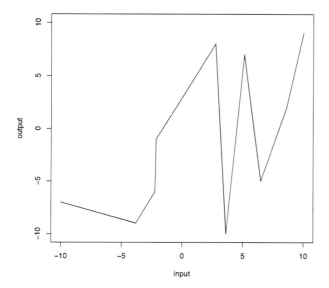

Figure 4: The target function to be learned.

ing over-fitting. The fitness function is defined as follows,

$$f(X) = \frac{1}{N} \sum_{i=1}^{N} [g(X_i) - Y_i], \qquad (8)$$

where X and Y are vectors containing the training set inputs and corresponding outputs, N is the number of training examples (30 in this case), and $g(x)$ is the piecewise-linear function as defined by the individual being evaluated.

An independent test set containing 30 examples is also generated at the beginning of a run. These play no role in the learning process, and are used solely to evaluate the learning process.

5.3 Choosing Quantitative Traits

When choosing quantitative traits for analyzing the operators, two goals should be kept in mind. First we would like our traits to be representative of the underlying phenotype, and second we want our traits to help lead us back to where problems are occurring in the genetic structure of our individuals.

For a Pittsburgh approach system, we considered two possible views of the phenotype: high-level behaviors, and the input-output map. The high-level-behavior view is particularly appropriate when one is working with an agent based model or robotics domain. Certain behaviors that seem important for the specific domain can be quantified. Things such as obstacle avoidance, navigation, goal seeking and tracking could all be quantified, often in terms of the frequency or duration of certain model events or situations. The advantage to this approach is that, with careful thought, the traits are very likely to accurately and comprehensively describe the phenotype space. The disadvantage is that they could be far removed from the underlying representation, making it difficult still to diagnose the actual problem.

Another way to think about the phenotype is as a mapping between inputs and outputs. This approach has the advantage of being much closer to the representational structure, thus having the potential to identify problems more easily. The disadvantage is that quantifying the entire input/output map is nearly impossible for anything but the most trivial of problems. The only hope is to sample points in the space and hope that they can provide enough information to be useful. This approach is most easily applied to very simple problems.

Given both the ease of implementation and the likelihood of producing relevant information, we chose to use the second approach of sampling the input/output space. We selected a set of 10 sample inputs that will be passed to each individual. These inputs are evenly distributed across the condition/input space. The corresponding output at each sample point is a quantitative trait, giving us 10 traits total. This decision influenced our choice of test problems as well, as we will see in the next section.

5.4 Looking Under the Hood

To get an initial sense of the behavior of the Pittsburgh (Pitt) 2-point crossover operator, we performed an experiment on the function approximation problem described in table 1. A population of 100 individuals was used, and all individuals were initialized to contain 10 rules, the ideal number needed to solve the problem. Crossover was performed at a rate of 1.0, and prior to individuals being passed to the crossover operator, Gaussian mutation is applied with a mutation rate of 1.0 and $\sigma = 0.05$. As was the case with the standard 2-point crossover, the effects of mutation on the phenotypic traits are not measured.

The standard 2-point crossover operator cannot change the size of an individual, but the Pitt crossover can and does. In order to control bloat (constant genome growth), parsimony pressure is applied in the form of a fitness penalty when the Pitt operator is used. We used a penalty of 0.01 per rule. All plots that display fitness show the raw fitness values, before the penalty is applied.

Thirty runs were performed, and the average metrics are displayed in figure 6. When compared with the metrics from the standard 2-point crossover in figure 3, we notice a couple of things. First, the perturbation curve is much higher than with the standard 2-point crossover, ranging from 1.5 at the beginning of the run, up to 2.0 by the end, indicating that this operator may be over-extending it's search. Perhaps more importantly though, the heritability curve is quite low, averaging around 0.3. This indicates that an EA using this operator may have problems converging past a certain point, limiting its ability to find good solutions.

While helpful, this analysis does not give us quite enough information to diagnose any issues with the crossover operator. Next we will analyze the relationship between the various traits to see if we can get a better understanding of what is causing the low heritability.

5.5 Identifying the Problem

Aggregated information about the traits, and the relationships between them, is all stored within the matrices. We thought that by carefully examining them, the source of our problem might become clear. We are particularly concerned with the heritability of the operator, so we chose to examine the $\mathbf{G'P^{-1}}$ matrix. We begin by examining the $\mathbf{G'P^{-1}}$ matrix for the standard 2-point crossover operator from the experiment shown in figure 3.

For each generation we calculated the 30 heritability matrices from each run, and then averaged them together, producing one matrix per generation. Below we provide part of the average matrix from generation 5, as an example. Note that the variances along the diagonal tend to have values near 0.5, while all the off-diagonal covariances are fairly negligible.

$$\begin{bmatrix} 0.523 & -0.005 & -0.005 & -0.003 & & -0.008 \\ -0.005 & 0.550 & -0.010 & -0.007 & \cdots- & 0.007 \\ -0.005 & -0.010 & 0.552 & -0.010 & & -0.007 \\ -0.003 & -0.007 & -0.010 & 0.520 & & -0.004 \\ & & \vdots & & \ddots & \\ -0.008 & -0.007 & -0.007 & -0.004 & & 0.542 \end{bmatrix}$$

When we compare this with the $\mathbf{G'P^{-1}}$ matrices associated with the Pittsburgh 2-point crossover, we noticed something interesting. In the early generations of the run, certain pairs of traits had much higher covariances than others. Based on this, we deduced that those traits were linked in some way. We provide a part of the average matrix from generation 5 below, as an example.

$$\begin{bmatrix} 0.528 & \mathbf{-0.122} & -0.014 & -0.003 & & -0.002 \\ \mathbf{-0.122} & 0.470 & \mathbf{-0.041} & -0.003 & \cdots- & 0.005 \\ -0.014 & \mathbf{-0.041} & 0.392 & \mathbf{-0.029} & & -0.004 \\ -0.003 & -0.003 & \mathbf{-0.029} & 0.391 & & -0.007 \\ & & \vdots & & \ddots & \\ -0.002 & -0.005 & -0.004 & -0.007 & & 0.420 \end{bmatrix}$$

Each trait is represented by both a row and a column in a covariance matrix, with row i and column i representing the the same trait. The numbers along the diagonal (shown in *italics*) are the variances of the each trait, and the other numbers are covariances between two different traits identified by the specific row and column. In the above example, the numbers displayed in **bold** indicate the unusually high values.

Our traits were all measured using probes at consecutive input values. This means that the high covariance values all appear to be between neighboring traits. Since we chose traits that would be closely related to the genes in our representation, we can infer that rules that have similar conditions tend to have higher linkages between them. A crossover operator that can reduce the frequency of cuts between highly linked genes should have a higher heritability.

5.6 An Improved Recombination Operator

Taking what we have learned into consideration, we decided to create what we call the "condition space crossover operator". Instead of performing cuts on the genome explicitly, our crossover performs cuts in condition space.

In the function approximation domain we have only one condition per rule. Our new operator first sorts the rules of both parents by the condition value. This sorting is not only done within each parent, but the rules of both parents are sorted relative to one another as well (see figure 5 for an illustration). This creates $l_1 + l_2 - 1$ possible cut points, where l_1 and l_2 are the lengths of the two parents. Two cut points c_1 and c_2 are then selected, and the rules falling between c_1 and c_2 in each parent are exchanged, creating the two offspring.

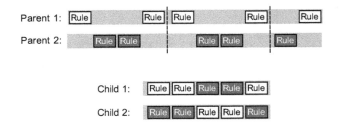

Figure 5: An illustration of the Condition Space Crossover operator. Rules are sorted by condition value both within and between parents. Crossover points are then selected such that only rules with similar condition values are exchanged between parents.

Figure 7 shows the metrics for an experiment run using the new crossover operator. As before, 30 runs were performed with a population size of 100, a crossover rate of 1.0, Gaussian mutation $\sigma = 0.05$ and a parsimony penalty of 0.01. As we can see, the single parent heritability has increased to an average of close to 0.4 throughout the run. In addition, the perturbation has decreased somewhat, especially early in the run, and leveled off roughly near 1.5. The population of selected parents has also converged more rapidly, and on a smaller volume than with the Pitt crossover operator.

Figure 10 shows a comparison of the single parent heritability measures $(\mathrm{m}(\mathbf{G'P^{-1}}))$ of the two operators. Whiskers are plotted showing the confidence intervals of these curves. The condition space crossover has a significantly higher heritability than the Pitt 2-point operator.

To give the operators a proper test, we used the 50 point test function described in section 5.2.2. We compared both operators using EAs that both had population size of 100, Gaussian mutation with $\sigma = 0.01$, parsimony penalty = 0.01, and individuals initialized with 50 rules each, instead of the normal 10. The best-so-far training results (Figure 8) and testing results (Figure 9) show that our new operator significantly outperforms the Pitt 2-point crossover. The increase in heritability and decrease in perturbation seems to have provided a more appropriate balance for achieving an effective search.

6. CONCLUSIONS

We have demonstrated that multivariate quantitative genetics theory can provide a framework for practitioners to answer questions about their algorithms, even when specific theories do not yet exist. Much of the effort in using this approach will be expended on developing an appropriate set of quantitative traits. For the practitioner though, this is a much less daunting task than developing new theory to address their problems. And as we saw in our example, even a subset of traits can yield the information necessary to make a diagnosis.

There are a number of steps we are taking at this point. With this successful proof of principle on rule representations/operators, we are now applying this approach to a second difficult representation/operator issue, finite state automata, to show its generality. We are also developing

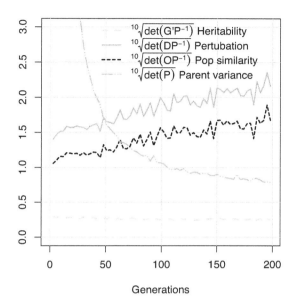

Figure 6: Pitt 2-point crossover on the function approximation problem shown in figure 4. A plot of $m(G'P^{-1})$, $m(DP^{-1})$, $m(OP^{-1})$ and $\sqrt[10]{\det(P)}$, averaged over 30 runs. Gaussian mutation was also used, but it's effects are not measured here.

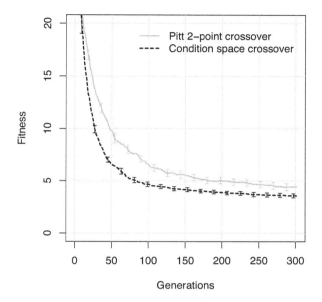

Figure 8: Average Best-so-far plot of training results.

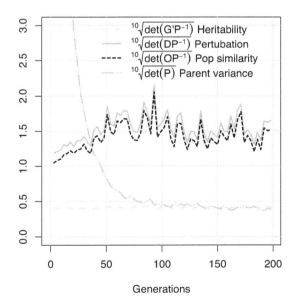

Figure 7: Condition space crossover on the function approximation problem shown in figure 4. A plot of $m(G'P^{-1})$, $m(DP^{-1})$, $m(OP^{-1})$ and $\sqrt[10]{\det(P)}$, Gaussian mutation was also used, but it's effects are not measured here.

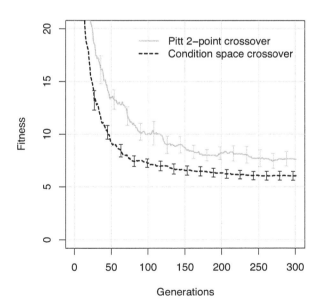

Figure 9: Plot of average test set results on best-so-far.

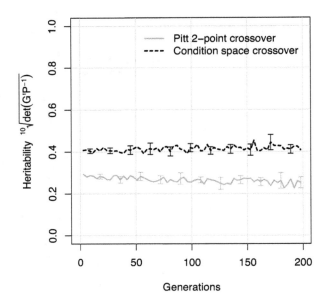

Figure 10: A comparison of the heritability of both Pitt approach crossover operators.

a covariance matrix similarity metric that addresses some of the short-comings of the one presented here.

7. REFERENCES

[1] L. Altenberg. The schema theorem and Price's theorem. In L. D. Whitley and M. D. Vose, editors, *Foundations of Genetic Algorithms III*, pages 23–49, San Francisco, CA, 1995. Morgan Kaufmann.

[2] S. J. Arnold. Multivariate inheritance and evolution: a review of concepts. *Quantitative Genetic Studies of Behavioral Evolution*, pages 17–48, 1994.

[3] H. Asoh and H. Mühlenbein. Estimating the heritability by decomposing the genetic variance. In Y. Davidor, H.-P. Schwefel, and R. Männer, editors, *Parallel Problem Solving from Nature – PPSN III*, pages 98–107, Berlin, 1994. Springer. Lecture Notes in Computer Science 866.

[4] J. K. Bassett, M. A. Potter, and K. A. De Jong. Looking under the EA hood with Price's equation. In K. Deb, R. Poli, W. Banzhaf, H.-G. Beyer, E. Burke, P. Darwen, D. Dasgupta, D. Floreano, J. Foster, M. Harman, O. Holland, P. L. Lanzi, L. Spector, A. Tettamanzi, D. Thierens, and A. Tyrrell, editors, *Genetic and Evolutionary Computation – GECCO-2004, Part I*, volume 3102 of *Lecture Notes in Computer Science*, pages 914–922, Seattle, WA, USA, 26-30 June 2004. Springer-Verlag.

[5] J. K. Bassett, M. A. Potter, and K. A. De Jong. Applying Price's equation to survival selection. In H.-G. Beyer, U.-M. O'Reilly, D. V. Arnold, W. Banzhaf, C. Blum, E. W. Bonabeau, E. Cantu-Paz, D. Dasgupta, K. Deb, J. A. Foster, E. D. de Jong, H. Lipson, X. Llora, S. Mancoridis, M. Pelikan, G. R.

Raidl, T. Soule, A. M. Tyrrell, J.-P. Watson, and E. Zitzler, editors, *GECCO 2005: Proceedings of the 2005 Conference on Genetic and Evolutionary Computation*, volume 2, pages 1371–1378, Washington DC, USA, 25-29 June 2005. ACM Press.

[6] D. S. Falconer and T. F. C. Mackay. *Introduction to quantitative genetics*. Longman New York, 1981.

[7] B. Flury. *Common Principal Components and Related Multivariate Models*. Wiley series in probability and mathematical statistics. Wiley, New York, 1988.

[8] E. T. Game and M. J. Caley. The stability of P in coral reef fishes. *Evolution*, 60(4):814–823, 2006.

[9] T. Jones and S. Forrest. Fitness distance correlation as a measure of problem difficulty for genetic algorithms. In L. Eshelman, editor, *Proc. of the Sixth Int. Conf. on Genetic Algorithms*, pages 184–192, San Francisco, CA, 1995. Morgan Kaufmann.

[10] R. Lande. Quantitative genetic analysis of multivariate evolution, applied to brain: Body size allometry. *Evolution*, 33(1):402–416, Mar. 1979.

[11] R. Lande and S. J. Arnold. The measurement of selection on correlated characters. *Evolution*, 37(6):1210–1226, Nov. 1983.

[12] W. B. Langdon. *Genetic Programming and Data Structures: Genetic Programming + Data Structures = Automatic Programming!* The Kluwer international series in engineering and computer science. Kluwer Academic Publishers, Boston, 1998.

[13] B. Manderick, M. de Weger, and P. Spiessens. The genetic algorithm and the structure of the fitness landscape. In R. K. Belew and L. B. Booker, editors, *Proc. of the Fourth Int. Conf. on Genetic Algorithms*, pages 143–150, San Mateo, CA, 1991. Morgan Kaufmann.

[14] H. Mühlenbein, J. Bendisch, and H.-M. Voigt. From recombination of genes to the estimation of distributions: II. continuous parameters. In H.-M. Voigt, W. Ebeling, I. Rechenberg, and H.-P. Schwefel, editors, *Parallel Problem Solving from Nature – PPSN IV*, pages 188–197, Berlin, 1996. Springer.

[15] H. Mühlenbein and G. Paaß. From recombination of genes to the estimation of distributions: I. Binary parameters. In H.-M. Voigt, W. Ebeling, I. Rechenberg, and H.-P. Schwefel, editors, *Parallel Problem Solving from Nature – PPSN IV*, pages 178–187, Berlin, 1996. Springer.

[16] H. Mühlenbein and D. Schlierkamp-Voosen. Predictive models for the breeder genetic algorithm: I. continuous parameter optimization. *Evolutionary Computation*, 1(1):25–49, 1993.

[17] M. A. Potter, J. K. Bassett, and K. A. De Jong. Visualizing evolvability with Price's equation. In R. Sarker, R. Reynolds, H. Abbass, K. C. Tan, B. McKay, D. Essam, and T. Gedeon, editors, *Proceedings of the 2003 Congress on Evolutionary Computation CEC2003*, pages 2785–2790, Canberra, 8-12 Dec. 2003. IEEE Press.

[18] G. Price. Fisher's 'fundamental theorem' made clear. *Annals of Human Genetics*, 36(2):129–140, 1972.

[19] G. R. Price. Selection and covariance. *Nature*, 227:520–521, Aug. 1970.

[20] S. H. Rice. *Evolutionary Theory: Mathematical and*

Conceptual Foundations. Sinauer Associates, Inc., 2004.

[21] J. Schäfer and K. Strimmer. A shrinkage approach to large-scale covariance matrix estimation and implications for functional genomics. *Statistical Applications in Genetics and Molecular Biology*, 4(1):1175, 2005.

[22] P. F. Stadler. Correlation in landscapes of combinatorial optimization problems. *Europhys. Lett.*, 20:479–482, 1992.

[23] E. Weinberger. Correlated and uncorrelated fitness landscapes and how to tell the difference. *Biological Cybernetics*, 63(5):325–336, 1990.

[24] B. Yuan and M. Gallagher. Experimental results for the special session on real-parameter optimization at CEC 2005: a simple, continuous EDA. In D. Corne, Z. Michalewicz, B. McKay, G. Eiben, D. Fogel, C. Fonseca, G. Greenwood, G. Raidl, K. C. Tan, and A. Zalzala, editors, *Proceedings of the 2005 IEEE Congress on Evolutionary Computation*, volume 2, pages 1792–1799, Edinburgh, Scotland, UK, 2-5 Sept. 2005. IEEE Press.

[25] B. Yuan and M. Gallagher. A mathematical modelling technique for the analysis of the dynamics of a simple continuous EDA. In G. G. Yen, S. M. Lucas, G. Fogel, G. Kendall, R. Salomon, B.-T. Zhang, C. A. C. Coello, and T. P. Runarsson, editors, *Proceedings of the 2006 IEEE Congress on Evolutionary Computation*, pages 1585–1591, Vancouver, BC, Canada, 16-21 July 2006. IEEE Press.

Towards the Geometry of Estimation of Distribution Algorithms based on the Exponential Family

Luigi Malagò
Politecnico di Milano
Via Ponzio, 34/5
20133 Milano, Italy
malago@elet.polimi.it

Matteo Matteucci
Politecnico di Milano
Via Ponzio, 34/5
20133 Milano, Italy
matteucci@elet.polimi.it

Giovanni Pistone
Collegio Carlo Alberto
Via Real Collegio, 30
10024 Moncalieri, Italy
giovanni.pistone@gmail.com

ABSTRACT

In this paper we present a geometrical framework for the analysis of Estimation of Distribution Algorithms (EDAs) based on the exponential family. From a theoretical point of view, an EDA can be modeled as a sequence of densities in a statistical model that converges towards distributions with reduced support. Under this framework, at each iteration the empirical mean of the fitness function decreases in probability, until convergence of the population. This is the context of stochastic relaxation, i.e., the idea of looking for the minima of a function by minimizing its expected value over a set of probability densities. Our main interest is in the study of the gradient of the expected value of the function to be minimized, and in particular on how its landscape changes according to the fitness function and the statistical model used in the relaxation. After introducing some properties of the exponential family, such as the description of its topological closure and of its tangent space, we provide a characterization of the stationary points of the relaxed problem, together with a study of the minimizing sequences with reduced support. The analysis developed in the paper aims to provide a theoretical understanding of the behavior of EDAs, and in particular their ability to converge to the global minimum of the fitness function. The theoretical results of this paper, beside providing a formal framework for the analysis of EDAs, lead to the definition of a new class algorithms for binary functions optimization based on Stochastic Natural Gradient Descent (SNGD), where the estimation of the parameters of the distribution is replaced by the direct update of the model parameters by estimating the natural gradient of the expected value of the fitness function.

Categories and Subject Descriptors

G.1.6 [**Mathematics of Computing**]: Optimization — *Stochastic programming*; G.3 [**Mathematics of Computing**]: Probabilistic algorithms (including Monte Carlo)

General Terms

Theory, Algorithms

Keywords

Estimation of Distribution Algorithms, Stochastic Natural Gradient Descent, Exponential Family, Stochastic Relaxation

1. INTRODUCTION

Estimation of Distribution Algorithms (EDAs) [23] are a family of algorithms for black-box optimization, often presented in the literature as an evolution of Genetic Algorithms (GAs), where the variational operators of crossover and mutation are replaced by statistical operators. Given a statistical model, either fixed a priori or learned at runtime, at each iteration an EDA evolves a population of feasible solutions to an optimization problem by performing selection with respect to the fitness of the individuals in the population (the sample), estimating the parameters of a distribution given the selected individuals (the observations), and sampling new candidate solutions (the offsprings).

From a theoretical point of view, an EDA can be modeled as a Markov chain defined over the distributions of a statistical model [18, Chapter 6], indeed each run of the algorithm describes a random sequence of densities that converges towards distributions with reduced support. At each iteration of the algorithm the empirical mean of the fitness function with respect to the population decreases in probability, until convergence, for this reason it becomes of interest to evaluate the gradient of the expected value of the function to be minimized with respect to the parameters that identify a density in the model, and in particular to study how the gradient field changes according to the function and the statistical model used in the relaxation.

In this paper we propose a geometric framework for the theoretical study of optimization algorithms that employ statistical models coming from the exponential family. In the Evolutionary Computation (EC) literature, we focus on EDAs based on the exponential family, and, in particular, on those algorithms that use statistical models that can be represented with undirected graphical models, such as Markov Random Fields, Markov Networks, and log-linear models. Examples of algorithms that belong to this class are FDA [29], MN-FDA [38], MN-EDA [39], and DEUM [41].

If we only consider strictly positive densities, i.e., distributions with full support where all probabilities are positive, or in other words we limit the analysis to the interior of the model used by an EDA, other algorithms that do not explicitly use the exponential family fit this geometric framework. This is the case of all EDAs based on the independence model, such as PBIL [6], UMDA [30], and cGA [20], and on the marginal product model of ECGA [19], which employs a factorization of the joint probability distribution based on the product of the joint distributions defined over the elements of a partition of the original set of variables. Moreover, if we consider the equivalence between Directed Acyclic Graphs (DAGs) and undirected graphical models [25], it is possible to represent the set of densities that factorize according to the DAG with an equivalent MRF. This is always the case for EDAs with bivariate models, such as MIMIC [13], COMIT [7], and BMDA [32], and easily applies to the Bayesian Networks used in BOA [31] and EBNA [14], when the undirected graph obtained by making all edges undirected is already moralized, i.e., all nodes that have a common child are connected [25].

Besides any algorithm whose dynamic is forced over a statistical model, population based algorithms can also be represented as a sequence of points within the probability simplex, by representing populations with densities, for example with maximum likelihood estimators. For instance, this is the approach developed by Vose in [44] for the study of the dynamics of Genetic Algorithms (GAs). From this perspective it is possible to compare the behavior of different algorithms, for example in case of small instances, by comparing the sequences of densities generated by each run.

The idea of finding the minimum of a function by employing a statistical model is well known in the combinatorial optimization literature. Among the others we mention the use of the Gibbs distribution in optimization by Simulated Annealing [22] and the use of Markov Random Fields in Boltzmann Machines [1]. An approach which is quite similar to EDAs, but has been developed independently, appears in the stochastic optimization literature under the name of Cross-Entropy method [37]. In [47], the authors describe some of these meta-heuristics as model-based search, to emphasize the use of a probabilistic models able to capture the interactions among the variables that appear in the fitness function.

The framework we propose is rather general and it can be also applied to the class of algorithms and techniques from integer and combinatorial optimization, whenever the original minimization problem is, implicitly or not, replaced by a new one, where the new variables are the parameters that identify a distribution in a statistical model. We refer to this approach to optimization as *stochastic relaxation*, i.e., to look for the minima of a function by minimizing its expected value over a set of probability densities in a statistical model. The name comes from the highly cited paper [16], where the authors describe an algorithm for image restoration based on the Gibbs distribution and an annealing scheme.

The Gibbs distribution belongs to the the exponential family and appears to be a common statistical model in combinatorial optimization. More recently, it has been explicitly analyzed in the context of EDAs, see for example [27, 28], where the authors discuss BEDA, an algorithms with nice theoretical properties, able to converge to the global minima of the fitness function, but that unfortunately cannot be used in practice due its computational complexity. We start with the discussion of this example, since most of re-

sults in the next sections aim to generalize such analysis to the exponential family.

EXAMPLE (GIBBS DISTRIBUTION) Let $f(x) \geq 0$ be a nonconstant function defined over a finite set $\mathcal{X}$, such that $f(x) = 0$ for some values in the domain. In order to find the minimum of f, we introduce the statistical model

$$p(x; \beta) = \frac{e^{-\beta f(x)}}{Z(\beta)}, \quad \beta > 0, \quad \text{with} \quad Z(\beta) = \sum_{x \in \mathcal{X}} e^{-\beta f(x)}.$$
$$(1)$$

In the statistical physics literature Equation (1) is know as *Gibbs (or Boltzmann) distribution*, $f(x)$ is usually called *energy function*, the parameter β the *inverse temperature*, and $Z(\beta)$ the *partition function*. The Gibbs model is not closed in the topological sense, indeed it does not include the limit distributions for β that tends to 0 and to $+\infty$, see for example [21]. As $\beta \to 0$, $p(x; \beta)$ tends to the uniform distribution over $\mathcal{X}$, since $\lim_{\beta \to 0} e^{-\beta f(x)} = 1$. On the other side as $\beta \to +\infty$ we have that $\lim_{\beta \to +\infty} e^{-\beta f(x)} = 1$ if $f(x) = 0$, and 0 otherwise, that is, the Gibbs distribution converges to the uniform distribution defined over the reduced support with zero (minimal) energy. Moreover we have $\nabla \mathbb{E}_\beta[f] = -\text{Var}_\beta[f]$, i.e., the derivative of the expected value of the energy function with respect to the β parameter is always negative, so that the expected value decreases monotonically to its minimum value as $\beta \to +\infty$.

The assumption on the non negativity of the energy function can be easily removed, and the Gibbs distribution is in principle a good candidate model for the stochastic relaxation, since it admits as limit a global optimum for the original optimization problem. However, the use of the Gibbs distribution poses some practical problems, since it requires an explicit formula for the fitness function, which may not be available in black-box contexts, and an efficient way to compute the partition function, which involves a sum over the entire sample space. To overcome these limitations, different approaches have been proposed in the literature, for example one possibility is to choose larger models such that the joint probability distribution could be factorized in a convenient and computationally tractable way, see for instance FDA [29].

We are interested in studying how difficult it is for an EDA to find the global minimum of the problem, by studying how the landscape of the expected value of the fitness function changes according to the choice of the model in the stochastic relaxation. In order to answer these questions, when the statistical model belongs to the exponential family, we propose to study the gradient of the expected value of the fitness function, as we did for the Gibbs distribution. We base our analysis on the assumption that the greater the number of local minima, the lower the probability to find the global minimum for an EDA, and similarly, for different algorithms that can be described within the stochastic relaxation framework.

The paper is organized as follows. In Section 2 we introduce the notation used in the remaining part of the paper, and we formally describe the approach to optimization based on stochastic relaxation. In Section 3 we review and generalize some properties of the exponential family, together with other results, such as the characterization of its topological closure and of is tangent space, that make this family of statistical models particular suited in the context of the stochastic relaxation. Next, in Section 4 we describe the stochastic relaxation of a function based on the exponential family as the general framework for the study of different algorithms and meta-heuristics in optimization that make use of these probabilistic models. In particular we provide a characterization of the stationary points of the relaxed problem, together with a study of the minimizing sequences with reduced support. The analysis developed in the paper aims at providing a better understanding of the behavior of different EDAs, and in particular their ability to converge to the global minimum of the fitness function. Nevertheless, the theoretical results we present in this paper lead to the definition of a new class of algorithms for binary functions optimization based on stochastic natural gradient descent, described in Section 5, for which we provide preliminary experimental results.

2. STOCHASTIC RELAXATION

In this section we introduce the notation what will be used in the rest of the paper, together with the formalization of stochastic relaxation in the context of optimization. We concentrate on the optimization of functions defined over binary variables, even if the generalization to the case of a finite set is straightforward. Such class of functions is known in mathematical programming literature as pseudo-Boolean functions [9] to underline that they take values over the real numbers, rather then in $0/1$.

A pseudo-Boolean function is a real-valued function defined over a vector of binary variables. These functions appear in many different fields and they are well studied in integer programming and in combinatorial optimization. The optimization of this class of functions is of particular interest, since it is NP-hard in the general formulation [46], and no exact polynomial-time algorithm is available in the literature. Often, pseudo-Boolean function optimization is referred also as *binary optimization* or *0/1 programming*.

In the following we introduce, for later convenience, an harmonic encoding based on the discrete Fourier transform instead of the standard $0/1$ encoding for binary variables, i.e., we map $y = \{0, 1\}$ to $x = (-1)^y$, so that $-1^0 = +1$, and $-1^1 = -1$. We introduce the set of indices $L = \{0, 1\}^n$, and we denote with $\Omega = \{+1, -1\}^n$ the search space, such that an individual (a point) $x = (x_1, \ldots, x_n) \in \Omega$ is a vector of binary variables. To provide a more compact notation we introduce a multi-index notation, i.e., let $\alpha = (\alpha_1, \ldots, \alpha_k)$ be a vector of non negative integers, we define $\|\alpha\| = \alpha_1 + \cdots + \alpha_k, \|\alpha\|_\infty = \max\{\alpha_1, \ldots, \alpha_k\}, \alpha! = \alpha_1! \cdots \alpha_k!$, and $y^\alpha = y_1^{\alpha_1} \cdots y_k^{\alpha_k}$. A pseudo-Boolean function $f : \Omega \to \mathbb{R}$ has a unique representation given by the square-free polynomial

$$f(x) = \sum_{\alpha \in I} c_\alpha x^\alpha, \qquad (2)$$

where $\alpha \in I \subset L$, since $x_i^2 = 1$. Any pseudo-Boolean function thus can be uniquely determined by a set I of exponents of the monomials, and the corresponding vector of real coefficients c. Each index α in I represents an α-*monomial interaction* among the variables of order equal to the degree of x^α. By Equation (2) we have that pseudo-Boolean functions belong to the broader class of Additively Decomposable Functions (ADF) [42], i.e., they can be expressed as the sum of more elementary functions given by the monomial interactions.

We can extend the multi-index notation to the random vector X, and denote with $\mathbb{E}_0[\cdot]$ the expected value with respect to the uniform distribution. As a consequence of the non standard harmonic encoding we introduced, $\{X^\alpha\}_{\alpha \in L}$ forms an orthonormal basis for the space of pseudo-Boolean functions with respect to the inner product $\langle f, g \rangle = \mathbb{E}_0[fg]$, as stated in the following proposition.

PROPOSITION 1. *Let* $\alpha, \beta \in L$, $\mathbb{E}_0[X^\alpha X^\beta] = 1$ *if and only if* $\alpha = \beta$, 0 *otherwise.*

To introduce the notion of stochastic relaxation, we need to define probability distributions over the elements of the sample space Ω. Let $X_i : \Omega \to \{+1, -1\}$ represent the i-th component x_i of x. From a probabilistic point of view, each X_i is a random variable and $X = (X_1, \ldots, X_n)$ a random vector defined over the observation space Ω. A probability distribution is a probability measure $\mathbb{P}$ over Ω and, since it is discrete, it corresponds to the probability density function of X, $p(x) = \mathbb{P}(X = x)$, that describes the density of probability for each x. We denote with $\mathcal{S}$ the set of all possible probability distributions for X, i.e., all $p(x) : \Omega \to [0, 1]$, such that $p(x) \geq 0$ for all $x \in \Omega$ and $\sum_{x \in \Omega} p(x) = 1$. A *statistical model* $\mathcal{M} \subset \mathcal{S}$ for X is a set of probability distributions, i.e., $\mathcal{M} = \{p(x)\}$. In case we deal with parametric statistical models, we write $\mathcal{M} = \{p(x; \xi)\} = \{p_\xi\}$, with $\xi \in \Xi$, to underline the dependence of p on the parameter vector ξ.[1]

Since we are interested in the limits of sequences of distributions in a model $\mathcal{M}$, we denote with $\overline{\mathcal{M}}$ its topological closure, i.e., the set of densities that are limit densities of sequences in $\mathcal{M}$ with respect to the weak topology, where, if $\{p_n\}_{n>1}$ and p are densities in $\mathcal{M}$, $\lim_{n \to \infty} p_n = p$ means $\lim_{n \to \infty} p_n(x) = p(x)$ for all $x \in \Omega$.

A natural parameterization for $\mathcal{S}$ is the vector of *raw parameters* or *raw probabilities* $\rho = (p_x)_{x \in \Omega}$, under which $\mathcal{S}$ coincides with the probability simplex Δ. Let $\mathcal{S}_>$ be the set of strictly positive distributions, i.e., all $p \in \mathcal{S}$ such that $p(x) > 0$ for all $x \in \Omega$. We define with $\text{Supp}\, p$ the *support* of a density p, i.e., the set of points in Ω with probability greater than zero. Densities in $\mathcal{S} \setminus \mathcal{S}_>$ have reduced support and lay on the faces of the probability simplex. In particular we denote with $\delta(x)$ the degenerate distribution where the support has cardinality 1 and coincides with x.

The combinatorial problem of finding the minimum of a non-constant pseudo-Boolean function f can be formalized as the unconstrained binary optimization problem

$$\text{(P)} \qquad \min_{x \in \Omega} f(x).$$

Let $\Omega^* \subset \Omega$ be the set of solutions of (P), with $\Omega^* \ni x^* = \operatorname*{argmin}_{x \in \Omega} f(x)$. We introduce the stochastic relaxation (R) of the original problem (P), by considering the functional $\mathbb{E}_p[f] : \mathcal{S}_\geq \to [\min f, \max f]$ and minimizing it over the set of all densities over Ω, i.e.,

$$\text{(R)} \qquad \min_{p \in \mathcal{S}} \mathbb{E}_p[f].$$

Let $S^* \ni p^*$ be a solution of (R), i.e., a probability density in the probability simplex. Once a proper parameterization

[1]For mathematical convenience, in the following we make some common regularity assumptions on $\mathcal{M}$, in particular we require that densities in the model change smoothly with the parameter vector ξ.

ξ that uniquely identifies densities in $\mathcal{S}$ is introduced, the relaxed optimization problem can be formulated as $\min_{\xi \in \Xi} \mathbb{E}_\xi[f]$.

The parameter vector ξ is the new vector of variables in (R), and since we restrict to continuous parameterizations, which is the case for a large class of models in statistics, both $\mathbb{E}_p[f]$ and (R) are continuous. Let Ξ^* the set of solutions $\xi^* = \operatorname*{argmin}_{\xi \in \Xi} \mathbb{E}_\xi[f]$ of (R), i.e., the set of parameters that identify distributions in Ω^*.

PROPOSITION 2. *Given the optimization problem* (P) *and the stochastic relaxation* (R)

(i) *they admit the same minimum, that is,* $\min_{x \in \Omega} f(x) = \min_{p \in \mathcal{S}} \mathbb{E}_p[f]$

(ii) *densities that are solutions to* (R) *have reduced support included in* Ω^*, *i.e.,* $\mathcal{S}^* \subset \mathcal{S} \setminus \mathcal{S}_>$

(iii) *they have equivalent solutions, i.e., a solution to either one determines a solution to both*

PROOF. A similar proposition appears in [24], where the approach to optimization based on stochastic relaxation is discussed in the more general setting of polynomial optimization. In particular, as to the equivalence of the solutions of (P) and (R), we remark that $\mathcal{S}^*$ can be obtained as the set of densities with support included in Ω^*, while solutions sampled from densities in $\mathcal{S}^*$ are in Ω^*. $\square$

The problems (P) and (R) have the same complexity which is exponential in n, indeed, even if under some parameterizations, such as the raw parameters, the relaxed function becomes linear in the new variables, on the other side in these cases the number of linear inequalities required to define the domain of the parameters is exponential in n. We are interested in constraining the densities used in the relaxation to a lower dimensional model which corresponds to a subset $\mathcal{M} \subset \mathcal{S}$ and study when (P) and the new optimization problem are equivalent.

DEFINITION 3. *The* stochastic relaxation *of* (P) *with respect to the statistical model* $\mathcal{M}$ *is defined as*

$$(\text{M}) \qquad \inf_{p \in \mathcal{M}} \mathbb{E}_p[f].$$

We take the infimum instead on the minimum, since in general $\mathcal{M}$ is not closed in the topological sense, and the minimum may not be attained. This is for example the case of the Gibbs distribution, discussed in Section 1 and in the conceptual algorithm BEDA, where the minimum is reached by the limit density when $\beta \to \infty$. Since for every $\mathcal{M} \ni p$, $\mathbb{E}_p[f]$ is lower-bounded by $\min f$, and $\mathcal{M}$ is closed in $\mathcal{S}$, a solution $p^* = \operatorname*{argmin}_{p \in \overline{\mathcal{M}}} \mathbb{E}_p[f]$ to (M) always exists. The problem of interest is under which conditions the minimum of (M) is equal to the minimum of (R), or equivalently of (P).

We now introduce a second example of a statistical model which plays an important role in optimization and in particular in the EDAs literature.

EXAMPLE (INDEPENDENCE MODEL) Let $\mathcal{S}_1$ be the *independence model* for X, that is, the set of densities that factorize as the product of the marginal probabilities, i.e,

$$p(x) = \prod_{i=1}^n p_i(x_i), \qquad (3)$$

where $p_i(x_i) = \mathbb{P}(X_i = x_i)$. A common parameterization for $\mathcal{S}_1$ is based on first order moments $\eta_\alpha = \mathbb{E}[X^\alpha]$, with $\|\alpha\| = 1$ (where on the left-hand side α appears as index for η), so that a density is uniquely identified by a vector η of n parameters called *expectation parameters*. The parameters are independent with respect to each other, and under the harmonic encoding their domain is $[-1, 1]$. In case of the usual $0/1$ encoding, the domain reduces to $[0, 1]$ and each parameter represents the marginal probability $\mathbb{P}(X_i = 1)$, cf. [3]. Under the expectation parameters, the independence model can be represented as an n-dimensional hypercube, where each of the 2^n vertices is one of the degenerate distributions $\delta(x)$. As a consequence the minimum of a stochastic relaxation based on $\mathcal{S}_1$ coincides with the minimum of (P). Moreover, since η is an n-dimensional vector, we can employ the multi-index notation, and write the expected value of f with respect to a density p in $\mathcal{S}_1$ as a pseudo-Boolean function itself, i.e.,

$$\mathbb{E}_\eta[f] = \sum_{\alpha \in I} c_\alpha \eta^\alpha. \qquad (4)$$

The independence model appears frequently in optimization in the context of stochastic relaxation. As far as EDAs are concerned, this is the case for all univariate EDAs, such as PBIL, UMDA, and cGA. These algorithms were the first to be proposed in the EDA literature. One of the reasons is that estimation and sampling with the independence model are computationally efficient, since they are linear operators in the number of variables. Unfortunately, the expected value of f under the η parameterization is a polynomial function defined over the hypercube $[-1, +1]^n$. The optimization of such class of functions is not trivial, and in the worst case it may admit an exponential number of local minima. By comparing Equation (2) and (4) we see that solving (M) corresponds to remove the integrality constraints over the binary variables, which is at the basis of rounding procedures and derandomization in pseudo-Boolean programing, e.g. [9].

We know that univariate EDAs are not well suited for the optimization of functions with higher-order interactions among variables, since they may get stuck in local minima, for this reason other algorithms that employ statistical models able to take into account such interactions have been proposed in the literature. In particular in this paper we are interested in models that come from the exponential family.

3. PROPERTIES OF THE EXPONENTIAL FAMILY

In the rest of the paper we will study the exponential family in the context of the stochastic relaxation. We introduce the k-dimensional exponential family $\mathcal{E}$

$$p(x; \theta) = \exp\left(\sum_{i=1}^k \theta_i T_i(x) - \psi(\theta) \right), \quad \theta \in \mathbb{R}^k, \qquad (5)$$

where the functions $T_1(x), \ldots, T_k(x)$ are the *canonical* or *sufficient statistics*, and $\psi(\theta)$ is the *cumulant generating function*. The parameters in θ are usually called *natural* or *canonical parameters* of the exponential family. Due to the exponential function, probabilities in the exponential family never vanish, so that only distributions with full support can be represented using this parameterization. As a consequence, statistical models that belong to the exponential family only include distributions in $\mathcal{S}_>$, i.e., points in the interior of the probability simplex.

The choice of such family is not too restrictive, since many models in statistics belong to the exponential family. Another advantage is the possibility to include in the model specific interactions among the variables, according to the choice of the sufficient statistics T_i. On the other hand, a limit is given by the fact that the exponential family includes only strictly positive distributions, differently from many models used in EDAs, for instance the independence model itself. In practice, this is not an issue, we sample finite populations and any limit distribution can be approximated with the desired precision with a sequence of distributions that converge in probability to the boundary of the model. On the other side, from a theoretical point of view it becomes important to characterize its topological closure and which distributions with reduced support may be obtained as limit of sequences of densities in the exponential family. Indeed if the model contains all degenerate distributions, the stochastic relaxation (M) and the original problem (P) have the same global minimum and thus equivalent solutions.

In the following we review some properties of the exponential family $\mathcal{E}$ and we introduce some generalizations of known results in the literature. In the first subsection we describe some known results that provide a characterization of the closure of the exponential family. These results are important to determine when the closure of the exponential family includes all degenerate distributions so that the minimum of f can be effectively determined. In the second subsection we describe some geometrical properties of the exponential family, according to the information geometry theory [4]. In particular, starting from a characterization of the tangent space of the exponential family, we provide a study of the gradient field associated to the expected value of a function defined over the sample space, in case it is finite. This analysis is important in order to study local minima of the stochastic relaxation based on the exponential family, as discussed in the next section.

Since these properties of the exponential family are general and apply not only when the sample space is Ω, we state the propositions and the theorems in case of a finite sample space $\mathcal{X} \ni x$. Similarly, limited to this section, we have $f : \mathcal{X} \to \mathbb{R}$. We refer to [8, 10] as monographs on exponential families.

3.1 Extended Exponential Family

The exponential family does not include densities with reduced support, and it is not closed in the topological sense, i.e., limit distributions are not included in the model. Nevertheless it is possible to characterize its closure by looking at the convex support [11, 10, 12], or marginal polytope [45, 34], of the exponential family. In the following, let $T(x) = (T_1(x), \ldots, T_k(x))$.

DEFINITION 4. *The* convex support *or* marginal polytope P *of the exponential family $\mathcal{E}$ is the convex hull of $T(\mathcal{X})$, i.e.,*

$$P = \left\{ \eta \in \mathbb{R}^k : \eta = \sum_{i=1}^k \lambda_i t_i, \lambda_i \geq 0, \sum_{i=1}^k \lambda_i = 1 \right\}$$

In order to state the theorems that provide a characterization of $\overline{\mathcal{E}}$ we introduce the following definitions.

DEFINITION 5.

(i) *A face F of the marginal polytope P is a subset $F \subset M$ such that there exists an affine mapping $A : \mathbb{R}^k \ni t \mapsto A(t) \in \mathbb{R}$ which is zero on F and strictly positive on $P \setminus F$*

(ii) *A subset $S \subset \mathcal{X}$ is exposed for the exponential family $\mathcal{E}$ if $S = T^{-1}(F)$ where F is a face of P.*

The closure of the exponential family $\mathcal{E}$, also known as *extended exponential family*, consists of the union of the exponential families with reduced support identified by the exposed face F of the polytope P, as a consequence of the two following theorems. We omit the proofs that can be found in [26], cf. [8, 36].

THEOREM 6. *Let θ_n, $n = 1, 2, \ldots$, be a sequence of parameters in $\mathcal{E}$ such that for some $q \in \mathcal{S}$ $\lim_{t \to \infty} p(\cdot; \theta_t) = q$, i.e., q belongs to the extended exponential model*

(i) *If the support of q is full, then q belongs to the exponential model $\mathcal{E}$ for some parameter value $\theta = \lim_{t \to \infty} \theta_t$*

(ii) *If the support of q is defective, then the sequence θ_n is not convergent, $\text{Supp } q$ is an exposed subset of $\mathcal{X}$, and q belongs to the trace of the exponential model on the support*

THEOREM 7. *If q belongs to the trace of the exponential family $\mathcal{E}$ with respect to an exposed subset S, then q belongs to the extended exponential family.*

In the choice of the model for an EDA, and more in general for any algorithm that fits the stochastic relaxation framework, you want to ensure that all degenerate distributions $\delta(x)$, with $x \in \mathcal{X}$, can be obtained as the limit of a sequence of distributions if $\mathcal{E}$, in other words by the previous theorems, that all points $T(x)$, with $x \in \mathcal{X}$, are exposed faces of P. This condition, which is satisfied by the independence model while not by the Gibbs distribution, as discussed in the previous examples, is sufficient but not necessary for the equivalence of (P) and (M). In the next section, see Theorem 13, we provide a sufficient condition for the equivalence of (P) and (M) for the exponential family in Equation (5), when the sample space is Ω, i.e., f is pseudo-Boolean.

The sequences of distributions in the exponential family that represent each run of an EDA are likely to converge in probability to densities with reduced support. Then, by Theorem 6 (ii), it follows that at least one of the natural parameters of the sequence will diverge to either $+\infty$ or $-\infty$. In case all θ parameters diverge, the population consists of individuals that are all equal.

3.2 Tangent Space and Gradient Vector

In our framework based on the stochastic relaxation of the original function, we introduced a new continuous optimization problem. Since in general the problem is nonlinear, we are interested in studying minimizing sequences of densities in the statistical model that converge in probability to a local minima of the stochastic relaxation. By studying the gradient vector, we determine at each point of the statistical model the direction of maximum decrement of the relaxed function. Such analysis is the starting point for determining the presence of local minima in the stochastic relaxation and thus to study the behavior of different algorithms, such as EDAs. Moreover, these results provide theoretical justification for the novel class of algorithms proposed in Section 5.

We now introduce a description of the exponential family, from a geometric point of view, presenting the approach described in [17, Part III and IV], which consists of a generalization to the non-parametric case of the information geometry theory presented in [4]. We provide an informal presentation, and we refer to the original papers for formal statements and proofs.

From a geometric point of view, a statistical model can be considered as a manifold of probability densities. In particular, the set of all strictly positive densities p, with respect to some reference measure μ, can be modeled as a differentiable manifold. A coordinate chart, or simply a chart, defines a local coordinate system at each point. In particular, we introduce a local chart in p, called *affine chart*, such that densities q are expressed with respect to the fixed reference measure p by $\frac{q}{p} - 1$. The affine chart has a dual chart, called *exponential chart* where densities q are expressed by $\log \frac{q}{p} - \mathbb{E}_p(\log \frac{q}{p})$. Here we only discuss the affine chart, even if the same results could be obtained using the exponential chart, since they are dually coupled [33]. We introduce a tangent bundle over the manifold, by defining at each p a tangent space T_p as the set of all random variables centered in p, i.e.,

$$\mathrm{T}_p = \{v : \mathbb{E}_p[v] = 0\}.$$

The tangent space T_p can be equivalently characterized as the set of tangent vectors to any curve that goes through p. Consider a curve $p(\theta)$ such that $p(0) = p$. It is easy to verify that $\frac{\dot{p}(\theta)}{p}$ for $\theta = 0$ belongs to T_p, since

$$\mathbb{E}_p\left[\left.\frac{\dot{p}(\theta)}{p}\right]\right|_{\theta=0} = \mathbb{E}_0[\dot{p}] = \frac{d}{d\theta}\mathbb{E}_0[p] = 0,$$

where $\mathbb{E}_0$ is the expected value with respect to the reference measure μ. We are interested in evaluating the tangent vector to the curve at any point, not only for $\theta = 0$, for this reason we require a moving coordinate system such that the reference measure p changes with θ and is equal to the point where the derivative is evaluated. As a consequence, the velocity vector along the curve corresponds to the logarithmic derivative $\frac{\dot{p}(\theta)}{p(\theta)} = \frac{d}{d\theta}\log p(\theta)$ and at each point belongs to the tangent space T_p.

The one dimensional exponential model

$$p(\theta) = e^{\theta T - \psi(\theta)}\mu \qquad (6)$$

can be represented as a curve in the manifold. By taking the logarithmic derivative, we obtain that the velocity vector of the curve corresponds to $T - \frac{d}{d\theta}\psi(\theta)$, which in turn is a vector in the tangent space expressed in the moving coordinate system. On the other side, given a vector field $U(p)$ defined at every point of the manifold, the vector in p belongs to T_p, so it must correspond to the tangent vector of some curve, i.e.,

$$\frac{d}{d\theta}\log p(\theta) = U(p).$$

We obtained a differential equation whose solution is a curve in the exponential model.

In case we deal with a finite sample space $\mathcal{X}$, the exponential family can be modeled as a finite dimensional manifold, where the natural parameters define a coordinate system for the manifold. In particular, it is possible to evaluate derivatives with respect to the natural parameters, and determine the direction of maximum decrement of a function defined over the manifold.

Let us start by introducing the definition of higher-order covariance between a set of random variables.

DEFINITION 8. *Let* $\overline{X}_i = X_i - \mathbb{E}_\theta[X_i]$. *The m-order covariance between m real valued-variables $X_1, \ldots, X_m$ is defined as*

$$\mathrm{Cov}_\theta(X_1, \ldots, X_m) = \mathbb{E}_\theta\left[\prod_{i=1}^m \overline{X}_i\right].$$

The previous formula generalizes the usual definition of covariance between two random variables. Some properties of the m-order covariance are proved in the appendix, in particular, see Proposition 15.

In the rest of the paper, to maintain a compact notation, we will write ∂_i for the partial derivative $\frac{\partial}{\partial \theta_i}$.

PROPOSITION 9. *Let* $f : \mathcal{X} \to \mathbb{R}$ *be a non-constant function and p_θ a density in $\mathcal{E}$*

(i) $\partial_i \mathbb{E}_\theta[f] = \mathrm{Cov}_\theta(f, T_i), i = 1, \ldots, k$

(ii) $\partial_i \partial_j \mathbb{E}_\theta[f] = \mathrm{Cov}_\theta(f, T_i, T_j), i, j = 1, \ldots, k$

(iii) *If all partial derivatives of $\mathbb{E}_\theta[f]$ up to order $m-2$ vanish at θ, then $\partial_{i_1} \cdots \partial_{i_m}\mathbb{E}_\theta[f] = \mathrm{Cov}_\theta(f, T_{i_1}, \ldots, T_{i_m})$ at θ, with $m > 2$*

(iv) *If all partial derivatives of $\mathbb{E}_\theta[f]$ up to order $m-1$ vanish at θ, then $\partial_{i_1} \cdots \partial_{i_m}\mathbb{E}_\theta[f] = \mathrm{Cov}_\theta(f, T_{i_i} \cdots T_{i_m})$ at θ, with $m > 1$*

REMARK First and second partial derivatives of $\mathbb{E}_\theta[f]$ can be expressed in terms of covariances between f and the sufficient statistics T_i's of the exponential family. For instance, the second-order Taylor expansion of $\mathbb{E}_\theta[f]$ in $\overline{\theta}$ reads

$$\mathbb{E}_\theta[f] = \mathbb{E}_{\overline{\theta}}[f] + \sum_{i=1}^k \mathrm{Cov}_{\overline{\theta}}(f, T_i)(\theta_i - \overline{\theta}_i)$$

$$+ \frac{1}{2}\sum_{i,j=1}^k \mathrm{Cov}_{\overline{\theta}}(f, T_i, T_j)(\theta_i - \overline{\theta}_i)(\theta_j - \overline{\theta}_j) + O(\|\theta\|^3).$$

By taking the logarithmic derivative of the exponential family $\mathcal{E}$ with respect to the natural parameters it is easy to verify that any tangent vector can be expressed as a linear combination of the centered statistics.

PROPOSITION 10. *The tangent space T_θ of the exponential family $\mathcal{E}$ at θ is spanned by the sufficient statistics centered in θ, i.e,*

$$\mathrm{T}_\theta = \left\{v : v = \sum_{i=1}^k v_i(T_i - \mathbb{E}[T_i]), v_i \in \mathbb{R}\right\}.$$

The direction v of maximum decrement of $\mathbb{E}_\theta[f]$ is the unit vector $v \in \mathrm{T}_\theta$ that maximizes the directional derivative of $\mathbb{E}_\theta[f]$.

PROPOSITION 11. *Let* $\mathrm{D}_v \mathbb{E}_\theta[f]$ *be the directional derivative of $\mathbb{E}_\theta[f]$ in the direction of the tangent vector $v \in \mathrm{T}_\theta$*

(i) $\mathrm{D}_v \mathbb{E}_\theta[f] = \mathrm{Cov}_\theta(f, v)$

(ii) If $f \in \mathrm{Span}\{T_1, \ldots, T_k\}$ the directional derivative is maximal when $v \propto f$

(iii) If $f \notin \mathrm{Span}\{T_1, \ldots, T_k\}$ then the directional derivative in maximal in the direction v given by the projection $\hat{f}_\theta$ of f onto T_θ, i.e.,

$$\hat{f} = \nabla \mathbb{E}_\theta[f] I(\theta)^{-1}(T - \mathbb{E}_\theta[T]) \qquad (7)$$

where $\nabla \mathbb{E}_\theta[f] = (\mathrm{Cov}_\theta(f, T_i))_{i=1}^k$ is the vector whose components are the partial derivatives $\partial_i \mathbb{E}_\theta[f]$, and $I(\theta) = [\mathrm{Cov}_\theta(T_i, T_j)]_{i,j=1}^k$ is the covariance matrix

PROOF.

(i) Let $v = (v_1, \ldots, v_k)$, we have

$$\mathrm{D}_v \mathbb{E}_\theta[f] = \sum_{i=1}^k v_i \partial_i \mathbb{E}_\theta[f] = \sum_{i=1}^k v_i \, \mathrm{Cov}_\theta(f, T_i)$$
$$= \mathrm{Cov}_\theta(f, v).$$

(ii) If f can be expressed as a linear combination of the sufficient statistics T_i's, by the Cauchy-Schwarz inequality we have

$$\|\mathrm{Cov}_\theta(f, v)\| \le \sqrt{\mathrm{Var}_\theta(f) \, \mathrm{Var}_\theta(v)},$$

which is maximum when $v \propto f$.

(iii) If f does not belong to the span of the T_i's, the direction of maximum decrement coincides with the orthogonal projection $\hat{f}_\theta$ of f onto the tangent space T_θ. Since $\hat{f}_\theta$ belongs to T_θ we have

$$\hat{f} = \sum_{i=1}^k \hat{a}_i (T_i - \mathbb{E}_\theta[T_i]). \qquad (8)$$

Moreover, in general the projection of f depends on θ, and to determine $\hat{f}_\theta$ we need to solve a system of linear equations. Since $f - \hat{f}_\theta$ is orthogonal to T_p, for every element of its basis T_i follows that

$$\mathbb{E}_\theta[(f - \hat{f}_\theta)(T - \mathbb{E}_\theta[T])] = \mathrm{Cov}_\theta(f - \hat{f}_\theta, T) = 0,$$

from which we obtain, for $i = 1, \ldots, k$,

$$\mathrm{Cov}_\theta(f, T_i) = \mathrm{Cov}_\theta(\hat{f}_\theta, T_i) = \sum_{j=1}^k \hat{a}_j \, \mathrm{Cov}_\theta(T_j, T_i).$$

As the Hessian matrix of $\psi(\theta)$ is invertible, we have

$$\hat{a} = \mathrm{Cov}_\theta(f, T)[\mathrm{Cov}_\theta(T_i, T_j)]^{-1} = \nabla \mathbb{E}_\theta[f] I(\theta)^{-1}.$$

The formula generalizes (ii), since in case f belongs to $\mathrm{Span}\{T_1, \ldots, T_k\}$, $\hat{a}$ correspond to the coefficients a of f, thus $\hat{f}_\theta = f$.

$\square$

The covariance matrix $I(\theta)$ is the Fisher information matrix and, from Equation (7), follows that the projection $\hat{f}_\theta$ of f over T_θ corresponds to the *natural gradient* $\tilde{\nabla} \mathbb{E}_\theta[f]$, i.e., the gradient of $\mathbb{E}_\theta[f]$ evaluated with respect to the Fisher information metric, cf. [15, 5].

THEOREM 12. *Let $f \in \mathrm{Span}\{T_1, \ldots, T_k\}$ and $q \in \mathcal{E}$, the one dimensional exponential family*

$$p(x; \theta) = \frac{q e^{\theta f}}{\mathbb{E}_q[e^{\theta f}]}, \quad \theta \in \mathbb{R} \qquad (9)$$

follows the direction of $\nabla \mathbb{E}_\theta[f]$, and $\lim_{\theta \to \infty} \mathbb{E}_\theta[f] = \min f$

PROOF. Consider the vector field defined over $\mathcal{E}$ that in each point associates the projection of f onto the tangent space T_p. From the definition of tangent vector as the velocity vector of a curve, see Equation (6), and the characterization of f as a linear combination of the centered sufficient statistics, see Equation (8), we have

$$\frac{\dot{p}}{p} = \frac{d}{dt} \sum_{i=1}^k \theta_i(t) T_i - \psi(\theta(t)) = \sum_{i=1}^k \dot{\theta}_i(t)(T_i - \mathbb{E}_{\theta(t)}[T_i])$$
$$= \sum_{i=1}^k \hat{a}_i(\theta(t))(T_i(x) - \mathbb{E}_{\theta(t)}[T_i]).$$

If the parameters θ are identifiable, i.e., if the centered sufficient statistics T_i are linearly independent, we obtain the following differential equation

$$\dot{\theta}(t) = \hat{a}(\theta(t)).$$

If the coefficients $\hat{a}_i$'s are constant, for instance if f belongs to the span of the T_i's, the vector field is constant and it corresponds to the centered random variable $f - \mathbb{E}_\theta[f]$. The differential equation reduces to

$$\frac{d}{d\theta} \log p(\theta) = f - \mathbb{E}_\theta[f].$$

Given an initial condition q, the differential equation admits as solution the one dimensional exponential family

$$p(\theta) = \frac{q e^{\theta f}}{\mathbb{E}_q[e^{\theta f}]}.$$

It is easy to show that independently from q, as θ goes to $-\infty$, the expected value of the limit converges to the minimum of f. On the order side, in case $\hat{f}_\theta$ changes with θ, we have

$$\frac{d}{d\theta} \log p(\theta) = \hat{f}_\theta - \mathbb{E}_\theta[\hat{f}_\theta]$$

that, differently from the previous case, does not admit an exponential model as solution. $\square$

The previous theorem generalize the example of the Gibbs distribution we discussed in Section 1. In particular, from Equation (9) the Gibbs distribution is obtained for $\theta < 0$, when q is the uniform distribution over the $\mathcal{X}$.

One of the most important consequences of the previous theorem, is that under a proper choice of the sufficient statistics of the exponential family, i.e., when the statistical model is able to take into account the interactions present in the functions to be minimized, there are no local minima in the stochastic relaxation where a local search techniques based on gradient descent may be trapped, indeed, from any distribution q in the model there exists a curve that follows that natural gradient $\tilde{\nabla} \mathbb{E}_\theta[f]$ that admits as limit the uniform distribution over the minima of f.

4. STOCHASTIC RELAXATION BASED ON THE EXPONENTIAL FAMILY

Given an exponential family $\mathcal{E}$, since the sample space is Ω, the sum of the sufficient statistics is a pseudo-Boolean function itself, and we have the following (exact) expansion of the log probabilities

$$\log p(x; \theta) = \sum_{\alpha \in L^*} \theta_\alpha x^\alpha - \psi(\theta), \qquad (10)$$

where $L^* = L \setminus \{0\}$. Statistical models of this form belong to the exponential family, they are known as (saturated) *log-linear models*, and are well studied in categorical data analysis for the analysis of contingency tables [2]. From Equation (10) it follows that, without loss of generality, we can consider exponential models where the sufficient statistics are α-monomials, i.e.,

$$p(x;\theta) = \exp\left(\sum_{\alpha \in M} \theta_\alpha x^\alpha - \psi(\theta)\right), \quad \theta_\alpha \in \mathbb{R}, \quad (11)$$

with $M \subset L^*$ and $\#(M) = k$. This allows to include in the model any order of interaction among the variables, by considering the proper monomial X^α among the set of sufficient statistics of the exponential family.

The following theorem provides a sufficient condition for the exponential family $\mathcal{E}$ such that (P) and (M) are equivalent.

THEOREM 13. *Given* (P) *and the stochastic relaxation* (M) *based on* $\mathcal{E}$, *if* $\{X_i\}_{i=1}^n \subset \{X^\alpha\}_{\alpha \in M}$ *there exists a sequence of distributions* $\{p(x;\theta_t)\}_{t\geq 1}$ *in* $\mathcal{E}$ *such that* $\lim_{t\to\infty} p(x;\theta_t) = q$ *and* $\mathbb{E}_q[f] = \min f$, *i.e.,* (P) *and* (M) *are equivalent*

PROOF. The exponential family includes only strictly positive distributions. Unless f is constant, the minimum is never attained, and at most $\min_{x\in\Omega} f(x) = \inf_{p\in\mathcal{M}} \mathbb{E}_p[f]$. By Theorem 7, we know that there exits a sequence in $\mathcal{E}$ that converges in probability to the $\delta(x^*)$ distribution if all points in Ω are exposed faces of the marginal polytope P. When the sufficient statistics coincide with the set of variables X_i, i.e., in the case of the independence model of Equation (3), P is the n-dimensional hypercube with vertices in Ω, where each of the 2^n vertices corresponds to a degenerate distributions $\delta(x)$. Since all monomials X^α are linearly independent and orthogonal, any marginal polytope generated by a subset of monomials that includes $\{X_i\}_{i=1}^n$ has the same number of vertices. In other words, since any X^α is a function of the X_i's, the new vertices are a lifting of the hypercube vertices, so they remain exposed. This implies, by Theorem 7, that there exists a sequence $\{p(x;\theta_t)\}_{t\geq 1}$ of densities in $\mathcal{E}$ such that $\lim_{t\to\infty} p(x;\theta_t) = \delta(x^*)$ and $\lim_{t\to\infty} \mathbb{E}_{\theta_t}[f] = \min f$. The convergence in probability ensures that when t is big enough, solutions to (P) can be sampled with probability as close as desired to 1 from distributions in such a sequence. $\square$

Sequences described in the previous theorem can be constructed in different ways. For instance, from a theoretical point of view, they could be obtained from a Gibbs distribution where the energy function admits x^* as minimum, but of course in practice we do not know it, unless we could efficiently use f as the energy function itself, as proposed in BEDA [28]. More in general EDAs try to generate sequences of this form, where the empirical mean of f with respect to the population decrease in probability from one iteration to the next, by iteratively selecting best individuals, learning a statistical model, estimating its parameters, and then sampling a new population. In Section 5 we propose a method to generate such sequences explicitly by estimating the natural gradient of f.

THEOREM 14. *Consider the stochastic relaxation* (M) *based on the exponential family* $\mathcal{E}$

(i) p_θ *in* $\mathcal{E}$ *is stationary if and only if* $\mathrm{Cov}_\theta(f, X^\alpha) = 0$ *for all* α *in* M

(ii) *if* f *can be expressed as a linear combination of the sufficient statistics of* $\mathcal{E}$

    1. $\nabla\mathbb{E}_\theta[f]$ *never vanishes*

    2. $\mathbb{E}_\eta[f]$ *is a linear function in the* η *parameters.*

(iii) *any stationary point of* $\mathbb{E}_\theta[f]$ *is a saddle point*

PROOF. (i) The result follows from Proposition 9.

(ii) We prove the result by contradiction. Suppose the gradient vanishes, i.e., $\mathrm{Cov}_\theta(f, X^\alpha) = 0$ for all α in M. Then we have

$$0 = \sum_{\alpha \in M} c_\alpha \mathrm{Cov}_\theta(f, X^\alpha) = \mathrm{Cov}_\theta(f, f - c_0) = \mathrm{Var}_\theta(f),$$

which leads to a contradiction unless f is constant.

(iii) In order to simplify the notation, we define an arbitrary total order of the sufficient statistic X^α of $\mathcal{E}$, and introduce the k-dimensional vectors $T = (X^\alpha)_{\alpha \in M}$ and $\theta = (\theta_\alpha)_{\alpha \in M}$. Let $\beta = (\beta_1, \ldots, \beta_k) \in N = \{0, 1\}^k$, the usual multi-index notation applies to the partial derivative operator D, such that $\mathrm{D}^\beta = \partial_1^{\beta_i} \ldots \partial_k^{\beta_k}$. Suppose $\bar{\theta}$ is a stationary point for $\mathbb{E}_\theta[f]$. In order to determine its nature we consider the Taylor series approximation evaluated in $\bar{\theta}$ and truncated at order m, i.e.,

$$\mathbb{E}_\theta[f] = \mathbb{E}_{\bar{\theta}}[f] + \sum_{\substack{\beta \in N: \\ \|\beta\| = m}} \binom{m}{\beta} \mathrm{D}^\beta \mathbb{E}_{\bar{\theta}}[f] \frac{(\theta - \bar{\theta})^\beta}{\beta!} + O(\|\theta\|^{m+1}),$$

where $m > 1$ is the smaller value such that at least one higher-order covariance of order m differs from zero. Under this hypothesis, when $m = 2$ by Proposition 9 (ii) we have that $\partial_i\partial_i\mathbb{E}_{\bar{\theta}}[f] = 0$, with $i = 1, \ldots, k$. Similarly, when $m > 2$ by applying Proposition 15 (iii) and (v), all non vanishing partial derivatives of order m have distinct indices. Finally by Proposition 9 (iv) follows that higher-order covariances reduce to covariances between two random variables, i.e.,

$$g(\theta) = \sum_{\substack{\beta \in N: \\ \|\beta\| = m}} \binom{m}{\beta} \mathrm{D}^\beta \mathbb{E}_{\bar{\theta}}[f] \frac{(\theta - \bar{\theta})^\beta}{\beta!}$$

$$= \sum_{\substack{\beta \in N: \|\beta\| = m \\ \|\beta\|_\infty = 1}} \binom{m}{\beta} \mathrm{Cov}_{\bar{\theta}}(f, T^\beta) \frac{(\theta - \bar{\theta})^\beta}{\beta!}.$$

Follows that g is a k-dimensional square-free homogeneous polynomial of degree m in θ, which is indefinite. Indeed in $\theta = \bar{\theta}$ the gradient vanishes and the Hessian matrix H has entries on the diagonal equal to zero. This implies that H has eigenvalues with different sign, since their sum must equal the trace of H, which is zero. Since H is not identically null, there must be at least a strictly positive and a strictly negative eigenvalue, so that the polynomial is indefinite. Follows that $\bar{\theta}$ is a saddle point. We conclude the proof by observing that under the hypothesis that all $\{X_i\}_{i=1}^n$ appear as sufficient statistics of the model, m must be less or equal to k. We prove that by contradiction. Suppose $m > k$, than we have

$$0 = \sum_{\alpha: \|\alpha\| \leq k} c_\alpha \mathrm{Cov}_\theta(f, T^\alpha) = \mathrm{Cov}_\theta(f, f - c_0) = \mathrm{Var}_\theta(f),$$

which leads to a contradiction unless f is constant. $\square$

The previous theorem, and in particular the statement that any critical point for the expected value of f is a saddle point, implies that a gradient descent heuristic will converge towards the boundary of the model, or in other words, that one of more of the θ parameters will diverge. In particular, if the model encodes the interactions of f, a local search method based on gradient descent can converge to the global optimum, independently on the starting point. Of course the evaluation of the exact gradient is not computationally feasible when n is large, thus in the next section we proposed a meta-heuristics based on stochastic natural gradient descent.

5. STOCHASTIC NATURAL GRADIENT DESCEND

By leveraging on the results presented in the previous sections, we propose an algorithm that updates explicitly the model parameters in the direction of the natural gradient of the expected value of f. This approach fits the framework of the stochastic relaxation, and the algorithm can be described as a sequence of points in a statistical model that converges towards the boundary of the model. Differently from most of the EDAs described in the literature, the parameters are not estimated from a selected population, rather what is estimated from the samples is the direction and the size the natural gradient.

From the analysis carried out in the previous section, the gradient of $\mathbb{E}_\theta[f]$ in the exponential family can be evaluated in terms of covariances, but since this evaluation requires a summation over the entire search space Ω, we replace the exact covariances with empirical covariances and estimate them from the current population. The basic iteration of an algorithm that belongs to the Stochastic Natural Gradient Descent (SNGD) meta-heuristic can be summarized in the following steps.

Algorithm 1: SNGD

1. Let $\mathcal{E}$ be an exponential model and $\mathcal{P}^0$ the initial population, set $t = 0$ and $\theta^t = 0$
2. Evaluate the fitness of $\mathcal{P}^0$
3. Evaluate the empirical covariances $\widehat{\mathrm{Cov}}(f, T_i)$ and $\widehat{\mathrm{Cov}}(T_i, T_j)$ from $\mathcal{P}^t$, and let $\tilde{\nabla}\hat{\mathbb{E}}[f] = \nabla\hat{\mathbb{E}}[f]\hat{I}^{-1}$
4. Update the parameters $\theta^{t+1} = \theta^t - \gamma\tilde{\nabla}\hat{\mathbb{E}}[f]$
5. Sample the population $\mathcal{P}^{t+1}$ from $p(x; \theta^{t+1}) \in \mathcal{E}$
6. Set $t = t + 1$
7. If termination conditions are not satisfied, GOTO 2.

The samples in $\mathcal{P}^0$ are usually generated randomly, but in case of prior knowledge about the function to be minimized, a non-uniform population can be employed. The parameters of the algorithm are the size of the population $\mathcal{P}^t$, and the step size γ, together with the number of iterations of the Gibbs sampler and the value of the initial temperature T. We included a vanilla version of the algorithm in Evoptool, an extensible toolkit for the implementation and evaluation of EC algorithms over a set of fixed benchmarks, available for download on the AIRWiki webpage, see [43].

We generated populations of different sizes, up to 150 times larger than n, and we set $\gamma = 1$, and the initial temper-

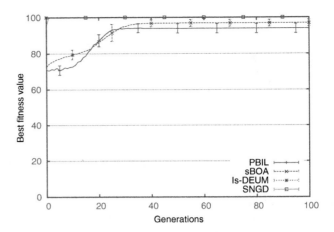

Figure 1: Experimental results over 30 runs for a set of 8x8 instances of a 2D Ising spin glass problems. Population size was set to 1024 for all algorithms. PBIL: learning rate = 0.99; sBOA truncation selection = 50%, elitism = 25%, maximum number of incoming edges = 4; Is-DEUM: Gibbs sampler cooling scheme $T = 1/(cr)$, c=0.0005, r=# of bit sampled; SNGD: Gibbs sampler iterations = 1, T=1, step size = 1.

ature $T = 1$. The value of the γ parameter much depends on the minimum and maximum value of the fitness function, that for these preliminary tests has been normalized between 0 and 100, in such a way that when the minimum of the benchmark problem is found, $f = 100$, on the other side, the maximum corresponds to $f = 0$. The choice of the value of the parameters comes from experimental evaluations, that we plan to extend and make more rigorous in the next implementations of the algorithm.

The advantage of such approach, compared to the single iteration of an EDA, is that the computation of the empirical covariances is relatively fast, since it is linear in the sample size, and quadratic in the number of parameters of the model. Other techniques, such as the solution of an overdetermined linear system via singular value decomposition, used to estimate the parameters of the model in DEUM, or for instance the calculation of maximum likelihood estimator, for the exponential family, are in general more computational expensive. As a drawback, in order to generate robust and accurate estimations of the covariances, this approach requires large populations.

We tested the algorithm to determine the ground states of a set of instances of a 2D Ising spin glass model, where the energy function is defined over a square lattice E of sites by

$$f(x) = -\sum_{i=1}^{n} c_i x_i - \sum_{i < j \in E} c_{ij} x_i x_j. \qquad (12)$$

The sufficient statistics of the exponential family $\mathcal{E}$ employed in the relaxation have been determined according to the lattice structure, in particular the have been chosen to match all the monomials in the expansion of f in Equation (12). We compared the performance of our algorithm with Is-DEUM [41], an implementation of DEUM specifically designed to solve spin glass problems, and with other two popu-

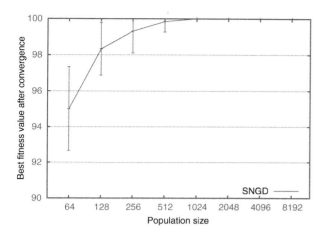

Figure 2: Experimental results over 30 runs for a set of 8x8 instances of a 2D Ising spin glass problems. SNGD: Gibbs sampler iterations = 1, $T = 1$, step size = 1.

lar EDAs, PBIL and sBOA. PBIL is a univariate EDA based on the independence model, while sBOA employs Bayesian Networks, estimated at each iteration form the selected population. We ran multiple instances of the algorithms, for different sizes of the lattice. Figure 1 shows the results of a set of experiments run over 8x8 instances randomly generated, where all algorithms employ the same population size. Preliminary results show that, similarly to Is-DEUM, our implementation of SNGD is able to find the ground state of the Ising spin glass after few generations.

The most critical parameter of the SNGD algorithm is the size of the population generated at each iteration by the Gibbs sampler. Clearly, the larger the sample size, the more accurate the predictions of the covariances are. Indeed, even if we are in the hypothesis of Theorem 12, so that there are no critical points in the model and there exists a unique basin of attraction, in case of small populations the algorithm may get trapped in local minima, since the closer to the boundary the distribution is, the smaller the variance of the sample. Figure 2 shows how the fitness of the best individual after convergence of the algorithm changes, for different values of the population size. In order to avoid premature convergence to non optimal solutions, the population size must be chosen according to both the problem size n and the number k of parameters of the model.

6. DISCUSSION AND FUTURE DIRECTIONS OF RESEARCH

In this paper we presented an approach to pseudo-Boolean optimization based on the idea of the stochastic relaxation. We introduced a parameterization based on the natural parameters of the exponential family and we discussed some properties of this family of statistical models. In particular we showed that the choice of a proper model in the relaxation becomes crucial to avoid the presence of critical points for the expected value of f. The analysis carried out in the paper leads to the definition of a class of algorithm based on stochastic natural gradient descent, called SNGD, where the gradient is estimated through the evaluation of empirical co-

variances. Preliminary experimental results are encouraging and compare favorably with other recent heuristics proposed in the literature.

We identified two promising directions of research. First, since we deal with a sample size that is much smaller than the cardinality of the sample space, the estimation of the co-variances is affected by large noise. For this reason it seems convenient to replace empirical covariance estimation with other techniques which proved to be able to provide more accurate estimation, such as shrinkage approach to large-scale covariance matrix estimation [40]. Such method offers robust estimation techniques with computational complexity which is often no more that twice that required for empirical covariance estimation.

Second, similarly to many multivariate EDAs, when the interactions of f are unknown, we can incorporate in the algorithm some model building techniques able to learn from the samples a set of statistically significant correlations between the variables in f. Often in many real world problems we deal with sparse functions, i.e., each variable interact with a restricted number of other variables, under this hypothesis, we propose to employ ℓ_1-regularized methods for high-dimensional model selection techniques [35].

The algorithm we proposed is highly parallelizable, both in the estimation of covariances and in the sampling step. The final aim is to develop an efficient and effective approach to adaptively solve very large pseudo-Boolean problems also in the black-box context for which the interaction structure among the variable is unknown.

7. REFERENCES

[1] E. Aarts and J. Korst. *Simulated annealing and Boltzmann machines: a stochastic approach to combinatorial optimization and neural computing.* John Wiley & Sons, Inc., New York, NY, USA, 1989.

[2] A. Agresti. *An Introduction to Categorical Data Analysis.* Wiley, New York, 1996.

[3] S. Amari. Information geometry on hierarchy of probability distributions. *IEEE Transactions on Information Theory*, 47(5):1701–1711, 2001.

[4] S. Amari and H. Nagaoka. *Methods of information geometry.* American Mathematical Society, Providence, RI, 2000. Translated from the 1993 Japanese original by Daishi Harada.

[5] S.-i. Amari. Natural gradient works efficiently in learning. *Neural Computation*, 10(2):251–276, 1998.

[6] S. Baluja. Population-Based Incremental Learning: A method for integrating genetic search based function optimization and competitive learning,. Technical Report CMU-CS-94-163, Pittsburgh, PA, 1994.

[7] S. Baluja and S. Davies. Using optimal dependency-trees for combinatorial optimization: Learning the structure of the search space. In *Proceedings of the 1997 International Conference on Machine Learning*, 1997.

[8] O. E. Barndorff-Nielsen. *Information and Exponential Families in Statistical Theory.* John Wiley & Sons, New York, 1978.

[9] E. Boros and P. L. Hammer. Pseudo-boolean optimization. *Discrete Applied Mathematics*, 123(1-3):155–225, 2002.

[10] L. D. Brown. *Fundamentals of Statistical Exponential*

Families with Applications in Statistical Decision Theory, volume 9 of *Lecture Notes - Monograph Series*. Institute of Mathematical Statistics, Hayward, California, 1986.

[11] N. N. Čentsov. *Statistical Decision Rules and Optimal Inference*. Number 53 in Translations of Mathematical Monographs. American Mathematical Society, Providence, Rhode Island, 1972. Translation 1982.

[12] I. Csiszár and F. Matúš. Closures of exponential families. *Ann. Probab.*, 33(2):582–600, 2005.

[13] J. S. De Bonet, C. L. Isbell, Jr., and P. Viola. MIMIC: Finding optima by estimating probability densities. In M. C. Mozer, M. I. Jordan, and T. Petsche, editors, *Advances in Neural Information Processing Systems*, volume 9, page 424. The MIT Press, 1997.

[14] R. Etxeberria and P. Larranaga. Global optimization with bayesian networks. In *Proceedings of the Second Symposium on Artificial Intelligence. Adaptive Systems (CIMAF 99)*, pages 332–339, Cuba, 1999.

[15] A. Fujiwara and S. Amari. Gradient systems in view of information geometry. *Physica D. Nonlinear Phenomena*, 80(3):317–327, 1995.

[16] S. Geman and D. Geman. Stochastic relaxation, Gibbs distributions, and the Bayesian restoration of images. *IEEE Transactions on PAMI*, 6(6):721 – 741, Nov 1984.

[17] P. Gibilisco, E. Riccomagno, M. P. Rogantin, and H. P. Wynn, editors. *Algebraic and Geometric Methods in Statistics*. Cambridge University Press, 2009.

[18] C. González, J. A. Lozano, and P. Larrañaga. Mathematical modeling of discrete estimation of distribution algorithms. In P. Larrañaga and J. A. Lozano, editors, *Estimation of Distribution Algoritms. A New Tool for evolutionary Computation*, number 2 in Genetic Algorithms and Evolutionary Computation, pages 147–163. Springer, 2001.

[19] G. R. Harik. Linkage learning via probabilistic modeling in ECGA. Technical Report IlliGAL Report No. 99010, University of Illinois at Urbana-Campaign, Urbana, IL, 1999.

[20] G. R. Harik, F. G. Lobo, and D. E. Goldberg. The Compact Genetic Algorithm. *IEEE Transactions on Evolutionary Computations*, 3(4):287–297, November 1999.

[21] C.-R. Hwang. Laplace's method revisited: Weak convergence of probability measures. *Annals of Probability*, 8(6):1177–1182, 1980.

[22] S. Kirkpatrick, C. D. Gelatt, and M. P. Vecchi. Optimization by simulated annealing. *Science*, 220, 4598:671–680, 1983.

[23] P. Larrañaga and J. A. Lozano, editors. *Estimation of Distribution Algoritms. A New Tool for evolutionary Computation*. Number 2 in Genetic Algorithms and Evolutionary Computation. Springer, 2001.

[24] J. B. Lasserre. Global optimization with polynomials and the problem of moments. *SIAM Journal on Optimization*, 11:796–817, 2001.

[25] S. L. Lauritzen. *Graphical models*. The Clarendon Press Oxford University Press, New York, 1996. Oxford Science Publications.

[26] L. Malagò and G. Pistone. A note on the border of an exponential family. SIS 2010, arXiv:1012.0637, 2010.

[27] H. Mühlenbein and T. Mahnig. Mathematical analysis of evolutionary algorithms. In *Essays and Surveys in Metaheuristics, Operations Research/Computer Science Interface Series*, pages 525–556. Kluwer Academic Publisher, 2002.

[28] H. Mühlenbein and T. Mahnig. Evolutionary algorithms and the Boltzmann distribution. In *Foundations of Genetic Algorithms 7*, pages 525–556. Morgan Kaufmann Publishers, 2003.

[29] H. Mühlenbein, T. Mahnig, and A. O. Rodriguez. Schemata, distributions and graphical models in evolutionary optimization. *Journal of Heuristics*, 5(2):215–247, 1999.

[30] H. Mühlenbein and G. Paaß. From recombination of genes to the estimation of distributions I. Binary parameters. In H.-M. Voigt, W. Ebeling, I. Rechenberger, and H.-P. Schwefel, editors, *Lecture Notes in Computer Science 1411: Parallel Problem Solving from Nature (PPSN IV)*, volume 1141 of *Lecture Notes in Computer Science*. Springer, 1996.

[31] M. Pelikan, D. E. Goldberg, and E. Cantú-Paz. BOA: The Bayesian Optimization Algorithm. In W. Banzhaf, J. Daida, A. E. Eiben, M. H. Garzon, V. Honavar, M. Jakiela, and R. E. Smith, editors, *Proceedings of the Genetic and Evolutionary Computation Conference GECCO-99*, volume I, pages 525–532, Orlando, FL, 13-17 1999. Morgan Kaufmann Publishers, San Fransisco, CA.

[32] M. Pelikan and H. Mühlenbein. The Bivariate Marginal Distribution Algorithm. In R. Roy, T. Furuhashi, and P. K. Chawdhry, editors, *Advances in Soft Computing - Engineering Design and Manufacturing*, pages 521–535, London, 1999. Springer-Verlag.

[33] G. Pistone. Algebraic varieties vs differentiable manifolds in statistical models. In P. Gibilisco, E. Riccomagno, M. P. Rogantin, and H. P. Wynn, editors, *Algebraic and Geometric Methods in Statistics*, chapter 21, pages 339–363. Cambridge University Press, 2009.

[34] J. Rauh, T. Kahle, and N. Ay. Support sets in exponential families and oriented matroid theory. Proc. of *WUPES'09*, submitted to IJAR, arXiv:0906.5462, 2009.

[35] P. Ravikumar, M. J. Wainwright, and J. D. Lafferty. High-dimensional Ising model selection using l_1-regularized logistic regression. *The Annals of Statistics*, 38(3):1287–1319, 2010.

[36] A. Rinaldo, S. E. Fienberg, and Y. Zhou. On the geometry of discrete exponential families with application to exponential random graph models. *Electronic Journal of Statistics*, 3:446–484, 2009.

[37] R. Y. Rubenstein and D. P. Kroese. *The Cross-Entropy method: a unified approach to combinatorial optimization, Monte-Carlo simluation, and machine learning*. Springer, New York, 2004.

[38] R. Santana. A Markov network based factorized distribution algorithm for optimization. In N. Lavrac, D. Gamberger, L. Todorovski, and H. Blockeel, editors, *Proceedings of the 14th European Conference*

on *Machine Learning (ECML-PKDD 2003)*, volume 2837, pages 337–348. Springer-Verlag, Dubrovnik, Croatia, 2003.

[39] R. Santana. Estimation of distribution algorithms with kikuchi approximations. *Evolutionary Computation*, 13(1):67–97, 2005.

[40] J. Schäfer and K. Strimmer. A shrinkage approach to large-scale covariance matrix estimation and implications for functional genomics. *Statistical applications in genetics and molecular biology*, 4(1), 2005.

[41] S. Shakya and J. McCall. Optimization by estimation of distribution with DEUM framework based on Markov random fields. *International Journal of Automation and Computing*, 4(3):262–272, 2007.

[42] R. K. Thompson and A. H. Wright. Additively decomposable fitness functions. Technical report, Dept. Comput. Sci., Univ. Montana, Missoula. MT, 1997.

[43] G. Valentini, L. Malagò, and M. Matteucci. Evoptool: an extensible toolkit for evolutionary optimization algorithms comparison. In *Proceedings of IEEE World Congress on Computational Intelligence*, pages 2475–2482, July 2010.

[44] M. D. Vose. *The Simple Genetic Algorithm: Foundations and Theory*. MIT Press, Cambridge, MA, USA, 1998.

[45] M. J. Wainwright and M. I. Jordan. Graphical models, exponential families, and variational inference. *Foundations and Trends in Machine Learning*, 1(1-2):1–305, 2008.

[46] L. A. Wolsey. *Integer Programming*. Wiley-Interscience, 1998.

[47] M. Zlochin, M. Birattari, N. Meuleau, and M. Dorigo. Model-based search for combinatorial optimization: A critical survey. *Annals of Operations Research*, 131(1-4):375–395, 2004.

APPENDIX

A. PROOFS

We first prove some properties for the m-order covariance.

PROPOSITION 15.

(i) $\mathrm{Cov}_\theta(T_1, T_2, T_3) = \mathrm{Cov}_\theta(T_1, \overline{T}_2\overline{T}_3)$

(ii) if $\mathrm{Cov}_\theta(T_1, T_2) = 0$ and $\mathrm{Cov}_\theta(T_1, T_3) = 0$, then $\mathrm{Cov}_\theta(T_1, T_2, T_3) = \mathrm{Cov}_\theta(T_1, T_2 T_3)$

(iii) $\mathrm{Cov}_\theta(T_1, T_2, T_2) = \mathrm{Cov}_\theta(T_1, T_2^2) - 2\mathbb{E}_\theta[T_2]\mathrm{Cov}_\theta(T_1, T_2)$

(iv) if $\mathrm{Cov}_\theta(T_1, \ldots, T_m) = 0$ and $\mathrm{Cov}_\theta(T_1, \ldots, T_{m-1}) = 0$, then $\mathbb{E}_\theta[\overline{T}_1 \cdots \overline{T}_{m-1}T_m] = 0$, with $m > 2$

(v) if $\mathrm{Cov}_\theta(T_1, \ldots, T_m) = 0$ and $\mathrm{Cov}_\theta(T_1, \ldots, T_{m-1}) = 0$, then $\mathrm{Cov}_\theta(T_1, \ldots, T_m, T_m) = \mathbb{E}_\theta[\overline{T}_1 \cdots \overline{T}_{m-1}T_m^2]$, with $m > 2$

PROOF

(i) $\mathrm{Cov}_\theta(T_1, T_2, T_3) = \mathbb{E}_\theta[(T_1 - \mathbb{E}_\theta[T_1])\overline{T}_2\overline{T}_3]$
$= \mathbb{E}_\theta[T_1\overline{T}_2\overline{T}_3] - \mathbb{E}_\theta[T_1]\mathbb{E}_\theta[\overline{T}_2\overline{T}_3] = \mathrm{Cov}_\theta(T_1, \overline{T}_2\overline{T}_3)$

(ii) $\mathrm{Cov}_\theta(T_1, T_2, T_3) = \mathbb{E}_\theta[\overline{T}_1\overline{T}_2(T_3 - \mathbb{E}_\theta[T_3])]$
$= \mathbb{E}_\theta[\overline{T}_1\overline{T}_2T_3] - \mathbb{E}_\theta[T_3]\mathrm{Cov}_\theta(T_1, T_2)$
$= \mathbb{E}_\theta[\overline{T}_1(T_2 - \mathbb{E}_\theta[T_2])T_3]$
$= \mathbb{E}_\theta[\overline{T}_1T_2T_3] - \mathbb{E}_\theta[T_2]\mathrm{Cov}_\theta(T_1, T_3)$
$= \mathrm{Cov}_\theta(T_1, T_2T_3)$

(iii) $\mathbb{E}_\theta[\overline{T}_1\overline{T}_2^2] = \mathbb{E}_\theta[\overline{T}_1(T_2 - \mathbb{E}_\theta[T_2])^2] = \mathbb{E}_\theta[\overline{T}_1T_2^2] +$
$- \mathbb{E}_\theta[\overline{T}_1]\mathbb{E}_\theta[T_2]^2 - 2\mathbb{E}_\theta[T_2]\mathbb{E}_\theta[\overline{T}_1T_2] =$
$= \mathrm{Cov}_\theta(T_1, T_2^2) - 2\mathbb{E}_\theta[T_2]\mathrm{Cov}_\theta(T_1, T_2)$

(iv) $\mathbb{E}_\theta[\overline{T}_1 \cdots \overline{T}_m] = \mathbb{E}_\theta[\overline{T}_1 \cdots \overline{T}_{m-1}T_m] +$
$- \mathbb{E}_\theta[T_m]\mathbb{E}_\theta[\overline{T}_1 \cdots \overline{T}_{m-1}]$,
from which it follows
$\mathbb{E}_\theta[\overline{T}_1 \cdots \overline{T}_{m-1}T_m] = 0$

(v) We apply *(iv)* and we obtain
$\mathbb{E}_\theta[\overline{T}_1 \cdots \overline{T}_m\overline{T}_m] = \mathbb{E}_\theta[\overline{T}_1 \cdots \overline{T}_{m-1}(T_m - \mathbb{E}_\theta[T_m])^2] =$
$= \mathbb{E}_\theta[\overline{T}_1 \cdots \overline{T}_{m-1}T_m^2] + \mathbb{E}_\theta[\overline{T}_1 \cdots \overline{T}_{m-1}]\mathbb{E}_\theta[T_m]^2 +$
$- 2\mathbb{E}_\theta[T_m]\mathbb{E}_\theta[\overline{T}_1 \cdots \overline{T}_{m-1}T_m]$
$= \mathbb{E}_\theta[\overline{T}_1 \cdots \overline{T}_{m-1}T_m^2]$

$\square$

The following proposition describes some properties of the exponential family, together with some generalizations to higher order partial derivatives.

PROPOSITION 16. *Let p_θ be a density in $\mathcal{E}$*

(i) $\partial_i\psi(\theta) = \mathbb{E}_\theta[T_i], i = 1, \ldots, k$

(ii) $\partial_i\partial_j\psi(\theta) = \mathrm{Cov}_\theta(T_i, T_j), i, j = 1, \ldots, k$

(iii) $\partial_i\partial_j\partial_k\psi(\theta) = \mathrm{Cov}_\theta(T_i, T_j, T_k), i, j, k = 1, \ldots, k$

(iv) *Let $i_1, \ldots, i_m$ be distinct indices in $1, \ldots, k$, if all partial derivatives of $\psi(\theta)$ up to order $m - 1$ vanish at θ, then $\partial\theta_{i_1} \cdots \partial_{i_m}\psi(\theta) = \mathrm{Cov}_\theta(T_{i_1}, \ldots, T_{i_m})$ at θ, with $m > 3$*

PROOF (i) and (ii) are well known results in the literature, see for example [10, Chapter 2]. As to (iii), we have

$\partial_i\partial_j\partial_k\psi(\theta) = \partial_k\mathrm{Cov}_\theta(T_i, T_j) = \partial_k(\mathbb{E}_\theta[T_iT_j] - \mathbb{E}_\theta[T_i]\mathbb{E}_\theta[T_j])$
$= \mathrm{Cov}_\theta(T_k, T_iT_j) - \mathbb{E}_\theta[T_j]\mathrm{Cov}_\theta(T_k, T_i) - \mathbb{E}_\theta[T_i]\mathrm{Cov}_\theta(T_k, T_j)$
$= \mathrm{Cov}_\theta(T_i, T_j, T_k)$

As to (iv), we notice that the derivative of the $(m-1)$-order covariance generates the m-order covariance and a sum of terms which are products of lower order covariances, i.e.,

$\partial_{i_m}\mathrm{Cov}_\theta(T_{i_1}, \ldots, T_{i_{m-1}}) = \partial_{i_m}\mathbb{E}_\theta[\overline{T}_{i_1} \cdots \overline{T}_{i_{m-1}}]$
$= \partial_{i_m}\mathbb{E}_0[\overline{T}_{i_1} \cdots \overline{T}_{i_{m-1}}p_\theta]$
$= \mathbb{E}_\theta[\overline{T}_{i_1} \cdots \overline{T}_{i_m}] + \mathbb{E}_\theta[\partial_{i_m}(\overline{T}_{i_1} \cdots \overline{T}_{i_{m-1}})]$
$= \mathrm{Cov}_\theta(T_{i_1}, \ldots, T_{i_m}) - \sum_{j=1}^{m-1} \mathrm{Cov}_\theta(T_{i_m}, T_{i_j})\mathbb{E}_\theta\left[\prod_{k=1, k\neq j}^{m-1} \overline{T}_{i_k}\right].$

Starting from $m = 4$, the derivative of $\psi(\theta)$ equals a sum of products of terms, that all vanish by hypothesis except for the 4th-order covariance. Similarly for higher order cases. $\square$

(i) $\partial_i \mathbb{E}_\theta[f] = \partial_i \mathbb{E}_0 \left[f \exp\left(\sum_{i=1}^k \theta_i T_i - \psi(\theta) \right) \right]$

$= \mathbb{E}_\theta \left[f \left(T_i - \partial_i \psi(\theta) \right) \right] = \mathbb{E}_\theta \left[f(T_i - \mathbb{E}_\theta[T_i]) \right] = \mathrm{Cov}_\theta(f, T_i)$

(ii) $\partial_i \partial_j \mathbb{E}_\theta[f] = \partial_j \mathbb{E}_\theta \left[f \left(T_i - \partial \theta_i \psi(\theta) \right) \right]$

$= \partial_j \mathbb{E}_0 \left[f \left(T_i - \partial_i \psi(\theta) \right) p_\theta \right]$

$= \mathbb{E}_\theta \left[f \left(T_i - \mathbb{E}_\theta[T_i] \right) \left(T_j - \mathbb{E}_\theta[T_j] \right) \right] - \mathbb{E}_\theta[f] \, \mathrm{Cov}_\theta(T_i, T_j)$

$= \mathbb{E}_\theta \left[f \overline{T}_i \overline{T}_j \right] - \mathbb{E}_\theta[f] \mathbb{E}_\theta[\overline{T}_i \overline{T}_j]$

$= \mathrm{Cov}_\theta(f, \overline{T}_i \overline{T}_j) = \mathrm{Cov}_\theta(f, T_i, T_j).$

(iii) The formula is true for $m = 3$, it is easy to show that

$\partial_i \partial_j \partial_k \mathbb{E}_\theta[f] = \partial_k \mathrm{Cov}_\theta(f, \overline{T_i T_j}) = \partial_k (\mathbb{E}_\theta[f \overline{T_i T_j}] - \mathbb{E}_\theta[f] \mathbb{E}_\theta[\overline{T_i T_j}])$

$= \partial_k (\mathrm{Cov}_\theta(f, T_i T_j) - \mathbb{E}_\theta[T_j] \mathrm{Cov}_\theta(f, T_i) - \mathbb{E}_\theta[T_i] \mathrm{Cov}_\theta(f, T_j))$

$= \mathrm{Cov}_\theta(f, T_i T_j, T_k) - \mathrm{Cov}_\theta(f, T_j) \mathrm{Cov}_\theta(T_k, T_i) +$

$- \mathbb{E}_\theta[T_i] \mathrm{Cov}_\theta(f, T_j, T_k) - \mathrm{Cov}_\theta(f, T_i) \mathrm{Cov}_\theta(T_k, T_j) +$

$- \mathbb{E}_\theta[T_j] \mathrm{Cov}_\theta(f, T_i, T_k)$

$= \mathrm{Cov}_\theta(f, T_i, T_j, T_k) - \mathrm{Cov}_\theta(f, T_k) \mathrm{Cov}_\theta(T_i, T_j) +$

$- \mathrm{Cov}_\theta(f, T_j) \mathrm{Cov}_\theta(T_k, T_i) - \mathrm{Cov}_\theta(f, T_i) \mathrm{Cov}_\theta(T_k, T_j)$

The derivative of the m-order covariance generates the $(m+1)$-order covariance and a sum of terms with are product of lower order covariances, i.e.,

$\partial_{i_m} \mathrm{Cov}_\theta(f, T_{i_1}, \cdots, T_{i_{m-1}}) = \partial_{i_m} \mathbb{E}_\theta[\overline{f} \, \overline{T}_{i_1} \cdots \overline{T}_{i_{m-1}}]$

$= \mathbb{E}_\theta[\overline{f} \, \overline{T}_{i_1} \cdots \overline{T}_{i_m}] + \mathbb{E}_\theta[\overline{T}_{i_1} \cdots \overline{T}_{i_{m-1}} \partial_{i_m} \overline{f}]$

$+ \mathbb{E}_\theta[\overline{f} \, \partial_{i_m} (\overline{T}_{i_1} \cdots \overline{T}_{i_{m-1}})]$

$= \mathrm{Cov}_\theta(f, T_{i_1}, \ldots, T_{i_m}) - \mathrm{Cov}_\theta(f, T_{i_m}) \mathrm{Cov}_\theta(T_{i_1}, \ldots, T_{i_{m-1}})$

$- \sum_{j=1}^{m-1} \mathrm{Cov}_\theta(T_{i_m}, T_{i_j}) \mathbb{E}_\theta \left[\overline{f} \prod_{k=1, k \neq j}^{m-1} \overline{T}_{i_k} \right].$

Starting from $m = 4$, the derivative of $\mathbb{E}_\theta[f]$ equals a sum of products of terms, that all vanish by hypothesis except for the 4th-order covariance. Similarly for higher order cases. (iv) The formula is true for $m = 2$, see Proposition 15 (ii). Starting from $m > 2$, before taking derivatives of covariances of order equal to 3, apply Proposition 15 (i), so that the m order derivative of $\mathbb{E}_\theta[f]$ is a sum of terms which are products of lower order covariances. By hypothesis all terms vanish, expect the covariance between f and the product of the sufficient statistics. $\square$

Convergence Rates of SMS-EMOA on Continuous Bi-Objective Problem Classes

Nicola Beume
Fakultät für Informatik,
Technische Universität
Dortmund, Germany
nicola.beume@tu-dortmund.de

Marco Laumanns
IBM Research – Zurich,
Switzerland
mlm@zurich.ibm.com

Günter Rudolph
Fakultät für Informatik,
Technische Universität
Dortmund, Germany
guenter.rudolph@tu-dortmund.de

ABSTRACT

Convergence rate analyses of evolutionary multi-objective optimization algorithms in continuous search space are yet rare. First results have been obtained for simple algorithms. Here, we provide concrete results of convergence rates for a state-of-the-art algorithm, namely the S-metric selection evolutionary multi-objective optimization algorithm (SMS-EMOA). We show that the SMS-EMOA produces the same sequence of populations as certain single-objective evolutionary algorithms on arbitrary problem classes. Thereby we are able to transfer known convergence properties for classes of convex functions. We especially consider the SMS-EMOA with populations of parents and offspring greater than one and different concepts for the choice of the reference point used for the internal calculation of the dominated hypervolume within the selection operator.

Categories and Subject Descriptors

F.2.1 [**Analysis of Algorithms and Problem Complexity**]: Numerical Algorithms and Problems; G.1.6 [**Numerical Analysis**]: Optimization; G.3 [**Probability and Statistics**]: Probabilistic algorithms

General Terms

Algorithms, Performance, Theory

Keywords

multiobjective optimization, convergence rate, dominated hypervolume, reference point

1. INTRODUCTION

Convergence rate analyses of evolutionary multi-objective optimization algorithms (EMOA) with continuous search space are yet rare. Results are known for simple algorithms

[9] only. Still there is justified hope to be able to transfer results from further developed analyses of single-objective evolutionary algorithms (EA). EMOA generate orders of (firstly incomparable) individuals to perform a selection among them. The key idea is to utilize the function generating the order as a fitness function in a single-objective EA.

In [1] first results on convergence rates for a state-of-the-art algorithm, namely the S-metric selection evolutionary multi-objective optimization algorithm (SMS-EMOA) have been established.

Here, we build on [1] and extend these results considerably. By modeling algorithmically equivalent single-objective evolutionary algorithms, we are able to transfer known convergence properties for certain classes of functions. We especially consider the SMS-EMOA with populations of parents greater than one and extend the selection concept to offspring populations greater than one. Three different concepts for the choice of the reference point used for the internal calculation of the dominated hypervolume within the selection operator are considered: adaptively depending on two points, adaptively depending on more than two points, and fixed throughout the optimization process.

The next section provides basic definitions and notation. Section 3 resumes basic concepts and helpful lemmas needed for the central convergence results, and summarizes results and ideas of proofs from [1] we build on. Section 4 deals with a new version of hypervolume selection based on pairwise comparisons of individuals. Thereby the SMS-EMOA is considered with populations of parents and offspring. The SMS-EMOA with an adaptive reference point for comparing more than two individuals is analyzed in Section 5 followed by a fixed reference point in Section 6. We finally summarize our work and point out future research in Section 7.

2. BASIC DEFINITIONS

2.1 Multi-objective Optimization

We consider unconstrained multiobjective optimization problems min $f(x) : \mathbb{R}^n \to \mathbb{R}^d$ where $f(x) = (f_1(x), \ldots, f_d(x))$ maps an n-dimensional vector of the search space to a d-dimensional vector of the objective space.

A strict partial order, called *Pareto dominance*, holds in the objective space based on the coordinate-wise total order: a point $p = (p_1, \ldots, p_d)$ *weakly dominates* a point q (written as $p \preceq q$) iff $p_i \leq q_i$ holds for all $1 \leq i \leq d$. A point p *dominates* q (written as $p \prec q$) iff $p \preceq q$ and $p \neq q$. Two distinct points $p \neq q$ are *incomparable* ($p \parallel q$) iff neither point dominates the other. Considering a set $A \subseteq \mathbb{R}^d$, points of A that are not dominated by any other point in A are referred to as *non-dominated in A* or the minima of A. Those points that are non-dominated regarding the whole objective space are *Pareto-optimal* and called the *Pareto front*. The set of their preimages in the search space is named the *Pareto set*.

The objective functions are typically conflicting so that the Pareto front indeed is a set and not a single optimal point. In the continuous domain only an approximation of the Pareto set or front can be expected to be achieved since Pareto-optimal points may not be sampled exactly and the Pareto front is typically an infinite set so that it cannot be obtained completely. In order to compare approximations of the Pareto front—e.g. the results of different EMOA—several quality measures exist, typically rewarding quantity, closeness to the Pareto front, and high diversity. Among these, the *hypervolume indicator* (or *S-metric*[1] or *Lebesgue measure*) by Zitzler and Thiele [10] is of outstanding importance due to its consistency with the Pareto dominance relation, cf. Zitzler et al. [11]. It is formally defined in the following subsection.

The quality measures express how valuable a Pareto front approximation is. Thus the idea to seek a set that is optimal with respect to this measure suggests itself. Indicator-based EMOA realize this by using the quality measures or indicators within their selection operator.

We exploit that convergence results for one EA algorithm can be transferred to another in case the algorithms behave similar. Therefore, we introduce the following definition:

Definition 1. Let $(X_t)_{t \geq 0}$ and $(Y_t)_{t \geq 0}$ be two stochastic sequences of states generated by two evolutionary algorithms A_X and A_Y. The EA A_X and A_Y are called *algorithmically equivalent* if $\forall t \geq 0 \colon X_t \stackrel{d}{=} Y_t$ holds for their associated state sequences, i.e. X_t and Y_t have the same distribution for all $t \geq 0$. □

In particular, two algorithms are algorithmically equivalent if both use the same probability distribution for probabilistic decisions, and their deterministic decisions are equal. We use the term in this way by assuming equal variation operators and showing that the deterministic selection operators produce the same output in case of the same input for certain classes of problems. We do not consider the computational resources of the EA operators but only the input-output-behavior, thus the state of the EA's population.

2.2 Dominated Hypervolume

Definition 2. Let $M = \{v^{(1)}, v^{(2)}, \ldots, v^{(m)}\} \subset \mathbb{R}^d$, $d \geq 2$ be a finite set of elements, which are mutually incomparable w.r.t. to the dominance relation $\preceq$. Let $r \in \mathbb{R}^d$ indicate the *reference point* with $v^{(i)} \prec r$ for all $i = 1, \ldots, m \in \mathbb{N}$. The quantity

$$H(v^{(1)}, \ldots, v^{(m)}; r) = \mathsf{Leb}\left(\bigcup_{i=1}^{m} [v^{(i)}, r] \right) \quad (1)$$

is termed the *dominated hypervolume* or *S-metric* where $\mathsf{Leb}(\cdot)$ denotes the Lebesgue measure in $\mathbb{R}^d$, and $[v^{(i)}, r]$ the

---

[1]Note that the term *S-metric* is archaic and the measure is not a metric in the mathematical sense.

hypercuboids spanned by the points in M and the reference point r. □

For bi-objective problems ($d = 2$), provided the elements $v^{(1)}, \ldots, v^{(m)}$ have been labeled in ascending order of their first component, i.e., $v_1^{(1)} < v_1^{(2)} < \ldots < v_1^{(m)}$, equation (1) specializes to

$$H(v^{(1)}, \ldots, v^{(m)}; r) =$$

$$(r_1 - v_1^{(1)})(r_2 - v_2^{(1)}) + \sum_{i=2}^{m}(r_1 - v_1^{(i)})(v_2^{(i-1)} - v_2^{(i)}).$$

Geometrically speaking, the hypervolume is calculated as a sum of the area of rectangles.

The hypervolume of a single point $v \in \mathbb{R}^d$ results in

$$H(v; r) = \prod_{i=1}^{d}(r_i - v_i)$$

and in

$$H(v; r) = (r_1 - v_1)(r_2 - v_2)$$

for the special case of a bi-objective optimization problem, so $v \in \mathbb{R}^2$.

In order to optimize the composition of a set, it is desirable to quantify the value of a single point within a set. To this end, we define the hypervolume contribution of a point to a set as the dominated hypervolume that is exclusively dominated by the point and thus gets lost when the point is excluded from the set.

Definition 3. The hypervolume contribution of v to M, with $v \in M \subset \mathbb{R}^d$ is defined as
$$H_\Delta(v; r) = H(M; r) - H(M \setminus \{v\}; r).$$ □

2.3 Convergence

To avoid misunderstandings it is necessary to equip the notion of "convergence" with a precise meaning.

Definition 4. Let X be a random variable and (X_t) a sequence of random variables defined on a probability space $(\Omega, \mathcal{A}, P)$. Then (X_t) is said to
(a) converge completely to X, if for any $\epsilon > 0$

$$\lim_{t \to \infty} \sum_{i=1}^{t} P\{|X_i - X| > \epsilon\} < \infty;$$

(b) converge almost surely or with probability 1 to X, if

$$P\{\lim_{t \to \infty} |X_t - X| = 0\} = 1;$$

(c) converge in probability to X, if for any $\epsilon > 0$

$$\lim_{t \to \infty} P\{|X_t - X| > \epsilon\} = 0;$$

(d) converge in mean to X, if

$$\lim_{t \to \infty} E(|X_t - X|) = 0.$$ □

The velocity of approaching a limit is expressed by the "convergence rate."

Definition 5. Let $(Z_k : k \geq 0)$ be a non-negative random sequence. The sequence is said to *converge geometrically fast in mean (in probability, w.p. 1) to zero* if there exists a constant $q > 1$ such that the sequence $(q^k Z_k : k \geq 0)$ converges in mean (in probability, w.p. 1) to zero. Let $q^* > 1$ be supremum of all constants $q > 1$ such that geometrically fast convergence is still guaranteed. Then $c = 1/q$ is called the *convergence rate*. A sequence with geometrically fast convergence is synonymously denoted to have a *linear convergence rate*. $\square$

Let $\rho(\cdot)$ denote a function that measures the performance of an EA's population X_k and ρ^* the target value. If the sequence $(Z_k)_{k\geq 0}$ defined by $Z_k = |\rho(X_k) - \rho^*|$ converges (in any mode mentioned above) to zero with a certain convergence rate, then the EA approaches the target performance value with this rate.

For example, let $\rho(X_k)$ be the best objective function value of the population at generation $k \geq 0$ of a single-criterion EA and ρ^* be the global minimum of the objective function. If Z_k converges to zero then the EA converges to the global minimum. Similarly, let $\rho(X_k)$ be the dominated hypervolume of population X_k and ρ^* the maximal dominated hypervolume in the multi-objective scenario then the population converges to the maximum dominated hypervolume if $Z_k \to 0$ as $k \to \infty$. For the convergence analysis in the sections 3.3 and 4 we consider the convergence of the population towards the Pareto front. Thereby, $\rho(X_k)$ denotes the distance to a certain point on the Pareto front.

2.4 Convexity

Definition 6. A set $S \subseteq \mathbb{R}^n$ is said to be *convex* if $\xi x + (1 - \xi) y \in S$ for all $x, y \in S$ and $\xi \in [0, 1]$. A function $f : S \to \mathbb{R}$ is termed
a) *convex* if $f(\xi x + (1 - \xi) y) \leq \xi f(x) + (1 - \xi) f(y)$,
b) *strictly convex* if $f(\xi x + (1 - \xi) y) < \xi f(x) + (1 - \xi) f(y)$,
c) *strongly convex* if

$$f(\xi x + (1-\xi) y) \leq \xi f(x) + (1-\xi) f(y) + \frac{L}{2} \xi (1-\xi) \|x-y\|^2,$$

d) (K, Q)-*strongly convex* if it is strongly convex and

$$\frac{K}{2} \xi (1-\xi) \|x-y\|^2 \leq \xi f(x) + (1-\xi) f(y) - f(\xi x + (1-\xi) y)$$

$$\leq \frac{L}{2} \xi (1 - \xi) \|x - y\|^2 \quad (2)$$

with $K, L \in \mathbb{R}^+, 0 < K \leq L < \infty$ and $Q = L/K$. $\square$

Definition 6 a) says that a function is convex if its epigraph (the set of points lying on or above its graph) is convex. For convex functions any local minimum is a global one, i.e. minima have equal function values. Strictly convex functions are convex with a unique minimizer. Strongly convex functions are a subclass fulfilling a tighter bound of the inequality, whereas for (K, Q)-strongly convex functions the relation of the terms is bounded from two sides. The inequalities become more precise with increasing values of the parameters K and L.

Lemma 1. The sum of a strongly convex function and a convex function is a strongly convex function.

Proof. Let $f : S \to \mathbb{R}$ be strongly convex and $g : S \to \mathbb{R}$ convex over a convex set $S \subseteq \mathbb{R}^n$. Set $h(x) = f(x) + g(x)$. Since

$$h(\xi x + (1 - \xi) y) = f(\xi x + (1 - \xi) y) + g(\xi x + (1 - \xi) y)$$

$$\leq \xi f(x) + (1-\xi) f(y) - L \xi (1-\xi) \|x-y\|^2 + g(x) + (1-\xi) g(y)$$

$$= \xi (f(x) + g(x)) + (1 - \xi) (f(y) + g(y)) - L \xi (1-\xi) \|x-y\|^2$$

$$= \xi h(x) + (1 - \xi) h(y) - L \xi (1-\xi) \|x-y\|^2$$

with some $L > 0$ for $\xi \in [0, 1]$ the function $h : S \to \mathbb{R}$ is strongly convex. $\square$

Finally, notice that $f(\cdot)$ is termed *concave* if $-f(\cdot)$ is convex.

3. PRELIMINARIES

3.1 SMS-EMOA

We have discussed that the S-metric has valuable theoretical properties and is regarded as a rather fair measure. So, plainly speaking, an EMOA is tended to be valued when its results gain high S-metric values. Taking this as a design principle, the S-metric selection evolutionary multi-objective optimization algorithm (SMS-EMOA) [2] explicitly aims at the maximization of the S-metric value of its population. It is a steady-state EMOA, i.e. performing $(\mu + 1)$ selection. The selection process starts with partitioning the $\mu + 1$ individuals by non-dominated sorting. From the worst set of mutually incomparable individuals one individuals is discarded. The hypervolume of the worst set is calculated and the individual with the least hypervolume contribution (cf. Def. 3) to this set is rejected. This minimizes the loss of the population's dominated hypervolume.

The SMS-EMOA does not specify a certain variation operator. It has mainly been considered using SBX recombination and polynomial mutation (see e.g. [3]). Here, we consider Gaussian mutation or uniform mutation on the surface of a hypersphere, both coupled with self-adaptation of the step size with the $1/5$ success rule.

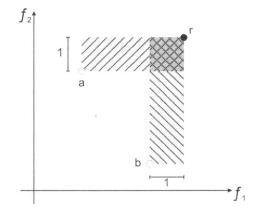

Figure 1: Dominated hypervolume of the points a and b w.r.t. the adaptive reference point $r(M)$, with $M = \{a, b\}$. The hypervolume contributions of a and b to M are shaded in light gray.

The calculation of the hypervolume requires the specification of a reference point r. It could be chosen and remain fix throughout the optimization process. Yet, in the original SMS-EMOA it is no exogenous parameter but calculated internally and adapted in each generation. We define this concept as the *adaptive reference point*:

Definition 7. Let $M = \{y^{(1)}, \ldots, y^{(m)}\}$ be a multiset with $y^{(i)} \in \mathbb{R}^d$ for $i = 1, \ldots, m$. The vector $\mathbf{r}(M) := r = (r_1, \ldots, r_d)$ with $r_k = \max\{y_k^{(i)} : i = 1, \ldots, m\} + 1$ for $k = 1, \ldots, d$ is termed the *adaptive reference point* of M. For short, we also use the objective vectors' subscripts as arguments, e.g.: $r(i, j) = \mathbf{r}\{y^{(i)}, y^{(j)}\}$. $\square$

Note that points that are the worst ones in the population regarding an objective function have a distance to the reference point of exactly 1 w.r.t. that worst objective (cf. Fig. 1). This fact has been exploited to gain the convergence result described in Section 3.3. Before resuming that result, we need to clarify the relation of the hypervolume and hypervolume contributions.

3.2 Properties of the Hypervolume

Lemma 2. The order of two points according to their hypervolume is equivalent to their order induced by their hypervolume contributions. This holds for arbitrary choice of the reference point and dimension of the objective space.

Proof. The hypervolume dominated by a set M with $|M| = 2$ consists of the contributions of the two points, i.e. the exclusively dominated parts, and a part that is dominated by both points (cf. Figure 2). The hypervolume of a single point is equivalent to its hypervolume contribution plus the hypervolume value of the part dominated by both points, which is equal for both parts. As the common dominated part adds the same constant to the hypervolume contribution of each point, the order of the hypervolume contributions is equal to the order of the absolute hypervolume values. $\square$

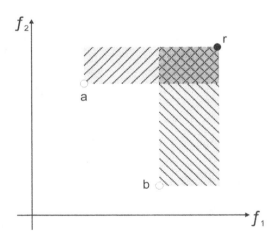

Figure 2: The striped areas depict the hypervolume contribution of the points. The checkered area is dominated by both points, so its value added to both contributions results in the absolute values. The order induced by both measures is equal.

Lemma 3. Let $f_1(x) = a'x + a_0$ and $f_2(x) = b'x + b_0$ be linear functions with $a, b, x \in \mathbb{R}^n$, with $a_0, b_0 \in \mathbb{R}$, and $n \geq 2$. The dominated hypervolume for a fixed reference point $r \in \mathbb{R}^2$ is a concave function if the matrix $a\,b'$ is negative semidefinite.

Proof Notice that the dominated hypervolume

$$H(x; r) = [r_1 - f_1(x)][r_2 - f_2(x)]$$

$$= [r_1 - (a'x + a_0)][r_2 - (b'x + b_0)]$$

$$= [(r_1 - a_0) - a'x][(r_2 - b_0) - b'x]$$

$$= (r_1 - a_0)(r_2 - b_0) - [(r_1 - a_0)b + (r_2 - b_0)a]'x + a'x \cdot b'x$$

$$= (r_1 - a_0)(r_2 - b_0) - [(r_1 - a_0)b + (r_2 - b_0)a]'x + x'(a\,b')x$$

is a quadratic form which is concave iff $a\,b'$ is negative semidefinite. $\square$

Example: ab' is negative semidefinite if $b = -a$ since aa' is positive semidefinite. Lemma 3 is used in Section 5.

3.3 Equivalence of $(1+1)$-ES and $(1+1)$-SMS-EMOA

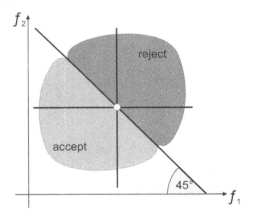

Figure 3: Regions of acceptance or rejection for the surrogate weighted sum function.

In [1] the algorithmic equivalence of the $(1 + 1)$-SMS-EMOA and a single-objective $(1 + 1)$-EA has been shown provided the variation operators of the algorithms are identical. Though the SMS-EMOA uses the hypervolume contribution as selection criterion, technically the proof has been performed considering absolute hypervolume values of the points. Lemma 2 assures us that this is a valid model since the measures behave equally in this scenario. The $(1+1)$-EA uses a weighted sum $f^s : \mathbb{R}^n \to \mathbb{R}$ with $f^s(x) = \frac{1}{2}(f_1(x) + f_2(x))$ as fitness function, also called *evenly weighted sum* in the following. The decisions of acceptance and rejection are depicted in Figure 3. A new point is accepted if it lies on or below the diagonal through its parent. This function exactly resembles the hypervolume for the considered scenario. For the selection operators it has been shown in [1] that whenever the $(1+1)$-SMS-EMOA accepts a point, then this point is also accepted by the $(1 + 1)$-EA. Analogously, points are rejected alike in both algorithms, so that their selection decisions are equal.

THEOREM 1. *The $(1 + 1)$-SMS-EMOA with adaptive reference point applied to a bi-objective optimization problem $\min\{f(x) : x \in \mathbb{R}^n\}$ is algorithmically equivalent to a $(1+1)$-EA applied to the minimization of the single-objective function $f^s : \mathbb{R}^n \to \mathbb{R}$ with $f^s(x) = \frac{1}{2}(f_1(x) + f_2(x))$, assuming equal variation operators.*

Proof. See [1]. □

THEOREM 2. *The* $(1+1)$*-SMS-EMOA with adaptive reference point and self-adaptation applied to a bi-objective optimization problem* $\min\{f(x) : x \in \mathbb{R}^n\}$*, with* $n \geq 2$ *approaches an element of the Pareto front with linear order of convergence if both objective functions are convex and at least one of them is strongly convex.*

Proof. The proof is analogous to the proof in [1] when taking into account Lemma 1 and the fact that [4, 5] actually covers the case of strongly convex functions. □

4. SMS-EMOA WITH SELECTION BASED ON PAIRWISE COMPARISONS

4.1 $(1, 2)$-SMS-EMOA

We show the algorithmic equivalence of the $(1,2)$-SMS-EMOA to the single-objective $(1,2)$-EA in order to transfer known convergence results. We assume equal variation operators for both algorithms. Despite the quite different selection concepts, we show that the selection among the offspring according to their dominated hypervolume in the SMS-EMOA equates to the selection in the EA according to the evenly weighted sum. This proof is analog to the one in [1] for the algorithmic equivalence of $(1+1)$-SMS-EMOA and the $(1+1)$-EA. In the $(1+1)$ case, the selection operator decides among the parent and the offspring and keeps the better one. The selection operators perform exactly the same task in the $(1,2)$ case as it decides among two individuals (the two offspring) without using any information how they have been generated or differentiating between parent and offspring. This results in the following theorem:

THEOREM 3. *The* $(1,2)$*-SMS-EMOA with adaptive reference point applied to a bi-objective optimization problem* $\min\{f(x) : x \in \mathbb{R}^n\}$ *is algorithmically equivalent to a* $(1,2)$*-EA applied to the minimization of the single-objective function* $f^s : \mathbb{R}^n \to \mathbb{R}$ *with* $f^s(x) = \frac{1}{2}(f_1(x) + f_2(x))$*, assuming equal variation operators.* □

Due to Theorem 3 we can transfer known properties of the $(1,2)$-EA as defined by Rudolph [8] to the $(1,2)$-SMS-EMOA as given in Algorithm 1. Hence, the convergence results by Rudolph [8] for the $(1,2)$-EA is directly transcribed:

THEOREM 4. *Let the* $(1,2)$*-SMS-EMOA with adaptive reference use variation by mutations due to a multivariate uniform distribution on the surface of a hypersphere with radius* $r > 0$ *and self-adaptation of the step-size (i.e., the radius)* r *via the 1/5-success rule (Procedure* adapt*) with the observation interval* $\delta > 0$*, the success probability* $p_s = \frac{1}{5}$ *and the adaptation factor* $\gamma > 1$*. Applied to a bi-objective optimization problem* $\min\{f(x) : x \in \mathbb{R}^n\}$ *the algorithm approaches an element of the Pareto front at most with linear order of convergence if both objective functions are convex and at least one of them is strongly convex.* □

4.2 $(1, \lambda)$-SMS-EMOA

To show algorithmic equivalence for the general case of the $(1,\lambda)$-SMS-EMOA and the $(1,\lambda)$-EA with $\lambda \geq 2$, we consider the selection behavior more formally. As the SMS-EMOA has been designed as a steady-state-algorithm, i.e. operating with $\lambda = 1$ as a $(\mu+1)$ algorithm, we first have to

enhance the concept of the hypervolume selection to the case of more than one offspring. The selection among offspring could be defined analogously to the original one using the hypervolume contributions. Yet we define it in a slightly different way to gain correspondence to the single-objective $(1,\lambda)$-EA. For the case of $\lambda = 2$ the concept is equivalent to the normal selection of the SMS-EMOA as described before; for $\lambda > 2$ the new concept is different.

The selection within the SMS-EMOA now is performed based on pairwise comparisons in a tournament modus. In each step two individuals are compared regarding their hypervolume with respect to the adaptive reference point (see Definition 7). The better individual is also better regarding the evenly weighted sum as shown in [1]. Those individuals that win the comparisons are again compared in pairs until the best individual is determined. By comparing the best ones iteratively, the individual with the maximal value regarding the evenly weighted sum is chosen. Thus, the algorithmic equivalence to the $(1,\lambda)$-EA is given.

COROLLARY 5. *The* $(1,\lambda)$*-SMS-EMOA with* $\lambda \geq 2$*, using the adaptive reference point and pairwise comparisons of hypervolume values within the selection, applied to a bi-objective optimization problem* $\min\{f(x) : x \in \mathbb{R}^n\}$ *is algorithmically equivalent to a single-objective* $(1,\lambda)$*-EA applied to the single-objective function* $f^s : \mathbb{R}^n \to \mathbb{R}$ *with* $f^s(x) = \frac{1}{2}(f_1(x) + f_2(x))$*, assuming equal variation operators.* □

Thanks to the algorithmic equivalence described in Corollary 5 the convergence result in [8] (p. 184) for the $(1,\lambda)$-EA can directly be transcribed:

THEOREM 6. *Suppose the objective functions* $f_1(x)$ *and* $f_2(x)$ *lead to a* (K, Q)*-strongly convex surrogate function via* $f^s(x) = \frac{1}{2}(f_1(x) + f_2(x))$ *with* $f^s : \mathbb{R}^n \to \mathbb{R}$*. Let the constant* M_λ *denote the expectation of the maximum of* λ *independent samples from a Beta distribution with support* $(-1, 1)$ *and parameters* $p = q = (n-1)/2$*. Then the convergence rate of the* $(1,\lambda)$*-SMS-EMOA,* $2 \leq \lambda < \infty$ *with adaptive reference point, pairwise comparisons, and variation operations as described in [8] (p. 184) is*

(a) $1 - M_\lambda^2$ *if* f^s *is quadratic, the Hessian matrix* $\nabla^2 f^s(x)$ *is known in advance and the length of the gradient in ellipsoid norm* $\|\cdot\|_{\nabla^2 f^s(x)}$ *can be determined;*

(b) $\leq 1 - M_\lambda^2/Q^{3/2}$ *if* f^s *is quadratic, the Hessian matrix* $\nabla^2 f^s(x)$ *is known in advance and the Euclidean length of the gradient can be determined;*

(c) $\leq 1 - M_\lambda^2/Q^2$ *if the largest Eigenvalue of the Hessian (or constant* L*) is known in advance and the Euclidean length of the gradient can be determined.* □

Evidently, the gradient and Hessian of the surrogate function follow from the gradients and Hessians of the objective functions:

$$\nabla f^s(x) = \nabla \left(\frac{f_1(x) + f_2(x)}{2} \right) = \frac{1}{2}(\nabla f_1(x) + \nabla f_2(x))$$

$$\nabla^2 f^s(x) = \nabla^2 \left(\frac{f_1(x) + f_2(x)}{2} \right) = \frac{1}{2}(\nabla^2 f_1(x) + \nabla^2 f_2(x))$$

Algorithm 1: (1,2)-SMS-EMOA with Self-Adaptation

1 choose $X^{(0)} \in \mathbb{R}^n$ and $\sigma^{(0)} > 0$, set $t = 0$ and $k = 0$
2 repeat
3   draw $Z^{(t,1)}, Z^{(t,2)}$ from a multivariate Beta distribution with support $(-1, 1)$ and parameters $p = q = (n-1)/2$
4 $Y^{(t,1)} = X^{(t)} + \sigma^{(t)} Z^{(t,1)} \; ; \quad Y^{(t,2)} = X^{(t)} + \sigma^{(t)} Z^{(t,2)}$
5 $R^{(t)} = (\max\{f_1(Y^{(t,1)}), f_1(Y^{(t,2)})\} + 1, \max\{f_2(Y^{(t,1)}), f_2(Y^{(t,2)})\} + 1)'$
6   **if** $f(Y^{(t,1)}) \prec f(Y^{(t,2)})$ **or**
       $\big(f(Y^{(t,1)}) \parallel f(Y^{(t,2)})$ **and** $H(f(Y^{(t,1)}); R^{(t)}) > H(f(Y^{(t,2)}); R^{(t)}) \big)$ **then**
7 $X^{(t+1)} = Y^{(t,1)}$
8   increment k
9   **else** $X^{(t+1)} = Y^{(t,2)}$
10 $\sigma^{(t+1)} = \mathtt{adapt}(\sigma^{(t)}, t, k\,; \delta, p_s, c)$
11   increment t
12 until *termination criterion fulfilled*
13 output: $X^{(t)}$

Procedure adapt$(\sigma, t, k\,; \delta, p_s, \gamma)$

1 if $t \bmod \delta \neq 0$ **then return** σ
2 $q_s = k/\delta \; ; \quad k = 0$
3 if $q_s \geq p_s$ **then return** $\sigma \times \gamma$ **else return** σ/γ

4.3 $(1+\lambda)$-**SMS-EMOA**

Analogous to the previous section, the algorithmic equivalence of the $(1+\lambda)$-SMS-EMOA and $(1+\lambda)$-EA using the evenly weighted sum as fitness function can be shown. Again the SMS-EMOA uses the adaptive reference point and pairwise comparison; here to determine the best individual among the set of the parent and the λ offspring.

COROLLARY 7. *The $(1+\lambda)$-SMS-EMOA, using the adaptive reference point and pairwise comparisons of hypervolume values within the selection, applied to a bi-objective optimization problem $\min\{f(x) : x \in \mathbb{R}^n\}$ is algorithmically equivalent to a single-objective $(1+\lambda)$-EA and applied to the single-objective function $f^s : \mathbb{R}^n \to \mathbb{R}$ with $f^s(x) = \frac{1}{2}(f_1(x) + f_2(x))$, assuming equal variation operators.* $\square$

Thus, a convergence result obtain in [8] (Th. 6.12) for the $(1+\lambda)$-EA can be transferred to the $(1+\lambda)$-SMS-EMOA.

THEOREM 8. *Suppose the objective functions $f_1(x)$ and $f_2(x)$ lead to a (K, Q)-strongly convex surrogate function via $f^s(x) = \frac{1}{2}(f_1(x) + f_2(x))$ with $f^s : \mathbb{R}^n \to \mathbb{R}$. If the Euclidean length of the gradient is available for all $x \in \mathbb{R}^n$ then the following property holds for the $(1+\lambda)$-SMS-EMOA with $1 \leq \lambda < \infty$, using the adaptive reference point, pairwise comparisons of hypervolume values, and mutation of a parent X_t via $X_t + \|\nabla f^s(X_t)\| \cdot Z$ where Z is a spherically distributed random vector with support $\mathbb{R}^n$: The algorithm converges almost surely and in mean to the to the Pareto front and the mean velocity of approach is geometrically fast (i.e., linear convergence rate) regardless of the actual choice of the distribution of Z and its parameterization.* $\square$

4.4 $(\mu+1)$-**SMS-EMOA**

For the $(\mu+1)$-SMS-EMOA with its original steady-state scheme, we have to discard one of $\mu + 1$ individuals. Again,

due to the total order of the hypervolume and the evenly weighted sum used by the single-objective $(\mu+1)$-EA a minimal element of a set of individuals is well-defined. Since this worst element is discarded by the SMS-EMOA as well as by the $(\mu+1)$-EA, the algorithmic equivalence of these algorithms is given.

COROLLARY 9. *The $(\mu+1)$-SMS-EMOA, using the adaptive reference point and pairwise comparisons of hypervolume values within the selection, applied to a bi-objective optimization problem $\min\{f(x) : x \in \mathbb{R}^n\}$ is algorithmically equivalent to a single-objective $(\mu+1)$-EA using the same arbitrary mutation operator and applied to the single-objective function $f^s : \mathbb{R}^n \to \mathbb{R}$ with $f^s(x) = \frac{1}{2}(f_1(x) + f_2(x))$.* $\square$

Due to Corollary 9, we are able to transfer known results for a $(\mu+1)$-EA to the $(\mu+1)$-SMS-EMOA, like the lower bound for the $(\mu+1)$ ES shown by Jägersküpper and Witt [6], resulting in the following theorem.

THEOREM 10. *Suppose the objective functions $f_1 : \mathbb{R}^n \to \mathbb{R}$ and $f_2 : \mathbb{R}^n \to \mathbb{R}$ lead to a surrogate function $f^s(x) = \frac{1}{2}(f_1(x) + f_2(x))$ with unique optimizer $x^* \in \mathbb{R}^n$. The $(\mu+1)$-SMS-EMOA, where $2 \leq \mu = poly(n)$, with adaptive reference point and pairwise comparisons of hypervolume values within the selection, optimizes such a bi-objective optimization problem where the number of steps until the distance to x^* has been halved is $\Omega(\mu n)$ with probability $1 - 2^{\Omega(n)}$ and also in expectation.* $\square$

5. REFERENCE POINT FOR GLOBAL COMPARISON

An alternative selection concept for the SMS-EMOA is to determine the reference point $r(M)$ subjected to a set M of more than two points, which is the standard selection scheme of the SMS-EMOA. Thereby the comparison is not performed pairwise but directly among all $|M|$ regarded

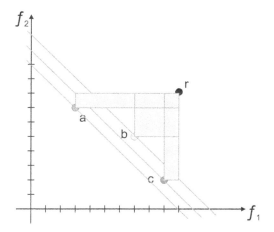

Figure 4: The adaptive reference point $r = r(\{a, b, c\})$ is chosen relative to the three points. In this example, the maximal and minimal elements according to the evenly weighted sum do not correspond to the minimal and maximal elements due to the hypervolume.

points. Consider the hypervolume of each point in M w.r.t the described reference point $r(M)$. We show by a counterexample that the order induced by the hypervolume values of the points is not equivalent to the order induced by the function f^s of the evenly weighted sum.

THEOREM 11. *The order of individuals induced by the weighted function $f^s = \frac{1}{2}(f_1(x) + f_2(x))$ differs from the order according to hypervolume values when the reference point is chosen adaptively depending on more than two points.*

Proof. In order to generate corresponding orders, the order of hypervolume values has to be inverse to the order of weighted function values. We show that contradictions already occur for a set of three points regarding the minimal and maximal values. Consider the set $M = \{a, b, c\}$ in Figure 5 with $a = (3, 7), b = (7, 6), c = (9, 2), r(\{a, b, c, \}) = (10, 8)$. The order of the hypervolume values and the evenly weighted sum function are:

$$H(c, r(M)) = 6 \quad < H(a, r(M)) = 7 \quad < H(b, r(M)) = 9$$
$$\Rightarrow \quad b \text{ p.o. } \quad a \text{ p.o. } \quad c$$
$$f^s(b) = 6 \quad > f^s(c) = 5.5 \quad > f^s(a) = 5$$
$$\Rightarrow \quad a \text{ p.o. } \quad c \text{ p.o. } \quad b,$$

whereas p.o. abbreviates "preferred over". Obviously, the orders of a, b, c differ, especially regarding the minima and maxima. □

From Theorem 11 it follows that the selection according to the hypervolume of a point in the SMS-EMOA and the selection of the EA according to the evenly weighted sum are in general not equivalent when the reference point depends on more than two points. This already holds for a set of three individuals, which can occur when the parent or the offspring population consist of more than one individual since the orders already differ in their minimal and maximal elements.

COROLLARY 12. *When the reference point of the hypervolume is chosen adaptively depending on more than two points, then for $\mu > 1$ or $\lambda > 1$ the $(\mu + \lambda)$-SMS-EMOA and the $(\mu + \lambda)$-EA with the evenly weighted sum as fitness function and using equal mutation operators are not algorithmically equivalent; as well as the (μ, λ)-SMS-EMOA and the (μ, λ)-EA with $\lambda > 2$.* □

6. (1+1)-SMS-EMOA WITH FIXED REFERENCE POINT

In the previous sections the reference point was chosen adaptively depending on the current positions of parents and/or offspring. Here, the reference point is chosen at the beginning of the optimization and kept fixed during the run. The reference point is chosen such that it is dominated by all individuals throughout the optimization process.

THEOREM 13. *The $(1 + 1)$-SMS-EMOA with fixed reference point $r \in \mathbb{R}^2$ for minimizing $f(x) = (f_1(x), f_2(x))'$ is algorithmically equivalent to the $(1 + 1)$-EA that maximizes the surrogate function*

$$f^s(x) = [r_1 - f_1(x)] [r_2 - f_2(x)], \tag{3}$$

assuming equal variation operators.

Proof. Let $x \in \mathbb{R}^n$ be the current parent. Both algorithms generate the offspring $y \in \mathbb{R}^n$ through the same mutation operation using identical step size rules. It remains to compare the selection operation. Fur this purpose fix some $r \in \mathbb{R}^2$.

If $f(y) \prec f(x)$ then the $(1 + 1)$-SMS-EMOA accepts y. If $f(y) \prec f(x)$ results from the fact that $f_1(y) < f_1(x)$ and $f_2(y) \leq f_2(x)$ then

$$f^s(y) = [r_1 - f_1(y)] [r_2 - f_2(y)] > [r_1 - f_1(x)] [r_2 - f_2(x)] = f^s(x)$$

and the $(1 + 1)$-EA would accept y since it is maximizing the surrogate function. If $f(y) \prec f(x)$ results from the fact that $f_1(y) \leq f_1(x)$ and $f_2(y) < f_2(x)$ the analogous argumentation leads to an acceptance of y.

Exchanging x and y in the reasoning above reveals that $f(x) \prec f(y)$ leads to a rejection of y by the $(1 + 1)$-SMS-EMOA (it accepts x) and by the $(1 + 1)$-ES since $f^s(x) > f^s(y)$.

If $f(x) \parallel f(y)$ then y is accepted by the $(1 + 1)$-SMS-EMOA if its dominated hypervolume is larger than that of x, i.e., if $H(y) > H(x)$. Suppose this is true. Since the hypervolume $H(\cdot)$ is identical to the surrogate function $f_s(\cdot)$ it follows that $f^s(y) > f^s(x)$ which in turn implies that the $(1 + 1)$-EA would accept y. Evidently, if $H(x) > H(y)$ then y is rejected by both algorithms.

Finally, if $f(x) \parallel f(y)$ and $H(x) = H(y)$ then both algorithms must use the same tie-breaking rule.

Summing up: Both algorithms generate as well as accept (or reject) a new point in the same manner. Therefore they are algorithmically equivalent under the conditions of the theorem. □

Based on this general result a convergence result can be derived.

THEOREM 14. *The $(1 + 1)$-SMS-EMOA with fixed reference point and variation by uniform mutations on the surface of a unit hypersphere and step sizes proportional to the* *length of the gradient maximizes the dominated hypervolume of the linear problem*

$$f(x) = (a'x + a_0, b'x + b_0)' \to \min!, \quad x \in \mathbb{R}^n$$

with convergence rate

$$c(x) = 1 - \frac{\kappa(x)}{\nu_1^2} \cdot \frac{0.405}{n}$$

where $0 \leq \kappa(x) \leq \nu_1^2$ and ν_1 is the largest eigenvalue of matrix $a\,b'$ provided that $a\,b'$ is negative semidefinite.

Proof. Owing to Lemma 3 and the preconditions of this theorem it is guaranteed that the surrogate function / hypervolume in (3) is a quadratic form whose Hessian matrix is negative semidefinite with rank 1. In order to invoke Theorem 13 for deriving a convergence result for the $(1 + 1)$-SMS-EMOA a convergence result for the $(1 + 1)$-EA for semidefinite quadratic forms is required. Apparently, such a result does not exist yet. Therefore, the remainder of the this section is devoted to establish such a result in Theorem 15 below. Since the maximization of a concave function is identical to minimizing a convex function the application of Theorem 15 completes the proof of this theorem. □

At first, some facts from matrix theory are required.

Lemma 4. Let $A : n \times n$ be a symmetric and positive semidefinite matrix with rank$(A) < n$.

a) The eigenvalues $\nu_1 \geq \nu_2 \geq \ldots \geq \nu_n \geq 0$ of A are nonnegative with $\nu_1 > 0$ and $\nu_n = 0$.

b) The eigenvalues of A^2 are ν_i^2 for $i = 1, \ldots, n$.

c) $\forall x \in \mathbb{R} \setminus \{0\} : 0 = \nu_n \leq \frac{x'Ax}{x'x} \leq \nu_1$.

Proof. See e.g. [7]. □

Next, a probabilistic result is of essential importance.

Lemma 5. If u is an n-dimensional random vector that is uniformly distributed on the surface of a unit hypersphere then $\|u\| = 1$ with probability 1 and $x'u = \|x\| \cdot B$ where B is a Beta random variable with support $[-1, 1]$ and parameters $p = q = (n - 1)/2$.

Proof. See [8], p. 22. □

Now we are in the position to prove the desired result.

THEOREM 15. *Let $f : \mathbb{R}^n \to \mathbb{R}$ be a quadratic function with positive semidefinite Hessian matrix whose rank is less than n. The $(1+1)$-EA with uniform mutations on the surface of a unit hypersphere and step sizes proportional to the length of the gradient minimizes $f(\cdot)$ with position-dependent mean convergence rate*

$$c(x) = 1 - \frac{\kappa(x)}{\nu_1^2} \cdot \frac{0.405}{n}$$

with $0 \leq \kappa(x) \leq \nu_1^2$.

Proof. It suffices to consider the case $f(x) = x'Ax$ where A is positive semidefinite with rank$(A) < n$. Let $r > 0$ be the deterministic step size and u an n-dimensional random vector that is uniformly distributed on the surface of a hypersphere (i.e., u is a random direction of unit length).

Let $x \in \mathbb{R}^n$ be the current position of the $(1+1)$-EA. The random fitness value of the offspring $x + r\,u$ is given by

$$
\begin{aligned}
f(x + r\,u) &= (x + r\,u)'A(x + r\,u) \\
&= x'Ax + 2\,r\,u'Ax + r^2\,u'Au \\
&= x'Ax + 2\,r\,\|Ax\| \cdot B + r^2\,u'Au \quad (4) \\
&\leq x'Ax + 2\,r\,\|Ax\| \cdot B + r^2 \cdot \nu_1 \quad (5) \\
&= f(x) + \frac{\|Ax\|^2}{\nu_1}\left(2\gamma \cdot B + \gamma^2\right) \quad (6)
\end{aligned}
$$

where (4) results from Lemma 5, (5) from Lemma 4(c), and (6) from setting $r = \gamma\,\|Ax\|/\nu_1$, with $\gamma > 0$. After selection the fitness value of the selected individual is

$$f(x_{t+1}) = f(x_t) + \frac{\|Ax_t\|^2}{\nu_1}\,\min\{0, 2\gamma \cdot B + \gamma^2\}$$

since a positive value of $2\gamma \cdot B + \gamma^2$ would lead to a rejection of the offspring. This in turn leads to the expected fitness value

$$
\begin{aligned}
\mathrm{E}\left(f(x_{t+1})\right) &= f(x_t) + \frac{\|Ax_t\|^2}{\nu_1}\,\mathrm{E}\left(\min\{0, 2\gamma \cdot B + \gamma^2\}\right) \\
&\leq f(x_t) - \frac{\|Ax_t\|^2}{\nu_1}\,c_n \quad (7)
\end{aligned}
$$

where

$$c_n = -\min_{\gamma > 0}\{\mathrm{E}\left(\min\{0, 2\gamma \cdot B + \gamma^2\}\right)\} \approx \frac{0.405}{n} > 0$$

for large n (see [8], p. 171f.). According to Lemma 4 inequality (7) can be further processed via

$$
\begin{aligned}
\mathrm{E}\left(f(x_{t+1})\right) &\leq f(x_t) - \frac{(Ax_t)'(Ax_t)}{\nu_1}\,c_n \\
&= f(x_t) - \frac{x_t'A^2 x_t}{\nu_1}\,c_n \\
&= f(x_t) - \frac{\kappa(x_t)\,x_t'x_t}{\nu_1}\,c_n
\end{aligned}
$$

where $\kappa(x) \in [0, \nu_1^2]$. Since $f(x) = x'Ax \leq \nu_1\,x'x$

$$
\begin{aligned}
\mathrm{E}\left(f(x_{t+1})\right) &\leq f(x_t) - \frac{\kappa(x_t)\,f(x_t)}{\nu_1^2}\,c_n \\
&= f(x_t)\left(1 - \frac{\kappa(x_t)\,c_n}{\nu_1^2}\right)
\end{aligned}
$$

which proves the theorem. □

7. CONCLUSIONS

This paper showed several convergence rates of the S-metric selection evolutionary multi-objective optimization algorithm (SMS-EMOA) applied to classes of continuously bi-objective optimization problems. We contribute to the understanding of the performance of this state-of-the-art EMOA and demonstrate how results from single-objective optimization can be transferred to multi-objective optimization.

We showed algorithmic equivalence of the SMS-EMOA to different single-objective EA by modeling a single-objective surrogate function such that it corresponds to the behavior of the S-metric (or dominated hypervolume) in the selection of SMS-EMOA. Three different concepts for the choice of the reference point have been considered. If it is chosen adaptively depending on two points only, the equivalence to a single-objective EA using an evenly weighted sum holds, resulting in convergence findings for the $(1, \lambda)$-SMS-EMOA, the $(1+\lambda)$-SMS-EMOA and the $(\mu+1)$-SMS-EMOA. For an adaptive reference point depending on more than two points this equivalence is not given. For a fixed reference point, the algorithmic equivalence of a $(1 + 1)$-SMS-EMOA to a single-objective $(1 + 1)$-EA is proved so that future results for certain problem classes obtained by analyzing the $(1+1)$-EA directly hold for that $(1 + 1)$-SMS-EMOA as well.

Future work shall deal with convergence properties of multi-objective problems with more than two objectives. Furthermore, other multi-objective optimization algorithms shall be considered.

8. REFERENCES

[1] N. Beume, M. Laumanns, and G. Rudolph. Convergence rates of (1+1) evolutionary multiobjective algorithms. In *Proceedings of the 11th International Conference on Parallel Problem Solving from Nature - PPSN XI*, LNCS 6238, Part I, pages 597–606, Berlin, Germany, 2010. Springer.

[2] N. Beume, B. Naujoks, and M. Emmerich. SMS-EMOA: Multiobjective selection based on dominated hypervolume. *European Journal of Operational Research*, 181(3):1653–1669, 2007.

[3] K. Deb, A. Pratap, S. Agarwal, and T. Meyarivan. A Fast and Elitist Multiobjective Genetic Algorithm: NSGA-II. *IEEE Transactions on Evolutionary Computation*, 6(2):182–197, 2002.

[4] J. Jägersküpper. How the (1+1) ES using isotropic mutations minimizes positive definite quadratic forms. *Theoretical Computer Science*, 361(1):38–56, 2006.

[5] J. Jägersküpper. Algorithmic analysis of a basic evolutionary algorithm for continuous optimization. *Theoretical Computer Science*, 379(3):329–347, 2007.

[6] J. Jägersküpper and C. Witt. Rigorous Runtime Analysis of a $(\mu + 1)$ ES for the Sphere Function. In *Proc. of the Genetic and Evolutionary Computation Conference (GECCO 2005)*, 2005.

[7] J. R. Magnus and H. Neudecker. *Matrix Differential Calculus*. Wiley, Chichester, UK, revised edition, 1999.

[8] G. Rudolph. *Convergence Properties of Evolutionary Algorithms*. Kovač, Hamburg, 1997.

[9] G. Rudolph. On a multi–objective evolutionary algorithm and its convergence to the Pareto set. In *Proceedings of the 1998 IEEE International Conference on Evolutionary Computation*, pages 511–516. IEEE Press, Piscataway (NJ), 1998.

[10] E. Zitzler and L. Thiele. Multiobjective optimization using evolutionary algorithms – a comparative case study. In *Proc. of the 5th Intl. Conference on Parallel Problem Solving from Nature (PPSN V)*, LNCS 1498, pages 292–304, Berlin, 1998. Springer.

[11] E. Zitzler, L. Thiele, M. Laumanns, C. M. Fonseca, and V. Grunert da Fonseca. Performance Assessment of Multiobjective Optimizers: An Analysis and Review. *IEEE Transactions on Evolutionary Computation*, 7(2):117–132, 2003.

Author Index